ECONOMIC DEVELOPMENT IN BURMA · 1951-1960

ECONOMIC DEVELOPMENT IN BURMA

1951–1960

BY LOUIS J. WALINSKY

THE TWENTIETH CENTURY FUND

NEW YORK · 1962

Copyright © 1962 by the Twentieth Century Fund, Inc.
Manufactured in the United States of America
By Connecticut Printers, Incorporated, Hartford, Connecticut
Library of Congress Catalog Card Number: 62–13330

TO

J. S. FURNIVALL, THADO THIRI THUDHAMMA
1878–1960

In appreciation of his profound scholarship,
humanity and wisdom, and of his dedicated service
to his beloved Burma over many decades.

*We must have the capacity to look for our past mistakes, and to learn from
those errors. If we do so, we shall at least enable our successors to avoid
those errors and follow the true path.*

U NU

The Pyidaungsu Policy, September 26, 1959

FOREWORD

To capture an individual's experience in the field of political and economic development, and to permit him to reflect upon its meaning while it is still fresh in his mind, has seemed to the Trustees of the Twentieth Century Fund a highly worthwhile objective. Mr. Louis Walinsky represented the case of a man who for several years had been closely involved in the development of post-war Burma; his intimate knowledge of the country's processes of growth and development placed him in a unique position to survey this scene, still comparatively little known to Americans.

The Fund's interest was increased by the fact of its being in the midst of a major survey, under the direction of Professor Gunnar Myrdal, of South Asia. The detailed elaboration of economic development in one South Asian country promised to be helpful to the larger study, now in preparation. Taken by itself, moreover, the study promised to be a significant contribution to understanding of the developmental process. The price many other countries will have to pay for development can be seen in the light of Burma's experience — a price to be judged not only in economic terms, but in terms of effort, sacrifice of old ways, and adjustment to novel methods and values.

Mr. Walinsky in his Introduction has explained the circumstances of his work in Burma. It involved the participation of an American firm of economic consultants, working in close consultation with the country's leaders and planners. The record here presented includes chapters on the social and historical aspects of Burma, on a canvas inevitably wider than the issues of practical, day-to-day planning. That an American economist should have combined his task with so large a perspective and so deep a concern for Burmese life as a whole is in itself encouraging.

Burma is a country which never really resigned itself to a colonial status and struggled against diverse forces to attain a true independence. Its success in creating durable institutions and achieving satisfactory progress is a matter of importance to the South Asian area and far beyond. The Twentieth Century Fund hopes that this record by a scholar objective and critical in his treatment, yet with a profound sympathy for the country, will make a contribution to American understanding of Burma and also, perhaps, to progress within Burma itself.

AUGUST HECKSCHER, *Director*
The Twentieth Century Fund

41 East 70th Street, New York
March 1962

ACKNOWLEDGMENTS

I am indebted to many persons for valuable assistance in connection with this study.

A number of friends and colleagues have been kind enough to review the manuscript, in whole or in part, and have given me the benefit of their criticism. Those who have read substantial portions of the manuscript include: U Thant, Acting Secretary General of the United Nations and former Secretary to Prime Minister U Nu (Chapters 1–5); U Hla Maung, former Executive Secretary, Economic and Social Board (Chapters 1–14); Dr. Tun Thin of the International Monetary Fund, former Director of the Central Statistical and Economics Department; Dr. Everett E. Hagen of the Center for International Studies at M.I.T., Chief Economist for Robert R. Nathan Associates in Burma from 1951 to 1953; Dr. John H. Adler of the International Bank for Reconstruction and Development; and Mr. Robert R. Nathan and Mr. A. J. Creshkoff of Robert R. Nathan Associates, the economic consultants to the Government of Burma from 1951 to 1959.

Dr. Antonin Basch of the University of Michigan and Mr. Edward Felder of the Agency for International Development reviewed Chapter 31; Dr. Richard Musgrave of Princeton University, who served as special tax consultant for Robert R. Nathan Associates in Burma on two short-term assignments in 1954 and 1958, reviewed Chapter 25; and Mr. Shigeharu Takahashi of the International Bank for Reconstruction and Development, agricultural economist on the Robert R. Nathan staff in Burma from 1952 to 1957, reviewed Chapter 16. I am grateful to all these gentlemen for their assistance.

I am especially indebted to Dr. Hagen, who read the entire manuscript and most generously cut into his own crowded work schedule to provide me with many helpful detailed and general comments; to Mr. Nathan, who provided me with office facilities and access to his organization's files; and to Mr. A. J. Creshkoff, who helped me locate various materials and prepare some of the statistical tables. Miss Jane Kemon, my secretary, provided unfailing patience, good cheer and research and editorial assistance, in addition to unusual competence and judgment.

I am indebted to many others, Westerners and Burmese alike, for help in filling gaps in my knowledge for the periods 1951–53 and February 1959 onward. Among these are: Dr. Frank Trager, Professor of International Relations, New York University, and onetime Chief of the T.C.A. Mission in Burma; Mr. Gerald McCarthy, partner in Tippetts-Abbett-McCarthy-Stratton (Formerly K.T.A.), consulting engineers; Col. Homer B. Pettit, onetime General Manager for K.T.A. in Burma; Messrs. John Alexander and Alfred Straus, who served with K.T.A. in Burma beginning in 1951; Messrs. Richard McCaffery and Walter Stoneman of the Agency for International Development; H.E. William P. Snow, H.E. Sir Richard Allen and H.E. E. Ben-Horin, who were respectively the United States, United Kingdom and Israeli Ambassadors to Burma as of early 1961; and many Burmese friends and civil servants to whom, though they shall be nameless here, I am no less indebted. I must, however, acknowledge with thanks the graciousness of the Hon'ble U Nu, the then Prime Minister, in making me his guest during my visit to Burma early in 1961, and the kindness of the Hon'ble U Raschid, the then Minister for Industries, Mines and Labor, in extending to me the facilities I required to bring this study up to date.

It may also be appropriate here to express my appreciation to my former colleagues of the Robert R. Nathan Associates field staff in Burma, whose names are listed in Appendix VII.

I am deeply grateful to the Twentieth Century Fund, which financed this study and made possible my visit to Burma early in 1961 to help complete it. I owe special thanks to Mr. August Heckscher, the Fund's Director, for his never-failing courtesy and consideration.

My wife, Dorothy Monie Walinsky, has enabled me to understand the full significance of the thanks so often expressed by authors to their wives in introductions to books like this. She has been a true partner in the writing of this book.

Lastly, I owe a tremendous debt to Burma, to her leaders and to the many civil servants who, throughout my period of service in Burma, shared with me their experience and insights and accorded me their confidence and friendship. Although this study is a highly critical one, I know they will recognize the sincere friendship and the desire to be of constructive help which motivate it.

LOUIS J. WALINSKY

Washington, D. C.

SOURCES AND USAGE

I have, for the most part, cited the sources for statistical data and other factual information. I have also drawn upon my personal diaries and files, the home office reports and correspondence, the Robert R. Nathan Associates files and my memory.

Certain of the repeatedly recurring source references are given in brief form in the chapters. These are spelled out below. The full names of government agencies that have been frequently designated by alphabetic symbols in the text are also given below. I have used, in tables and elsewhere, the Burmese measures — the crore, the lakh and the kyat. As will be seen from the list which follows, they are simply converted to more familiar measures, and the reader, I trust, will soon find them also familiar.

SOURCE REFERENCES

K.T.A. Preliminary Report

> *K.T.A. Preliminary Report on Economic and Engineering Survey of Burma for Burma Economic Council,* Knappen Tippetts Abbett Engineering Co. associated with Pierce Management, Inc. and Robert R. Nathan Associates, Inc., January 1952.

K.T.A. Comprehensive Report

> *K.T.A. Comprehensive Report, Economic and Engineering Development of Burma,* prepared for the Government of the Union of Burma by Knappen Tippetts Abbett McCarthy, Engineers, in association with Pierce Management, Inc. and Robert R. Nathan Associates, Inc., 2 vols., August 1953.

Economic Survey of Burma (various years)

> This is an annual survey, published by the Superintendent of Government Printing and Stationery of the Union of Burma, Rangoon.

BURMESE GOVERNMENT AGENCIES

A.R.D.C. Agricultural Resources Development Corporation (also later called, Agricultural and Rural Development Corporation and Land Resources Development Corporation — L.R.D.C.)

B.P.I. Burma Pharmaceutical Industry

C.D.C. Commerce Development Corporation

C.S.E.D. Central Statistical and Economics Department

C.S.M.B. Civil Supplies Management Board

E. and S.B. Economic and Social Board

E.S.B. Electricity Supply Board

I.D.C. Industrial Development Corporation

I.W.T.B. Inland Water Transport Board

M.N.P. Ministry of National Planning

M.R.D.C. Mineral Resources Development Corporation

N.H.B. National Housing Board

R.E.S.B. Rangoon Electricity Supply Board

S.A.M.B. State Agricultural Marketing Board

S.T.B. State Timber Board

COMMON BURMESE MEASURES

1 crore = 100 lakhs = 10 million
1 lakh = 100,000
1 kyat (written K 1) = 1 rupee = U. S. 21¢ = 1 shilling sixpence
K 1 lakh = $21,000 = £7,500
K 1 crore = $2.1 million = £750,000
$1 = K 4.76
£1 sterling = K 13.33 = $2.80
To convert (in the case of dollars, crudely):
From K crores to dollars, multiply by 2 million;
to £ sterling, multiply by ¾ million;
From dollars to kyats, multiply by 5;
From million dollars to K crores, divide by 2;
From £ sterling million to K crores, multiply by 1⅓.

The Burmese ton is the long ton of 2,240 pounds, except in the case of timber, in which round tons are used for logs, and cubic tons for processed timber.

CONTENTS

INTRODUCTION   *page* xxi

PART I BACKGROUND

Chapter 1 Geography and Basic Resources   3
         2 A Glimpse of the Pre-British Society and Economy 10
         3 British Rule   17
         4 Profile of the Economy Before World War II   31
         5 Independence and Economic Aspirations, Plans and
            Policies   56

PART II THE EIGHT-YEAR DEVELOPMENT
PROGRAM

Introduction to Part II   80

Chapter 6 The American Consultants and Their Preliminary
            Report   83
         7 The Pyidawtha Conference   96
         8 The K.T.A. Comprehensive Report: Economics, Policy
            and Administration   110
         9 The K.T.A. Comprehensive Report: The Sector Programs 134

PART III IMPLEMENTING THE PROGRAM IN A
CHANGING ECONOMIC SETTING—AN OVERVIEW

Chapter 10 The Fight for a Feasible Rate of Program Implementa-
            tion — 1953–54   153
        11 The Fight for Economic Stability: The Foreign Exchange
            Side — 1954–55   163
        12 The Fight for Economic Stability: The Domestic Inflation
            Side — 1955–56   185
        13 The Fight for Central Responsibility, Program Priorities
            and Better Performance — 1956–57   217

14 Political Split, Crisis and Change — 1957–58   237
15 Cleanup and Consolidation: The Military Regime —
    September 1958–March 1960   252

PART IV IMPLEMENTATION BY MAJOR SECTORS
AND PROJECTS

Chapter 16 Implementation of the Agriculture and Irrigation
            Program   269
        17 Implementation of the Program for State Manufacturing
            Industry   299
        18 Implementation of Other Public Sector Programs 318
        19 Implementation by the Private Sector   336
        20 Outcomes and Impact of the Development Program 352

PART V MAJOR PROBLEMS IN PROGRAM IMPLE-
MENTATION

Chapter 21 The Problem of Defects in the Basic Plan   371
        22 The Problem of Internal Security   382
        23 Problems of Cultural Adaptation   388
        24 Problems of Specialized Manpower   400
        25 Problems of Finance   409
        26 Problems of Annual Budgeting and Programing   432
        27 Problems of Management in the Public Enterprises 448
        28 Problems of Supervision and Coordination   465
        29 Problems of Public Administration   477
        30 Problems of Central Economic Policy   491
        31 Problems of Foreign Aid   507
        32 Problems of Technical Assistance   546

PART VI CONCLUSIONS AND APPRAISALS

Chapter 33 Significance of the Experience for Burma's Further Eco-
            nomic Development   565
        34 Significance of the Burma Experience for Economic
            Development in Other Countries   584
        35 Significance of the Burma Experience for U. S. and
            Western Aid Policy   605

APPENDICES   613
INDEX   663

APPENDICES

I Prime Minister's Report to the People on National Economy,
September 27, 1957   613

II "Our Goal and Our Interim Programme," Economic Policy
Statement, 1953   634

III Investment Policy Statement of the Council of Ministers,
June 8, 1955   647

IV Text of the Union of Burma Investment Act, 1959   650

V Membership of Important Working Economic Committees, as
of 1955–56   653

VI Agenda of the Economic and Social Board, 1955–56   655

VII Robert R. Nathan Associates Field Staff in Burma,
September 1951–February 1959   659

VIII Selected Economic Indicators in Burma, 1938–39 to 1959–60   660

ILLUSTRATIONS
(in back pocket)

Map of Burma

Map of Development Projects

Organization of the Central Government in July 1953

Diagram of the Eight-Year Development Plan

LIST OF TABLES

Selected Economic Indicators in Burma, 1938–39 to 1959–60   *page* 660

1   Distribution of Workers by Major Census Classification, 1931   33

2   Percentage Distribution by Race of Male Earners Grouped by Selected
Economic Functions, 1931   35

3   Income Data on Sample Basis, 1957   37

4   Urban Family Income, 1957   38

5   Agricultural Acreage and Production, 1936–37 to 1940–41 Average   41

6   Number of Factories and of Workers Employed, 1940   46

7   Foreign Trade Balance, 1901–41   49

8   Exports, 1938–39   49

9   Sea-Borne Export Trade with Principal Countries, 1938–39   50

10   Government Revenue and Expenditures, 1938–39   51

11   General Development Goals in 1950–51 Prices   112

12   Government and Private Capital Formation, 1953–54 to 1959–60   114

13   Governmental Receipts, by Source, Including Estimated Net Income of
Governmental Enterprises, 1938–39 and 1951–52   122

14   Requirements for New Skilled Manpower, by Type of Worker,
1953–59 (Cumulative)   130

15   K.T.A.-Planned Project Expenditures by Sector   135

16   K.T.A.-Planned Expenditures for Transportation and Communications   141

17   Foreign Exchange Transactions and Reserves, 1952–53 to 1959–60   165

18   Direction of Rice Exports, by Tonnage, 1954 through 1959–60   169

19   Direction of Rice Exports, by Value, 1954 through 1959–60   170

20   Proposed Imports in 1955–56, by Country and Economic Sector   188

21   Proposed Private Imports in 1955–56, by Commodity and Area of Origin   189

22   Proposed Private Imports from Barter Sources in 1955–56, by Commodity and Country of Origin   191

23   Import Program of the Civil Supplies Management Board, 1955–56   192

24   Consumer Price Index and Value of Imports, 1953–54, 1954–55 and
1955–56   198

25   Imports by Type of Commodity, 1953–54, 1954–55 and 1955–56   212

26   Imports by Major Category and Structure of Payments, 1953–54, 1954–55
and 1955–56   213

27   Consumer Price Index for a Worker's Family in Rangoon, 1953–54,
1954–55 and 1955–56   213

28   Interim Consumer Price Index for Low-Income Households in Rangoon
(Revised April 1958), Selected Components, 1953 through 1958–59   214

29   Consumer Price Indexes in Rangoon, 1941–60   *page* 215
30   Government Capital Expenditures, 1952–53 to 1955–56 and Estimates for 1956–57 to 1959–60 as Presented in February 1957 by the Ministry for National Planning   221
31   Public Capital Expenditures for Agriculture and Irrigation, 1952–53 to 1959–60   270
32   Capital Expenditures for Agriculture and Irrigation, by Major Program Component, 1952–53 to 1955–56   271
33   Government Loans to Agriculturists, 1952–53 to 1959–60   292
34   Land Nationalization and Redistribution, 1953–54 to 1957–58   293
35   Public Capital Outlays in the Industrial Sector, 1952–53 to 1959–60   300
36   Public Capital Outlays in the Industrial Sector, by Major Category, 1952–53 to 1959–60   301
37   Investment in Major State Manufacturing Plants (Exclusive of Working Capital), 1952–53 to 1959–60   302
38   Selected Financial Data for Government Manufacturing Enterprises   313
39   Current Operating Surplus or Deficit, Selected State Manufacturing Industries, 1957–58 to 1960–61   314
40   The Teak Production Cycle, 1953–54 to 1956–57   321
41   Growth of Power Capacity, Generation and Consumption, 1951–52, 1957–58 and 1959–60   328
42   Power Generation and Consumption in the Rangoon Electricity Supply Area, 1952, 1957–58 and 1959–60   329
43   Power Generation and Consumption in the Rest of Burma, 1951–52, 1957–58 and 1959–60   329
44   Agricultural Production, Pre-war, 1951–52 and 1959–60   339
45   Paddy Yields per Acre, 1936–41 and 1951–52 to 1959–60   339
46   Crude Petroleum Production, 1939 and 1951 to 1959–60   341
47   Production of Petroleum Products, 1951–52 to 1959–60   341
48   Production of Selected Minerals, 1939 and 1952 to 1959–60   341
49   Percentage Distribution of Public and Private Imports, 1954–55 to 1959–60   343
50   Estimated Industrial Production, Employment and Number of Establishments, by Type of Industry and Product, 1953–54 and 1956–57   344
51   Cottage Industry: Percentage Increase from 1953–54 to 1956–57 in Number of Establishments, Employment and Output, by Type of Product   346
52   Production and Employment in Manufacturing Establishments Employing Ten or More Persons, 1953 and 1957   347
53   Value of Manufacturing Output, by Product, 1953 and 1957   348
54   Growth of Private Industrial Production, 1953–57   348
55   Public Capital Expenditures by Economic Sector, 1952–53 to 1959–60   353
56   Percentage Distribution of Public Capital Expenditures by Economic Sector, 1952–53 to 1959–60   354
57   Gross Domestic Product in 1947–48 Prices, 1938–39 to 1959–60   355
58   Eight-Year Development Plan, Major Economic Targets and Achievements   357

59 Gross Capital Formation, Public and Private, 1949–50 to 1959–60 *page* 358
60 Gross and Net Capital Formation, 1949–50 to 1959–60 359
61 Programed and Actual Capital Formation, January 1952 to 1959–60 359
62 Public and Private Capital Formation, Programed and Actual, January 1952 to 1959–60 361
63 Gross Capital Formation as Per Cent of Gross Domestic Product, Programed and Actual, 1952–53 to 1959–60 361
64 The Use of Resources, Pre-war and 1950s, a Percentage Distribution 361
65 Comparison of Selected Program Goals and Achievements 362
66 Health Facilities and Personnel, 1938–39, 1952 and 1959–60 365
67 Enrollment in State Schools, 1952 to 1959–60 366
68 Number of State Schools, 1952 to 1959–60 366
69 Rice Production, Exports, Proceeds and Prices, Selected Data, 1952–53 to 1959–60 372
70 The Union Government Budget, 1952–53 to 1959–60 413
71 Comprehensive Budget of the Public Sector, 1952–53 to 1959–60 414
72 Cash Consolidated Budget of the Union Government and Its Effect on the Privately Held Money Supply, 1953–54 to 1959–60 416
73 Resources Available for Public Capital Expenditures, 1952–53 to 1959–60 417
74 Financing of Public Capital Expenditures, 1952–53 to 1959–60 419
75 Union Government Budgetary Receipts, 1952–53 to 1959–60 422
76 Current Income and Expenditures of Larger State-Owned Boards, 1956–57 426
77 The Union Government Budget, 1954–55 to 1959–60, Program and Actual 444
78 Comprehensive Budget of the Public Sector, 1954–55 to 1959–60, Program and Actual 445
79 Cash-Consolidated Budget of the Union Government and Its Effect on the Privately Held Money Supply, 1954–55 to 1959–60, Program and Actual 446
80 Selected Pay Scales in the Public Service, 1954 482
81 Chronological Highlights of the Foreign Aid Experience 508
82 Major Foreign Aid Agreements, 1951–60 510
83 Aid Commitments and Deliveries Through September 30, 1960 511
84 Chronology of U. S. Project Loan Agreements 529
85 Implementation of the $25 Million U. S. Development Loan: Status of Projects as of September 30, 1960 531
86 Burma's Credit Position with the U.S.S.R., 1955–56 to 1959–60 539
87 Sources of Foreign Specialists Assisting the Government as of September 1957 548
88 Foreign Specialists Assisting the Government as of September 1957, by Field of Activity 550
89 Government Agencies Utilizing Services of Foreign Specialists, as of September 1957 551

INTRODUCTION

This study in a sense completes a mission I undertook in Burma in September 1953 — a mission which was still incomplete when I left Burma in February 1959. During that time, as General Manager and Chief Economist of the field staff provided by Robert R. Nathan Associates, Inc., economic consultants to the Government of Burma, I served as chief economic advisor to the Government. The job of our field staff, with the advice, assistance and general supervision of the Robert R. Nathan home organization, was to help the Government in carrying out the comprehensive long-term economic and social development program which had just been completed with the assistance of the so-called K.T.A. combined engineering and economic planning team. (The Robert R. Nathan firm had been the economic arm of that combined team from 1951 to 1953, and I had participated in that effort as well, although on a part-time consulting basis.)

The job required our team to advise and assist the Government in periodic adaptations of the long-term development plan; in annual budgeting and fiscal, foreign exchange, capital investment, import and other programing; in formulating central economic policies; in measuring and evaluating program progress; in improving program implementation; and also to perform numerous staff functions, as in foreign exchange control operations and assistance in loan, joint venture and other negotiations; and, in general, to make ourselves as useful as possible. In performing these services, our relations with the Government, its leaders, its organizations and agencies and its officials were continuous and intimate. Our organizational attachments were to the Economic and Social Board and to the Ministry of National Planning, both of which, for most of the period, were headed by the Prime Minister. We were, in effect, part of the Prime Minister's Office, and participated — sometimes as advisors, sometimes as members, sometimes as staff — in every important central standing or *ad hoc* committee concerned with economic affairs, up to and including the Economic and Social Board itself. The agenda and papers for such meetings, when not initiated by our group, almost always included our advisory opinions and comments.

This study is, therefore, unusual in that it has been done, so to speak, from the inside. It has the advantages, but also the possible disadvantages, which derive from the fact that I was a participant — even a partisan — in the experience I have attempted in this study to describe and appraise objectively. But while I have tried to be objective, the reader is entitled to approach the work with some doubt as to my success on this score.

This raises also the question of motivations. Why did I undertake this work? Perhaps I should state first some possible motivations which were not involved. I did not write this book to describe or justify the roles which the Robert R. Nathan firm, my colleagues on the field staff, and I played. These roles would make an interesting story, but the telling of that story is not my purpose here. Our part in the experience does enter into the account, as it must, but to — I believe — a less than warranted degree. Nor was it my desire to "reveal all" in a "Now it can be told" account. Readers who hope to find the study spiced with personal tidbits and revelations will be disappointed. They will find here nothing which, I believe, the chief *dramatis personae* would object to as extraneous or inessential to a serious analysis and appraisal of Burma's economic development experience in the 1950s. This also applies to the very few citations I have made from key memoranda in my own files.

I undertook this work chiefly because it was a matter of personal necessity, but also because I thought that a case study of Burma's unique experience in the 1950s would make a useful contribution to the literature on economic development.

Our firm left Burma in February 1959, on the advent of General Ne Win's Caretaker Government, with its job not yet done. The political split and crisis of 1958 had made it impossible for the A.F.P.F.L. Government to rectify its economic policies, strengthen its public administration, improve its management of the public enterprises and, in general, more effectively implement its development program. Unfortunately the crisis had occurred just when the accumulated experience of the previous years gave promise that the Government would be more receptive to action along these necessary lines. (The Ne Win Government did carry out many such actions, but by then we were no longer there.) This accounts for the feeling of incompletion with which I left Burma. I wanted to think through the experience, attain as much perspective as I could, and derive from it whatever lessons might be useful to Burma in her further efforts to achieve economic development. Only thus, I felt, could I be truly finished with the job.

This was not, however, my sole motivation. I had had some exposure to problems of economic reconstruction and development elsewhere and, although I had not been able, during my service in Burma, to keep up with the rapidly growing literature to the extent I should have liked, I had a keen interest in this field. I hoped through this study to acquire — particularly by a consideration of how much of the Burmese experience was of a general, rather than a particular, significance — a better understanding of economic development problems in other countries, and of problems of United States and Western aid policy and practice.

These motivations explain the organization of the study. Since relatively few Americans know very much about Burma as it was before World War II, Part I of this book is devoted to background material — including information on geography and resources, the days of the kings, the British occupation, the structure of the economy just before World War II, and the economic aspirations which accompanied the independence struggle. This material rests on a few sources only and makes no pretense to authority. Part II deals with the formulation in the post-independence period of development plans and programs, culminating in the so-called Comprehensive Development Plan of 1953. Part III presents a chronological account of the changing emphases and central problems which concerned the policy-makers and planners from 1952 through 1960. Part IV is devoted to the implementation experience in the public and private sectors, and to the total outcomes and impact of the program. Part V analyzes the many problems — insecurity, manpower, finance, administration, etc. — which affected implementation in all fields. And Part VI, finally, considers the significance of the experience — for Burma, for other countries seeking economic development and for U. S. and Western aid policy and practice.

The book is a long one — perhaps too long. I thought, however, that a full documentation and illustration might be welcomed by two groups of readers — those interested in comparing the Burmese experience with others they know better, and those interested in having an ample basis for drawing their own conclusions. My own involvement in the experience gave especial weight to the latter of these considerations. It occurred to me also that many readers might not wish to wade through the entire book. I thought, therefore, that the several parts should each be full-bodied, so that selective reading might still do justice to that part of the experience with which it deals.

As I reflect on the job I have done, I am conscious that it may convey a distorted picture. I have been so intent upon seeking out and analyzing the weaknesses of Burma's effort that I have failed adequately to portray its many positive accomplishments. The net effect, I fear, despite the record presented in Chapter 20, may be to convey the impression that the entire effort was hopelessly botched, mismanaged and wasted. This was not the case. Much was accomplished. Progress was made. The essential failure of the effort was not that it accomplished nothing; it was that it could — and should — have accomplished so much more than it did. I have concentrated on the weaknesses and failings of the experience, not because I wished to misrepresent it, but because it was from them that the lessons I sought to learn were chiefly to be found. I hope my Burmese friends, when they read this book, will keep this in mind. I believe many of them will share the view of the former Minister who exhorted me, when I visited Burma early in 1961, to "Make your book really critical. Only in this way can you help."

I complete this study with the conviction that countries seeking economic development, and others interested in helping them achieve it, can learn much from Burma's experience. This conviction was bolstered, while I was engaged on the study, by such reading in the literature as I was able to do, by many discussions with friends and colleagues familiar with development problems in other underdeveloped countries, and by the reactions expressed by a number of young people from these countries. I had the opportunity to speak to these young people about economic development problems in Burma, in connection with their professional studies in this country, and they said to me, in effect, "This all sounds very much like our own problems, at home." The conviction derives even more, however, from the attempt I have made to probe through successive levels of causation from the surface down in order to get to the root causes which explain the shape and course of Burma's experience. These causes, I am sure, are common to most underdeveloped countries which have recently embarked, or are about to embark, upon major economic development efforts.

It is not strange that this should be so. What Burma has in common, in greater or lesser degree, with most underdeveloped countries extends far beyond the much-cited cycle of low income, low savings and low investment; the poor literacy and ill health; the shortages of skilled labor and technicians; the embryonic middle-class and limited entrepreneurial capacities; the tropical or semi-tropical climate unconducive to persistent effort; the economy geared to the use of barter in exchange transactions; and the primitive agricultural sector — all of which are commonly taken as bench marks of underdevelopment.

Burma also shares with the most significant of these underdeveloped countries — particularly with many in Asia and Africa — a colonial heritage; an independence achieved only after World War II; an electorate and leadership unschooled in the ways of democratic self-government; a tendency to equate colonialism with imperialism and capitalism and, hence, strong socialist tendencies and ideology; a strong animus toward foreign influence and position in their economies; an identification of industrialization with development and progress; a civil service and public administration weakened by independence and heavily burdened by new tasks; a desire for a position of neutrality in the international power struggle; and a number of debilitating illusions about the nature and difficulty of the development process.[1] In political terms, Burma also shared with many of these countries a one-party domination of the political scene, a leadership pledged to produce welfare and a

1. India and a few other countries may be exempt from some of this series.

political need to "deliver" it. Finally, Burma has, as do these other countries, a unique and complex set of traditional attitudes, values, behavior patterns and social relations which are, for the most part, not conducive but are even inimical to economic development. (Burma differs in her development problems from most of these countries chiefly in the abundance of her natural resources relative to population, in the considerable World War II damage she sustained, in the civil insurrection she has suffered since shortly after independence, and in her long-term prospects for a favorable balance of international payments.)

These and similar common factors act as built-in brakes on economic development in these countries and offset to a considerable degree the energizing fuels pumped into their development engines in the form of capital investment and technical know-how. While the importance of many of these built-in brakes is fully recognized, the significance of others is not. Among the latter, special attention needs to be given to the roles of ineffective and corrupt public administrations, inadequate civil service organizations and staff, poor management in the public enterprises, misdirected economic policies, lack of appreciation — even when animus is not present — of the contribution to development goals which private individuals and firms can make, impractical personnel and other requirements imposed on foreign investors, and, even more importantly, discrimination against resident alien and minority groups who frequently possess more capacity and initiative for economic activity than do indigenous populations. Also less than adequately appreciated are such factors as the contempt displayed for manual or dirty work, the exaggerated respect and deference paid to seniors, the extended family principle, and the many religious customs, taboos and values, especially those which abhor the taking of animal life and which emphasize giving rather than accumulation.

Reflection on Burma's experience has convinced me that problems of economic development would be eased enormously if some of the hard truths underlying the process were more generally understood in the underdeveloped countries. It would be extremely helpful if they could come to realize that development is not a simple, quick or easy process; that economic development can take place only as part of a broader social and cultural change; that independence does not automatically bring welfare in its wake; that planning, investment and technical assistance, in the absence of effective implementation, do not suffice; and that development cannot enable them, in the next five, ten or even twenty years, to modernize and transform their economies, much less to "catch up with the West." Within such a time span, they cannot even reduce, in absolute terms, the ever-widening gap between productivity and income which exists between the advanced and underdeveloped countries.[2]

2. If a country with an annual per capita income of $50, for example, could achieve a growth rate of 4 per cent per year in that income, this would amount initially to an income increase of only $2 per capita per year — as compared with the $20 per capita increase in annual income

It is equally important that the underdeveloped countries realize the need for realistic goals and approaches; for patient, persistent and unremitting determination and effort; for sacrifices of present consumption in favor of savings and investment; and for numerous structural and cultural accommodations in their societies and in their ways of life to clear the way for, and to stimulate and foster, the growth process. It is in fact essential that they realize at how high a price development comes. Only as this realization takes hold can their desires and determination to achieve development become truly significant.

But the lack of these awarenesses is itself one of the conditions of underdevelopment. And the communication of such understandings to the people and leaders of the underdeveloped countries is as difficult and challenging a problem as any the West has to solve in its efforts to assist the underdeveloped world. It is my hope that this study may make some contribution to these understandings.

LOUIS J. WALINSKY

Washington, D. C.
June 1961

POSTSCRIPT

In concluding my appraisal, in Chapter 33, of what Prime Minister U Nu's Pyidaungsu government had learned, and failed to learn, from the experience of the 1950s, I wrote, in May 1961: "Some of the important lessons of the past, it appeared, had been learned only too well; others appeared not to have been learned at all. The confidence of the citizenry had been severely shaken ... And a new failure might see a new, and this time more permanent, military take over, with unforeseeable consequences for the future of democratic government."

While this book is still at press, early in March 1962, this possibility has been realized. General Ne Win has once again seized control of the government. But whereas his earlier assumption of power in September 1958 observed, at least superficially, constitutional forms, and was pledged, as soon as fair and free elections could be held, to surrender power once again to a duly elected civilian government, the recent action was in open violation of the Constitution and clearly envisages a prolonged period of military rule.

---

which a Western country would achieve with only a 2 per cent increase in per capita income starting from a base of $1,000 per year, or the $40 per capita increase in annual income which the United States would achieve with the same 2 per cent increase in per capita income, starting from a base of some $2,000 per year. The only feasible near-term reduction in the "gap" then is in the rate of growth. Absolute reduction in the per capita income gap, within say a twenty-year time span, is not foreseeable at all.

Superficially, return of the military government would once again contribute to at least greater national unity, more decisive government and decision-making, improved law and order and social discipline, and more efficient operation of the public services and enterprises, although the realization of even these prospects will depend on the continued passive acceptance by the Burmese people (including the minority groups) of the new dispensation, and on the continued unity and integrity of the ruling military elite. More fundamentally, this unhappy *finis* to Burma's post-independence development effort within a framework of democratic consent should serve as one more dramatic warning to the newly emerged and emerging nations that are currently embarking on the quest for development. It is a warning that the lack of realism and clarity in development goals, ineffective and irresponsible leadership, confused policies and poor administration and implementation, all aggravated by the lack of political accountability in a one-party government, will endanger not only the success of their development efforts, but the very existence of democratic government as well.

Louis J. Walinsky
March 6, 1962

Part I

BACKGROUND

CHAPTER 1

Geography and Basic Resources

GEOGRAPHY[1]

Shaped roughly like a diamond kite some 500 miles across and 800 miles from north to south, and with the long, narrow Tenasserim coastal strip extending like the kite's tail another 500 miles down the Malay Peninsula, Burma sits on the Bay of Bengal and the Andaman Sea, bounded on the land side by East Pakistan, India, China, Laos and Thailand. Her 20 million people occupy an area of 262,000 square miles, about that of Texas, a little larger than that of France and nearly double that of Japan. Lying between 10 and 28 degrees north latitude, about two thirds of the country is in the Tropical Zone, one third in the Temperate Zone. The land boundaries are for the most part mountainous and extremely difficult of passage. The water boundaries on the south form a deep recess between the Indian sub-continent to the west and the Malay Peninsula and the East Indies to the east and southeast. Sea routes connecting these areas bypassed Burma in earlier centuries. These geographic features have contributed greatly to Burma's historic isolation from the world.

The Tibetan mountain ranges, which set off the land barriers of the country as a whole, carry through to a series of lesser hills within the country. The Arakan Yomas separate the Arakan coastal strip from the rest of the country, and the Pegu Yomas divide the lower central plain. The highland plateau of the Shan Hills sets the east central region apart. Surrounding all of these is the horseshoe of hills which mark the land frontiers. This varied topography is linked with distinctive climatic and other features in several areas. The major divisions are the Lower Delta, where rainfall averages about

---

1. Except where other sources are cited, this chapter relies for the most part on the K.T.A. Comprehensive Report.

100 inches a year; Central Burma, the Dry Zone, where rainfall is something less than 40 inches a year; Northern Burma, where rainfall is like that in the Lower Delta; the Shan Plateau in the east central area, with rainfall of about 60 inches a year; and the Arakan and Tenasserim coastal strips in the southwest and extreme southeast respectively, where the average annual rainfall reaches 200 inches.

Burma has three main seasons: the monsoon or rainy season, lasting for about six months from mid-May to mid-October; the "cold" season, lasting from about mid-November to some time in February; and the hot season, which follows and lasts until the onset of the rains. A minor transitional season of extremely humid weather follows the rains and lasts about a month. This general climatic pattern varies considerably from area to area, depending upon the configuration of the land and the intensity of the monsoon. In the valleys and the Delta, the temperature rarely falls below 60 degrees (Fahrenheit) during the "cold" season — and then only at night. Daytime temperatures range from 80 to 90 degrees. In the rainy season the temperatures are mostly in the upper eighties and lower nineties, and the air is extremely humid. Hot-season temperatures are not frequently below 90 degrees, and often exceed 100 degrees. On the Shan Plateau and in the hills, temperatures are lower, and in the cold season frost forms at night.

When the Burmese first arrived on the scene in the ninth century, reportedly from the Tibetan area, they settled in the Dry Zone. The Lower Delta in those days was for the most part jungle and swampland inhabited by the Mons as the Kingdom of Pegu. The Arakanese, with a considerable admixture of Indian blood, occupied the Kingdom of Arakan. The Mons extended from Pegu down into the Tenasserim. The Shans, essentially a Siamese people, overran the country in the thirteenth century. They were thrown back onto the plateau only in the early part of the sixteenth century, after which they lived there in relative isolation, paying annual tribute to the Burmese kings.

In the middle of the eighteenth century the Burmese conquered the Mon Kingdom of Pegu, laying waste to and depopulating the country. They annexed Arakan only as recently as 1785. Indeed, it was not until this venture into the southwestern part of the present Union of Burma that they made their first noteworthy contacts with the British in India. Out of this contact arose the irritations which led some years later to the beginnings of the English occupation. Bordering what the English called "Divisional Burma" or "Burma Proper" in the northern frontier hills are found the Chins, the Kachins and the primitive Naga and Wa tribesmen. Cutting across some of the areas in Burma Proper are the Karens, who live in three major groups in the Lower Delta, on the Delta-Tenasserim border and in the Southern Shan States. A diversity of peoples and of language, culture and customs has thus matched Burma's topographic and climatic differences. The Union of Burma of today is a union of diverse areas, peoples and ways of living.

NATURAL RESOURCES

Burma is rich in agricultural, fishery, timber, mineral and water resources. Of these, the most important are the agricultural resources. Burma has never had a food problem.

Of Burma's total land area of 163.3 million acres, 41 million acres are general crop land; 15 million, paddy land; 34 million, grazing land; and 70 million, forest land. Approximately 23 per cent of the land resources were found to be in use in a land-use survey made in 1956.[2]

The most important single crop is rice, for the production of which Burma has great natural advantages. Burma, especially the Lower Delta, is a great rice bowl; before World War II, her rice exports exceeded 3 million tons per year. Though current exports are only some two thirds of pre-war, Burma is still the world's largest exporter of this important food grain. Other food crops, in approximate order of importance, are groundnuts (peanuts), sesamum, sugar cane, beans and other pulses, onions, millet, chilli, maize, potatoes and wheat. Tea and coffee are grown. Fruits — limes, mangoes, papayas, bananas, jackfruit, mangosteens, durians and many others — are abundant, and are found in most areas. Cattle, water buffaloes, horses, sheep, goats, pigs, geese and chickens are the chief livestock[3] and poultry raised. Among the non-food crops tobacco, rubber and cotton are the most important.

Apart from rice, which, though concentrated in the Lower Delta, is the major crop throughout the country, the most important items of agricultural production in the various regions are groundnuts, pulses, sesamum, millet and cotton in the Dry Zone; rubber in the Tenasserim; and livestock, wheat, potatoes, fruits and tea in the Shan States.

Fishing is carried on for the most part in the coastal areas of the Arakan, the Lower Delta and the Tenasserim, and ranks as an important industry in those areas. Bectie, the best-known local fish, is delicious eating. A considerable amount of river and lake fishing is also carried on. Abundant supplies of deep-sea fish are available at offshore fishing banks, but these have not been adequately exploited by the Burmese, who have yet to develop a widespread taste for deep-sea fish.

The best-known timber resource is teak. Before the war, Burma exported annually some 200,000 sawn tons of this unique hardwood, harvested on a

2. *Report of the Land and Agricultural Planning Commission,* Rangoon, 1956.

3. Cattle and oxen are used mostly as draft animals. Post-war prohibitions against cattle slaughter outside the Shan States were maintained till early in 1959, owing chiefly to the need to restore the depleted stock of draft animals and to Buddhist abhorrence of slaughter, and beef was not generally available in the rest of Burma. General Ne Win revoked the ban in 1959 but it was reinstated by U Nu when he resumed office in 1960.

sustained-yield basis. Valuable though less well-known hardwoods of other kinds abound and have widespread domestic uses. Their total output, in fact, substantially exceeds that of teak. Bamboo is also abundant, and forest items such as cutch, lac and various kinds of resins and gums are important products.

Minerals are a significant component of the resource picture. Central Burma has substantial reserves of petroleum. The Northern Shan States are the home of the famous Bawdwin Mines, which have produced large quantities of lead, zinc, silver and other concentrates. The Mawchi Mines in the Kayah (former Karenni) State have long been famous for their tin and tungsten, which are also mined in quantity in the Tenasserim area. Substantial reserves of sub-bituminous coal exist at Kalewa in the Chindwin area of northwestern Burma, and coal deposits have been located in other areas as well. Burma is famous for its rubies, sapphires and jade. Building stone and road metals, salt and natural gas are produced in quantity. Iron, copper, antimony and other ores have been found.

The major rivers are the Irrawaddy, the Salween and the Sittang. All three run roughly from north to south. Together with their tributaries and other river systems, they make possible low-cost north-south water transport and provide ample sources for hydroelectric power. They present at the same time major obstacles to east-west communications. The Irrawaddy-Chindwin River System provides the chief means of inland water transport, affording some 1,500 miles of waterways commercially navigable throughout the year.

POPULATION AND POPULATION CHARACTERISTICS

From approximately 4 million in 1824,[4] Burma's population has grown to about 20 million at the present time. The population density of about 75 per square mile creates no strain on her natural resources, and with her moderate population increase of perhaps 1.5 per cent per year, population pressure does not threaten to create a strain on available resources in the foreseeable future.

The racial composition of the present population cannot precisely be established. The last complete census, taken in 1931, enumerated language groups rather than races. Most of the details of the 1941 census were lost during the Japanese invasion. Sample censuses taken in 1953, 1954 and 1957 did include a racial distribution, but again on the basis of the language spoken. The 1931 census, in which the total population count was approximately 14.7 million, showed less than 9.9 million, or approximately two thirds of the total, as speaking Burmese; close to 3.5 million, almost one quarter of the total, as speaking other indigenous languages;[5] over one million, more than 7 per cent, as

4. G. E. Harvey, *British Rule in Burma, 1824–1942,* Faber and Faber, London, 1946, p. 14.

5. The non-Burmese-speaking indigenous group comprised approximately 1.3 million Karens, 1 million Shans, 344,000 Chins, 305,000 Mons, 176,000 Palaung-Was, 154,000 Kachins and 145,000 "all other" indigenous language groups.

speaking Indian languages; and about 178,000, or 1.2 per cent, as speaking Chinese. The most recent census data indicate that of an estimated 20 million total population, some 17 million, or 85 per cent, were Burmese by the language test; a little over 2 million, some 10 or 11 per cent, were other indigenous peoples — Karens, Shans, Chins, Kachins, and so on; approximately 700,000, or 3.5 per cent, were Indians and Pakistanis; approximately 250,000, or 1.25 per cent, were Chinese; and other races were negligible.

Differences in fertility rates and in health conditions, as between the Burmese-speaking and the non-Burmese-speaking indigenous peoples, may account in part for the greater relative size of the Burmese group in the data of the 1950s than in the 1931 data. The larger part of the change in proportions, however, is undoubtedly due to cultural assimilation and to the fact that the sample rural censuses of 1953 and 1954 were taken, for security reasons, in those villages lying closest to the towns, where the proportion of non-Burmese-speaking indigenous peoples is probably somewhat smaller than it is elsewhere. The decline shown in the Indian-speaking population, in absolute as well as in relative terms, may also reflect in part a degree of cultural assimilation. But the permanent departure of many Indians during and since World War II and their lower birth rate (an unusually high percentage of this population has historically been comprised of unmarried males) suggests that there has been a decline of significant magnitude in this population.

The Indians, Pakistanis and Chinese are heavily concentrated in urban areas. As a result, while Burmese-speaking people constitute roughly three quarters of the urban population, they constitute roughly seven eighths of the population outside the towns.

In 1957, some 3,267,000 persons, or about 16 per cent of the total non-institutional population, lived in the 252 towns listed by the census. The heaviest concentrations of population are naturally found in the Irrawaddy basin and the Lower Delta, the lightest in the Tenasserim, the Shan States and the frontier hill regions.

By common agreement of foreign observers,[6] the Burmans are a laughter-loving, generous, charming and hospitable people. They also impress foreigners with their inherent dignity and courtesy, their tolerance, their improvidence, their love of games, gambling and finery, and their quick-tempered capacity for sudden violence.

The geographic and climatic factors which have made agriculture and, within that agriculture, rice cultivation the central feature of Burmese economic life have affected also the work patterns and characteristics of the

6. See, for example, W. J. Grant, *The New Burma*, George Allen and Unwin Ltd. London, 1942; C. J. Richards, *The Burman, An Appreciation*, Burma Pamphlets No. 7, Longmans, Green & Co., Ltd., Calcutta, 1945; G. E. Harvey, *British Rule in Burma 1824–1942*, Faber and Faber, London, 1946; J. Russell Andrus, *Burmese Economic Life*, Oxford University Press, London, 1948; John F. Cady, *A History of Modern Burma*, Cornell University Press, Ithaca, 1958.

people. The agricultural cycle intermittently requires periods of intensive work and permits periods of relative ease and leisure. This pattern seems to have permeated deeply the culture, working habits and attitudes of the people. Closely related to this is the fact that throughout Burma minimum levels of living can be achieved without sustained hard work. Not only can harvests, fish and fruit be obtained with relative ease, but the climate, at the same time that it frequently deters hard work, permits essential clothing and shelter requirements to be satisfied with even greater ease. The village Burman can obtain the minimum protection he requires from the weather by building a hut of bamboo and thatch to be had from the forests almost for the asking, by the expenditure of a few days' labor time.[7] His minimum clothing needs can be satisfied with ten yards or less of cotton cloth per year. Thus nature has imposed little compulsion upon the Burman to work hard. Nor does his Buddhist religion provide him with a philosophy of life that ranks the accumulation of wordly goods high in his scale of values.

If the Burman is inclined to be indolent because of the climate, nature's bounty, his relatively few requirements and his scheme of values, this tendency seems also to have been fostered historically by his use of defeated peoples as slaves, and more recently by his dependence during the British days on immigrant Indian coolie labor for the performance of hard and menial tasks, in both town and countryside.

The Burman is willing, cheerful and cooperative when he works. He displays a manual dexterity and a talent — even an inventiveness — in handling mechanical things. But he tends to shy from fixed routine; and his culture has not impressed him with the importance of maintenance, perhaps because so much of what he has had and dealt with has been of a perishable or, at most, semi-durable nature. He tends to be satisfied with the makeshift, however temporary it may be. In the case of a machine or automobile in which a part has become defective, he will tend to improvise cleverly a temporary expedient to overcome the difficulty, but not concern himself particularly about the replacement necessary to ensure continued performance.

Although rudimentary education and literacy have always been widespread due to teaching in the monasteries, the level of education is low. An increasing number of boys and girls attend the state primary schools, but the percentage completing primary school is small, and the percentages entering and completing the middle and high schools and the colleges are progressively smaller. Despite recent progress, the number of Burmans with professional or technical education is still extremely small. Under the British colonial regime, most of the important posts, both in Government service and in the private sector,

---

7. Even in Rangoon, a one-family basha (bamboo and thatch) hut could be provided commercially in the 1950s for 250–350 kyats, or, say, two to three months' wages for a semi-skilled worker.

were held either by the British or by Indians. The lack of education and experience in these skills represents a serious lack so far as economic development is concerned.

The health of the population is fairly good compared to the general level existing in, say, India. The low average life expectancy of not much more than thirty years which prevailed till recently was due chiefly to a very high rate of infant mortality.[8] The life expectancy of infants who reach the age of one year is thus much higher than the average life expectancy. Despite the abundance of food, there is considerable malnutrition due chiefly to a diet lacking in vitamins, proteins and calcium. Malaria, dysentery, tuberculosis and venereal diseases have been the chief health scourges, and leprosy has also been pronounced. Considerable progress has, however, been made in recent years in reducing these health hazards.

The Indians, Pakistanis and Chinese are important elements in the population resource pattern. They contribute know-how and experience in trade, commerce, industry, the professions and the handicrafts. More important perhaps than this, they display drives to achieve success in these fields — possibly because it is only in this way that they can hope to attain social status[9] — which make them the more dynamic element in the private sector of the economy.

The status of women in Burmese society is unusually free, and this extends to the economic sphere. Many of the most able of the Burmese traders, shopkeepers and salespeople are women. Women are entering increasingly into the legal and medical professions. Even when they are not engaged in commercial activities outside the home, Burmese women exert a strong though not ostentatious influence on the economic decisions of their husbands, who almost invariably take counsel with them and generally follow their advice.

8. On the basis of incomplete census figures, infant mortality declined from 350 per 1,000 live births in 1949 to 170 per 1,000 in 1956. *1957 Sample Census, Population, Housing and Cottage Industry*, C.S.E.D., Rangoon, 1958, p. 64.

9. I am indebted to Professor Hagen of M.I.T. for this concept, which is discussed in Chapter 34.

CHAPTER 2

A Glimpse of the Pre-British

Society and Economy

THE MONARCHY[1]

Up to the early years of the nineteenth century, immediately prior to the first step in the British annexation of the country, Burma was an absolute monarchy, and the structure of her village-based agricultural society was essentially feudal.

The authority of the king was not based, as had been the case in Western Europe, on any theory of divine right, but rather on his occupancy of the royal palace, which was conceived to be the very center of the universe; on his role as supreme protector and promoter of the Buddhist faith; and on the magical ceremonies and regalia which created about the monarch an aura of divinity. Brahman priests, numerologists and astrologers selected auspicious dates and locations for the palace and capital city, which were moved repeatedly. The fundamental Buddhist tenet of Karma, which held that the deeds performed in previous existences determined one's present status, provided a basic religious prop to occupancy of the throne. This prop was all the stronger when the monarch displayed piety and modesty, when he patronized the Buddhist clergy and shrines, and when he built great pagodas. The mystic

1. My chief source for this chapter has been John F. Cady's excellent *A History of Modern Burma* (Cornell University Press, Ithaca, 1958), Part I. I have also used: G. E. Harvey, *British Rule in Burma 1824–1942* (Faber and Faber, London, 1946); D. G. E. Hall, *Michael Symes, Journal of his Second Embassy to the Court of Ava in 1802* (George Allen & Unwin Ltd., London, 1955); J. Russell Andrus, *Burmese Economic Life* (Stanford University Press, Stanford, 1957); and Everett E. Hagen, *The Economic Development of Burma* (N.P.A. Planning Pamphlets No. 96, 1956). Anyone wishing to go more deeply into this period should study J. S. Furnivall's *An Introduction to the Political Economy of Burma* (Peoples' Literature Committee & House, Rangoon, 1957) and *Colonial Policy & Practice* (Cambridge University Press, Cambridge, 1957).

white elephant and the white umbrella were key symbols of his status and authority.

The king in theory was absolute master over the lives, the property and the services of all his people. This theory underlay much of the structure and functioning of the entire society. The king was expected at the same time, however, to be moderate, wise, truthful, just and considerate. Custom required that learned Brahman priests be maintained at court not only to advise the king on ceremony, regalia, administration and public relations, but also to instruct him in personal modesty. Succession to the throne was within the royal family, but did not automatically go to the eldest son. The king could designate any one of his numerous sons (by a number of wives) or brothers, or any of his near relatives, as his successor. Such designation was frequently an invitation to assassination, and succession to the throne was a constant problem. Nor was succession held to oblige the new king to fulfill treaty obligations undertaken by his predecessor.

GOVERNMENT

Royalty was hereditary, but the Burmese nobility was not. It was based rather on royal appointment and service to the king.

The central administration was vested in a small group of Wungyis, or ministers, whose council was called the Hlutdaw. This council acted on all matters of state, whether legislative, executive or judicial, subject to the king's approval. Royal edicts were issued in its name. Each Wungyi was assisted by a Wundauk, who appears to have functioned as something less than a deputy and something more than a secretary.

Provincial governors — known as Myowuns — represented the king and the Hlutdaw in the several provinces, having both military and civil jurisdiction. They exercised the police, the judicial and the tax authorities. Local officials operated under and subject to their review.

At the next lower governmental level came the hereditary township chiefs — the Myothugyis — who were the bridge between the monarchy and the people. Each township consisted of a circle of villages, and constituted a kind of service regiment under the Myothugyi. Military or non-military services were rendered in lieu of taxes. This pattern was the dominant one in the Kingdom of Burma (Upper Burma). In Lower Burma, the former Kingdom of Pegu, where there were large Mon, Karen and migrant populations, many of the communities were non-service in character, and paid taxes instead. In these cases, the pattern of administrative authority became territorial rather than regimental. Service or Ahmudan population, however, owed their allegiance and their service to their own Myothugyi, even if they migrated to other areas. The Myothugyi recruited and assigned services, led his military or non-military service regiment, maintained law and order, dispensed justice, and was the key figure in the social life and relations of his group. Since communications were difficult, local communities were relatively isolated, and the village circle lived very much a life of its own.

The feudal relations which permeated the society, and which inculcated a profound sense of respect for superiors, were embodied in an elaborate and fixed set of sumptuary conventions. Each family's status governed the kind of house its members could live in, the clothing or finery they might wear, the size and lavishness of the shinpyu[2] and ear-boring ceremonies they might hold for their children, the number of servants or retainers they might engage, the caparison of their animals, and so on. Furnivall says that "even the funeral ceremonies and types of coffin were similarly regulated."[3] Myothugyis, for example, were entitled to occupy a house of some size and style, be accompanied on tour by ten to fifteen armed retainers, caparison their horses or oxcarts, and use silver utensils and red umbrellas. These sumptuary conventions, rigidly enforced, obviously affected attitudes toward the acquisition and accumulation of wealth.

RELIGION

Buddhism supplemented the unifying role of the feudal structure in the society. Except for the frontier hill peoples and the Karens, most of whom also were animists before the advent of the missionaries, all Burma's people — Mons and Arakanese as well as Burmans — were Buddhists. Every Buddhist boy undertook a novitiate in the clergy for some weeks at least, during which time, with shaven head, he wore the saffron robe, carried his begging bowl and fasted daily from noon till dawn. Even the child's parents prostrated themselves before him when he first donned monk's attire at the shinpyu initiation ceremony. Though access to some lower levels of the monkhood was easy, and though idlers and sometimes criminals sought such refuge, misbehavior in those wearing the robe was frowned upon and strictly controlled by the monastic order or Sangha, by disrobing if need be. The order was headed by a primate designated by the king, assisted by a commission. Though non-political in nature, the order exerted tremendous influence because of the reverence in which monks were held. Piety, self-denial, generosity, tolerance and gentleness were the way of life they propagated. There were, however, many critical junctures in Burmese history when monks intervened in temporal affairs, always enlisting a large measure of popular support.[4] Religious functions pertaining to government were performed, oddly, not by Buddhist monks, but by Brahman priests from India.

But Buddhism had been acquired by the Burmans only some centuries after

2. The ceremony which attends initiation into monkhood.
3. J. S. Furnivall, Foreword to Andrus, *op. cit.*
4. Cady (*op. cit.,* pp. 52–53) cites a number of such instances.

they came to Burma. It was superimposed on an animistic faith which peopled the mountains, the forests and particular localities with a variety of spirits called nats and which relied on magical arts and incantations. People could be buried alive underneath city gates or palace walls, so that their spirits would forever stand on guard. Tattooing was relied upon to ward off arrows, or bullets or snakebite. The old animist beliefs were never far below the surface of the people's Buddhist practices, and sometimes shone through like copper beneath a worn silver plating.[5]

MINORITY GROUPS

The Shans, the Karens, the Kachins, the Chins, the Arakanese and the Mons — each a distinct racial, cultural and language group — had all within fairly recent history been defeated or subjugated, or both, by the dominant Burmese group. Arakanese and Mons in particular, after much back-and-forth fighting with the Burmans, had finally been defeated during the latter half of the eighteenth century. Many were slaughtered, driven off or taken into slavery, and their villages razed to revert to jungle. The Chins were cowed, the Shans placed in vassalage and the Karens persecuted. Only the hardy Kachins, marauding into the valleys from their mountain retreats, maintained a degree of independence. The history of these minority peoples and their frequently unhappy relations with the Burmese is woven into the social fabric of contemporary Burma.

TRADE

Transportation was by river boat and by oxcart. Trade was dominantly local. Apart from local fairs and bazaars, trade was largely by caravan, overland with southern China and riverine with Lower Burma. Chinese caravans brought gold leaf, paper, raw silk and floss, satins, velvets, cordage, arsenic, tea, spirits, honey, dried fruits, walnuts and preserves. The caravans carried back seeded raw cotton, amber, ivory, precious stones, betel nuts, edible birds' nests and drugs. For many years also, the Chinese mined silver at the famous Bawdwin Mines near Namtu.

From Lower Burma by cargo boat came rice, fish paste, dried fish, salt and a few European-manufactured wares. Downstream traffic comprised sugar, cooking oils, cotton and some petroleum from the primitive oil wells at Yenangyaung.

While the trade of the Kingdom of Burma was chiefly with Lower Burma and with China, and to some extent with the Shans, sea trade with the outside world was conducted by the Arakanese and the Mons in Lower and Coastal Burma. From England came textiles, hardware and glassware; from

5. H. Fielding Hall's *The Soul of a People* (Macmillan and Co., Ltd., London, 1913) is the classic study of Buddhist beliefs and practices in Burma.

India, yarn and cotton cloth. Arab ships brought woolen goods, velvets and opium. Spices and porcelains came from the East Indies and China. The outgoing trade consisted of silver, rubies, timber, beeswax, forest products, precious stones, ivory, tin, lead, copper and sugar. Significantly, the export of rice from Lower Burma was prohibited before the British occupation.

REVENUES

The basic tax was a household tax paid by the non-service personnel throughout the countryside to the king's officials. Theoretically this tax was in lieu of the services owed by everyone to the king. But in practice it was apportioned roughly on the basis of ability to pay and amounted to 10 to 15 per cent of the annual crop. Usually the governors collected more than the normal levies, and forwarded perhaps 60 to 80 per cent of their authorized collections to the royal treasury. The making of presents to officials at every level in order to sue for favor or consideration constituted an informal tax system complementary to the formal one. In addition, a heavy flat-rate capitation tax was imposed on backward and migrant peoples and others not assimilated into the regular system of government. This tax was considered a mark of subjection as well as of discrimination.

The king had title to all ivory and to the output of all silver, amber, ruby and sapphire mines. The Shan vassal princes paid him annual tribute in silver and horses. The king claimed the proceeds of the 10 per cent tariff on imports and a 5 per cent levy on exports. Duties imposed on up-river traffic also accrued to the royal treasury. Wealthy merchants were required to pay periodic extortion in the form of presents to the king at festival times.

Other minor royal taxes were levied on fruit trees, fishing and timber operations, brokerage, ferries, landing stages and court fees and fines. Rights to a sizable portion of the king's revenues had been granted, over the years, to relatives, ministers and other high officials. These Myosa — royal "eaters of towns" — were frequently entitled to the revenues of whole townships or districts.

VILLAGE LIFE[6]

While the typical Burmese village was devoted to agricultural pursuits, there were many villages whose primary occupation was logging, fishing or mining. Villages were enclosed for security purposes within a stockade which embraced not only the bamboo-and-thatch huts, but also a monastery, pagodas, a well or wells, water tanks, a threshing floor, a recreation space and perhaps a rest house for travelers. A family's dwelling place was always within

---

6. The description of village life rests almost entirely on J. S. Furnivall, *An Introduction to the Political Economy of Burma*, Peoples' Literature Committee & House, Rangoon, 1957 (3rd ed.), Chapter 3.

the village enclosure rather than on the adjacent cultivated land. Family-size farms were the rule. Land tenure was secure, and the sale of land was virtually unknown. In fact, the very concept of sale was strange. Land could be mortgaged. The lender might have the use of it during the life of the loan, but he could not foreclose the mortgage and become its owner. In the rare cases in which land was sold, it was established that the family of the seller could always buy it back, for the same price. It was also established that the total amount of interest paid on a loan could not exceed the original principal.

In addition to their agriculture or other basic pursuit, villages tended to become specialized in a handicraft. While almost every household contained a loom for the weaving of cloth, each village tended to specialize in the manufacture of some other product as well, whether paper, lacquer ware, footwear, umbrellas, fishing nets, harnesses, mats, pottery, or any one of a number of other articles in common use. These provided a basis for trade with other villages in the area.

Village life was a cooperative life in many ways. The people of each village circle owed joint services through their Myothugyi, or headman. In individual villages, the men took turns standing watch at the village gates and shared fire and police duties. A complex set of customs governed the use of communal facilities such as the threshing floor and the water supply. Other conventions governed the settlement and use of vacant land within the village. Occupation and use over a period of time were equivalent to ownership. All the male children attended the kyaung, or monastery school, where they learned to read, write and reckon, and were taught the basic tenets of their faith.

In the village as well as in the town, women had from the earliest times enjoyed a status virtually equal to that of the men. Marriage was by mutual consent and was performed by a simple civil ceremony in the presence of elders. Women enjoyed separate property rights and rights of inheritance. They were free to engage in trade and other activities. Divorce could be simply effected by declaration and registration with the village-circle headman.

Work in the fields was seasonal. It called for intensive labor during the plowing, transplanting, harvesting and threshing, but also provided periods of relative ease. There was ample time for communal celebrations like the annual Water Festival, which came at the end of the hot season, before the rains, and the Festival of Lights, which followed them at the end of Buddhist Lent, before the onset of cold weather. The home handicrafts, petty trade and gossip provided welcome diversions within this leisurely pattern, as did the occasional traveling show, or pwe, the ceremonies which marked the initiation of each boy into monkhood and the ear-boring ceremony held in due course for every girl. Traveling fairs or bazaars, which in many areas were held at five-day intervals, provided opportunities for exchange and trade among neighboring villages. Every full moon was the occasion of some sort of festival. The periodic visits on tour of the Myothugyi, of the tax collector or even occasionally of provincial officials, with their entourages, were important events in the normally placid village life. Excitement was introduced when the men were called up to suppress dacoit bands in the neighborhood, to fight floods or fires, or to go off to war. But every day the monk and his novices came in saffron-robed procession with their begging bowls to be filled with rice, and always there was the tinkling of pagoda bells in the distance.

CHAPTER 3

British Rule

THE BRITISH ANNEXATIONS

The British annexed Burma in three bites over a period of some sixty years, from 1824 to 1885. The first bite, coming at the end of the War of 1824-26, resulted in the annexation of the Arakan and the Tenasserim coastal strips. The second, in 1852, took Lower Burma, the former Kingdom of Pegu. The third, in 1885, engulfed Upper Burma.

In each case the British action was taken in consequence of an incident or incidents considered provocative. Thus the action in 1824 followed on a number of incidents in which Burmese soldiers crossed the Arakanese border into British India in pursuit of Arakanese rebels seeking refuge there. The 1852 action was triggered by the imposition of a heavy and perhaps arbitrary fine by the Myowun in Rangoon on the captain of a British ship for alleged violation of port rules. The action in 1885 was taken pursuant to the imposition of a heavy fine on the Bombay-Burmah Trading Company in which an arbitrary court procedure was used to enforce the payment of a large "loan" demanded by King Thibaw.

The underlying motives for these actions went much deeper. In 1824 the basic reason seems to have been that, with the conquest of the Arakan, the Burmese had become neighbors to a Western sovereignty and culture with which they simply could not, within their own conventions, communicate. Thus, says Harvey,

. . . now there were no fewer than 50,000 terror-stricken folk from Arakan alone seeking refuge in our territory, with Burman commanders in pursuit ordering English officers not only to surrender the fugitives but also to tell the viceroy of India he'd better hurry up and pay homage to the king of Burma or it would be worse for him.

The viceroy sent envoys to Burma, hoping to arrange a *modus vivendi,* six envoys, over a series of years. He never received even a reply. The envoys were lodged on a scavengers' island and often they returned without having been granted an audience. The king of Burma could not receive ambassadors from a mere viceroy: he must have them from the king of England himself.[1]

On this point Harvey footnotes wryly: ". . . he did not know where England was, he had no ship in which to send a return embassy."

Affirming that the British motivations in the several annexations were not even economic, Harvey emphasizes that the 1852 action was severely criticized in England, and that the 1885 action was motivated by a desire "to keep out the French," while at the same time "Humanitarians in England desired the downfall of Thibaw's bloodthirsty regime."[2]

These explanations seem too simple. Surely the rapid growth of population, of rice acreage and of rice exports in the Arakan and Tenasserim areas, and the lucrative exploitation of teak in the Tenasserim as well, inspired British commercial interests in the period 1826–52 with a lively interest in the economic potential of Lower Burma, which promised also to be a feasible avenue toward the development of trade with China through Yunan. Again, the rapid development of Lower Burma after the annexation in 1852 made almost inevitable the extension of British hegemony to the remainder of Burma.

ECONOMIC DEVELOPMENT

The experience in British Burma — from 1825 in the Arakan and the Tenasserim and from 1852 in the Lower Delta, right up to the annexation of Upper Burma — followed the same general pattern. Previous restrictions imposed by the Kingdom of Burma on rice exports[3] were abolished. Rice acreage, production and exports grew apace. Populations in these areas, reduced in previous decades by wars, slaughter and flight to adjacent areas, but augmented now by immigration both from India and from Upper Burma, kept pace with and made possible the agricultural growth.[4]

Several events in the outside world during this period had major significance for the rapid development of rice cultivation in British (Lower) Burma. The Indian mutiny in 1857–58 and the advent of steam navigation at about

1. G. E. Harvey, *British Rule in Burma 1824–1942,* Faber and Faber, London, 1946, pp. 18–19.
2. *Ibid.,* p. 64.
3. To ensure low rice prices in Upper Burma.
4. According to John F. Cady (*A History of Modern Burma,* Cornell University Press, Ithaca, N.Y., 1958), population in the Tenasserim doubled in the seventeen years following 1835, and rice acreage increased 50 per cent in the seven years from 1845 to 1852. In the Arakan, rice acreage increased approximately 350 per cent from 1830 to 1852. According to J. Russell Andrus (*Burmese Economic Life,* Stanford University Press, Stanford, 1957) population in lower Burma rose from approximately 1.5 million in 1856 to about 4 million in 1885. J. S. Furnivall (*Colonial Policy and Practice,* Cambridge University Press, Cambridge, 1957) shows an increase in rice acreage in Lower Burma from approximately 1.3 million in 1856 to roughly 4 million in 1885.

that time were followed by the cutoff of supplies of rice from Carolina to Europe during the American Civil War, and not long afterwards (in 1869) by the opening of the Suez Canal. Over time, it was the opening of the Canal and the rapid growth of population in India which were to have the greatest continuing influence on rice production in Burma. The rates of increase of population and rice acreage after the annexation of Upper Burma in 1885 were no greater than they had been in the period following 1852. The increase in absolute terms was of course much larger. From 1885 to 1941, population in Lower Burma grew from about 4 million to roughly 9 million. Rice acreage at the same time grew from about 4 million to some 10 million. The rise in rice exports, however, was much greater in percentage as well as in absolute terms during the latter period. They rose only from some 400,000 tons in 1865 to 520,000 tons in 1881, and to 817,000 tons in 1891; by 1921 they had tripled to 2.5 million tons, and by 1941 they were in excess of 3 million tons.[5]

During the latter part of the British occupation of Lower Burma there was a very considerable construction and development of railways, roads, inland water transport and agricultural embankments. These economic developments were accompanied by developments in the governmental and administrative spheres — developments that exerted a profound influence on the social structure, relations and culture.

The beginning of a sizable immigration from India has already been noted. Some of this immigration was permanent; some of it was only seasonal. Along with the influx of Indians and of British administrators trained in India came the Indian applications of English law and the form of colonial administration developed in India. Under British district officials, there were set up not the old Burmese Myothugyis — the township or circle of village headmen — but, first, Taikthugyis who administered on a territorial basis rather than on a basis of personal relationship, and, later, individual village Thugyis or headmen. In place of the Burmese customary law there was now substituted a highly complex and impartial rule of law, founded on the sanctity of contract, comprehensible to English-trained lawyers only. The Arakanese, the Karens and the Mons had utilized the opportunities afforded by the several British invasions to turn against their Burmese oppressors. Thus racial and minority antagonisms were exacerbated. The English refused to recognize the authority of the ecclesiastic code or of the chief Buddhist primate and the monastic order. All knowledgeable observers and students of Burmese history, British included, agree that out of this combination of circumstances a social disintegration set in. The introduction of the rule of British law and the sanctity of the written contract was perhaps basic to this disintegration.[6]

5. Again, the population and rice export figures are from Andrus (*op. cit.*) and the rice acreage figures from Furnivall (*op. cit.*).
6. J. S. Furnivall is the father of this thesis.

Central to this process were the developments on the new agricultural frontier in Lower Burma. Under the British, as in the Burmese times, the occupancy and cultivation over a period of years of previously unoccupied land was accepted as the means of acquiring ownership. Under the British, twelve years working of the land was required before a certificate of title could be obtained by the cultivator. However, the tax receipt which covered the first payment of land revenues on the new land was considered equivalent to a certificate of occupancy and carried the presumption that title in due course would be granted. The tax receipt, therefore, soon came to serve as the prime security for cash loans, or it — and occupancy — could be sold outright for cash.

Clearing the land of jungle and bringing it into productive cultivation involved a considerable input of labor over several years. Few cultivators could get through this period of initial difficulty without borrowing heavily. While quite a few worked a piece of land just long enough to get their tax certificate, only to sell it for cash and move on to settle another plot, the great majority of the new cultivators went increasingly into debt. The debt problem was aggravated by another circumstance. The sumptuary restrictions that prevailed in the feudal Kingdom of Burma had never been as prevalent among the Mons and the Karens of Lower Burma. The uprooted immigrants who flocked in from Upper Burma were now free of the sanctions of their traditional Myothugyi headmen and, provided the cash was available, could dress and live as lavishly as they pleased, all with borrowed money. They were not aware that as they borrowed, whether against tax receipts or land title, they could be foreclosed in a court of law, and driven off their land or forced into tenant status. This had not been the case under Burmese customary law. Thus the problems of land alienation and farm tenancy found their inception in the early years of the Delta's development.

The Taikthugyis — circle headmen — were no effective substitute for the former Myothugyis, or regimental leaders. They tended to become mere collectors of land revenue. The new Thugyi, or village headman, never succeeded in winning the loyalty, respect or full cooperation of the village folk, who rapidly became a highly mobile population. The refusal of the British to recognize the Buddhist primate and the authority of the Sangha resulted in progressive deterioration within the Buddhist order. The monkhood became increasingly a refuge for irresponsible people and criminals, and their conduct could not be controlled. The British, and the Indians who came with them, preempted all positions of importance, not only in the Government administration but also in trade, commerce and the professions. A knowledge of English soon became essential to the achievement of any degree of status in the society. While the British attempted at first to improve instruction in the monastic schools, the monks would not cooperate with them, because the more modern education was mundane, and for nationalist reasons as well, and this effort soon foundered. Lay schools were started by the Government, but relatively few of them. The boys educated there tended to become superior and disrespectful to their elders, and frustrated in relation to their masters and prospects.

Meanwhile, in the Kingdom of Burma from 1852 to 1878, one of the better kings, Mindon, made a sober effort to improve conditions. He tried to improve the public administration by placing all high officials on salary, in contrast to the former system of Myosas, or revenue fiefs. This move he attempted to finance by a tax reform designed to replace the previous service system by a universal household tax based roughly on ability to pay. He introduced in 1861 a coined money and stimulated foreign trade. He sponsored the development of river transport, of manufacturing and of mining activity, and hired foreign technicians. He introduced telegraphic communications between the capital and Lower Burma, using a Morse code adapted to the Burmese alphabet, and sent young men to Europe for training. A devout king, he also built many pagodas, organized the Fifth Buddhist Synod in 1871[7] and engaged in the construction of Mandalay as a new capital city. Mindon made no attempt to strike back at the British in Lower Burma, as many urged him to do at times when the British were being sorely tried elsewhere[8] and might not have been able effectively to resist. He took a posture which would eventually result, he seems to have hoped, in the return to the Kingdom of Burma of the annexed provinces. Despite all this, the British resented his attempts to enter into independent and sovereign negotiations with foreign powers, particularly the French, and British commercial interests pressed increasingly for the annexation of Upper Burma to develop improved avenues of trade with China. When Mindon was succeeded in 1878 by King Thibaw, the end of independent Burma was in sight. Thibaw's misrule led to intolerable corruption, internal dissent, banditry, rebellion and virtual anarchy in the Kingdom of Burma. Under these conditions the British soon found the occasion for war. The annexation of Burma was completed in 1885.

The annexation of Upper Burma was followed very quickly by the liquidation of the monarchy and the Hlutdaw, and by the introduction of the same institutions and methods as had already been introduced into lower Burma. The resulting social disintegration and disorder were initially greater than those which followed the earlier annexations. Under King Thibaw, anarchy had spread so far that almost every village had armed its men and sent them out foraging and looting in the countryside. The British attempted to suppress this disorder by drastic measures which included the shooting outright

7. This Synod reduced the Buddhist scriptures to stone tablets and purified them at the same time.
8. As during the Indian Mutiny in 1857–58.

of anyone caught in the possession of arms, and the burning of whole villages. This action only fed the fires of rebellion. Of the 35,000 troops maintained in the country in those days by the British, fully 30,000 were required in Upper Burma. Gradually some order was brought out of the anarchy. The course of social disintegration, however, was not halted.

The development of the agricultural frontier in Lower Burma continued at a hectic pace, accompanied by increasing violence. Accounts of it are reminiscent in many ways of the stories told of the gold rushes in California and Alaska. Intimidation and outright violence on the part of strong men and their armed retainers drove many a timid cultivator off his claim. Others, more subtle, bribed minor officials, after paying taxes on unoccupied land for some years, to give them title to land they had not cleared or developed. Still others, armed with capital, adopted the loan-and-foreclosure technique to acquire sizable land holdings. Native moneylenders were soon followed by professional Indian moneylenders — the Chettyars — who in time took over virtually the entire financing of agriculture in Lower Burma, and who increasingly took over ownership through foreclosures. Widespread conditions of this kind affecting the major economic activity of the country could not help but permeate the social structure in almost every conceivable way.

Nevertheless, the country continued to develop. With the increase in rice and timber production came expansion of the rice-milling and sawmilling industries. Railroads and inland water transport were extended and improved, better roads and communication facilities were built and established, the ports were greatly improved, the oil industry was developed and exports grew. The famous Bawdwin lead, zinc and silver mines in the Northern Shan States, the Mawchi tin and tungsten mines in the Southern Shan Kayah (former Karenni) State and a considerable tin and tungsten output in the Tenasserim were similarly developed. Substantial investments were made in tea and rubber plantations. Medium-scale manufacturing plants in cement, sugar and other industries were built. Banking, insurance and similar services were introduced. The economy was increasingly placed on a cash basis, and a growing import of consumer as well as capital goods rounded out the picture.

ECONOMIC AND SOCIAL PROBLEMS

What concerned and even alarmed the more serious and perceptive of the British administrators was the tremendous increase in social mobility and unrest and the growth of crime and corruption which accompanied this economic development. As time went by, they appreciated increasingly that some of their own actions — notably the abolition of the Myothugyis, their contribution to the deterioration of the Sangha and the monkhood, and their introduction of the rule of law and the sanctity of contract which made land alienation possible — were in large part responsible for these evidences of social disorganization. It was not, however, until the impact of the world-wide depression of the 1930s struck in Burma that they became fully aware of the degree to which the Burman farmer had become a landless tenant in his own country. By this time, fully two thirds of the agricultural land in Lower Burma had been lost to absentee landlords, most of them Chettyar money-lenders.

Of all these observers, it was J. S. Furnivall who perceived with the greatest sensitivity and insight just what British rule in Burma had done to the Burman. Not only were land ownership, the Government, the civil service, and trade and commerce almost entirely in foreign hands; there had been, in effect, a leveling down of all Burmans, and a destruction of the existing social relations and values. There were no posts of importance to which a Burman could aspire; nor did the means exist for training and experience by which the Burman could equip himself for advancement. Furnivall stressed also that the increasing inflow of cheap consumer goods from abroad was destructive of the small-scale manufacturing, home industry and artisan trades which had flourished before the English occupation. The resulting sense of frustration and loss of status was bound to find expression in crime. If the Burmese youth could not advance, he could at least display his daring and his prowess by joining up with a dacoit band and thus release his frustrations in acts of violence against persons and property.

Similarly, the elaborate system of law, and its respect for the sanctity of contracts set up by the British, encouraged crime and corruption, as well as land alienation. In courts where only lawyers flourished, where the testimony of witnesses could easily be distorted by bribed interpreters, where witnesses could be intimidated by dacoits and "bad hats," and where the great majority of officials entrusted with judicial functions accepted bribes, the guilty frequently went unpunished, and prospective litigants were encouraged to take the law into their own hands. Although side by side with the Indian Civil Service there was developed an indigenous so-called Class II Burma Civil Service, its trainees — who frequently became contemptuous of their own people and elders and lost contact with their own community — were not accepted by the British community and soon found themselves operating in a social limbo. This was the background out of which there inevitably developed after World War I a resurgence of the Burmese nationalist spirit.

THE GROWTH OF BURMESE NATIONALISM

Psychological, racial and ideological factors, as well as economic factors, promoted the rapid growth of the nationalist spirit. Sparked by mixed feelings of national pride, humiliation and religious affront during a time of war-born economic distress, it was encouraged by slogans of democracy and self-determination, stimulated by Gandhi's fight for home rule in India, nourished by increasing mistrust of British motives, exacerbated by the consequences of the world-wide depression of the 1930s and stoked by the prolonged failure of the British to cope constructively with the basic economic problems which beset the country. Only a relatively few extremists became dedicated to Marxism, and only a few others were tempted by the leadership principles of Fascist Germany and Japan. The movement remained basically a nationalist movement. It was only in the late 1930s and finally in the crucible of World War II and its concomitant fight for freedom that a group of recent students imbued with a socialist ideology took over leadership from the educated moderates and, later, the fiery political monks who dominated the movement, and won responsibility for government in the independent Burma that came into being in 1948.

The organizational embryo for the nationalist movement was the Young Men's Buddhist Association, organized in 1908 by a small group of educated Burmans, moderate in their views. Dedicated originally to the discussion only of religious and cultural subjects, as membership grew pressures increased for the consideration of political questions. The economic impact of World War I was felt most severely in Lower Burma. A shortage of ocean shipping, aggravated by the priority given to minerals, timber and oil exports, limited severely the export of the rice surplus from Lower Burma. While other prices rose, the price of rice dropped sharply. Moneylenders called in their loans, the pace of foreclosures quickened and economic distress became widespread. Tax delinquency became a serious problem, with only tardy and inadequate relief on the part of the Government.

In this setting, a Burmese campaign in 1916, directed toward the prohibition of the wearing of shoes by westerners on pagoda premises, caught on like wildfire. The many branches of the Young Men's Buddhist Association united in support of this cause, and by 1918 the situation had become quite tense as nationalist sentiment crystallized on the issue. This was perhaps because "the issue became a symbol of anti-British political sentiment. It provided an occasion in which the Buddhist Burman could tell the British overlord that there was something the latter could not do."[9] The Government finally resolved the question with a concessionary ruling to the effect that the monk in charge of each local pagoda could decide the question as he chose.

This period also saw the publication of a report by a Committee on the Imperial Idea, organized by Lieutenant Governor Sir Spencer Harcourt Butler, which, in effect, told the Burman that the Anglo-vernacular schools and educational system should serve the Imperial Idea. This report made it all the more difficult for the Burmese nationalists to accept the implications of the White Paper Report of the Joint Committee on Indian Constitutional Reform

9. Cady, *op. cit.*, p. 190.

which followed shortly in 1918. While the initial reaction of the Y.M.B.A. leadership to the White Paper was to request the separation of Burma from India, they soon realized that the English felt Burma's progress toward self-government would have to be slower than the pace considered suitable for India. By the time the protests, negotiations and debate over this question were over, the nationalist spirit in Burma had been given a tremendous impetus; and Burmese ideas as to the degree of self-government they desired, still further stimulated by the initiation of Gandhi's non-cooperation movement in India, had been considerably enlarged. "From 1920 to 1922, political agitation ceased to be the exclusive concern of the Burmese Western-oriented intelligentsia. The popular revolution for political freedom had begun."[10] The Young Men's Buddhist Association was soon metamorphosed into the more general and more popular General Council of Burmese Associations, with a leadership much closer to the people.

The next big nationalist issue arose out of the University Act of 1920 and the British program to establish higher standards for the proposed university in Rangoon by stiffening the high-school final and college-entrance examinations. Considerable resentment already existed in Burma because of the difficulties previously encountered by Burmese students in meeting the entrance requirements of the Indian colleges, and because of the alien culture which prevailed in the Anglo-vernacular schools. The opening of the Rangoon University (Burma's first) followed shortly after participation by the Burmese nationalist leaders in the election boycott initiated in India, and at a time when strikes and unrest were in the air. The newly entered students at the university were persuaded to go on a strike, which enlisted widespread popular support. They demanded complete home rule for Burma and denounced the governmental reforms proposed by London. The strike spread to all Government schools, and the monks were soon demanding a complete system of national schools free from British support or control. "The political grievance behind the University strike was the conviction that the British had decided to give Burma a second-class constitution on the basis of the country's small number (less than 400) of university degree holders and had then decided to perpetuate this disability by abruptly raising the standards of instruction and removing them from possible Burmese alteration."[11]

National schools were quickly organized to take care of the striking students, but encountered great difficulties in finance, faculty and discipline. The strike petered out during 1921. Its political effects, however, were great. Students and pongyis had entered upon the political arena as factors of great potential significance. The importance which the Burmese themselves attribute to this strike of 1920 is indicated by the fact that December 4 — the

10. *Ibid.*, p. 212.
11. *Ibid.*, p. 219.

date on which it was called — is celebrated in independent Burma as National Day.

During the war the British had constituted a Rice Control Board to stabilize domestic rice prices. The spread between these artificially depressed domestic prices and high export prices had enabled the Board to accumulate a very sizable profit, to the natural resentment of the cultivators and moneylenders in Lower Burma. When the question arose as to how these profits were to be used, the Government of India took the view that since they were amassed as the result of the high prices paid by Indian consumers, these profits should be spent outside Burma. Although they apparently were spent ultimately on railroad, road and other improvements within Burma, this issue had aggravated the previously existing situation. By the time the Burma Reforms Committee, established by the Parliament, arrived in Burma in the fall of 1921 to inquire into the governmental reforms appropriate to the situation, feelings were already such that the General Council of Burmese Associations had decided to boycott the Committee's sessions and to refuse all cooperation "except where it might contribute to the speedy attainment of home rule."[12] The Burmese nationalists now demanded complete home rule.

It was 1923 before the dyarchy system recommended by the Reforms Committee was approved by the Parliament and introduced into Burma. But "The reform was at best a makeshift, opportunist measure which had little relevance to Burma's wishes or needs. It was destined to prove futile in practice because it was incapable of tackling the country's urgent economic problems."[13]

Under dyarchy, the most pressing questions in the economic sphere arose out of the twin burdens of agricultural debt and taxation. The Government insisted that agricultural tax levies be increased in spite of many reports by its land settlement officers that tax relief was necessary. One such general report, prepared by Mr. Furnivall in 1922, urged that consideration be given to a number of circumstances which would in effect reduce the cultivators' tax burden. These reports were not accepted, and Mr. Furnivall shortly thereafter resigned from the civil service.[14]

Economic distress in the countryside did much to stimulate the organization and growth of village political associations, called the Athins, which provided a fertile ground for the agitation of politically minded pongyis (monks). Outstanding among these was U Ottama, who began his agitational career upon his return from India in 1921. His major appeals consisted in attacks upon dyarchy and in alleging affronts to monks, to the Buddhist faith and to the dignity and pride of the Burmese nation. In demanding home rule he also incited to violence. Other pongyis fomented village folk to turn

12. *Ibid.*, p. 224.
13. *Ibid.*, p. 230.
14. *Ibid.*, p. 238.

against tax collectors, police, headmen and the Government. U Ottama was imprisoned three times. Each of these occasions served further to agitate nationalist sentiments. U Wisara, another pongyi leader, was sent to jail after leading a movement against agricultural taxation. When he died in 1929 in consequence of a hunger strike, popular emotions were raised to fever pitch. Because of the influence of political pongyis like these among the village organizations, the nationalist politicians were of necessity soon forced to compromise with and were even dominated by the pongyis.

Declining rice prices in the latter part of the 1920s, the collapse in 1928–29 of the cooperative agricultural credit societies which accompanied the price decline, and the death of U Wisara provided the inauspicious setting for the visit of the Simon Commission in 1929 to review the operations of government under dyarchy. A sharp split occurred at this point between those nationalists in favor of separation from India and the pongyi-led nationalists, in close touch with the Indian Congress, who favored non-separation.

As they had done with the earlier Reforms Committee, the Burmese boycotted the Simon Commission. Its recommendation that Burma be separated from India was unfortunately not accompanied by clear assurances that a separated Burma would be granted a degree of self-government fully equal to that which might be granted to India. The report therefore touched off a bitter debate which lasted until the introduction of responsible though limited cabinet government in Burma in 1937.

These, of course, were also the years of deep world-wide depression. The catastrophic drop in rice prices in 1930 and the years following, far exceeding in impact the drop at the end of World War I, accelerated and aggravated agricultural distress, land alienation and unrest in Lower Burma. It led also to increasing competition between Burmese and Indian labor and to a series of violent inter-racial explosions. The most notable of these was in connection with the dock strike of 1930, in which Burmese laborers brought in as strike breakers eventually engaged in battle with the Indian strikers demanding to recover their jobs. "Fighting spread quickly throughout Rangoon and raged unchecked for two days. The tattoo *sayas* did a flourishing business. Rough Burmese mobs decorated with magical charms hunted down panic-stricken Indians in a savage, fanatical frenzy. The official report indicated around 100 killed and about 1,000 injured, almost all Indians; contemporary observers reported from 300 to 500 killed."[15]

Other race-motivated riots occurred in the Rangoon jail, against Chinese and Indian traders and cultivators. Nationalist feeling now began to find expression also in anti-British manifestations of a personal kind. The whitewash report presented by the official Enquiry Committee into the operations of the "Bullinger Pool" — a buying cartel of large British millers and exporters which

15. *Ibid.*, p. 305.

had engaged in collusive buying of paddy in the previous decade — occasioned many such attacks, and contributed to the growing popular hostility against the European firms. "Behind these more obvious grievances was the growing awareness among the better informed that European firms, who continued to pay handsome dividends even during the depression years, were for the most part opposed to constitutional concessions, ameliorative economic regulations, and limitation of Indian labor immigration."[16] What especially irritated the more thoughtful of the Burmese leaders was the awareness that the British, at the same time that they failed to perceive the underlying economic and nationalist causes of growing unrest, made use of the evidences of this unrest as an excuse for not granting to Burma a greater degree of self-government.

The Saya San Rebellion, which broke out at the very end of 1930, fed on agrarian discontent over the debt and tax burdens and the denial to poor farmers of free access to forest reserves for supplies of firewood and bamboo. A former pongyi and political organizer, Saya San, organized a rebellion which utilized the traditions, panoply and ceremonies of the Burmese kings to capture the popular imagination. His primitive army was assembled in secrecy and drilled in the hills. At an auspicious moment selected by the astrologers, Saya San was crowned, armed with the sword of victory, and covered by the white umbrella. His initial force of 1,500 men was equipped with only thirty guns, but with enough charms, amulets and tattooing for the army to consider itself invulnerable. The rebellion spread with amazing rapidity. It took an army division and more than a year to quell it. Though the rebellion never succeeded in achieving a widespread popular participation, it did completely win the sympathy, even the admiration, of the Burmese public. Even those Burmans who considered Saya San a charlatan admired his daring and courage.

From 1930 to 1936, one quarter of the paddy land in Lower Burma had been foreclosed, and the British Government recognized, belatedly, the enormous extent to which land alienation had progressed. Now, in addition to the slogans of democracy and self-determination which had served them as popular catchwords since the early 1920s, some nationalist leaders began to be attracted by other alternatives. "The revival of Germany under Hitler suggested that leadership rather than democracy was the key to national progress, and Japan seemed to illustrate the same principle. In striking contrast, but equally effective, was the rise of Russia under communism with its new interpretation of democracy. Some began to look to Japan and others to Russia, while not a few were willing to flirt with both."[17]

16. *Ibid.,* p. 309.

17. J. S. Furnivall, Introduction to Thakin Nu's *Burma Under the Japanese,* MacMillan and Co. Ltd., London, 1954, pp. xxii–xxiii.

These newer ideas were mainly in evidence at the University of Rangoon, where, for some time, politically conscious students had taken to calling each other Thakin.[18] In 1935, U Nu and a group of Thakins, including U Aung San, U Kyaw Nyein and U Raschid, captured control of the Rangoon University Students Association. In the following year, their aggressive actions provoked disciplinary action by the university against both U Nu and U Aung San. The Thakins quickly replied with a students' strike, which had tremendous impact throughout the country. As in the case of the 1920 strike, this one spread to many other schools and required the postponement of the high-school final tests as well as of the university examinations. "Burman sentiment generally made heroes of the strikers and accorded them full moral and material support. The transformation of a student protest against disciplinary authority into a political event of province-wide impact was the achievement of the Thakins and the Student Movement leadership."[19] Eventually a number of the students' demands were met.

In 1937 the new Constitution was introduced, accompanied by separation from India. The new Constitution provided for responsible cabinet government and an elected legislature. It reserved, however, control over defense and foreign and monetary affairs to the British governor, and reserved to the governor the right to final veto over any action of the legislature. Serious anti-Indian riots broke out in 1938. In 1939, U Ba Swe and U Kyaw Nyein formed the secret Burma Revolutionary Party (later to become the Socialist Party). The Government belatedly turned its attention to agrarian problems, enacting tenancy and other agricultural legislation. But World War II came too soon thereafter to enable these efforts to be tested. The British entry into the war was opposed by all Nationalist leaders except a few of the older men. A so-called Freedom Bloc was formed, the object of which was to resist any attempt to enlist Burmese aid unless such aid were paid for by complete independence.

The story of Burma's wartime fight for independence is for the most part the story of the Thakins. An informed appraisal of their ideology and motivations at this time may therefore be in order. During this period, says Mr. Furnivall,

They [the Thakins] grew rapidly in numbers and influence. They were enthusiastic for the diffusion of enlightenment and strongly attacked the prevalence of corruption in public life and Government service; their political objective was unconditional independence as soon as possible by any possible means. They were attracted by the Japanese catchword of co-prosperity, and most of them were not

18. In Burmese "Thakin" means "master," a term which under British rule had been reserved for the British. The students' use of the term was intended to demonstrate their equality with the English and their determination to be masters in their own house.
19. Cady, *op. cit.*, p. 380.

averse from Japanese assistance in obtaining independence, but only a few, and these dissidents from the main group, seem to have been in touch with the Japanese. The Japanese onslaught on China repelled them and their warmest sympathies lay rather with Russia. None of them, however, knew anything about Russia except from books, and none had ever come into contact with Russians or other practising communists. Communism attracted them because it provided a plausible explanation of foreign capital in Burma and seemed to offer a short-cut to independence. But they were offended by its doctrinaire repudiation of religion. Burma was closely identified with Buddhism; they were Buddhists, some of them very devout Buddhists, and they saw that communism could make no headway in Burma unless it came to terms with Buddhism. Only two or three went so far as to call themselves communists, and even these had no practical acquaintance with its working. Before the war communism in Burma was purely academic.[20]

20. Furnivall, *loc. cit.*, pp. xxiii–xxiv.

CHAPTER 4

Profile of the Economy
Before World War II

GENERAL MEASURES

In 1938–39, the last full year unaffected by the outbreak of World War II in Europe, the total output of the Burmese economy (measured in 1947–48 prices converted to dollars) is estimated to have been a little over $1 billion. This represented a per capita output of about $63. More than half of the total was accounted for by agriculture and fisheries, forestry and mining: approximately 40 per cent by agriculture and fisheries, 7 per cent by forestry, and 5.5 per cent by mining. Rice marketing accounted for an additional 13 per cent.[1] Industry, including cottage and home industry, contributed perhaps 10 per cent. Trade and marketing of products other than rice added 10 to 12 per cent of the total. The remainder of the gross domestic product was made up of small contributions by construction, transport, power, government services, other services and the rental value of housing.[2] Thus the economy was largely extractive in nature.

Only five sixths of the total output was used in Burma; the rest was transferred abroad, either as income paid (6 per cent) or toward the accumulation of reserves (11 per cent). Of the domestic uses, consumer expenditures accounted for 63 per cent of total resources and current governmental expenditures for something less than 8 per cent, while close to 13 per cent went into

---

1. Since collusive buying by exporters and millers reportedly operated to depress paddy prices below free market levels, part of the income ascribed to rice marketing undoubtedly was contributed by agriculture.

2. *Economic Survey of Burma 1959*, Tables 2 and 4, pp. 5 and 9.

capital formation.[3] In comparison with per capita output of approximately $63, per capita consumption amounted to approximately $41.[4] Investment was mostly private, and almost half of it was accounted for by depreciation. If the total national output was approximately $1 billion, net capital formation amounted to less than $70 million.[5] Gross domestic capital formation in Burma thus exceeded only slightly the amount of reserves accumulated abroad.

DISTRIBUTION OF THE LABOR FORCE

The data bearing most closely on occupational distribution in the pre-World War II period are those provided by the 1931 census, since the 1941 census tabulations were lost in the Japanese invasion. The distribution of 6.2 million workers shown in Table 1 is not believed to be significantly different from that of 1938–39.

Roughly two thirds of all workers were engaged in agriculture. These workers together with those engaged in forestry, animal raising, fishing and hunting comprised seven tenths of the entire working population. Nearly 11 per cent of all workers were engaged in industry, including cottage industry, mainly in textile production. Trade, with 9 per cent of all workers, was the next largest group. The remaining workers were scattered among minerals and petroleum production, transport, the public services, domestic service and the professions and liberal arts.

A certain degree of fluidity exists among certain of the occupations. Thus, many of the workers shown by the census as engaged in cultivation worked in the rice mills as well as on the land, depending on the season. By far the greatest part of the employment shown in industry and cottage industry represents unpaid family members who worked only part time and at home. The professions and liberal arts group, with nearly 200,000 workers or 3.2 per cent of the total, included 128,000 monks. Unregistered healers undoubtedly accounted for most of the 29,000 workers shown in the medicines category.[6] It has not been possible to establish how many of the 20,900 persons included under the heading "arts, sciences, entertainment, astrology, etc." were astrologers.

Of the total working population of 6.2 million, female workers, including working dependents, numbered close to 2 million, or 32 per cent of the total. About one third of the agricultural workers were women. In most handicraft occupations, women predominated; they accounted for 96 per cent in the textile category, over 70 per cent in pottery and earthenware, and more than

3. *Economic Survey of Burma 1953*, Table 2, p. 4; *The National Income of Burma 1958*, Rangoon, 1958, Summary Table 1B, p. 5.

4. *Economic Survey of Burma 1959*, Table 4, p. 9.

5. *Economic Survey of Burma 1953*, Table 4.

6. There were in Burma before the war only 1,599 doctors, 956 nurses and 1,513 midwives (George E. Harvey, *British Rule in Burma 1824–1942*, Faber and Faber, London, 1946, p. 45).

Table 1

DISTRIBUTION OF WORKERS
BY MAJOR CENSUS CLASSIFICATION, 1931

Classification	Number (*Thousands*)	Per Cent
Total	6,211.0	100.0
Exploitation of animals and vegetation	4,321.4	69.6
Ordinary cultivation	4,009.1	64.5
Special crops	118.6	1.9
Forestry	52.7	.9
Animal raising	79.9	1.3
Fishing and hunting	61.0	1.0
Exploitation of minerals	21.9	.3
Exploitation of petroleum	17.6	.3
Industry (incl. cottage industries)	644.4	10.7
Textiles	233.2	3.7
Sawyers	21.3	.3
Metals	21.6	.3
Ceramics	13.5	.2
Chemical products	18.5	.3
Rice processing	63.3	1.1
Other food industries	78.2	1.3
Articles of dress	60.0	1.0
Misc. construction and wood crafts	101.5	1.6
Misc. industry	53.3	.9
Transport	222.1	3.5
Water transport	73.7	1.2
Roads and bridges	35.0	.5
Road transport	80.5	1.3
Rail transport	27.8	.4
Other	5.0	.1
Trade	557.2	9.0
Banks, insurance, brokerage, etc.	13.2	.2
Textiles	18.8	.3
Wood (excl. firewood)	14.9	.2
Trade in foodstuffs (incl. hotel, etc.)	446.7	7.3
Other trade	63.8	1.0
Public administration	49.9	.8
Professions and liberal arts	198.9	3.2
Religion	128.3	2.1
Medicines (incl. unregistered healers)	29.1	.5
Instructions	20.7	.3
Arts, sciences, entertainment, astrology, etc.	20.9	.3
Domestic service	44.7	.7
Miscellaneous	118.1	1.9

Source: 1931 Census, Part II, from K.T.A. Preliminary Report, p. 10.

55 per cent in lacquerware, baskets and other woody materials. Women also comprised more than half of all workers engaged in trade. They participated only to a small extent in minerals exploitation, in transport and communications and in the public service.[7]

Data on the functional distribution of employed workers in 1931 are available for male workers only. These data, covering nearly 3.8 million workers of all races, are given in Table 2, which also gives the distribution of jobs or functions by racial group.

As might be expected, over two thirds (nearly 70 per cent) of the male workers were occupied in agriculture — 31 per cent as cultivating landowners, 14 per cent as cultivating tenants and 24 per cent as agricultural laborers. (If we take all agriculturists as equal to 100, 45 per cent were cultivating landowners, 20 per cent were cultivating tenants and 35 per cent were agricultural laborers.) Unskilled and semi-skilled laborers, at 11.5 per cent of the total, were the next largest group. Traders and shop assistants, at 6.5 per cent of the total, and craftsmen, at 5.1 per cent, were the only other sizable groups. Managers and officials of organized industrial undertakings accounted for less than one tenth of one per cent of the total.

The racial distribution shows that while Burmans comprised 53 per cent of all male workers, they accounted for 68 per cent of all cultivating tenants and an almost identical percentage of all agricultural laborers. Sixty-one per cent of the rentiers were Burmans, as were some 57 per cent of the craftsmen. Burmans accounted, however, for only a minority of the unskilled and semi-skilled laborers, the clerical workers and military and police personnnel.

Indigenous races other than Burman, comprising only 29 per cent of the male working population, accounted for more than half of all cultivating landowners. This fact was undoubtedly due to the concentration of these people outside Lower Burma, in areas where land alienation had not progressed as far as it had in Lower Burma. As tenants, agricultural laborers, rentiers and military and police personnel, their distribution was roughly comparable to their numbers. In other occupations, however, this was not the case.

Indians born outside Burma, who constituted one eighth of all male workers, concentrated heavily in the military and police forces, in the clerical occupations, in trade and in the handicrafts, yet they provided Burma at the same time with virtually her entire force of menial sweepers and scavengers. The participation of Indians in agriculture and as rentiers was far below their population proportion. The Chinese, forming only 2 per cent of the male working force, tended to concentrate in trading, craft and clerical occupations. They also provided management officials well in excess of their population proportion. The "other races" group, which would include such westerners as

7. 1931 Census, from K.T.A. Preliminary Report, p. 9.

Table 2

Percentage Distribution by Race of Male Earners Grouped by Selected Economic Functions, 1931

	Number of Workers— All Races	Per Cent						
		Total	Burmans Proper	Other Indigenous Races	Indians Born Outside Burma	Indians Born in Burma	Chinese	Other Races
All male earners[a]	3,778,336	100	53.3	29.2	12.1	1.9	2.1	1.3
Cultivating landowners	1,174,584	100	44.6	51.7	1.1	.9	1.1	.6
Cultivating tenants	535,695	100	68.2	25.0	3.4	2.5	.1	.8
Agricultural laborers	917,212	100	67.5	23.8	5.1	2.6	.2	.9
Unskilled and semi-skilled laborers (excl. sweepers and scavengers)	435,293	100	38.2	9.5	45.4	2.1	3.4	1.5
Sweepers and scavengers	6,995	100	3.5	.3	90.4	5.5	.2	.2
Traders and shop assistants	246,065	100	40.3	9.9	31.0	2.5	13.3	3.1
Craftsmen	191,689	100	56.9	9.7	23.2	2.0	5.9	2.3
Clerical workers	47,341	100	39.1	8.3	37.9	4.4	4.0	6.5
Rentiers	44,048	100	61.1	27.8	5.2	1.8	1.4	2.7
Army, navy, air force and police	32,569	100	29.6	20.4	41.1	1.9	.3	6.7
Managers and officials of organized industrial undertakings	3,347	100	51.3	6.4	17.9	3.6	6.0	14.7

Source: 1931 Census, Part I, p. 155, and Part II, p. 300, from K.T.A. Preliminary Report, p. 10.

a. Excludes male working dependents and all female earners and working dependents.

were in Burma, concentrated heavily in management, in the military and police forces and in the clerical occupations.

WAGES AND INCOME

Data on wages and income in 1938–39 are available but fragmentary. Agricultural workers were paid largely in kind. Typical pay for agricultural laborers was ten months' board and lodging for the season's work, plus 100 baskets of paddy.[8] The number of factory workers was small. In the relatively highly paid government service, a peon (or office boy) received 16 rupees[9] per month, a lower-division clerk 50 rupees, an upper-division clerk 100 rupees and a superintendent 320 rupees. These amounts would have to be multiplied three or four times to arrive at their equivalent purchasing power today. This would make their present value in dollars equivalent to, say, $11 per month for the peon, $35 for the lower-division clerk, $70 for the upper-division clerk and $235 for the superintendent. Most workers in clerical and trading occupations just preceding the war were paid a wage somewhat above that of a peon, but well below that of a lower-division clerk. Better-paid workers in the few large factories and skilled workers in the mines and oil fields received wages comparable to those of the lower-division clerk. The considerable number of persons occupied in so-called cottage industry were almost all self-employed and family workers who engaged in production only on a part-time basis. Their annual income, essentially a supplementary income, probably averaged not more than the current equivalent of $50 or so per year.

The data on national income that have been developed since World War II indicate current average per capita consumption to be only 80 per cent of the pre-war level. Undoubtedly some of the extremes in the pre-war income distribution have since been leveled out, so that living levels at the lower end of the income scale are today somewhat higher in relation to pre-war than is indicated by the more general measure. This comparison suggests that such data on wage and income levels as have become available in recent years afford a reasonably good indication of the wage and income structure before the war.

Crude data from a sample of 108,000 households in Rangoon in January 1950 showed roughly one third of the households receiving incomes of less than 100 rupees ($21) per month, and another 27 per cent receiving from 100 to 200 rupees. Close to 13 per cent fell in the income class from 201 to 300 rupees per month. One half of all the households had combined incomes equal

8. A basket is equal to 46 pounds of unmilled rice. One hundred baskets of paddy would translate roughly into some 3,300 pounds of milled rice.

9. Although a separate Burmese currency was established after separation from India in 1937, only some time after independence did the rupee become the kyat. The exchange rate of each has always been 13.3 to the pound sterling. With the pound at $2.80, rupees and kyats are worth one shilling sixpence, or 21 cents.

Table 3

INCOME DATA ON SAMPLE BASIS, 1957

(*Based on 1.1 Million Persons*)

Average Annual Income	Per Cent of Total Sample	Number of Persons 11 Years and Over Who Had Done Some Work During Year (*Thousands*)
Total	100.0	1,108.7
Under K 250	8.8	97.2
K 250–K 499	14.9	164.9
K 500–K 749	17.2	190.6
K 750–K 999	12.2	134.4
K 1,000–K 1,999	32.9	364.2
K 2,000–K 2,999	6.3	70.0
K 3,000–K 3,999	3.9	43.1
K 4,000–K 4,999	1.2	13.3
K 5,000–K 7,499	1.4	15.9
K 7,500 and over	1.0	11.5

Source: *1957 Sample Census, Population, Housing and Cottage Industry*, C.S.E.D., Rangoon, 1958, Table XVIII, p. 44.

to no more than $35 per month, three fifths fell below $42, and more than seven tenths were below $63. Indications were that unskilled laborers in Rangoon earned the equivalent of $14 to $18 per month, while skilled factory workers earned from $23 to $32.[10]

Figures for 1951 published in the *Burma Labour Gazette* gave average monthly wages for close to 50,000 workers in some 763 establishments in various occupations. These averages were: railway transport, with close to 19,000 workers, 115 rupees ($24.15) per month; rice milling, with some 8,000 workers, 91 rupees ($19.11); sea and river transport, with approximately the same number of workers, 118 rupees ($24.76); oil extraction, with over 4,000 workers, 178 rupees ($37.38); sawmilling, with over 3,400 workers, 82 rupees ($17.22). The highest monthly average wage was in banking, with some 1,300 workers; it was 213 rupees ($44.73).[11]

The 1957 census gathered data on population, housing and cottage industry for the 252 centers classified as towns. These towns had a total population of close to 3.3 million and contained 708,000 households. Income data were taken on a sample basis from the 1.1 million persons eleven years of age and over who had done some work during the census year. (See Table 3.) If these figures are converted to dollar equivalents, it will be seen that nearly 9 per cent reported annual incomes below $52.50 per year, 15 per cent below $105, 17 per cent below $157.50, 12 per cent below $210, and 33 per cent below $420. Thus two fifths of the urban working population earned less than $157.50 per

10. K.T.A. Preliminary Report, p. 14.
11. *Ibid.*

Table 4

URBAN FAMILY INCOME, 1957

Average Annual Income	Number of Families (*Thousands*)	Per Cent
Total	677	100
Below K 500	80.7	12
K 500–K 2,499	463.5	68
K 2,500–K 4,999	82.5	12
K 5,000–K 9,999	39.5	5.8
K 10,000 and over	10.8	1.6

Source: Adapted from *1957 Sample Census, Population, Housing and Cottage Industry,* C.S.E.D., Rangoon, 1958, Table VI, p. 53.

year, more than half less than $210 per year, and more than 85 per cent less than $420 per year, or $35 per month.

According to the 1957 sample household income tabulation (Table 4), 12 per cent of all households had annual incomes below 500 kyats ($105) per year, 80 per cent below 2,500 kyats ($525), and 92 per cent below 5,000 kyats ($1,050). Approximately 80 per cent of all households in the towns thus had a monthly income of less than $44.

The median income of the urban population in the towns was 696 kyats ($146) per year.

HEALTH

The span of human life in pre-war Burma was short, standards of sanitation were extremely low, infectious disease was widespread, medical services and facilities were very limited and infant mortality rates were very high.

The pre-war data, obviously unreliable, show a birth rate of about 35 per 1,000 and a death rate of about 25 per 1,000.[12] The average life expectancy at birth was approximately 31 years. This low expectancy was due chiefly to a very high infant mortality rate of 204 per 1,000.[13] Malaria, cholera, smallpox, plague, dysentery and respiratory diseases (including tuberculosis) were the most common diseases. Malaria and dysentery, both bacillary and amoebic, were particularly widespread. Yaws, beriberi, trichinosis, skin diseases and leprosy were also quite common.

In the entire country, according to figures given by Andrus, there were 315 hospitals and dispensaries, with a little more than 9,000 free beds, for a popula-

12. The apparent annual population increase of 10 per 1,000 indicated by these figures is belied by the relatively reliable census data, which show an average population increase of 14 per 1,000 in the decades preceding World War II (J. Russell Andrus, *Burmese Economic Life,* Stanford University Press, Stanford, 1957, pp. 283–85).

13. Harvey, *op. cit.,* p. 44.

tion of nearly 17 million people.[14] Harvey reports that qualified medical personnel consisted of some 1,600 doctors, less than 1,000 nurses and approximately 1,500 midwives. Two thirds of the doctors were Indian, only one doctor in five was Burmese.[15] Only ten qualified dentists were listed, all of whom practiced in Rangoon, Moulmein and Maymyo.[16]

EDUCATION

Simple literacy was widespread in the pre-war years. More than one half of all males and about one sixth of all females could read and write. Literacy among Burmese-speaking peoples — that is, excluding the Shan States and the hill peoples — was even higher: more than seven tenths of all males and more than one fifth of all females were literate. Since most of the boys had been taught in monastic schools, which had been deteriorating for some time, the levels of literacy achieved were, however, quite rudimentary.[17] There were in all something over 7,000 recognized schools in 1935, with a registration of 516,000. Of those enrolled, 443,000 were in the primary schools, 52,000 in the middle schools and 13,000 in the high schools. There were also some 2,000 students at the collegiate level.[18]

These figures indicate that less than one in four of Burma's more than 30,000 villages had a school of any standing. In addition to the recognized schools, there were, according to Grant, more than 18,000 unrecognized institutions accommodating more than 200,000 pupils. These were for the most part monastic schools. Taking Grant's figures on the population of recognized schools against the age distribution of the population, it would appear that perhaps one fifth of all children in the five- to ten-year-old age group, and perhaps one twentieth of all children in the ten- to fifteen-year-old age group, were enrolled in such schools.

There were only 250 middle and high schools in the entire country.[19] Many of them were run by missionaries. Since nearly one third of the secondary-school pupils were concentrated in Rangoon, a number of the urban centers classified as towns by the census must have lacked a middle or high school. The Anglo-vernacular schools at the higher levels would seem to have been devoted largely to the training of clerks,[20] and the educational system was evidently productive of much frustration and discontent.

The single University of Rangoon, with colleges of arts and science, medicine, education and agriculture, and departments of engineering and law,

14. Andrus, *op. cit.*, p. 288.
15. Harvey, *op. cit.*, p. 45.
16. Andrus, *op. cit.*, p. 291.
17. *Ibid.*, pp. 36–37, and Harvey, *op. cit.*, pp. 45–56.
18. W. J. Grant, *The New Burma*, George Allen and Unwin Ltd., London, 1942, p. 135.
19. Harvey, *op. cit.*, p. 46.
20. J. S. Furnivall, *Colonial Policy and Practice*, Cambridge University Press, Cambridge, 1957, pp. 123–30.

had by 1938–39 an enrollment of about 3,000 students. Relatively few of these studied medicine and engineering; the heavy concentration was in the arts and law faculties. According to Andrus, a one-time professor of economics at the university, "The scholastic standard of the University was held rather high."[21] Harvey[22] disputes this. According to him, entrance standards to the university were progressively lowered on the insistence of Burmese politicians ("two thirds . . . should never have been admitted"), so that standards deteriorated sadly, and discipline as well.

Curricula in the schools were not adjusted to the requirements of the modern world. Hagen reports that "the education offered was largely devoid of vocational, technical or scientific content. Nor were the few high school graduates properly prepared for a cultural college education, for the high schools taught almost nothing about social or political institutions."[23] Finally, at the higher levels of education, Indians rather than Burmans predominated. In 1937, out of 421 advanced students, only 126 were Burmans.[24]

AGRICULTURE

Close to 70 per cent of Burma's pre-war population lived and worked on farms, of which there were some 1.7 million with a total acreage somewhat in excess of 19 million. These farms were powered by approximately 5 million oxen and 1 million buffaloes.[25] Making allowance for animals below working age, the data support the adage that the typical farm in Burma is a "one-yoke farm" — two draft animals on a 10-acre farm. The Season and Crop Reports cited by Andrus show also 971,000 plows and 785,000 carts, averaging out at one plow for every two farms and two carts for every five farms. The acreage under irrigation, mostly in the Dry Zone, was roughly 1.5 million, or less than 8 per cent of the total.

Of the total acreage planted to crops, more than 60 per cent was planted to paddy, as is shown in Table 5, which gives the production, as well as acreages, of the major crops. The paddy yield was less than 1,300 pounds per acre, one of the lowest of any major rice producing country. This yield, equivalent to some 27.5 bushels per acre, compared with 49.7 bushels in the United States, 52.5 in China, 75.4 in Japan, 103.9 in Italy and 124.4 in Spain.[26]

Nearly half of all the farm land — 48 per cent — was farmed by tenants. Of this land, 34 per cent was owned by non-agriculturists and 14 per cent by other farmers; the remaining 52 per cent was farmed by owner-cultivators. The

21. Andrus, *op. cit.*, p. 38.
22. *Op. cit.*, pp. 47–48.
23. Everett E. Hagen, *The Economic Development of Burma*, N.P.A. Planning Pamphlet No. 96, Washington, 1956, p. 22.
24. *Ibid.*, p. 23.
25. Andrus, *op. cit.*, Table X, p. 53.
26. K.T.A. Preliminary Report, p. 47.

Table 5

AGRICULTURAL ACREAGE AND PRODUCTION,
1936–37 TO 1940–41 AVERAGE

	Acres (Thousands)	Production (Thousands of Long Tons)
Total	19,166	
Paddy	12,832	7,426
Groundnut	808	181
Sesamum	1,401	45
Cotton	452	21
Pulses	1,329	250
Sugar cane	64	1,000[a]
Millet	475	78[b]
All other	1,805[c]	—

Source: *Economic Survey of Burma 1959*, Tables 7, 9, pp. 13, 17.

a. Reduces to sugar in the approximate ratio of 10:1.

b. Production figure includes wheat, acreage does not.

c. Included in 1940–41 (in thousands of acres): maize, 214; grain, 275; chillies, 123; tobacco, 134; fodder crops, 190; vegetables, 96; plantains, 60; miscellaneous cereals, 164; and fruit gardens, 377. (J. Russell Andrus, *Burmese Economic Life,* Stanford University Press, Stanford, 1957, p. 51.)

picture is quite different when viewed separately for Upper and for Lower Burma. In Upper Burma, 68 per cent of the land was farmed by owner-cultivators, and less than half of the 32 per cent operated by tenants was owned by non-farmers. In Lower Burma, only two fifths of the land was operated by owner-cultivators; of the 59 per cent operated by tenants, non-agriculturist absentee landlords owned the predominant share.[27] The rate of turnover among agricultural tenants was very high.[28]

A number of interesting characteristics of Burmese agriculture were revealed for the first time by the first-stage census taken in 1953. While these are sample data covering only some 47,000 farms and are not altogether typical (they were taken in connection with the population census of 252 towns and represent either farms within those towns or farms operated by residents of those towns), they nevertheless afford informative insights into the structure of agriculture. The characteristics shown may be taken as reasonably valid for the pre-war period.

The 47,000-odd farms had a total area of some 482,000 acres, of which 54 per cent was tenant-operated. While the average size of these farms was just over 10 acres, 40 per cent were farms of less than 5 acres. Farms of this size accounted for only 6 per cent of the acreage. Twenty-two per cent of the farms, with 15 per cent of the acreage, were in the 5–10-acre size group; 16 per cent,

27. *Report on Land Administration of Burma (1938–39)*, cited in K.T.A. Comprehensive Report, Vol. I, p. 134.

28. Andrus, *op. cit.*, pp. 71–72.

with 18 per cent of the acreage, in the 10–15-acre size group; 7 per cent, with nearly 12 per cent of the area, in the 15–20-acre size group; and 14 per cent, with 49 per cent of the area, were 20 acres or more in size. The large proportion of farms of less than 5 acres undoubtedly reflects the atypical nature of the urban farm sample.

There was no very significant variation in ownership or tenancy between farms of different sizes. Of the rented farms, 65 per cent were on a fixed-rent basis, and 8 per cent on a share-of-produce basis. The others were rented under special arrangements in which consideration was given to felt obligations towards relatives and friends.

In yields, the paddy farms in the size group under 5 acres were in the lead, reflecting a more intensive cultivation. The cattle population reported showed an average of two working animals per farm and an average of 9.9 acres per team. The meat-animal and poultry population was most heavily concentrated in the farms under 5 acres in size, indicating that an important element in the operations of this group was the production of meat and poultry for sale in the urban communities in or near which they are located.

Among the most interesting of the data are those which report the receipts, expenditures and net income of the farm operators. Average annual receipts per farm for the entire group were 1,139 kyats ($239); average expenses, 716 kyats ($150). The latter consisted of operating expenses of 520 kyats,[29] interest of 70 kyats, rent of 81 kyats, and land tax of 45 kyats. The average net income per farm was 423 kyats, or less than $89 per year.[30]

The range in average net income among farms of various sizes was not what one would expect, except for the farms of 20 acres and more. In fact, the average net income on the small intensive farms under 5 acres in size was substantially larger than that of the 5–10-acre and the 10–15-acre farms, and equaled that of the 15–20-acre farms.

Of equal interest in the economics of Burmese agriculture are the detailed data on loans received and interest paid by the farm operators. Some 28,000 out of the 47,000 farms covered by the survey reported borrowing 8.7 million kyats and paying interest of 3.3 million kyats, or 38 per cent of the money borrowed. Since the average loan period was less than a full year, the annual interest rate was obviously higher than 38 per cent. The loans were extended both by government agencies and by private lenders. The latter provided

29. Average farm operating expenditures were distributed as follows:

	Per Cent
Wages	53
Livestock feeding	20
Cattle and implement hire	7.4
Repairs	6.5
Seed purchase	5.8
Transport costs	3.8
All others	3.5

30. However, for roughly one half of all farms which reported as part of their income consumption on the farm, indicated net cash income was only two thirds of this figure.

roughly three times as much credit as the former, and at a very much higher rate of interest. Whereas the rate paid for government credit was less than 8 per cent, that paid to private lenders was well over 50 per cent.[31] Since the average interest paid per farm for a private loan of some 300 kyats was in excess of 160 kyats, and since the average net income per farm was only 423 kyats, it is plain that the provision of credit at modest rates of interest could increase average net farm income by one third.

FISHERIES

Together with rice, salt and tea, fish and fish products constitute the essential elements in the Burmese diet. Owing to a lack of refrigeration facilities, most of the catch is dried or salted, and much of it is pounded into ngapi, a fish paste eaten with rice. The coastal areas, rivers and streams, the inland lakes, and even the rice paddies contribute to the catch. Deep-sea fishing is relatively neglected.

The 1931 census listed 61,000 persons as engaged in fishing and hunting. Undoubtedly a great many others were part-time fishermen in the off-agricultural season.[32]

TIMBER

With some 53,000 workers engaged in forestry, the timber sector was responsible for 7 per cent of the country's total output in 1938–39, and for some 7 per cent of the value of all exports. The value of timber exports matched that of all agricultural produce (cotton, pulses, rubber, oil cakes, etc.) other than rice.

The chief timbers were teak, with an annual production of more than 450,000 round tons, and non-teak hardwoods, with slightly more than 500,000 tons. Over 200,000 tons of trimmed teak were exported in the form of squares, mostly to India. Firewood was also an important product, being used as a fuel in river transport, on some sections of the railway, in some local sawmills and factories and for small-scale electricity generation, as well as for heating in the hilly areas. Converted to charcoal, it was the chief cooking fuel in urban areas. Among lesser forest products were bamboo, canes, lac, cutch and thitsi. Bamboo has a number of important applications. It is used for housing, utensils, baskets and rafting, and also in bridgemaking and, as pulp, in crude-paper making. Lac, useful in varnishes, sealing wax, etc., and cutch, used in tanning, were both exported in some quantity.

Two important aspects of the teak industry are the long production cycle

31. U Tun Wai (*Burma's Currency and Credit*, Orient Longmans Ltd., Calcutta, 1953, pp. 96, 148) places effective rates of interest on "Sabape" loans (repayable in kind) at 200 and more per cent.

32. From the Rangoon golf course during the monsoon season, the author has often seen people from the nearby villages wading in the chaungs which serve the course as water hazards, and fishing either with poles or with their hands.

and the dependence on elephant power. Since green teak is too heavy to float, the trees are first girdled — that is, ringed to the heartwood — in the forest. Only after two years can a girdled tree be felled. It is then dragged by elephants to a stream and must wait there until the high waters during the monsoon float it to the river. On the river journey the logs are rafted. Two to four years may elapse between the felling and the arrival of the logs at Rangoon or Moulmein, where they are milled and made ready for export. The production cycle, beginning with girdling, is commonly reckoned at six years. Widespread insurrection in the post-war period seriously deterred girdling work, and this interruption largely explains why it took so long to effect a substantial revival of the teak export trade. Loss of animal power was another serious deterrent to the revival of the industry. Elephants are used not only to bring the logs to stream-side but also to break log jams on the river. Before the war, the companies engaged in teak operations used some 6,000 elephants as motive power. These herds were badly depleted during the war, and many animals were subsequently lost to the insurgents.

MINING

With something over 50,000 workers,[33] mining contributed 5.5 per cent to the value of total output and approximately 35 per cent to the value of all exports.

The most important mineral product was crude petroleum, with an output of 276 million imperial gallons, of which more than 200 million were exported. Other important components of minerals production were some 4,300 tons of tungsten concentrates, 5,400 tons of tin concentrates, 5,600 tons of mixed tin and tungsten concentrates, 77,200 tons of lead and lead concentrates, 59,300 tons of zinc concentrates, and 26,000 tons of iron ore. Production also included more than 6 million ounces of silver, 1,000 ounces of gold, 212,000 carats of rubies, 11,000 carats of sapphires, 18,000 carats of spinel, 17 tons of jadeite, 84 pounds of amber, and minor tonnages of copper matte, galena, nickel speiss and antimonial lead.[34] Petroleum exports alone accounted for some 23 per cent, and other mineral exports for some 12 per cent, of the value of all exports.[35]

33. The 1931 census showed close to 18,000 workers engaged in petroleum extraction, and about 22,000 in other minerals production. However, Harvey reports that just before the war some 23,000 workers were engaged in oil production, and about 35,000 in minerals production at the Bawdwin and Mawchi mines and in the Tenasserim. He places a labor force of 11,000 at the Bawdwin Mines, and states that 24,000 were engaged in tin and wolfram production at the Mawchi Mines and in the Tenasserim. These figures make no provision for other minerals production. (Harvey, *op. cit.*, pp. 61–63.)

34. The figures on amber, jadeite, spinel, copper matte, galena, nickel speiss and antimonial lead refer to 1953 production.

35. The source for most of the production and export figures shown above is the *Economic Survey of Burma 1959*, Tables 16 and 17. Other data are derived from an official Government of Burma document, *Economic Analysis, Burma's Economic Conditions, Plans and Prospects*, pre-

Three British firms monopolized the oil industry: the Burmah Oil Company (accounting for three quarters of the output), the Indo-Burma Petroleum Company (12 per cent), and the British Burmah Petroleum Company (9.5 per cent).[36] In the ten-year period 1928–38, the average yield of the Burmah Oil Company on its ordinary stock was 22 per cent.[37] In 1937 the dividend was 30 per cent.[38] According to Harvey, only one third of the large labor force in the oil industry was Burmese a generation before the war. Burmese, however, comprised half of the labor force by 1927, and three fifths ten years later.[39]

The Burma Corporation, a British concern, operated the great silver, lead and zinc mines at Bawdwin, employing Gurkhas and Indians as underground workers and Sino-Shans and Chinese in work above ground. As of 1940, it was estimated that half of the known reserves of the Bawdwin Mines had already been extracted. The depleted state of the reserves, which would have provided for only eight to ten years of production at the pre-war level, was responsible for the reluctance of the post-war joint venture with the Burmese Government to replace at high cost more than one third of the previous capacity of the mill that was destroyed during the war.

The British-owned Mawchi Mines ranked as the largest individual tungsten-producing mine in the world.[40] It supplied roughly half of Burma's tin and tungsten production. As at Bawdwin, the labor force was made up largely of Gurkhas and Indians. The proven reserves ensured many years of full-scale operations. A number of smaller mining companies in the Tenasserim accounted for the other half of Burma's tin and tungsten output. The more important of these were also British-owned and supplied the major part of that region's output.

Reported production at the ruby and sapphire mines at Mogok in the Shan States has undoubtedly been vastly understated by the industry. The finest jade in the world is said to have been produced in Burma. Jadeite was never cut and polished domestically, but was exported in low-cost slabs, chiefly to Hong Kong and China.

INDUSTRY AND MANUFACTURES

Analysis of national income data for the pre-war period suggests that manufactures contributed 11 to 12 per cent of the total national product. This total was made up approximately as follows: industry (other than rice processing),

pared for the World Bank Mission in January 1955 by Robert R. Nathan Associates, Inc., Tables 8–11, pp. 38–42.

36. Andrus, *op. cit.*, pp. 117–18.
37. Harvey, *op. cit.*, p. 61.
38. Andrus, *op. cit.*, p. 120.
39. Harvey, *op. cit.*, p. 62.
40. Andrus, *op. cit.*, p. 126.

Table 6

NUMBER OF FACTORIES AND OF WORKERS EMPLOYED, 1940

	Establishments	Workers Employed (*Thousands*)
Total	1,027	89.4
Rice mills	673	41.6
Sawmills	116	11.6
Petroleum refineries	10	7.5
Cotton gins	54	3.8
Railway workshops	12	3.3
General engineering	19	3.0
Printing	19	2.7
Dockyards, etc.	9	2.2
Matches	5	2.0
Vegetable oil mills	29	1.5
Cotton mills	1	1.3
Hosiery and underwear	2	1.1
All other[a]	78	7.8

Source: Adapted from J. Russell Andrus' *Burmese Economic Life* (Stanford University Press, Stanford, 1957, Table 21, p. 142), which was in turn condensed from the Annual Report on the Working of the Factories Act, 1940.

a. Includes woolens, ordnance, ice and aerated water, rubber goods, rope, soap, jewelry, starch, cement, etc.

4 per cent; rice processing, 3.4 per cent; cottage industry, 3 per cent; and ngapi manufacture, 1 per cent. The 1931 census showed some 664,000 workers engaged in industry and cottage industry. This number would have been, say, 10 per cent larger by 1938–39. However, the Annual Report on the Working of the Factories Act for 1940 showed less than 90,000 workers employed in a little over 1,000 factory establishments.[41] Close to 650,000 workers must have been engaged in smaller establishments and in home production, most of them in the latter and working part time.

The chief types of factory production in 1940, together with the number of establishments and the number of persons employed in them, are shown in Table 6.

Two thirds of all establishments qualifying as factories were rice mills, which employed more than 46 per cent of all factory workers. More than 10 per cent of the establishments were sawmills, which employed 13 per cent of the workers. Petroleum refining accounted for 8.4 per cent of all factory employment. Thus, together rice milling and sawmilling accounted for three fifths and, with petroleum refining, almost seven tenths of all factory employment.

41. A factory is defined for the purposes of the Act as "premises in which power is used in aid of the manufacturing process and where 20 or more workers are employed." (Andrus, *op. cit.*, p. 142.)

Nearly half of the factory workers were employed within Rangoon and its industrial suburbs. Most of the important factories were owned by British interests, while a few of the medium-sized establishments were owned by Indians or Chinese. Except for the small upcountry rice mills, Burmese ownership was not a significant factor in the manufacturing industry.

The relative importance of the various handicraft industries is indicated in the employment data tabulated in the 1931 census, as reported by Andrus.[42] According to these data, approximately 230,000 workers were engaged in cotton spinning, sizing and weaving; 66,000 in lacquer ware and related production; 51,000 in tailoring and dressmaking; 42,000 in carpentry and similar occupations; 36,000 in palm-toddy production; 24,000 in cheroots production; 22,000 in jewelry production; 13,000 in blacksmithing and metalworking; and 12,000 in pottery making.

TRANSPORT AND COMMUNICATIONS

With the exception of early international air travel,[43] international passenger and freight traffic to and from pre-war Burma was almost exclusively by sea. Internally, transport was by the railways, the waterways and the highways, which ran more or less parallel to one another in a generally north-south direction.

The railways operated a little more than 2,000 miles of meter-gauge line, utilizing 358 locomotives, 762 passenger cars, 384 other coaches and 7,583 wagons. They carried less than 20 million passengers and more than 4 million tons of freight per year. The average passenger haul was about 24 miles; the average freight haul, 172 miles. More than 60 per cent of the officers of the Burma railways were English; only 16 per cent of them were Burman. The remaining officers were Anglo-Burmans, Anglo-Indians and Indians.

Organized inland-water transportation was mainly in the hands of the Irrawaddy Flotilla Company. This Scots concern carried 7 to 8 million passengers and 1.3 million tons of freight annually in its 263 power craft and 383 dumb craft (non-powered barges). Its steamer crews numbered 5,500, its dockyard employees 3,000 and its clerical staff 500. Data on passenger and freight miles are not available. Also, most of the large firms in the rice, timber, petroleum and other industries had their own vessels. Their craft were augmented by thousands of individuals and small firms operating anything from small sampans to small steamers. The total traffic carried on the rivers is estimated to have been several times that carried by the Irrawaddy Flotilla Company. Total inland water traffic probably exceeded that carried by the Union of Burma Railways.

42. *Op. cit.*, pp. 133–36.
43. Imperial Airways, KLM, Air France and the China National Aviation Corporation operated one to three services per week, according to Andrus (*op. cit.*, pp. 249–50).

Highways in the pre-war period consisted of approximately 17,000 miles of vehicular roads. Of these, little more than 6,000 miles were metaled, surfaced and motorable in all seasons. Another 6,000 miles or so were earth or gravel roads motorable in the dry season only. Close to 5,000 miles of earth and gravel roads were designed for ox-cart travel and were not motorable at all. There were fewer than 20,000 registered vehicles in the entire country.

The ports were well developed. The largest port was, of course, Rangoon, with Moulmein, Akyab and Bassein vying for second place. Some 828 ocean-going vessels were recorded as having entered Burmese ports in 1940. Counting coastal traffic, Rangoon port alone had more steamers than this. Freight imports and exports at the port of Rangoon were 1.4 million tons and 3.7 million tons, respectively.

Coastal shipping and trade were important, particularly between Rangoon and Akyab to the west and Moulmein to the east.

Communications facilities on the whole were quite limited. A reasonably adequate telegraph system with more than 8,000 miles of line and more than 33,000 miles of wire operated out of 656 telegraph offices and covered the entire country. The Rangoon telephone system had only some 2,800 subscribers, augmented by some 1,270 connections maintained by the Government itself. Telephone systems in other towns were very small even by comparison with the Rangoon system, and inter-town communications were limited. There were thirteen radio stations, thirty-two receivers and two broadcast transmitters. Of the country's 6,000-odd radio sets, more than half were in Rangoon and more than half of these were western owned. There were 372 post offices, and the postal service is said to have been reasonably satisfactory.[44]

FOREIGN TRADE

The outstanding characteristics of Burma's foreign trade in the pre-World War II period were (a) the unusual degree to which the economy was dependent on foreign trade; (b) the unusually favorable balance of that trade; (c) the predominance of rice and oil among exports; (d) the importance of India as a trading partner with respect to both exports and imports; and (e) the degree to which both the import and the export trade were dominated and controlled by foreigners.

For the five-year period 1936–41, the average value of exports was nearly one half the value of the total domestic product. The average value of imports was nearly one quarter the value of the total domestic product. The value of exports and imports combined was approximately seven tenths that of the total output of the country.

---

44. The source for most of the information on transport and communications has been Andrus (*op. cit.,* Chapters 15–20). Some of the data used, however, have been drawn from the K.T.A. Comprehensive Report and from the *Economic Survey of Burma 1954.*

Table 7

FOREIGN TRADE BALANCE, 1901–41

Years	Millions of Kyats			Percentage Excess of Exports
	Exports	Imports	Excess of Exports	
1901–06	210.6	145.1	65.5	45
1906–11	304.8	184.0	120.8	66
1911–16	356.8	211.8	145.0	68
1916–21	457.6	282.3	175.3	62
1921–26	660.2	365.7	294.5	81
1926–31	661.2	362.6	298.6	82
1931–36	485.6	201.3	284.3	141
1936–41	519.2	250.8	268.4	107

Source: K.T.A. Comprehensive Report, Table III–4, p. 45.

Over a series of five-year periods, beginning with 1901–06 and ending with 1936–41, exports substantially exceeded imports in each five-year period. The excess ranged from a low of 45 per cent to a high of 141 per cent. For the period 1936–41, average exports were 107 per cent in excess of average imports. (See Table 7.) This surplus on trade account was paid abroad in the form of profits and remittances, for depreciation reserves and capital repatriation, and for shipping, insurance and other services.

Rice accounted for nearly half of the value of all exports, oil for less than a quarter. Combined, they accounted for nearly seven tenths of all exports. Metals and ores and timber were the next in importance, while a group of agricultural products other than rice contributed nearly as much as did timber to the export balance. The predominance of rice and oil in the export picture is apparent from the 1938–39 data in Table 8.

Table 8

EXPORTS, 1938–39

	Millions of Kyats	Per Cent	Cumulative Per Cent
Total	478	100.0	
Rice	223	46.7	46.7
Oil	109[a]	22.8	69.5
Metals and ores	57	11.9	81.4
Timber	33	6.9	88.3
Other agricultural products	32[b]	6.7	95.0
All other	24	5.0	100.0

Source: Adapted from *Economic Survey of Burma 1959,* Table 30, p. 43.

a. Oil exports have been separated from the "all other" figure of K 133 million shown in the source table, but are a 1937–41 average figure rather than the 1938–39 figure.

b. Includes cotton, 8; pulses, 7; rubber, 6; oil cakes, 5; and all other agricultural products, 6.

Table 9

SEA-BORNE EXPORT TRADE WITH PRINCIPAL COUNTRIES, 1938–39

Country	Per Cent of Total
Total	100.0
India	54.3
United Kingdom	12.7
Ceylon	5.6
Straits Settlements	5.6
Japan	1.8
Germany	3.8
Malaya	1.3
United States	0.2
China	0.4
Others	14.3

Source: Foreign Commerce Yearbook, 1939, based on *Seaborne Trade of Burma*, as cited in J. Russell Andrus, *Burmese Economic Life*, Stanford University Press, Stanford, 1957, p. 167.

In that same year the total value of imports was 216 million kyats, less than half the value of exports. Of the import total, in the official classification used in the *Economic Survey of Burma 1959*, consumer goods accounted for 168 million kyats, or nearly four fifths, and capital goods for 48 million kyats, or just over one fifth. Food items made up the largest category, with clothing items running an important second. Provisions, fish, vegetable oils, spices, sugar and flour were among the most important of the foodstuffs. The clothing items comprised mostly cotton goods and thread and yarns, with apparel and woolen goods far behind. Hardware was the main component of the household goods imported.

Iron and steel products, other metal goods, machinery, jute gunny bags, instruments, coal and coke, motor vehicles and gasoline were among the principal capital and production goods.[45]

More than half of all the exports — 54 per cent — went to India (Table 9). One eighth went to the United Kingdom. Other British Empire destinations — Ceylon, Straits Settlements and Malaya — also received one eighth of the total. Since India took the largest part of the rice, petroleum and teak exports, she was of necessity Burma's largest purchaser. India, again with 54 per cent, and the United Kingdom, with 18 per cent, accounted for more than seven tenths of Burma's total imports in 1938–39.

The chief imports from India were cotton textiles, iron and steel, coal and coke, flour, fish, tea, cigarettes and jute gunny bags. Japan, with less than 7 per cent of the total, was the next largest source of foreign supply.

British and Indian merchants dominated the rice export trade, while the British had virtually a monopoly in petroleum, timber and minerals exports.

45. Andrus, *op. cit.*, Table 25, p. 174. For a unique classification of these imports see Furnivall, *op. cit.*, Appendix I.

Table 10

GOVERNMENT REVENUE AND EXPENDITURES, 1938–39

	Million Kyats	Per Cent of Total
Revenues, total	164.3	100.0
Land revenue	54.2	33.0
Forest revenue	14.3	8.7
Customs	36.4	22.2
Excise duties and excises	23.0	14.0
Income taxes	19.1	11.6
Other	17.3	10.5
Expenditures, total	157.9	100.0
Current expenditures	141.8	89.8
Revenue collection	10.3	6.5
Civil administration	52.6	33.3
Social development	16.7	10.6
Economic development	13.6	8.6
Defense	18.6	11.8
Other	30.0	19.0
Capital expenditures	16.1	10.2

Source: Adapted from K.T.A. Preliminary Report, Tables III and IV, pp. 27–28.

Indian and Chinese merchants shared with a few Burmese exporters the trade in lesser agricultural commodities. The structure of the import trade was similar. British and Indian trading firms predominated, and Chinese merchants played a lesser role. The role of the Burmese in the import trade was negligible.

PUBLIC FINANCE, MONEY AND BANKING

The central Government before World War II disbursed revenues amounting to approximately 11 per cent of the gross domestic product. The chief sources of revenue and the chief avenues of expenditure are shown in Table 10.

Total revenues of 164 million rupees were derived from five major sources. The largest of these were land revenue and customs, which contributed 33 per cent and 22.2 per cent of the total, respectively. Customs revenues, as Andrus points out, did not at that time include any duties on imports from India, Burma's largest single supplier, for until 1941 such imports were not subject to tariff duty.[46] The land revenue included revenues from fisheries, and petroleum and mining royalties. Since excise duties were imposed largely on imported goods, duties on these goods contributed substantially more than is shown by the customs figure alone. The minor role of the income tax in the revenue structure is accounted for not only by the low level of personal in-

46. Andrus, *op. cit.,* p. 321.

come but also by difficulties in the administration and collection of such a tax.

Of the expenditures, one third went to civil administration, and less than one eighth to defense. The classification shown in the table, while interesting in relation to economic and social development, conceals several noteworthy specifics. Police expenditures accounted for 15.5 million rupees, jails for 3.4 million, education for 9.8 million, medical expenditures for 4.5 million, and pensions for 14.7 million. Thus, outlays for police and jails combined were double the outlays for education and four times those for health. Pension payments alone were half again as large as those for education, and approached those for defense.[47]

District and local finance, in the sense of autonomous revenues and expenditures, were virtually non-existent.

After the separation of Burma from India in 1937, the Burmese currency was managed by the Reserve Bank of India through its branch in Rangoon. There were thirty-eight banks in the entire country in 1941, twenty-one of which were located in Rangoon. Of the Rangoon banks, eighteen were foreign banks or branches of foreign banks; only three were native to the country.[48] The commercial banks were engaged predominantly in the financing of foreign-exchange transactions and were commonly termed "Exchange Banks."

Other sources of credit were the Chettyars, previously described, who were the dominant source of agricultural credit; the pawn shops, operated mainly by Chinese; the cooperatives, chiefly agricultural credit cooperatives; and the Government.

The commercial banks catered mostly to the larger foreign firms, both in export and in import. Data indicating the scale of their operations before the war are not available. Total deposits of these banks are reported to have been some K 123 million, with advances and bills discounted of K 47 million.[49] (As of December 1952, the twenty-three commercial banks then in operation in Burma had total deposits of 293 million kyats, advances of 146 million, bills of 4.5 million and investments of 36 million, of which 25 million were Government and Government-guaranteed securities.)[50] The scale of lending by Chettyars is indicated by the estimate that places their pre-war investment in Burma at £56 million (747 million rupees), of which two thirds to three quarters are said to have consisted of agricultural loans.[51] This, however, appears to have been supplemented by some £7 million of deposits and bank advances.[52] Their loan funds thus amounted to some £63 million or 840 million rupees, of which two thirds to three quarters were loaned to agriculturists, and

47. *Ibid.*, Table 38, p. 322.
48. K.T.A. Preliminary Report, p. 6.
49. U Tun Wai, *op. cit.*, pp. 177–78.
50. K.T.A. Comprehensive Report, p. 67.
51. Harvey, *op. cit.*, p. 68, and U Tun Wai, *op. cit.*, p. 50.
52. U Tun Wai, *op. cit.*, p. 45.

the balance to trade and industry. Not all of this would have been loaned for current purposes. Annual agricultural credits, some of them extended by non-Chettyar lenders, might have amounted to 350 to 450 million rupees. After the depression of the early 1930s, most of the capital of the Chettyars was tied up in foreclosed land, and their current agricultural lending declined to about 100 million rupees for the remainder of the decade.[53]

Neither the cooperatives nor the Government was an important source of credit. The less than 1,500 agricultural cooperatives had a total paid-up capital of less than 1 million rupees.[54] Negligible deposits and loans from banks had, in 1938, added not much more than their own capital. The loans made by the banks during that year amounted to little more than one half million rupees, and their total loans outstanding amounted to less than 4.7 million rupees. Government loans to agriculture and to small-scale industry were negligible in amount and significance. The credits extended by hundreds of pawnshops were undoubtedly more substantial than both of these combined.

Interest rates were high. Rates of interest paid for agricultural loans have already been described in the section on agriculture. Bank rates were 8 to 10 per cent to the relatively small group of preferred borrowers. Others paid 15 to 24 per cent on solid security. Pawnbrokers and individual moneylenders charged 3 to 5 per cent per month, with gold and precious jewelry as security. On unsecured personal loans, the rate was usually 10 per cent per month.

FOREIGN INVESTMENT

Andrus places total foreign investments in Burma just prior to World War II at approximately £155 million sterling.[55] This is accounted for by Indian Chettyars, £56 million; foreign corporations, £47.2 million; Government and municipal bonds, £45 million; urban real estate, £3.25 million; Chinese investments, £2.8 million; and Indian industrial investments, £1 million.

Of the £56 million "invested" as loan capital by the Indian Chettyars, roughly two thirds, it is said, consisted of agricultural loans, the other third of trade and industrial loans. Combined with the £45 million of Government and municipal bonds, the loan capital would appear to have comprised a little more than half of the total. The £47.2 million figure for foreign corporations includes investments of £18 million in oil, £11 million in mining, £9 million in timber and £3 million in rice.[56] Harvey, citing the same source as does Andrus, points out that the investment figures do not reflect the reinvestment of profits over the years. He estimates reinvestments in the neighborhood of £20 million. Both Andrus and Harvey admit the difficulty of estimating

53. *Ibid.*
54. K.T.A. Preliminary Report, p. 38.
55. Andrus, *op. cit.*, p. 184.
56. Harvey, *op. cit.*, p. 68.

Chinese and Indian investments, and these figures may considerably under-state the actual amounts. It may be generalized, therefore, that foreign in-vestments totaled £160 to £180 million or, at the then rate of exchange, some $800 to $900 million. The value of those investments in terms of 1960 pur-chasing power would almost surely be around $2 billion, or approximately double the then total national output.

STAGNATION IN THE ECONOMY

Although no national-income estimates for years prior to 1938–39 have ever been framed, the major evidences point very strongly to the conclusion that Burma's economy in the period between World War I and World War II was a stagnant one.

During this period, agricultural acreage increased at a rate far below that of population growth. For example, in the decade from 1930 to 1940, acreage under rice increased from 12.4 to 12.8 million, a little over 3 per cent, while population grew 14 per cent. The dominant role of agriculture, forestry and mining in the total national output, and the very large share of the export values of these commodities in the total national product, have already been mentioned. Comparative exports from Burma in the two decades prior to World War II would, therefore, be a major indicator of the economy's growth. Data cited earlier in another connection (Table 7) have shown that the average value of exports by five-year periods dropped from 660 million kyats in 1921–26 and 661 million kyats in 1926–31 to 486 million kyats in 1931–36 and 519 million kyats in 1936–41. Despite price changes, it is plain that the output and surplus of Burma's major productive sectors had leveled off. The leveling off in agricultural acreage has already been noted. Timber produc-tion for some years had been controlled through forest reserve areas and placed on a stabilized sustained-yield basis. Minerals output, virtually all of which went into export, had also leveled off at a peak in the early 1920s. Little new industrial investment and production was in evidence in the inter-war period.

Supporting evidence is found in the facts known about the foreign firms that accumulated most of the savings in the Burmese economy. The practice of these firms was to pay out a large part of their earnings in the form of dividends. Dividend payments of 20 to 40 per cent were common. It was also their practice to make liberal provision for depreciation and to accumulate substantial reserves. It was not their practice to plow back a large part of earnings into plant expansion and modernization. Thus the estimated 6.7 per cent of the gross domestic product which went into net capital formation in 1938–39 may reasonably be considered to have applied generally during the inter-war period. Assuming a 3:1 ratio of capital input to income response, this would indicate an average annual increase of 2 per cent in the output of the economy during those years. With population growing at an average annual rate of 1.4 per cent, the increased output per capita would appear to have been little more than one third of one per cent per year. It is by no means clear that even this exceedingly modest increase in per capita output was generally shared among the population. Furnivall, for example, has argued rather convincingly that the living level of the Burmese cultivator actually experienced a decline over the pre-World War II decades.

Finally, indirect corroboration of the relative stagnation of the Burmese economy before World War II may be found in the stagnant educational system, in the growing incidence of crime and in the increasing political dissatisfaction and frustration of the population.

CHAPTER 5

Independence and Economic

Aspirations, Plans and Policies

WAR AND INDEPENDENCE

World War II made it possible for Burma to achieve early independence. It also created circumstances which gravely endangered that independence as soon as it was achieved. The war inflicted great physical damage on the country, first in 1942 when the Japanese invaded, and then in 1945 when the Allies bombed and fought their way back in. The Burmese people experienced a rude shock when the Japanese, whom they first viewed as liberators, subjected them to tyranny, humiliation and privation far more severe than they had ever known. War uprooted and displaced the population, and caused much fertile agricultural land to revert to jungle. It sharpened internal ideological conflicts and, as part of the tactics of the independence fight during and immediately after the war, it provided large segments of the population with arms which were later to become the weapons of insurrection. By cheapening the value in which life was held and the respect for law and order, it intensified a disposition to rely upon violence and terror as means of achieving political ends — what was later called "the cult of the gun."

The British withdrawal in 1942 was preceded by damaging Japanese bombings and was accompanied by a scorched-earth policy. Railways and waterways were stripped of their rolling and floating stock, mines were flooded, oil refineries were dynamited, oil wells sabotaged, bridges blown up, ports blocked, roads damaged and power stations demolished. Under Japanese occupation, hopes of the nationalists for independent action within the "greater co-prosperity sphere" were quickly dashed. Religious sentiments were outraged and personal dignity was subjected to serious affronts. Imports of required consumer goods were scanty. Textiles were virtually unobtainable. Moreover, the Japanese ruthlessly exploited for their own purposes such domestic production as was available and preempted the limited transport facilities for military use. Internal distribution of consumer supplies was disrupted. Domestic vegetable oils were requisitioned for use as lubricants. The draft cattle population, so important to agriculture, was depleted not only by disease but also by requisitions for meat and leather for the Japanese military forces. Labor was put to work in "sweat battalions" and paid in worthless military currency, sometimes for killing tasks such as the construction of the Burmese-Siamese Railroad. Some younger people were, however, sent to Japan for technical training, and some attempts were made by the Japanese military to encourage small-scale local production. The greatest benefit, fortuitously, was the pre-invasion flight of the Indian moneylenders and landowners which left the Delta cultivators free of their rent and interest burdens.

The physical damages sustained by Burma are difficult to evaluate in monetary terms. It is estimated that at least one half of the country's man-made wealth was destroyed. Collis quotes the military administration's "Handing Over Report" as stating: "We do not think it any exaggeration to say that no British possession has suffered so much damage."[1] According to Hagen, "World War II destroyed a larger share of the nation's physical wealth than was destroyed in any other country of the world except perhaps Greece."[2]

Monetary estimates of the extent of the damage have varied considerably. The Burmese War Damage Claims Commission in 1948 reported the total claims of private individuals at K 2.4 billion. A Burmese civil servant, Mr. Barber, estimated agricultural losses alone at K 624 million. Miss Peter Ady estimated a requirement of K 9.5 to K 11 billion in post-war prices to rehabilitate the economy. A Ministry of Finance tabulation calculated war damages at K 12.7 billion, and a Ministry of Foreign Affairs paper tabulated a total of K 50.5 billion. A paper prepared by Robert R. Nathan Associates, consulting economists to the Government, to assist in reparations negotiations with Japan in 1954, concluded that "Approximately K 14 billion in current prices would seem to be a reasonable statement of Burma's physical damages. An additional K 3 to K 5 billion, again in current prices, would seem to be a reasonable equivalent of the goods and services taken by the Japanese in exchange for an eventually worthless Japanese-issued currency."[3]

The Burmese nationalists initially assisted the "liberators" and participated broadly in the puppet government set up by the Japanese. Before long, their

1. Maurice Collis, *Last and First in Burma*, Faber and Faber, London, 1956, p. 253.
2. Everett E. Hagen, *The Economic Development of Burma*, National Planning Association, Washington, D. C., 1956, p. 31.
3. *Burma's Reparations Claims Against Japan*, Robert R. Nathan Associates, Inc., June 5, 1954, p. 2.

shock and disillusionment led them to plot against their new masters and to prepare for the day when they could turn against both the new and the former masters. As, at this juncture, the tides of war began to turn against the Axis, the formulation of a clear-cut English policy with respect to post-war Burma became a matter of increasing urgency. Governor Dorman-Smith, who, together with the remnants of his staff and a group of Burmese advisors, had established a Government-in-Exile at Simla in India, worked hard to prepare reconstruction plans. He tried to persuade the Government in London to enunciate basic policies which would be acceptable to Burma at the war's termination. He was convinced that England should make crystal-clear, while the conflict was still in progress, that (a) within a specified and limited period of years after the war, home rule would be granted on terms no less favorable than those accorded India; (b) England would assist in the reconstruction, thus making good her failure to protect the country from the invader; (c) the Chettyar moneylenders and landowners would not return, and immigration from India would be under Burmese control; (d) the large European firms would not be allowed to re-establish themselves on the former basis; and (e) the Burmese would in general determine basic economic policies affecting their own country. Detailed plans were also worked out at Simla for the rehabilitation and reconstruction of the basic services and sectors of the economy.

The British Government, however, was initially disinclined to accept Dorman-Smith's recommendations. Above all, it refused to place a time limit on the period of post-war British rule, to endanger the status and influence of the British firms, or to accede to the proposed post-war exclusion of the Chettyars and control of Indian immigration by the Burmese. British commercial interests meanwhile argued vigorously for what was essentially a return to the *status quo ante*. The British White Paper of 1945, while more conciliatory, was a great disappointment not only to the Burmese but to those friends of Burma in England, particularly in the Labour Party, who realized that England's policies now must be accommodated to the political realities of nationalist Burma. The recommendations which finally came out of Simla in 1945 were so divorced from the earlier recommendations prepared there that they were denounced as "rubbish" even by Burmese moderates at Simla who were keenly opposed to the extreme nationalists in Rangoon.[4] The determination of the nationalists to fight for immediate independence was confirmed.

The support of the Burmese people by this time had been consolidated under the banner of the Anti-Fascist People's Freedom League led by Aung San, U Nu and other Thakins. As the time of the British reinvasion ap-

4. John F. Cady, *A History of Modern Burma*, Cornell University Press, Ithaca, N.Y., 1958, p. 498.

proached, the A.F.P.F.L. stood firmly for complete sovereignty and independence. Its stand was facilitated by the military considerations as well as the apparent sympathies which influenced Lord Mountbatten, the Supreme Allied Commander for the area. His negotiations with the A.F.P.F.L. to insure its participation in the final fight against the Japanese were indirect recognition that the League represented the Burmese people, and helped it finally to force this position on the civil Government when the latter took over control from the army.

When the British returned to Burma in the spring of 1945, the economy was prostrate. The degree of privation experienced by the people is suggested in an early intelligence report quoted by Collis: " 'The people are in rags. There is no salt, matches, cooking oil. They have barely enough to live on, as the Japs have taken away all their rice, poultry, pigs and cattle. They are suffering from small-pox, skin diseases and malaria, as there are no hospitals and medicines. Shortage of bullocks has made rice cultivation impossible.' "[5] Indeed, wartime privations provided much of the motivation for later decisions to establish cotton-textiles and pharmaceuticals plants.

Initial responsibility for economic affairs was taken over by the Civil Affairs Service (Burma) as part of the military administration. Its primary job was to establish law and order, to bring in emergency supplies of foods, medicines and clothing, and to restore transport, communications and other essential services. C.A.S.(B.) also set up a projects section to restore activity in rice, timber and other main sectors. The largest and most significant of the projects was the rice project and its complementary Rice Marketing Board. The prewar commercial firms were enlisted in this quasi-public effort, with funds advanced by the British Government.[6] But progress could be made only very slowly. And the resumption of civil responsibility by Governor Dorman-Smith in October resulted in a curtailment of lend-lease and other military-financed supplies, to the detriment of Burma's speedy relief and recovery.[7]

No estimates of the levels to which total output had sunk by the war's end have ever been made. These levels must have been very low indeed, for even in 1946–47, the second full year after the war, total output was still down approximately 40 per cent from the 1938–39 level.[8] With 2 million acres of paddy land reverted to jungle and hundreds of thousands of miserable agricultural refugees in the towns, agricultural output was down two fifths, the rice export surplus by a great deal more. Mining and oil production and exports had virtually been eliminated. Timber production was less severely affected.

5. Collis, *op. cit.*, p. 217.

6. Hugh Tinker, *The Union of Burma*, Oxford University Press, London, 1957, p. 18.

7. Mountbatten was reluctant to hand over responsibility so quickly but Dorman-Smith, out of sympathy with the status accorded Aung San and his group by the military, insisted on immediate take-over. (Cady, *op. cit.*, pp. 511–15.)

8. *Economic Survey of Burma 1951*, Table III, p. 3.

Transport was still virtually at a standstill, and the flow of supplies was a trickle. These were the conditions when, in December of 1946, Clement Attlee announced a new policy with respect to Burma. General Aung San went to London in January 1947 to sign an agreement which ensured independence within one year.

This decision had not been easily won. The A.F.P.F.L. position had been pressed not only by blunt demands and general strikes but also by thinly concealed threats, as in the open drilling of military units loyal only to the A.F.P.F.L. Arms parachuted into Burma under Mountbatten's orders to assist in driving out the Japanese had not been turned in as requested. They were cached and ready for use in armed rebellion if the negotiations with the British did not turn out as desired. Moreover, the A.F.P.F.L. itself was not unified in terms of ideology and policy. Its leaders included some men who were primarily nationalists, others who were confirmed socialists, and others, including some of the ablest leaders, who were dedicated Communists. Each of these groups had internal divisions held precariously together only until independence was clearly in sight. Even before it was achieved, the Communists, after splitting among themselves, made their bids for power.

The split between the Red Flag Communists led by Thakin Soe, who wished to conduct armed rebellion against the British, and the White Flag Communists led by Thakin Than Tun, whose line was to work within and capture the A.F.P.F.L., came in March 1946. It was not long before Thakin Soe's group went underground and began active sabotage against the A.F.P.F.L. The reply to this was the expulsion of his group from the Freedom Coalition. The June 1947 assassination of Aung San, whose leadership till then had been unchallenged except by the Communists, was a further and most serious blow. It resulted, however, in a rallying of all other groups around U Nu, who inherited the leadership responsibility.

If "before the war Communism in Burma was purely academic," it had by now become both real and threatening. Thakins Than Tun, Soe, Thein Pe and others were intelligent, hard-working and able, as well as dedicated leaders. To the debt-ridden, dispossessed and land-hungry cultivators their appeal was exceedingly strong. Moreover, in the fight for freedom from the "imperialist yoke," the mental transfer from "imperialism" to "capitalism" involved but a short and easy step.[9] This step was made by many, and the Communist feeling was strong. In the post-war setting, the spectrum of ideological thinking among the influential leaders ranged from democratic socialism on the right to Trotskyism on the left. There was no leadership influential in its

9. "Burma has been for over a century under Imperialist domination, and Capitalists have during the entire period been regarded as the handmaids of Imperialism. During the entire course of our struggle for freedom therefore Capital and Imperialist domination have been closely associated in the minds of all of us who have taken part in that struggle, and it has been impossible to view the two in isolation." (Thakin Nu, *From Peace to Stability* [a collection of speeches], Ministry of Information, Rangoon, 1951, p. 75.)

following to the right of the moderate socialist position. Virtually all the leaders were agreed on socialist goals and objectives: on nationalization and state and/or cooperative ownership of the means of production; on assumption of trade by the Government and/or cooperatives; and on Burmanization (i.e., exclusion of foreigners from roles of influence) of the economy.

The chief differences in economic policy between the leaders were whether capitalist properties, when expropriated, should be compensated; whether foreign investment should be encouraged or taken into partnership, and under what conditions; and whether the country was ready to proceed at once with full-scale nationalization and socialization. A moderate socialist like U Nu had to compromise with more doctrinaire socialists like U Ba Swe and U Kyaw Nyein, and, in his public speeches and statements, be mindful always of the impact which the misrepresentations and more extreme appeals of the Communists exerted upon his audience. In this setting, the economic principles and provisions written into the Constitution, and into the early economic plans and programs, were surprisingly moderate in substance and in tone.

ECONOMIC ASPIRATIONS

The economic aspirations of independent Burma, as written into the Constitution and approved by the Constituent Assembly in September 1947, were those of a planned welfare state dedicated to the material and cultural uplift of the people and to their protection from monopoly exploitation, insecurity and abuse. Specifically, the Constitution provides for (1) social and economic (and, of course, political) justice for all citizens, and for equality of status and opportunity before the law (Preamble); (2) "equality of opportunity for all citizens in matters of public employment and in the exercise or carrying on of any occupation, trade, business or profession" (Section 14); (3) "the right of private property and of private initiative in the economic sphere," except that no one shall have the right to use private property to the detriment of the general public, that monopolistic organizations and practices are forbidden, and that private property, enterprises or sectors of the economy may be nationalized or acquired by the state "in accordance with law which shall prescribe in which cases and to what extent the owner shall be compensated" (Section 23); (4) ultimate ownership by the state of all lands, the right to resume possession and distribute them "for collective or cooperative farming or to agricultural tenants," and the prohibition of large-scale landholdings (Section 30); (5) planning of the economic life of the Union "with the aim of increasing the public wealth, of improving the material conditions of the people and raising their cultural level" (Section 41); (6) operation of all public-utility undertakings and exploitation of all natural resources, by the state, local bodies or peoples' cooperative organizations (Section 44, subsections 1 and 2).

The Constitution also provides for (7) equal pay for similar work to all women (Section 15); (8) the right of citizens to form associations and unions, to acquire property and to follow any occupation, trade, business or profession (Section 17); (9) the right to work, to maintenance in old age and during sickness or loss of capacity, to rest and leisure, and to free and compulsory primary education (Section 33); (10) special attention to the young (Section 34); (11) promotion of the education and economic interests of the weaker and less advanced sections of the people and their protection from social injustice and exploitation (Section 35); (12) regard for the strength and health of workers and the interests of nursing mothers and infants (Section 37); (13) material assistance to economic organizations not working for private profit, with preference being given to cooperatives and similar organizations (Section 42). In addition, Section 36 provides (14) that "The State shall regard the raising of the standard of living of its people and the improvement of public health as among its primary duties."

Under the circumstances, the Constitution was moderate, yet there is no doubt that its framers intended it to serve as an instrument for the creation of a socialist state. And, with Thakin Than Tun, his Communist followers and many other strongly leftist members in the Constituent Assembly, it is not surprising that U Nu, rising to move approval of the draft Constitution, should have described it in broadly Marxist terms as providing a "leftist" foundation for the soon-to-be-independent country and the basis for a new social order.

I might say, at once, that it will be Leftist. And a Leftist country is one in which the People working together to the best of their power and ability strive to convert the natural resources and produce of the land, both above ground and below ground into consumer commodities to which everybody will be entitled each according to his need. In a Leftist country there will be no such thing as a handful of people holding the monopoly over the inexhaustible wealth of the land while the poor and the starving grow more and more numerous. Then again, in such a country the aim of production is not profit for the few but comfort and happiness of a full life for the many. Lastly in a Leftist country there will be no distinction between the employer class and the employed class, or to put it simply there will be no such thing as the master-class and the slave-class, the governing-class and the governed-class. That briefly put, Sir, is what I mean by a Leftist country.

*   *   *

The wealth of Burma has been enjoyed firstly by the big British capitalists, next the Indian capitalists, and next the Chinese capitalists. Burmans are at the bottom, in poverty, and have to be content with the left-over and chewed-over bones and scraps from the table of foreign capitalists.

... All along, whether they liked it or not, the Burmese people have had to bow to this state of affairs. You see, they had not the political power to put an immediate end to that state of affairs. The moment we have the power, we will have to do away with this unfair, one-sided economic system. But that will not be all. I want the House to bear in mind that we will have to construct new economy in the place of the one to be abolished.

* * *

We are out to crush that evil economic system whereby a handful of people hold the monopoly, while the masses of Burma remain in endless poverty. It is immaterial as to who cause the perpetuation of this evil system—British, Indian, Chinese or Burman. The evil system must go.[10]

The guarded idealism and language of the Constitution itself undoubtedly owed much to the practical experience and judgment of men like U Mya and U Tin Tut. The Burmese people, however, had another and more ingenuous view of their prospects. In U Nu's own words, "Throughout the long period of resistance against the British, politicians had repeatedly brought home one sole theme 'Once we are freed from British domination, the Burmese people will be prosperous.' The masses kept this assumption very close to their hearts, perhaps more closely than any other assumption. That's why everybody is asking the same old question, 'Independence is here. Where are its attendant benefits?' "[11] U Nu himself was most optimistic. In a speech delivered on National Day, November 8, 1947, not long after the Constitution was approved, he said:

We must show ourselves equal to the rich natural resources of our country. For our masses to come up to standards of living befitting the natural wealth of our country we must all work to the limit from this day and hour. If we can all resolve to do so with one mind I shall predict that within five years at the longest this country of Burma, bountifully provided by nature, with a united and independent people working out their destiny on the soundest of political foundations, will see once again such a golden age as Pagan in the days when Shin Izza Gawna was exercising the magic of his alchemy.[12]

Even as late as 1952, U Nu could still speak publicly of that time in the not too distant future when every family in Burma would possess a house, a car and an income of 800 to 1,000 kyats per month. "Your country," he said, "is rich enough to provide these amenities."[13] While U Nu was conscious of, and mentioned, the need for hard work, the people as a whole were not. In fact, this naïve tendency of the average Burman to expect welfare and abundance to flow automatically from the new-found independence was to persist and provide a major obstacle to real economic advance for some time to come.

10. U Nu, *Towards Peace and Democracy* (a collection of speeches), Ministry of Information, Rangoon, 1949, pp. 2–4, speech at the eighth-day sitting of the third session of the Burma Constituent Assembly on Sept. 24, 1947.
11. Burmese New Year Message, April 16, 1948, *loc. cit.*, p. 70.
12. *Loc cit.*, p. 19.
13. Tinker, *op. cit.*, p. 104.

THE TWO-YEAR PLAN

The welfare-statism[14] of the Constitution was also embodied in the country's first economic plan — the Two-Year Plan of Economic Development for Burma, completed in April 1948. This plan developed out of the Rehabilitation Conference called by General Aung San at the Sorrento Villa shortly before his death, "to co-ordinate and concentrate on the speedy rehabilitation of the country and getting its economy back to pre-war level, . . . the tragic assassination of our national heroes, including our late Bogyoke, who was at the head of the Co-ordination Section [of the Conference] left the work unfinished. This, however, was quickly taken up as soon as possible when the Economic Planning Board was instituted, charged with the function of drawing up a restricted Two-Year Plan of Economic Development. The Plan incorporates most of the valuable material from the "Sorrento Plans," but not all . . ."[15]

While neither comprehensive nor thorough, the Two-Year Plan of 1948 is significant in a number of ways. It was, till 1960, the only attempt at comprehensive economic planning made by independent Burma without the assistance of foreign advisors. It was a first attempt to formulate specific ways and means of achieving the principles and goals stated in the Constitution. It defined the current thinking about economic policies and projects. And it in fact shaped basic agricultural and industrial planning and policy for a number of years thereafter.

Starting with agriculture, the Plan first defined the Government's three basic policies in this field. These were, first, to eliminate landlordism, to return alienated land to the peasants and to prevent further land alienation; second, to insure that land would be cultivated and organized on modern scientific lines and that the cultivator would get a fair share of its produce, be protected against "the caprices of a fluctuating market" and achieve "a standard of living which will enable him to live a full life and enjoy the amenities of modern civilization"; and, third, to regain the pre-war position in rice export and "become self-sufficient in as wide a range of other crops as possible."

The Plan set 1951–52 as the target year for achievement of the pre-war rice position. This was to be accomplished by a cultivation drive (details of which were to be worked out) whereby unrented land would be allocated to tenant farmers and Government loans would be provided toward the reclamation of the paddy lands now reverted to jungle. Targets were set, again for 1951–52, for the desired production of oil seeds, cotton, beans and pulses, onions, chillies and white sugar, but without specific recommendations as to how

14. The term is Frank N. Trager's, in *Building a Welfare State in Burma, 1948–56*, Institute of Pacific Relations, New York, 1958, p. 4.

15. *Two-Year Plan of Economic Development for Burma*, Supt., Govt. Printing and Stationery, Rangoon, 1948, p. 1. Aung San was the Bogyoke (General) referred to in the quotation.

these targets were to be achieved. The Plan favored the regulation of rents on agricultural lands. Stressing the importance of agricultural credit at moderate rates of interest, it recommended the formation of a central state agricultural bank, crop loans, state cattle and improvement loans and cattle insurance. It recommended that at least K 5 crores ($10.5 million) of such credits be provided for the 1948–49 season. In addition, the Plan discussed various policies and methods for improving agricultural output and recommended the stabilization of paddy prices, state control of agricultural exports, the establishment of eight experimental mechanized and collective farms of 2,000 to 3,000 acres each, consideration of tractor stations, additional agricultural research, the standardization of weights and measures, a Bureau of Agricultural Information and an Institute of Agricultural Engineering.

With respect to industrial development, the Plan first recognized the need for resource surveys and for the rehabilitation of the former industries. It recommended an industrial policy under which state ownership and operation would be mandatory for basic industries and preferred even for light consumer-goods industries. The latter, however, might be permitted to private enterprise under appropriate safeguards if state ownership was found impracticable. The Plan recommended the creation of a committee to assist cottage industry in organizing itself into associations, in obtaining technical assistance, in marketing, and the like. But it was about new industry that the Plan was most specific. It recommended the immediate setting up of a tile factory, a paper and chemicals (sulphuric acid, salt, caustic soda, chlorine) factory, a spinning and weaving factory with 20,000 spindles and 200 looms, two sugar mills with a capacity of 24,000 tons per year, a sawmill with a capacity of 30,000 tons of converted timber per year, a steel rerolling factory based on scrap metal, a rubber factory capable initially of producing bicycle tires and rubber shoes, and pilot plants for the production of soap and dairy products. It recommended also additional investigation of "favorable prospects" for still other plants for the production of basic chemicals, paints and varnishes, vegetable oils, industrial alcohol, drugs and pharmaceuticals, glass, porcelain insulators and leather tanning. It called further for additional testing of the Kalewa coal fields and their development if the tests proved satisfactory. With respect to the privately owned rice-milling industry, the Plan stated that "Endeavors shall be made to increase and improve the milling power in order to cope with increased production, and to reduce the percentage of broken rice produced at the existing mills."

Proposals regarding electric power, while general, were far-reaching. Noting that the nationalization of all electric power generating facilities had already been decided upon, the Plan recommended the creation of an Electricity Supply Board. Referring to a hydroelectric project already decided upon by the Government at the Bagawta Chaung, it urged that further survey work necessary for this project be carried out expeditiously, and recognized that for such a survey consulting engineers would have to be engaged. It referred also to the consideration being given to a hydroelectric project at Saingdin Falls, in connection with which the proposed paper and pulp plant was mentioned. The Plan called for still other broad surveys and the formulation of a long-term plan for the utilization of all sources of electric power and the electrification of transport and industry, and held that experts would again be necessary to assist in these. Finally, the Plan called for the generation and supply of electric power to a number of specific towns in the near future.

Other sections, including that dealing with transport and communications, were exceedingly brief. The Plan mentioned the urgent effort needed to restore transport and communications facilities, the desirability of extending new rail lines to hitherto non-accessible hill areas, and the need for several specified new highways. The inland-water transport services were to be nationalized and their employment Burmanized.

In the field of forestry, the Plan recommended that pre-war output targets be achieved by 1951–52, that state exploitation of the forests be conducted in accordance with sound conservation practices, that there be a gradual takeover of the extraction and milling processes and that state export controls be continued.

The fisheries recommendations were restricted to the creation of a research staff and laboratory and the inauguration of pilot training schemes in fishing and in the use of refrigerated transport facilities.

The Plan recognized the need for financial reconstruction, and stated somewhat ambiguously that "financial policy shall also be brought in line with the general policy of state socialism." It recommended the creation of a state bank, the inauguration of a decimal currency, the reorganization of the audit department, a savings campaign and compulsory life insurance for state employees.

Other sections of the Plan briefly discussed labor policies and relations, the need for further surveys of natural resources and the need for economic research.

Within a total of fifty-five pages, the Plan devoted fourteen to its discussion of agriculture, three to forestry, seven to industrial development, one to fisheries, six to technical education, three to electricity, five to labor, two to transport and communications, two to finance, six to surveys of natural resources, two to economic research and a page or less to other subjects. Much of this space was given over to the description of the pre-war and the current situations, and to statistical data concerning them.

Although the Plan started with the basic policy of state socialism as given, and was a fragmentary mixture of policies, plans and programs rather than a comprehensive plan, it does give evidence of a responsible attitude on the part of the people who framed it, a certain cautiousness of approach, a knowledge of agriculture, specific ideas about industry and a healthy awareness of the need for a great deal of additional investigation, research and expert assistance before much further progress could be made. It displays, however, not the vaguest notion of the magnitude of the task it was laying out, or of the time that would be required to complete it. For example, the following language and space are devoted to the major task of railways rehabilitation: "Urgent efforts must therefore be made to restore railway communications to normal as rapidly as availability of materials and technical personnel will permit."[16] And the following is the full treatment accorded docks and ports: "The building and repairs of Dockyards, Port facilities, etc., shall also be expedited."[17] Furthermore, the Plan does not betray the slightest notion of the magnitude of the financing that would be required, let alone consider how such an expenditure might be financed.

The Plan stands, therefore, more as an outline of what needed to be done than as a plan for getting it done, a statement of the "what" rather than the "how." It is a peculiar mixture of the down-to-earth and the unrealistic, of the knowledgeable and the naïve. In the industrial field, however, it broke new ground. The projects it recommended for early implementation were more or less identical with those incorporated into the comprehensive development program some years later.[18]

In many ways, the Two-Year Plan was the precursor of the "Comprehensive Development Plan" (as it came to be called) prepared in 1951–53. It recognized the huge basic rehabilitation job which had to be done in the transport and communications fields. It seemed to take completely for granted the similar task in oil and mining, on which it was completely silent.[19] It treated agriculture and forestry in dual terms which embraced the recovery of production to pre-war levels and the reorganization of tenure and operations. It called, although in quite general terms, for a broad electrification program, and in very specific terms for a large-scale industrialization program within the public sector. While the cost of these programs was not estimated at the time, it would certainly have approximated in magnitude the public sector investment estimates later prepared in conjunction with the "comprehensive" program. When the American consultants arrived in 1951, the Burmese already knew pretty well what they wanted — rehabilitation, better balance and structural reform in agriculture, rehabilitation and improvements in

16. *Ibid.,* p. 44.
17. *Ibid.,* p. 45.
18. *Ibid.,* Part IV, p. 21. The major exception was the large jute mill which was suggested only later.
19. The reference to the Kalewa coal fields involved new development, not rehabilitation. Undoubtedly the planners were counting on the large English firms to rehabilitate mining, perhaps in partnership with the Government.

transport and communications, and sizable new development in manufacturing industry and electric power, all within the context of state socialism.

THE INSURRECTION

Any progress which might have been made under the Two-Year Plan was stopped in its tracks by the insurrection. Even while the work on the Two-Year Plan was still under way, Thakin Than Tun and the White Flag Communists adopted in February 1948, shortly after independence, a revolutionary program directed to the overthrow of the Government. In the following months they went underground and into active revolt. Not only did the leftist unity program, which U Nu formulated in May in the attempt to reunite the coalition, fail to bring back the Communists; even the P.V.O.'s, the Marxist-minded organized remnants of the wartime Burmese independence army, refused to accept it. In the months which followed, a number of army units defected to the rebels, and the P.V.O.'s themselves went underground. Karen revolts broke out in September, with a separate Karen state as their objective. In December, the powerful Karen National Defense Organization (K.N.-D.O.) was formed, and it too went into active revolt.

So desperate did the situation become that within a month, January 1949, the Socialist members of U Nu's Cabinet were negotiating with the Communists and the P.V.O.'s in an effort to obtain their cooperation in the fight against the Karens. At this point the Union of Civil Service Employees challenged the salary cut which the Government had felt forced to impose as a result of its disrupted finances and sharply reduced revenues. With the K.N.D.O. forces camped on the very outskirts of Rangoon at Insein, the Government's civil servants early in February went on a strike in which the students and railway employees soon joined. By March, according to one historian,[20] the Socialist members of the Cabinet were offering to capitulate to the Communists and to turn control of the Government over to them. The only conditions they asked were that U Nu should remain as Prime Minister and that the new Government's "People's Courts" should not bring any charges against the Socialists for actions taken by them while in office. Even these pathetic conditions were declined by the Communists, and in April 1949 the Socialists resigned from the Cabinet. This was the newly independent country's darkest hour.

Tinker states that U Nu had not been aware of the Socialist negotiations, and that when he found out about them he repudiated the Socialist offer. Other historians of the period do not accept this version.[21] In any event, form-

20. Tinker, *op. cit.*, p. 43.

21. Cady (*op. cit.*, pp. 594–96) states there is evidence that the "seeming defection" was made with U Nu's consent. Furnivall (*The Governance of Modern Burma*, Institute of Pacific Relations, New York, 1960, p. 117) states that the Socialist resignation was intended to "facilitate a reconciliation between U Nu and and his critics."

ing a new Government with General Ne Win as Deputy Prime Minister at a time when the Government's authority extended scarcely beyond the boundaries of Rangoon, U Nu stood firm. This proved to be the turning point. By June the Government was already recapturing some of the towns which had been in the hands of the various insurgent forces. Late in the year the Government was able to take the initiative, and by the end of 1950 the position was more or less consolidated. All large concentrations of rebels had by that time been broken up, and the major threat to the Government removed. From then on, the fight against insurgency became a process of attrition.

The size of the insurgent forces at their peak was stated by U Nu to have been in excess of 15,000, made up as follows: fully armed Communists, over 5,000; Army mutineers, mostly Karens, more than 4,800; Union Military Police personnel, 2,000; Police and Special Police Reserves, over 1,700; and Sitwundans (locally organized protection units), over 1,500.[22]

By the end of 1950 it was estimated that the damages inflicted by the insurrection to public property had amounted to K 42.5 crores, that extra defense expenditures had amounted to K 40 crores and that damage to private property had amounted to K 100 crores. Estimates made almost a year earlier had indicated losses at that time of K 20 crores in Government revenues and K 1.25 crores in treasury lootings. The estimates of February 1949 also stated that some 30,000 persons had lost their lives in the insurrection.[23] The larger losses, however, must be measured by the impact of the insurrection on the economy as a whole. Total output, which had risen from 61 per cent of the pre-war level in 1946–47 to 72 per cent in the following year, declined to 65 per cent of the pre-war level in 1948–49 and to 61 per cent in 1949–50. Thus, four years after the war's end the economy had been driven back to virtually the early post-war level of output. It was not until 1951–52 that total economic output again reached and slightly surpassed the high point of 1947–48.[24]

THE EVOLUTION OF ECONOMIC
POLICIES AND PROGRAMS

Even as the authority and the very life of the young state were being assaulted and gravely endangered, the economic goals and aspirations incorporated in the Constitution were reaffirmed, economic principles and policies were further evolved, and steps were taken to relieve distress, reorganize the economy and make progress towards the country's basic economic objectives.

These principles and policies reflected two disparate points of view. The first and more moderate of these was the one reflected in the Constitution and in the Two-Year Plan. While devoted to socialist ideals and objectives, it was also

22. U Nu, in *From Peace to Stability*, p. 202.
23. *Ibid.*, p. 134, and *Towards Peace and Democracy*, p. 132.
24. *Economic Survey of Burma 1956*, p. 6.

firmly dedicated to democratic procedures, oriented to the western democracies, appreciative of the clear distinction between goals and ways and means,
and aware of the great practical difficulties which confronted the nation in
achieving its objectives. The other point of view, more doctrinaire and extreme, was impatient of compromise and delay, was oriented to the Soviet
Union, and catered to the illusions, miseries and passions of the economically
distressed populace. The sympathies of U Nu clearly were with the more
moderate view. As a statesman seeking to re-establish internal peace, however,
he was of necessity sensitive to the demands of the extreme left. Consequently,
the policies formulated and the measures taken went as far as they could in the
direction of a program on the basis of which "Leftist Unity" could be achieved
as a "keystone of the arch of national unity."

Thus, a fifteen-point compromise program announced in May 1948 proposed, *inter alia:*

(1) To secure political and economic relations with Soviet Russia and the democratic countries of Eastern Europe in the same way as we are now having these
relations with Britain and the United States.

(2) To nationalize monopolizing capitalist undertakings, and to administer the
resulting national undertakings by partnership between the State and the workers,
. . . the question of compensation to be considered only after these undertakings
have been nationalized.

(3) The State to take into its own hands the export and the import trade, in
fact all foreign trade.

* * *

(5) The refusal of any foreign aid of a kind which will compromise the political, economic and the strategic independence of Burma.

* * *

(7) To abolish private ownership of land and to distribute the land only among
the tillers of the soil.

(8) To draw up a plan for the industrialization of the country with a time-
table and to begin work on it at once.[25]

The proposed program was not accepted by the dissident groups. The Communists, as we have seen, did not return to the fold. The P.V.O.'s hesitated,
and then defected. The insurrection went from bad to worse. The Government, however, did not withdraw from its maximum compromise position.
The concessions which the moderates had offered were to influence policy
profoundly throughout the next decade.

The key economic policies stressed during the following period were concerned chiefly with industrialization, economic self-sufficiency, Burmaniza-

25. Thakin Nu, "The Programme," a statement made on May 25, 1948, in *Towards Peace and
Democracy*, pp. 92–94.

tion, the application of socialist principles, the role of private enterprise (both domestic and foreign) in the economy, and policy with respect to foreign aid.

Several motives underlay the urge for industrialization. Paramount among these were the belief that only through modernization and industrialization could the country's economic potentials be realized, and the companion belief, reinforced strongly by wartime privations, that industrialization was necessary to economic self-sufficiency. The first of these motivations was expressed by U Nu in June 1948 as follows:

the [Leftist Unity] Programme provides that a plan should be drawn up and work begun for the industrialization of the country. We cannot become a modern State until our factories, our electrical installations and our railways are increased a hundredfold or even a thousandfold. It is only when we reach this stage that the prosperity of the people will be in consonance with the country's wealth and natural resources. That is why it is necessary that we should begin working for the industrialization of the land, to draw plans and to carry out these plans. Government's Two Year Plan represents their initial effort in this direction.[26]

The second motivation was also stated by U Nu, in July 1949, but with far less clarity:

The primary concern of every citizen is to achieve economic self-sufficiency of the Union. Other problems pale into insignificance compared to it. Look at the countries of the world. However big a country may be its chief problem is that of self-sufficiency. It occupies top priority in the programme of any Government. Even in the United States of America, the world's wealthiest country, this principle holds good. England, France and the idol of the leftists — Soviet Russia — are no exception to the rule.[27]

These motivations were reinforced by the Socialists' belief that industrialization was necessary to the creation of a socialist state and by the healthy desire to reduce the economy's dependence on rice. Undoubtedly considerations of national pride and prestige also played a role. The confused element in the thinking about industrialization was the self-sufficiency idea. There was evident here a real confusion between economic self-sufficiency and economic independence. The Burmese believed, soundly, that their newly won political independence needed to be bolstered by a complementary economic independence. They failed to recognize, however, that economic independence lay in a combination of basic self-support and native control over the economy,

26. Thakin Nu, "The Nature of Leftist Unity," speech at the B.A.A. Ground on June 13, 1948, *loc. cit.,* p. 135.

Repeated reference is made here and subsequently to U Nu because, as President of the A.F.P.F.L. and Prime Minister, he was the official voice of party and Government policy. It was U Nu's practice to submit his important policy statements in draft to the Central Executive Committee of the A.F.P.F.L. and to the Cabinet for prior approval. These statements must therefore be regarded as reflecting far more than his personal views.

27. "Peace Within One Year," *loc. cit.,* p. 224.

rather than in an ability of the economy to produce anything and everything they might desire.

The object of the Burmanization policy was to displace foreigners — English, Indians and Chinese — from positions of economic control and influence. This was desired both as an adjunct of economic independence and as a salve to the personal humiliations experienced under foreign rule. Since the policy was directed to all sectors of the economy — to industry as well as agriculture, timber, trade and commerce, and the professions and civil services — the nationalism which underlay Burmanization policy provided a powerful impetus to industrialization policy.

It is only fair to point out that U Nu himself did not subscribe to the Burmanization policy with the same extremism and passion as many of his colleagues and followers. As early as September 1947, in addressing the Constituent Assembly, he emphasized that the important issue was not that of foreigner versus Burman, but rather that of exploiter versus the people.

Thus, in presenting the draft Constitution, he stated:

The question then arises as to whether this [the creation of a new economy] can be effected by the substitution of Burman capitalists in the place of foreign capitalists and whether by this means it will be possible to convert that unfair one-sided bad economy into fair and equitable good economy. At first glance, it might seem that it will be something to the good if Burmans are to enjoy now what formerly foreign capitalists enjoyed.

. . . Actually it would be, as they say, "The new Presbyter is the old Priest writ large." Mere change of garb will not mend matters. The only difference so far as I can see is that the blood-sucking "trousers and dhoties" will be replaced by "pasoes."[28] This however is not what we want, not by any means.[29]

With respect to the selection of ways and means by which socialist goals were to be achieved, the moderates were again on the defensive. Time and again U Nu attempted to educate his people to the fact that the techniques employed in the Soviet Union and other Communist or socialist countries were not necessarily well suited to the Burmese situation, and to distinguish between socialism and nationalization. He stressed repeatedly also that socialism could not be built overnight.

Thus in a May Day speech in 1948 which addressed a triple warning to the leftists, U Nu argued against the blind emulation of Communist techniques. Referring to an ancient Burmese allegory concerning the magical tree which produced abundance, he said:

28. The dhoti was the garb of the Indian merchants, while the pasoe is the dress-up, as compared with the everyday, longyi or skirt worn by well-to-do Burmans.

29. "Sowing the Seeds of Freedom," speech at the eight-day sitting of the third session of the Burma Constituent Assembly on Sept. 24, 1947, *loc. cit.*, pp. 3–4.

It behooves us therefore to use, with all our energy, this Leftism as a means by which we shall bring to Burma that magic tree. But when we plant the tree there are many points which we must remember. One important point to remember is that when we plant that tree, we should not be guided by books of words but plant the seed in relation to Burmese soil, Burmese water and Burmese climate. We should not attempt to read books on how such trees are planted in England, or in Russia, or in China and try to emulate these efforts. The methods which achieve success in other countries may not achieve success in Burma and what is written in books cannot be blindly followed. The effects of Burmese soil, Burmese water and Burmese climate, must be carefully considered if the tree is to grow. Lenin and Stalin when building up Russia did not use everything which they found in the writings of Karl Marx. They adopted what was suitable for Russia.[30]

In a Martyr's Day speech in July 1950 entitled "Our Policy and Programme," U Nu referred to the lamentable misunderstanding of the socialist creed "among certain quarters in our country" and attributed this misunderstanding to "the colossal ignorance of some socialist propagandists, their debased moral character, conceit and tactlessness." He added: "Many of us consider that socialism is nothing but the nationalization of all wealth and industries of the well-to-do. Nationalization itself is not an end but only a means in the socialist scheme of things."[31]

And in a National Day speech in November 1948, he said: "If any one asked me if I wanted to transform Burma into a Leftist country, I would, without hesitation, answer in the affirmative. If again I am asked whether Burma could be transformed overnight into a Leftist country, I would, without hesitation, answer in the negative. Burma cannot be transformed overnight into a Leftist country."[32]

The policy toward free enterprise was clearly related to the foregoing in a speech to the Burma Chamber of Commerce and Industries in December 1948. In this speech, U Nu said:

Although we are very keen to transform the Union into a Leftist country, we have a firm conviction that it cannot be done overnight. At such a time of transition from one epoch to another the Union Government, with a view to rehabilitate the shattered economy and to start new commercial enterprises, is keenly desirous of the co-operation of all businessmen, great and small, who own capital or the necessary business experience or both. On behalf of the Union Government, I wish to state that we enthusiastically desire the co-operation of all businessmen to lay firm economic foundations of the Union, by individual enterprise wherever possible, by collective enterprise where individual enterprise is impossible, by in-

30. "Warning to Leftists," *loc. cit.,* p. 79.
31. *From Peace to Stability,* p. 86.
32. "Three Major Problems," in *Towards Peace and Democracy,* p. 161.

vesting capital in those enterprises . . . in which they are proficient but for which financial aid is necessary.[33]

Thus, at the outset, and for a number of years after, the stated policy was to encourage private initiative and investment on an interim basis, pending socialization of the economy. The response was not impressive.

By the spring of 1949, when the fortunes of the Government in its fight with the insurgents were at their lowest ebb, an official report put the need for private enterprise on a note of desperate urgency:

> It is necessary to stress the fact that the present economic situation of Burma is very dangerous and almost desperate . . . production is less than one half the prewar level . . . Yet a larger population is trying to maintain a higher standard of living than before the war. This cannot last . . . the end must inevitably be inflation, hurried efforts at retrenchment, unemployment and general collapse. Something *must* be done urgently to save us from economic ruin with the almost inevitable resulting loss of political independence . . . We must increase *production*.[34]

The report argued for austerity, savings and capital formation, for priority in imports to raw materials for home industry, for a "Buy Burmese" campaign and for throwing all fields of enterprise, with but few exceptions, open to the private sector: ". . . we cannot take over all the foreign enterprises all at once, and it is a waste of time to discuss the nationalization of nonexistent industries. In our present economic situation we have no time to waste. We must do all we can as quickly as we can to encourage enterprise." Since in the opinion of the reporting committee *"all that State and private Burman enterprise can do for many years to come will be quite inadequate to develop industrial production in Burma,"* it was necessary to seek the help of foreign enterprise. "We need foreign enterprise to assist in the industrial development of Burma, and we should impose on it only such restrictions as are necessary for the national welfare of Burma," the committee said.

And in June 1949, in a statement of Government policy laid before the Parliament by U Nu, he declared: "Since we do not possess either the capital or the technical resources necessary for industrialization, we must enlist the help of foreign capital and technicians."[35]

The enforced evolution of policy with respect to private foreign investment was matched by a corresponding development with respect to foreign national aid as well. The Leftist Unity program of May 1948 had stated the position in negative terms — "the refusal by Burma of any foreign aid which would be detrimental to the political, economic and strategic freedom of Burma." Be-

---

33. *Loc cit.*, p. 165.
34. *Report of the Industrial Development Committee on Industrial Policy*, Laid on the Table of Parliament on September 28, 1949, Supt., Govt. Printing and Stationery, Rangoon, 1949, p. 5.
35. Tinker, *op. cit.*, p. 96.

hind this lurked a suspicion "that by debts do we become enslaved" and the belief that through unity, work, production and exports there would be no need to seek foreign loans or aid "with humble demeanor."[36] By February 1950 this tone had changed. "We are convinced," said U Nu, "(a) that Burma cannot progress without financial and technical assistance of foreign countries, and (b) that our declared policy in regard to foreign affairs of not aligning ourselves with any power bloc does not exclude us from co-operating closely with the Democracies in matters relating to economic development."[37] And in January 1951, in replying to critics who questioned a recent Commonwealth loan of £6 million and a $10 million grant from the United States, he reaffirmed, "We will accept aid from any country so long as such aids are beneficial to our Union and do not affect directly or indirectly the sovereignty of our country."[38]

Two additional policies, political in character but with great significance for economic development, must also be mentioned. From the beginning the A.F.P.F.L. had firmly stated and repeatedly reiterated that it would adhere only to democratic principles and practices in seeking to build the Socialist State. It repudiated the violence and the tyranny of communism. Secondly, with respect to its policy for dealing with the insurrectionists, U Nu repeatedly made clear that:

We are not fighting them [the Communists] because they hold views differing from those of the A.F.P.F.L. nor are we fighting them because unity cannot be achieved with them, but only because they are attempting to overthrow the Government by force of arms. . . .

Let the Communists discard their policy of seizing power by violence and announce that they will follow the methods of democracy and end the insurrection. Government will at once issue orders for the "cease fire." . . .

But we must divide them into three classes in respect of treatment: (i) those who have not yet been engaged in armed insurrection, (ii) those who have been so engaged, and (iii) those who, under the cloak of Communism, have committed dacoity, rape or murder.

We shall take no action against those in the first category; we shall take action against those in the second category, but deal with them leniently. Those in the third category will be dealt with firmly in accordance with the law. . . .

I do hope very much therefore that Communists who have faith in their own beliefs, in their leadership and in the masses will leave the darkness, quit the insurrection, and emerge into the light of day.[39]

36. Thakin Nu, "The Nature of Leftist Unity," June 13, 1948, in *Towards Peace and Democracy,* pp. 133–34.
37. "Economic Problems," speech at the Burma Chamber of Commerce, Feb. 23, 1950, in *From Peace to Stability,* p. 76.
38. "Our Achievements," speech at the Union Youth Rally, Jan. 8, 1951, *loc. cit.,* p. 154.
39. "The Nature of Leftist Unity," June 13, 1948, in *Towards Peace and Democracy,* pp. 125–26.

The "lenient" treatment promised those who had engaged in insurrection was to go so far in practice as to lose all significant deterrence value.

The evolution of Government economic policy was accompanied by economic action on a number of fronts. The most important steps were those directed towards the relief of agrarian distress and towards agrarian reform. Tenancy arrangements were placed under Government supervision and control, annual rent payments were limited to twice the inflation-depleted value of the land-revenue tax, moratoria were declared on taxes due, agricultural credits were liberally extended, further land alienation was prohibited and a land-nationalization and distribution program was enacted. Rice and timber exports were placed under the control of Government monopolies, and imports of essential consumer goods in the hands of another Government organization, the Civil Supplies Management Board. The generation and distribution of electric power were nationalized and placed under the authority of an Electricity Supply Board. Inland-water transport was nationalized under a corresponding board, as was teak timber extraction and processing. An energetic effort was made to revivify and strengthen both agricultural and consumer cooperatives. It was even contemplated for a time to place under the control of these cooperatives the respective state monopolies for rice exports and consumer goods imports.

So long as the insurrection continued on a large scale, neither these economic policies and measures nor any others could have made much contribution towards reviving the economy. Villagers were still fearful in many areas of going out into the fields or the forests. Foreign capital would not undertake sizable expenditures to rehabilitate the mines, oil fields and former industries. Domestic investment was at a virtual standstill. The still-shattered internal transport systems could not function at more than a crawl. Trade and commerce languished. Not until 1950–51, as the tides of the insurrection began to recede, could the economy sluggishly begin to show signs of revival. And only with the advent of 1951–52, when economic output had once again reached the 1947–48 level, could serious efforts toward economic rehabilitation be made.

Even as the first signs of revival appeared, the Government took steps to marshal technical and other assistance from abroad, so as to prepare itself for the major effort ahead. A modest loan of £6 million was arranged for in London in June 1950. An economic cooperation agreement was concluded with the United States three months later which called for an initial grant of $10 million to be provided chiefly in technical assistance. Arrangements were made for a group of English economists to visit Burma in March–April 1951, and for a combined team of American consulting engineers and economists to make a comprehensive two-year survey and recommendations for Burma's development beginning later that year, the dollar costs to be covered within the United States grant.

The survey and recommendations of the American consultants, and the history of the program they helped to formulate and execute, are part of the major concern of this book, and will be dealt with in subsequent chapters. Brief attention, however, should be given here to the contribution of the British economists[40] as the final element in the introductory setting.

This contribution took the form of a group of seven papers on major economic problems prepared under considerable time pressure, and of a set of tentative national product accounts for 1947–48, which were presented for discussion to a special conference in April 1951 held under the auspices of the National Planning Ministry. Among the findings and recommendations of the group were: (1) the ebb of the insurrection tide made rehabilitation and developmental action possible; (2) though intensive work needed to be started on an economic survey and related research, action could not await its completion; (3) the effect of the Government's then existing fiscal operations was deflationary and should be countered by early investment on public projects (roads and buildings) which did not require much study, planning or expert assistance; (4) the Government should not hesitate to borrow, if necessary, for sound self-liquidating projects; (5) the Government need not be unduly alarmed about inflation; (6) while the outlook for the balance of payments was bright, the Government should build up state controls over imports, since such control would be of strategic importance later on; and (7) the rigid currency standard, based 100 per cent on foreign exchange holdings, should be made more flexible.

Far more important than any of the foregoing, however, was the analysis that a program of industrialization was the only productive means of absorbing the annual increment of some 50,000–60,000 men of working age to the labor force. "If all this increase has to be absorbed in agriculture sooner or later the standard of living of Burmese people must decline," it was stated. "This is the strongest single argument, indeed the overriding argument, in favour of industrialization on a scale at least sufficient to absorb into the industrial and service sector the annual increment in numbers of working men."[41] The size of industrial and related investments required to do this absorption job, on the basis of the preference for capital-extensive industries recommended, was estimated at K 40 to K 50 crores ($84 million to $105 million) per year.

40. The economists were G. D. N. Worswick, Dudley Seers, Peter Ady, K. Martin and F. A. Burchardt. Though they were frequently referred to as "The Oxford Economists," Martin was actually from the University of Manchester.

41. *Conference Papers on Current Economic Problems of Burma 1951*, Supt., Govt. Printing and Stationery, Rangoon, 1951, p. 4.

I do not intend to discuss here the validity of this analysis, although I believe that the premise of early declines in the marginal productivity of added investments in Burma's then existing state of agriculture, on which it rests, is open to grave question. The importance of the recommendation, as Burma girded herself for a major economic development effort, is that it confirmed and gave additional emphasis to her determination to industrialize.

Part II

THE EIGHT-YEAR
DEVELOPMENT PROGRAM

INTRODUCTION TO PART II

Burma's comprehensive eight-year economic and social development program was prepared by a combined group of two engineering firms and one economic consulting firm, engaged in the United States for that purpose by the Burmese Government with funds provided under the Technical Cooperation Administration Program. Representatives of these firms — the Knappen Tippetts Abbett engineering firm, Pierce Management, Inc., mining engineers, and Robert R. Nathan Associates, Inc., consulting economists — arrived in Burma in the fall of 1951.

The comprehensive program was formulated over a period of more than two years ending early in 1954. Three distinct steps were involved in the process. First, in January 1952 the group of consultants submitted a preliminary report and recommendations — the so-called K.T.A. Preliminary Report. Second, in August 1952 the Government held a major economic conference, known as the Pyidawtha Conference, which endorsed the main economic targets recommended in that report and accepted in principle its recommendations for immediate action to invest some K 108 crores ($227 million) in the basic sectors of the economy. This conference also adopted major programs for agriculture, land nationalization, transport and communications, housing, education and health, as well as programs for locally developed improvement projects and a plan for more democratic local administration. Third, the consultants submitted in August 1953 their final Comprehensive Report on the Economic and Engineering Development of Burma.

This report provided an economic framework which embraced not only the specific programs recommended by the consultants for public action in the productive and essential-services sectors of the economy, but also the Government's own plans for social investment and anticipated investment by the private sector. The Government's acceptance of this report in February 1954 gave it a comprehensive development plan. There remained yet, however, a fourth and less distinct step in the process, occurring over a period of time as the Government made decisions which substantially altered the program's size and composition.

The eight-year program has popularly been identified, even within Burma, as the K.T.A. Program. Actually, the participation in its formulation was much broader than that name implies. The real beginning had been made with the Two-Year Plan of 1948. In addition, as was pointed out in the *Economic Survey of Burma 1953,*

A United Nations Social Services Mission has surveyed the social welfare needs of the country and submitted recommendations for development of social services. Another group of United Nations technicians has made recommendations concerning the development of cottage industries and has initiated programmes of technical advice in this field. Individual technical advisors have been available in almost every field of economic activity. The Department of Agriculture has prepared a five-year programme for the expansion of agricultural output and the production of new crops. The Ministry of Land Nationalization has prepared an eight-year plan. The Irrigation Department has planned a number of projects, in collaboration with K.T.A. engineers. In similar manner other agencies of the Government have prepared programmes relating to their specific fields of activity. Government is evolving its development programme in the light of the over-all recommendations of the consulting engineers and economists and of the specific programmes proposed by other consulting groups and by the various Government agencies.[1]

The development program finally adopted was, therefore, an amalgam of Burmese and foreign planning in which even on the foreign side a variety of sources had participated.

Economic development did not stand still while the process of formulating and finalizing the program was going on. A 20,000-spindle cotton spinning mill had been set in motion by the Two-Year Plan and was about to start operation at the time the K.T.A. group arrived in Burma. Contracts had been let, and construction was already under way on a modern airport at Rangoon. Most of the preliminaries for setting up a large brick and tile factory had already been completed, and machinery and equipment had been ordered abroad. With T.C.A. help, rehabilitation of the Port of Rangoon was going forward. Preparatory work was in process toward the erection of a large modern hospital in Rangoon, again with T.C.A. help.

The K.T.A. Preliminary Report itself made a number of recommendations for immediate or early action which were soon translated into investment activity. The Pyidawtha Conference approved these and gave added impetus to investment, especially in the social sectors. From 1950–51, immediately prior to the K.T.A. Preliminary Report, to 1952–53, at the end of which the K.T.A. Comprehensive Report was submitted, annual capital formation practically doubled. Gross public fixed capital formation increased from K 13.3 crores to K 25.9 crores, or 95 per cent. Total net fixed capital formation in the economy

1. *Economic Survey of Burma 1953,* p. 57.

increased from K 20.3 crores to K 39.7 crores, also 95 per cent.[2] It will be understood therefore why the so-called K.T.A. Eight-Year Plan did not begin with the financial year 1953–54, the beginning of which coincided with the submission of the Comprehensive Report, but rather with January 1952, immediately following the submission of the Preliminary Report. That was when the accelerated investment program really began.

This program — hailed by Prime Minister U Nu as being "of supreme importance . . . for the creation of a new state and ushering in of a new era for the people"[3] — dominated the economic and social life of Burma throughout the remainder of the decade, and the fumbling of it contributed in 1958 to a political crisis of major proportions. How the program came into being, and what it was, will be examined in the following chapters.

2. *Economic Survey of Burma 1956,* Table 5, p. 10.
3. *The Pyidawtha Conference, August 4–17, 1952, Resolutions and Speeches,* Ministry of Information, Rangoon, Dec. 18, 1952, Introduction.

CHAPTER 6

The American Consultants and

Their Preliminary Report

THE AMERICAN CONSULTANTS

U Nu has described the origin of the K.T.A. contract arrangements in the following way:

I want to say a few words on the history of the economic projects, generally known as the K.T.A. Report. Since the time when we, as politicians, were struggling for independence, we were particularly enamoured of the various projects being implemented in other independent countries. We had built castles in the air after reading about such projects. We had vowed that we would draw up similar projects once independence was achieved. But, on the eve of independence our leaders fell in one swoop at the hand of the assassins, and barely three months after independence multi-coloured rebels started widespread insurrections. We were therefore, constrained to wave aside whatever projects we had in mind and we were only set on the restoration of law and order.

While we were thus engaged in the suppression of the insurrections, my attention was drawn to a news item in which I had been all along interested. It appeared in one of the English newspapers and it was on Iran. According to that news, the Government of Iran entrusted to a foreign firm the task of surveying and reporting on the economic resources of that country, and that firm, after a detailed survey, submitted a report to the Iranian Government. It was then that I asked Secretary U Hla Maung to find a suitable firm worthy of being entrusted with the task of submitting a similar report on the economic resources of the country.

We found two or three firms with creditable experience in that line, and we chose the firm of K.T.A. (Knappen Tippetts Abbett Engineering Co.) as our

Government believes that it was the best of the lot. As the magnitude of the task was stupendous, the cost of securing the services of that firm was also very great, and the Union Government requested the United States Government to bear the expenses of K.T.A. out of E.C.A. funds, to which that Government kindly agreed.[1]

Apparently the report on Iran referred to by U Nu was not that prepared by Morrison-Knudson engineers in 1947, but that of the Overseas Consultants consortium in 1949. Both of these, however, were engineering firms or groups of such firms. The idea of engaging a combined engineering and economic team to conduct a joint survey of Burma evidently originated with U Hla Maung, at that time Secretary both to the Ministry of National Planning and to the Ministry of Finance. U Hla Maung had been a member of the Indian Civil Service before the war and was now not only among the most senior officials in the Government service but also the man on whom Prime Minister U Nu leaned most heavily regarding economic questions. U Hla Maung had been educated in the United Kingdom as well as in Rangoon, and had studied economics sufficiently to develop a considerable grasp of and a profound respect for Keynesian and macro-economics and for the national-planning techniques based on them. It was he who had been responsible for bringing to Burma, earlier in 1951, the five British economists who were to advise on development policy and to frame an initial set of national-product accounts. U Hla Maung viewed the tentative national-product accounts drawn up by the English economists as providing the necessary basis for modern economic planning, and he was no doubt a factor in the selection of Robert R. Nathan Associates of Washington, D. C., to take responsibility for the economic side of Burma's forthcoming planning effort.

He was influenced in this selection by Mr. Nathan's reputation as a wartime economic planner in the United States and his subsequent planning activities in behalf of Israel and with Jean Monnet in France. Nathan's reputation as a liberal New Dealer and his support for the economic positions and policies of organized labor in the United States made him even more acceptable to the socialist-oriented Burmese leaders than would otherwise have been the case.

U Hla Maung was impressed with the new technology as well as with the new economics. Regarding the United States as the citadel of modern technology and engineering techniques, he was extremely desirous that the engineers selected to assist Burma in the formulation and implementation of a development program be from the United States. The conclusion of the T.C.A. aid agreement in 1950 and the willingness of the U. S. Government to use part of the grant aid funds to pay for the kind of comprehensive survey and program desired by Burma made such an arrangement financially feasible in the Burmese view. Actually, a specific suggestion that such a survey be made seems

1. "Implementation of Economic Projects," speech at meeting of Secretaries and Heads of Departments, Jan. 11, 1954, in U Nu, *Forward with the People* (a collection of speeches), Ministry of Information, Rangoon, 1955, pp. 107–08.

to have come from Mr. Griffin, leader of a U. S. mission to Burma early in 1950 which brought about the conclusion of the aid agreement.

The arrangement that the U. S. Government would pay the dollar costs of a survey made by consultants engaged directly by the Government of Burma was a felicitous one. No group of technicians on the U. S. Government payroll that might have been provided to the Government of Burma could have achieved the degree of acceptance and trust which grew out of the direct-hire arrangement. The Government of Burma felt from the outset that the consultants they had engaged were responsible in the first instance to them, rather than to the U. S. Government. The staff of the consultants came more and more to be regarded as members of the family rather than outsiders seeking to further the purposes of a foreign power.

The rather unusual arrangement whereby two engineering firms and one economic consulting firm collaborated in the preparation of a comprehensive economic and engineering survey and report warrants some explanation here of their working arrangements and responsibilities. Knappen Tippetts Abbett Engineering Co. was, so to speak, the prime signator to the contract with the Government of Burma. Pierce Management, the mining engineers, and Robert R. Nathan Associates, the economic consultants, were not, however, subcontractors to K.T.A. They were designated as Associated Companies and were also signatories to the contract with the Government. While each firm was responsible for the work within its own field, the basic and over-all responsibility was undertaken by K.T.A., which was responsible also for liaison with the Government and for general administration. The General Manager of the project, designated by K.T.A., was the official channel through whom all three firms communicated with the Government in the planning period from 1951 to 1953.

Within this general arrangement, Robert R. Nathan Associates was responsible for broad economic analysis and for developing the economic framework for the comprehensive development program. This included the appraisal of over-all resources and development potentials, the selection of aggregate targets for economic growth, the determination of investment required, the allocations of that investment by major sectors of the economy, the projections of financial and foreign-exchange resources that would be available, the changes in economic institutions, structure and policies that would be required, and the central organizational, manpower and administrative aspects of planning and executing the proposed program. Pierce Management had, naturally, responsibility for the mining sector. Knappen Tippetts Abbett retained direct responsibility for all other sectors of the economy — agriculture and irrigation, forestry, transport and communications, manufacturing industry and electric power — as well as general coordinating and over-all supervisory responsibility. The working arrangements called for the economists to provide to the engineering firms such economic data, analyses and projections as would be helpful to the latter in working out their own sector and project studies. Thus, in the case of manufacturing industry, the economists supplied the engineers with data or estimates on potential markets or, in the case of ports and railways, with projections of future volumes of traffic requiring those facilities.

The chief problems which arose under these arrangements were with regard to the agricultural and industry sectors, where the basic approach and views of the engineers and the economists were quite different. The economists exercised during this planning period no real influence in the formulation and determination of the manufacturing industry program which was finally recommended. They did, however, take issue with the engineers with respect to the recommendations to be made in the field of agriculture, and the recommendations contained in the Comprehensive Report represented a somewhat unsatisfactory reconciliation of rather sharply divergent views. Some of the questions and issues here suggested will be further pursued later in this section.

THE K.T.A. TERMS OF REFERENCE

The contract concluded in August 1951 between the Government and K.T.A. and its associated companies called for a variety of services ranging from the preparation of surveys and reports to the preparation of applications for financing, services in connection with specific projects to be implemented, general engineering consultative and economic advisory services, purchasing services and the training of Burmese technicians. The contract stated the general purpose of the employment very broadly to be that:

. . . it [the consultants] shall act as the technical secretariat to the Burma Economic Council, and perform all services required to that end, including advice with respect to various important aspects of the country's economy and engineering problems and assistance in solving practical operating difficulties which may occur while CONSULTING ENGINEER[2] is in Burma, in the particular fields in which CONSULTING ENGINEER is to supply personnel hereunder. . . .

The services will be performed under the direction and supervision of GOVERNMENT with a view to assisting the Burma Economic Council in programming and implementation of its plans for an over-all development program.[3]

The surveys and reports required called first for a preliminary survey of the national economy (to be completed within twenty weeks) which would:

appraise the suitability and practicability of GOVERNMENT's general economic development program for accomplishing the objectives of its planning policy, and ascertain and make recommendations concerning the scope and feasibility of re-

2. This and other contract references to "CONSULTING ENGINEER" embrace the associated companies.

3. "Agreement between the Government of the Union of Burma and Knappen Tippetts Abbett Engineering Company," executed August 8, 1951, Article I.B., p. 2.

construction, expansion and improvement of existing facilities and services, and of establishing new facilities and services, all within the framework of the over-all planning policies of GOVERNMENT . . .[4]

The contract called next for an indeterminate number of project surveys and reports, both of projects tentatively recommended in the Preliminary Report and of others which might be designated by the Government, with an eye to determining their technical and economic feasibility and desirability. An interim report was to be presented to the Government at the end of the first year of the associated companies' service, summarizing and analyzing their work during the first year and submitting a program of activities for the ensuing year. But most importantly, at the conclusion of the two-year contract period, the consultants were to:

present a written report recommending a comprehensive, integrated program for the over-all development of the resources of Burma and governmental and private measures in addition to those which may already have been taken, designed to place such program in operation, presenting detailed reasoning and justification for such program and implementing measures, in the light of the desire of the GOVERN-MENT to improve the productivity, production, and standard of living of the people of Burma as rapidly as possible and to achieve a diversified and balanced economy appropriate to the national and economic independence of Burma.[5]

Despite the extremely broad terms of reference, the contract actually precluded the consultants from considering and making recommendations with respect to agriculture — the basis of the entire economy — and the social services. This was because the Burmese believed themselves better equipped to deal with agricultural problems, and because they wished to utilize U. N. advice in the health, education, housing and other welfare fields. The exclusion of agriculture was rectified, upon the recommendation of the consultants, soon after completion of their Preliminary Report. The social services remained outside the scope of their responsibility and staff specialization.

THE K.T.A. PRELIMINARY REPORT

The Preliminary Report — produced within twenty weeks by a group of six consultants and fifteen field staff engineers and economists — posed a challenge to the Government and the people of Burma to undertake a bold and ambitious economic development program which would realize her "impressive" potentials for greatly increased production and higher levels of living and welfare. After surveying broadly the pre- and post-war positions inherent in Burma's basic resources, the consultants made rough judgments as to the increase in national output which might be achieved over the remainder of the decade and the amount of total investment, public and private, which

4. *Ibid.*, Article I.C.1.a., p. 3.
5. *Ibid.*, Article I.C.1.c., "Comprehensive Report," p. 7.

would be needed to achieve that goal. Finally, they outlined an initial investment program of some K 75 crores ($157 million) in the fields of transport
and communications, power, water resources, manufacturing and mineral
industries; assured the government that its financing would involve no near-
future problems; and urged that early and determined action be taken on it
and on the other recommendations contained in the report, if the desired goals
were to be reached in time.

Noting the structure and nature of the Burmese economy before the war
and the retarded nature of its development, the report found most significant
in the pre-war economy "the absence of forces tending to accelerate development and thereby to afford opportunities for a more abundant life to the
people of Burma."[6] It also noted the great damage wrought by the war and,
subsequently, by insurrection, and the decline in the total product of the economy to perhaps 60 per cent of the pre-war total. The report held, however, that
Burma's potentials for development were bright:

Burma has a great potential for a vastly increased output and levels of living far
higher than those she has ever before achieved. This potential is solidly based on
Burma's economic geography and population—on her fertile farm lands; her
climate, so suited to paddy production; her rich and diversified mineral resources;
her vast forests; her natural waterways and power sites; her growing population
and labor force and the capacities of her people for education and for work —
skilled, managerial and technical work included.[7]

With natural and human resources in hand, the necessary productive equipment and managerial know-how could be acquired or developed.

The report emphasized that realization of this potential depended on the
effective implementation of some basic policy decisions. "The termination of
civil unrest," it held, was "an absolute prerequisite to substantially higher output."[8] It added: "The supply of managerial, technical and skilled workers
may well be the next most limiting factor in the increase of total production
and must therefore be greatly increased." There was need also for

a basic plan for economic development which encompasses (a) an intensive survey
and appraisal of the resources of Burma, (b) ambitious yet feasible goals which
take into account both the resources of the country and the wants of her people,
and (c) economic policies and engineering projects essential to achieve the goals.
Plans are of little value unless they are implemented. Therefore, a development
program must include organizational measures designed to best assure the maximum execution of the program.[9]

In considering the broad goals which might tentatively be established, the
report made certain basic assumptions. Paramount among these was the as-

6. K.T.A. Preliminary Report, p. 2.
7. *Ibid.*, p. 3.
8. *Ibid.*, p. vii.
9. *Ibid.*

sumption that "civil order will be fully established by the beginning of 1954 and that peace will prevail thereafter. This means the virtual stoppage of the insurrection within two years. To the extent that peace comes more quickly, the progress will be more rapid. Conversely, persistence of disorder will further delay progress."[10]

Additional assumptions were that the Government would give reasonably prompt effect to the policies and actions recommended in the Preliminary Report, that additional projects and policies recommended as the survey continued over the next two years would similarly be implemented, that Government policies would seek to direct the maximum feasible portion of current production into capital facilities and that substantial funds for financing the program would be forthcoming from external sources as needed.

In setting, on the basis of these assumptions, the goal for maximum increase in total output, the report held that total output could be doubled by the end of the decade from the then-estimated level, bringing it to some 30 per cent above the pre-war total. The annual rate of total production at the beginning of 1952 was then believed to be between K 300 and K 350 crores. The report recommended a total production goal of some K 700 crores in then-current prices. This goal was to be achieved in three steps. It looked to an annual rate of output of some K 400 crores by the beginning of 1954, when it was assumed civil order would be fully restored. It looked to a further increase in output to a level of some K 550 crores within two to three years after the end of the insurrection. The third step was to see the realization of the target of K 700 crores in 1959.

The total proposed increase in gross domestic product in the magnitude of 100 or more per cent within an eight-year period appears at first to be extraordinarily high. Achievement of such an increase would call for an increase of some 8 per cent per year, a remarkable rate of growth for a normal economy. When it is taken into consideration, however, that the Burmese economy was then operating at some 60 per cent of its pre-war level, and that the proposed increase of 100 per cent from that distressed level would take it in total only to 30 per cent over pre-war — and on a per capita basis only to 4 per cent over pre-war — by 1959, the degree of performance called for was not an extraordinary one at all. While undoubtedly difficult, any target involving a lesser increase could scarcely have been considered a challenge.

To achieve this projected increase in total national output would require, it was tentatively estimated, an investment of some K 750 crores. This estimate took as a point of departure the rather general relationship between total new investment and increased production in many countries — roughly speaking, a 3:1 ratio — but took into account also two factors which it was thought would operate in Burma to reduce this ratio. These were the very large com-

10. *Ibid.*, p. 5.

ponent of reconstruction and rehabilitation investment within the total, to which the income response might be considerably higher than normal, and the very considerable production increases which might be expected in the depressed agriculture, timber and mining sectors owing to the improved security conditions assumed. Of the total of K 750 crores of investment required, it was further estimated that two thirds could be financed domestically, provided that one eighth of the total output of the country were channeled into investment. One third of the total requirement, it was anticipated, might have to be financed by borrowing abroad. In any case, the report stressed that "these are suggested as tentative goals. They are based on an over-all preliminary appraisal, which is believed to be reasonably conservative, and are certainly subject to review and revision as the survey group explores more fully the resources of Burma and evolves a more comprehensive program for the most efficient and maximum utilization of these resources. . . . For the present, they should serve as moderately ambitious and certainly attainable objectives."[11]

The broad findings, conclusions and recommendations stated above derived out of a detailed examination which covered the following section headings: "The People of Burma and Their Welfare"; "The Fiscal, Monetary and Credit System"; "Agriculture"; "Forestry"; "Mineral Industry"; "Industries"; "Transportation (Ports and Waterways, Railway Transportation, Highways, Airways)"; "Communications"; "Water Resources"; and "Power Development." Since many of the findings presented in the Preliminary Report are descriptive of facts and situations already set forth in earlier chapters, mention will be made here only of those which are either not redundant or which seem to merit restatement.

As regards population, the report held that while any significant improvement in general health conditions would result in an increased rate of growth in population and labor force, it did not foresee any problem of over-density relative to available resources. It noted that the labor force was not effectively utilized. In addition to considerable total, part-time and seasonal unemployment, there existed a widespread under-employment. The income of cultivators was perhaps lower relative to that of the total population than it had been before the war. The report held that "Far more training is required not only in basic education but also in practically every category of training designed directly to enhance the productivity of workers."[12] The report stressed also that much progress was necessary and possible in the field of health.

With regard to finance, the report held — as had the British economists — that the recent fiscal policy of the Government had had a deflationary effect, and that more vigorous and realistic fiscal policies would be required. It considered the tax system to be on the whole well conceived and progressive. It noted that the most important single source of revenue for the Government

11. *Ibid.*, p. 6.
12. *Ibid.*, p. viii.

was the profits of the State Agricultural Marketing Board (the Government monopoly for rice exports). Finding that Burma's monetary and banking system was entirely inadequate to meet the requirements of an expanding economy, it supported then-pending draft legislation to provide needed monetary reforms and central bank controls. It advocated more effective and permanent measures than had yet been taken to provide agricultural credit to the cultivators at reasonable rates of interest. Finally, it indicated the need for improvement of short-term financing facilities for trade and industry, and the need for new institutions to fill the void created by the virtual absence of long-term financing facilities and savings.

Although a study of the agricultural resources of the country was not included among the responsibilities of the survey group, the report stated that agricultural production could be more than doubled by a major program of improvement and expansion. Among the measures which such a program would embrace, it specified the opening up of new lands, the general use of high-quality seeds, the greater use of fertilizers, the more extensive use of irrigation, new crop possibilities, modern farming methods and reasonable rates of interest for agricultural credit.

In the field of minerals, the report found ample evidence that Burma could rehabilitate the oil and base-metals industries. It stated also that "Investigation has disclosed that Burma could become a substantial producer of antimony metal, could probably produce its domestic needs of non-coking coals, and could substantially increase its lead and zinc exports."[13]

Industrial development, it was held, "is urgently needed to provide productive work opportunities for the growing population and labor force, to reduce Burma's excessive dependence on the production and export of rice and a few other key items, to increase per capita productivity and output, to conserve foreign exchange, and most importantly, to make larger quantities and more varied supplies of goods available to her people."[14] The report cautioned, however, that

There is little prospect of or need, with few exceptions, for entering into the production at this time of manufactured items necessitating large-scale enterprises or complex processing. Industrialization is inevitably a gradual process in which industries grow in relation to those on which they depend for supplies and in relation to others which in turn are dependent on them. Burma needs to initiate selected industries which will benefit from the natural advantages of local raw materials and local markets. Careful selection, based on sound criteria, will help achieve successful operations, which in turn will encourage other industries.[15]

As regards transportation, the report advised that a special commission should be established to achieve proper coordination of the four basic trans-

13. *Ibid.*, p. x.
14. *Ibid.*
15. *Ibid.*

portation modes — waterways, railways, highways and airways. Ports, waterways and railways all required a great deal of rehabilitation and new facilities. The highways had suffered from excessive use and deficient maintenance since 1941. Communications were disrupted, limited in personnel and administration and still seriously affected by insurgency.

A coordinated water-resources program which would encompass waterways, irrigation, land reclamation and drainage, hydroelectric power, flood prevention, prevention of soil erosion, and adequate and safe water supply and sanitation, was badly needed. The existing water program was hampered by the lack of systematic collection of data on surface and ground water and of plans for multi-purpose reservoirs.

As regards power, the report estimated that demand would increase from 10 to 20 per cent per year, and listed a number of favorable sites which appeared feasible from the point of view both of economic generation and of markets for electric power.

As regards organization within the Government, the report found serious deficiencies both in statistical information and in trained Burmese personnel required for effective planning. The staff of the Ministry of National Planning was inadequate both in size and in experience to do its job. Doubt was expressed as to the organizational structure and relations of the Government ministries, departments, boards and their subdivisions, as to the allocation of functions among them, as to their personnel and wage-salary practices and, in general, as to the ability of the Government, as then organized and manned, to carry out effectively the large-scale development program proposed. Finally the report stressed that "The needs of the economic development program demand more efficient private organization as well as more efficient public organization. The government can assist greatly in developing improved efficiency in the sphere of privately organized enterprise."[16]

RECOMMENDATIONS OF THE
PRELIMINARY REPORT

Recommendations for immediate action were made for all the sectors covered in the survey. The more important are listed below.

General recommendations called for the development of improved economic statistics in a variety of fields as soon as possible; a comprehensive program of education and training to prepare the skilled personnel required for the development program; improved systems of primary and secondary education; expansion of facilities for professional training; great emphasis on expanded programs for technical and vocational training; more teacher-training schools; more liberal provisions in the budget for education and train-

16. *Ibid.*, p. 222.

ing; development and implementation of a comprehensive national health program; and a broadly conceived housing program. Serious consideration was urged for the revision of basic pay scales within the Government service.

Recommendations in the financial area called for an expansionary fiscal policy; adoption of draft legislation for central banking and monetary reforms; expansion of the commercial banking system; specific tax changes; a number of urgently needed studies of the revenue structure, tax administration, and economics of rice growing and marketing; establishment of a state agriculture bank; and the administration of foreign-trade controls.

As regards mineral industries, the consultants recommended establishment of a Minerals Development Corporation; the development of antimony mines; further testing and studies of the Kalewa Coal Project; and a program for mineral exploration and training.

Manufacturing-industry recommendations included establishment of an Industrial Development Corporation; early action to modernize the rice-milling industry; and the establishment of an integrated fishing industry, a salt-extracting plant, a bamboo-pulp and paper mill, a cigarette factory, a roofing-tile plant, three integrated sawmill and millwork units, and a rubber-products plant. Further study and investigation of a number of other manufacturing industries was also recommended, as was a review of Government tax, trade and other policies to ensure that they would stimulate and facilitate industrial development.

Transportation recommendations included the establishment of a commission to coordinate the basic transport modes; immediate action to rehabilitate the ports; implementation of the railways rehabilitation program; the expediting of rehabilitation work on damaged bridges; major rehabilitation and maintenance of national trunk and main roads; the construction of certain new roads; the inauguration of a program of planning and reorganization within the building and roads department; a training program in the Airways Board; expansion of the wireless-telegraph network; the introduction of an automatic dial-telephone system in Rangoon; and detailed field investigation and design of several water-storage projects and further study of others.

Power recommendations called for detailed field investigations and for the design and construction, where justified, of three hydroelectric projects and further consideration of a number of others.

In connection with Government organization, recommendations included retention, by the Prime Minister, of the National Planning Board portfolio; improved coordination between the Ministry of National Planning and other Government ministries and departments, especially the Ministry of Finance; reorganization of the Ministry of National Planning; establishment of the appropriate composition and responsibilities of the top Economic Council; and the inauguration of a progress-reporting system on development progress.

The recommendations stressed that the autonomous development corporations recommended in the fields of mining and industry "should be set up and run on a businesslike basis and that same basis should apply to the new autonomous enterprises they set up or sponsor."[17]

In an endeavor to balance the socialist Government's obvious concentration on the public sector, the report stressed that the Government could and should render general assistance to private enterprise by developing cheaper sources of fuel and power; by providing better transportation and communication facilities; by developing the natural resources and basic industries; by beneficial relaxation of import controls and tariffs; by fostering cheaper credit and creating greater mass-purchasing power; by providing research and technical assistance; by eliminating unnecessary delays and difficulties which business men encountered in dealing with the Government; by providing inducements to new and desirable investments through tax incentives, accelerated amortization, loans, financial participations and similar means; by conducting training programs to develop skilled workers and technicians needed by industry; and, in general, by creating an atmosphere of security and confidence which would encourage private investment and enterprise.

Finally, the report suggested a specific program for immediate investment in the amount of K 74.5 crores (approximately $157 million), composed as follows:

	K Crores
Transport and communications	28.2
Railroads	22.2
Ports and waterways	1.1
Highways	3.5
Airways	.3
Communications	1.1
Power	30.0
Water resources	7.1
Manufacturing industry	8.5
Mineral industries	.7

The reaction of the Government of Burma to the Preliminary Report was highly favorable. The Government was pleased both by the sympathy displayed towards its aspirations and by the consultants' expression of confidence that Burma could make large forward strides within the decade towards their achievement. The growth and investment goals suggested were considered entirely feasible, although it was emphasized that their timely attainment would require changes in thinking, attitudes and public administration.

All ministers, members of the Economic Council, Government secretaries and heads of departments were invited to a meeting at the residence of the

17. *Ibid.,* p. xx.

Prime Minister on March 3, 1952 to "consider and discuss" — actually, to hear — the major recommendations contained in the Preliminary Report. In a memorandum prepared by U Hla Maung, Secretary of the Ministry of National Planning, and distributed to all participants in the conference, the following statements were made:

> The general economic framework within which the Consulting Engineers suggest that economic development during the next ten years should be set is basically sound. A program of development of the order recommended . . . involving a capital investment of approximately Rs. 750 crores . . . may appear unpractical and idealistic if judged in the light of the actual rate of investment and capital formation which Burma has been able to achieve in the past. But when it is remembered that even such an ambitious programme could increase the gross national product of Burma by only 30 per cent as compared with pre-war and very little on a per capita basis, it becomes clear that no matter how impossible or ambitious that program may seem in view of past achievement, the difficulties must be overcome . . . From this point of view, the Preliminary Report constitutes a challenge to the people of Burma.[18]

The memorandum went on to discuss the availability of resources and manpower for the objectives recommended and to consider the extent to which Burmese thinking would need to be adapted, and the administrative system geared, in order to achieve a development program of this magnitude. Expressing assurance on all these counts, provided the proper efforts were made, the memorandum promised the executive agencies of the Government that if they would only get on with the job, the Government would see to it that the necessary resources were available. Significantly, U Hla Maung stressed the danger of the restrictions and inhibitions inherent in a bureaucratic system, and stated that a firm decision was necessary "that *all* development projects will be undertaken on business principles and with an organization which assumes more of the character of a large-scale business organization than a watch-dog Department of Government." For this reason he expressed gratification with the report's recommendation that autonomous development corporations be organized in the industries and mineral fields. Finally, he suggested that a number of subcommittees be set up to consider the specific project and other detailed recommendations presented, and to recommend to the Government whether or not they should be accepted, rejected or modified.

The conference confirmed and accepted the general analysis, approach and goals recommended by the consultants. Explicit confirmation was given to the recommended target increase in national output to K 700 crores by 1959 and to the recommended total investment target of K 750 crores needed to achieve it. In the months that followed, action was initiated on a broad front to put into effect many of the projects and policies recommended.

18. "Memorandum for the Economic Council," February 29, 1952.

CHAPTER 7

The Pyidawtha Conference

Pyidawtha means, literally, "happy land." U Nu has explained the term as follows: "Pyidawtha, which is our common goal, is one [a land] which not only possesses good roads, good railways, good bridges, good houses and abundant production, but one which also does away completely with the evil system of class exploitation, of crimes, of disease, of retrogression, of ignoramuses and of exploitation."[1]

It was at a conference called by the Government in August 1952 that the designation "Pyidawtha" was first used to denote the objective of Burma's development program. As the official report of that conference puts it:

> For the first time in the history of Independent Burma, there was held for a period of fourteen days from August 4 to August 17 this year, the history-making Pyidawtha Conference which was convened by the Union Government for discussions "of supreme importance for major programmes for the creation of a new state and ushering in of a new era for the people" . . . To fully discuss the ten development plans enumerated below, nearly one thousand delegates including Members of Parliament, Commissioners and senior Government officials and representatives of the *ludu* [the people] from the A.F.P.F.L., and A.B.P.O., etc. came from all the seven administrative divisions in the Union . . . to confer with Cabinet Ministers and high ranking officials of the Union Government. . . .
>
> All these plans are aimed at radically changing the colonial system of exploitation as existed under the foreign power, to one of sincere benevolent democratic Government of the Burmese people by the Burmese people.
>
> . . . the holding of the Conference was actually a ceremony for laying the foundation of a true Pyidawtha.[2]

---

1. "Burma's Goal," speech of Aug. 24, 1953, in U Nu, *Forward with the People* (a collection of speeches), Ministry of Information, Rangoon, 1955, p. 50.
2. *The Pyidawtha Conference, August 4–17, 1952, Resolutions and Speeches,* Ministry of Information, Rangoon, Dec. 18, 1952, Introduction.

The conference was a major effort by the Government to mobilize its key officials and mass organizations in support of its forthcoming development effort. The mass organizations represented were the Anti-Fascist People's Freedom League (A.F.P.F.L.), the nationalist coalition, and the All Burma Peasants' Organization (A.B.P.O.), the units of which extended parallel with those of the Government from the center in Rangoon down to the village level.

Among the ten programs adopted unanimously by the Pyidawtha Conference, the key program was that which embodied the targets for increased investment and national output recommended in the K.T.A. Preliminary Report and the immediate investment program recommended by the K.T.A. (Since the presentation of the Preliminary Report, this had grown from some K 75 crores to a total of K 101 crores, or $212 million.) The resolution adopted on this program and the supporting speech presented by the Minister for Industry and Mines were sober and restrained in tone.

It was noted, for example, that the proposed increases in national output aimed at a per capita consumption only slightly in advance of the pre-war level. This increase the Minister regarded as "not substantial" but, he added, under the circumstances "We must be realistic, and we cannot afford to set up a goal which no matter how desirable may be impossible of achievement under present conditions."[3] Stressing the many practical difficulties involved in carrying out any development program, the country's limitations in technical personnel and other resources, the considerable effort that would be required, and the program's dependence on the detailed studies and investigations then being carried out, the Minister cautioned: "We cannot therefore say that the programmes *will* be fully implemented. Every effort will be made to carry them out, and as much as is practicable will be carried out. But if we fail to reach the targets set in time, there should be no disappointment."[4]

He then warned that "A programme of economic development on this scale cannot be undertaken by Government under the present administration set-up, which was designed not as an instrument of development and welfare but for the maintenance of foreign rule. The system must accordingly be changed and the ideas and attitudes of mind which prevail amongst all working within this system must also undergo a major change." In this connection the Minister anticipated that a considerable contribution toward the necessary administrative changes would result from the decision to set up four development corporations — in the fields of industry, minerals, agriculture and transport.[5] These corporations, he said, "will be set up on business principles,

3. *Ibid.*, p. 38, Resolution No. 4, "Target for Economic Development," presented by the Hon'ble U Kyaw Myint, Minister for Industry and Mines, on August 11.
4. *Ibid.*, p. 41.
5. The decision to set up a development corporation in the transport field, tentative at that time, was subsequently reversed.

and will operate on business lines using methods and procedures adopted by large-scale business organizations. They shall be free from departmental rules and restrictions which are now an effective barrier to carrying out any work of development. It is hoped that these Corporations will develop into an effective instrument for the achievement of the development goals stated in the Resolution."

Finally, the Minister emphasized that an absolute prerequisite to the successful execution of the program was a willingness on the part of both the Government and its key officials to make bold decisions. While recognizing that every effort needed to be made to prevent unnecessary, wasteful or reckless spending on ill-considered and inadequately investigated projects, he stressed that indecision based on fears of one kind or another "is probably as big a crime as embarking on ill-considered projects which involve Government in loss and wastage."[6] A certain amount of waste would be inevitable. "In such cases, decisions must give full consideration to the good faith of those responsible for carrying out the projects. Only then would they be willing to act boldly and with expedition."

Whether this speech was prepared by the Minister himself or by National Planning Secretary U Hla Maung, whose earlier memorandum it echoed, it certainly pointed realistically, analytically and with prescience to a number of key considerations which the Government would have done well to remember and to act upon in the years that followed.

The work of the conference went far beyond its approval of the economic goals of the K.T.A. Preliminary Report and its immediate investment recommendations. A number of other programs were adopted which were to be of major significance in the comprehensive economic and social development program. These included a five-year program for agricultural production, an eight-year program for land nationalization, a major program for transport and communications, a substantial public-housing program, major education and health programs, and a village-district community-improvement program, also called "Pyidawtha." The conference also made a gesture toward a development program for those hill areas which even within the Burmese context were considered "underdeveloped areas." Finally, it approved a plan for the democratization of the colonial type of local administration which still prevailed.

Brief descriptions of these other programs adopted by the conference follow.

THE AGRICULTURAL PROGRAM

The Agricultural and Rural Development Five-Year Plan, so called because it aimed to raise agricultural output in five years to the value it had before the war, was geared explicitly to the broad economic framework outlined in the

6. *Ibid.*, p. 42.

K.T.A. Report. It aimed by the end of the decade to increase the total value of agricultural output from K 150 crores to K 265 crores, an increase of K 115 crores. It anticipated also that the resulting increased value of agricultural processing would make for a total increase in agricultural output of K 130 crores. Agriculture would thus contribute roughly 40 per cent of the total increase in national output proposed by the consultants for 1959.

The agricultural program aimed chiefly at restoring the pre-war export surplus of rice, and at achieving self-sufficiency in a number of other commodities the production of which was then badly depressed, and had in most cases been deficient before the war. Among these the most important were groundnuts, cotton, beans and pulses, sugar cane, onions, chillis, jute, tobacco, tea, coffee, coconuts, dairy products and fish and fish products. Specific targets were outlined for each of these commodities, along with methods for achieving them, such as land reclamation, the opening up of new lands, double cropping, improved land use, improved cultivation practices, better breeding practices, etc. Costs were estimated by project only for the first year of activity. The plan envisaged also the establishment of an agricultural bank, a number of irrigation projects, the repair and reconstruction of bunds (dikes) in the paddy-growing areas, the increased use of fertilizer, partial mechanization where applicable, various types of aids and incentives for the cultivators, and arrangements for continued research and planning.

Of the several crop programs, the rice program was by far the most important. The 2.5 million acres of paddy land lost to cultivation through war and insurgent activities were to be reclaimed and rehabilitated; an additional half million acres of new land were to be brought under paddy cultivation with the aid of irrigation projects; improved seeds and improved cultivation practices, including increased use of fertilizers, were also to be relied upon to achieve the target.

While the five-year program embraced fisheries, it was strangely silent about forestry.

THE LAND NATIONALIZATION PLAN

In sharp contrast to the clearly defined agricultural program, the so-called and long-discussed land nationalization plan was not a plan at all. It was rather a confused and poorly defined expression of intent, accompanied by an elaborate outline of the organizational structures that would be built to achieve its cloudy objectives. The Constitution had, of course, already provided that the state, as the ultimate owner of all lands, would see to their equitable distribution among the landless peasantry. The Land Nationalization Act of 1948, enacted shortly after independence, had had only a short trial in one area of significance before the developing insurrection made further attempts to implement it impracticable. However, that initial experience had apparently not been a happy one[7] and a new and quite different act would be legislated only in September 1953. The Pyidawtha Conference disclosed how murky and inchoate was the thinking about land nationalization in mid-1952.

As there presented, the plan proposed for immediate action the setting up of a central committee for land nationalization, the building of a district-level staff and its training, a program of research, the gathering and mapping of information that would be essential to later distribution operations, and the establishment of model mechanized farm colonies and collectives for experimental purposes. It proposed also a few sample land distributions in order to gain experience with the problems that would later be encountered. For the longer term — that is, beginning with the following year — the plan proposed the organization of district and village land-nationalization committees in selected areas, the building and training of local staff as well as of the committees, and the beginning of land distribution — which would ultimately comprehend some 9 million acres of agricultural land — on a one-yoke farm basis to landless farmers. This distribution would be accompanied by the organization of the newly landed farmers into agricultural cooperatives and collective farms. The plan listed, without further explanation, a number of additional and presumably complementary plans which would embrace agriculture, health, rural development, social considerations, electricity, housing, transport and communications, finance, democratic administration, cultural affairs, etc.

The plan made no attempt to define what the maximum permissible size of farms would be, what compensation might be paid to former owners, on what bases land might be transferred to agriculturalists, what, if anything, those agriculturalists would pay for the land received, whether they would indeed be the actual owners of the land transferred to them, how much land might ultimately be transferred, or any of the many other practical and frequently perplexing questions obviously connected with a land distribution program. It is not altogether surprising, therefore, that the land nationalization program, as later formulated and put into effect, was neither carefully worked out in all important aspects nor well calculated to make a substantial contribution to the reconstruction of agriculture and to increased agricultural production.

TRANSPORTATION AND COMMUNICATIONS

The transportation and communications program adopted by the Pyidawtha Conference proposed to carry out, within the three years ending 1954–55, some two thirds of the reconstruction work required to bring the system back to its pre-war condition and efficiency. Estimating that the total rehabilitation job, which incorporated a substantial amount of long deferred maintenance as well as rebuilding and replacement of equipment, would re-

7. Hugh Tinker, *The Union of Burma,* Oxford University Press, London, 1957, pp. 95–96.

quire the expenditure of K 50 to K 60 crores ($105 to $126 million), the program envisaged the expenditure in three years of close to K 40 crores ($83 million), of which K 20 crores ($42 million) would be spent for railways alone.

Explaining that recent attempts at rehabilitation had been delayed by the inability to procure ships, steel rails and other equipment — perhaps because of the Korean War then in process — the plan envisaged the restoration of 384 miles of railway out of the 546 miles of pre-war lineage then inoperable, and the acquisition of 171 passenger coaches and 1,400 freight cars, as compared with then existing deficiencies of 714 and 3,175 respectively. The entire deficit of 56 locomotives was to be filled within the three-year period, and major railway stations which still required restoration were to be restored. Of a deficit of 86 passenger launches for river transport as compared with pre-war, 26 would be procured at a cost of approximately K 2 crores ($4.2 million). Six new airstrips would be constructed in addition to the major airport construction project going on in Rangoon, and the necessary airdromes or terminals to accompany them would be built. Some K 4.7 crores ($9.9 million) would be spent to acquire ships for coastal and ocean service. A somewhat lesser sum — K 3.7 crores ($7.8 million) — would be spent on the restoration of the port of Rangoon, and some K 38 lakhs ($800,000) on still-required rehabilitation of the lesser outports. One dramatic new project proposed was the installation of a dial telephone system in Rangoon at a cost of K 3.2 crores ($6.7 million). Fully 250 local post office buildings would be constructed to restore the number to the pre-war total of 640, at a cost of K .5 crores ($1 million). Finally, small wireless sets would be installed in important district headquarters, and land telegraph lines would be restored in areas where security conditions made such activity practicable.

Noteworthy in the presentation of this program by the Minister for Transport and Communications was his overt admission of the existence of widespread corruption in both the railway and the inland water transport services, and his rather naïve and plaintive plea to the public to refrain from giving bribes to corrupt personnel and to report to the proper authorities such evidences of corruption as they might observe.

HOUSING

The housing program was presented by the outstandingly able and energetic U Raschid, newly designated Minister for Housing and Labor, and Vice Chairman at that time of the recently established National Housing and Town and Country Development Board, the agency through which the housing program would be implemented. Stressing that housing construction in recent years had failed in large measure to make good the wartime and insurrection losses and the extensive fire damage, let alone to provide for the growing population, U Raschid presented a three-pronged program of extensive housing construction in the towns, construction of model villages in the countryside and development of indigenous building materials. For Rangoon, which presented a special problem because of its size and because of the large number of refugees whose hutments had encroached onto the streets, the plan envisaged the construction of a satellite town at Kande, as well as many other housing projects within the city and the planned removal of refugee hutments into a transit camp and permanent village at Thingangyun. A large Government office building would be constructed which would permit the return of many requisitioned private dwellings to their owners. Incentives would be given to private builders, and steps would be taken to augment and improve the town's water supply. Comparable action was promised in the near future in at least five other towns, including Prome, Akyab, Mandalay and Magwe. At least one model village was proposed to be built in each of the thirty-six districts. These villages would be laid out in an orderly manner, with adequate water supply and sanitary provisions. In each the Government would establish a community center which would include a health center, some cottage industry and, wherever practicable, an agricultural station. As part of the scheme, the Housing Board would construct a large factory capable of meeting the country's needs for roofing tile.

Additional contributions to the use of indigenous materials would be made by the building-materials department attached to the Housing Board and by a research unit to be installed at the Industrial Research Institute. The Board had decided to make loans available in modest amount to those who were interested and were able to undertake housing construction for their own use. For those building bamboo huts, financial advances would be made in the form of aluminum-sheet roofing materials, or C.G.I. sheets. U Raschid stressed also that personnel would be trained, both abroad and at home, at all levels from architecture and town planning to simple carpentry. Research instruction in the use of hand machines and various materials would be supplemented by socioeconomic research in housing conditions, income levels, etc. He advised that the 1951–52 budget provided K 3.5 crores ($7.4 million) for the Housing Board program and that the budget for the following year was then in preparation.

In addition to its own program, the Housing Board undertook a wide variety of construction activities for other agencies, acting, for example, as the executive agency for the Health and Education departments in the construction of hospitals and schools.

The housing plan, although it called for a start to be made in a field in which action was urgently needed, was seriously defective in at least two important respects. It made no assessment whatsoever of the total size of the job which needed to be done, or of how much of that job it intended to undertake and at what cost. Also, it gave no overt recognition to the questions of what kind of housing should be constructed in the towns, of what the average unit cost would be, and of whether such construction should be on a subsidized or a self-liquidating basis. Obviously the questions involved in both these major problem areas had not been seriously tackled, if they had been considered at all. The unanimous approval accorded to this plan by the Pyidawtha Conference without debate or discussion left both sets of questions wide open for *ad hoc* implementation by the Housing Board and Ministry. The only way in which the central planners were able to deal with the housing program was in terms of the annual budget review, never in terms of the relation of the proposed annual appropriation to a clearly envisaged longer-term plan.

THE MEDICAL AND PUBLIC HEALTH PLAN

The Medical and Public Health Plan reflected the contributions of World Health Organization and U. S. technical-assistance specialists in the painstaking analysis which had been made of the problem, and in the well-thought-out and comprehensive measures proposed for dealing with it. Underlying the plan were the dismal facts. The death rate in Burma was the highest in the world — 30 per 1,000 population. Infant mortality was 195 per 1,000, while the mortality of mothers in childbirth was from five to ten times greater than in more advanced countries. The chief health scourges were malaria; gastro-intestinal infections such as typhoid, dysentery, cholera and diarrhea; respiratory diseases such as tuberculosis, pneumonia and asthma; and contagious diseases such as smallpox, plague, measles and whooping cough. Unbalanced diet was another main cause of poor health. Shortages of medical personnel, facilities and supplies were important factors. The country had only 294 hospitals and dispensaries, with a total of only 8,546 beds — one per 1,980 persons. There were 552 doctors in the medical services of the state and about 700 doctors engaged in private practice — one per 13,580 persons. There were 404 nurses in the state service, and 650 engaged in private practice — one per 16,130 people. Pre-war facilities for the manufacture of vaccines against smallpox, cholera, typhoid, paratyphoid and rabies had been destroyed.

A five-pronged program was set forth for dealing with this situation: (1) the mounting of organized and well-planned campaigns for combatting malaria, venereal disease, tuberculosis and leprosy, for promoting maternal and child welfare and for improving environmental sanitation; (2) the improvement of medical facilities and services; (3) provisions for the domestic manufacture of biologicals, drugs and preparations; (4) the training of medical personnel; and (5) the promotion of a national-fitness movement.

The anti-malaria campaign was based on spraying; the VD campaign on blood testing and treatment; and the TB campaign on vaccination, X-ray treatment, education and environmental procedures. The maternity and child welfare effort would be based on a large number of maternity and child health centers staffed by woman health visitors and trained midwives. In the leprosy campaign, new leper colonies and central clinics and hospitals would be established. The hospital program envisaged key hospitals in Rangoon and Mandalay, completely equipped to treat all diseases; regional hospitals with 200 to 500 beds in Moulmein, Bassein, Akyab, Mitkyina, Taunggyi and Magwe; district hospitals with 150 to 200 beds in each of the thirty-six district headquarters; and township hospitals with 25 to 60 beds in every township. It envisaged also a large number of rural health centers below the township hospital, on the basis of one for every fifteen village tracts or district council circles with populations from 15,000 to 40,000. It was estimated that approximately 800 such rural health centers would be required, each staffed by a public health assistant, a vaccinator, a woman health visitor and five midwives. These centers, it was thought, would treat simple diseases and refer other cases to the nearest township hospitals. A number of child health clinics and mobile health vans would also be brought into the plan.

While the plan envisaged steps to increase the domestic manufacture of biologicals, drugs and preparations, it did not at that time contemplate the large-scale drugs and pharmaceuticals plant which later became part of the program. The Pyidawtha program anticipated that the necessary manufacture would be taken care of by the already existing Harcourt Butler Institute and by the office of the Chemical Examiner. It did envisage, however, the processing and public distribution of vitamin tablets, without indicating the auspices under which the processing would take place. Plans for the training of medical and health personnel encountered their greatest difficulty with respect to doctors. In spite of increased enrollments at the medical college and plans for the opening of a second medical college, the deficiency would still be great, and large numbers of foreign doctors would therefore be engaged on short-term contracts to meet immediate needs. Training programs for nurses, public-health nurses, woman health visitors, midwives, health assistants and inspectors, vaccinators and compounders, it was thought, would be capable of turning out the necessary personnel during the life of the plan.

The chief job of the National Fitness Council would be to promote health-building and provide facilities and equipment for sports activities.

Cost estimates had been worked out for some parts of the health program, chiefly in their early phases, but not for the entire program. It was clear that the largest single costs would be for environmental sanitation and for hospital construction. The former, it was thought, would require the sinking of 75,000 wells to supply reliable water, and the construction of some 3 million latrines throughout the country at a cost of more than K 10.5 crores ($22 million). The cost of the hospital program was not even tentatively approximated. The proposed 1952–53 budget was K 6.6 crores (nearly $14 million), of which K

3.8 crores ($8 million) would be for recurring expenditures and K 2.8 crores (nearly $6 million) for non-recurring expenditures. As in the case of the Housing Plan, this well-thought-out and essential program was undertaken with only a limited notion of the nature of the capital costs that would be required over a period of time, and without any reliable estimate of the impact which the large numbers of additional personnel contemplated would make on the Government's current budget.

THE EDUCATION PLAN

The Education Plan, prepared with the assistance of a special educational advisory commission which had the benefit of a recent study made by a U.N.E.S.C.O. mission and of the participation of an outstanding Burmese educator, U Kaung, was organized around five basic principles or objectives laid down by the Government. These were, first, to insure that all citizens should have a basic education in the three R's; second, to train the requisite number of technicians for the realization of Pyidawtha; third, to train for responsible citizenship; fourth, to eradicate illiteracy and promote the five (Buddhist) strengths;[8] and, fifth, to train the citizenry for democratic ways of living. Simultaneously the plan foresaw the expansion of facilities at all levels, the training of teachers and other specialized personnel, a reorganization of the curriculum so as better to achieve the stated objectives, and the use of special institutions and techniques to supplement the work of the schools.

To ensure basic education in the three R's for all, 1,000 additional state primary schools were to be opened each year. Assistance in furniture, books and equipment would be provided for 1,000 monastery schools each year for an indefinite period of time. A campaign against adult illiteracy would be undertaken by the Mass Education Council. The two existing teacher-training colleges would be supplemented by three new ones. It was not considered practicable to attempt compulsory universal education, even at the primary-school level. However, compulsory primary education was already being experimented with in one pilot project in Rangoon, and a similar project would be undertaken in a rural township. The curriculum in the primary schools would be enriched by training in arts and handicrafts, school gardening and general science.

Technical training was to begin at the middle school level, in the fifth standard, in which instruction in English as a second language would also begin. Middle schools in urban areas would introduce a technical and commercial bias into their curricula, whereas the middle schools in village areas would introduce a rural or agricultural bias. The high schools would introduce specialized classes for those preparing for the study of medicine, and general workshops and homemaking and business-training courses. A few specialized

8. Intellectual, physical, moral, economic and social strength.

agricultural and technical high schools would also be established. Training at the university level would be supplemented by specialized technical institutes and vocational institutes for forestry, veterinary medicine and agriculture. For adults, evening classes, trade schools and part-time schools would be provided. Outside the structure of public education would be the monastery schools and private institutions at higher levels. The educational administration would be reorganized in accordance with the requirements of the enlarged and reorganized educational system. The estimated cost for 1952–53 was placed modestly at K 1.4 crores ($2.9 million).

The cost of adding 5,000 primary schools over a five-year period was estimated at K 8.3 crores ($17.4 million), or a very modest 1,660 kyats ($349) each. These could obviously be little more than large huts with either thatch or C.G.I. sheet roofing, lacking running water or toilet facilities and perhaps not even provided with electric lighting. The cost of the program as a whole, however, was not estimated, on either the capital or current expenditures sides. In comparison, subsequent estimates for the engineering college, the polytechnic high school and the agricultural, veterinary and forest research institutes alone totaled more than K 2 crores ($4.2 million), and actual costs for these projects were substantially greater.

Despite the restraint and modesty of the approach, the education plan was still a third example of program determination in the social-investment area which was "wide open" in terms of the potential claims it might make on the limited resources available for capital development.

PLAN FOR THE DEVOLUTION OF
POWERS (THE PYIDAWTHA PLAN)

The Pyidawtha Plan, which took its name from that given to the conference as a whole, was aimed simply at bringing local communities into the development effort. It provided that annual development grants of K 50,000 ($10,500) would be made to each township in the Union. These funds would be spent for projects proposed by township Pyidawtha committees, subject to review by district and division-level Pyidawtha committees. Local communities were encouraged to supplement the Government's allotment with voluntary contributions of cash, labor or materials. It was anticipated that the projects undertaken by the local committees would reflect the felt needs of the people in those communities, and that the funds would be spent mostly for minor projects in the provision of roads, bridges, irrigation, drainage, tanks and ponds, wells and other sanitary facilities, and in some instances for schools and other community facilities. Since there were some 200 townships in the Union, approximately K 1 crore ($2.1 million) annually would suffice to finance this program.

While the scale of the program was exceedingly modest, the basic idea which underlay it was good. A fundamental defect in the organization of the committees at the various levels, however, was that they were composed almost entirely of Government officials. The only non-Government officials were the one or two members of each committee designated by the local A.F.P.F.L. or party organization.

THE DEMOCRATIZATION OF
LOCAL ADMINISTRATION

Democratization of local administration involved no plan for capital expenditure or development but dealt rather with public administration. Since a large-scale public-investment program must of necessity be executed largely by the existing governmental administrative machinery, the structure and quality of that machinery are highly pertinent to the prospects for effective implementation of public programs. An examination of the then existing administration and the plans for democratizing it is therefore pertinent here.

Burma had made no effort since acquiring independence to change in any important way the basic structure of public administration inherited from the British rule. At the center in Rangoon were the ministries and the Secretariat. The Secretariat consisted of the Government secretaries and their staffs. Not integrated with these were the operating departments, which were administratively responsible to the respective ministries for policy, for review and approval of programs and budgets and for various types of administrative clearance. Leaving apart the Shan, Kayah and Kachin states, Burma Proper was divided into seven administrative divisions, each under a commissioner. Each division was subdivided into two or more districts, each of them headed by a deputy or district commissioner (D.C.). Districts were again divided into subdistricts with subdivisional officers (S.D.O.'s), and these in turn into townships, administered by township officers (T.O.'s). The next step below the township was the village, administered by the headman and the village elders. This administrative apparatus in the field was responsible to the Government through the Home Ministry, which controlled all appointments.

The structure of the Government was colonial not only in form but in spirit. As in colonial days, appointments were made from the top down, and only at the village level was there a semblance of self-government. The only exceptions were those towns of sufficient size to have been granted a civic charter.

Each of the major central departments with national or field responsibilities had representatives in the field attached to the various district and township headquarters. Thus, the health, education, irrigation, buildings and roads, excise, agricultural, veterinary and other departments all maintained officers of appropriate rank in each of the district headquarters, although they did not in all cases maintain lesser officers in the township headquarters. These specialized officers had a dual responsibility — to their own departmental superior and to the local township officer or deputy commissioner, as the case might be. Their budget, policy and program direction was departmental. Their authority for implementation could derive, however, only out of the sanction and support of the central Government official to whose headquarters they were attached.

The democratic process in Burma consisted chiefly in voting for members of Parliament. The citizen did not, except in cities which had been granted self-governing charters, participate in any way in local government or in the selection of local officials.

The central administration functioned laboriously. "Cases" were made of each matter that arose. These became part of a file which included all earlier precedents or related cases and moved upwards within the Secretariat through layers of minor officials, each of whom entered painstaking notes or comment called "minutes." Eventually the papers reached the desk of the Secretary in charge, who entered his own decision or referral, after which they proceeded on their tortuous rounds. The average case was not disposed of for many months, and for the most part no urgency was involved. Some cases might remain pending for years, and many were lost or completely forgotten. The entire system seemed calculated to produce delays or vetoes, rather than to expedite action. This leisurely procedure, inherent in the colonial administration and attitude, was particularly ill-adapted to the requirements of a major economic development effort, and was perhaps the most debilitating of the legacies which the British left to independent Burma.

The purpose of the plan for the democratization of local administration was to introduce the beginnings of local self-government. Each village was to be governed by an elected village council. In towns and cities, comparable committees would be elected in each ward, and an urban council would then be formed by representatives of the ward committees. At the next level, township councils would be formed, composed of representatives from the village and urban councils. At the district level, there would also be a council, composed of four or more representatives from each township council in that district. The village headmen, township officers, subdivisional officers and deputy commissioners, who until that time had been centrally appointed, would be attached as executive officers to the respective councils or committees.

Authorization for this plan was to be enacted by the Parliament, after which it would be inaugurated on a trial basis in a few districts.

SIGNIFICANCE OF THE
PYIDAWTHA CONFERENCE

What, then, was the significance of the Pyidawtha Conference? It represented, first, an attempt by the Government to develop a widespread public understanding and to enlist widespread public acceptance, support and participation in the broad economic program and goals which the Government itself had already accepted some months earlier when the K.T.A. Preliminary Report was presented. Second, it adopted a five-year program for the basic agricultural sector and recommitted the nation to a major land nationalization program, which was vague as to methodology and ultimate objectives. Third, it approved a program for rehabilitation in the important field of transport and communications which was to require a larger share of public investment than any other sector of the economy. Fourth, it embraced large-scale programs in health, education and housing without any clear definition or concept of what their total costs would be, and in the housing field at least, without coming to grips with some of the basic criteria necessary to the formulation of a clear-cut program.

For the sectors with which it specifically dealt, the Pyidawtha Conference blocked out major programs and major requirements for public investment which the consultants would have to embrace and incorporate within the scope of their Comprehensive Plan. The silence of the Pyidawtha Conference in relation to forestry, mining, electric power, water resources and manufacturing industry permitted the consultants somewhat more latitude in these sectors. Even in these areas, however, the Burmese thinking, whether formulated in the Two-Year Plan of 1948 or later, was to play a decisive role in the comprehensive program which was actually brought into being.

CHAPTER 8

The K.T.A. Comprehensive

Report: Economics, Policy

and Administration

THE K.T.A. COMPREHENSIVE REPORT

The K.T.A. Comprehensive Report was submitted in August 1953, within the two years envisaged under the contract, some eighteen months after the submission of the Preliminary Report and one year after the Pyidawtha Conference. During the interim several developments had occurred which affected, some favorably and some adversely, the prospects for Burma's successful execution of the comprehensive program foreseen in the Preliminary Report.

On the negative side, the progress made toward suppression or pacification of the insurrection, while perceptible, was far less than had been assumed in timing the program. While indigenous insurrectionist groups had been brought under better control, the K.M.T.[1] elements had become an increasing problem. Closely related to internal disorder was the sizable increase in the budgetary requirements of the defense forces, which constituted a heavier drain on resources than had been anticipated.

On the plus side were the more favorable prices being obtained for rice and other primary products in export markets and, consequently, the improved outlook for foreign exchange and budgetary receipts for the remainder of the program period, as compared with earlier expectations. Also on the plus side

1. These were Kuomintang troops that had retreated across the southern border into Burma at the time of the general retreat to Formosa.

was the generally favorable reception accorded by the Government to the recommendations made in the Preliminary Report and the positive actions which had already been taken. The Government had moved with relative vigor on the recommended King's Highway road project from Rangoon to the new airport at Mingaladon, on railways and waterways rehabilitation, on the procurement of vessels for the Shipping Board, on rehabilitation of the port of Rangoon, on exploration and testing of the Kalewa coal deposits, on the brick and tile factory and on a number of Housing Board projects, including construction of model villages and of a large new Government office building in Rangoon. On the organizational front, the Government had formed two development corporations in the fields of industry and mining, as recommended in the Preliminary Report, and had added a third in the field of agriculture. It had also organized a State Agricultural Bank.

These developments were taken as evidence of the Government's determination to embark on the kind of program recommended, and as assurance of its vigorous support of such a program in the future. On the whole, therefore, the consultants saw no reason to modify in a more conservative direction the broad scope and nature of their earlier recommendations.

THE ECONOMIC GOALS

The Comprehensive Report made no change in the basic output and investment goals earlier recommended. The target for total production (in 1950–51 prices) remained at K 700 crores, and that for net capital formation at K 750 crores. These goals, however, were made somewhat more conservative by two factors. First, the target date was slightly extended from the end of the calendar year 1959 to the end of the fiscal year 1959–60, adding eight months to the program's duration. More significant, however, was the refinement made since the preparation of the Preliminary Report in the gross domestic product estimates for the 1950–51 base period. At the time of the earlier report, output for 1950–51 had been estimated crudely at K 300 to K 350 crores. Thus the target of K 700 crores called for an increase of 100 to 133 per cent in gross national product during the program period. Output for the base period was now calculated at K 371 crores. The target of K 700 crores would require, therefore, a lesser increase of 88 per cent, and over a somewhat longer time period.

The over-all economic development goals of the Comprehensive Report for gross domestic product and for consumer purchases are shown both in total and on a per capita basis in Table 11.

Two aspects of the recommended goals merit attention here. First, while the output and consumption goals represented sizable increases from the base period 1950–51 and from the figures for 1952–53 (as estimated at the time the Comprehensive Report was completed), they represented quite modest in-

Table 11

GENERAL DEVELOPMENT GOALS IN 1950–51 PRICES

	1938–39	1950–51	1952–53	1959–60	Percentage Increase to 1959–60 from:		
					1938–39	1950–51	1952–53
Gross domestic product							
Total (million kyats)	5,337	3,710	4,295	7,000	31	88	63
Per capita (kyats)	326	201	226	340	4	69	50
Consumer purchases							
Total (million kyats)	3,382	2,693	2,964	4,663	38	74	58
Per capita (kyats)	206	146	156	224	8.5	54	44
Consumer purchases as per cent of G.D.P.	63.3	72.6	62.7	66.6			

Source: K.T.A. Comprehensive Report, Vol. I, Table II–1, p. 22.

Note: Data for 1952–53 were projected estimates at the time the table was prepared. Official series data have since been converted to 1947–48 prices, and comparison of the 1952–53 projected data with later revised data, both in 1950–51 prices, cannot be made using official data.

creases in relation to the pre-war achievement. On a per capita basis, the target increases for 1959–60 were only 4 per cent for output and 8.5 per cent for consumption over the pre-war levels. It had been from the beginning the consultants' view that any targets less ambitious than these would not provide adequate incentives, in terms either of Burma's potentials or of the Government's aspirations. This view had been confirmed by the reactions expressed to these goals at the Pyidawtha Conference. At the same time, the goals were considered sufficiently ambitious to require real effort. The second point worthy of note is the larger increase in per capita consumption relative to per capita output implicit in the targets. Whereas consumer purchases in the base period 1938–39 were estimated to be only 63.3 per cent of gross domestic output, it was anticipated that by 1959–60 they could take 66.6 per cent. This larger share did not mean that a smaller part of the national output would be set aside for investment. It was based rather on the changed structure of ownership and income distribution in the economy which would result in the virtual disappearance of the portion previously paid abroad to foreign enterprises. Before the war, close to 7 per cent of the gross domestic product had been paid abroad in dividends. The liquidation of this obligation, it was thought, would permit part of that share to go to domestic consumption and still permit a somewhat larger proportion of the national product to flow into investment channels.

With respect to the original goal for net capital formation of K 750 crores during the program period, a good deal of additional analysis was done. Estimates were made of the probable division of this investment as between the public and private sectors, and the investment was projected year by year through the program period in relation to the projected gross domestic product. Gross as well as net public and private investment was estimated and similarly distributed and related. These estimates or projections are shown in Table 12. The estimated data for January–September 1952 and for 1952–53 are separated in the table from the programed figures for the years 1953–54 through 1959–60. But this has been done only to accentuate the fact that the estimated actual data were being incorporated into the entire program. They will be treated as additive to those for the programed years in the comments which follow.

First, combined public productive and social net capital formation was estimated at K 402 crores, or 54 per cent of the total of K 750 crores. Unplanned private investment was counted on to make up nearly half the total. Second, Government gross capital formation (including defense) throughout the program period was estimated at approximately K 520 crores, or slightly less than half the K 1,067 crores of total gross capital formation. (The slightly disparate share of public investment in net and gross capital formation was

Table 12
GOVERNMENT AND PRIVATE CAPITAL
FORMATION, 1953–54 TO 1959–60

Year 1	Gross Domestic Product 2	Government Capital Formation		Private Capital Formation		Per Cent Col. 4 to 2 7	Per Cent Col. 6 to 2 8
		Productive and Social— Net 3	Productive and Defensive —Gross 4	Net 5	Gross 6		
Grand Total		4,020	5,225	3,470	5,440		
1952, Jan.–Sept.	4,121	150	230	255	385	5.6	9.3
1952–53 (est.)	4,650	220	375	265	460	8.1	9.9
Programed, total		3,650	4,620	2,950	4,595		
1953–54	5,200	390	565	265	470	10.9	9.0
1954–55	5,550	550	695	280	495	12.5	8.9
1955–56	5,950	605	745	345	570	12.5	9.6
1956–57	6,300	605	740	410	645	10.7	10.2
1957–58	6,600	540	670	490	735	10.2	11.1
1958–59	6,800	490	615	560	815	9.1	12.0
1959–60	7,000	470	590	600	865	8.4	12.4

Millions of Kyats

Source: K.T.A. Comprehensive Report, Vol. I, Table III–7, p. 50.

due to the somewhat larger element of depreciation in the private sector.) Beginning with 1953–54, the schedules anticipated that gross capital formation would require the allocation of approximately one fifth of the gross domestic product annually. Within this total, the share of public investment was expected to rise quickly to a peak of 12.5 per cent in 1954–55 and 1955–56 and decline substantially thereafter to 8.4 per cent by the end of the program period. The role of gross private capital formation was expected to rise steadily to a peak in 1959–60, approximating the earlier peak to be achieved by the public sector.

Not shown in the table is the judgment that of the total net capital formation of K 750 crores, approximately K 550 crores, or 73 per cent, would be for productive investments, while some K 200 crores, or 27 per cent, would be invested in the social area. Of the total of K 365 crores shown in the table as being programed for public investment from 1953–54 through 1959–60, it was anticipated that approximately K 300 crores would be spent for planned projects in the productive areas with which the engineering consultants were concerned, while the remainder would be invested in schools, hospitals, housing and other social projects. Finally, it was estimated that of the total public and private gross investment, close to two thirds would be spent domestically, while a little more than one third would be spent abroad and would thus require foreign exchange.[2] Repeated references in the report suggested that the figures cited for public capital expenditure were offered as maxima, and the private investment figures as minima. It was particularly stressed that some of the planned public investment in the manufacturing-industry sector might actually be implemented by the private sector, either independently or in joint ventures with the Government, and that the private sector might also account for a substantial portion of the social investment anticipated, especially housing. Thus, while public investment was shown to account for slightly more than half of the net investment requirement, the report contemplated that the public share might in fact fall to less than half of the total.

The emphasis which the economic consultants placed on the contribution to be made by private enterprise not only represented their conviction that the job could not and should not be done by the Government alone, but enabled them to express, albeit indirectly, their views on a problem which had persisted in the background since their work in Burma had begun two years before. They had undertaken to formulate a comprehensive development plan for a government socialist in its economic convictions, highly mistrustful of private enterprise and unaware of the constructive roles played by the market and competition in a regulated but relatively free economy. While the economists had conceived it to be neither necessary nor appropriate to challenge directly the Government's basic political and economic convictions, they were naturally aware that these would exert an important influence on the kind of program likely to be adopted, and, because of the degree of state ownership and operation which would be involved, on the efficiency with which it could be carried through. The tactic they adopted, therefore, was to avoid any direct reference or challenge to socialist ideas as such, and to consider specific policies and projects strictly in terms of whether they would work. If a given proposal were challenged on the ground that in the given circumstances it was not likely to work satisfactorily, rather than because it originated out of a given ideological position, the Government might consider the question on its merits rather than on ideological grounds. This continued to be the economists' position and tactics in the rationale of the Comprehensive Report, and helps explain the emphasis it placed on certain ideas and concepts.

For example, in discussing the proposed economic goals, and recognizing the Government's propensity to aim at the equalization of incomes, the report stressed the limitations of this objective and the importance of increasing total output.

The degree to which redistribution of income can advantageously be effected is limited. The prospect of increasing one's income is a powerful incentive to invest-

2. K.T.A. Comprehensive Report, Table III–2, p. 41.

ment and to efficient production, and if progressive taxation is so heavy that it makes it difficult for the owner of the enterprise to increase his income after taxes, or if other measures reduce too greatly his incentives, private investment will dwindle, production will be less efficient, prices will be higher, and the mass of the people will suffer.

However, the most absolute limitation on the redistribution of income as a method of raising the standard of living is that it cannot bring about an increase sufficient to make a significant contribution to living levels in general. If the entire income of the wealthy in Burma were taken in taxes, and distributed in government services or in cash among the nineteen million people of Burma, the increase in income per person would be very small. The wealthy are few and the poor are many. Burma simply does not produce enough goods to yield a high income. Maximum production of which Burma is capable with present methods of production cannot yield a high level of living, no matter how equitably the income from it is distributed. The benefits from optimum distribution of income will be small compared to those from a comprehensive development program.[3]

Having emphasized the necessity for increased output and having pointed out the contribution which the restoration of normal employment would make to increased output, the economists then stressed that the need for increased productivity prevailed throughout the economy, in existing as well as in new industries, and in the private as well as in the public sector. Agriculture, forestry, mining, cottage and manufacturing industry, trade, commerce and government would all have to contribute toward this objective, even though it was recognized that the concomitants of increased productivity "will not invariably be welcomed."[4] The argument also took into account the obvious propensity of the Government to equate industrialization with progress, and its disposition, therefore, to venture heavily into state-owned manufacturing industry. The report emphasized consequently the reasons why "The consumers market for industrial products will be limited for some time" and pointed out that "only a fairly small number of new industries will be efficient in Burma at present." Primary emphasis needed to be placed on agriculture.

The introduction of this limited number of industries will itself raise the average level of income . . . the extent to which industry can feed on itself in this way is limited. The development in Burma of an increasing market for industrial products therefore depends on an increase in per capita income throughout the entire economy. For this increase, agriculture offers the dominant opportunity. Income in agriculture is now low, but the potential exists to increase it substantially. A fundamentally important step in the industrialization of Burma must therefore be a comprehensive, well organized and determined program to achieve a con-

3. *Ibid.*, p. 24.
4. *Ibid.*, p. 30.

tinuing increase in productivity and in the standard of living of Burma's agriculturalists.[5]

The great emphasis which the Comprehensive Report placed on the importance of the agricultural sector is worthy of special note, not only on substantive grounds but also because of the criticism commonly made later that it had neglected or underestimated the importance of agricultural development.

In presenting the recommended economic goals, the report called attention to four main problems which stood as obstacles to the program proposed, and which "must be overcome if the program is to succeed." The first of these was the problem of internal security. The second was that "which arises from the acute shortage of skilled technicians and experienced managers and administrators. Indeed, it would not be overstating the case to say that the success of the development program hinges more on this than on any other single factor."

The third bottleneck was

that which arises in the organization and administration within Government itself, where established modes and procedures are in tune with the more leisurely pace of another day, having developed in response to a relatively static rather than a dynamic way of life in Burma. Organization, administration, and personnel in the government ministries, agencies, departments and boards must be brought into step with the dynamic requirements of the development program.

and

Finally, determination, vigor and daring must be displayed by those charged with responsibility for the execution of the development program. There has been no opportunity to evaluate as yet the degree to which these qualities will be forthcoming. It is to be hoped that they will be present, for it is clear that the program will falter without them.[6]

These were indeed to be the factors most responsible for the difficulties encountered in executing the program.

FINANCING THE PROGRAM

Whereas the Preliminary Report had anticipated that Burma might have to borrow abroad approximately one third of the funds required to finance the recommended program, the improvement in rice export prices since that time and the outlook for the continuation of relatively favorable rice prices for the remainder of the program period now led to the conclusion that Burma could

5. *Ibid.,* p. 35.
6. *Ibid.*

probably finance the entire development program out of her own resources. In mid-1953, Ngasein Small Mills Special (42 per cent broken), Burma's dominant export rice grade, was selling on a government-to-government basis at £60 sterling per ton. Private sales were being consummated at £70 and more per ton. The projections of the economists anticipated a rising level of exports from their then abnormally depressed volumes and only a moderate decline in prices to not less than £50 per ton by 1959-60. These overly optimistic expectations, frequently criticized since as having led Burma to undertake a larger program than would otherwise have been the case,[7] were the most important single factor leading to the conclusion that the foreign exchange requirements of the K 750 crores program could be financed without assistance from abroad.

Because the profits of the rice export trade accrued to the Government either as income taxes paid by the State Agricultural Marketing Board or as "rehabilitation contributions" made to the treasury by that Board, rice prices and profits were extremely important in the budgetary, as well as in the foreign exchange, picture. Rice prices and profits did not, however, make an important contribution to the highly important domestic financial needs, for they originated in foreign exchange rather than in domestic currency revenues. They could contribute importantly to domestic finance only if transactions of the private sector abroad were on the whole in a deficit position, so that the private sector would have to buy foreign exchange from the Government and thereby reduce the privately held domestic money supply.

Because of the importance of foreign trade to the economy, the analysis of Burma's capacity to finance the proposed program was divided into separate analyses of her ability to finance its foreign exchange and its domestic currency requirements. On the foreign exchange side, it was estimated that requirements would roughly double during the program period as compared with the then existing level of foreign exchange expenditure. This was based on calculations that the foreign exchange component of the planned public investment would be close to half of the total investment requirement, that the proportion of total gross public and private development expenditures required to be spent abroad would be something more than one third and that the propensity of the public to purchase consumer goods from abroad at the higher levels of income anticipated would be substantial. Expectations with respect to foreign exchange earnings, while based chiefly on rice, looked to substantial increases in revenues from a higher level of timber, minerals and other exports as well. These, however, were expected to contribute little more than one fifth of the total increase of K 90 crores in foreign exchange receipts anticipated.[8]

7. This criticism is not valid. On this point, see the discussion in Chapter 21.
8. *Ibid.,* Table III–6, p. 48.

The report presented[9] two sets of estimates showing the calculations entering into the future value of rice exports. The more optimistic of these envisaged a somewhat greater recovery in rice acreage and production, and anticipated that as much as 2.5 million tons might be exported by 1959–60, at an average price of £55 per ton in that year. The less optimistic schedule illustrated the results which might be expected from a somewhat more modest recovery in acreage and output, and an export peak of approximately 2.3 million tons by the end of the program period, at an average price of £50 per ton in that year.[10] The indicated results of even the more conservative of these estimates was not only that the foreign exchange requirements as calculated could be met, but that the already large foreign exchange reserves would be substantially increased.[11]

The dependence of these estimates on the Government's success in dealing with the insurrection was explicitly recognized: "The more rapidly complete civil order is restored, and rice, mineral and timber production and exports increase, the larger will be Burma's foreign exchange earnings. The progress of restoration of civil order is therefore of first importance as a determinant of Burma's foreign exchange position."[12]

The possibility that the comforting foreign exchange analysis presented might prove ill-founded was not excluded. In this event, it was pointed out, three alternatives would be available to supplement inadequate foreign exchange earnings. The first would be the use of the existing reserves in excess of K 120 crores, of which less than one third were then required by statute as currency backing, and of which as much as half might safely be drawn down if necessary. The second alternative would be the restriction in some degree of imports for private use.[13] The third alternative would be the obtaining of loans from abroad. The report concluded therefore that "In view of the very favorable earnings prospects and the availability of these supplementary procedures, it is hardly conceivable that Burma will not have adequate foreign exchange to finance the full development program which has been recommended. She should proceed with her development program with no hesitation whatsoever on this score."[14]

The report anticipated no difficulty on the part of the private sector in financing the private investment contemplated for it. Pre-war figures indicated that the private sector had then saved 14.2 per cent of the gross domestic

9. *Ibid.*, Tables III–5A and 5B, p. 46.

10. The export tonnage goals may be compared with a pre-war peak export of close to 3.5 million tons and an average export volume for the five years preceding the war of more than 3 million tons.

11. *Ibid.*, Table III–6, p. 48.

12. *Ibid.*, p. 40.

13. This possibility would of course be limited by the possible need to use consumer goods imports as an offset to domestic inflation.

14. *Ibid.*, p. 49.

product. Private activity before the war included, of course, a number of industries or functions which had since been wholly or partly nationalized. Nevertheless, it was considered that the private sector would still be able readily to finance investment at the level envisaged for it of 9 to 12 per cent of the gross domestic product, at the higher levels of output expected to prevail.

The domestic financing of the public capital formation program was not expected to be so easy. Because a substantial part of the Government's revenue was derived from its monopoly of rice and timber exports, an unusually large proportion of its revenues were in the form of foreign exchange rather than of domestic currency. The Government's current expenditures within Burma were already in excess of its revenues from within Burma, and this situation was expected to continue. However, the Government's net non-budgetary receipts — chiefly the net domestic surpluses of the state-owned boards and corporations on current account which were not comprehended within the formal budget of the Ministry of Finance and Revenue — were already sizable, and could be expected to increase. These might be supplemented by private saving in excess of private capital formation, thus increasing the non-inflationary resources available for public expenditure programs. Taking these factors into account, and assuming that the Government's current budgetary expenditures could be kept from growing much larger, it appeared that the Government might run only a modest domestic deficit on a cash-consolidated basis through the program period.[15] These deficits might be offset, at least in part, by an excess of private imports as compared with private exports, thus moderating the growth of the privately held money supply. The projected trend in the privately held money supply even thus calculated showed that this might almost double by the end of the program period. However, in relation to the increased gross domestic product, it might rise only from approximately 16 per cent to 20 or 22 per cent.

These estimates and projections assumed that the current expenditures of the Government during the remainder of the decade would not rise higher than K 70 crores per year, as compared with the K 65 crores budgeted for 1952–53. "The figure is held at K 70 crores because it is believed that the Government must hold it at approximately this level if enough resources are to be available for the development program."[16] Even on the basis of this assumption, the economists concluded that it was impossible to forecast whether domestic currency requirements could be financed on a non-inflationary basis without substantial alterations in the tax structure. The report was realistic in stating that "the precise trend of events five or six years in the future is so uncertain that it would be absurd to assume that the precise turn

15. *Ibid.*, Table III–11, p. 54.
16. *Ibid.*, p. 53.

of developments now projected for that period has significance for future policy. . . . The conclusions drawn may require considerable modification as the development program progresses."[17]

The situation, it was clear, would have to be watched and reappraised from year to year. The execution of the comprehensive development program would have to be accompanied by "equally comprehensive planning of economic policies." The final conclusion was that there existed nothing in the financial picture, foreign or domestic, to prevent the Government from embarking with confidence on the program recommended.

CENTRAL ECONOMIC POLICIES

The consultants next analyzed the problems of central economic policy, government organization and specialized manpower that would have to be reckoned with, and made recommendations for dealing with them. The discussion which follows will concentrate on those recommendations which will later be of significance in analyzing the execution of the program.

In approaching the question of fiscal policy, the Comprehensive Report first stressed the necessity for much-improved fiscal information. This included the need for a cash consolidated budget which would reflect and anticipate the impact of the totality of the Government's fiscal relations with the public; for estimates of Government expenditure divided more accurately between domestic and foreign outlays; for the more prompt submission of badly lagging budgetary accounts by the spending agencies and departments; and for the introduction into the budgetary procedure of expenditure authorizations as well as expenditure estimates. Two major emphases were made as regards fiscal policy — one, already noted, that tendencies continually to increase the level of current budgetary expenditures be strongly resisted; and, two, that in current budget review special consideration be given to technical and related training programs, the need for higher pay for skilled and responsible administrative workers, the agricultural extension service, and other items which would assist materially in the execution of the development program. These two objectives do not appear to be altogether compatible. Had the consultants, however, known then some of the things they learned later on, they might well have pointed out at the time that overstaffing and inefficiency in the public service were so pronounced as to afford opportunity to achieve both objectives.

The discussion of tax policy examined the tax structure from the point of view of its equity, its adequacy in providing revenues and its effect on incentives. It pointed up one extremely interesting problem relating to equity and a number of deficiencies so far as incentives were concerned. Levels of taxation in general were considered adequate to the then existing needs, and

17. *Ibid.,* p. 57.

Table 13

GOVERNMENTAL RECEIPTS, BY SOURCE,
INCLUDING ESTIMATED NET INCOME OF
GOVERNMENTAL ENTERPRISES, 1938–39 AND 1951–52

Type of Revenue	Millions of Kyats		Per Cent of Total	
	1938–39	1951–52 (Rev. Est.)	1938–39	1951–52 (Rev. Est.)
Total	164.3	812.0	100.0	100.0
Land revenue	54.2	21.5	33.0	2.6
Profits of state enterprises (est.)	—	370.0	—	45.6
Customs	36.4	193.0	22.2	23.8
Excises and excise duties	23.0	34.8	14.0	4.3
Sales tax	—	23.0	—	2.8
Taxes on income	19.1	44.5	11.6	5.5
Other taxes	5.7	24.1	3.4	3.0
Forest revenue	14.3	13.0	8.7	1.6
Other revenue	11.6	88.1[a]	7.1	10.8
Gross domestic income	1,460	4,116		

Source: K.T.A. Comprehensive Report, Table IV–1, p. 63.

a. Excludes non-cash transfer of K 30 million from the International Monetary Fund, matched by an equal non-cash payment to the Fund, the two together canceling out.

the structure of the system was such as to promise adequate increases in relation to anticipated increases in output and income. However, an intensive study of the tax structure was needed, as was expert assistance in improving the obvious weaknesses of tax enforcement.

The major problem in the equity of the tax structure arose out of the degree of dependence which it placed on the profits of the State Agricultural Marketing Board, the Government's rice export monopoly. These profits derived from the huge margin which prevailed between the low controlled price paid to the cultivator for his paddy and the very high price at which the milled rice was sold in export abroad. The magnitude of this problem is illustrated in Table 13.

As Table 13 shows, profits of state enterprises in 1951–52 were estimated to amount to K 370 million (K 37 crores), or nearly 46 per cent of total Government revenues. While part of these profits derived from the operations of the State Timber Board — the Government teak export monopoly — and from profits of the Civil Supplies Management Board, which imported consumer goods for sale to the public, the lion's share was contributed by the S.A.M.B. Under the circumstances, these profits represented in large part an indirect tax upon the paddy cultivator. Because of the abnormally high price commanded at the time by rice in international markets, part of the profit could rationally be regarded as a windfall, paid by the buyer abroad rather than the cultivator at home. However, to the extent that the Government-imposed ceiling on paddy prices prevented them from rising at least in correspondence with the prices of other commodities bought by the paddy cultivator, they could also be considered an indirect and discriminatory tax on the country's rice producers. In considering the question of equity and, incidentally, the political feasibility of maintaining this situation over the years to come, countervailing tendencies also needed to be taken into account.

As indicated in Table 13, the land revenue taxes paid by the cultivators had declined sharply even in absolute terms, simultaneously with domestic inflation, and now represented less than 3 per cent of the total tax burden, in comparison with 33 per cent before the war. Further, reform legislation had placed strict limits on the rents paid by tenant farmers, and conditions were such that many cultivators paid neither their rents nor their land revenue taxes. Liberal Government loans to the cultivators were seemingly impossible of collection and were virtually a subsidy to the farmers. Finally, many of the farmer's costs of production (as in the case of seasonal labor) were paid in kind rather than in cash and therefore tended to hold down his production costs. These factors undoubtedly did much to mitigate the seeming gross inequity inherent in the Government's fixed paddy purchase price. Yet it was quite remarkable that the cultivators did not agitate in an organized way against the maintenance of this heavy indirect tax burden. The failure of the A.B.P.O. (All Burma Peasants' Organization) and of the farm cooperative movement to protest this exploitation more vigorously can be explained only by the farmers' general docility and the subservience of the farm organizations to the dominant political party.

Table 13 illustrates also the extreme importance of indirect taxation in the Burmese tax structure and the very minor role of income taxation, even as compared with the pre-war period. The latter is partly due to the generally low levels of personal income and the difficulties of administration and enforcement of personal and business income taxation, except in the case of salaried employees of the Government and the larger enterprises. It is also due the diminished role of larger private companies in the economy, as compared with pre-war years.[18]

The seeming regressivity of the tax structure inherent in the relatively important role played by indirect taxation is not quite accurate. This is because the customs, excises and excise duties and sales taxes were progressive in nature, ranging from little or nothing on essential goods consumed by low income groups to fairly steep rates on luxury goods. The sales tax on imported goods, collectible at point of entry, had actually been introduced be-

18. The reclassification of Government revenues some time later brought income taxes paid by Government enterprises within the income-tax classification. While this appeared to give the income tax greater relative importance than before, the difference was not real.

cause of the consultants' earlier recommendations in place of the previous much-evaded and uniform turnover tax.

The recommendations with respect to banking and credit policy stressed the vital importance of affording adequate credit facilities at reasonable rates of interest to the country's agriculturalists at the village level. The expansion of the commercial banking system through branch banking would help solve this problem, but the major contribution toward its solution would have to be made by the newly established State Agricultural Bank operating through a system of village banks. Since these could be developed effectively only in conjunction with soundly organized village cooperatives and the training of necessary staffs, this process would take time. Meanwhile, direct loans through the Department of Agriculture would have to be continued on a more soundly administered basis. Development of a village banking structure would, of course, serve the needs of cottage industry, petty trade and personal loans, as well as those of agriculture itself.

It would be difficult to overestimate the importance of the objectives here sought. The exceedingly high interest rates prevailing in the countryside not only drained the incomes of the borrowers and retarded the growth of village economic activity; they also served as a powerful magnet which attracted savings away from potential industrial investment.

Because it was expected that the foreign exchange position would be easy, recommendations with respect to foreign exchange and foreign trade policy were of a liberal nature. The economists, however, had here to deal with at least one novel situation. Whereas the foreign exchange position and outlook, as they saw it, permitted free or uncontrolled imports, the Government, because of its desire to Burmanize trade, had introduced an import licensing system. Most commodities were under an "open general license" permitting imports by anyone in any amount. However, a number of commodities were under special license, in the issue of which Burmese nationals were granted priority. This situation had already led to a number of undesirable consequences, including political favoritism in the issue of licenses, the emergence of a great many bogus traders whose sole business was the obtaining and sale of licenses, and the consequent forcing up of consumer prices to cover the price paid for the licenses. Further, inefficient administration by the licensing authorities resulted in poor timing of the license issue, and licenses issued were not always used. Consequently, supplies and prices tended to fluctuate abnormally.

If the consultants had been able to foresee the foreign exchange difficulties which were later to develop, the dangers which attended the Burmanization of trade policy could have been foreseen, and undoubtedly the issue would have been squarely faced. Since they anticipated an easy foreign exchange situation, however, the consultants were content at the time to recommend that if the licensing system were continued for reasons of Burmanization policy, license issue should be so liberal as to approximate the conditions which would obtain in a free market. They also recommended, as a positive alternative to import licensing, that constructive steps be taken to aid Burmese traders in establishing efficient contacts with foreign suppliers and efficient trading procedures. Burmanization policy, it was stressed, should not protect inefficiency, and the Government should be fully aware of the costs as well as the advantages (in its view) of the policy.

ORGANIZATION FOR COORDINATING
THE PROGRAM

The economic consultants viewed the central coordination of the program as divided into four closely related steps — planning, programing, implementation, and progress reporting and expediting. The planning function embraced not only the determination of development goals and plans for achieving them, but all major aspects of the nation's economic activity and the formulation of appropriate central economic policies necessary to facilitate achievement of the planning objectives. The programing function centered on the annual programs which would adjust to changing circumstances and to modifications in the over-all plan. These closely related functions were to be vested in the Ministry of National Planning, which was to work in close cooperation with a strengthened Ministry of Finance and Revenue and with the operating ministries, departments, boards and corporations primarily responsible for the investment programs in their respective areas. The consultants particularly stressed the need to integrate the planning process with the annual budgeting process and to develop, with respect to the latter, a perspective of several years at least, which would take into account not only resource patterns but also the continuing financial claims of current spending authorizations. The implementation function involved responsibility for the final review and approval of programs and policies, the reconciliation of differences between the Ministry of National Planning and the operating agencies, and the supervision and coordination of program execution. This function was vested in the Economic and Social Board, which had only recently been created for this purpose, pursuant to recommendations made in the Preliminary Report. Its members were the key economic ministers for Agriculture, Industry, Finance, Mines, Trade Development and National Planning, as well as the Chairman of the Central Bank and the Executive Secretary of the board itself. Its Chairman was the Prime Minister. While the Board was presumably junior to the Cabinet in decision-making authority, it constituted, in fact, a super-cabinet because its membership included, in addition to the Prime Minister, the three next most powerful Cabinet members — U Ba Swe, U Kyaw Nyein and Thakin Tin. The progress reporting function was intended to keep track of progress in the execution of the development program, to anticipate and locate bottlenecks and to provide information which would enable the Economic and Social Board to take necessary corrective or expediting action.

U Hla Maung, the former Secretary for National Planning and for Finance and Revenue, had by this time surrendered those posts in order to become Executive Secretary to the Economic and Social Board. The Prime Minister had surrendered the National Planning portfolio on assuming the chairmanship of the Economic and Social Board. The new Minister for National Planning, U Win, had responsibility also for the ministries of Religious Affairs and Union Culture. He had, however, accepted the Planning portfolio only on the understanding that the Prime Minister would in reality continue to function as Planning Minister, which proved to be the case. Thus, for some time, the ultimate responsibility for central coordination, both in planning and in implementation, was vested in one person, the Prime Minister. And since the Executive Secretary of the board was the former Planning Secretary, intensely interested in the planning function and close to the Prime Minister, there was a natural tendency for the planning function to be performed increasingly at the Economic and Social Board, rather than within the Planning Ministry. The fact that U Tin Pe, the new Secretary for National Planning, was relatively uninterested in the planning function and soon became involved in the bustle of program execution, facilitated this process.

Meanwhile, with the completion of the Comprehensive Report, the two-year contract of the K.T.A. and its associated companies had lapsed. The Government had also renounced further U. S. technical assistance because of the K.M.T. issue.[19] Robert R. Nathan Associates, the economic consultants, were now engaged separately by the Economic and Social Board, and Knappen Tippetts Abbett, the senior engineers, were retained by the Ministry of National Planning. In both cases the Government was now paying the consultants' costs out of its own pocket, rather than with grant funds. While the Nathan staff was engaged by the Economic and Social Board, it was to service also the Ministry of National Planning, the members of the indigenous staff of which — the Central Statistical and Economics Department — were youthful and inexperienced. The Nathan group, therefore, were obliged to act not only as advisors but also as an economic staff to both the Planning Ministry and the Economic and Social Board. Since interest and receptivity were

19. After desultory attempts at raids across the Chinese border, during which they lived off the countryside, the Kuomintang troops gradually extended their area of occupation and depredation within Burma, in some cases collaborating with native insurrectionists. The view is widely held in Burma that the K.M.T.'s, supplied in part by air drop from bases outside, were sustained with United States help. It was certainly believed that the United States, if it wished, could have prevailed upon Formosa to withdraw these troops. The voluntary termination of United States aid was considered a necessary moral preliminary to the charges Burma was shortly to present to the United Nations.

greatest at the Board, it was only natural that they should function chiefly through it rather than through the Ministry of National Planning. Later on, with U Hla Maung gone from the Board and an interested and dynamic new Secretary, U Mo Myit, at the Ministry of National Planning, this situation changed. Still later, when U Mo Myit assumed responsibility for both posts, it made little difference which "hat" the consultants wore.

ADMINISTERING THE PROGRAM

While the consultants felt reasonably confident that the central coordination of the program would be adequately handled, they were quite concerned about the way in which the program would be administered. Their concern here was not only with the ministries, with the newly organized development corporations in the fields of agriculture, industry and mining and with the many other government boards which were responsible for a wide variety of economic activities, but also with the quality of the public service generally and with the impact of Government administration on the private and mixed sectors of the economy. They urged, consequently, a number of actions needed to improve the Government's administrative posture and performance.

For the twenty-six ministries, certain obvious consolidations were suggested, as was the reorganization of internal structures within the ministries to clarify lines of responsibility and improve coordination and performance. "A number of the ministries," the Comprehensive Report stated, "seem rather to be organized in such a way as to foster undue deliberation, an excessive number of lateral clearances, delays and blurred responsibility and accountability. It has been stated that, in some instances, nobody seems to be clearly in charge of anything. The internal structure within each ministry should be one which encourages the orderly delegation of responsibility, prompt action and sharply focused accountability for results in specific areas of responsibility."[20]

As regards the development corporations, which had tremendously significant roles to play in the development program, the consultants urged that these be granted adequate autonomy for operations within the policy lines laid down by the Government, that the boards of directors of these corporations provide adequate representation to non-government officials and delegate adequate authority and responsibilty to their managing directors, and that they avoid direct involvement in individual projects by creating appropriate bodies which would be responsible for their implementation. If, for example, the Industrial Development Corporation wished to initiate a pulp and paper plant, it should set up an autonomous, businesslike, publicly owned corporation to do the job. If that was not feasible, it should make appropriate arrangements for a joint venture or insure in some other way that the project would be executed. It should not itself become engaged in direct operations,

20. *Ibid.*, p. 84.

but confine itself to the "initiation, financing and subsequent exercise of such controls as would be appropriate to any large owner of an enterprise, to insure that it was well managed and efficiently operated." In this connection, the consultants warned that "If the development corporations go beyond the exercise of such functions, and extend themselves into the sphere of actual operations, they will become hopelessly bogged down in detail, and they will be unable to carry on their development activities on the scale and with the objectivity required for satisfactory performance."[21] They also cautioned that the development corporations, though engaged in the initiation and guidance of new development projects, should not neglect the equally important job of encouraging and fostering modernization and expansion by existing private enterprises. Their recommendations also covered the needs of the development corporations for funding powers, for adequate and capable staff, for effective internal organization and, finally, for an imaginative and dynamic approach to their respective tasks, unhampered by fears of petty criticism from higher authority.

Even more important than the new development corporations in the total economic picture were the already existing state boards which dealt with the public. Such boards were responsible for rice and teak exports, for the large-scale importation of essential consumer goods, and for the operation of the basic utilities and public services — rail, water and air transport, the port of Rangoon and the generation and distribution of electric power. A number of boards had only recently been separately created to execute specific projects. These included the Paper Board, the Mingaladon Airport Board, the Brick and Tile Factory Board and the Cotton Spinning and Weaving Board. Other boards, such as the Cement Board, the Sugar Board and the Tariff Board, also existed for operational or regulatory purposes. The current revenues and expenditures of these boards, quite apart from their capital investment activities, amounted to approximately K 200 crores per year in an economy whose gross domestic product was something less than K 500 crores.[22] Clearly their efficient operation was essential to the achievement of economic development and growth. Here again the consultants urged the Government to take measures to assure effective organization, management and operation, concluding, "The problem of the quality of management of existing and prospective state enterprises is crucial."[23]

Somewhat more generally, and with respect to the public administration as a whole, the consultants stressed and made specific recommendations for improved training, recruitment practices, conditions of work, and personnel

21. *Ibid.*, p. 85.
22. This comparison of magnitudes is not intended to suggest that the contribution of the state boards to the gross domestic product even approached in magnitude their level of current operations.
23. *Ibid.*, p. 86.

and administrative management. Finally, they re-emphasized the various actions on the part of the Government needed to improve the scale and efficiency of economic activity in the private and mixed sectors of the economy. These included the provision of cheaper fuel and power, the improvement of transport and communications facilities, the development of natural resources, the fostering of low-cost and adequate credit, the provision of research and technical assistance, the elimination of unnecessary restrictions on business activity, the more expeditious treatment of business in regulatory matters, the provision of incentives to investment, the inauguration of training programs and, above all, the creation of an atmosphere of security and confidence. The consultants also called on the Government to clarify earlier statements of policy vis-à-vis the private sector:

> If the Government makes clear that it is not, in principle, hostile to private economic activity in spheres which Government has not reserved to itself, and if it indicates further that it welcomes the contributions which private economic activity can in the non-reserved sectors make to the economic development of the country . . . , it may be anticipated with confidence that private economic activity will increase in volume and in efficiency. If so, it will contribute in major degree toward the realization of economic development goals.[24]

MANNING THE PROGRAM

The problem of manning the program was one of specialized manpower. There was an abundant labor supply, and a small nucleus of skilled workers. Literacy was relatively widespread and increasing. The experience of large employers of labor indicated that the Burmese national was adept at assimilating modern industrial skills. The over-all situation, therefore, was one of a relatively undeveloped force which possessed a potential for rapid upgrading. The development program, however, would generate needs for specialized types of manpower either non-existent or very scarce in Burma. These included many kinds of professional workers, technicians, skilled workers, managers and administrators. It was the lack of specialized personnel of this kind which constituted in the consultants' opinion "the critical manpower factor and the greatest obstacle to the development program. . . . Unless the needs for such persons are appreciated in their full significance, and unless adequate steps are taken to assure their availability in time, the fulfillment of the development program itself within the time contemplated will not be feasible."[25]

Estimates were made of requirements for specialized manpower. These were prepared to show separately requirements for the planned public projects and for the economy as a whole. (See Table 14.)

24. *Ibid.,* p. 91.
25. *Ibid.,* p. 94.

Table 14

Requirements for New Skilled Manpower, by Type of Worker, 1953–1959 (Cumulative)[a]

Type of Worker	1953–54	1954–55	1955–56	1956–57	1957–58	1958–59	1959–60
Total skilled workers							
Planned projects	6,470	10,167	11,702	12,709	13,119	12,836	13,115
Entire development program	13,270	18,040	22,539	25,815	28,443	29,584	32,138
Managerial and supervisory							
Planned projects	382	531	718	905	972	982	1,037
Entire development program	692	851	1,128	1,375	1,502	1,532	1,657
Professional							
Planned projects	430	545	630	688	699	667	688
Entire development program	730	855	1,000	1,098	1,149	1,152	1,203
Sub-professional							
Planned projects	1,224	1,708	2,006	2,240	2,170	2,088	2,116
Entire development program	1,824	2,328	2,716	3,040	3,070	3,018	3,166
Carpenters							
Planned projects	754	1,173	1,269	1,011	1,012	834	785
Entire development program	3,754	4,773	6,469	7,411	8,612	9,184	10,485
Masons							
Planned projects	268	404	430	369	360	320	320
Entire development program	1,268	1,654	2,230	2,619	3,060	3,320	3,620
Electricians							
Planned projects	378	584	670	723	796	842	929
Entire development program	578	794	950	1,053	1,176	1,242	1,379
Machinists							
Planned projects	108	169	185	193	193	191	181
Entire development program	168	231	261	277	280	281	281
Mechanics							
Planned projects	440	692	795	816	888	889	855
Entire development program	640	902	1,075	1,136	1,223	1,239	1,255

Table 14 (Continued)

Type of Worker	1953–54	1954–55	1955–56	1956–57	1957–58	1958–59	1959–60
Pipe fitters							
Planned projects	313	534	609	578	591	558	560
Entire development program	513	744	889	908	971	978	1,010
Foundry workers							
Planned projects	93	154	170	183	196	198	205
Entire development program	128	190	218	238	253	258	274
Smiths							
Planned projects	173	294	352	390	406	409	436
Entire development program	248	372	457	510	531	539	586
Power plant operators							
Planned projects	124	220	241	273	277	281	303
Entire development program	164	262	297	337	344	356	383
Processing plant operators							
Planned projects	0	25	122	522	560	700	705
Entire development program	5	30	129	528	568	708	714
Drivers							
Planned projects	1,648	2,883	3,184	3,401	3,490	3,351	3,451
Entire development program	2,348	3,723	4,294	4,746	5,070	5,121	5,431
Miscellaneous skilled workers							
Planned projects	135	251	321	419	509	526	544
Entire development program	210	331	426	539	634	656	694

Source: K.T.A. Comprehensive Report, Vol. I, Tables VII–2 and VII–3, pp. 96–98.

a. The figure for each year represents the total requirements above the 1952–53 level; figures for successive years are not additive.

Requirements for the planned public program were calculated by the K.T.A. engineers, on the basis of the total planned projects program recommended. The figures for the economy as a whole incorporated these estimates and added to them estimates of the specialized workers needed in relation to the additional investment output anticipated. The broader manpower estimates were thus less reliable than those for the planned projects only.

Although the skilled-manpower requirements as estimated for the planned projects showed an increase over the program period — from more than 6,000 such workers needed in 1953–54 to more than 13,000 workers by 1959–60 — the greatest numerical deficiencies were for more easily trained workers, such as artisans, machine operators and drivers. Deficiencies of really key personnel — the managerial and supervisory, professional and sub-professional workers — ran from approximately 2,000 in 1953–54 to less than 4,000 in 1959–60. Similarly, while the total of skilled manpower needed for the entire development program was indicated as growing from some 13,000 in 1953–54 to more than 32,000 in 1959–60, the total estimated to be required in the three key categories rose only from a little over 3,000 in 1953–54 to roughly 6,000 in 1959–60. If the needs for sub-professional workers are eliminated from the internal totals just calculated, as presenting no particularly difficult training problems, the needs for managerial, supervisory and professional personnel for the economy as a whole were indicated as increasing from some 1,400 in 1953–54 to less than 3,000 in 1959–60. Assuming that the estimates even crudely approximated the prospective situation, and granted the importance of such deficiencies, the magnitude of the problem posed was not insuperable, given a will to come to grips with it.

To deal with this problem, the consultants recommended a comprehensive approach which included expanded university and other higher-level training programs within Burma, an expanded program of foreign study for qualified Burmese, the hiring for some years to come of professional and technical personnel abroad, and a number of training programs at the sub-professional, artisan and skilled-worker levels. Coordination of training authorities and activities was recommended, as was a special emphasis on the training of qualified instructors for vocational training and the development of in-service training in the various Government organizations. It was also urged that the Government establish a commission to evolve a fully comprehensive and integrated technical training program.

The economic consultants gave consideration also to more general problems of increasing labor productivity on the job, but gave special attention to the need for able management. After commenting on the importance of management, they stressed the broadness of its nature and the kinds of judgment and experience involved. In this connection they observed that "the experience of colonial Burma with respect to management could easily be misleading. In colonial Burma large-scale mining and trading enterprises were managed by resident staff who were primarily operational in character. Policy management, while invisible, was provided by the home office [in the U. K.] and by directorates of these corporations. In contrast to these arrangements, management in Burma will now be required to assume much broader responsibilities."[26]

Citing recent development in the Philippines, Ceylon and Turkey, the Comprehensive Report highlighted the lessons to be learned from these countries, whose experiences confirmed broadly many of the points the consultants had already made. The report then suggested a number of possible solutions to the management problem. "Perhaps the most important of the lessons which this experience has provided is that adequate authority must be granted to personnel charged with managerial responsibilities."[27] Attention was focused on the new development corporations in terms of their priority requirements for able management. Finally, the various arrangements under which foreign managerial assistance could be obtained were examined and appraised. Of all the possibilities, the consultants were of the view that in the case of larger and more complex enterprises undertaken by the Government, a joint venture with a private firm was the most desirable. If such an arrangement was not feasible, the consultants advised that management contracts with foreign companies would probably be the most effective alternative.

26. *Ibid.,* p. 112.
27. *Ibid.,* p. 115.

CHAPTER 9

The K.T.A. Comprehensive

Report: The Sector Programs

The remainder of the Comprehensive Report was devoted to the major sectors of the economy — agriculture and irrigation, transportation, telecommunications, power and industry (including forest and mineral industry). In each case the existing position was analyzed in comparison with the pre-war, potentials were appraised, and a recommended program was presented which included specific projects, policies, institutional changes and changes in existing government administrative organizations, where these were considered to be required. The projects and programs recommended for these areas came to a total of K 352.5 crores, distributed as shown in Table 15. In a number of cases, however, parts of the recommended program extended into the years beyond 1959–60. For the program period ending in 1959–60, the recommendations involved an outlay of some K 300 crores. This was the figure used in the earlier discussion of investment goals to establish that part of the total public spending which would be planned at the outset.

It will be noted that the planned projects concentrated most heavily on the transportation and communications field, which accounted for fully half of the total. Within this category, the highways were allocated the largest share, followed by the ports and waterways. Power development, with 27 per cent of the total, was next in value, followed by irrigation, industry and mining, in that order. Other than irrigation projects, no agricultural projects were proposed as such by the K.T.A. engineers in their summary list of recommended projects. This was partly because agriculture had not been included in their original terms of reference. Other reasons were that a fertilizer plant and various forestry projects were included under manufacturing industry, that some

Table 15

K.T.A.-PLANNED PROJECT EXPENDITURES BY SECTOR

	K Crores	Per Cent
Total	352.5[a]	100.0
Irrigation	45.1	12.8
Mining	11.5	3.3
Industry	23.0	6.5
Transport and communication	176.6	50.0
Railways	27.3	7.7
Ports and waterways	56.8	16.1
Highways	82.0	23.3
Airways	7.5	2.1
Telecommunications	3.0	.9
Power	96.3	27.3

Source: K.T.A. Comprehensive Report, p. 840.

a. Some of these costs ran beyond 1959–60. The total for the period ending 1959–60 is K 300 crores.

of the power projects recommended would be multi-purpose projects of benefit to agriculture, and that a number of the important recommendations made with respect to agriculture involved annual outlays of a current budgetary or turnover kind (as in the case of expanded agricultural extension services or the use of improved seeds) rather than capital projects. The principal reason, however, was that the biggest single job which needed to be done in the agricultural field — the restoration of some 2.5 million acres of paddy land which had reverted to jungle — was dependent primarily on the restoration of civil order in the countryside, rather than on a program of capital investment.

Since health, education, housing and the social welfare area generally had also been excluded from the K.T.A. terms of reference, and since the Government had already formulated and adopted plans for these areas at the Pyidawtha Conference, the consultants offered no recommendations for them.

AGRICULTURE

Of all the sector discussions and programs, that for agriculture was unique in that it was the only one which was prepared jointly by the economic and engineering consultants. It reflected, not unnaturally, divergent approaches and points of view. The economists were more concerned to pursue problems of land tenure, marketing, price policy, cooperatives, credit, extension, research, land nationalization and the existing Government organization for administering the program. Their basic approach to the question of increased production and yields was through an expanded and developed extension service, research, experimental and demonstration farms, the use of approved seeds, better manuring practices, insect and pest control, improved credit facilities, improved storage and marketing practices, etc. The engineers' approach concentrated on big irrigation projects, the use of chemical fertilizer and mechanization. Their calculation was that an annual input of some K 9 crores towards a more intensified agriculture would yield an annual increment of some K 13 crores in excess of these costs.

These rather sharply divergent approaches had implications which went beyond methodology. Within the context of the land nationalization program adopted by the Government, a mechanization program, quite apart from its other merits or demerits, could be carried through only if it was accompanied by the consolidation of small farming units into cooperative or collective farms. Proposals for rapid mechanization would therefore lend themselves to the purposes of those who desired to promote the rapid socialization of Burmese agriculture — an outcome which would probably have horrified the politically conservative engineers. As the economists saw it, there were many other reasons why a program of rapid mechanization would not have made very good sense at that time. These included the low cost of labor, inexperience in equipment use, problems of machinery maintenance and repair, the investment needed to level out and join small farms, and probable farmer resistance to such a change. The recommendations presented to the Government represented a not altogether satisfactory reconciliation of these divergent views. Since the core of the program for agriculture was the five-year program for expanded production already adopted by the Pyidawtha Conference, and since the consultants were in accord with this program, it was taken as a point of departure for their comments.

Fully 2.5 million acres of paddy land had reverted to jungle during the war and insurrection. At the then prevailing yields of about 1,200 pounds per acre, this represented about 1.5 million tons of paddy or 1.1 million tons of rice, all of which was lost from the export surplus until a reasonable degree of security could be established. In the areas where these lands were located the cultivators would not venture forth to clear the brush and bring the fields back into cultivation. Insecurity also resulted in lesser yields on some of the land still under cultivation, because the cultivators would not put in a full quota of work on those lands which lay furthest from their villages. During the height of the plowing, transplanting and harvesting seasons, the cultivators were accustomed to camp out in their fields at night and work from daybreak to nightfall, but now they were afraid to do so. By leaving their villages only at daybreak by slow oxcart and returning to them before nightfall, they lost much valuable working time. Finally, in many cases insecurity was influential in reducing the amount of necessary maintenance work done on the bunds and dikes which retained water or prevented flooding of the fields.[1]

1. Insecurity was not the only influence here. Before the war, the maintenance of dikes and

While yields were pathetically low and improved farming practices could, over a period of time, make a tremendous contribution to increased output, it was clear that the largest and quickest advance toward that end could be made on the security front. The reclamation of paddy land from jungle would indeed require some capital outlay, primarily for brush clearance. But these costs would range only from K 10 to K 30 ($2.10 to $6.30) per acre, and would be a one-time, short-run and not heavy capital expenditure. Unless it was subsidized, it would be private, not public, investment. More than 600,000 acres had been brought back into paddy cultivation in 1952–53, when the Government paid a subsidy of K 10 per acre for reclaimed land. How much of this increase resulted from payment of the subsidy, and how much would have occurred in any case solely because of the improvement in security conditions, could not be determined.

The land nationalization program about to be carried out by the Government gave much cause for concern, quite apart from the Government's idea that the resumption and distribution of land should be only a preliminary to the collectivization of farming. The determination to confiscate all agricultural land holdings except those up to 50 acres, provided the entire 50 acres were worked by the owner and his family, and to take up similarly all holdings in excess of one-yoke-sized farms (roughly 10 acres) if the excess was not operated by the owner, had at least two serious disadvantages. In the first place, there was simply not enough land to go around. Many owners, in order to retain possession, would begin to work land themselves, thereby forcing tenants off the land and making landless laborers of them. Under existing conditions of tenure, this was expected to be a major problem in Upper Burma. The other deficiency was that the arbitrary limitation on the maximum size of holdings would in a number of cases lessen possibilities for long-run development of efficient mechanized production by owner-operators. Further, in no case would tenants be permitted to work a farm larger than ten acres. In many areas, such a farm would be below the minimum size required to support a family at existing levels of productivity. The economists therefore recommended that the initial land distribution be limited to cases of absentee ownership only. This would minimize changes in the management unit and concentrate primarily on changes in land holding rights.

Recommendations made with respect to short- and longer-term agricultural credit, agricultural taxation, marketing, domestic farm price policy, cooperatives, farming methods, research, extension, Government organization, etc.,

---

bunds had been the responsibility of the landlord. Foreign landowners had already fled the country, and many domestic but absentee landlords were unable to collect their rents, hence they no longer performed this maintenance work. Tenants were not disposed to do the work at their own expense, so long as questions of tenure and ownership remained unresolved.

were far too numerous and detailed to mention here. The conclusions with respect to the State Agricultural Marketing Board, however, require some comment at this point.

Approximately two thirds of all rice exports were at that time being sold by the S.A.M.B. on a government-to-government contract basis. Prices had risen from £50 sterling per ton in the early part of 1952 to £55 per ton in the second half of that year, and to £60 per ton in 1953. The one third of the surplus which was being sold through private traders (acting generally as agents for foreign buyers or governments) was being sold at prices substantially higher than the government-to-government prices. The consultants emphasized that while rice export prices could be counted upon to remain relatively favorable, they had undoubtedly reached their peak and could be expected to decline at least moderately from that point on. Emphasis should therefore be placed, they recommended, on concluding sales for successive new crop surpluses as early as possible, and on continuous and determined efforts to improve the quality of rice produced. They recommended also that the Government seek to conclude long-term contracts with its major buyers to protect itself against prospective price declines. The Government accepted this recommendation and concluded several large-scale long-term agreements, notably with Ceylon and Japan.

One other aspect of the drive for increased output is of interest here. This concerns the use of chemical fertilizer in the production of paddy. Under the Government's fixed buying price for paddy, the cultivator got a maximum of K 280 per 100 baskets of approximately 46 lbs. each, or approximately K 140 per long ton of paddy. At an equivalent of less than $30 per ton for his product, the increased yields which he could expect from using chemical fertilizer would fall considerably short of his added cost. At the same time, the price the Government was getting for the milled rice in export was so far in excess of the price received by the cultivator that the cost of fertilizer would be well repaid from the point of view of the economy as a whole. What was required to stimulate the use of fertilizer was either an increase in the Government's paddy buying price or a subsidy which would bring the cost of fertilizer within the cultivator's reach. The latter alternative was recommended.

IRRIGATION

The irrigation program recommended by the consulting engineers called for four projects, two of which — the Mu River Project and the Yamethin District Project — were major. It aimed at increasing the gross acreage irrigated by nearly 1.7 million acres at an estimated total cost of K 45 crores ($94.5 million), as shown in the tabulation which follows.

Project	Gross Acres (Thousands of Acres)	Estimated Total Cost (Crores)	Indicated Ratio Annual Benefits to Costs
Total	1,675.0	45.0	
Mu River	999.4	17.5	15.5:1
Yamethin District	609.5	26.1	2.2:1
Loikaw Area	50.5	.7	3.1:1
Kandaw Village	15.6	.7	1.5:1

The recommendations called also for a reorganization of the Irrigation Department.

ELECTRIC POWER

The electric power program was quite ambitious. It proposed a number of hydroelectric projects (including one in association with the Mu River Irrigation Project); the installation of diesel-powered small generating plants in some thirty-six towns; and a network or grid of transmission lines which would initially connect the diesel stations and which would later serve to distribute hydroelectric generated power. The estimated total cost of the projects recommended was K 96.3 crores ($202 million), distributed as follows:

Project	Estimated Cost (K Crores)
Pegu	18.9
Panglaung	15.6
Saingdin Falls	15.5
Myingyan steam plant	9.2
Mu River	6.7
Lampha Chaung	5.2
Balu Chaung	2.1
Kalewa steam plant	.4
Diesel plants (36 towns)	13.1
Transmission lines	9.6

The electric power program was closely related to the industrial program to be described later, which envisaged the development of three industrial centers, one at Rangoon, one at Akyab in the Arakan District and one centering around Myingyan in the Dry Zone.

The Saingdin Falls hydroelectric project, with a 40,000 KW capacity, was intended to supply the power needed by the Akyab industrial complex, while the Myingyan steam plant, with a 30,000 KW capacity, was to be the core of the proposed industrial complex of the same name. The Pegu hydroelectric plant, with a 30,000 KW capacity, was intended to provide supplementary power for the Rangoon industrial complex.

The dieselization scheme for thirty-six towns did not originate with the consulting engineers. It had been developed at the Electricity Supply Board and had a powerful political motivation. U Kyaw Nyein, the Minister for Industries and at that time perhaps the chief political strategist of the A.F.P.F.L., was already looking forward to the next general elections in 1956. The early introduction of low-cost electric power in these towns and its distribution to the surrounding villages would be very helpful in marshaling the rural vote. Since the diesel generators could presumably be installed and operating by the time of the elections, whereas the hydroelectric stations could not, this consideration weighed powerfully in the decision to go ahead with them. Another consideration was that once hydroelectric power came onto the distribution lines, these small diesel generating stations would either be placed on a stand-by basis or else moved to towns not reached by the transmission grid. While it is highly doubtful that the engineers would themselves have proposed this plan, it had sufficient rationale for them to accept it and incorporate it into their own program.

What the consulting engineers' plan did not include, and what subsequently became an important factor in the total electric power plan, was the scheme of the Rangoon Electricity Supply Board — by now nationalized and made an organizational subsidiary to the Electricity Supply Board — for modernization and expansion of its own thermal electricity generating facilities in Rangoon.

TRANSPORTATION AND COMMUNICATIONS

The chief expenditure components of the recommended transportation and communications program are shown in Table 16.

Within the railways program, the civil engineering works component included, most importantly, rail renewals, track restorations and improvements and major bridge repairs. The mechanical works and rolling stock category included solely freight and passenger cars, locomotives and parts.

Within ports and waterways, the next major category, the program for the port of Rangoon called chiefly for the reconstruction of wharves and docks, with a substantial outlay for additional flotilla as well. The Shipping Board program merely made budgetary provision for four vessels which the newly established Shipping Board had already placed on order, two for the coastal trade and two for the coal-rice trade with India. The sizable inland waterways program provided chiefly for flotilla for general passenger and cargo traffic, and also for specialized flotilla and related facilities for the coal and

Table 16

K.T.A.-PLANNED EXPENDITURES FOR TRANSPORTATION AND COMMUNICATIONS

(*K Crores*)

Railroads	27.3
Civil engineering works	17.6
Mechanical works and rolling stock	6.3
Diesel locomotives	2.4
Other	1.0
Ports and waterways	56.8
Port of Rangoon	27.1
Outports	2.0
Shipping Board	5.0
Inland waterways	22.7
Airways	7.5
Airport improvements	6.1
Aircraft	1.4
Highways	81.9
Rehabilitation—major roads	27.0
Rehabilitation—district roads	28.7
Farm-to-market roads	20.0
Special-access roads	5.0
General	1.2
Telecommunications	3.0
Rangoon automatic	1.4
Other	1.6

petroleum trades. The coal haul was new, and dependent on the proposed development of the Kalewa coal fields. The petroleum haul was designed to substitute for the traffic previously carried by the now damaged pipeline, the repair of which was not considered feasible because of its vulnerability to continued damage by the insurgents.

The airways program was designed chiefly to effect necessary airport improvements and for the eventual replacement of the DC-3 domestic airways fleet.

The very sizable highways program contemplated major rehabilitation and reconstruction of the main trunk and district roads, improvement and construction on a fairly large scale of farm-to-market roads, and the construction of a few special-access roads in connection with projects contemplated in other sectors.

The modest provision for telecommunications contained one major project only, namely, the installation of an automatic dial telephone system in Rangoon. The remaining allotment covered a number of proposed minor outlays including the use of microwave equipment to effect inter-town telephone communications.

The program as a whole was almost exclusively one of rehabilitation and reconstruction. In a number of cases the job would of course permit a certain amount of replanning and upgrading — diesel locomotives would replace old steam locomotives, a dial telephone system in Rangoon would replace outmoded facilities, and so on. It remained, however, essentially a job of repair and replacement, and was for the most part built around the rehabilitation programs already prepared by the Burmese Government's operating agencies in the several transportation and communications fields.

The recommendations of the consultants went, however, far beyond the investment programs described above. They examined also questions of the organization and operation of the Government agencies concerned, problems of personnel, training, accounting, traffic codes, methods and a host of other operating questions and policies, and offered recommendations with respect to all of them.

MINERALS

The action program recommended by the mining consultants took into account the fact that the three most important single projects necessary to the rehabilitation of the mining industry would be carried out by private firms, either alone or in joint venture with the Government. These projects were the Bawdwin Mines operated by the Burma Corporation, which produced chiefly lead, zinc and silver, the Mawchi Mines, in territory still controlled at that time by the insurgents, which was the big tin-tungsten producer, and the oil fields at Chauk operated by the Burmah Oil Company. For immediate action by the Government, the consultants recommended the development of the Kalewa coal deposits and the establishment of a zinc smelter and refinery at Myingyan, at the following costs:

	K Crores
Total	11.5
Kalewa coal project	7.3
Myingyan zinc project	3.7
Lough Keng zinc development	.5

The Kalewa coal project called for the annual production of more than 700,000 tons of run-of-mine coal to be converted into some 415,000 tons of marketable coal and briquets, whose chief users, it was anticipated, would be the Burma Railways, industries and the Rangoon thermal electricity generating plant. The zinc smelter and refinery would form, it was thought, part of the proposed industrial complex at Myingyan. They were conditional on the Kalewa coal development, since they would depend on cheap coal from Kalewa to generate electric power. The zinc ores would be supplied as concentrates from the Bawdwin Mines and as ore from the Lough Keng deposits, whose development was also proposed.

The consultants also recommended further exploration and studies of other projects, the organization and administration of the Mines and Geological departments, the organization and operation of the newly established Mineral Resources Development Corporation and changes in existing mining laws, taxation and development policies in the minerals field. In addition they re-called earlier recommendations that the Minerals Resources Development Corporation be relatively autonomous, that it operate as a private enterprise and that its executive head possess some technical knowledge and wide busi-ness experience. "Unless these recommendations are implemented," they stressed, "achievement of the Corporation's objectives will be greatly prej-udiced."[2] The occasion for this reiterated caution was that the M.R.D.C., though recently established, had already afforded ample evidence that these recommendations were being disregarded.

MANUFACTURING INDUSTRY

Manufacturing industry, together with irrigation and electric power, pre-sented an opportunity to do something new. Whereas other sectors called primarily for reconstruction and rehabilitation, the Government attributed, as we have seen, great importance to manufacturing, which symbolized to the leaders the new Burma they desired to build, and which, they thought, held out the greatest hope for higher levels of living and welfare. Moreover, U Kyaw Nyein, the then Minister of Industries, was not only one of the out-standing socialist and political leaders but also a highly imaginative and dynamic individual. U Hla Maung, in 1952 still the Secretary to the Ministry of National Planning, had urged the consulting engineers to do an intensive job in the manufacturing sector and had authorized them to bring out more staff to work on this sector than on any other.

The greatest single need was of course the modernization and improvement of the nation's rice mills. India, Burma's largest single rice customer, had al-ways been a purchaser of low-grade rice. This had contributed to the lack of emphasis on rice-mill improvement in the past. Now, however, India was purchasing less than historic quantities, and this loss could be compensated for in other markets only through better quality. Besides, the lack of proper grading equipment caused much rice of superior grades to be mixed and sold with poorer grades, and at lower prices. The consultants had taken note of this problem and had supported the many recommendations made for im-provement of the rice-milling industry by a T.C.A. consultant. The rice mills, however, were privately owned, and any program of modernization and im-provement could be carried out only by the millers themselves, with such in-centives, guidance and aid as the Government might provide. Unfortunately, the Government's generally hostile attitude toward private business, its an-

2. K.T.A. Comprehensive Report, Vol. II, p. 684.

nounced general policy to socialize the means of production after an interim period of indefinite duration, and its known intentions to nationalize rice mills and turn them over to the cooperatives, effectively paralyzed any desire which the millers might have had to make additional investments in their mills. The unrealistic price schedules established by the S.A.M.B. for the milling of various grades of rice on S.A.M.B. account also contributed importantly to this result. This explains why the K.T.A. program for Government investment did not include a specific rice-mill improvement project.

The engineers' approach was first to consider what industries could be developed on the basis of the raw materials available in Burma, taking into account the planned fuel, power and other developments proposed, and to cull these on the basis of the domestic market for their products. They then considered the interrelations of this range of feasible industries in terms of geographic location and of time-phasing. Out of this process there first emerged a group of forty-five industries in three clusters — twenty-eight in the Rangoon district, ten in the Myingyan district and seven in the Akyab area. Of these, the engineers recommended initially the following group of basic industries, which contained a heavy emphasis on construction materials, for Phase I implementation during the program period ending in 1959–1960:

	K Crores
Total	22.9
Fertilizer factory	7.0
Bamboo pulp and paper mill	5.9
Steel products plant	4.2
Integrated forest industries (sawmill and wallboard, plywood, joinery and furniture plants)	1.7
Sulfuric acid plant	1.5
Jute bag and twine mill	.7
Cement mill expansion	.6
Rice bran oil plant	.4
Asbestos-cement-plant	.2
Others	.7

On its face, the recommended program seemed reasonable. Chemical fertilizer was certainly needed and would make a substantial contribution to agricultural production. The suitability of bamboo for the manufacture of pulp and paper had been proven in similar mills in India and Pakistan, and the growing domestic market was adequate to support a mill of economic size. Sulfuric acid was needed in many industrial processes. The Government rice export monopoly could alone utilize a far larger output of jute bags and twine than would be possible in the recommended mill, and experiment had demonstrated that jute could be grown economically in Burma. Domestic cement production was not adequate to meet the already existing requirements. Integrated forest industries would be based on Burma's huge timber supplies, and would utilize sawmill waste as well. Rice bran oil would substitute for imported vegetable oils. Only the 20,000-ton-per-year steel-products plant would appear to raise serious doubts. And the engineering consultants included this project only because of virtual insistence by the Government.

There were, however, other weaknesses in the program. The proposal for a fertilizer factory called for the annual production of some 43,000 tons of ammonia and 157,000 tons of superphosphates. But there had not been enough research and experimentation in Burma to establish precisely which fertilizers would be most effective, and so little was used that years of patient education of farmers would be required before a sizable demand existed. The proposal for an integrated forest industry which would process Burmese timbers and utilize existing waste products could at that time serve only to divert the attention and energies of the limited number of key officials in the forestry field from the far more important task of restoring pre-war levels of teak output and exports.

A far more serious weakness was the fact that while the program attempted to give due weight to questions of economic and technical feasibility, it was seemingly unaware of the grave problems which any program for manufacturing industry would involve if the industries concerned were to be state owned and operated. As the engineers saw it, the plants would be planned, designed and built by foreign firms who would hand over a completed "turnkey" job to the Government and provide personnel to train workers and supervise production during the break-in period. The subsequent problems they saw primarily as production problems which could be solved by hiring foreign technicians and production supervisors for as long as would be required to train Burmese personnel.

This view oversimplified the problem on two counts. It assumed that the laborious machinery of the Government administration could function with reasonable promptness in matters of supervision, direction and policy. More importantly, it lacked awareness of the serious difficulties involved in the determination of policy for such enterprises, particularly when these were monopolistic in nature. Even in an advanced industrial society with a highly capable and even sophisticated civil service, the operation of state-owned enterprises would raise many problems of price, wage, profit, tariff, tax, labor relations and other policies which would be extremely difficult to solve. In the Burmese setting these problems would be aggravated by the more fundamental problem of administrative efficiency. In combination, these problems should have raised grave doubts as to whether the Government should venture into the field of manufacturing industry at all, no matter how desirable on other grounds particular industries might have appeared to be.

In considering the problems of management which would be encountered, the economic consultants had been careful to point out that questions much broader than those concerned only with production would be involved. They had advised that the broad problem of management could perhaps best be solved in joint venture with private enterprise. This was one of the points at which the integration between the work of the economists and that of the engineers broke down.

SALIENT CHARACTERISTICS OF
THE K.T.A. PROGRAM

Stressing increased production rather than increased equalization of income as the necessary key objective of Burma's development efforts, the K.T.A. program proposed an increase in national output of nearly 90 per cent in the eight and one half years ending in 1959–60. Ambitious though it was with respect to the levels of output prevailing at the time, the major objective certainly appeared to be feasible in relation to the levels of output achieved in 1938–39. The investment requirements for the economy as a whole were based on the income increases sought rather than on an initial calculation of resource availability. The feasibility of financing the program was, however, tested in relation to both the foreign exchange and the domestic finance positions and outlook. Within this broad economic framework, and on the basis of explicit assumptions with respect to restoration of internal security and the steps which would be taken to ensure effective implementation and to solve problems of specialized manpower, the K.T.A. Report proposed specific programs for the productive sectors of the economy. The investment required for its planned program comprised less than three sevenths of the total net capital formation proposed. The economics of the program thus left ample room for additional public investment both of a productive and of a social nature, and for private investment as well. In this respect it was at the same time comprehensive and flexible. In terms of basic policy, it emphasized strongly the importance of private investment and of Government action to encourage and facilitate such investment.

Basically the K.T.A. Report did three things. It offered a comprehensive plan; it suggested a number of the components in such a plan, implicitly embracing within its own investment schedules the health, education, housing and welfare programs already adopted by the Government, and those which would be carried out by the private sector; and it tried to anticipate problems of central economic policy, coordination, supervision, administration, specialized manpower and management, and indicated how they might be solved. Similarly, it tried to anticipate specific operational problems which would arise in implementing the sector programs and indicated how these, too, should be dealt with. It thus provided the broad targets, a comprehensive statement of what should be done and a guide to how to do it.

GOVERNMENT INFLUENCE ON
THE K.T.A. PROGRAM

Since the K.T.A.'s terms of reference called for the consultants to serve in a technical advisory capacity to the Government, and since in any event it would have been only natural for the Government to attempt to influence them in the formulation of the program, it may be appropriate to consider at this point the degree to which such governmental influence was in fact exerted. The Government's general policy of socialization was of course pervasive, and provided the context within which the consultants had to work. So far as the basic economic framework and analyses were concerned, there was no attempt whatsoever by the Government to influence the conclusions reached or the recommendations made. The Government's influence was, however, felt in three particulars — the Burmanization of trade policy already discussed, the land nationalization program and the composition of the manufacturing industries program.

The consultants would undoubtedly have taken sharper issue with the land nationalization program then proposed had they not been cautioned that a sharp criticism of this policy and plan would be regarded as indicative of a lack of sympathy with the Government's objectives and policies, and that this in turn would inevitably color the Government's reactions to other elements in the consultants' report. As to the manufacturing industry program, it has already been mentioned that the recommendation for a small steel mill was made only on the Government's insistence. The Government had also indicated its own very favorable views concerning the establishment of a hydroelectric power plant and a mill for bamboo pulp and paper in the Arakan district, and concerning the proposal previously made by the U. N. technicians for an integrated forest industry. These expressions were certainly influential in the priority treatment accorded these projects by the engineering consultants. Finally, although the consultants did not include a project for a pharmaceuticals plant in their summary list of initially recommended manufacturing industry projects, the determination had already been made at a very high political level to go ahead with such a plant, and the text of the consultants' report was amended to include such a plan among the group of projects initially to be implemented.

Nevertheless, it may be said that the Government of Burma exercised an unusual and even admirable degree of restraint in permitting the consultants to arrive at their own findings and recommendations, with only a minimal degree of interference or pressure on the part of their sovereign client.

FURTHER CHANGES IN THE ECONOMIC
DEVELOPMENT PROGRAM

The fourth step in the formulation of the comprehensive economic development program, as has already been indicated, was not a distinct process. It occurred during the implementation process over the years, and consisted in changes made in the scale and composition of the program as the changing resource picture imposed limitations on the program's size, as modified thinking or changing circumstances caused deletions and substitutions and as organizational weaknesses smothered certain programs at their birth. This part of the account belongs properly to the implementation analysis to be made later in this study and will be presented there. It will, however, help to place the K.T.A. program in perspective if we anticipate briefly some of these developments, as they affected the composition of the development program.

The main changes were made within a few months after the Comprehensive Report was presented, and affected chiefly the programs for manufacturing industry and electric power. The first step towards modifying the K.T.A. manufacturing industry program was to expand the list of forty-five recommended industries to a list of sixty-five industries. The second and more significant step was to ignore the K.T.A.'s recommendations for priorities within this group. This made possible a manufacturing industry program of far greater size and far different composition. Of the K.T.A.'s priority group of fourteen projects, only the steel mill and the jute mill were undertaken during the program period, and the Government's jute mill project was four times the size of that recommended by K.T.A. The industries built by the Government were with one exception (the jute mill) those which had previously been included in the Two-Year Plan of 1948. While the K.T.A. program for electric power had centered on hydroelectric projects at Saingdin Falls and at Pegu and on a steam plant at Myingyan, the program adopted by the Government abandoned all these projects and centered instead on a large hydroelectric project at Balu Chaung, thermal generation in the towns upcountry, and a large-scale expansion of thermal facilities in Rangoon. The actual programs in manufacturing industry and electric power were thus virtually independent of the K.T.A. recommendations. The substantial irrigation and highways programs recommended by K.T.A. never really got started. What finally emerged, therefore, was a comprehensive investment program which was almost entirely a Burmese development.

The agricultural program was in essence the Five-Year Agricultural Plan adopted by the Pyidawtha Conference (which in turn resembled closely the skeleton agriculture component of the Two-Year Plan of 1948) plus the independently developed land nationalization program. As has just been noted, and for reasons which will later be made clear, activity in irrigation and highways never got effectively under way during the remainder of the decade, and K.T.A.'s sizable programs for them remained stillborn. While investment in transportation and communications comprised the largest single share of the capital expenditures incurred, and while the K.T.A. recommendations in this area were voluminous and detailed, the job done was for the most part, and of necessity, a pre-determined rehabilitation and reconstruction job. This had already been envisaged in its major details (except for highways) in the Two-Year Plan of 1948 and in the programs developed within the respective agencies of the Government and approved by the Pyidawtha Conference. The wholesale changes made by the Government in the electric power and manufacturing industry programs have just been noted. And programs for health, education, housing and local improvements, as has been pointed out, had been prepared by the Burmese with United Nations and United States technical assistance and approved by the Pyidawtha Conference.

To what extent, then, were the K.T.A. program and the comprehensive development program actually undertaken by the Government identical? Their chief and almost only important point of correspondence was the economic framework within which both were cast — namely, the goal of an increase in total output to some 30 per cent over the pre-war output by the end of the decade and the concept of a total net capital formation of K 750 crores. This was the unique contribution of the K.T.A. Plan. Its additional values — and they were many — lay not so much in the development of original project or program ideas as in the detailed and factual analyses of conditions and problems in the various sectors of the economy; in the pulling together of these documented studies within a single comprehensive plan where their magnitude and interrelations could be perceived and appreciated; in the preliminary engineering and economic studies made of probable costs and potential benefits by sector and by projects for all the projects which had been till that time considered, and for others which still needed to be considered; in the appraisals made of the Government departments and institutions which would be responsible for the work undertaken and of the changes in governmental organization, relations and procedures which would be required to do these jobs effectively; and in the emphases placed on the policy changes which would be needed to facilitate the execution of a program of the magnitude contemplated.

What the K.T.A. survey contributed, in essence, was a goal, an approach, and a demonstration of the kinds of analysis, organization, procedures and policies necessary to do the job. The effectiveness of this contribution was limited by an incapacity or unreadiness on the part of those whose appreciation was most required to realize its full implications.

Part III

IMPLEMENTING THE PROGRAM IN A CHANGING ECONOMIC SETTING—AN OVERVIEW

CHAPTER 10

The Fight for a Feasible Rate of Program Implementation— 1953-54

The Burmese Government had been waiting a long time, and with increasing eagerness, to get started on its comprehensive economic and social development program. Fortified with the "blueprint" provided by its experts, and urged by them to attack development with vigor and even with daring, the Government now prepared itself psychologically and procedurally to get on with the job. Important moves were made even before the consultants submitted their Comprehensive Report. And submission of the Report, on the eve of the fiscal year 1953–54, was swiftly followed by an intensive agency review of its recommendations and by a top level implementation conference, early in 1954, at which program determinations were made, responsibilities assigned, and procedural steps initiated to accelerate progress. Enthusiasm at the center was soon communicated to the operating agencies. Their budget demands for the fiscal year 1954–55 (submitted in May and June of 1954) were so ambitious as to be obviously neither feasible nor consistent with economic stability. Having worked for the better part of two years to persuade the Government to adopt an ambitious and aggressive approach, the economic consultants were now obliged to try to persuade it not to go too fast. This first battle was lost. The capital program adopted for the fiscal year 1954–55 was larger by at least one third than the maximum recommended by the economic consultants. Consequences of this initial push were felt in many ways throughout the remainder of the program period.

The Government had taken significant action to improve its organizational readiness following the submission of the consultants' Preliminary Report. It had set up development corporations, as recommended by the consultants, for industry and mining, and on its own initiative established a similar corporation for agriculture. It had created the Economic and Social Board to serve as the key agency for review and determination of development programs and related policies, and to supervise program implementation. It had also set up a Central Statistical and Economics Department in the Ministry of National Planning, and passed enabling legislation to make it possible for this new department to develop the statistical data necessary for planning and programing purposes. The Government took two further steps while the final report of its consultants was still in the drafting stage. The first of these was of an operative kind. In March 1953 a purchasing mission under the leadership of Bo Min Gaung, Minister for Rehabilitation and Public Works, was dispatched to Hong Kong, Japan, the United States, the United Kingdom and Europe to place large-scale orders for machinery and rolling stock in anticipation of program requirements. The second step, in mid-1953, was approval of a capital budget of some K 56 crores for the fiscal year 1953–54. This was geared to the long-term program recommendations still in process of preparation, and provided for the necessary intermediate step-up in the rate of capital expenditure.

The procedural approach to implementation was carefully thought out and quite comprehensive, if not altogether practical. Upon submission of the consultants' report in August 1953, their recommendations were distributed in whole or in appropriate part to ministries, departments, boards and corporations throughout the Government for review and comment. Over the following weeks, agency reactions were submitted to the Ministry of National Planning and meetings were held to resolve various questions which arose. At the end of 1953 the Prime Minister's office issued a directive[1] to all Government agencies concerned, which analyzed the implementation problem and instructed the agencies how to proceed.

Implementation was divided into four categories — the K.T.A. projects and policy recommendations, other departmental projects, social projects and implementation by the private sector. With respect to the first three, the agencies were directed first to distinguish between projects to be executed in

1. "Programme of Implementation of Development and Reconstruction Projects," December 30, 1953. While the final report of the consultants was distributed to the agencies by the Ministry of National Planning and the initial responses of the agencies to the recommendations were made through that Ministry, the subsequent issuance of a directive by the Prime Minister's office — in this connection, the office of the Executive Secretary of the Economic and Social Board — was quite significant. It was the first overt recognition that interest in and capacity for planning as well as for implementation resided organizationally at that time in the Economic and Social Board rather than in the Ministry of National Planning.

the fiscal years 1953–54 to 1955–56 and those planned for the four fiscal years beginning with 1956–57. They were also directed to resolve, if possible, such differences as they still might have with the consultants' recommendations, again through the Ministry of National Planning. On accepted projects, they were to proceed at once. "Most of the recommendations have been accepted without qualification, and the Departments and Ministries concerned have accordingly assumed responsibility in regard to the carrying out of these projects and recommendations." If the necessary information was already available for near-term projects, the agencies were to prepare lists of the equipment needed and call for tenders. If the information was not yet available, engineering help was to be enlisted to draw up detailed plans and specifications. The agencies were also directed to classify near-term projects according to whether they could be executed mostly with local materials and local technical personnel, or whether the bulk of the materials and technical services would have to be obtained from abroad. They were directed, further, to report what, if any, organizational changes would be needed; how many and what kinds of foreign technicians would be necessary; what training programs should be initiated and what management arrangements would be desirable. They were instructed to state also the additional budgetary allotments they would need, and how much of these funds would be required in the form of foreign exchange. The information was to be supplied within one month. It is clear that the directive raised questions which needed to be raised. Whether the agencies were capable of dealing with them adequately, and in the time allotted, was something else again.

Moreover, the directive did not neglect the policy recommendations made in the consultants' report. "Each Ministry or Department concerned shall report to the Economic and Social Board by January 31, 1954, which of these recommendations they are unable to accept and the reasons therefor. Others shall be implemented as indicated."[2]

The directive stated that as soon as the information was supplied by the several agencies, another purchasing mission would be chosen (in addition to the Bo Min Gaung Mission, which had already been dispatched) to make arrangements abroad for purchase of plant and equipment, engagement of firms of consultants and recruitment of technical personnel.[3] Finally, the

2. It may be appropriate to note that the original draft of the directive did not call upon the agencies to indicate their views on the *policy* measures recommended by the consultants. It was only upon a representation by the economic consultants to the effect that the policies were of great importance to the implementation process that specific provision was made in the directive for their review and adoption. Since U Hla Maung, the then Executive Secretary of the Economic and Social Board, was undoubtedly more aware of the importance of economic policy than any of his successors in that office, his initial neglect to call for such a review was indicative of the lack of appreciation within the Burmese Government of the role of economic policy.

3. In sending general purchase missions abroad, the Government was evidently motivated by a number of considerations. The Central Purchasing Board was notoriously slow and inefficient; the Government feared graft and chicanery on the part of its own officials, and wished large-scale purchasing activities to be carried out under the direct supervision of trusted ministers; and

directive called for certain measures to insure implementation of the program for the private sector.

To describe the measures set forth with respect to the private sector it is necessary to go back a few weeks to pick up another development. On National Day in November 1953 Prime Minister U Nu had made a statement, "Our Goal and Our Interim Programme." After reaffirming the ultimate objective of creating a socialist state, and describing the development program as an interim step toward that objective, U Nu stressed the very large contribution to the "Interim" program — an investment program of some K 240 crores — needed from the private sector.

The achievement of the programme . . . requires that we institute measures which will enable the people in the private sector to carry out their part of the development programme. It is necessary that we encourage them to make this investment and to equip themselves for carrying out this programme. . . .

We have accordingly directed the Economic and Social Board to submit detailed recommendations for achieving the above objectives in the fields both of commerce and industry and for overcoming the difficulties and handicaps under which our nationals labor at present.[4]

The recommendations made by the Economic and Social Board in response to the Prime Minister's directive were embodied in a resolution adopted at its fourth meeting.[5]

As regards Burmese traders, the Board recommended that those who had established direct contact with foreign manufacturers and suppliers and had specialized in certain commodities be granted import licenses on a more liberal basis, and that the number of import licenses be adjusted to the anticipated demand for the various commodities so that import flows would approximate those under uncontrolled conditions. It recommended also that an attempt be made to divert commodities more or less monopolized by foreign agents into "national" trade channels, and that the Government strengthen its staff of commercial attachés abroad to assist national importers to establish direct contacts with foreign suppliers. More important, it recommended that the Government set up joint corporations with indigenous interests and subscribe a large part of the capital required. "Such corporations will thus be free from financial handicaps, and share the credit and prestige of Government in establishing foreign contacts and securing adequate business."[6]

---

it also believed that by dealing directly with manufacturers, it could eliminate dealers', distributors' and agency charges. Actually, direct purchases made it necessary for the Government itself to carry replacement parts, and resulted in the absence of adequate service facilities ordinarily provided by distributors.

4. "Our Goal and Our Interim Programme," Supt., Govt. Printing and Stationery, Rangoon, 1953, p. 5.

5. *Ibid.*

6. *Ibid.,* p. 10.

With respect to private industry, the Board recommended that indigenous investment be facilitated by publication of a list of fields in which private investment would be welcomed, by liberal loans at low rates of interest to "those national interests who are willing to set up industries and give proof of their ability to organize them and run them as profitable enterprises," by joint ventures with private individuals or firms in suitable cases, by facilitation of the import of necessary raw materials, by the setting up of a Tariff Board with powers to determine the amount and duration of the protection to be granted to each industry, and by tax relief for initial periods.[7]

The implementation directive then called upon the Ministry of Commerce[8] to create a Commerce Development Corporation and otherwise implement the Board's trade recommendations. It asked the Ministry of Industries to publish a list of industries in which private investment would be welcomed and to create a Tariff Board. It directed the Industrial and Mineral Resources Development Corporations to implement the policy of liberal loans. The directive, in fact, went so far as to state that individuals contemplating investment might be accorded financial assistance to retain consulting firms.

The Prime Minister's Implementation Conference, held in continuous session over an eight-day period beginning February 15, 1954, was the catapult from which the Development Program was formally launched. Programs, projects and policies recommended by the consultants[9] were reviewed, most remaining differences were resolved, and the basic determinations were made. Actually, recommendations already accepted by agencies and ministers were not carefully examined at the Conference. Consideration was reserved for the most part for recommendations concerning which questions or objections still remained. In some cases, particularly with respect to the program for the port of Rangoon, recommendations were accepted only "subject to field investigations and detailed working out with [the port's own] consulting engineers." And in the case of the industries program, as has already been noted (Chapter 9, p. 148), the consultants' list of forty-five projects was expanded to some sixty-five projects, and the recommended priorities

---

7. The economic consultants had had no opportunity to express their views on the questions before the Economic and Social Board or on the recommendations adopted by it. They first learned of the recommendations only on publication of the resolution. It was of course clear that the concept of the program as an "interim" measure of indefinite duration on the road to a socialist state could not provide the desired incentive for private investment. The consultants did state their negative views on the joint ventures proposed in the trade field vigorously, and were perhaps instrumental in deferring action along these lines until the issue again arose in 1956 as an anti-inflation measure. At the time, the consultants were informed that the Government was prepared to lend up to 100 per cent of the capital required for new private ventures. They of course maintained strongly that any loan applicant should be required to put up at least minimal equity capital of his own. But this was only one among many dichotomies in the policies of a socialist government.

8. Subsequently called the Ministry of Trade Development.

9. Described in Chapters 8 and 9.

were abandoned. With these major exceptions, however, the consultants' recommendations were accepted by and large across the board.

The Conference did not, however, review the health, education and housing programs adopted by the Pyidawtha Conference, even though the December directive was broad enough to encompass them. The review was, therefore, essentially a review only of the consultants' recommendations. The Conference put the Government's formal imprimatur on these recommendations, and gave the green light to implementing action. The Commerce Development Corporation and a Tariff Board were established. The agencies of Government attacked their programs with renewed vigor. A new procurement mission, under U Tin, the Finance minister, departed. The program was now under way.

THE PUSH FOR A BIG PROGRAM

One additional measure inaugurated late in 1953 was the introduction of progress reporting by the Economic and Social Board. The object was to enable the Board to keep track of progress by project, program and agency, so that it might take action, when necessary, to coordinate and expedite the programs, and even anticipate bottlenecks. The basic report was a quarterly one providing data on both physical progress and expenditures. For various reasons, it was the expenditures reporting which proved to be the most useful.

The first big push for rapid implementation came in May–June 1954 in the form of tremendous agency capital budget demands for fiscal year 1954–55. Swollen especially by the manufacturing, electric power, transportation and social service sectors, and with modest demands from very few, total requests came to some K 120 crores — more than double the budget approved for 1953–54 and 1.7 times the K 69.5 crores scheduled for 1954–55 gross public capital expenditure in the eight-year program. The economic consultants had recommended a public capital program for 1954–55 no larger than K 74 crores, including K 5 crores for agricultural loans. This recommendation, supported by the Ministry of National Planning, was accepted for the most part by the Economic and Social Board, which approved a moderately higher program of K 78 crores. When this decision subsequently came before the Cabinet, a storm of protest arose from ministers whose budget demands had been severely reduced, and the capital budget issue was opened for reconsideration. By Cabinet action the program was increased to some K 107 crores. When the economic consultants protested, they were requested to review their position in the light of two questions: "How large a capital investment programme are the Ministries, Departments, Boards and Corporations capable of carrying out, if authorizations and funds are granted?" and "How serious would be the danger of inflation, if such a larger programme were approved?"

The consultants then executed a tactical, but not substantive, retreat. Treating the first question as speculative, they concentrated on the second. A program of K 85 crores might be authorized, they held, in view of the attrition of at least 10 per cent reasonably to be expected in its execution, without too serious danger of inflation. They expressed concern not only with the immediate inflationary dangers of a larger program, but also with the quickened pace to which it would lead in the years immediately following, and the degree to which this would aggravate the exceedingly difficult problems of domestic finance and economic stability already anticipated for those years. On this point, they stated:

It remains finally to ask: Is this [inflationary] risk worth taking? What is to be gained? What is to be lost? In our judgement, there is little to be gained, much to be lost. The most that could be gained would be a shortening of the duration of the development programme. Indeed, the sharply higher levels of capital expenditure sought by the operating agencies would of necessity require comparably high or higher capital programmes in 1955-6 and 1956-7, to continue the work undertaken in 1954-5. This could only have the effect of bringing forward the target year of the programme from 1959-60 to say 1957-8. But this is simply not feasible. Resources do not permit it. With the optimum schedules already laid out for achievement by 1959-60, we face an increasingly serious problem in domestic financing, which may have to be met in 1955-6 or the year after. The enlarged programme now proposed for 1954-5 might not bring about inflation, or serious inflation, next year. It would however tremendously increase the difficulties which will have to be encountered and solved in the later years of the programme. It might make those problems unsolvable. For this reason, if for no other, the risk of inflation posed in 1954-5 by an *actual* capital programme of the magnitude of [say] K 900 million is not worth taking.[10]

These considerations led the Government to review the position once again. The Prime Minister, after a number of lengthy discussions with the consultants,[11] expressed his concern to the ministers responsible for major programs, and requested their participation in a further reappraisal.

It is now clear to the Hon'ble Prime Minister that the full programme asked for by all Ministries, Departments, Boards and Corporations cannot be sanctioned without the danger of serious inflation, and the Hon'ble Prime Minister therefore desires to reappraise all projects from the point of view of their essentiality and balance, in order that the programme as a whole will be in balance and within the limits of feasibility. The Hon'ble Prime Minister hopes that such reappraisal will enable a decision as to which projects can be postponed and which of them may be spread over a longer period of time.

10. "Alternative Capital Investment Programmes for 1954-5," memorandum, submitted to the Executive Secretary, Economic and Social Board, Rangoon, by Robert R. Nathan Associates, Inc., July 16, 1954, pp. 10-11.

11. Mr. Robert R. Nathan, president of the economic consultants' firm, was especially requested to come to Burma on very short notice to participate in these discussions, and to advise on the extraordinary measures and policy actions which the larger program, if adopted, might necessitate.

The Hon'ble Prime Minister desires to undertake this review on the following basis: —

(a) from the point of view of whether it will be physically possible to carry out all the projects within the period contemplated, taking into consideration the availability of material and personnel resources. The discussions in this respect will be based not only on the feasibility of the projects from the point of view of each Department, but also from the point of view of whether the *total* resources available are sufficient to meet the demands of all Departments — whether e.g. there is any danger of Departments, Boards and Corporations competing with each other for such limited resources as may be available within the country to a degree which will hamper the total programme;

(b) the contribution each proposed project is expected to make to either the earning or the conserving of our foreign exchange resources;

(c) the relative importance of the foreign exchange and domestic expenditure components of each project; and

(d) whether domestic resources such as raw materials, man-power, etc. are available for the successful execution of each project.[12]

In a series of meetings held August 13–18, well after the budget documents had gone to press with a capital program of K 85 crores, the major programs were reviewed. Reductions effected from the Cabinet-approved program, chiefly in the railways, electricity, public works and Housing Board programs, came to something less than K 10 crores, and the program finally approved was K 97.5 crores. The consultants had lost their fight. They had succeeded, however, in impressing on the Prime Minister that a number of highly significant policy actions would now be required if the program were to be carried through without serious consequences. They were invited to restate their views for further consideration.

The economic consultants' response emphasized primarily the need to increase rice production, to improve rice qualities, and to market rice more effectively through more flexible pricing and quantity discounts. Specific programs for increasing minerals, timber and non-rice agricultural production were also urged. Foreign exchange savings, they said, should become an important criterion in establishing industrial priorities; meanwhile, a liberal import policy was advisable to offset the inflationary effects of large-scale domestic spending by the Government, and this policy should not be influenced unduly by short-term fluctuations in the foreign exchange position. Other recommendations called for early steps to broaden the tax base, in order to lay the foundation for increased revenues in the years ahead; for pricing policy in the various government enterprises appropriate to their varying types and circumstances; for special efforts to anticipate and deal with potential shortages and bottlenecks in program implementation; for im-

12. Memorandum, U Hla Maung, Executive Secretary, Economic and Social Board, Prime Minister's Office, Rangoon, August 12, 1954, pp. 1–2.

provement of statistical data needed for planning, control and management purposes; and for special emphasis on management problems. Specific steps were recommended for implementation of all these policy measures.[13] It seemed quite clear that unless effective action were taken by the Government along the lines suggested, its ambitious investment program was destined to run into serious trouble.

The trouble erupted sooner than expected and not quite in the form expected. It struck first in the form of a severe decline in foreign exchange reserves. So hard did this hit that it dominated policy thinking and investment practice for a considerable time to come. In view of this, it will be in order to review the situation as it appeared in July–August 1954, while the battle over the size of the 1954–55 capital program was being waged, and to explain why, in the face of this emerging situation, more attention was not given to this important factor.

Rice export prices had reached their peak about a year before, in the spring of 1953. The termination of the Korean War, bumper crops and U. S. disposal of surplus wheat and rice in Asia had contributed to a sharp break in rice and other commodity prices in the months following. The Burmese Government did not, however, reduce its own prices. Sales and shipments declined, and stocks rose sharply during the remainder of 1953. These developments of course occasioned much concern, especially because India, the largest buyer, was then claiming to have achieved self-sufficiency so far as rice was concerned.

The first break in this situation came in September 1953, when the Government concluded a four-year sales agreement with Ceylon, calling for annual deliveries of at least 200,000 tons of rice at substantially reduced prices. Instead of the previous £60 per ton, the prices for the four years beginning 1954 were to be £50, £48, £46 and £44 per ton respectively. A similar arrangement with Japan was concluded in December 1953. But India remained the big problem. She would not buy at the price established in the Ceylon-Japanese contracts. And it was felt that, if India were allowed to buy at a lower price, Burma would have to grant an equal reduction, retroactively, to Ceylon and Japan. Finally, in March 1954 a way was found out of the impasse. An agreement was reached for the delivery in two years of 900,000 tons of rice at an average price of £48 per ton. Of this, £13 per ton would be credited towards the settlement of the partition debt to India, making the cash price £35 per ton.

Thus, although there had been a decline of nearly K 20 crores in Burma's foreign exchange reserves from September 1953 to March 1954, the expectation at the time budget-making for the fiscal year 1954–55 began was that the

13. These recommendations were first submitted under the date of August 21, 1954, as "Policy Determinations Related to Fiscal Year 1954–55 Program," and, in more detail, under the date of October 1, 1954, as "Economic Policies for Fiscal Year 1954–55 and Specific Recommendations for Policy Implementation."

flow of rice exports and receipts would step up considerably in the second half of the year, and that foreign exchange losses for the year as a whole would not be excessive. During the following months, as the budget-making process continued into August, the reserves continued to decline. For a number of reasons, this issue did not seriously enter even then into the capital program decision. Part of the loss had been of a non-recurring nature, the result of settlement of the debt to the United Kingdom for £7.3 million (nearly K 10 crores) and a substantial payment for the Government's one-third interest in the Burmah Oil Company. The purchasing missions were making substantial advance payments against orders placed for future delivery. And the data on hand were not current. While data on the monetary reserves held by the Union Bank were available, figures on government holdings and holdings of the commercial banks lagged badly. Since large transfers had been made on Government account to its financial offices in London, and reports from that office on payments and holdings were tardy, the current state of the total reserves, as against the monetary reserves only, was not known in Rangoon. It was known that receipts for rice shipments were lagging behind the value of the shipments, although the disorderly accounting at the State Agricultural Marketing Board did not permit precise appraisal of the amounts outstanding. Further, the Government expected additional resources from abroad. Preliminary negotiations with the Japanese looking toward a substantial reparations settlement had been completed, and an early settlement was considered likely. And the Government had already decided to seek loan assistance from the World Bank. Finally, a reappraisal of the foreign exchange outlook had resulted in the conclusion that the possibilities ranged all the way from a sizable surplus to a large deficit for the eight-year program period, and that a determined drive to increase rice output, qualities and sales, even at lower prices, would insure adequate foreign exchange earnings over the long run. All these factors, combined with the then very comfortable size of the reserve holdings and the value of the rice stocks in hand, contributed to the negligible weight given to near-term foreign exchange considerations in the decision on the 1954–55 capital program.

Although they were overshadowed by the foreign exchange "crisis" soon to erupt, other noteworthy influences of the big 1954–55 program persisted. Many large-scale projects and programs were initiated, and contract commitments made, from which it was difficult to withdraw later. Administrative and managerial resources were spread very thin. A considerable imbalance was introduced into the total program, and inevitably there was a good deal of waste and inefficiency in the form of discontinuous and poorly correlated development activity. But it is time now to turn the spotlight on developments in the foreign exchange field, and on the fight for economic stability which ensued from efforts to deal with foreign exchange stringency.

CHAPTER 11

The Fight for Economic Stability: The Foreign Exchange Side—1954-55

The fiscal year 1953-54 drew to a close with a number of important developments. A constructive reparations agreement was concluded with Japan, calling for the payment over a ten-year period of $200 million in Japanese goods and services, and for the provision of an additional $50 million "Economic Cooperation" fund for the loan financing of joint Burmese-Japanese (public, private or mixed) economic projects. Public capital spending had more than doubled the level reached in the previous year, rising from K 23 crores to K 53.8 crores (exclusive of debt repayments), or 95 per cent of the level programed. Despite a disappointing harvest — estimated paddy output was only 5.5 million long tons, as compared with 5.7 million the previous year, and the index of total agricultural production did not rise at all — gross national output increased by nearly 4 per cent over 1952-53. Domestic prices fell slightly during the year. The unsettling economic factors were the decline in rice export prices, the excessive rice stocks — despite large shipments to India, these amounted to some 1.5 million tons, for much of which adequate storage facilities did not exist — and the decline of nearly K 43 crores in the foreign exchange reserves, which brought total holdings at the beginning of the fiscal year 1954-55 to some K 76 crores.[1]

1. The citation of the general measures here does not mean that all these data were on hand at the time. Many important statistical indicators became available only months after the fact, and policy had to be based for the most part on tardy data, crude "guesstimates," and scanty sample data.

On the personal side, U Tin Pe, Secretary to the Ministry of National Planning, was killed in an air crash. U Hla Maung, abroad on a mission, was replaced as Executive Secretary of the Economic and Social Board by U Thant, until then Secretary to the Prime Minister.

Rice prices in 1953-54 had centered around the £50 sterling per ton for S.M.S. (Small Mill Special) grade set in the Ceylon and Japanese contracts. Export shipments had amounted to 1.27 million long tons, valued at K 84 crores — an average yield of something less than £50 per ton. This compared with an export value of K 102 crores the previous year for a slightly smaller tonnage. However, the cash price of £35 per ton for 1953 rice, established in the India sale agreement, indicated that there would have to be a further downward adjustment in 1954-55 prices. Ceylon and Japan were making it quite plain that in the coming year they did not propose to be bound by the terms of the four-year sales contracts negotiated a year before. And the appreciable accumulation of stocks during 1953-54 confirmed the conclusion that prices would have to be further reduced.

Burma entered the fiscal year 1954-55 with carry-over stocks of 1.5 million tons of highly perishable and deteriorating rice and the prospect of a new export surplus of approximately 1.8 million tons. Thus, total availabilities for the year amounted to some 3.3 million tons, of which it was urgent that the largest possible portion be sold and shipped. Deficiencies of handling facilities, both in internal transport and at the ports, placed an indeterminate limitation on how much rice could actually be shipped even if it were sold. Effectively handled, shipments could reach a total of, say, 2 to 2.5 million tons. This would be possible, however, only if sales agreements were concluded early in the season, so that the maximum possible tonnages could be moved before the advent of the rainy season in April-May. This was why the economic consultants had urged in their policy memoranda of September and October that an intensive effort be made to achieve early results on the rice export front. It also explains why, in 1954 and in succeeding years, belated action in adjusting prices and in concluding sales agreements adversely affected total tonnages shipped.

As the fiscal year 1954-55 began, thinking in Burma was not yet fully oriented to the radical change in the international rice market. Despite the increase in stocks on hand and numerous quality disputes with large buyers, particularly India and Ceylon, which were slowing up shipments and payments, the Government was still reluctant to act boldly to achieve high-volume export sales at the cost of sharply lower prices. The tendency was, rather, to seek new markets or devices which would make it possible to keep prices as close as possible to recently prevailing levels. Thus in October 1954 Prime Minister U Nu proposed to U. S. Ambassador Sebald that the U. S.

Table 17

FOREIGN EXCHANGE TRANSACTIONS AND RESERVES,
1952–53 TO 1959–60

(*K Crores*)

Fiscal Year	Receipts	Payments	Surplus or Deficit	Foreign Exchange Reserves— End of Period
1952–53	134.7	109.9	+24.8	
1st half	62.8	47.0	+15.8	111.1
2nd half	71.9	62.9	+ 9.0	118.6
1953–54	107.7	151.3	—43.6	
1st half	50.3	67.7	—17.4	99.1
2nd half	57.4	83.6	—26.2	76.0
1954–55	99.0	123.0	—24.0	
1st half	47.8	62.3	—14.4	61.3
2nd half	51.2	60.7	— 9.5	51.6
1955–56	134.2	110.2	+24.0	
1st half	66.4	53.4	+13.0	71.0
2nd half	67.8	56.8	+11.0	74.6
1956–57	125.0	157.6	—32.6	
1st half	55.9	69.4	—13.5	64.1
2nd half	69.1	88.2	—19.1	56.0
1957–58	114.5	111.3	+ 3.2	
1st half	51.5	65.1	—13.6	51.4
2nd half	63.0	46.2	+16.8	68.2
1958–59	111.7	106.2	+ 5.5	
1st half	39.6	46.3	— 6.7	67.7
2nd half	72.1	59.9	+12.2	78.5
1959–60	131.2	135.2	— 4.0	
1st half	72.1	65.4	+ 6.7	71.0
2nd half	59.1	69.8	—10.7	76.7

Sources: *Economic Survey of Burma,* various years through 1960, and *Selected Economic Indicators,* C.S.E.D., Rangoon, November 1960.

Government buy Burmese rice for redistribution to the hungry peoples of Southeast Asia.

The extent of the decline in the foreign exchange reserves during 1953–54 now began to occasion a good deal of concern, particularly at the central bank (Union Bank) and at the Ministry of Finance and Revenue. As has already been pointed out, the foreign exchange position and outlook were not regarded as an important factor during the period May-August 1954, when the large 1954–55 capital program was in process of formulation. At that time, however, it had been thought that the last months of the fiscal year 1953–54 would produce something of a surplus in the balance of payments and reduce the losses in foreign exchange incurred up to that time. This did not prove to be the case. The loss in foreign exchange during the fourth quarter of the fiscal year 1953–54, ending September 30, had been larger than that of any of the three preceding quarters. Then the early months of the fiscal year 1954–55 witnessed a continued decline, though at a somewhat lower rate. What was disturbing was not the level of the reserves. The foreign exchange reserves required for monetary cover amounted to only some K 25 crores (this would of course increase with the anticipated increases in money supply during the year), and at the end 1953–54 monetary reserves held by the Union Bank (as distinct from total foreign exchange holdings) were some 2.5 times that amount. It was the direction and rate of the movement of the foreign exchange reserves that constituted the problem. So negligible a factor had foreign exchange been considered that plans for the 1954–55 fiscal year had not included even an informal foreign exchange budget. This was the general situation out of which a number of developments were now to ensue.

The question of foreign exchange was first raised at the newly formed Council of Economic Advisors.[2] Dr. Hla Myint proposed that a stop be put

2. The Council of Economic Advisors was created by order of the Economic and Social Board in August 1954 on the recommendation of U Hla Maung, Executive Secretary of the Board. The Board's order stated that "It will be the duty of the Council to consider all problems of economic policy, either on reference by the Economic and Social Board or on its own initiative, and advise the Economic and Social Board. It will also be its duty to consider whether economic research, collection of statistics and administrative procedures and arrangements within government are adequate to provide a reliable basis for the formulation of economic policy, and advise the Economic and Social Board. The Council will confine itself to consideration of economic problems only."

Appointed to the council were Mr. J. S. Furnivall, Chairman, U Hla Maung, Deputy Chairman, Dr. Hla Myint, Dr. Tun Thin, U Thet Su and the author. Mr. Furnivall was of course the dean of all foreign advisors in Burma. He had had a long, distinguished, and (to the Burmese) sympathetic career as an officer in the Indian civil service prior to independence. After independence, he was invited to return to Burma as planning advisor. By now elderly and semi-retired, he enjoyed universal respect by virtue of both his record and his age. Dr. Hla Myint, English-educated, had already made something of a name for himself in the field of welfare and development economics. He had assisted the Government in 1947, 1948 and 1949 but, apparently frustrated, had then left Burma to teach at Oxford. Then U Hla Maung persuaded him to come to Burma for the year 1954–55, under United Nations auspices, to serve as economic advisor. Dr. Tun Thin had recently become head of the Department of Economics at Rangoon University after taking his doctorate at Harvard University, where he won the distinguished Wells Prize for an outstanding dissertation. He had also assisted in the reparations negotiations and acted as Economic Advisor to the Socialist Party leaders at the Asian Socialist Congress. U Thet Su had recently completed a term of service as Chairman of the State Agricultural Marketing Board, and was widely known in international rice circles as "Mr. Rice." The author was Chief Economist of Robert R. Nathan Associates, the economic consultants to the Government.

In recommending the creation of the Council of Economic Advisors, U Hla Maung was probably motivated by two major considerations. The theoretical and policy issues which had been raised in connection with the 1954–55 program and budget had been difficult for many of the ministers to comprehend. U Hla Maung may have felt that he was being too closely identified in the minds of some of the ministers with the foreign economic consultants, whose views were communicated to the Government through him. He may therefore have believed that a broadening of the advisory base to include Mr. Furnivall and professional Burmese economists might counteract such an impression. Also, he may have believed that a Council of Economic Advisors would help the ministers to develop a greater appreciation of the importance of economic policy.

The Council of Economic Advisors was not destined to last very long. It functioned really only during November and the first days of December 1954. Shortly thereafter Mr. Furnivall took an extended leave to lecture in the United States and U Hla Maung, after intermittent absences, was designated Ambassador to Yugoslavia. The remaining council members were reluctant to functo further foreign exchange commitments by the purchasing missions abroad and by the operating agencies working on the development program. This action, however, seemed over hasty to other members of the Council, especially because the details of the end-1953–54 position were not yet known and it was not yet possible either to understand why the reserves had dropped as much as they had or to project with reasonable accuracy what was likely to happen in the months ahead. It was also held that a foreign loan was preferable to curtailments in the long-term program.

Despite intensive efforts, a complete picture of the 1953–54 balance of payments could not be developed for several months. Customs figures available showed total exports of K 107 crores and imports of K 95 crores — a favorable trade account balance of K 12 crores. Since Burma generally ran an unfavorable balance on non-trade account of less than K 10 crores per year, the known debt repayment to India and the United Kingdom during 1953–54, amounting to some K 15 crores, only partially explained the deficit of close to K 44 crores in the balance of payments. It was this lack of clarity which underlay the reluctance of the Economic Council to take hasty action.

It was of course clear that rice export earnings would be the controlling factor. Here the Council was confronted by the extremely conservative projections supplied by the State Agricultural Marketing Board and the Ministry of Trade Development responsible for S.A.M.B. operations and the far more optimistic views of the economic consultants on what could be done if the Government pursued aggressive policies on the rice export front. The Council therefore advised the Government on November 15 that:

immediate attention be directed toward expediting the sale of rice and improving arrangements for shipping, and that an immediate review be made of the prospect of rice sales and shipments during the present financial year;

. . . that an immediate review be undertaken of the programme of Government foreign expenditures, including payments made to date and the schedule of payments committed and to be committed during the present financial year, and of other relevant factors affecting the foreign exchange position. This review should be of such a character as would facilitate the establishment of foreign exchange allocation . . . if required . . .[3]

This review was to be completed by the end of November so that the Economic and Social Board could make such decisions as might be required.

The Union Bank, whose capable General Manager, U San Lin, had been invited by the Council of Economic Advisors to participate in its review, now

---

tion as a council during the absence of these two men. In the early part of 1955, the intended functions of the Council were in any event more or less taken over by a committee composed of economic secretaries to government.

3. "Resolution of the Council of Economic Advisors," November 15, 1954.

submitted a memorandum projecting large cash and foreign exchange deficits during 1954–55 and recommending that the Government substantially reduce the rate of proposed investment to insure financial stability. This memorandum was referred to the economic consultants. Their comments, submitted on November 26, 1954, agreed that sizable deficits would be incurred in 1954–55, although they believed that these would be more moderate than those projected by the Bank. They differed, however, with the thesis implicit in the Bank's recommendation that the size of Burma's long-term capital program should be governed only by the resources which she herself could muster. The consultants believed that the Government should seek loans from abroad to supplement its own resources. They recommended also that the Government approach the problem of rice marketing with vigor, with the object of shipping some 2 million tons of rice during 1954–55 and more thereafter; that it take equally vigorous steps to improve the mechanisms for the processing, handling, routing and shipping of rice, so as to make possible exports of as large a volume as could be sold; that it adopt and energetically implement the economic policies they had recommended in October; that it expedite arrangements for the flow of reparations goods and services from Japan under the recently concluded agreement; that it seek the extension of capital loans from the World Bank to provide additional safeguards for the foreign exchange position; and that it establish more precisely the foreign exchange components of approved capital program expenditures and take steps to insure that foreign exchange expenditures did not exceed the totals implicit in those programs. These recommendations were productive of some results.

U Raschid, one of the most capable ministers in the Government, was now placed in charge of the Ministry of Trade Development with responsibility for rice sales and exports. Also during November, a sales agreement was concluded with People's China for 150,000 tons of 1954 crop rice at £40 per ton, mostly on a barter basis. The sale of 1954 crop at £40 per ton suggested that prices in agreements for 1955 new crop rice would be somewhat above but not much higher than that level. This indicated, of course, a further and rather substantial reduction in the price of export rice, but it was doubtful whether it would be adequate to move the quantities desired.[4] Other steps included the presentation of a list of possible loan projects, totaling some $163 million, to the World Bank Mission then visiting Rangoon and considerable activity directed toward placing as much as possible of the procurement needed for the approved capital development program on the Japanese reparations schedules.

4. In this connection it may be noted that the decision of the Council of Economic Advisors to "wait and see" was based on the assumption that 1.8 million tons of rice and rice products would be shipped during 1954–55 at an average price of £44 per ton. This, they had estimated, would result in a deficit of some K 20 to K 30 crores in the balance of payments for the year.

Table 18

DIRECTION OF RICE EXPORTS, BY TONNAGE,
1954 THROUGH 1959–60

(*Thousands of Tons*)

Country	1954	1954–55	1955–56	1956–57	1957–58	1958–59	1959–60
Total sales	1,530	1,631[a]	1,931	2,005	1,463	1,614	2,080
Barter as per cent of total	0	23.3	25.0	14.5	8.7	5.3	5.9
Cash sales	1,530	1,331	1,449	1,715	1,335	1,529	1,958
Asia	1,281	1,118	1,158	1,474	1,102	1,248	1,632
India	627	562	127	584	385	266	390
Pakistan	—	—	60	153	168	127	256
Japan	309	238	262	104	50	26	46
Malaya	30	158	232	62	77	71	52
Singapore	—	—	—	75	107	130	102
Ceylon	175	123	132	260	160	240	213
Indonesia	140	37	345	236	155	388	573
Europe	123	146	86	64	72	87	144
United Kingdom	81	82	57	57	52	45	72
Mauritius	32	36	23	58	48	49	47
Ryukyu Islands	40	31	30	30	20	32	31
Other countries	54	—	151	89	93	113	104
Barter sales	1	380	482	290	128	85	122
U.S.S.R.	—	34	212	107	—	30	45
China	—	115	105	98	10	} 55	12
Czechoslovakia	—	} 231	165	} 85	83	} 55	4
Yugoslavia	—	} 231	165	} 85	29	} 55	28
Other Eastern Europe	—	} 231	165	} 85	} 6		26
Israel	—				} 6		7

Sources: *Economic Survey of Burma*, 1956 through 1960, and *Quarterly Bulletin of Statistics*, First Quarter, 1958; data for 1959–60 from S.A.M.B.

a. Individual country data add up to 1,711 thousand tons, but published total is 1,631 thousand tons.

The Bank "credit-worthiness" mission headed by Dr. Antonin Basch appeared, however, to take a rather dim view of both the highly ambitious size of the development program and the economics of some of its components (notably the manufacturing and electric power programs). It also seemed to feel that insufficient attention was being directed toward the primary agricultural, mining and timber sectors. Loan prospects therefore did not appear to be bright. As regards reparations, the operating agencies which had been asked to indicate which of their requirements could be met from Japan had exhibited considerable misunderstanding; in many cases they had put forward additions to their already over-large approved capital programs for 1954–55. This was the position when the Ministry of Finance and Revenue, on January 14, 1955, submitted a memorandum pointing to the Government's dwindling cash and foreign exchange balances, and calling for savings on both the domestic and foreign exchange fronts.

The measures proposed by the Ministry were quite drastic: a 25 per cent

Table 19

DIRECTION OF RICE EXPORTS, BY VALUE,
1954 THROUGH 1959–60

(*K Crores*)

Country	1954	1954–55	1955–56	1956–57	1957–58	1958–59	1959–60
Total sales	95.2	84.5[a]	87.7	89.5	66.3	71.6	83.5
Barter as per cent of total	0	22.8	25.9	13.7	8.0	5.9	6.3
Cash sales	95.2	70.1	65.0	77.2	61.0	67.4	78.2
Asia	82.7	62.3	51.1	65.9	51.0	56.0	67.3
India	39.4	34.2	5.6	25.5	16.6	11.8	16.6
Pakistan	—	—	—	7.0	8.4	5.7	11.0
Japan	21.6	15.1	14.0	5.6	2.7	1.4	2.4
Malaya	.9	4.2	7.7	2.9	3.9	3.1	1.9
Singapore	—	—	—	2.5	4.4	4.1	3.0
Ceylon	11.2	6.5	7.0	11.5	7.5	11.8	8.6
Indonesia	10.6	2.3	16.8	10.9	8.0	18.1	23.8
Europe	3.0	3.7	2.5	1.7	1.7	2.5	3.6
United Kingdom	1.8	1.9	1.5	1.4	1.0	1.2	1.8
Mauritius	2.6	2.3	1.2	3.0	2.6	2.5	2.3
Ryukyu Islands	2.8	1.8	1.5	2.0	1.1	1.7	1.5
Other countries	4.1	—	8.7	4.6	4.6	4.7	3.5
Barter sales (total)	—	19.3	22.7	12.3	5.3	4.2	5.3
U.S.S.R.	—	1.8	10.5	4.6	—	1.6	2.4
China	—	6.0	5.1	4.1	.5		.3
Czechoslovakia	—						.1
Yugoslavia	—	11.5	7.1	3.6	4.8	2.6	1.5
Other Eastern Europe	—						.7
Israel	—						.3

Sources: Economic Survey of Burma, 1956 through 1960, and *Quarterly Bulletin of Statistics,* First Quarter, 1958; data for 1959–60 from S.A.M.B.

a. Individual country data add up to K 89.4 crores, but published total is K 84.5 crores.

cut in current governmental expenditures by wholesale, "across-the-board" reductions in personnel; reduction by a similar percentage of expenditures for diplomatic and consular establishments; and complete suspension of relatively unimportant departments and projects. To save foreign exchange, the Ministry proposed restrictions on the import of luxury goods. Somewhat plaintively, it pointed out that "previously, whenever a reduction in Government spending was recommended by the Finance Ministry and a conflict arose with other ministries, the Council of Ministers had always overruled Finance." This memorandum was also referred to the economic consultants for comments.

The consultants were satisfied that the objectives of the Ministry of Finance and Revenue should be supported even though some of the specific measures it proposed were unacceptable. They had not been fully reconciled to the large program adopted over their protests the previous August, and they had seen no evidence since that time that the Government was determined to move promptly on the policy measures which they had urged as necessary complementary steps following adoption of the 1954–55 program. The time lost, especially in making sales commitments for the new rice crop and a substantial part of the carryover stocks, now led the consultants to anticipate a deficit of up to K 30 crores in the balance of payments during 1954–55, unless countervailing action were taken. Such a decline might break through the minimum currency cover required by law and, in their view, could not be permitted. After appraising the factors involved in both current and capital expenditures on both the domestic currency and foreign exchange sides, the consultants recommended: first, that current governmental expenditures be reduced moderately by approximately K 5 crores to the level originally recommended, the cuts to be selective rather than across-the-board as proposed by the Ministry of Finance and Revenue; second, that the policy measures recommended in October be adopted and vigorously implemented; third, that it be made clear to the Government agencies that reparations credits could be used only *within* their modified approved capital programs, not as additions to them; and, fourth, that K 15 to K 20 crores be established as the maximum tolerable foreign exchange loss for 1954–55, and that a committee of ministers be designated to implement this objective.[5]

Two special considerations were involved in this last recommendation. First, in the special capital program review of the previous August, it had proved exceedingly difficult to cut the capital programs of the agencies to tolerable levels, and it seemed clear that a control over their foreign exchange expenditures might be a much more effective device for achieving the desired result. Second, it seemed quite clear also that there were bound to be very substantial shortfalls in the domestic spending of the agencies for development purposes, and that these shortfalls were unlikely to be matched by corresponding cuts in their foreign exchange expenditures, which involved only purchases easily made abroad. It appeared therefore that in the absence of foreign exchange control machinery, equipment and raw materials would pile up in the warehouses or on the docks and be subject to pilferage and deterioration, while foreign exchange reserves would be run down to an unnecessary degree.

The retrenchment proposal of the Ministry of Finance and Revenue came before the Economic and Social Board at its meeting on January 28. Since Minister of Finance U Tin stated that his Ministry wished additional time to study the alternative proposals of the consultants, the question was referred to the Finance Subcommittee of the Cabinet (U Ba Swe, U Kyaw Nyein and U Tin) and to the four-Ministry committee recommended by the consultants (Finance and Revenue, National Planning, Trade Development and the

5. Memorandum submitted to the Economic and Social Board by Robert R. Nathan Associates, Inc., January 26, 1955.

Economic and Social Board). When the combined committees met on February 2, the Ministry of Finance and Revenue finally gave up on its proposal for an across-the-board cut in Government personnel in the face of the argument that so blind a cut would be destructive of efficiency. However, the senior ministers decided to try to effect savings of some K 30 crores in domestic and foreign exchange expenditures combined. They appointed a subcommittee composed of U Thant, Dr. Hla Myint, U Kyaw Nyun (Secretary of the Ministry of Finance and Revenue), U Hla Maung and the chief economic advisor to work out a program.

The subcommittee met the next week to consider the many possibilities, held intensive discussions with the operating agencies to determine where cuts in the capital program were feasible, and reported back to the ministers. The latter were in general agreement with the subcommittee's findings that the 1954–55 capital program should be reduced by roughly K 12.5 crores (with savings of approximately K 6 crores in foreign exchange), that current governmental expenditures should be moderately curtailed and that moderate cuts should be imposed on private imports and governmental imports for private use. The Economic and Social Board on February 11 approved in principle the proposed reductions of K 10 crores in domestic and K 20 crores in foreign exchange expenditure for 1954–55, but deferred decision on the means of achieving this goal.[6] By the time the Economic and Social Board met again on the retrenchment proposals on March 6 the consultants had submitted another memorandum spelling out the details of the proposed savings — an approximate K 12 crores reduction in capital programs (7 crores in foreign exchange), a reduction of K 3 to K 5 crores in current governmental expenditures, a reduction of K 2 crores in imports for private use by the Civil Supplies Management Board and a saving of approximately K 7 crores in private imports. In addition, they recommended the setting up of a foreign exchange control authority to manage foreign exchange expenditures and commitments by Government agencies. These recommendations were approved, as were additional recommendations: that policy on private investment be clarified; that International Monetary Fund and U. S. Government loans be considered in addition to the pending World Bank Loans; and (the oft-repeated earlier recommendation) that rice and other foreign exchange earnings be emphasized.[7] It seemed therefore that some of the necessary decisions had been made, that others would shortly follow, and that the remainder of fiscal year 1954–55 would witness a healthy consolidation. However, one of the recommenda-

6. Rather inconsistently, that same meeting of the Economic and Social Board approved the proposal made by the Union of Burma Airways to purchase three expensive Viscount aircraft for international operations.

7. Memorandum, "Comments and Recommendations on Financial Retrenchment in 1954–55," Robert R. Nathan Associates, Inc., February 21, 1955.

tions adopted provided the springboard for a quite unexpected and serious development when it was publicly announced.

The subcommittee had been mindful of the serious speculative and inflationary potentials inherent in any drastic curtailment of private imports. It had therefore tried to minimize the dangers by preserving the open general license category of imports and by dealing moderately with other licensed items. With respect to the latter categories of goods, the recommendations were that the volume of new licenses to be issued be curtailed, and the validity of the very substantial volume of import licenses already issued be cut from 12 to 6 months, with the proviso that only one half of their face value might be imported during the first six months of the year.[8] When the decision of the Economic and Social Board was announced by the Ministry of Trade Development on the evening of March 6, it was stated that orders placed by importers against existing licenses up to March 7 would not be subject to the new limitation. On the following day, March 7, traders besieged the banks to open letters of credit, and cables sped overseas placing new orders against them.[9] Banks worked late into the evening, and in many cases well beyond midnight, writing letters of credit. At the same time something of a panic developed in local markets. Intensive speculation and inventory building led to sharp rises in prices. And the trading community, anticipating that restrictions might shortly be imposed on O.G.L. (Open General License) commodities, started a letter of credit run on these as well. An emergency meeting of the Cabinet was held March 10 to consider how to deal with this situation. Foreign exchange reserves by now had dropped approximately another K 15 crores from the October 1 level. Unfortunately, the Prime Minister and U Raschid, the most knowledgeable member of the Cabinet on these matters, were both away in Bangkok. The Cabinet decided to suspend the O.G.L. list to stop the run on foreign exchange.

This decision was of course debatable, and it was debated at great length. On the one hand, it appeared quite possible that the traders' scare and the run on foreign exchange would prove to be short-lived and that, if permitted to do so, it might quickly run its course, especially if the Government were to issue a reassuring statement to the effect that the O.G.L. List would not be suspended. Imports had been flowing in freely and in considerable quantity, and stocks in the country were thought to be in easy supply. Also, abolition of the O.G.L. List, which had until then accounted for more than two thirds of all private imports, and establishment of a complete licensing system would

8. For open general license items, it was also recommended, on the suggestion of U San Lin of the Union Bank, that traders be required to place substantial deposit margins against letters of credit. This recommendation was not accepted by the Board.

9. The Board had of course intended "up to March 7" to mean *through* March 6. The Attorney-General, consulted in haste, ruled otherwise.

obviously impose very severe strains on the personnel and the administrative procedures of the Ministry of Trade Development. It was highly doubtful whether the Ministry would be able to handle this additional burden effectively. On the other hand, there was no knowing how far the run on foreign exchange might go, if unchecked. On balance, the consultants favored riding out the scare, but the Government decided to play it safe. Undoubtedly the decision was a difficult one to make, and could presumably best be made by those familiar with the psychology of the Burmese trading community.

The O.G.L. suspension decision constituted the climactic action of the first half of fiscal year 1954-55 and set the stage for a number of developments that plagued the economy for the next two years, the influence of which is still felt. It may be useful, therefore, to summarize the position as it then appeared and offer a perspective on the further action considered necessary at the time, as stated in a memorandum submitted by the economic consultants on March 15, 1955, under the heading "Selected Economic Policies and Programs for Priority Attention."

After referring to the defensive short-run measures recently approved by the Government for dealing with the foreign exchange situation, the consultants urged the necessity for longer-run policies and measures directed to the same objective. They once again recommended the highest priority for efforts to achieve higher levels of production and exports of rice, timber and minerals; expeditious action on foreign loans; the preparation of a foreign exchange budget; immediate action to control foreign exchange spending in accordance with the approved budget; specific measures with respect to private imports; and active consideration of tax and savings measures.

In connection with these recommendations, a few brief observations may be in order. First, in commenting on rice exports and on plans and procedures for the programing of imports, the economic consultants were not yet aware of additional but not yet publicly announced rice barter agreements concluded the month before with Czechoslovakia, Hungary and East Germany, or of still other barter deals concluded later which may have been pending at that time.[10] These deals were to complicate enormously the problem of foreign exchange allocation and use, and reduce substantially the value in use of Burma's apparent foreign exchange earnings. Second, because of the inexperience of Burmese governmental administration, the consultants were being drawn into the "how" of foreign exchange spending by Government agencies and import programing and controls, as well as into the "what" of policy. Third, the sharp rise in the prices of many commodities following the O.G.L.

10. Although the consultants enjoyed the confidence of the Government, they were not consulted about contemplated barter deals, or most other questions in which Soviet bloc nations were concerned. Whether this was because, as Americans, they were not expected to take an objective view, or whether it was because the Government wished to spare them possible embarrassment, is uncertain. Perhaps both considerations had a bearing.

suspension indicated that the trading community would enjoy huge windfall profits for some time to come. This suggested that improved tax enforcement as well as changes in tax structure already recommended should be emphasized. Finally, the memorandum sharply focused the dual character of the program needed — the short-run negative measures required to curtail expenditures in 1954–55, and the longer-term positive measures needed to increase export earnings and mobilize foreign aid. In the nature of the case, the latter measures would require more time. It was the restrictive measures which stood out in 1954–55 and for most of 1955–56.

It was only at about this time, some six months after the fact, that the major details of foreign exchange transactions in the previous fiscal year 1953–54 became known, and it became possible to appraise with accuracy the reasons for the unexpectedly large deficit in that year. An aside on this question may be appropriate here before proceeding with the chronological account.

The Customs data, it will be recalled, had shown exports of K 107 crores and imports of K 95 crores, or a favorable balance of K 12 crores on trade account in 1953–54. The balance of payments data now showed export proceeds at K 100 crores and import payments at K 113 crores. These differences accounted for K 25 crores of the K 56 crores difference which needed explanation (K 12 crores balance of payments surplus in the Customs figures plus K 44 crores of deficit on total balance of payments account). The difference on the export side was accounted for by a lag in collections against rice shipments. Under the sales agreements, the Government purchasers paid 90 per cent against shipment, withholding 10 per cent for possible settlement of quality disputes. Over and above these withholdings, the State Agricultural Marketing Board fell behind in its invoicing and consequently in collections. The larger difference, however, was on the import side, where the payments figures were K 18 crores larger than the customs figures. A small part of this difference was in the private imports, indicating forward payments. Payments for Government imports, however, were K 15 crores larger than the Customs data indicated. Investigation disclosed that this huge difference was accounted for chiefly by two factors: certain Government imports, notably defense items, were for some reason classified by Customs as non-trade items. Second, the Customs practice was to register Government imports only when duty was paid on them. When payment of customs duties was deferred at the request of the agencies concerned, the imports were not included in the customs figures until later. The large deficit on non-trade account which made up the remainder of the difference was the large debt repayment to the United Kingdom and the debt settlement with India, of which the planners of course had been aware. Thus, of the "alarming" decline of K 44 crores in the foreign exchange reserves, some K 18 crores were due to non-recurring items, some K 5 crores represented accounts receivable, and a large but indeterminate amount represented advance payments on both private and governmental account. The condition, while serious, had certainly not warranted panic.

The most notable developments in the third fiscal quarter, ending June 30, concerned import and export trade, the control over governmental foreign exchange spending, foreign loans and the over-all economic development plan.[11]

The return of Prime Minister U Nu and Trade Minister U Raschid shortly after the suspension of the O.G.L. led to an early modification of the extreme measures for control of imports. The O.G.L. was restored, although on a much more limited basis, and included goods of the type recommended by the consultants for automatic licensing. U Raschid also issued a statement to the trade which did much to allay the apprehension that had been created.

Developments on the rice export front, however, were less encouraging. In addition to the barter deals with China, Czechoslovakia, Hungary and East Germany previously mentioned, discussions were under way with Ceylon and China looking toward a triangular trade deal in which China would buy rice from Burma on barter account and then exchange it for rubber with Ceylon. Because Ceylon would in turn ship rubber to People's China, the arrangement might prejudice a possible U. S. loan to Burma. The outlook for rice exports was in any case dim, not because the potentials themselves were limited, but because the State Agricultural Marketing Board and the staff of the Ministry of Trade Development seemed disinclined to fight for shipments of much more than 1 million tons. It was this spirit of defeatism which led the economic consultants to propose to the Prime Minister early in April that responsibility for rice export sales be given to private trade, even though they were aware that the socialist elements in the Government might find the proposal highly offensive. When this proposition was, at the Prime Minister's suggestion, put to U Raschid, the responsible minister, he declared that such a move would be politically unacceptable and could not be considered.

Real progress, however, was made toward controlling the foreign exchange commitments and expenditures of Government agencies. The four-ministry committee constituted for this purpose turned the operational responsibility over to a Committee of Deputies who were in fact secretaries to the ministries concerned. Working with the Executive Secretary of the Economic and Social Board, members of the Rangoon University Economics Faculty and the economic consultants, these officials reviewed the foreign exchange commitments of all Government agencies, established foreign exchange allocations for them for the fiscal year and reviewed all major proposed commitments with an eye to determining whether they were in fact essential or could

11. During this time U Tin Maung replaced U Thant as Executive Secretary of the Economic and Social Board.

be postponed.[12] Because of the need to allocate reparations and barter credits as well as free foreign exchange, U Soe Tin, who was responsible for reparations scheduling in the Foreign Office, was appointed staff director for the coordinated foreign exchange control operation. Information gathered in response to a questionnaire distributed by the control authority and in subsequent meetings with the key agencies made it possible to impose very substantial cuts on their proposed uses of foreign exchange. Agency foreign exchange commitments and proposals for further commitments during 1954–55 were K 63.4 crores. Actual payments for the fiscal year, under control, turned out to be K 43.5 crores, a reduction of roughly one third. This result could not have been achieved in the absence of the control.

On the foreign loan front developments were inconclusive. The Economic and Social Board had approved in broad the recommendation that foreign loans be sought from the International Monetary Fund and other governments (the United States had been specifically mentioned), as well as from the World Bank. The Finance Subcommittee of the Cabinet was now asked to review the need for a foreign loan. After at least two lengthy meetings and a hearing of the economic consultants' views, it made a positive finding on the question. At about the same time the U. S. Government indicated informally through its Embassy in Rangoon that it would give every possible consideration to any loan request which Burma might make. The Prime Minister, however, was reluctant to act upon this invitation. He was aware of the provisions of the Battle Act restricting U. S. aid to nations which sold strategic commodities to Iron Curtain countries, and was unwilling either to tie Burma's hands in connection with arrangements for the sale of her rubber or to jeopardize the excellent state of U. S.-Burmese relations by accepting a loan which might occasion future reproaches. Also, he was scheduled to depart shortly on a long trip which would include several weeks in the United States. He perhaps had it in mind to explore there the possibility he had raised the previous October, that the United States might buy some of Burma's surplus rice. In any event, no further action on this front developed at this time.

Although an action program had been developed to deal with the foreign

12. U Mo Myit, who had replaced the late U Tin Pe as Secretary, Ministry of National Planning, some time before, became an important figure in the coordinating machinery which was now developing, along with U Kyaw Nyun, the Secretary of Finance and Revenue; U Tin Maung, Secretary, Economic and Social Board; U Tun Thaung, Secretary, Ministry of Industries; Dr. Tun Thin, Director, Central Statistics and Economics Department; and U Soe Tin, Director, Economics Division, Foreign Office.

Other secretaries to government participated from time to time (notably U Ba San of the Ministry of Trade Development), as did officials of various Departments and Boards in matters concerning their agencies. So far as the Burmese Civil Service was concerned, however, it was the first-named six men who increasingly carried the planning, programing, coordinating and control responsibilities, with the assistance of the economic consultants, and subject to the policy decisions of the Government.

exchange problem in 1954–55, there remained the problem of the following years. U Raschid was concerned with this. He was keenly dissatisfied with the rationale of the development program as a whole, which he called a spending program but not a plan, with many of the projects included in it, and with what he considered the poor performance of the Ministry of National Planning. On May 26 he therefore submitted a memorandum proposing a broad review of existing economic and social development plans. In view of the new appraisal of resource availabilities, he called for the reappraisal of projects, for the establishment of clear priorities and for a rephasing of the entire program in the light of them. He also urged that the Economic and Social Board concern itself to a far greater extent than it yet had with the various questions involved in both planning and program implementation, that the Board's membership be reconstituted and that a Committee of Experts be created, composed for the most part of secretaries to the ministries represented on the Board, to screen and make recommendations on all matters coming before the Board. The Board itself, he said, should meet every two weeks.[13] Finally, he proposed either a reactivation and strengthening of the Planning Ministry or its abolition and transferral of its functions to the Economic and Social Board.

U Raschid's proposals were considered on the eve of the Prime Minister's departure for Israel, Yugoslavia, the United Kingdom, the United States and Japan. It was decided not to abolish the National Planning Ministry. However, an Economic Planning Board was constituted under the chairmanship of U Ba Swe to review the entire development program as suggested and to function as the Economic and Social Board during the Prime Minister's absence. U Ba Swe now directed that a review of the entire development program along the lines suggested by U Raschid be conducted within a two-week period ending June 15. When it was suggested that an adequate review could not be carried out within so short a period and that the most which could be hoped for would be a quick review of the 1955–56 program, the time allotted was extended by ten days.

The Committee of Experts thereupon circulated a questionnaire calling on the agencies to submit within two weeks their proposed capital expenditures for each year through 1959–60. Each was to report: (a) its approved long-term program; (b) the program as the agency now believed it should be modified, giving due weight to its experience in the initial phases; and (c) the agency's minimum essential program, on the assumption that foreign exchange would continue to be extremely tight over the next five years. This information was to be supplied for each major project within the agency's

13. Meetings of the Board had been held irregularly, and sometimes as much as a month or two apart, depending on the presence of, and pressure of business on, the Prime Minister. Since little of economic importance could be decided without reference to the Board, this point was one of increasing importance.

program (agencies like the Industrial Development Corporation and the Agricultural Resources Development Corporation had scores of projects), showing proposed domestic and foreign exchange expenditures separately. Detailed data were also requested on each project to make possible a considered review of its economic and technical feasibility. On the suggestion of the economic consultants it was decided to review also the production and export programs of the major revenue or foreign exchange producing agencies so as to cover the resource as well as the spending side of the program. The Committee of Experts split into two subcommittees to deal simultaneously with both aspects.

The report of the Committee of Experts was made on schedule at the end of June.[14] As was to be expected, it had found that it could not deal with anything but the 1955–56 outlook in the allotted time, and this only in general terms. This outlook was indeed a dismal one, chiefly because the outlook for rice exports as presented by the Ministry and agency responsible was for earnings of some K 69 crores, of which K 22 crores would be in barter credits and only K 47 crores in free foreign exchange. In reviewing the capital programs of the agencies, the Committee had given special consideration to the degree to which projects were committed (and the waste which the curtailment of committed projects would involve), to projects which promised to be productive of foreign exchange earnings or important to internal security, to projects of clear essentiality and to projects which could use substantial quantities of reparations and barter credits. Review on this basis resulted in a capital program of K 82 crores for 1955–56 and an availability of only K 40 crores for all imports for private use, whether imported under private or governmental auspices. Implicit in this program was a huge governmental deficit with the private sector and an increase of some two thirds in the private money supply.

On the spending side, the Committee recommended continued strict control over governmental foreign exchange expenditures; specific allocations of foreign exchange for capital projects; imports of K 40 crores for private use; import of consumer goods, particularly textiles, from Japan, either through reparations or credit arrangements or both; negotiation of deferred payments with suppliers and contractors wherever possible; and reduction in current departmental budgets. It clearly chose, however, a large-scale capital program rather than a level of consumer imports which would prevent serious inflation.

On the production or receipts side, the Committee took into account some of the recommendations of the economic consultants. It urged that the State Agricultural Marketing Board be run as a business concern and placed in the charge of an individual invested with very broad powers; that the S.A.M.B. initiate as soon as possible sales of rice by tender or auction to the private

14. *Report of the Expert Committee,* June 29, 1955.

trade and engage commission agents in all important buying countries; and that a number of specific steps be taken to increase output and exports of timber, minerals and non-rice agricultural produce.

The economic consultants, committed by representation on the Board of Experts to an apparent concurrence in all its views, entered a minority report. This report differed with that of the Committee in three important particulars. It insisted that the volume of imports for private use could not be cut to the proposed austerity level of K 40 crores without disastrous inflation, and held that these imports must be maintained at a minimum level of K 65 to K 70 crores. It stated therefore that the Government had no choice but to seek a sizable foreign loan if it pursued the other measures recommended by the Committee. Finally, it asserted flatly that the State Agricultural Marketing Board was not competent to achieve the improvements in paddy quality, milling, marketing, shipments and earnings necessary and possible under the circumstances. These objectives could be achieved "only if private trade is permitted to participate in paddy purchasing, milling, storage, sales and shipping arrangements in far greater degree than at present." It advocated, therefore, that rice exports be returned to the private trade, and that Government rely on an export tax to produce the revenues for which the S.A.M.B. was then responsible.

Events now moved swiftly. The Economic Planning Board was plainly shaken by the experts' report of the dour outlook for 1955–56 and the inflationary implications. It ignored, however, the experts' recommendations that S.A.M.B. operations be placed under the control of one strong man, that responsibility for rice exports be returned to private trade and that a foreign loan be urgently sought. (It seemed quite clear that on this last point the members of the Board were merely complying with what they understood to be the position of the Prime Minister rather than reflecting their own views.) In substance, approval was given to the experts' report and the proposals for a high level of capital program and a disastrously low level of imports for private use. More constructively, the Planning Board accepted the thesis that exports and export earnings simply had to be increased. After a strong plea by the economic consultants that two million tons of rice exports be established as a major national "must" target for 1955–56, it rejected the projections of the agencies for an export program of 1.5 million tons and approved instead a target of 1.7 to 1.8 million tons, which would yield approximately K 80 crores in foreign exchange. It also approved specific measures to achieve the higher target, including a more aggressive export pricing policy and an upward revision of the prices paid to millers for quality grades.[15] Approved

15. Paddy purchased by S.A.M.B. was milled by private millers on S.A.M.B. account. The rates then paid for the milling of various grades made it more profitable for the millers to mill lower grades. Hence this point was important.

as well were higher export targets for timber and minerals and specific measures for achieving the increases, including the provision of adequate security
for the girdling of teakwood. The experts' group was directed to follow
through with the agencies concerned to insure performance on these increased
export targets.[16]

Toward the end of the month the Prime Minister returned from his prolonged trip abroad. While in the United States he had explored without result
the possibilities of exchanging some of Burma's surplus rice for funds to be
used in the employment of U. S. technicians.[17] He had also discussed the possibilities of encouraging private investment from the United States and had
talked to high officials of the World Bank. He was, however, still averse to
the idea of a U. S. loan.

Meanwhile a second round of capital program and related reviews had been
held. Whereas in the first review a number of capital projects had been approved, not because of their essentiality but rather because they seemed capable of utilizing reparations and barter credits, these were now eliminated from
the program on the assumption that it would be possible to use the reparations and barter credits previously allotted to them for the importation of
either consumer or capital goods required by the private sector. This second
review brought the capital program down from K 82 crores to K 60 crores.
The proposed level of imports for private use was correspondingly increased
from K 42 crores to K 55 crores. The picture, while easier than it had appeared some weeks before, was still extremely serious in terms of its prospective impact on domestic prices.

When the Prime Minister was briefed on the position and outlook, he
quickly agreed that further steps were necessary. His directives resulted in
further cuts in the 1955–56 capital program, which brought it down to K 56
crores, and in an increase in the program of imports for private use, which
brought it up to K 75 crores.[18] These changes, it was thought, would be
adequate to prevent further sharp increases in domestic prices during 1955–
56. There would remain, however, some danger on the foreign exchange side,

16. As a symptom of the Government's earnestness, U Ba Swe, at that time Minister of Mines,
as well as Chairman of the Planning Board and Minister of Defense, called a large-scale minerals
conference, attended by the industry representatives as well as district and agency officials, to
instill vitality in the minerals production and export drive.

17. This failure was, significantly, soon followed by the conclusion of a rice barter sales
agreement with the U.S.S.R. for 150,000 to 200,000 tons for 1956.

18. This compared with the peak level of K 86 crores in 1953–54, when imports were relatively uncontrolled. The concept "imports for private use" was intended to include private imports (both licensed and O.G.L.), imports by the Civil Supplies Board for sale to the public, and
certain imports made under special arrangements. These included industry requirements approved
by the Industries Department, coal and coke supplies for the Railways and Electricity Boards, special supplies for the petroleum and mining ventures and gunnies for the State Agricultural
Marketing Board. The term "private use" is not, therefore, exact. Nor does it match the Customs
classifications.

and the Prime Minister now agreed that a foreign loan should be sought as protection against a possible shortfall in rice exports and earnings below the target level. This would make possible an increase in the level of imports for private use to above K 75 crores, if necessary. The loan was not to be sought from the United States, but from India, and U Raschid was dispatched to negotiate it. But when U Raschid's first reports from New Delhi indicated that India was prepared to make only K 5 crores available immediately, and possibly another K 5 crores later on, the Prime Minister promptly decided to seek a loan from the United States, and cables went to Ambassador Barrington in Washington.

What Burma requested from the United States was a loan of $50 million to bolster her balance of payments position. Only some days later, on U Raschid's return from India, did it become clear that India's initial response had been based on a misunderstanding. India was willing to lend as much as Burma would undertake to repay within a three-year period beginning 1959. It was decided, therefore, to request a loan of K 15 or K 20 crores from India on this basis. Meanwhile initial reactions from the U. S. Government indicated that a balance of payments loan was unlikely, that all other possibilities were being carefully explored and that it would in all probability be possible, failing other alternatives, for the United States to render substantial assistance under Public Law 480 in the form of sale of surplus agricultural commodities for local currency. Since Burma's largest imports were cotton textiles and yarns, a P.L. 480 program centering on U. S. surplus cotton could be very useful in augmenting scarce foreign exchange. At about this time a Burmese mission was preparing to depart for the annual meetings of the World Bank and the International Monetary Fund where, it was hoped, talks with officials might facilitate the conclusion of early loan agreements. Thus, although the fiscal year 1954–55 had involved a continuous semi-crisis over the foreign exchange problem, as the year drew to a close it appeared that early relief was in sight.

Indeed, agreement in principle was reached in Washington by the end of September on a $20 million P.L. 480 program, and an understanding was reached with India within the following month for a combined loan and credit of K 20 crores.

At the central governmental planning and control level, 1954–55 had been a difficult and trying year. In some respects, however, it was a year of considerable accomplishment. Gross domestic product, in real terms, increased by 6.4 per cent despite a very small increase in agricultural production. Increases occurred in all sectors of the economy, most notably in state marketing. Rice exports rose substantially to 1.63 million tons from 1.27 million tons the year before. While total rice stocks had not been reduced, their composition had changed. Much old rice had been shipped. That part of the 1955 crop

which had not been sold was held in the form of unmilled paddy, less liable to
spoilage. Despite the sharp drop in average price per ton received (from
£49.7 to £38.9), the value of shipments actually increased slightly from K 84
crores to K 84.5 crores. The decline in the foreign exchange reserves was held
to K 24 crores. The year-end holdings were K 52 crores, slightly above what
was considered the safety level. But rice export proceeds had been well below
the value of shipments. S.A.M.B. receivables had increased close to K 10
crores during the fiscal year, and were now some K 13–15 crores. The official
foreign exchange holdings therefore considerably understated the real position. Public capital expenditures, held down by two rounds of program cuts
and by a rigorous control over foreign exchange commitments and spending, reached a new high level of K 61 crores (net of foreign debt repayments).
Another important step forward was the adoption by the Cabinet of a statement of policy to encourage private investment both foreign and domestic.

Of the general economic measures, only those for the privately held money
supply and consumer prices occasioned concern. Privately held money supply
had increased by K 20 crores from the level of K 89 crores of a year before — a
rise of more than 22 per cent. While the austerity index of consumer prices
for low income families in Rangoon had increased only 7 per cent from the
previous September, the clothing component had risen by 55 per cent, reflecting hoarding and speculation in cotton textiles and yarns. The food
component, up only 3 per cent from the previous year, did not reflect the
very substantial increase in the prices of imported foodstuffs and provisions
seldom bought by low income families. Price increases from March 1955,
when the O.G.L. was suspended, to September 1955 were, however, much
larger, since prices at that time were well below the levels of the previous
September because of large-scale imports and seasonal factors. The total cost
of living index rose 14.7 per cent, textile prices 60 per cent, and food costs 18
per cent in the second half of the year. On the reparations front, most of the
year had been spent in protracted negotiations with the Japanese on implementation of the agreement. The increasing volume of rice export
sales on open or barter account was disturbing. And on the most important
front of all — internal security — progress was disappointing.

Nevertheless, the government now looked forward to the remainder of the
program period with renewed confidence. The capital program for 1955–56
had been cut to the maximum degree consistent with commitments. Reasonably adequate provision for consumer imports had been made. Some
determination had been instilled into the export drive. More realistic rice
export pricing would be practiced, and was expected to result in increased
export volume and earnings. The deferred decision to seek more foreign
loans had been made, the necessary steps had been taken, and early results
could be anticipated. While 1955–56 would undoubtedly be another year of

stringency, the period beyond would be easier. With many presently committed capital projects then completed (some of them substantial foreign exchange savers), the capital program could be adjusted with greater flexibility to resource availabilities as they then appeared. This was the substance of the confident message which Prime Minister U Nu gave to the nation in his speech of September 28, 1955.

For these reasons, I am convinced our financial situation is basically sound and under control. Our financial future, as well as our physical and spiritual future, is not gloomy, but bright. We face a period of temporary financial stringency, as I have stated, in the next financial year, after which conditions will ease. The fact that after a period in which expansion of Government expenditures was encouraged, economy is now to be practiced, does not constitute a financial crisis. Neither does the fact that private and consumer imports may, for a period of a year, require to be limited to essential goods, constitute a crisis. In fact, Gentlemen, there is no crisis. There is only an adjustment — a moderate adjustment — to the facts of life as we know them. We are in a position of a man who, when his income was high, and in anticipation of high continued earnings, bought himself a large expensive automobile. His income now having been somewhat reduced, but still considerably in excess of his current requirements, he may have to give up the more expensive car in favour of a less expensive one. Things may be a bit tight until the changeover is made — but his is no crisis either.

A unique combination of circumstances, centering on the import situation, was, however, to result in a powerful domestic inflationary development in the coming year, reversing almost completely the face of the economic coin as it had appeared in 1954–55, and prolonging the tension to which the economy had been subject. The fight for economic stability, initially on the foreign exchange front, now became for a time a fight against domestic inflation.

CHAPTER 12

The Fight for Economic Stability: The Domestic Inflation Side— 1955-56

The fiscal year 1955–56 opened auspiciously with substantial progress in the mobilization of foreign resources. With an understanding already reached with the U. S. Government for the purchase of approximately $20 million worth of surplus U. S. agricultural commodities (chiefly cotton), to be paid for in local currency, negotiations continued on matters of detail. Further negotiations with India improved the initial understanding that India would extend a loan of K 10 crores and a credit of an additional K 10 crores. An agreement signed in mid-October modified this to provide that the entire K 20 crores would be in the form of a loan freely convertible into all sterling area currencies. The rate of interest was to be 4 per cent, and the principal was to be repaid in eight half-yearly installments, beginning March 1959. Negotiations were being conducted simultaneously in Washington with the International Monetary Fund, looking to a draw of dollars against Burmese currency, and discussions indicated a favorable outcome. Indeed, the only question seemed to be whether Burma would be permitted to draw only two thirds of her maximum quota (up to that time the maximum draw permitted to any member country) or allowed to draw 100 per cent. Finally, the World Bank had undertaken to send another mission to Burma in November, this time to consider specific loans, chiefly for the railways and the port of Rangoon. In the light of previous discussions with the Bank there was every reason to anticipate that the results of this mission would be positive.

The other important element in the foreign exchange picture was of course the rice exports, where a disposition to continue with barter deals was increasingly evident. The inconclusive talks which Prime Minister U Nu had conducted earlier in the year with the U. S. Government on the exchange of rice for the services of U. S. technicians seemed to have led to the conclusion that Burma had no alternative but to sell more of her surplus rice to the Soviet bloc.[1] The Prime Minister departed in mid-October on a one-month trip to the Soviet Union, Poland and several other nations. In November three-year rice barter agreements were concluded with Czechoslovakia and Poland for the annual sale of 100,000 tons and 50,000 tons respectively. The following month another one-year agreement was concluded with People's China, also on barter account, for 150,000 tons.

The mobilization of foreign resources and the continuation of rice export sales on open or barter account to Soviet bloc countries were, however, not the only considerations as the Government approached the all-important problem of arranging for an adequate flow of imports for private use in 1955–56. There was no question of the Government's desire to arrange for such a flow. General elections were scheduled for April. The Government was keenly aware that since the modification of the Open General License System the previous March there had been substantial increases in the prices of imported goods — chiefly textiles — and that this might well have an important influence on the vote. It therefore wished to arrange for the importation of a large volume of consumer goods in the first half of the fiscal year to contain prices and, if possible, to reverse their direction.

This desire led to two broad decisions — one, since the total volume of such imports would have to be modest, to cut out inessential goods and bring in large volumes of the more essential commodities; and two, to shift responsibility for importing and distributing some of the most essential goods from the private sector to the Civil Supplies Management Board, the Government monopoly for essential consumer goods imports. Higher-priced textiles, various foods and provisions and a number of other commodities were among those somewhat hastily adjudged to be of the luxury or non-essential type and slashed from the import program. Low-priced textiles, edible oils (an important element in consumer goods imports), cement, wire nails and C.G.I. and asbestos-cement sheets for roofing were among the commodities added to the import and distribution program of the Civil Supplies Management Board.[2]

---

1. Since the potential tonnages involved in such an arrangement with the United States were very small — the agreement later consummated involved only 10,000 tons — the logic of such a conclusion is not clear.

2. Since the P.L. 480 program then under final negotiation would provide mostly cotton textiles — the total import program called for K 12 crores of textiles and K 6 crores of cotton yarns and P.L. 480 would provide K 8 crores of cotton textiles, or two thirds of that program — P.L. 480 was vital to the import program for the year.

At the same time, responsibility for the importation and distribution of electrical appliances and supplies was taken from private trade and assigned to the Government-owned Electricity Supply Board and its Rangoon subsidiary.

These changes in the composition of imports and in the structure of importing and distribution itself were of course in addition to the major structural change already made the previous spring. Whereas formerly two thirds of all privately imported goods had been under the automatic Open General License, less than one third would now be brought in under it. This last change had two important implications. On the administrative side, it meant a great deal more work for the Ministry of Trade and Development on the issuance of licenses. On the importers' side, it meant that the newly licensed goods would have to be imported by inexperienced Burmese traders whose major business heretofore had been the selling of licenses rather than the importation and distribution of goods.

On top of all this, the decision to allocate barter credits for the importation of consumer goods required that import licenses would somehow have to be tied, in part at least, to specific foreign exchange allocations. This meant that inexperienced importers would be buying from government monopolies in Soviet bloc countries where availabilities and choices were limited, where new procedures had to be worked out for every phase of the procurement operation, where qualities were inferior and where prices were non-competitive.

The highly involved scheduling, programing and allocations involved in the 1955–56 import program are illustrated in Tables 20–23. The derivation of the K 16 crores of barter credits proposed for utilization in the private use imports program may be seen from Table 20. Of the K 21 crores of private licensed imports, some K 9 crores were to be purchased from barter countries, some K 8 crores from other countries and over K 3 crores from India (Table 21.)

Responsibility for dealing with this formidable complex of problems rested primarily with the Ministry of Trade Development. The Committee of Experts — each of whom had his own full-time job to do — was heavily engaged in still another review of the long-term capital program and in negotiations with the World Bank Mission, which had by this time arrived. The review was directed to the formulation of a revised three-year capital program beginning 1956–57, which would be compatible with Burma's lower foreign exchange earnings. Concern was expressed to the Ministry of Trade Development and to the Economic and Social Board, chiefly by the economic consultants, about the difficulties into which the import program seemed to be heading. It seemed even then that there was inadequate provision for textiles, food and provisions and building materials.

What the consultants questioned most seriously, however, was the decision nearly to triple the import program of the Civil Supplies Management Board

Table 20

Proposed Imports in 1955–56, by Country and Economic Sector

(K Crores)

	Total Barter Credit	Purchase Missions and Defense	Total Private	License[a]	O.G.L.	Civil Supply[b]	Industry	B.O.C. and Mines	Coal and Coke	B.A.H.B.	Misc.
Total			76.72	21.12	18.10	21.50	8.00	2.50	1.80	3.00	0.80
Barter countries	35.73	19.55	16.18	9.08	—	7.05	0.05	—	—	—	—
U.S.S.R.	9.96	6.71	3.25	2.00	—	1.25	—	—	—	—	—
Czechoslovakia	8.00	5.25	2.75	2.00	—	0.75	—	—	—	—	—
East Germany	2.70	2.00	0.70	0.70	—	—	—	—	—	—	—
Hungary	0.66[c]	0.23	0.43	0.13	—	0.30	0.05	—	—	—	—
China	8.91[d]	2.86	6.05	3.00	—	3.00	—	—	—	—	—
Yugoslavia	2.50[f]	2.50[e]	—	—	—	—	—	—	—	—	—
Poland	2.50[f]	—	2.50	1.25	—	1.25	—	—	—	—	—
Israel	0.50[f]	—	0.50	1.25	—	0.50	—	—	—	—	—
Non-barter sources:											
India			10.70	3.31	0.35	2.20	0.65	—	1.29	3.00	—
Dollar countries			0.63	0.53[g]	—	—	0.10	—	—	—[h]	—
Others			49.21	8.20	17.75	12.25	7.20	2.50	0.51	—	0.80

Source: 1955–56 Import Program, as submitted to Economic and Social Board by Trade Development and Planning ministries.

a. For proposed breakdown see Table 23.
b. May request Civil Supplies for breakdown.
c. Includes K 13 lakhs of additional rice sales in exchange for textiles.
d. Includes credit of K 91 lakhs from last year's account.
e. Includes debit account of K 50 lakhs of last year.
f. Under negotiation.
g. K 20 lakhs have been provided for motor spare parts and accessories, printed books and periodicals from dollar countries.
h. K 20 lakhs from K 1 crore of the original allocation have now been provided for dollar areas.

Table 21

Proposed Private Imports in 1955–56, by Commodity and Area of Origin

(K Lakhs)

Description	Total	Barter Countries	India	Dollar Countries	Other Countries
1. Paper, all sorts	100.00	85.00	15.00	—	—
2. Fountain pens	10.00	4.00	—	—	6.00
3. Bicycles and tricycles	20.00	2.50	—	—	17.50
4. Records	3.00	—	—	—	3.00
5. Chinese raw medicines	1.00	1.00	—	—	—
6. Textiles	700.00	285.70	200.00	—	214.30
7. Foodstuffs	250.00	25.00	78.00	—	147.00
8. Provisions, all sorts	30.00	—	—	—	30.00
9. Household goods	70.00	53.50	—	—	16.50
10. Lubricants (dollar)	15.00	—	—	15.00	—
11. Medicines (dollar)	18.00	—	—	18.00	—
12. Motor vehicles	100.00	30.00	—	—	70.00
13. Tires and tubes for cycles and cars	100.00	4.80	30.00	—	65.20
14. Machinery	300.00	146.00	—	—	154.00
15. General hardware	100.00	100.00	—	—	—
16. Building materials	120.00	105.00	5.00	—	10.00
17. Photographic goods	25.00	10.30	—	—	14.70

Table 21 (Continued)

Description	Total	Barter Countries	India	Dollar Countries	Other Countries
18. Electrical goods	50.00	50.00	—	—	—
19. Requisites for sports and games	13.00	2.30	—	—	10.70
20. Saccharin	—	—	—	—	—
21. Soap	14.00	—	—	—	14.00
22. Beedi leaves	3.00	—	3.00	—	—
23. Miscellaneous	10.00	2.40	—	—	7.60
24. Watches	10.00	—	—	—	10.00
25. Toilet requisites	10.00	—	—	—	10.00
26. Radio, radiograms	10.00	—	—	—	10.00
27. Liquor	10.00	—	—	—	10.00
Subtotal	2,092.00	908.00	331.00	33.00	820.00
28. Printed books and periodicals (dollar)	2.00	—	—	2.00	—
29. Motor spare parts and accessories (dollar)	18.00	—	—	18.00	—
Grand Total	2,112.00	908.00	331.00	53.00	820.00

Source: 1955–56 Import Program, as submitted to Economic and Social Board by Trade Development and Planning ministries.

Table 22

Proposed Private Imports from Barter Sources in 1955–56, by Commodity and Country of Origin

(K Lakhs)

Description	U.S.S.R.	Czecho-slovakia	East Germany	Hungary	China	Yugo-slavia	Poland	Israel	Total
1. Paper, all sorts	—	30.00	3.50	—	45.00	—	6.50	—	85.00
2. Fountain pens	—	—	—	—	4.00	—	—	—	4.00
3. Bicycles and tricycles	—	2.50	—	—	—	—	—	—	2.50
4. Records	—	—	—	—	—	—	—	—	—
5. Chinese raw medicines	—	—	—	—	1.00	—	—	—	1.00
6. Textiles	—	45.00	23.50	13.00	170.00	—	34.20	—	285.70
7. Foodstuffs	—	—	—	—	25.00	—	—	—	25.00
8. Provisions, all sorts	—	—	—	—	—	—	—	—	—
9. Household goods	—	25.00	3.50	—	25.00	—	—	—	53.50
10. Lubricants (dollar)	—	—	—	—	—	—	—	—	—
11. Medicines (dollar)	—	—	—	—	—	—	—	—	—
12. Motor vehicles	10.00	20.00	—	—	—	—	—	—	30.00
13. Tires and tubes for cycles and cars	—	1.30	3.50	—	—	—	—	—	4.80
14. Machinery	103.00	18.50	—	—	—	—	—	—	146.00
15. General hardware	20.00	22.00	13.00	—	20.00	—	25.00	—	100.00
16. Building materials	30.00	30.00	10.00	—	10.00	—	25.00	—	105.00
17. Photographic goods	7.00	1.30	2.00	—	—	—	25.00	—	10.30
18. Electrical goods	30.00	.70	10.00	—	—	—	9.30	—	50.00
19. Requisites for sports and games	—	1.30	1.00	—	—	—	—	—	2.30
20. Saccharin	—	—	—	—	—	—	—	—	—
21. Soap	—	—	—	—	—	—	—	—	—
22. Beedi leaves	—	—	—	—	—	—	—	—	—
23. Miscellaneous	—	2.40	—	—	—	—	—	—	2.40
24. Watches	—	—	—	—	—	—	—	—	—
25. Toilet requisites	—	—	—	—	—	—	—	—	—
26. Radio, radiograms	—	—	—	—	—	—	—	—	—
27. Liquor	—	—	—	—	—	—	—	—	—
Total	200.00	200.00	70.00	13.00	300.00	—	125.00	—	908.00

Source: 1955–56 Import Program, as submitted to Economic and Social Board by Trade Development and Planning ministries.

Table 23

IMPORT PROGRAM OF THE CIVIL SUPPLIES MANAGEMENT BOARD,
1955–56, BY COMMODITY

(K Lakhs)

Sugar	150
Tinned milk	175
Infant milk	65
Cotton yarn	600
Silk yarn	100
Textiles	500
Cement	30
Gunnies	50
Building materials	180
Groundnut oil	70
Sewing thread	60
Fishing nets and twine	10
Staff shop, miscellaneous, etc.	55
Subtotal	2,000
Canned fish	120
Enamelware	30
Total	2,150

Detailed Breakdowns: Textiles and Building Materials

Textiles (monopoly)	
Plain grey cloth	35
Plain grey sheeting	20
White long cloth and shirting	250
White mulls (Moyaman)	15
Dyed shirting twill	180
Total	500
Building materials (monopoly)	
Asbestos	10
Corrugated sheets	150
Steel wire nails	20
Total	180

Source: 1955–56 Import Program, as submitted to Economic and Social Board by Trade Development and Planning ministries.

(from approximately K 8 crores to approximately K 21.5 crores) at the expense of private importers, at a time when efficient implementation of the import and distribution program was of paramount importance. A program increase of this magnitude would pose serious problems for even a long-established, efficient commercial organization. It seemed clear that to assign such a task to a relatively untried Government organization restricted by red tape was simply to invite unnecessary trouble. These warnings did receive some consideration. They resulted, however, not in a decision to curtail the planned expansion of the Civil Supplies program, but rather in a weak attempt to make provision for some of the distribution problems that the enlarged program would necessarily involve.

But the problem of import license issue to the sharply curtailed private sector was the most difficult of all. This was dealt with entirely within the Ministry of Trade Development, and the planning authorities became privy to its procedures only several months later. Importers had been invited some months before to register themselves for up to six lines of trade. There were something over 3,200 registered importers to deal with in connection with licensed goods, and only K 21 crores worth of licenses were to be issued. The largest registration for any single line of goods was for textiles, with something over 1,000 registrants. Import licenses were to be allotted to applicants in the ratio of ten or five times their paid-up capital, depending on the category into which they fell. Obviously, any attempt to distribute the limited value of the import licenses — out of a combined textiles and yarns program of some K 18 crores, private importers were to be assigned a total of K 7 crores only — would mean issuance of licenses so ludicrously small on the average as to be practically impossible of utilization.[3]

U Raschid, the Minister of Trade Development, was aware of this. He attempted to reduce the number of registered importers by issuing a questionnaire designed to establish whether the applicants were bona fide importers or only fly-by-night operators interested in obtaining import licenses for sale, but this came to nothing because of pressure from the Burmese trading community. The difficulty was compounded by the naïveté and insecurity of the officials at the Ministry of Trade Development, which prevented them from using common-sense methods in the allocation of foreign exchange to the import licenses. Since most import licenses were for a few thousand kyats only and both sterling and barter credits had to be allotted, a formula was needed for the allocation of either sterling or barter credit in a given country to individual licensees. Only in this way could the further chopping up of licenses be avoided. Since, however, free foreign exchange was obviously much more desirable, and even within the barter-credit category licenses issued on countries like Czechoslovakia or East Germany would be far more desirable than would be those, say, on Hungary or Poland, the Ministry officials, in the effort to be fair and to avoid complaints, "solved" this problem by giving proportionate shares of all these credits to each licensee. Finally, since each license had to be laboriously computed and completed by hand in four original copies — the Ministry of Trade Development had no computing machines or duplicating equipment (other than typewriters and mimeograph machines) and refused to make carbon copies of the licenses — the mere mechanics of license issue was simply hopeless. The operation was an administrative monstrosity.

Import licenses for textiles for the six months beginning October 1, 1955 in

3. The K 4.5 crores of textile licenses later issued for the first half of the year to, say, 1,000 importers meant an average license value of some K 45,000 or about $9,500. While many licenses would be larger than average, others of course would be smaller. These values were reduced by foreign exchange allocations. Obviously, import procurement could not be efficiently conducted in such small lots.

the amount of K 4.5 crores were issued only on December 26, when half the period had already gone by. As if all this were not enough, the P.L. 480 agreement, which had been counted upon to finance two thirds of the total cotton textile import program in 1955–56 (partly for private importers and partly for the Civil Supplies Board), had run into a number of snags. At the end of 1955 it had still not been concluded. Yet, since final agreement was expected from day to day, the officials concerned continued to wait — as did that portion of the import program.

Mention should be made here of several other significant economic developments during the closing months of 1955. One of these was the inauguration of a "hire-purchase scheme." Under it the Industrial Development Corporation undertook to import equipment from the barter account countries and sell it to local enterprisers on the installment plan. This represented not so much a modification in the Government's attitude toward the private sector as recognition of the need to utilize the credits piling up as a result of rice exports on open account. It was the fact, however, rather than the motive, which was significant. Ironically, Burma's sale of rice to the Soviet bloc nations was responsible for the first substantial assistance the Government accorded in the independence period to indigenous non-farm producers.

A second development was the genesis of the later "exchange of gifts" between the U.S.S.R. and Burma. Shortly after the Prime Minister's return from his trip to the Soviet Union, Messrs. Khrushchev and Bulganin repaid his visit in Rangoon, with the result that an agreement was reached on the spot, providing for Soviet agricultural and industrial aid in return for Burmese rice.[4] The U.S.S.R. would also make Burma gifts of a technological institute and a transport plane.

Another noteworthy development was the conclusion of a rice sales agreement for 1956 with Japan at prices 12 per cent below those of the previous year. This also liquidated the previously established price differential between the higher-priced grades bought by Japan and the standard S.M.S. (42 per cent broken) grade, which meant that S.M.S. prices could be reduced even more than 12 per cent without affecting the Japanese contract. Thus an element of flexibility was introduced into Burma's rice marketing which had been sadly lacking before. Marketing developments by this time were such that U Raschid had become hopeful that 2 million tons of rice might be sold and shipped in the fiscal year 1955–56. These prospects encouraged Burma to take the stand that the barter countries could not purchase Burmese rice for resale to other Burmese markets.[5]

It was not until late in January 1956 (the fourth month of the fiscal year)

4. This arrangement cut across an understanding already reached with the World Bank that it would bring an agricultural mission to Burma. The news that the Soviet Union would provide experts led the World Bank to cancel its own plan.

5. A number of instances of resale at market-breaking prices had already come to light.

that planning officials became aware of the distressing lag in the import program and of many of the complexities and difficulties which had developed in it. The occasion was a meeting of the Foreign Exchange Control Subcommittee, called for the purpose of reviewing the foreign exchange position. U Ba San, Secretary of the Ministry of Trade Development, reported that the total of private import licenses thus far issued for 1955–56 was less than K 5 crores, out of a total of over K 21 crores. Of these, he reported, less than K 3 crores were for textiles imports, out of a total of K 7 crores for the private sector. It was immediately clear that much valuable time had been lost and that steps of an emergency nature were needed to expedite the lagging import program.[6] Current and complete data on prices were of course not at hand. It was, however, common knowledge that textile import licenses were selling in the market place at a premium of 150 per cent over their face value. Spot retail prices of many textile and imported food and provision items, as well as of such items as soap, photographic film, razor blades, sewing thread, bathtubs, electric fans, tires and tubes, and any number of other goods were being quoted at double and triple their prices of some time ago. U Ba San revealed the difficulties encountered in the issue of import licenses, and frankly admitted that his Ministry did not know how it could speed up issue with its existing staff.[7] It was concluded that emergency action on textiles imports was needed, increasing the total textile program from K 18 to K 22 crores; that extraordinary measures should be taken to speed up license issue and imports of consumer goods; and that additional clerical staff should be authorized for the Ministry of Trade Development. In order to enable the recipients of import licenses of small value to utilize them, it was also decided to permit groups of holders to consolidate their licenses and treat them as one larger license. These recommendations were brought immediately to the Trade Minister.[8]

The meeting with U Raschid, the Trade Minister, confirmed the recommendations. He decided to increase the size of the textiles import program immediately by approximately K 4 crores, divided equally between Civil Supplies and private importers. No time would be required for the issue of additional private import licenses, since the value of those already issued could be increased by announcement on the part of the ministry. Meanwhile, the Civil Supplies Board would be given an additional foreign exchange allocation so that it would not have to wait for consummation of the P.L. 480 agreement.

---

6. It was also clear that it would no longer be possible to arrange for the import of sufficient quantities of consumer goods to achieve the previously hoped-for impact on prices in time for the general elections.

7. It had not, however, requested budgetary approval for the additional clerks needed.

8. A check made on the progress of the Civil Supplies Management Board import program revealed that this too was badly lagging, mostly because the P.L. 480 resources allocated to Civil Supplies for its textiles import program had not yet become available.

These were of course partial measures only. Coincidentally, the Cabinet asked the economic consultants for advice on how prices might be contained and for their views on certain measures which had been considered within the Cabinet itself. This request made it possible for the consultants to bring the entire import question to the Cabinet, as the supply side of the problem, and to urge the necessary remedial measures.[9]

Their recommendations stressed swift action to increase the issue of private import licenses to the program level, particularly those for textiles; to reduce the Civil Supplies import program in favor of more private licensing and imports; to expedite to the maximum extent the procurement and distribution of the reduced Civil Supplies imports; to conclude and implement the P.L. 480 agreement with the United States; to utilize the India loan to implement the import program to the extent necessary; to try to get the Soviet bloc countries to ship the goods required from them against Burma's rice credits at an early date and at reasonable prices; and to set rice prices at levels which would permit the cash sale of all the rice Burma was able to ship. On the demand side, the consultants recommended: efforts to eliminate waste and inefficiency in the Government, particularly in public enterprises; improved enforcement of existing tax laws and strengthening of the tax structure; development of schemes to increase and mobilize private savings; and discipline with respect to future capital expenditures. They also urged action to expedite loan arrangements with the World Bank and, once again, intensified efforts to improve rice, timber, minerals and other export production and earnings.[10]

The Government by this time was too preoccupied with preparations for the forthcoming general elections to give the price and supply problems the full attention they required, but a number of useful steps were taken. The issue of private import licenses was speeded up. In the first four months of the fiscal year only some K 5 crores of private import licenses had been issued; in the next six weeks, the figure was K 7 crores. Finance Minister U Tin and Supply Minister Bo Min Gaung were dispatched on emergency procurement missions to India and Japan respectively, and arranged for substantial

---

9. In considering the price increases which had taken place, the Cabinet was evidently unaware of the serious lags in the import program and of their effect on prices. The Cabinet attributed price increases to speculation, hoarding and "black money" resulting from profiteering and tax evasion. The Government had, therefore, considered such "remedial" measures as the purchase of gold abroad for domestic resale at very high prices, the granting of tax and other amnesties to "illegal and black market money" to bring it out of hiding and get it deposited in banks, the imposition of price controls and possibly the requisitioning of private import shipments for resale by the Government. The economic consultants, for perhaps obvious reasons, saw no merit in the first three of these proposals.

10. "A Programme for Dealing with Higher Prices," Robert R. Nathan Associates, Inc., February 2, 1956. The consultants did not recommend at this time (as they later did) that action be taken to reduce radically the number of registered importers. They and the central planning and control authorities were now "moving in" on Ministry of Trade operations for the first time, and did not yet appreciate the importance of this factor.

early deliveries from those countries, chiefly of cotton textiles. The Government, having recognized the contribution which prolonged negotiations over the P.L. 480 agreement was making to delays in the planned import program, now cut through the remaining red tape and on February 8 concluded arrangements with the United States for the purchase of $20.8 million worth of surplus commodities, including $17.5 million worth of cotton.[11]

Civil Supplies procurement was also stepped up. Important, though belated, was the Government's decision to reduce the price of export rice S.M.S. grade to £36 per ton on a government-to-government basis — a somewhat greater reduction than had been made for Japanese grades — and to give preference to cash buyers. Impressed by the contributions which such a decision might make to the fight against price inflation, it also decided in principle, on the advice of the economic consultants, that the Government enterprises under construction should be organized into separate corporations and that shares in these companies should be offered for sale to the private sector.[12]

It was at this time that the idea of joint ventures in the import field, previously decided upon by the Economic and Social Board in December 1953, came under consideration again. Fleeting consideration was even given, for the first time, to the recommendations on tax reform presented by Dr. Musgrave under Robert R. Nathan Associates auspices in September 1954. This was a result both of the interest awakened in U Kyaw Nyein, the Industries Minister, in this idea and of a savings scheme suggested by the economic consultants. No action, however, was taken on these fronts.

By the middle of February, newspaper reports indicated that substantial declines in prices had occurred. Textile prices had dropped 30 per cent from their recent highs and textile licenses, which had been commanding premiums of 150 per cent, now brought premiums of "only" 50 per cent. The Government's actions, and the publicity given them, had indeed had some effect. This respite was unfortunately destined to be of short duration only.

At about this time a rather interesting question arose on the pricing of commodities by the Civil Supplies Management Board. Since most imported commodities were selling in the market place at substantial markups over C.I.F. prices and the Civil Supplies Board was selling comparable goods at far lower prices, there was naturally a considerable run on Civil Supplies items at their retail outlets and at the consumer cooperatives which acted as major distributors for them. Civil Supplies met this problem by rationing the quantities which one purchaser could buy at a given time. There was no doubt, however, that the commodities so purchased were being resold at far

11. Approximately half of the cotton so purchased was to be used to pay third countries for processing the remaining cotton into textiles which would be imported into Burma.

12. Attempts to implement this decision bogged down in the following months for a variety of reasons to be described later.

Table 24

CONSUMER PRICE INDEX AND VALUE OF IMPORTS,
1953–54, 1954–55 AND 1955–56

| | | 1954–55 | | 1955–56 | Percentage Change | |
	1953–54	March	Sept.	March	1953–54 to 1954–55	March 1955 to March 1956
Consumer price index (1941 = 100):						
Total	305	284	326	313	+ 6.8	+10.2
Clothing	340	330	527	585	+55.0	+77.3
Food, drink, edible oils	344	305	355	328	+ 3.1	+ 7.5

| | | | 1955–56 1st Half (Annual Rate) | Percentage Change | |
	1953–54	1954–55		1953–54 to 1954–55	1953–54 to 1955–56
Imports in K crores:					
Total	94.7	90.6	83.0	— 4.3	—12.4
Consumer goods	70.5	62.1	53.6	—11.9	—24.0
Textiles	17.8	12.4	8.6	—30.3	—51.7
Foods and provisions	16.2	16.9	11.4	+ 4.3	—29.6

Sources: Quarterly Bulletin of Statistics, Supt., Govt. Printing and Stationery, Rangoon, Second Quarter 1956, p. 91, and First Quarter 1958, p. 135; *Economic Survey of Burma 1957,* Table 29, p. 39.

Note: The 1941 = 100 index is shown here because it was the one used at the time. The index was changed twice thereafter, first to a 1952 base, and then to a 1958 base.

higher prices in the bazaars. To recapture these windfall profits which were bound to persist so long as goods remained in short supply, and for fiscal reasons, the economic consultants recommended that Civil Supplies prices for the less essential commodities be adjusted upward to a point moderately below prevailing market prices. While this idea had some appeal to the Government, decision on it was postponed until after the general elections.

The general position at the end of March 1956 with respect to consumer goods prices and imports is shown in Table 24.[13] The consumer price index showed a total increase of 10.2 per cent from March 1955 to March 1956, with increases of 77.3 per cent for clothing and of 7.5 per cent for food, drink and edible oils. As has previously been observed, this index for a workers' family in Rangoon — the only consumer price index then available — reflects the prices of imported goods adequately only in its clothing component. The data on consumer goods imports explain the increases in considerable degree.

13. Citation of March 1956 data at this point should not be taken to mean that the data were available shortly after the end of that month. They were obtained under emergency pressure only toward the end of May.

From 1953–54 to 1954–55 consumer goods imports declined 11.9 per cent, with textiles imports dropping 30.3 per cent. From 1953–54 to the first half of 1955–56 (annual rate) consumer goods imports declined 24 per cent, with textiles imports declining 51.7 per cent and food and provisions 29.6 per cent.

The price effect of the decline in imports was compounded by increases in the privately held money supply. Each additional crore of planned imports would have meant the surrender of 1 crore of domestic currency for the purchase of foreign exchange. Conversely, each lag of 1 crore in the volume of private imports meant that much more domestic currency in circulation. From March 1955 to March 1956 the privately held money supply increased from K 101 crores to K 138 crores, or about 37 per cent. At the same time foreign exchange reserves had increased from 51.6 crores at the end of the fiscal year 1954–55 to 71 crores by the end of March 1956. A little more than one third of this increase was accounted for by the new reserves obtained by the March draw from the International Monetary Fund. The remainder represented an increase neither planned for nor desired. It had accrued largely as a result of lags in the planned import program.

It may be useful at this point to mention briefly a number of other developments of economic significance which occurred during the January–March 1956 period. The so-called Three-Year Plan for the period beginning 1956–57 was finalized and presented to the Economic and Social Board. The basic idea was to add a new third year to the forward schedules each time the first year went into implementation, and thus to have a continuously revolving, near-term, realistic plan. Predicated on a conservative outlook for rice export proceeds of some K 75 crores per year, the plan envisaged that only some K 25 crores of foreign exchange per year would be available for capital expenditures, and called for a maximum capital program of some K 45 to K 50 crores per year.[14] It worked out suggested allocations within these totals for the major agencies and projects. The industry, electric power, transportation and social programs — being the largest — were of necessity the hardest hit. The Three-Year Plan, however, never received formal approval by the Government. Two factors were chiefly responsible for its still birth. The first was the progress being made in the mobilization of foreign resources, which modified the resource picture even as the Three-Year Plan was in its final stages. The second was that the Prime Minister was dissatisfied with the austere nature of the Three-Year Plan, which provided no funds for the new Rangoon hospital and other projects to which he was attached, and had begun to think of a new four-year plan consistent with the emerging resource pattern which would have a life span comparable to the period between general elections.

14. So great was the emphasis placed on foreign exchange in the program's formulation that no analysis was made at the time of its domestic currency implications.

The Three-Year Plan did, however, serve a number of useful purposes. It probed many weak spots in the capital program. It established more clearly the facts about commitments already entered into by the operating agencies and the degree of flexibility which remained for adjusting and re-phasing the program. It helped the operating agencies to understand the programing process better and to improve their programs, and it provided a better analysis of the foreign exchange requirements of the long-term capital program than had been available before. Finally, it indicated to the World Bank that Burma was serious about adjusting her capital expenditures to her resources, and was undoubtedly an important factor in the Bank's decision not long after to extend two important loans.

During these months the report of the Land and Agricultural Planning Commission, organized more than a year before, was nearing completion. The Commission, composed of a number of capable Burmese officials and assisted by the economic consultants and a number of other foreign specialists, was engaged in a massive effort to bring together all the pertinent facts bearing on Burma's agriculture and to develop major policies and programs. Undoubtedly its most important contribution was the reaffirmation of the previously accepted goal of restoring rice production and exports to their pre-war level. The severe declines in rice export prices since this goal was accepted by the Pyidawtha Conference had shaken the Government's confidence in its feasibility, and certain influential ministers had even suggested that Burma should perhaps seek to curtail her production of paddy in favor of other commodities. The L.A.P.C. report helped to counteract such sentiments.

Perhaps the most important of the non-price developments during this period were those on the foreign loan front. Sometime in January, even before the conclusion of the P.L. 480 agreement, talk of a U. S. development loan to Burma had been revived, first with the U. S. Embassy and later with Howard Jones and Kenneth Young of the State Department in the course of their separate visits to Burma.[15] These discussions covered three possibilities — the future use of U. S. kyat proceeds from P.L. 480 sales for domestic currency development loans; the exchange of some 10,000 tons of Burmese rice for the services of U. S. technicians; and a new dollar development loan. The figure mentioned by the Burmese for a new dollar development loan was $150 million. This, it was held, would make possible an increase in capital expenditures, for the remainder of the long-term program period, from the annual level of K 50 crores, which it then appeared Burma could finance, to the annual level of some K 70 crores she desired. These discussions contributed to positive results in the following months. Furthermore, in March arrangements were concluded with the International Monetary Fund for a draw of $15 million.

15. Howard Jones was Deputy Assistant Secretary for Far Eastern Economic Affairs; Kenneth Young was Director, Division of Philippine and Southeast Asian Affairs.

This was the first time the I.M.F. had accorded any member country the privilege of a draw equal to 100 per cent of quota.

Also of interest during this period was the negotiation of an agreement with Israel, with whom a barter agreement covering 10,000 tons of rice had been concluded in the closing months of 1955. The 1956 Israeli negotiating mission was headed by the dynamic Mr. David Hacohen, who had been Israel's first minister to Burma. The Israelis proposed a number of joint ventures to the Burmese. These included a highly imaginative and ambitious plan to put one million acres of land in the Shan States under wheat cultivation, the output to be purchased by Israel; a joint construction company, in which the Israeli partner would be the Solel Boneh; a joint shipping company; joint ventures in a rubber products plant and an oil paints and varnish factory; and various other ventures. After only a few weeks of negotiations, agreement was reached in principle on most of the proposals. The most notable exception was the joint shipping company, in connection with which the Burmese feared an awkward situation vis-à-vis Egypt over Suez Canal passage.

At about this time, word came from the World Bank that it was now ready to negotiate details of specific railway and port loans, and a mission was dispatched to Washington for this purpose. In March the U. S. Government made it known, at long last, that it was prepared to purchase 10,000 tons of Burmese rice to help meet emergency food shortages in East Pakistan. The proceeds of this purchase, amounting to approximately $1 million, would be used by Burma to procure the services of American technicians. This proposal was inadequate, and it came too late.

At the very end of March Mr. Mikoyan visited Burma. His visit continued and broadened the discussions carried on late in 1955 with Messrs. Khrushchev and Bulganin. The result was a four-year agreement with the U.S.S.R. for the annual sale, mostly on a barter basis, of 400,000 tons of rice. Taken in conjunction with other barter arrangements already concluded, this brought Burma's potential annual shipments on barter account to some 800,000 tons of rice — 50 per cent of the previous year's shipments. The earlier understanding that the U.S.S.R. would make Burma the gift of a technological institute now mushroomed suddenly to include six major projects — the technological institute, a hospital, a hotel, an industrial exposition hall and grounds, an agricultural exposition and grounds and a sports stadium complex. The "gift" agreement was of a vague and general kind. While Burma had volunteered to make "gifts" of rice in return, there was no indication whether these would be on a token or an equivalent value basis. No cost estimates of the Soviet "gifts" had been made. Further, it was not clear whether the Russian contribution would cover only the foreign exchange cost of these projects or the entire cost; nor was it specified when Burma would pay in rice for these "gifts."

The first weeks of the third quarter of the fiscal year (beginning April 1956) constituted almost a hiatus in the supervision and control process. The ministers were almost completely preoccupied with the general elections. U Tin Maung, the Executive Secretary of the Economic and Social Board, U Kyaw Nyun, the Secretary of the Ministry of Finance and Revenue, and Dr. Tun Thin, the Director of the Central Statistical and Economics Department, were in Washington for the World Bank negotiations. U Mo Myit, Secretary of the Ministry of National Planning, had called up all the operating agencies of the Government pursuant to new instructions from Prime Minister U Nu, and requested them to submit once again revised requests for the new four-year program which was to be coterminous with the life of the new government.

With the United States P.L. 480 agreement, the International Monetary Fund draw, the India loan arrangement and an indeterminate but substantial Soviet credit for a number of major projects, the resource picture had been substantially improved. On top of this, and spurred no doubt by the gift exchange arrangement with the U.S.S.R., the U. S. Government now offered to provide an initial development loan of $25 million and to lend to Burma the domestic currencies which would accrue to the United States from the P.L. 480 sales agreement. The Prime Minister, therefore, instructed the agencies to submit their capital program requests for the next four years on the basis of what they believed was really needed, rather than in the light of a restrictive resource pattern such as had been imposed on them in the development of the stillborn Three-Year Plan. With the Ministry of National Planning thus occupied and other key administrators away, there was little action on the price front. One special problem, however, must be described.

Under the terms of the P.L. 480 agreement with the United States, some $17.5 million worth of U. S. cotton was to be sold to Burma for domestic currency. This was designed to provide imports of cotton textiles in equivalent value to Burma; that is, Burma would make arrangements with third countries to process roughly half the cotton provided by the United States, and pay for the processing with the remainder of the cotton. Negotiation of the P.L. 480 agreement itself had taken more than four months after agreement had been reached in principle the previous September.[16] While all this

---

16. This prolonged delay was due to a number of factors. The Burmese, quite understandably, were somewhat cautious in dealing with a completely new kind of arrangement, and numerous questions occurred to them during the course of the negotiations. The political implications of the arrangements were such that decision on the Burmese side had to take place at the cabinet level. Each time a question was raised — whether on modification of the commodity composition of the program, what was meant by the United States requirements to avoid disruption of normal international trade patterns or the use of private trade channels in procurement and distribution — it was taken up by the Burmese Embassy in Washington and referred back to Rangoon for decision. Perhaps all these questions could have been resolved in one short week had a U. S. mission with adequate authority come to Rangoon.

was going on, however, the Ministry of Trade Development, which was responsible for ultimate implementation of the agreement, took no action to arrive at preliminary understandings with the nations which were ultimately to process the U. S. surplus cotton. The decision had been made to arrange for the processing with four countries — Japan, India, the United Kingdom and West Germany. But negotiation of processing agreements began only after the U. S. agreement had been concluded, and the procedure was to negotiate with the processing countries seriatim. Once again, excessive caution on the part of officials resulted in prolonged delays in reaching agreements.

The general elections of 1956 were held in April. Because of insecurity in some parts of the country, they were not held simultaneously in all districts, and returns were somewhat slow in coming in. Even on the basis of early returns late in April, the results were keenly disappointing to the Government. While there was no doubt that the A.F.P.F.L. coalition would return a strong majority to the parliament, it seemed clear that the A.F.P.F.L. would get something less than half of the total vote cast and that the National United Front — the newly formed opposition coalition which included many strongly leftist elements — would win perhaps one third of the total vote and between 40 and 50 seats. This outcome was variously laid to terrorism on the part of the insurgents, financial aid from the Soviet and Chinese embassies, the public's irritation with higher prices, and a growing disaffection in the countryside because of the arrogant behavior of corrupt local A.F.P.F.L. party machines. The Government evidently gave some weight to all three of these explanations. Its initial response was to determine that topmost priority would have to be given henceforth to control of the insurrection and to action to contain and reduce prices. This view was further strengthened in May, when the final election returns confirmed the earlier ones. The consultants were once again asked to prepare a paper on what should be done.

It seemed that this time the Government really meant business, and the consultants exerted every effort to bring together the facts bearing on the case. As of the middle of May the latest available data on prices, imports, foreign exchange transactions and other relevant indicators were those for the previous November or December. The Central Statistical and Economics Department of the Ministry of National Planning was pressed to run special emergency tabulations to bring the necessary data through March.[17] Toward the end of May the consultants' paper was ready.[18]

17. This emergency merely highlighted once again a situation which had persisted throughout the planning and early implementation periods, in that current data required for planning, programing and management purposes were simply not readily available. The consultants used this occasion to request U Mo Myit, the Secretary of the M.N.P., to issue a directive to the C.S.E.D. requiring that organization to produce, no later than the 15th of the month following the end of each preceding month, a new internal Government publication called "Economic Indicators," which thereafter did much to improve the earlier statistical deficiency.

18. "A Note on Anti-Inflation Measures," Robert R. Nathan Associates, Inc., May 29, 1956.

At about this time Trade Minister U Raschid returned from India, where he had just concluded an important agreement for the sale of 2 million tons of rice over a five-year period.[19] The economic consultants' paper on methods of dealing with the inflation problem was then in process of duplication, and U Raschid was in substantial accord with their recommendations. He urged the Prime Minister to give them his immediate and personal attention. This led to a lengthy meeting with the Prime Minister and with U Kyaw Nyein on the evening of June 1, at which the recommended program was carefully reviewed.

The consultants' recommendations were not very different from those they had made almost four months before. This time, however, they put more stress on short-term action on the supply side of the problem, since the soon-to-be-considered Four-Year-Plan would deal with the longer-term demand side. The May recommendations also went further than those of February in that they urged the liquidation of all commodity monopolies held by Civil Supplies, the addition of a number of essential short supply items to the O.G.L. list, and early action on 1956–57 licensing and procurement. They also urged Burma to seek free transfer of credits from any country in the Soviet bloc to any other country in it.[20]

The Prime Minister, once he had assured himself that the country could afford the foreign exchange drain which might be involved in the implementation of these measures, was prepared to approve them *in toto*. U Kyaw Nyein, however, objected quite strenuously to two of the recommendations — termination of Civil Supplies monopolies over essential commodities and inclusion on the O.G.L. list of some of the items then handled by Civil Supplies on a monopoly basis. He particularly objected to such treatment for tinned milk and cotton yarn. It was quite clear that the Civil Supplies monopoly was important in U Kyaw Nyein's thinking in two primary respects — one, as a device for squeezing Indians, Chinese, Pakistanis and other foreigners out of the import and distribution trade and, two, as a technique for broadening socialization of the economy. It was decided that tinned milk, cotton yarn and possibly one or two other items should be retained as Civil Supplies monopolies, and that Civil Supplies procurement and distribution of these items should be augmented. Other Civil Supplies monopolies would be terminated, and the items transferred to the O.G.L. list.

The Prime Minister decided to act swiftly on these matters. The entire

---

19. India would take 300,000 tons in 1956, 500,000 tons in 1957 and again in 1958, and 350,000 tons in 1959 and again in 1960. The price would be £34 for 1956, £33 for 1957 and £32 for 1958. Prices for 1959 and 1960 were left open for future negotiation.

20. Credits established in People's China and Czechoslovakia had proved to be readily usable. In the case of other countries, particularly the Soviet Union, the reverse was true. The sale of rice to the U.S.S.R., designed to help Burma, had resulted in effect in the extension of a no-interest $20 million credit to the Soviet Union.

program would be placed before the Executive Committee of the A.F.P.F.L. the following day and before the Cabinet on June 4. Full publicity on the anti-inflation program was to be released to the press immediately following the Cabinet's decision. Finally, the Prime Minister decided to assign responsibility for implementing the decisions to a new Executive Subcommittee for the Implementation of Anti-Inflation Measures.[21]

The newspapers of June 5 featured the story of the Government's new program to contain and reduce prices. Particularly stressed were the decisions to speed up the issue of import licenses, to expedite actual imports, to conclude cotton-textile processing arrangements required by the P.L. 480 program, to terminate Civil Supplies monopolies on many essential consumer goods, to place under the Open General License a number of essential commodities whose prices had risen sharply in recent months and to take timely action to insure a large volume of imports for private use in 1956–57. It was also announced that a high-powered committee had been constituted to carry out this program.

The new Executive Subcommittee did indeed get to work at once. It moved swiftly to expedite cotton textile-processing arrangements with Japan, the United Kingdom and India. Whereas in the four months since the conclusion of the P.L. 480 agreement with the United States only one processing agreement — that with West Germany — had been concluded, the three remaining agreements were negotiated within the space of a few short weeks. A review of the Civil Supplies monopoly position resulted in agreement at the committee level that the Board's import and distribution monopolies on low-priced textiles, cement, fishing nets and twine, tires and tubes, asbestos and C.G.I. sheets and wire nails should be terminated, and that only monopolies on sugar, condensed milk, infant foods and cotton and silk yarns should be retained for the time being. These recommendations were accepted by the Prime Minister. The Cabinet, however, approved only the termination of monopolies on asbestos sheets and on one grade of cotton textiles.[22]

21. Within recent weeks the Prime Minister, convinced by now of the need for improved performance by Government agencies engaged in economic activities, had set up still another committee, the Standing Committee for Supervision and Coordination. The six members of this committee were U Tin Maung, Executive Secretary of the Economic and Social Board; U Win Pe, the Cabinet Secretary; U Mo Myit, Secretary of the Ministry of National Planning; U Kyaw Nyun, Secretary of Finance and Revenue; U Chan Tha, Director of the much-feared Bureau of Special Investigation; and U Ba Khin, Director of Commercial Audit (and also Chairman of the State Agricultural Marketing Board). The duty of the S.C.S.C. would be to supervise the operations and insure the integrity and efficiency of the state-owned boards and corporations. With the exception of U Chan Tha, committee members — in addition to their other duties — were already variously heavily engaged in the Committee of Experts to the Economic and Social Board, the Foreign Exchange Control Committee and various other *ad hoc* committees. These six civil servants, together with the chief economic consultant, were now to compose the executive anti-inflation subcommittee.

22. The economic consultants had of course argued vigorously for the termination of the Civil Supplies monopoly on all items. The basic argument put forward on the other side was that the

The consultants had meanwhile come up — renewing U Raschid's earlier intention — with the recommendation that the list of registered importers should be severely "vetted" or reduced. This proposal was approved, and referred to the Ministry of Trade Development for action. Progress was also made on other fronts. The Government's efforts to achieve an understanding that credits it had established anywhere within the Sino-Soviet bloc could be used anywhere else within that bloc were partially successful. The U.S.S.R. agreed that K 5 crores of the credits to Burma's account in the U.S.S.R. might be used in Czechoslovakia.[23] Preliminary action was taken towards a large import program for 1956–57. Arrangements were made to schedule import license issue for 1956–57 to preclude delays in implementing the larger program. And it was decided to decentralize Government procurement so as to permit the operating agencies responsible for carrying out the capital program to procure directly all their requirements except common user items, responsibility for which would remain with the Ministry of Supply.[24]

One very important obstacle to the effectiveness of the anti-inflation program had developed at its very inception. A key element was the decision to add to the Open General License list a number of items in short supply whose prices had sky-rocketed. These included dried fish and prawns, onions, cocoanut oil, tires and tubes, machinery and selected building materials. The Government's press release of June 5 had indeed declared that such action would be taken. This news naturally was distressing to the Burmese traders, who enjoyed priority privileges in the issue of import licenses and would lose it were these commodities placed under Open General License. The traders now argued that the move would permit Indian and Pakistani traders to use the imports as an instrument for capital flight, and thus result in a rapid rundown of the foreign exchange reserves.[25]

These objections of the Burmese trading community, coinciding as they did with the Government's long-established Burmanization policy and its fear and suspicion of the alien traders, were responsible for the introduction

---

Civil Supplies Board could not survive without some monopoly privileges. Since the sole argument for the entire Civil Supplies operation was that it would insure the supply of essential commodities to consumers at lower prices than would be the case with private trade, this position was completely without logic.

23. Several attempts to arrange for the utilization of Burma's U.S.S.R. credits in People's China met with no success.

24. Centralized procurement had been put into effect some time before on the insistence of Prime Minister U Nu in order to minimize opportunities for graft and corruption. As in the case of the too suddenly enlarged procurement and distribution program of the Civil Supplies Management Board, the Central Purchasing Board had not been able to discharge this expanded responsibility adequately. Program implementation, already highly inefficient, was further affected by the poor flow of supplies.

25. It was widely believed that alien traders evaded foreign exchange controls on remittances and capital transfers by collusive underpricing of exports and over-invoicing of imports. Such collusion with overseas associates was undoubtedly practiced, but notions of the extent of the practice were probably highly exaggerated.

of a radical innovation in the structure of the import trade. The Government was, of course, unwilling to leave matters as they had been up to that time; however, it was equally unwilling to press forward with its earlier decision to place the commodities concerned under Open General License. Going back to the National Day speech of Prime Minister U Nu in December 1953 and the Fourth Resolution of the Economic and Social Board, the Government determined to enter into joint venture corporations with the Burmese traders and to give these corporations a monopoly on the importation of the goods in question. This decision was made on the evening of June 12[26] at a meeting with representatives of the Burmese trading community and their chambers of commerce, over the strong protests of the economic consultants.

The hasty decision to form joint venture trading companies for the importation of textiles (other than those grades reserved to the Civil Supplies Board), foods and provisions (including dried fish and prawns and edible oils), hardware and selected building materials items, etc., had not been thought through. In the ensuing weeks it was determined that each of the new trading corporations would be assigned responsibility for two or more commodities, so that at least a modicum of competition could be maintained between them; that their capital would be equally provided by the Government and the private partners; that the amount of capital any single individual or firm could subscribe to any of the new trading corporations would be limited; and that distributors and retailers would be permitted to subscribe.

These determinations did little to counteract the basic weakness of the original decision. It was poor policy to establish additional monopolies in the import and distribution of scarce commodities. It was even worse policy to share these new import monopolies with private individuals and firms. On top of this, the Government made the serious mistake of thinking that it would be possible to organize the new joint venture trading corporations within the space of a few short weeks and to have them assume responsibility for the imports assigned to them forthwith. In fact, it was many months before the first of the joint venture trading corporations came into being, and many weeks after that before it was ready to operate. In the meantime the Government issued no licenses to other traders for importation of the goods, with the result that supply deficiencies and rising prices persisted in these fields well into the following fiscal year.

The anti-inflation subcommittee had meanwhile continued its efforts to control inflation but they had become increasingly desultory, and had met with something less than success. This was not surprising. All through this period the key members of the subcommittee had been engaged also in de-

26. A week earlier Prime Minister U Nu had declared his intention to resign from office for a period of eight months, in order to devote himself to correcting the organizational weaknesses and internal abuses which had developed in the A.F.P.F.L. He had, earlier on the day of the meeting, formally turned the reins of government over to U Ba Swe.

velopments in connection with the new Four-Year Plan, in the budget review and capital program for 1956–57, in matters concerned with the U. S. and other loans, and in their foreign exchange control duties, as well as in their individual ministerial or other organizational duties. Furthermore, although the subcommittee had been given a nominally executive character, it could in fact make no important decisions on its own and had to await opportunities to present its views to the political leaders for approval. Finally, the subcommittee could not of course look continuously over the shoulders of the officials in the Ministry of Trade Development, the Civil Supplies Management Board and other agencies to insure that they were carrying out the policies and measures efficiently and in all respects. For example, the committee declined to force upon reluctant Trade Ministry officials a simplified import license issue procedure devised by the economic consultants. It did, however, take action when the Civil Supplies Board, declining to procure textiles in the U.S.S.R. because of the inferior quality, limited choice and high prices, refused at the same time to permit these textiles to be allocated to private importers.

Toward the end of September, which marked also the end of the fiscal year 1955–56, the economic consultants, pointing to this disappointing progress, recommended that U Kyaw Nyein, who held by now the title of Deputy Prime Minister for National Economy, be designated Chairman of the Executive Subcommittee to give greater authority to the committee and to supervise implementation of its decisions. This recommendation was approved. It is worth noting that the implementation of anti-inflation measures was least effective with respect to the proposed reduction in the excessive number of registered importers. While the Ministry of Trade Development officials concerned had given assurances that the "vetting" process would be completed by a special board set up for the purpose within some three months, virtually no action had been taken by the end of the fiscal year. Indeed, no substantial action along this line was taken during the remaining life of the A.F.P.F.L. Government, which endured until September 1958.

It is time now to pick up the threads of other important economic developments, previously described up to March–April of 1956. Sometime in May the Government accepted the March offer of the U. S. Government to pay $1.1 million for 10,000 tons of Burmese rice to relieve distress in East Pakistan, the money to be used to engage the services of American technicians, and the agreement was concluded shortly thereafter. Also in May, the World Bank granted two long-awaited development loans, a total of $19.35 million ($14 million to the port of Rangoon and the balance of $5.35 million to the Burma Railways). The strength shown by the opposition in the general elections had made it extremely difficult, however, for the Burmese Government to respond positively to the U. S. $25 million April development loan offer, particularly because of the restrictions which then existing U. S. legislation (the so-called "Battle Act" amendment) would impose on Burma's economic relations with the Soviet bloc countries. Prime Minister U Nu was nevertheless desirous of accepting a U. S. development loan, if this could be done in a manner consistent with Burma's position of neutrality and would not tend to create further irritations in Burmese-U. S. relations. This interest was communicated to the United States at the highest level. The "Battle Act" restrictions were of course unacceptable; Burma would not undertake to restrict her freedom of action vis-à-vis the Soviet bloc nations. If, however, the United States would still be willing to grant the loan, and any future action on Burma's part should make it necessary for the United States to terminate the loan, Burma would understand the necessity and would not regard the termination as an unfriendly act.[27]

The highly important five-year, two-million-ton rice sales agreement with India has already been mentioned. Still another May development was the arrival at Rangoon port of massive shipments of cement from the Soviet Union, which brought the port operations almost to a standstill. On one of his several procurement missions Bo Min Gaung had placed orders for some 100,000 tons of cement in the Soviet Union, apparently because cement was the only commodity available in quantity for early shipment, and because it was desired to utilize the credits which were piling up to Burma's account in the Soviet Union. The inexperienced Burmese had unfortunately given no thought to the problem of scheduling deliveries, and the Soviets apparently thought they were meeting their customer's wishes by shipping all the cement off as quickly as possible. On its arrival — unhappily coincident with the onset of the monsoon — storage facilities were simply not available, and distribution plans had not been worked out so that it could rapidly be transported away from the docks. Ultimately, a sizable portion of the shipment spoiled in the rains.

Other experiences with the barter countries, not quite as dramatic, were leading Burma to take an increasingly dim view of further rice sales on open account to Soviet bloc countries. Trade Minister U Raschid confirmed the

27. The Prime Minister was indeed disposed to view generously the actions of the United States, even when these directly affected Burma's economic interests. Such actions were primarily U. S. disposal of surplus wheat and rice to Asian countries under the same P.L. 480 arrangements as had been made available to Burma with respect to cotton. Undoubtedly, U. S. disposal of rice and wheat to India, Pakistan, Indonesia and other countries in the region did affect Burma's commercial rice marketings adversely during the previous years. Yet, when an informal inquiry was made at about this time by the U. S. Embassy about Burma's attitude toward a then contemplated U. S. P.L. 480 disposal of rice to Indonesia, the reaction of the Prime Minister was that Burma had no wish to express an opinion or to intervene. His reasoning — not communicated — was that Burma should not interfere in any action which might bring food to the mouths of the hungry peoples of Asia; that the United States was perfectly capable of forming an adequate judgment on such transactions; and that in any event any opinion expressed by Burma might not seriously influence any decision made by the United States.

complaints of the Burmese importing community about poor availabilities and higher prices. And Prime Minister U Nu made a public statement in which he declared that Burma's decided preference was of course for cash sales, and that sales on barter account had been made only as a result of unhappy necessity. In fact, on the eve of his departure for India to negotiate the long-term rice sales agreement, U Raschid had already ordered the State Agricultural Marketing Board to go slow on any further barter account sales. This, however, did not affect the conclusion of sales agreements with Hungary and Bulgaria for 50,000 and 20,000 tons respectively, which had been under negotiation for some time.[28]

Prime Minister U Nu's resignation from office in June did not signal any radical changes in Government policy or program. Indeed, the policy statement issued shortly after his resignation by U Ba Swe's new Government had been prepared at U Nu's direction and approved by him. In broad, the Government now declared that its major objectives would be to reduce the civil insurrection, maintain the established policy of neutralism in international affairs, and strive to reduce domestic price levels. In pursuit of this last objective it would shun new development projects and trim capital expenditures to the level of available resources.

Early in July the U. S. Government responded to the communication regarding its $25 million loan offer and in effect eliminated "Battle Act" restrictions. Other questions remained, particularly those concerning requirements imposed in the Mutual Security Act legislation for audit and end use checks and controls by U. S. representatives. These questions were satisfactorily settled, and some time in September the Government indicated to the United States its acceptance of the $25 million loan offer.[29]

Preparation of the Four-Year Plan requested by the then Prime Minister U Nu the preceding April had continued throughout the remainder of the fiscal year. In its later stages, this work had coincided and been coordinated with the 1956–57 budget review. The Four-Year Plan as now prepared took into account the added foreign resources already mobilized and in process of mobilization. The prospect of continued substantial deficits on the domestic currency side, however, had prevented any substantial increase in the prospective capital program above the level of K 45 crores earlier incorporated in the Three-Year Plan. The Four-Year Plan now proposed average capital expenditures through 1959–60 of about K 50 crores per year. Even this modest

28. The economic consultants had submitted notes as early as March and April 1955 warning of the dangers inherent in the rice barter deals then being made, and had continued to criticize them thereafter. The improving outlook for selling rice to cash customers at lower prices now made it possible for them to point out that the continuation of already existing barter sales arrangements threatened to cut into potential cash sales and earnings. This put the matter in quite another light so far as the Burmese Government was concerned.

29. The agreement was not, however, formally signed until March 1957.

level, it was held, would require not only continued reliance on foreign resources, but also major efforts to increase domestic resources through vigorous action on the tax front and greater efficiency in the public enterprises. The plan gave increased emphasis to agriculture, timber and mining. Significantly, it provided for a large-scale land reclamation program to restore some two million acres of land to paddy cultivation, and for much needed improvement of rice storage facilities.

The operating agencies had submitted requests for a capital program of some K 85 crores in 1956–57. Their budget demands were reviewed by the work-horse Committee of Experts under the chairmanship of the new Deputy Prime Minister for National Economy, U Kyaw Nyein. This review resulted in a proposed 1956–57 capital program of K 65 crores.[30]

The economic consultants were convinced that the recommended program for 1956–57 was considerably in excess of prospective resources and that, if approved, it would contribute substantially to continued inflationary pressures in the following fiscal year. They urged, therefore, that K 55 crores be established as the maximum permissible capital program for the following year and again affirmed that even such a reduced program would require vigorous governmental action on the tax front and equally vigorous action to reduce inefficiency in governmental operations. These views were accepted by the Government, and the capital program finally approved was limited to K 56.5 crores.[31] Several of the tax measures recommended by the consultants were also adopted, as was the recommendation of a record-breaking program of imports for private use, K 90 crores as compared with the K 75 crores

30. The year 1955–56 had been a disappointing one to U Kyaw Nyein insofar as his plans for industrial development were concerned. The Three-Year Plan had severely slashed funds for the industries sector. The World Bank had indicated that it would not consider any applications for industrial loans for enterprises which were to be state owned and operated. Finally, the Four-Year Plan deferred funds for new industrial projects until after 1956–57. Although the new Government's policy statement had been explicit in stating that new projects would not be undertaken, U Kyaw Nyein was not reconciled to such an outcome. He was thinking in terms of expanding the small 20,000-ton steel mill then under way to perhaps 200,000 or 300,000 tons capacity, so as to achieve economies of scale. He was thinking also, *inter alia,* of seven additional cotton textile mills which would give Burma a self-sufficiency in these goods, and of a large pulp and paper plant, a large fertilizer factory and a large truck and tractor assembly plant. The K 65 crores capital program for 1956–57 approved by him for submission to the Economic and Social Board did not make provision for any of these projects. It did provide, however, for a start toward doubling the capacity of the existing 20,000-spindle textile mill and for tripling the capacity of the existing 60,000-ton cement factory. And the plan provided, in later years, for a further sizable expansion in textile plant capacity, for a fertilizer plant and for joint ventures in tire and tube, glass, paint and ceramic factories.

31. In acting on the capital program for 1956–57, the Economic and Social Board made no decision with respect to the remaining three years of the draft Four-Year Plan. It was U Raschid who once again voiced basic dissatisfaction with the nature of the long-term plans. The Four-Year Plan as presented was indeed, as he stated, a program for capital expenditures rather than a plan, even though it was set in a resource, fiscal and policy framework. The central and sector plan objectives posited in the Comprehensive Plan of 1953 had not been modified in the light of changed circumstances. The Board now requested that the Four-Year Plan be re-worked to conform to the objections raised.

originally approved for 1955–56. Since it was anticipated that there would be a substantial carry-over of imports originally programed for 1955–56 into 1956–57, the decision to approve additional imports was bound to result in a tremendous wave of imports for private use in the following year, and it was confidently expected that this would finally break the back of the inflation which had been mounting since the early months of 1955. This decision was supported by the increase of some K 23 crores in the foreign exchange reserves during the course of 1955–56.

One more battle remained to be fought in connection with the 1956–57 program. U Ba San, the Trade Ministry Secretary, proposed to ship some 550,000 tons of rice to the barter countries. Demonstrating that, because of shipping limitations, so large a volume of barter shipments would cut severely into the volume of potential cash sales and shipments, the consultants opposed the proposed schedules, and they were fortunately successful in having them cut substantially. They were less successful when they advocated that the Government seek to conclude a three-year P.L. 480 agreement with the United States, as India had just done. The long delay in concluding and implementing Burma's first P.L. 480 agreement suggested that it was not too soon to commence negotiations, if a hiatus in the flow of P.L. 480 supplies was to be prevented in the future. The Government, it seemed, could not

Table 25

IMPORTS BY TYPE OF COMMODITY,
1953–54, 1954–55 AND 1955–56

(K Crores)

	1953–54	1954–55	1955–56 Total	1955–56 1st Half	Percentage Change 1953–54 to 1955–56
Total imports	94.7	90.6	87.2	41.5	− 7.9
Consumer goods	70.5	62.1	58.6	26.8	−16.9
Food, drink, edible oils	16.2	16.9	10.1	5.7	−37.7
Textiles	17.8	12.4	12.0	4.3	−32.6
Medicines	2.1	2.8	4.5	2.4	+114.3
Fuel	3.5	4.1	5.7	2.4	+62.9
Raw and semi-processed materials	8.1	6.9	8.7	3.9	+ 7.4
Others (including tires and tubes)	22.7	19.0	17.7	8.2	−22.0
Capital goods	24.2	28.5	28.6	14.7	+18.2
Building materials	11.2	11.1	8.7	4.4	−22.3
Machinery, etc.	7.3	7.9	11.9	6.4	+63.0
Private autos	1.2	.8	.4	.1	−66.7
Bicycles and parts	.9	.7	.4	.2	−55.6
Other transport equipment	2.6	6.6	5.6	2.9	+115.4
Others	1.0	1.4	1.5	.6	+50.0

Source: Economic Survey of Burma 1957, Table 29, p. 39.

Table 26

IMPORTS BY MAJOR CATEGORY AND STRUCTURE OF PAYMENTS,
1953–54, 1954–55 AND 1955–56

(*K Crores*)

	1953–54	1954–55	1955–56	Percentage Change 1953–54 to 1955–56
A. Total imports	94.7	90.6	87.2	— 7.9
Consumer goods	70.5	62.1	58.6	—16.9
Capital goods	24.2	28.5	28.6	+18.2
Private	78.0	68.0	49.0	—37.2
O.G.L.	51.0	45.4	23.8	—52.3
B. Payments for imports	113.1	96.1	82.8	—26.9
Private imports	81.1	69.4	45.8	—43.5
Government imports	32.0	26.7	37.0	+15.6

Source: Economic Survey of Burma 1957, Tables 29 (for customs data, part A of table) and 30 (for payments data, part B of table).

Note: The sizable discrepancy between customs and payments figures for imports in 1953–54 is due almost entirely to the failure of Customs to record almost half of the volume of Government imports. Customs data for private imports differ very little from payments data for the same category. The differences between customs and payments data in 1954–55 and 1955–56 are not significant, since they offset each other when the two years are combined, showing that the difference in 1954–55 must have reflected advance payments in that year.

Table 27

CONSUMER PRICE INDEX FOR A WORKER'S FAMILY IN RANGOON,
1953–54, 1954–55 AND 1955–56

	Total	Clothing	Food, Drink, Edible Oils
Index (1941 = 100)			
1953–54	305	340	344
1954–55: Mar.	284	330	305
Sept.	326	527	355
1955–56: Mar.	313	585	328
Sept.	343	695	363
Percentage Increase			
1953–54 to 1955–56	12.5	104.4	5.5
1953–54 to 1954–55	6.8	55.0	3.1
1954–55 to 1955–56	5.3	31.9	2.3
Mar. 1955 to Sept. 1956	20.8	110.6	19.0
Mar. 1955 to Sept. 1955	14.7	59.7	18.0
Mar. 1955 to Mar. 1956	10.2	77.3	7.5

Source: Quarterly Bulletin of Statistics, Supt., Govt. Printing and Stationery, Rangoon, Second Quarter 1956, Table IX(5), p. 91; First Quarter 1958, Table X(5), p. 135.

Note: See note to Table 24.

Table 28

INTERIM CONSUMER PRICE INDEX FOR LOW-INCOME HOUSEHOLDS IN
RANGOON (REVISED APRIL 1958), SELECTED COMPONENTS,
1953 THROUGH 1958-59

(1952 = 100)

| | | Foods and Beverages | | | |
	Total	Total	Oils and Fats	Fish and Fish Products	Clothing
1953	102.3	101.2	91.7	97.5	104.1
1954	99.2	94.1	98.9	91.1	110.6
1954–55					
March	100.3	94.0	81.3	85.6	114.6
June	103.6	98.0	82.0	96.4	121.1
Sept.	108.3	106.2	90.2	106.9	125.9
1955–56					
Dec.	108.8	106.5	86.7	99.4	133.9
March	112.3	105.7	80.5	112.8	160.2
June	121.0	118.2	101.9	135.2	163.5
Sept.	116.0	110.3	89.7	120.9	164.1
1956–57					
Dec.	115.9	110.3	105.8	106.6	165.8
March	114.9	110.3	119.0	106.9	160.9
June	120.8	122.9	115.8	149.2	138.4
Sept.	116.9	120.7	127.3	143.2	111.2
1957–58					
Dec.	110.0	112.8	108.7	111.7	107.6
March	109.6	109.9	102.1	115.5	108.9
June	116.2	118.1	111.8	136.2	115.8
Sept.	115.4	117.8	—	—	115.8
1958–59					
Dec.	102.1	98.4	98.3	94.7	112.6
March	96.5	91.7	—	—	103.6

Sources: Interim Consumer Price Index, Central Statistical and Economics Department, Rangoon, April 1958; and *Selected Economic Indicators,* various issues.

Note: The interim index is shown here because quarterly data for 1954–55, 1955–56 and 1956–57 are not available in the later index. The commodity categories shown are the most significant. Most other categories show little change through the period.

bring itself to regard this matter as urgent, and deferred action until it was too late.

The import and price story for 1955–56 may be read, in perspective, in Tables 25–27.

Commodity imports as a whole decreased only in minor proportion over the two years 1953–54 to 1955–56. Within that declining total, however, capital goods imports rose substantially and consumer goods imports declined by about one sixth. In the consumer goods category, the brunt of the decline was shared by two major groups — textiles and food, drink and edible oil items —

Table 29

CONSUMER PRICE INDEXES IN RANGOON, 1941–1960

	1941 = 100	1952 = 100	1958 = 100
1941	100		29.6
1951	365		100.8
1952	352	100.0	94.8
1953	340	102.3	92.5
1954	330	99.2	88.3
1955	326	104.4	91.8
1956	359	115.2	97.9
1957		115.6	103.9
1958		112.4	100.0
1959			88.9
Nov. 1960			100.7

Sources: Selected Economic Indicators; The Interim Consumer Price Index; and *A New Consumer Price Index in Rangoon,* all from Central Statistical and Economics Department, Rangoon.

Note: The 1941 index was for a Burmese worker's family; the interim index based on 1952 was introduced in April 1958 for low-income families; and the latest index, 1958 = 100, was introduced in 1959 for low- and middle-income families with monthly incomes up to K 400.

each of which declined by one third or more. And in the case of textiles, the rate of imports for the first half of 1955–56 represented a decline of more than 50 per cent from the 1953–54 rate. Within the total increase in capital goods imports, there was a decline of more than one fifth in the import of building materials.

The changes in the structure of imports shown in Table 26 are equally significant. While total imports declined less than 8 per cent, private imports declined by about two fifths, and imports under Open General License — which may be equated with imports by relatively more experienced traders — declined by more than half.

Finally, the cost-of-living index for low income groups in Rangoon, which reflects the increased prices of imported goods only in its clothing component, and at best only partly in its foods and beverage component, showed a total increase of one eighth over the two-year period, due almost entirely to a doubling of clothing prices. The increases from March 1955, when the Open General License system was first suspended and radically changed, were even larger. The March to September measurement, however, introduces a seasonal exaggeration into the measurement, particularly in the food component, and it is therefore not as significant as the end-year to end-year measurements. (The price perspective beyond this period is shown in Tables 28–29, in terms of improved indices subsequently developed and introduced.)

In broader terms, the gross domestic product increased by 3.2 per cent in 1955–56 in constant prices. The sectors accounting for the largest part of this increase were state marketing and agriculture. Rice exports increased from

1.63 to 1.93 million tons, with barter sales accounting for one quarter of the tonnage. Proceeds from rice export shipments rose from K 66 crores to K 88.9 crores, while the value of shipments rose only from K 84.5 crores to K 87.7 crores. This disparity reflected collection of payments deferred in the previous year. Proceeds from timber, minerals and other exports also rose, increasing the value of total exports from K 112 crores to K 117 crores. Imports data have already been cited. With a larger surplus on foreign trade account, the reported foreign exchange reserves rose by K 23 crores to K 74.6 crores. (It later transpired that approximately K 10 crores of this increase was an illusion due to delayed bookkeeping on accounts with barter countries.) Capital expenditures, under tight controls, declined sharply to K 48.3 crores from K 61 crores the previous year.

The fight against inflation did not end with formulation of the 1956–57 fiscal and import programs. It continued in the years that followed. But the emphasis was now to shift to other and even more basic problems. The foreign exchange crisis of 1954–55 and the inflation of 1955–56 raised fundamental questions of central fiscal responsibility, of development priorities and of better performance throughout the entire area of governmental activity, at all levels. It was these questions, and the attempts to deal with them, which were pervasive in 1956–57 and which will be described in the following chapter.

CHAPTER 13

The Fight for Central Responsibility, Program Priorities and Better Performance—1956-57

The fiscal year 1956–57 opened with a number of circumstances conducive to optimism. The capital program had been cut down to a reasonable size and fitted into a sound fiscal program. If implemented, this fiscal program would virtually balance the comprehensive budget of the public sector and, aided by a large volume of private imports, would halt further increases in the privately held money supply. The prospects were for an excellent rice crop which, at the slightly reduced price of £34 sterling per ton for S.M.S., would make it possible to sell most of the surplus to cash markets and reduce substantially the tonnages sold on barter account. A change in the hitherto inept management at the highly important Agricultural and Rural Development Corporation gave promise that progress soon would be made in expanding and balancing agricultural production. Prime Minister U Ba Swe, at a special meeting called for the purpose, urged all ministers, officials and agencies responsible for agricultural, minerals and timber production and exports to exert every effort to reach the targets set. The Government at long last took action to add a number of essential commodities, such as dried fish and prawns, tires and tubes, paper and selected toilet articles, to the O.G.L. list.

It also decided to treat applications for the import of industrial raw materials and machinery very liberally and to permit the Civil Supplies Board to buy as much cotton yarn as the market would absorb. The Soviet Union made arrangements for K 5 crores of relatively frozen credits to be utilized in Czechoslovakia.

Perhaps more important than any of these was the agreement expressed separately by the most important political leaders — U Nu, U Ba Swe and U Kyaw Nyein — with the policies urged by the economic consultants in the closing weeks of the fiscal year 1955-56. These had placed great emphasis on the need to improve public administration at all levels, through more delegation of authority and responsibility, improved executive direction of the Government-owned boards and corporations, autonomy for the commercial-type state enterprises, removal of the threat of B.S.I. criminal action for honest mistakes, and higher pay scales in the public service. They emphasized also that the added resources to be derived from greater efficiency should be supplemented by increased tax revenues, obtained primarily through improved administration and enforcement, but also through new tax measures; that the unsatisfactory flow of reparations should be expedited; that a vigorous program to expand paddy production was imperative; and, above all, that substantial progress in the further elimination of civil unrest in the countryside was needed, if general economic progress was to be assured.

Since such a program would make it possible for the Government to sustain an annual capital program in the amount of approximately K 50 crores for the next several years, the additional foreign resources already in view indicated that it was now possible to raise the investment targets above this level. The Indian loan of K 20 crores had not yet been used to any degree. The United States loan of $25 million had now been offered on terms acceptable to Burma, and only the final arrangements remained to be made. There seemed good reason to expect that a three-year P.L. 480 arrangement might be concluded in the value of approximately K 30 crores. A new medium-term credit of some K 8 crores had just been arranged with West Germany. All these, in combination with the Soviet gift arrangement, suggested that average capital expenditures for 1957-58, 1958-59 and 1959-60 might be raised from about K 50 crores to about K 65 crores.

The consultants advised the Government that consideration could now be given to such an enlarged capital program, provided satisfactory progress in paddy expansion was achieved during the fiscal year 1956-57, boards and corporations became more efficient, tax enforcement and revenue measures were implemented effectively and there was continued action on the anti-inflation front. Revision of the investment program was undertaken on this basis.

As the months went by, however, these hopes were dissipated. The dry season brought no significant advances on the security front. Apart from the contribution made by good weather to paddy production, primary production languished. This was especially apparent in the Tenasserim area — so important for tin and tungsten production — where a determined security effort on the part of the Government could have made a substantial contribution to increased mineral output. No effective action was taken to increase the efficiency of the Government-owned boards and corporations. The civil servants who made up the Standing Committee for Supervision and Coordination and who had been assigned responsibility for improvements lacked authority to take effective action.

Although the new Government had declared it a basic policy that new enterprises would not be undertaken, and although adequate management and staff arrangements had not yet been made for the first wave of Government manufacturing plants now nearly completed, the Ministry of Industries was still somewhat inconsistently seeking inclusion in the four-year plan of a number of new and costly industrial projects — notably a large expansion in steel capacity, a large fertilizer plant and a large truck and tractor assembly plant. So apathetic was the Government about the arrangements with the Soviet Union for the implementation of the "gift projects" agreement that only a strong representation by the consulting economist led it to include a provision in this agreement that designs and cost estimates would be subject to review by the Burmese Government.[1]

Although the Government had approved the recommendation that a special effort be made to improve tax enforcement — the windfall profits accruing to traders as a result of swollen margins above C.I.F. prices clearly indicated a potential tax bonanza on this score — the Income Tax Department denied that such prospects were in sight or that any special efforts were called for.

While the decision to inaugurate a group of joint venture corporations in the import trade had been made in June 1956, these corporations were not ready for action as of January 1957. Despite this, the Trade Minister declined to issue import licenses for 1956–57 for the goods concerned until the J.V.C.'s were ready to function. Declared Government policy that the importation of certain commodities should proceed freely under Open General License was negated by the foreign exchange control department at the central Union Bank. Bolstered by its close connection with the Bureau of Special Investigation, it arrogated to itself the right to review applications for letters of credit and to cut these down as far as it chose. Consequently, imports of consumer goods during the first half of 1956–57 were at an annual rate below even that of the previous fiscal year. Textile imports, the most crucial component of the import program, were at an annual rate of K 8.6 crores in the first half of

---

1. The apathy resulted from the feeling on the part of Prime Minister U Ba Swe and Deputy Prime Minister U Kyaw Nyein that the "gift" agreement was U Nu's "baby," and that there was little they could do about it.

1956–57, compared with K 12 crores for 1955–56 and K 17.8 crores in 1953–54. Although it had been established several times at top levels that the swollen lists of registered importers would be winnowed down to practical proportions, no effective action had been taken on this score. The Government agencies which had been given new responsibility for the monopoly import of electrical appliances and supplies had been tardy in procurement and were displaying rank favoritism and political preference in the distribution of these scarce commodities.

Despite informal indication by U. S. sources in September 1956 that the U. S. would look with favor on a three-year P.L. 480 arrangement (precedent for such a long-term agreement had been established in the case of India), the Trade Ministry shrugged off repeated urgings to initiate negotiations until December. Then it was learned that the U. S. was no longer in a position to comply with such a request, or indeed to negotiate even a new one-year agreement, pending legislative action by the U. S. Congress. At the Electricity Supply Board, repeated efforts had failed to bring about orderly procedures and financial planning. Finally a team of Canadian experts had been brought in with the assistance of the World Bank under Columbo Plan auspices, but the accounts and records were in such a mess that it was almost impossible for them to be of any assistance.

Not least among the items making for an increasingly dour appraisal of the outlook was the difficulty in finding opportunities to present the problems to the policy-makers. The Economic and Social Board was the established forum for such questions. It met, however, only infrequently, and permitted its agenda to be cluttered up with all kinds of trivia at the cost of important questions. When it did sit on the important questions, all too often it deferred decision or sent the problems back to the Committee of Experts, which was not in a position to take action on them. This, in effect, was the situation when, in February 1957, the Ministry of National Planning submitted its revised proposals for the four-year plan to the Economic and Social Board.

The revised four-year plan presented by the Ministry of National Planning called for capital expenditures of K 58 crores in 1956–57, K 60 crores in 1957–58, K 64 crores in 1958–59 and K 69 crores in 1959–60. Of the K 251 crores for the four years, it was estimated that K 138 crores would be required in foreign exchange and K 113 crores in domestic currency. As against the financial requirements of the plan, which made provision for large-scale imports for private use throughout the four-year period, the resource appraisal indicated prospective deficits of some K 42 crores of foreign exchange and about K 34 crores of domestic currency. The indicated foreign exchange deficit, it was pointed out, was well within the total of additional resources anticipated (the $25 million U. S. loan, additional P.L. 480 arrangements of some K 30 crores, the K 21 crores Soviet credit, the West German credit of K 8 crores and pos-

Table 30

GOVERNMENT CAPITAL EXPENDITURES, 1952–53 TO 1955–56 AND
ESTIMATES FOR 1956–57 TO 1959–60 AS PRESENTED IN FEBRUARY 1957
BY THE MINISTRY OF NATIONAL PLANNING

Agency Sectors	Expended 1952–53 to 1955–56		Programed 1956–57 to 1959–60	
	Amount (*K Crores*)	Per Cent of Total	Amount (*K Crores*)	Per Cent of Total
Total	170.9	100.0	251.3	100.0
Agriculture	11.7	6.9	34.8	13.8
Irrigation	2.1	1.3	4.6	1.8
Forestry	2.1	1.2	3.6	1.4
Mining	1.1	.6	14.1	5.6
Transportation	33.1	19.4	42.1	16.8
Communications	9.5	5.5	16.0	6.4
Power	18.5	10.8	24.5	9.8
Industry	19.5	11.4	17.7	7.1
Pyidawtha grants	3.2	1.8	2.0	.8
Building construction	26.9	15.8	29.0	11.5
State government	—	—	6.0	2.4
Social services	4.8	2.8	12.5	5.0
Miscellaneous	2.0	1.2	6.2	2.4
Defense	36.4	21.3	38.2	15.2

Source: "Four-Year Program" (1956–57 to 1959–60), Ministry of National Planning, Rangoon, Feb. 18, 1957.

sibly additional World Bank loans). The prospective domestic currency deficit, however, would require vigorous Government action to improve tax enforcement, strengthen the tax structure, improve the operating efficiency of the state-owned boards and corporations, adjust the price policy of state enterprises, and other measures to mobilize resources as well. "If the proposed level of capital expenditures is accepted," stated the Ministry, "Government must accept the responsibility for adopting the policies and measures necessary to provide the resources without further inflation."[2]

The Ministry also pointed out that the plan should be considered a flexible one, subject to adjustment at each budget-making time in the light of developing circumstance, and that the expenditure schedules incorporated into it were in process of being converted to the full-scale plan requested by the Economic and Social Board.

The program envisaged an increase of almost 50 per cent in the volume of public investment as compared with that of the preceding four years, with the largest increases going to agriculture, mining, transport and communications, power and social services. (See Table 30.) With the exception of manufacturing industry, the absolute amounts proposed for investment in all im-

2. Transmittal, "Four-Year Program" (1956–57 to 1959–60), Ministry of National Planning, Rangoon, Feb. 18, 1957.

portant categories showed substantial increases. In percentages, investments proposed for agriculture and mining increased most significantly in relation to the previous four-year period, while that for industry showed the most significant relative decline.

Although the economic consultants had been responsible in major degree for the resource appraisals and the proposed investment schedules, they had by now arrived at the point where they felt very serious doubts about the new program. Having repeatedly urged upon the Government, without apparent success, the policies and courses of action they held to be necessary concomitants of an ambitious capital development program, they now considered whether to restate their position once again in the strongest possible terms or to state flatly that the Government should curtail investment activities to a minimum until it had demonstrated substantial progress along the required lines. After much deliberation, and not without some internal difference of opinion, the consultants chose the former course.

Their comments were addressed to three major questions: Was the proposed investment program desirable and sound? Could it be financed without inflation? Should it be adopted as a feasible program?

As to the first question, they held that the proposed program was on the whole desirable and sound. A program of approximately such a size and composition was required if Burma was to make the forward strides in output and productive capacity of which she was capable. The proposed program gave increased and appropriate emphasis to the primary sectors of the economy — agriculture, timber and mining — and to projects which would save and earn foreign exchange. While looking to near-term results, it attempted to build a sound base for future development as well. Essential loans to stimulate activity in the private sector were also provided for within the program. For the most part, the economic and technical justifications for the projects proposed had been established.

Within this broad context the program did contain, it was emphasized, certain elements of weakness. Some of the major projects, notably the Kalewa coal project, required more adequate economic and technical justification. Others, such as the aircraft acquisition program, would require more specialized personnel and better management arrangements than seemed to be in prospect. Much of the programed building construction, as in the case of the Russian "gift projects," seemed to be relatively inessential. Some of the programs, as in the case of irrigation and highways, appeared to be beyond the executive capacities of the departments responsible for their implementation. These points, however, were regarded as subsidiary to the major questions of financing and feasibility.

In the consultants' opinion, the proposed program *could* be carried through without inflation. Success on this score, however, would require determined and efficient action by the Government along a number of related lines. Paramount among the requisites was a considerable volume of borrowing abroad (much of which had already been arranged for); successful implementation of a large-scale program of imports for private use as an offset to inflationary pressures; measures to improve substantially the collection of revenues from existing taxes and the introduction of new tax measures or higher rates on existing taxes, where necessary; more effective administration of Government enterprises to reduce current deficits and increase current profits; pricing policies in the Government enterprises, where appropriate, designed to produce larger revenues; and the more effective mobilization of domestic savings.

On the whole, the consultants stated, recent experience and the policies pursued by the Government offered little to justify the expectation that these conditions would be met. They concluded, therefore, that while the proposed program could be financed without serious inflation, it was not likely to be so financed in the continued absence of real determination on the part of the Government to do what was necessary.

In considering whether the proposed program should be adopted, the consultants emphasized that it had two aspects. It was both an investment program and a financing and implementing program. Without determination to carry out the latter part of it with expedition and vigor, the former part should not be adopted. The consultants stressed that the measures required would have to be accompanied by more delegation of authority and responsibility throughout the Government apparatus, with appropriate accountability and rewards and punishments; and that experienced and able management in Government enterprises of the commercial type should be permitted substantial autonomy. They emphasized the need for unrelenting effort to improve security throughout the countryside and to improve supervision and coordination of the implementation effort. On this last score they stressed particularly the need for the Economic and Social Board to meet weekly to review the operations of all key boards and corporations, all major economic areas and all major projects. Because of the burden such a schedule would impose on the Prime Minister, they suggested that an Executive Vice Chairman be designated to assist him.

Finally, the economic consultants affirmed that the budget preparation period, March–August, should be considered a test period during which the Government would appraise its determination and ability to carry through the course of action required. If the progress made was not satisfactory, the capital program would have to be reduced commensurately.

These views were soberly considered at a meeting of the Economic and Social Board during the latter part of February under the chairmanship of Prime Minister U Ba Swe. In the discussion the consultants laid great stress on the responsibility of the Economic and Social Board for initiating and seeing to the execution of the policies necessary and the consequent importance of weekly meetings. Both the Prime Minister and Deputy Prime Minister for National Economy U Kyaw Nyein stated that the Government was prepared to accept this responsibility. The Economic and Social Board, it was decided, would henceforth meet at least every two weeks in order to cope with the challenge. Decision on the Four-Year Plan itself was temporarily deferred while reconsideration was given to the resource appraisals it incorporated, which Finance Minister Bo Khin Maung Gale had taken exception to as being too optimistic.

Before the next meeting of the Board, the consultants held separate talks with U Ba Swe, U Kyaw Nyein and U Nu in which they spoke even more frankly and stressed even more emphatically the crucial nature of the decisions the Government was about to make. More important, on March 1 U Nu returned to the prime-ministership. Although it appeared that, in contrast to the situation prevailing before his resignation from office in June 1956, U Ba Swe would now continue to function as Chairman of the Economic and Social Board and as Minister for National Planning, it was scarcely to be expected that Prime Minister U Nu would refrain for long from direct participation in and supervision of economic development planning and implementation.

U Nu's absence of some nine months from the prime-ministership to concern himself primarily with party problems[3] had afforded him time and perspective in which to reflect on development. His own reflections and observations, the repeated and by now grave warnings of the economic consultants and developments within the A.F.P.F.L. itself determined him to make a major attempt to restore order in economic planning and implementation, to inaugurate new policy and priority emphases and to insist on better performance in Government. In March, when the Economic and Social Board rejected the more conservative resource appraisal submitted by the Minister for Finance and Revenue and approved the Four-Year Plan submitted to it by the Planning Ministry in February, U Nu refused to bring the plan before the Cabinet for final approval. He indicated that he would call for a thoroughgoing review in terms of criteria and directives he had under consideration.

U Nu's reflections had led him to the conclusion that the Government had made a great mistake in tackling a major economic development program without first restoring law and order. He was impressed with the debilitating effects of lack of integrity and adequate motivation in public administration generally and in the Government's many enterprises in particular. He felt

3. He had, of course, continued during this period as President of the A.F.P.F.L.

more strongly than ever that new enterprises should not be undertaken until order had been introduced into those already in existence, that the Government could operate enterprises efficiently only in joint venture with the private sector, and that public participation should be sought in the new Government enterprises through the sale of shares. Underlying all this was the realization that the weakness of the human element was the Achilles' heel in the Socialists' approach to economic development. Even if the Government were to acquire the necessary experience and know-how, venality and personal self-seeking would continue to be major stumbling blocks for which he saw no cure. U Nu had also been greatly impressed by the widespread fire which destroyed some 18,000 hutments in May in the Kamayut section of Rangoon, and had determined that extraordinary measures should be taken to reduce dry season urban fire hazards throughout the Union.

On the political side, the Prime Minister was influenced by the rift which had for some time been developing within the A.F.P.F.L. This was expressed in an exchange of letters between U Nu and U Kyaw Nyein at the time of U Nu's demission from the prime-ministership in June 1956.[4] The split was aggravated by circumstances attendant upon U Nu's return to office in March 1957 — circumstances which apparently led him to conclude that there had been a conspiracy on the part of some of his colleagues, led by U Kyaw Nyein, to prevent his return to office and to capture control of the A.F.P.F.L. The internal differences within the A.F.P.F.L. which culminated in the split of May 1958 have been described at considerable length elsewhere[5] and it is neither necessary nor appropriate to dwell on them here.

The accounts explain the split primarily in terms of personal rivalries and power conflicts. They fail to give appropriate weight to the very real differences in economic policy and program. Some of these have just been suggested. U Nu's growing dissatisfaction with state enterprise, particularly of the commercial type, constituted a basic policy difference with U Kyaw Nyein and, to perhaps a lesser extent, with U Ba Swe. His dissatisfaction with inefficiency, corruption and nepotism in the party and in the Government was also stronger than that of the other leaders, who were more inclined to view them as necessary concomitants of continued political unity and success. There was certainly sharp difference between the leaders over U Nu's insistence on centralized control over Government procurement and over the use of the Bureau of Special Investigation to insure honesty, both of which had been carried to extremes. U Kyaw Nyein and U Ba Swe had also been critical of the broader Soviet gift project arrangement into which U Nu

4. This exchange, which was circulated within the Party, was made public only in 1958.
5. For example, see: Sein Win, "The Split Story," *The Guardian* (Rangoon), March 23, 1959; Frank N. Trager, "The Political Split in Burma," *Far Eastern Survey*, October 1958, and "Political Divorce in Burma," *Foreign Affairs*, January 1959; and J. S. Furnivall, *The Governance of Modern Burma*, Institute of Pacific Relations, New York, 1958, Chapter V.

had entered impetuously without adequate consultation. These were substantive issues. In any event, it subsequently became clear, U Nu returned to the prime-ministership in March 1957 with the conviction that some of his Socialist colleagues did not desire his return any more than they had approved his retirement to clean up the A.F.P.F.L., and that before long he might be faced with an open fight for the control of the party and the Government. This conviction must inevitably have influenced his reaction to the then pending Four-Year Plan, particularly because he now felt somewhat fenced off from direct supervision over economic affairs.

U Nu did not make his now famous speech and issue his directives on the Four-Year Plan until June 8. In the meantime the Ministry of National Planning, with the assistance of the consultants, proceeded to convert the February version of the Four-Year Plan approved by the Economic and Social Board from a resource, capital expenditure and fiscal framework into an articulated plan which set forth targets for the economy as a whole and sector-by-sector, as requested earlier by U Raschid. The consultants prepared a detailed agenda for future meetings of the Economic and Social Board designed to bring before it in a systematic way the situations, problems and issues requiring review and decision.

During this period, foreign exchange again occasioned some concern. Chiefly because of upward revisions of K 15 crores in the import program for private use which had been made since the beginning of the fiscal year, discovery of the over-statement of K 10 crores in the end 1955–56 foreign exchange reserve position and a new lag in collections by the State Agricultural Marketing Board, the stated reserves had again substantially run down. The monetary reserves looked even worse than the total because of a large tranfer from the central Union Bank to the State Commercial Bank. After six months of relatively small imports due to protracted delays in the organization of the Joint Ventures Trading Corporations, imports had begun to arrive in great quantity. The price of imported commodities, particularly textiles, now broke rather sharply. Significantly, however, some commodities supplied by domestic production in whole or in substantial part continued to rise in price. This was especially true of fish and edible oils.

Attempts were made to spur previously agreed-upon action to set up the new Government manufacturing enterprises on an autonomous basis, without success. A test was made of the readiness of the Economic and Social Board to review and improve policy in connection with the arbitrary foreign exchange control and remittance policies practiced by the Union Bank Comptroller. This matter, too, was referred back to the secretary's level. Also significant was the news that the U. S. Government was still not in a position to undertake firm commitments on future P.L. 480 arrangements. Attempts were therefore made to get an interim program under way pending new legislative action by the U. S. Congress. These attempts centered on the use of P.L. 480 rupee funds, held by the U. S. Government in India under Section 104 (b) of the Act, to permit Burma to secure some $5 million worth of cotton textiles in India and pay for them with U. S.-owned rupees.

The Joint Venture Trading Corporations having got under way on a basis broadly competitive with one another, it was now proposed that each of the corporations be assigned responsibility for distributing goods in a different region of the country, without realization that such an arrangement would reintroduce the monopoly element previously eliminated by the over-lapping of commodity responsibilities. This proposal, fortunately, was not difficult to scotch. U Kyaw Nyein, addressing the Burmese Chamber of Industries, indicated that a substantial change had taken place in his views when he stated that the Government should place primary emphasis on the development of light industry, and that it should seek to have the private sector take the main responsibility in this field. A survey made of the operational and managerial readiness of the newly completed state industrial enterprises revealed serious weaknesses in the case of every one of them.

U Nu's speech of June 8 and its accompanying directives constituted a major attempt on his part to put the country's economic house in order, eliminate weaknesses and abuses, place first things first and, generally speaking, promote better performance at all levels of Government activity.

Dividing the problems into three categories — law and order, the national economy and social welfare — he affirmed that the Government, with himself largely responsible, had been guilty of two terrible blunders in undertaking a large-scale development program without first re-establishing law and order in the country, and in launching development plans without systematic preparation. These errors, he said, must now be corrected. Law and order must be established at all costs. New governmental enterprises would not be undertaken. Emphasis would be placed on the correction of weaknesses in existing projects. Economic production, he asserted, could not be entrusted only to salaried Government employees. Responsibilities should be extended also to people motivated by the desire to earn profit, and the profit motivation should be introduced by joint ventures with foreign and indigenous investors, and by selling shares in the Government enterprises to the workers employed in them and to civil servants. The morale of civil servants should be boosted by establishing department stores which would sell consumer goods at low prices exclusively to them, and by enabling them to obtain personal loans at low rates of interest. Japanese reparations and investment funds available after the requirements of essential Government projects were met should be used to finance private industry. With regard to the recently established Joint Venture Trading Corporations, U Nu stated that the Government should convert its equity share in these corporations into loans.

Resident alien businessmen should be permitted to exercise their legitimate economic rights by investing in the country's enterprises. Greater emphasis should be placed on agricultural production. Government concessions to the cooperatives should be progressively reduced to force responsibility and self-reliance upon them. Special plans were required to relieve the insufficiency of water supply in drought areas and to prevent the scourge of fire, which in every dry season burned down thousands of hutments. An integrated, realistic educational plan was needed. A special plan was required for the rehabilitation of the town of Rangoon. Public health was a priority problem. Priority would also be given to mass education projects to improve citizenship and to efforts to improve the accounts of the Government boards and corporations. Finally, U Nu called upon all Government servants to vow self-improvement and, once again, on the insurgents to "come out of the darkness into the light."

The Prime Minister's accompanying directives spelled out in varying degrees of detail the questions which needed consideration in connection with his new objectives and priorities, and set up a number of inquiry committees to deal with them. Committees were named for law and order, the morale of Government servants, law courts and laws, the national economy, water conservation and fire prevention, education, the rehabilitation of Rangoon, health, communications, post and telegraphs, buildings, mass education and auditing of boards and corporations. These committees were to conclude their inquiries and report back to him by the end of the month.

There was, of course, truth in the Prime Minister's criticisms and merit in the objectives he stressed. But in calling for a new Four-Year Plan he was confusing planning with policy and implementation. His basic criticisms were really directed to poor policy and even poorer administration and implementation, rather than to economic planning as such. The "terrible blunder" had not been in undertaking development without first completely restoring law and order, but rather in not pressing vigorously to suppress civil disorder while economic development was going forward. The twin efforts were complementary and each would have contributed to the other.

The lack of systematic preparation for development projects was a weakness on the implementation side. Weaknesses in the execution of projects reflected poor administration at the project, agency, ministerial and supervisory levels, rather than planning weaknesses. In the case of industrial and commercial projects, they also reflected basic errors in nationalization policy. Weak morale in the Government service resulted from many factors, prominent among which were nepotism, party interference, poor organization and supervision, lack of adequate delegation of authority, unnecessary red tape and inadequate pay scales. Excessive paternalism, political interference and lack of responsible local self-government were root causes of deficiencies in local water supply, urban fire hazards and the deplorable physical condition of Rangoon.

To emphasize these weaknesses, to call for these new policies and objectives, it had not been necessary or even meaningful — political considerations apart — to call for a new Four-Year Plan. What was necessary was that the Government apply itself to persistent effort to correct the accumulated abuses and weaknesses of the past. By calling for a new Four-Year Plan in the then existing context, U Nu confused rather than clarified the issues. At the same time he ignored the then pending Four-Year Plan painstakingly developed over the preceding year at his own request before he left office. He was attempting to achieve by directive within a period of three weeks a number of objectives which could not adequately be dealt with except over a much longer period of time, and not by committee reports. He was, thereby, guilty again of the hasty action without systematic preparation which he deplored in the very same speech. And he also unwittingly opened the door to foreign exchange collapse and domestic inflation, which were only narrowly averted in the weeks that followed.

In his comments on the national economy, the Prime Minister had given no thought to resources. He perhaps anticipated that compliance with his directive to abandon all thought of new enterprises would free sufficient resources to make provision for the new priority demands. This, of course, was not the fact. His reference to new enterprises was directed particularly to those in the manufacturing industry and minerals production fields, rather than to other types of projects. In any case, the then existing Four-Year Plan made little provision for new projects of any kind. In almost all cases the projects incorporated in the plan had already been initiated and were in various stages of completion. Of the largest programs, the transport and communications programs were made up almost entirely of rehabilitation projects, and the electric power program was in mid-passage. Even in the industry sector, the funds allotted for new enterprises amounted to less than K 3 crores per year.

When the various committees set up by the directives started their deliberations, it soon became apparent that the claims on resources which would emerge would be completely beyond the bounds of feasibility. In the National Economy Committee, of which the chairman was U Kyaw Nyein, the operating agencies seized the opportunity to demand an increase of approximately one third in the sums allocated to them under the Four-Year Plan, concerning the feasibility of which the consultants had already expressed so dim a view. The special law and order program, it soon became clear, would present demands for an additional K 40 or more crores over and above the sums already allocated. In regard to fire prevention (U Nu had designated himself Chairman of this committee), it was decided to insist on the removal of every hut with a bamboo thatch roof from every town or the reroofing of such huts with galvanized sheet metal. It had hastily been estimated that 30 million C.G.I. sheets would be required for the reroofing of all the thatched hutments, which, at K 6 kyats per 6′ x 3′ sheet, would amount to K 18 crores. Orders were actually given for the immediate procurement of this quantity, and only by chance intervention on the part of the economic consultants was a calculation made of the maximum potential requirement, which resulted in curtailment of this order by two thirds.

It was only within U Kyaw Nyein's National Economy Committee, where they had the opportunity to participate, that the consultants were able to elicit concern for the resource question. So occupied was this committee with the resource problem and with the program claims submitted by the operating agencies that it was able to give little time and attention to the reform and policy emphases enunciated by the Prime Minister. The consultants' efforts in this connection concerned ways and means to improve performance and management in the state enterprises; the sale of shares in these enterprises; and measures necessary to increase agricultural output. Again, these efforts were not very productive.

At the same time the consultants made still another attempt along related lines. Their suggestion to the National Economy Committee for improving efficiency in the state-owned boards and corporations had stressed primarily the need to set these up on a relatively autonomous basis with specific responsibilities and authority, and to subject them insofar as possible to competitive pressures, so as to create the basic conditions under which improved management might be achieved. To the Prime Minister they suggested a more concrete approach. This was to utilize the foreign technicians whose services were available to the Government under various auspices — direct hire, United Nations, Ford Foundation, Public Administration Service, and so on — to set up two or three task forces, composed in each case of engineering, economic, management and accounting talent, and to assign them responsibility for helping individual Government enterprises to achieve a better operating and management posture. The Prime Minister approved this proposal for the state industrial projects. The consultants urged, however, that the effort be made on a broader front and cover all state-owned boards and corporations, whether engaged in manufacturing, essential public services, foreign trade or intra-governmental service. This broader concept was approved by both the Prime Minister and U Kyaw Nyein.

Toward the end of June, when the reporting deadline was near, deliberations of the National Economy Committee became chaotic. The Committee was of course in no position or mood to reduce the swollen program claims submitted by the operating agencies. It decided merely to pass these on with only minor "vetting" to the Prime Minister's office. Suggestions made by private traders and industrialists were desultorily considered. U Kyaw Nyein, still desirous of continuing with a large-scale industrialization program by any means possible, unrealistically suggested that, if the Ministry of Industries could continue its proposed new industrial projects without making any financial claims either in foreign exchange or in local currency (!) upon the Government's resources, it should be permitted to do so. However, the Committee did recommend that the Government jute factory and other industrial plants be converted to public limited companies (to make possible the later sale of shares), that an Industrial Loan Bank be organized to help finance private industrial development, that an Investment Act be passed further to spur private investment and that the number of commodities handled by the Civil Supplies Board for sale to the public be reduced.

Over the protests of the consultants it recommended that the Civil Supplies Board should inaugurate a number of department stores or staff shops for the sale of goods to Government employees. Quite apart from any other considerations, the question of how an organization which had been unable to handle the distribution of ten to fifteen commodities effectively could now engage in the distribution of the thousands of items involved in department store operation was not even considered. Potentially valuable was the recommendation that the Task Force approach advocated by the consultants for the improvement of management in the Government boards and corporations be approved.[6]

But the most important concern of the National Economy Committee by this time was the question of resources. So strongly had the consultants harped upon this problem and so grim were the figures they had presented to the Committee on resource deficits to be expected in view of the claims then emerging, that a number of ministers felt the situation was hopeless. Confessing his own inability to impress the Prime Minister with the gravity of the position, U Kyaw Nyein requested that the economic consultants attempt to do so.

Not until early in July, when the Prime Minister met with his key economic secretaries (including those who had served as secretaries for the Law and Order, National Economy and Social Service Committees) and the consultants to review the major findings of the Committees, did he appreciate the nature, size and implications of the Pandora's box of demands he had opened. Warned that the situation created now threatened to end in catastrophe, U Nu recognized that his directives had misfired. His purpose had been to achieve law and order; improved efficiency, management, accounts and morale in the Government enterprises and in the Government service

6. The recommendations of the National Economic and other committees may be found in the Appendices to *Premier Reports to the People on Law and Order, National Solidarity, Social Welfare, National Economy, Foreign Affairs,* translation of speech by the Hon'ble Prime Minister U Nu in the Chamber of Deputies on Sept. 27, 1957, Director of Information, Rangoon, Jan. 9, 1958.

generally; increased participation by the private sector in development activity; accelerated agricultural development; fire prevention and water conservation; improved education and health; and the improved distribution of consumer goods. Now he found himself confronted with a number of demands for vastly increased expenditures superimposed on a hard core program already considerably in excess of what Burma could afford. For the non-extraordinary agency demands he accepted the position that there was neither time nor need to review these requests. They had been reviewed many times before and been found to be either non-essential or not financially feasible. It was clear that the previously prepared Four-Year Plan had to be treated as the point of departure for the present review. Increased outlays for law and order, fire prevention, and other priority objectives would have to be compensated for either by additional resources not previously contemplated in the Four-Year Plan or by curtailments in that plan.

In a series of intensive sessions ordered by the Prime Minister, the economic secretaries and the consultants slashed the previously approved capital program for 1957–58 to the bone. Among the projects eliminated were three of the six U.S.S.R. "gift" projects. The current budget for 1957–58 was also reduced, and steps were taken to review more carefully and substantially reduce the costs of the law and order program, which had been prepared separately. The Prime Minister also decided to seek special assistance from the U. S. Government for the law and order program. This eventually took two forms — first, a loan of $10 million to purchase supplies and equipment needed for the police forces and, second, the purchase, for $2 million worth of domestic currency, of surplus U. S. Army equipment worth perhaps ten times as much. Finally, the Prime Minister, again on the urging of the consultants, directed that a new tax program be prepared to muster the remainder of the resources necessary for maintenance of economic stability.

The Government had failed since 1954 to face up realistically to the need for more adequate domestic resource mobilization. The 1957 crisis was productive of the first substantial move in this direction. Even now the program adopted was something less than adequate. The tax program centered on increases in selected tariff rates, an increased excise tax on cigarettes, a reduction in the excise tax exemption allowed domestic enterprises and a substantial increase in the fees paid by foreigners for registration and for extension of stay permits.[7] Additional revenue measures proposed were improved income tax enforcement, greater efficiency in the boards and corporations, improved pricing policy on the part of the Civil Supplies Board, and the institution of tuition fees at the University of Rangoon. It was also proposed that a number of other previously recommended measures be studied with an eye

7. On the vigorous opposition of the consultants, the Prime Minister cut in half the proposed new rates. Even after this cut, the increases levied were severe and discriminatory.

to possible future action. It was estimated that the program recommended would yield an additional K 9.8 crores annually.[8]

The Prime Minister accepted the measures proposed and subsequent meetings of the Economic and Social Board and of the Cabinet gave approval to this program for the fiscal year 1957–58. The capital program, not including special provisions for law and order, came to K 50.2 crores. The Government's current budget had been curtailed substantially from the level earlier approved by the Ministry of Finance. Negotiations with the United States on the special arrangements previously mentioned were well under way. The one big early result of all the proposals made by the Prime Minister in his June speech was the program to strengthen the personnel and equipment of the armed forces and their auxiliary police. Most of the other objectives were neglected, temporarily at least, because of the financial crisis. For the rest, the entire Government apparatus had been subjected to a tremendous strain, and the Government had come very close to superimposing on its existing commitments additional obligations which would, in effect, have "broken the bank." In fact, had the U. S. Government not been willing to extend a loan for police purposes and to accept token payment for a large quantity of armed forces material, a desperate economic situation would have been precipitated.

In mid-June, shortly after the Prime Minister's directives, the consultants had completed for the Ministry of National Planning a fully-articulated Four-Year Plan corresponding to the February resource and expenditure schedules. So great had been the confusion caused by the Prime Minister's speech of June 8 that it was generally believed the Four-Year Plan was a dead letter. Even the Planning Ministry officials, who had worked on it for a year, were convinced of this. Indeed, the June 1957 Four-Year Plan was never subsequently submitted to the Government for official approval, nor was it ever published. Henceforth there would be only annual programs and budget reviews. No subsequent attempt was made within the period here reviewed to formalize a longer-term plan.

In the months that followed, U Nu had time once again to reflect on the over-all picture, and to prepare once again for the efficiency breakthrough which had gone awry in June. On September 27, 1957, he made one of his greatest speeches, the so-called "Marathon Speech" to the Parliament.[9] This speech, which took five hours to deliver, dealt with law and order, national solidarity, social welfare, the national economy and foreign affairs. The section dealing with the national economy reviewed at length the progress made since independence, the Eight-Year Pyidawtha Plan, the lessons learned from the experience of the previous years, the Four-Year Plan for capital expendi-

8. "Committee Recommendations on the 1957–58 Fiscal Program," Ministry of National Planning, Aug 8, 1957.
9. *Premier Reports to the People,* cited above.

tures and the Government's revised plans for better implementation and policy.[10] In this speech U Nu emphasized the progress made in recent years. This progress he summarized as follows:

Mr. Speaker, Sir, how then shall we sum up the progress which has been made in the national economy since Independence? We have finally restored production until it is now very close to that of pre-war. We have established a better balance in the economy, so that we shall no longer be as dependent as we were before on the production of a few key commodities for export. We have made great strides toward the restoration of our essential services in transport, electric power, communications, etc. We have raised standards of living and welfare. We have been making large capital investments in transport and communications, electric power, industry, social services, etc., which will contribute greatly to future production and welfare. We have begun to encourage private investment, both domestic and foreign, to contribute to our national output and well-being. We have kept our finances sound. We have kept price increases within reasonable bounds, and have contained them.

In short, considering the conditions from which we began and the difficulties which have plagued us, we do not need to be ashamed of what we have accomplished in these years. In fact, I think that on the whole we can take a considerable amount of pride in our achievements. Please recognize that when I say this I find no room for smug complacency. On the contrary, I think we must be highly self-critical of these accomplishments, because we could and should have achieved even more than we did. But our weaknesses were not the fault of indifference and lack of effort. They resulted for the most part from over-ambitiousness and over-eagerness to do everything at once. Fortunately, we have learned from this experience.[11]

The Prime Minister stressed that

What I called for in my June speech and directives was not the formulation of a new Four-Year Plan for capital expenditure — this we already had — but rather a modification of it to ensure better implementation and policy, with greatly increased emphasis on law and order, fire prevention, efficiency, morale, education, investment policy, and the like. This will involve, to be sure, modifications in the Four-Year Capital Programme. But it is aimed primarily at utilizing the lessons learned in recent years in achieving even greater progress in the years immediately ahead.[12]

The Prime Minister then emphasized that the chief lessons of Burma's experience in attempting to achieve accelerated economic development were: (1) that without the complete restoration of law and order efforts at economic and social development could not succeed; (2) that agriculture, timber and minerals, the basic sectors of the economy, must be restored to at least pre-war output before satisfactory gains in other important sectors of the economy

10. For the section on the national economy, see Appendix I.
11. *Ibid.*, pp. 15–16.
12. *Ibid.*, pp. 17–18.

could be achieved and sustained; (3) that new industrial ventures require intensive preparation, organization, supervision and management in order to be successful; (4) that until radical steps were taken to improve the morale of public servants, all governmental efforts toward economic and social betterment would be badly retarded; (5) that strenuous efforts were called for to achieve higher levels of efficiency throughout the Government and particularly in the state-owned boards and corporations; (6) that overcentralization and a lack of delegation of authority and responsibility resulted inevitably in "managerial constipation"; (7) that Government should undertake only those tasks which were appropriate and necessary, leaving other tasks to cooperative organizations and the private sector; (8) that if the nation was to carry out a large-scale economic and social development program and at the same time avoid inflation, the people of the country would have to contribute in reasonable degree to its financing; and (9) that an important concomitant of a high rate of development activity was large-scale import of consumer goods to counteract the inflationary influence of large-scale Government expenditures.

In order to profit from these lessons and achieve better implementation and policy, the Government, he declared, would henceforth: (1) give priority to the establishment of law and order and (2) emphasize the restoration of production and exports for the primary agriculture, timber and minerals sectors; (3) go slow on new state-owned industrial ventures until a reasonable state of efficiency had been achieved in industries already constructed; (4) improve efficiency in the Government boards and corporations by greater delegation of responsibility, strengthening of their management, improved accounting and the assistance of special task forces; (5) encourage the private sector by the enactment of special investment legislation, the establishment of a development bank, the liberalization and improved operation of foreign exchange and of remittance controls and the non-discriminatory treatment of resident foreign minority groups. (In this connection he explained that in his view socialism was no longer necessarily identified with Government ownership and operation. Socialist objectives of welfare, economic justice, maximum output, security and equal opportunity might be better achieved without nationalization than with it.) (6) Increase domestic revenues and savings through greater production, improved efficiency and lower costs in the public enterprises, improved tax enforcement and necessary tax measures; and (7) insist on improved work attitudes and responsibilities.

This speech had great potential significance for Burma's economic development effort. At long last the Government had incorporated in a formal statement to the parliament and to the people of Burma a sober and objective appraisal of its errors and failings, and affirmed in specific terms how it proposed to correct them. In this instance, as in the case of all his other important public addresses, U Nu's speech had previously been submitted to the Executive Committee of the A.F.P.F.L. and to the Cabinet for review and approval.[13] Hence it represented far more than the personal convictions of the Prime Minister himself.

It therefore appeared that the ensuing period might witness the inauguration of new priorities and new emphasis on greater efficiency, greater reliance on the private sector, and generally improved performance in project implementation and in resource mobilization. This was not yet to be. The rift within the A.F.P.F.L. was destined to widen in the succeeding months, and the attention and energy of the leaders were to be pre-empted by preparations for the A.F.P.F.L. Congress to be held early in 1958, by the split in the party which followed not long thereafter, and by the political rivalry and change in Government which then ensued. The impact of these internal party affairs and conflicts on the economic development effort will be the subject of the next chapter.

Before going on, other major economic outcomes of the year 1956–57 may be briefly reviewed. Spurred chiefly by large increases in agricultural production and in the industry sector, the gross domestic product rose by nearly 9 per cent in constant prices. Under the influence of good weather, the index of agricultural production based on pre-war figures rose from 81 to 93. Paddy production made the greatest contribution to this increase, rising from 5.8 to 6.4 million tons. Rice exports rose from 1.93 million tons to the long-sought goal of 2 million tons. Despite slightly lower average prices, the value of rice exported rose from K 87.7 crores to K 89.5 crores, and the percentage of rice exports sold to the barter countries declined, in terms both of tonnage and value, from approximately one quarter in 1955–56 to approximately one seventh. Swelled by tremendous, long-deferred volume in the second half of the year, imports rose sharply from K 87 crores in 1955–56 to K 132 crores in 1956–57. Consumer goods alone rose from K 58.6 crores a year earlier to K 93.6 crores. Imports of textiles actually exceeded in value those of 1953–54. For the first time since the economic development program had been inaugurated, the Union Government budget proper and the comprehensive budget of the public sector were in surplus. By the end of the year there had been a reduction of almost K 15 crores in the privately held money supply. Only sharp increases in the retail prices of oils and fats, fish and fish products and certain other food products maintained the general cost of living for low income families at the level of the previous year. Textile and clothing prices, hitherto the most aggravating component of the price index, declined by more than one third. The huge volume of imports had not been achieved, however, without a sizable decline in the foreign exchange reserves. These dropped from K 74.6 crores at the end of the previous year to K 56 crores, bringing the reserves to a point not far above the low level of 1954–55.[14]

13. In fact, that part of the speech dealing with socialism had been substantially redrafted to comply with the views of some of his colleagues.

14. Some K 10 crores of this decline, however, was of a bookkeeping nature only, involving an adjustment of the error made in the accounts of the previous year.

CHAPTER 14

Political Split, Crisis and

Change—1957-58

The political leaders devoted the opening months of the fiscal year 1957-58 chiefly to quiet preparations for the third A.F.P.F.L. Congress scheduled for January. The two earlier congresses had been held in January 1946 and December 1947. The forthcoming congress would, therefore, be the first in more than ten years and would provide a test both of relative strength and of the leaders' ability and desire to reconcile their differences. The activity, however, took place behind the scenes.

More visibly, the Economic and Social Board was liquidated in favor of the newly organized National Planning Commission, with largely the same membership. The significant difference was that the National Planning Commission was organized within the Ministry of National Planning. U Nu having resumed this portfolio, the National Planning Commission became more subject to his personal control than the Economic and Social Board had been.[1] Another feature of this change was the designation of U Raschid as Executive Member of the National Planning Commission, presumably with authority to make administrative decisions between meetings. On the efficiency front so clearly faced by the Prime Minister in his September 1957 speech, the most noteworthy development was the organization of Task Forces composed of foreign technicians and spearheaded by the economic consultants to investigate and make recommendations on the jute mill, the cotton mill and the pharmaceuticals plant; the operations of the Union of

---

1. Since in previous years consideration had several times been given to a merging of the Economic and Social Board with the Ministry of National Planning, it is more reasonable to consider this reorganization as the culmination of these earlier discussions than as a political move on the part of U Nu to consolidate his control over economic affairs.

Burma Airways; and factors retarding tin-tungsten mining in the Tenasserim. These were to be only the first steps in a series of such investigations,
which would cover all the important boards and corporations during the
year. Also noteworthy were a large-scale surrender of insurgents in November and the conclusion of agreements with the United States for the first two
projects to be financed under the $25 million U. S. development loan. These
were a land reclamation project and a mechanized timber extraction unit.
But by far the most significant economic development in the opening months
of the fiscal year 1957–58 was the sharp decline in the indicated size of the
paddy harvest.

Because of bad weather, it appeared that the new paddy crop would be
almost a million tons smaller than that of the previous year. The implications
of such a decline for rice exports, foreign exchange earnings, budgetary
revenues and the execution of the capital and fiscal programs were most serious. As further reports on the progress of the crop confirmed the earlier findings, it became clear that countervailing actions were needed. The most obvious response to the new situation was to slash the program of imports for
private use. This program had been set at K 104 crores for the year — higher
even than the initial record-breaking program for 1956–57. As a first step, this
program was cut to the level of K 90 crores. It was determined also that a
close review would be made of the Government's current and capital spending activities with a view to selective cuts.

The short crop also raised questions as to how much paddy the State Agricultural Marketing Board should procure for export and how the reduced export tonnages should be allocated. The sales of S.M.S. grade already con-
tracted to India (500,000 tons) and Ceylon (200,000 tons) would virtually
exhaust the anticipated availability of this staple grade, quite apart from
sizable contractual obligations to Pakistan, Indonesia and other buyers. Another important question was that of price. The only commitment Burma
had made for 1957–58 was to grant India a price of £32 per ton. The first question, therefore, was whether India should be given the entire 500,000 tons called
for by the contract or asked to take a lesser pro rata share of the total S.M.S.
availability along with other contractual buyers for whom prices had not been
set. A further question was whether other buyers should be supplied on the
basis of the contract price established for India or required to pay a higher
price more in line with market conditions. The consultants felt that with
huge foreign exchange losses in view as a result of the short crop, Burma
should, in fairness to herself as well as to other buyers, prorate the limited
availabilities to all contractual buyers, and charge buyers other than India a
price based on prevailing market conditions.

Early in January, conflicting revised estimates indicated an export surplus
of from 900,000 to 1.3 million tons of paddy, compared with 1.8 million tons

in the previous year. Despite the moral scruples of Prime Minister U Nu, the National Planning Commission decided that price increases would be sought from buyers other than India, Ceylon and Pakistan. The availabilities would, however, be prorated to India as well as to other buyers, and Ceylon and Indonesia would be supplied at £33 per ton, only £1 more than India. Other buyers would be asked to pay £37 or £38 per ton. All buyers, including India, would be asked to increase the down payment made on shipment from 90 to 97.5 per cent.[2]

It soon became clear that these measures would not suffice to protect the foreign exchange position, and a second round of cuts was imposed on the import program, reducing it from K 90 crores to K 80 crores. Since imports under Open General License were running at a rate far higher than the program estimate, it became necessary to reinstitute the Union Bank's control over letters of credit opened in connection with such imports. To prevent arbitrary action on the part of the Foreign Exchange Comptroller as between various categories of goods under Open General License, these imports were also programed.[3]

The long-awaited A.F.P.F.L. Congress had meanwhile taken place in January. U Nu opened it with another marathon speech — this time on Marxism. Affirming that much of Marxist economics was valid, he nevertheless repudiated the broader aspects of Marxist theory and declared, contrary to the position taken some time before by U Ba Swe, that Marxism and Buddhism were incompatible. In this ideological position U Nu was far closer to the convictions held by his political opponent, U Kyaw Nyein, than he was to those of Thakin Tin and Thakin Kyaw Dun, his political supporters in the fight with U Kyaw Nyein. Significantly, U Nu also stated that the A.F.P.F.L. was no longer a coalition but a party. He went on to discuss at length the goals of the A.F.P.F.L., what it had done to attain them and what it yet needed to do. He again affirmed that the chief goal was the building of a socialist welfare state and again admitted that many mistakes had been made in working toward this goal. The important thing, he declared, was to see that honest mistakes did not recur. In discussing the needs of the future, he

2. The difference between full cost and down payment was the margin provided for quality disputes between seller and buyer.

3. In the previous two years, imports of many categories of goods under Open General License had increased tremendously as compared with earlier experience and estimates. This increase was due both to loopholes and abuses of the O.G.L. system and to the development of large-scale smuggling of O.G.L. items into Thailand, China, Pakistan and India. Loose provisions in the Burmese regulations permitted wines and alcoholic tonics, for example, to be imported as drugs and pharmaceuticals, and residential air-conditioning units to be brought in under the heading of machinery, both on Open General License. Abuse of the O.G.L. system came in the form of hoarding. In the case of talcum powder, included among selected toilet articles on the O.G.L. list, the distributors for Yardley's were amazed when they received, within a few months, orders equal to seven to ten years' supply at their historic rate of sales. And since many goods on Burma's O.G.L. list were under import restrictions in neighboring countries, overland smuggling developed to take advantage of the resulting price differentials.

emphasized internal peace, world peace and the strengthening of democratic processes.

With respect to internal peace, his statement was surprisingly mild. The previous September he had stated, "We must be determined to stamp out and eradicate this social cancer that is eating away the vitals of our country."[4] Now he said:

I wish, at this Congress, to say to the insurgents, just three things. They are:

1) Let us not argue who has been in the wrong or in the right, between yourselves and ourselves;

2) I would request tolerance for any mistakes on our part, and we are ready to overlook your mistakes.

3) Although yourselves and ourselves may not agree as to ideology and programme, there are many tasks on which we can co-operate together for the good of the people of the Union of Burma. Therefore, come into the light, and let us work together on these tasks.

And he continued:

If it is unavoidable, we will have to expand our armed forces and carry on the fight anyway. But if it can be avoided, I would like to avoid it.[5]

Affirming the existence of democracy in Burma, U Nu appealed to the A.F.P.F.L. leaders at all levels to exercise self-discipline, to be ready to make sacrifices for others, to recognize their faults and to correct their deficiencies of character and conduct. Significantly, he requested: "Do not gather strength, in the form of followers and supporters, for yourself. But, gather strength for the A.F.P.F.L. . . . I urge the leaders to gather strength for the entire organization, and not for themselves separately."[6]

This marshaling of strength was, however, precisely what had been going on in the months prior to the congress. It was reflected now in the struggle over who was to be Secretary-General of the A.F.P.F.L. U Nu supported the candidacy of U Kyaw Dun. U Kyaw Nyein and his supporters were adamant that U Kyaw Dun should not be elected. At least two major considerations were involved in this issue. The first was that U Kyaw Dun was said to have warned U Nu of the alleged plot to prevent his return to the prime-ministership in March 1957. U Kyaw Nyein, for this and other reasons, considered U Kyaw Dun, together with Thakin Tin, a major enemy within the party. The second consideration involved the circumstances under which U Nu

---

4. *Premier Reports to the People on Law and Order, National Solidarity, Social Welfare, National Economy, Foreign Affairs*, speech by the Hon'ble Prime Minister U Nu in the Chamber of Deputies on Sept. 27, 1957, Director of Information, Rangoon, Jan. 9, 1958, p. 24.

5. Translation of U Nu's speech to the A.F.P.F.L. Congress, January 29, 1958, printed in *The Nation*, February 8, 1958, p. 51.

6. *Ibid.*, pp. 61–62.

resigned the prime-ministership in 1956 to devote himself to full-time party work. At that time, he had demanded that his colleagues who retained political office should give up, at least for the time being, their leadership in constituent party organizations. U Kyaw Dun, a minister in the Government, was apparently being exempted from this rule. U Kyaw Nyein felt that U Kyaw Dun's activity as Secretary-General would permit U Nu to consolidate his hold on the party, and insure his victory in the internal struggle.

In this tense situation, it was U Ba Swe who played the mediator's role. After warning that he would fight like a "tiger" anyone who ventured to split the A.F.P.F.L., Ba Swe effected a compromise on the U Kyaw Dun issue. The arrangement reportedly was that U Kyaw Dun would be elected Secretary-General by the A.F.P.F.L. Congress, but that he would voluntarily resign from that post within forty-five days thereafter.[7]

Another significant decision was made at the A.F.P.F.L. Congress. U Kyaw Nyein had felt for a long time that he was at a disadvantage in relation to other party leaders because he lacked an organizational mass following within the party. Thakin Tin was the head of the constituent All Burma Peasants' Organization, in which Thakin Kyaw Dun also held an important leadership post. U Ba Swe was head of the Trades Union Congress. Thakin Pan Myaing, another of U Nu's followers whose political star seemed to be on the rise, was head of the constituent Federation of Trade Organizations. Of the chief leaders of the A.F.P.F.L., only U Nu and U Kyaw Nyein lacked personal organizational followings within the coalition. One of the decisions taken at the congress which mollified U Kyaw Nyein was that he should form an A.F.P.F.L. youth organization.

The congress concluded without further issue or incident. It was clear, however, that U Kyaw Nyein and his supporters would insist that U Kyaw Dun fulfill his pledge. In the interim, U Kyaw Nyein went off on a lengthy trip to the U.S.S.R. and People's China in response to a long-standing invitation.

The Task Forces had by this time brought in several reports. These covered the jute, cotton textile and pharmaceuticals factories; the operational problems of the Union of Burma Airways; and the problems of the tin-tungsten miners in the Tenasserim area. In each case a number of serious problems had been uncovered, and a number of constructive measures had been recommended for dealing with them. However, it was exceedingly difficult to get high-level action on these situations. The studies had been conducted under the aegis of the Deputy Prime Minister for National Economy, U Kyaw Nyein, and even after his return from the Soviet Union and People's China, he was not disposed to concern himself with these problems. Since the Task Force

7. One report has it that this understanding was reached by U Ba Swe and U Kyaw Dun, and that U Nu was not a party to it.

recommendations went to basic issues and called for policy decisions which could be made only at the highest political level, U Kyaw Nyein's unreadiness to deal with them precluded further consideration. His capable secretary, U Tun Thaung, was at a loss as to how to proceed. U Mo Myit, the dynamic Secretary of the Ministry of National Planning and Executive Secretary of the National Planning Commission, hesitated to take over the Task Force reports for review by the National Planning Commission, for this would have appeared to be an invasion of a responsibility delegated to U Kyaw Nyein. And U Nu had other matters on his mind. The Task Force effort, for the time being at least, was stalled.

U Nu did, however, display in the period immediately following the congress a keen interest in the status of the development program. This reflected his new interest in achieving better performance, not a desire to expand the development effort, and came about in response to requests for consideration of a further U. S. development loan. By March, Burmese officials had reached preliminary agreement with I.C.A. representatives in Rangoon on a number of loan projects in addition to the land reclamation and mechanical timber extraction unit projects agreed upon in December. Such projects, totaling $19 million in value, had been passed on to I.C.A. Washington for approval. It was clear that within a short time the entire $25 million U. S. loan would have been obligated.

Informal discussions had, therefore, been initiated at the secretarial level with the U. S. representatives, looking toward the presentation of a further loan request. The tentative plan was to request the United States for a further loan of $75 million to be utilized over a period of perhaps three years. This was in line with the discussions which had led up to the $25 million loan; originally it had been contemplated that this loan might be merely the first of a series, and a $75 million loan could be considered a series of three loans of $25 million a year. Since the utilization of any further loans would have to be tied to specific projects, consideration of the request involved also the preparation of a tentative list of projects. It was the submission of a new list of proposed loan projects which sparked the Prime Minister into action at this time.

It was clear that U Nu did not wish to approve a new loan list, whether for U. S. or World Bank consideration. (The Bank had once again sent a mission to Rangoon, headed this time by Martin Rosen.) U Nu was seemingly unaware that the projects proposed were in almost every case projects previously approved by the Government. In only one or two cases were they new projects, and for these there was excellent justification. Deferring decision, U Nu plunged into an intensive review, with the economic secretaries, of the progress made in all important economic sectors over the past four years. Having completed this review, which required lengthy daily sittings over a period of some time, the Prime Minister requested the consultants to prepare an evaluation of the capital program of the previous four years.

That the Prime Minister was thinking not only of the need for emphasis on greater efficiency but also of possible significant modifications in the Government's economic policies and procedures was evident from the other matters on which he also requested the consultants' views. These included the principles which should guide the state enterprises in their pricing, financing and related policies; the particular problem of the Electricity Supply Board's financing and rate structure; the feasibility of using private agencies to manage the commercial side of the Union of Burma Railways operation; the feasibility of developing private channels for the marketing abroad of Burma's timber, rubber, minerals and possibly rice; the feasibility of joint ventures with foreign firms for both imports and exports; the considerations involved in assigning greater responsibility for mining operations to the private sector; and the desirability of certain joint shipping ventures then under consideration. The Prime Minister also ordered that a questionnaire be sent to all Government agencies asking whether they could not, by improving their efficiency, surrender part of their budgetary allotments.

Still another evidence of U Nu's preoccupation with efficiency and cost reduction was the innovation he introduced into the budget review process for 1958–59. He announced that the budget review would be conducted by a twelve-man committee designated by him. Apart from Chief Secretary U Khin Maung Pyu, now appointed Chairman of the Budget Committee, and U Ohn, the Prime Minister's advisor, the Budget Committee was composed of the same group of economic secretaries who functioned as the Committee of Experts, the Foreign Exchange Control Committee, the Anti-Inflation Committee, the Standing Committee for Supervision and Coordination, etc., and the chief economic consultant. Significantly, this Budget Committee was assigned responsibility for reviewing not only the capital budget but the current budget as well.[8]

During this period, negotiations were started on a second P.L. 480 arrangement with the United States. At the suggestion of the Government of India, negotiations were undertaken looking to the negotiation of a five-year trade clearing agreement with that country. Shimon Peres, of the Israel Defense Ministry, and General Dayan made a courtesy visit to Rangoon, followed shortly thereafter by Minister of Commerce Sapir as head of a trade mission which made a number of interesting proposals for further economic cooperation between the two countries. The first financial reports of the joint-venture trading corporations became available. These showed, for periods of operation ranging from six to nine months only, average profits of approximately 17 per cent on sales and approximately 40 per cent on investment! Arrangements with the United States for a loan to strengthen the police force and for the

8. Up to this time, the capital budget had been reviewed by the Committee of Experts under the auspices of the Economic and Social Board or the Planning Ministry. The current budget had always been reviewed by the Ministry of Finance. It may be noted that Bo Khin Maung Gale, the then Finance Minister, was close to U Kyaw Nyein.

sale of surplus military equipment to Burma were formally concluded. The "police loan" was for $10 million. At the same time, Burma was to be permitted to purchase, for $2 million worth of local currency, surplus military material worth perhaps ten times that much. U Kyaw Nyein, while in the Soviet Union and People's China, had made tentative arrangements for Soviet credits for the construction of dams and a Chinese credit for the construction of a textile mill. And the visit of the World Bank Mission under Martin Rosen brought to a head some fundamental questions involved in the Bank's relationship with the Government of Burma.

For some time there had been a feeling at the Bank that its relationship with the Government of Burma left something to be desired. The essence of this was that the Government had not taken the Bank fully into its confidence and that it did not fully welcome the Bank's advice. The Rosen mission hoped to establish a closer and more satisfactory relationship, on the basis of which the Bank could feel justified in participating in far greater measure in Burma's development effort than it yet had. The Government, however, was not ready for such a move. Prime Minister U Nu was not interested in new projects or expansion of the development program. And U Kyaw Nyein made it quite clear that, so far as he was concerned, Burma did not desire a close relationship with the World Bank. The Bank, he made plain, was essentially a capitalist institution incapable of viewing the problems and aspirations of a socialist state sympathetically. Nevertheless, by the time the World Bank Mission left Rangoon, it had inquired into a number of additional loan possibilities and had displayed some interest in several of them.

The most significant developments of the period April–June 1958 were on the political front, within the A.F.P.F.L. Significantly, U Kyaw Dun had not resigned from his post as Secretary-General of the A.F.P.F.L. as he had presumably indicated he would to U Ba Swe. U Kyaw Nyein's response was to organize a mass meeting of some 10,000 A.F.P.F.L. youths in the Insein district immediately north of Rangoon, and the size of the meeting was particularly noteworthy because Insein was considered U Kyaw Dun's political stronghold. A marked increase in crimes of violence and kidnaping in the Insein region followed. U Nu had already ordered the police to make a number of arrests of local A.F.P.F.L. officials in the Tharawaddy district, where the U Kyaw Nyein following was strong. He now ordered large-scale arrests of A.F.P.F.L. officials in the Insein district who were accused of complicity in many of the criminal acts. This naturally caused much comment.

While the Prime Minister was able to point out that he had impartially ordered the arrests, on the one hand, of followers of U Kyaw Nyein and, on the other, of followers of U Kyaw Dun, he wished to demonstrate that future police actions of this kind would continue to be completely impartial and non-political. He therefore took the extraordinary step of creating a four-man committee of civil servants to whom he entrusted complete supervision of the police forces in their attempt to restore law and order. In addition to the Inspector General of Police, this four-man committee included three highly respected civil servants — Chief Secretary U Khin Maung Pyu; Mr. James Barrington, the Permanent Secretary of the Foreign Office; and U Tun Thaung, the then Secretary to Deputy Prime Minister U Kyaw Nyein. The first three were considered apolitical. The designation of U Tun Thaung was perhaps intended to assure U Kyaw Nyein that supervision and administration of the police efforts would continue to be impartial. U Nu shortly followed this action by deposing the Minister for Home Affairs, Thakin Tha Kin, who was one of U Kyaw Nyein's closest supporters, and taking over the portfolio himself. This, he stated, was necessary to insure that control of the police would not fall into the hands of either A.F.P.F.L. faction. But U Kyaw Nyein did not accept U Nu's impartiality. It was U Nu's last action in taking personal charge of the ministry in control of the police forces which finally precipitated the A.F.P.F.L. split.

U Kyaw Nyein and his chief supporters in the A.F.P.F.L. — notably Thakin Chit Maung and U Tun Win, both of whom were certainly among the ablest members of the Cabinet — decided that they must fight back at what they obviously considered a declaration of political war. Even before the meeting which shortly took place between U Nu and U Kyaw Nyein, the Prime Minister told U Ba Swe that he had already decided to split the A.F.P.F.L. and to side with the Thakin Tin–Kyaw Dun group. According to this account[9] U Ba Swe had requested U Nu to reconsider this decision, and to postpone any split, at least until the general elections due in 1960. The split, however, was decided upon April 27, at a meeting between U Nu and U Kyaw Nyein. After their initial agreement to continue the Cabinet until the August session of the Parliament, and after U Ba Swe's decision to join forces with the Kyaw Nyein group, the Cabinet decided on May 5 to call a special emergency session of the Chamber of Deputies on June 5 to determine which faction should be invested with responsibility for forming a new government. The die was cast.

In the months that followed, charge and counter-charge flew between the "Clean" faction (also called the Nu–Tin group) and the "Stable" faction (the Swe–Nyein group). The entire country was beset with fears that whichever faction won the parliamentary test, the other would resort to violence. Fearing the worst, people rushed to the bazaars to stock up on rice, chilli, ngapi and other staples, and prices jumped sharply. The N.U.F. (National United Front), the Communist-minded opposition to the formerly united A.F.P.F.L., now declared for U Nu, charging that U Kyaw Nyein was

9. Sein Win, "The Split Story," *The Guardian* (Rangoon), March 25, 1959, p. 24.

merely a stooge for Western imperialist powers. Both factions, however, pledged themselves to acceptance of the parliamentary mandate and to non-violence. As the fateful day approached for the convocation of Parliament, June 5, U Ba Swe and U Kyaw Nyein demanded that U Nu resign prior to the parliamentary test. They also demanded that he pledge himself not to dissolve the Parliament in the event that the verdict went against him.

It was expected that the Swe–Nyein faction would obtain a large majority of the A.F.P.F.L. votes. U Nu would have a minority of A.F.P.F.L. votes, plus the votes of the N.U.F. The Swe–Nyein forces realized that the Shan and other Hill People's vote would never go against U Nu so long as he was Prime Minister. They hoped that, if he resigned prior to the vote, they might pick up some of it. And, of course, if U Nu resigned prior to the vote he would no longer be in a position to dissolve the Parliament. The status of the one remaining small bloc of votes, that of the Arakanese National Union headed by U Kyaw Min, was unclear. On the eve of the parliamentary sitting, however, the A.N.U.O. bloc declared for U Nu on his promise that, if elected, he would give serious consideration to its demand for separate state-hood for the Arakan. The Arakanese decision came in the midst of an intensive public debate over the constitutionality of a possible dissolution of Parliament by U Nu in the event that he failed to win a majority. This debate, occasioned by U Nu's refusal to announce in advance that he would under no circumstances dissolve the parliament (as U Ba Swe and U Kyaw Nyein had demanded), created renewed fears of violence on the part of the general public.

After the minimum of four days required by the Constitution, the parliamentary decision was taken on June 9. For the first time in the history of Burma, the final debate and roll call were broadcast over the radio. It was perhaps this decision to broadcast the activities — surely a felicitous one — which resulted in the restrained conduct of both sides during these climactic moments. The final vote was 127 to 119 in favor of U Nu. But 44 of U Nu's 127 votes had been cast for him by the N.U.F., on whose continued support his tenuous majority would henceforth depend.

In the immediate aftermath of the Parliament's decision, the "Stable" A.F.P.F.L. members constituted a new Supreme Council of the A.F.P.F.L., and voted to expel U Nu and all his followers. The new "Clean" A.F.P.F.L. Cabinet was especially noteworthy for the designation of U Kyaw Min, the leader of the Arakanese bloc and a former Secretary of Finance, as Finance Minister, and for the appointment of the able and devoted U Raschid as Minister for National Planning.

Once again U Nu called upon the insurgents to disarm and surrender, promising them the most lenient of treatment. He undertook among other things to declare a general amnesty for all crimes committed in the course of the insurrection and to call a national convention which would formulate a new "Charter for Democracy." He also assured the insurgents that, once they had surrendered their arms, he would permit the Communist Party to contest the forthcoming elections.

The N.U.F. joined U Nu in calling upon Thakin Than Tun to give up the insurrection. Than Tun, however, emboldened by the new turn of events which had placed the Government in a position of dependence on his aboveground supporters, strengthened his former demands. Not only did he continue to insist on negotiations with the Government prior to any surrender; he now boldly insisted that his "army" be permitted to retain its arms and that it be incorporated in the armed forces of the Government. Undoubtedly these demands — which U Nu did not accept — plus the arrogant behavior of the P.V.O. insurrectionists who did come in and form the People's Comrade Party, contributed much to the apprehension within the army.

There is little doubt that by this time the army had determined to take control if such action should become necessary to prevent the undue exercise of communist influence over the Government and possibly over the army. There was reason to think that U Nu already felt some concern over such a possible turn of events. This would certainly have been fortified by reports that U Ba Swe, as well as others of his group, were publicly claiming to have the support of the army, and stating that they would not be out of power very long.

Meanwhile, there were indications of a new trend in Burma's political life. In a number of cases, non-political independents were coming forward to declare that they would stand for Parliament in the forthcoming elections, which at this time were expected to be held either in November or the following March.[10] Dissension and splintering occurred among the left-wing groups which comprised the N.U.F. Various defections took place also in the two A.F.P.F.L. groups, with U Nu's "Clean" faction gaining on balance. Considerable doubt was expressed that the conventional August–September Budget Session of the Parliament would take place. Many considered that the "Clean" A.F.P.F.L. government could not face a budget session without serious danger of being voted out.[11] Although the Government first announced that the session would be held, it soon reversed itself and announced that it would defer the session and enact the budget by presidential decree.

In September, a conference of the "Clean" A.F.P.F.L. stalwarts provided a forum for a number of vociferous attacks upon the army. It was alleged that, in a number of areas, army colonels had displayed rank favoritism on

10. November would be just prior to the harvest, while March would be immediately following it.

11. Such a session would make possible numerous motions — for example, one against U. S. loan or P.L. 480 programs — on which at least part of the N.U.F. group would undoubtedly vote against the Government, and defeat it.

behalf of the Swe–Nyein faction, and that supporters of the "Clean" faction had been discriminated against and persecuted. It was even charged that the army was the "Number One Enemy of the People."[12] U Nu, who was not present at these sessions of the three-day conference, promptly disavowed these charges and expressed confidence in the integrity and impartiality of the army. Nevertheless rumors became widely current that the army was preparing to stage a *coup d'état,* and the army felt these rumors were sufficiently serious to warrant a formal denial. By mid-September the crisis had become acute. The split within the A.F.P.F.L. had been matched by analogous splits in the party's constituent organizations and in the trade unions, and open fighting took place between rival workers' groups, notably at port installations and the railway shops. The Cabinet vote to dissolve the Parliament, to enact the budget by decree and to hold general elections in November was followed by intense and dangerous maneuvering on all sides.

Neither A.F.P.F.L. faction trusted the other. Fears of assassination were expressed. Some of U Nu's followers, who commanded loyalties among the military police and other armed groups, had forces moved into strategic positions for possible action. Similar or counter moves were apparently made on the other side as well. The army, apprised through its intelligence of these movements and alleged plots, prepared for any eventuality. The Prime Minister, returning to Rangoon from an upcountry tour, was confronted by military leaders with the facts of the explosive situation as they saw them. It may be, as some reports have it, that the army demanded that U Nu oust certain of the chief troublemakers in his Cabinet and form a coalition with Ba Swe. Or it may be, as other versions have it, that U Nu requested the military to establish martial law, that the army demanded his resignation or that the army insisted that he call a budget session of the Parliament to demonstrate his Government's adherence to the Constitution. U Nu's version, the formally accepted one, is that he himself hit upon the plan to request the Parliament to turn responsibility for government over to General Ne Win for a period of six months, during which a caretaker government would concentrate on restoring law and order and make it possible to hold free elections in the country. On September 26, the Prime Minister addressed the country over the radio, quoting verbatim an exchange of letters which had that day taken place between himself and General Ne Win, in which he proposed such an arrangement and General Ne Win accepted it. On October 28, an emergency session of the Chamber of Deputies unanimously elected General Ne Win Prime Minister, and the period of uninterrupted A.F.P.F.L. rule was ended.

The impact of these political developments on the efficiency efforts pledged to the country has already been described for the period through March. The account may now be resumed for the period April–September.

12. Sein Win, *op. cit.,* p. 75.

The interest which U Nu had evidenced in March in evaluating development progress in the past four years had been followed in April with plans for a retrenchment drive in the Government. Over the years foreign technicians and advisors had made a number of suggestions looking toward much needed reforms in the Government's administrative apparatus and procedures. These had run more or less parallel with the stress placed by the economic consultants on improved administration and management in Government enterprises and essential services. The most dynamic of the United Nations public administration experts in Burma had been Brigadier Sydney Divers, who had recommended a number of basic steps needed in the public administration field, and who had succeeded in setting up within the Home Ministry a division aimed at improving public administration. This division was headed by U Chit Pe, a former Secretary of Agriculture and one of the more able and dedicated people in the Civil Service. U Chit Pe had been successful in bringing before the Cabinet an efficiency program aimed at reorganization — the elimination of duplicate branches in departments and their respective ministries and the liquidation of artificial patterns of organization and staffing which no longer corresponded to the Government's operational needs. This program, mistakenly called a retrenchment program, was taken up by the Prime Minister and approved by the Cabinet in April. But the May split in the A.F.P.F.L. caused the Government to defer action.

Prior to the split, for reasons which have been explained, the five Task Force reports prepared in the opening months of the fiscal year had waited in vain for action. After the split, jurisdiction over the Task Force effort automatically reverted to the Ministry of National Planning and its National Planning Commission. Indeed, in the Cabinet formed in June there was no longer a Deputy Prime Minister for National Economy, to whose office the Task Force effort had previously been assigned. The Prime Minister, however, was far too preoccupied with the developing political crisis to give his personal attention or that of the National Planning Commission to these reports. Thus there was little point in further Task Force operations, and the studies were discontinued.

An action program for the National Planning Commission prepared by the economic consultants — essentially an updating of the action agenda earlier prepared for the Economic and Social Board during U Ba Swe's prime-ministership — was similarly ignored, as were the several policy-position papers prepared at the Prime Minister's specific request. Although a special *ad hoc* committee of six ministers was constituted to consider import and price policies, particularly with respect to the Joint Venture Trading Corporations and the Civil Supplies, it took no action on them. The major report prepared by the economic consultants at the request of the Prime Minister, an Evaluation of the Capital Program 1952–53 to 1957–58, completed in July, found no reception at all. The Prime Minister displayed not the slightest interest in it. Having been prepared on his direct instruction, the report could not very well be submitted to anyone else, nor was anyone else in a position to use it effectively. The all-important fact was that U Nu's actions were of necessity geared to the fight for his political life. It was obviously for political reasons that he organized a General Planning Conference in July, in which he sat in intensive daily sessions with representatives of various functional groups in the economy — traders, producers, workers, students, clergymen, artists, etc. — and heard out their statements on what the Government should do for them. It was clear that action by the Government on any of the many policy recommendations already before it would have to wait upon consideration of the recommendations to be submitted as a result of the General Planning Conference. And if past experience was a reliable guide, little attention would be paid to these as well.

One positive result of U Nu's earlier resolve to seek increased efficiency in the Government was the inauguration by U Ba Khin, Director of Commercial Audit as well as Chairman of the State Agricultural Marketing Board, of a large-scale training program for government accountants. In a final effort to get something done on the efficiency front, the economic consultants submitted to the National Planning Commission a series of proposed directives which required only the stamp of approval to take effect. The directives put forward the fundamental measures most needed to improve the operation of the state-owned boards and corporations and the two actions considered the most crucial for the encouragement of private-sector investment. They would have set up the Government boards and corporations on an autonomous basis, provided for appropriate boards of directors and delegation of authority, established new accounting methods and procedures, taken initial steps to establish an industrial bank and simplified and liberalized the administration of foreign exchange controls. This final effort was shortly lost in the political tidal wave which brought a new government into office.

STATISTICAL HIGHLIGHTS OF 1957–58

Primarily because of the serious short-fall in paddy production, the index of agricultural production declined to 82 in 1957–58 from 93 the previous year. The gross domestic product declined in consequence by 5 per cent. Rice exports fell to 1.46 million tons from 2 million tons the year before. The value of rice shipments declined similarly from K 89.5 crores to K 66.3 crores. Within these totals, the tonnage and value of rice shipped on barter account declined from approximately 14 per cent of the total in 1956–57 to less than 9 per cent in 1957–58. As a result of measures taken early in the fiscal year to offset anticipated declines in rice production, exports and earnings, imports declined to K 111 crores from K 132 crores the year before. Consumer goods imports fell from K 94 crores to K 63 crores. However, capital goods imports, at K 48 crores, were substantially higher than the K 39 crores in the preceding year. Bolstered by foreign loans and a large flow of reparations, foreign exchange reserves increased by K 12 crores to K 68.2 crores at the end of the fiscal year, while the privately held money supply increased only moderately from K 121 crores to K 130 crores. Capital expenditures, programed at K 56.7 crores, amounted to K 52.3 crores, or practically the level of the year before. Consumer prices on the average held steady, the interim consumer price index actually declining one point from 116 the year before. Within this total, however, there had been a sharp decline of about one third in clothing prices, while food prices, sparked by sharp increases in the prices of oils and fish and fish products, increased by roughly 9 per cent.

CHAPTER 15

Cleanup and Consolidation:

The Military Regime—

September 1958–March 1960

Although General Ne Win formally took office as Prime Minister only on October 28, 1958, his regime, in effect, took power upon his acceptance on September 26 of Prime Minister U Nu's offer to turn responsibility for a caretaker government over to him. As of that date, the "Clean" A.F.P.F.L. Government virtually ceased to function, and General Ne Win plunged immediately into intensive planning and organizing preparatory to discharging his new responsibilities.

U Nu's letter proposing that General Ne Win take over stated that the primary purpose of the new Government would be "to provide all the necessary conditions and requirements that would ensure the holding of a free and fair General Election before the end of April 1959." U Nu also requested assurances that Government servants and members of the armed forces would abstain from "any encroachment or interference in the political field," that lawless acts committed by some military personnel would be suppressed, that particular attention would be given to the suppression of crime, that internal security would be established and that the Government's traditional policy of neutrality in foreign relations would be continued. General Ne Win's letter of acceptance specifically agreed to these stipulations, which were to constitute the priority objectives of his caretaker government. In accepting confirmation by the Parliament on October 31 of his designation as Prime

Minister, General Ne Win added to the above pledges his promise to take "severe action" against the "economic insurgents" who were responsible for high prices, and pledged himself to bring down the cost of living.[1]

In actuality, the goals of General Ne Win and his chief lieutenants in the armed forces went far beyond these objectives. Over the years they had been increasingly concerned over the "mess" the politicians had made of the country. Their sense of order had been offended by the slackness, indiscipline, waste and disorder which pervaded the society. Their patriotism had been outraged by the primacy given to personal and political interests as against the national interest. Filled by now with an ill-concealed contempt for the "politicians" who had brought about this sorry state of affairs, they were fairly bursting with impatience to attack and clean up the mess. This, for them, meant primarily the injection of discipline, order and morale into the body politic; the tightening up and de-politicalization of the public administration; and the elimination of waste and abuses in public activities. What they desired involved basically a clean break with the manner in which things had been done in the past. They were determined to conduct a thorough housecleaning with a broad and stiff broom. Once this was done, they planned to return to the barracks, but continue to keep a watchful eye on the politicians to insure that they would not again permit the nation to relapse into the intolerable conditions of the past.

In the initial act of choosing his Cabinet, General Ne Win made it quite clear that efficiency rather than politics was to be the key criterion. In place of the twenty-odd ministers who had formed the previous Government, he appointed only thirteen in addition to himself. Of these, only five ministers were politicians, and these represented the respective state governments, as was required by the Constitution. Of the other eight, two were jurists, five were respected former civil servants and one was an educator. Only two of these had responsibility for one ministry only. Each of the others, and the General as well, were responsible for three ministries or more.

The Cabinet, however, was not to be the significant decision-making body in this Government. Of more importance was the Military Staff Council, presided over by Brigadier Aung Gyi and Colonel Maung Maung, and composed for the most part of colonels and other officers assigned to key administrative and operating posts. It was by this Military Staff Council, reportedly, that the important decisions were made, subject only to the approval of General Ne Win. Had General Ne Win sat as Chairman of the Military Staff Council there would have been no need for the Cabinet at all, except as a vehicle for civilian appeals against military decisions. These decisions came

---

1. This exchange of letters, and General Ne Win's speech of acceptance to the Parliament, are to be found in the *Government in the Union of Burma, 1958 Nov.–1959 Feb.*, Director of Information, Rangoon, pp. 2–10.

before the Cabinet for confirmation, to be sure, but only to preserve the constitutional form. The Cabinet was, in effect, a constitutional "cover" and a sounding board before which General Ne Win could express his reactions to the proposals of his military aides — with whom he was not always in agreement — and make his decisions. The ministers well understood the real power position; they knew that the power resided elsewhere, and were fearful of opposing it.

In dealing with economic questions, the Military Staff Council took advantage of the experience of civil servants who had been most closely concerned with economic matters under the preceding Government. Some of these, notably U Kyaw Nyun, the Finance Secretary, U Mo Myit, the National Planning Secretary, and U Soe Tin, Executive Secretary of the Foreign Office, who had been responsible for reparations programing and foreign exchange controls over Government expenditures, sat as members of a new Economic Advisory Committee to the Cabinet, in which Brigadier Aung Gyi, Brigadier Tin Pe and Colonel Maung Maung also participated. Thus the military men were able to acquire background information and ascertain the views of these able civil servants.

The housecleaning, nation-building task which the military had set for itself was vast. There was no prospect at all that it could be achieved within the six months allotted to the caretaker government — the maximum which could be assigned to nonmembers of Parliament under the Constitution. It is not surprising, therefore, that the initial efforts of the military were directed not primarily to pacification of the insurrection but rather to economic, administrative, morale and housekeeping problems. Thus, at the February 1959 session of Parliament at which arrangements for the April elections were presumably to be made, General Ne Win had to advise the Parliament that the existing state of affairs would not permit free elections to be held so soon. He thereupon resigned in compliance with the terms of reference under which he had been elected, and avowed his willingness to carry out the duties which would be assigned to him as Chief of Staff if the Parliament should decide to hold elections as previously planned. But he also stated his willingness to continue in office, if the Parliament would vote the necessary amendment to the Constitution, until the conditions essential to the holding of free elections were established. The amendment was voted, and the Ne Win Government continued in office through March 1960.

The views which motivated the military regime were, in fact, well-founded. There was, after ten years of A.F.P.F.L. rule, a tremendous need to re-establish law and order, to improve the public administration, to increase the efficiency of the state-owned enterprises, to eliminate undue political influence and abuses, to instill among all elements and organizations in the society a greater sense of social responsibility and discipline and to place the national interest clearly above personal and party considerations.

So far as the cost of living was concerned, the unselective emphasis placed on the lowering of all prices by the Ne Win Government was somewhat off the mark. Prices had been stabilized for more than a year. True, prices of a number of commodities were out of line with prices in general, but quite special reasons were involved — chiefly ineffective or delayed procurement of certain imported commodities by Government agencies, unwise interference by the Government in the normal structure of the import trade and, in a few cases, seasonal or cyclical factors. For the most part, forces already in motion could be expected to moderate these out-of-line prices before long. Specific steps could be taken, to be sure, to hasten this outcome in specific commodity situations. More important, however, was "a modification in the structure of the import trade to make it less restrictive, less monopolistic, more competitive and more consumer-directed."[2]

A most important current economic problem which faced the new Government, and to which insufficient attention was paid at the time, was the export of the new rice crop surplus. Despite the traditional underestimation of the size of the new crop surplus by the Ministry of Trade Development and the State Agricultural Marketing Board, indications were that this surplus would amount to at least 2 million tons, and might range as high as 2.5 million tons. Combined with the carry-over from the previous year of some 800,000 tons, this meant an export availability of at least 2.8 million tons of rice and rice products for 1958–59. There were also indications that People's China might enter the international rice market with exports of perhaps 1 million tons. It was essential that the pricing of the new crop be realistic, with discounts for quantity purchases, and that every effort be made to market the crop as early as possible before potential buyers fully appreciated the international demand-supply position. In any event, early sales were essential to make large-scale shipments physically possible during the course of the year.

Also to be considered was the effect on domestic money supply of the purchase by S.A.M.B. of the record post-war crop anticipated, and the importance, therefore, of large export shipments, which would insure the foreign exchange needed to support an adequate flow of imports. The military, however, did not at first appreciate this problem. They were more concerned with locating and disposing of some 170,000 tons of old and spoiling stocks, which to them symbolized the slack operations of the previous Government. Their failure to appreciate the importance of early new crop disposal contributed to a low volume of rice shipments for the year (1.6 million tons), to a low level of imports in the first half of the year (only K 41 crores) and to a tremendous increase in the privately held money supply (K 27 crores). This

2. "What Should Be Done About the Cost of Living?," a memorandum submitted to the Economic Sub-committee of the Cabinet, by Robert R. Nathan Associates, Inc., November 7, 1958.

was the major economic failure of the military regime during its first year in office. But it is time to turn to a more orderly examination of how the Ne Win Government set about accomplishing the tasks it had set for itself, and to appraise its achievements.

ADMINISTRATION

The first and most significant administrative step taken by the Ne Win Government was to place colonels[3] and other high-ranking military officers in charge of almost every important Government operation. This meant, in the first instance, the state-owned boards and corporations, the public utilities, the state import and export trading enterprises, the manufacturing enterprises and the development corporations. It meant, also, the assignment of military officers to key Government posts in many of the old-line Government departments. In many cases these officers became directors-general or chief executive officers of the organizations. In others they took rank as deputy. In still others they were installed as observers or advisors. But in all these cases, they reported in fact to the Military Staff Council and only nominally to the ministers concerned, and they wielded the real power.

Simultaneously with this wave of new authority, the Government announced unequivocally that slackness and indiscipline in the Government services would no longer be tolerated. Throughout all Government offices, all personnel from the secretaries down were to report to work at 9:30 A.M. sharp, and to remain on duty until the close of the office day at 4:30 P.M. All personnel were to sign in on arrival, and attendance lists were to be brought to the secretaries for personal perusal a few minutes after the beginning of the day's work. Personnel who went out during working hours were to leave word where they had gone and for what purpose. A new note of obligation to duty was introduced. It was combined with a new sense of apprehension as well.

In the state enterprises, decision, efficiency and action were the order of the day. The colonels were impatient. They would brook no delay. Armed with clear authority from the Military Staff Council and confident of its support, their decision-making was crisp and their drive authoritative. They fairly vied with one another in "cleaning up messes." Cost reduction, revenue increases, improved accounting and higher standards of performance were enforced as best the colonels could understand and achieve them.

Throughout the Government establishment, personnel records were examined to determine whether jobholders met with minimum qualification requirements, and orders were issued to discharge some 3,000 employees whose qualifications were below the established standards. Laborers em-

3. After General Ne Win, there were only three or four Brigadier Generals in the Burmese Army. The next highest ranking officers were colonels.

ployed by the Government were required to disassociate themselves from labor unions controlled by politicians, and to be represented only by independent unions which would concern themselves with economic questions only. Well-to-do merchants and businessmen who, through political "protection," had been permitted to become delinquent in tax and loan payments were compelled under threats of foreclosure to settle up promptly. Student demonstrations and political meddling were sternly suppressed, and higher educational standards imposed. In such diverse ways was administration tightened and greater discipline enforced in every phase of the national life.

This emphasis on improved administration was best symbolized and most apparent to the general public in the administration of the city of Rangoon itself. The former municipal administration was rudely pushed aside as incompetent — which it was — and its functions were taken over by a military commissioner. The results were immediate and apparent to all. Details of military personnel and civil service employees were organized to clean streets and parks. After the initial cleanup, volunteers were called out to assist in finishing the cleanup and maintaining their neighborhoods. Vendors' stalls, which had encroached on the sidewalks and streets, were demolished in favor of new bazaars. Squatters' basha (bamboo and thatch) huts in crowded kwetthits (concentrations of such hutments) all over the city were taken down and moved, with military assistance, to the new satellite towns of Okkalapa and Thaketa, rehousing nearly 200,000 persons. Clogged and festering sewers and drains were cleaned. Garbage disposal, which had been intolerably ineffective, was organized and maintained. Rigid supervision of bus, taxi and pedi-cab transportation effected swift improvements in service. Pariah dogs began to disappear from the streets. Within the space of a few short weeks the city began to take on a new look and tone. And, after some months, it could be reported that even the death rate and the incidence of fires had been substantially reduced.

THE COST OF LIVING

The Ne Win regime wasted little time in taking the severe measures it had promised against those it had labelled "economic insurgents." In the belief that high consumer prices were due in large part to speculative hoarding by importers and distributors, a series of sudden raids sealed stores and warehouses in Rangoon. Books of accounts were requisitioned for examination, and merchants were required to produce evidence of ownership and legal importation and to demonstrate that they were not hoarding or profiteering before their goods and books were released. In concurrent action, safe-deposit boxes in all the Rangoon banks were sealed, and their owners were required to open them in the presence of the authorities. While not very much by way of illicit foreign currency or gold holdings was uncovered, these measures struck terror into the trading community. In neither case had the military troubled to obtain court orders. Yet such was the atmosphere of fear created that no one ventured to challenge the legality of these actions. Finally, in a number of cases resident alien merchants were arrested and deported, virtually without notice, as undesirable elements, without the formality of court orders, hearings or trial.

Steps taken to augment the supplies of high-priced goods were more constructive. One of the first acts of the regime was to terminate the ban which the A.F.P.F.L. Government had maintained on the slaughter of cattle. The effects of this were immediate. As cheap beef entered the bazaars, prices of mutton, poultry and fish declined markedly. Navy boats were used to augment and transport the fish catch. Military vehicles were used to haul firewood into the town.

Concurrent with these actions to improve supply were steps to improve distribution. The army itself set up a number of retail distribution points. The Civil Supplies Management Board, the cooperatives and the joint venture trading companies were also pressed to open new retail distribution facilities.

Price ceilings were imposed on a number of domestic goods and services. These not only included foodstuffs, firewood and cigarettes; even the price of taxi and pedi-cab rides and motion picture theater admissions were "voluntarily" reduced. Profit margins or markups were also imposed on essential imported commodities. These permitted markups of 5 to 7½ per cent for importers and wholesalers and 10 to 15 per cent for retailers. Retailers were required to post the ceiling prices on these commodities in plain sight.

Still further steps were taken with respect to the import and distribution of imported goods. A vigorous campaign was conducted to de-register spurious importers, and approximately two thirds of all registered importers were disqualified. Two of the joint venture trading companies through which producers had been required to purchase their industrial materials requirements, and which had proved clearly ineffective, were liquidated. Other joint venture trading companies were required to set aside a substantial portion of their available supplies for distribution in the districts. Many of the items previously included under the open general import license were placed under specific license. And toward the end, the Ne Win Government ruled that, effective June 1, 1960, all private agency imports into Burma could be arranged for only through Burmese firms.

The measures taken by the Ne Win Government were effective in reducing living costs, but not to the extent shown by official price indices. From September 1958, the index of consumer prices for low income families in Rangoon declined each month until, by February 1959, it had fallen by about 18 per cent. The largest declines were in the important food and beverages component of the index. While the seasonal low, established in February 1959, was not held, by the following September average living costs were still 12 per cent lower than they had been a year before. However, by March 1960, when the Ne Win Government concluded its term in office, the index was already some 11 per cent higher than it had been in March 1959 — a rather clear indication that the price reductions achieved in the early months of the regime had been due in substantial part to stock liquidation and to Government measures too severe, arbitrary and extreme to be permanent in their effect. There is, moreover, real question as to the accuracy of the reported price reductions. The lower prices did prevail in the bazaars — so long as supplies lasted. But the stalls were cleaned out early in the day, and many who had queued up were turned away with empty shopping baskets. It is only reasonable to conclude that a black market existed, and that average prices paid by consumers were higher than those reported in the Government statistics.

LAW AND ORDER

The record of the Ne Win Government in re-establishing law and order is impressive. Within nine months after the establishment of the caretaker regime, it was reported that the number of insurgents had decreased from some 9,300 to 6,365. The official data report almost 3,500 insurgent casualties — 1,176 killed, 1,362 wounded and 915 captured. They report, in addition, 2,304 surrenders during the same period.[4] The 15-month record shows a further reduction in the number of insurgents to a total of some 5,000; casualties of over 5,000 (1,872 killed, 1,959 wounded and 1,238 captured); and 3,618 surrenders.[5] The total of serious crimes reported for the first nine months — murder, dacoity, robbery and kidnaping — was 4,604, compared with 6,452 in the comparable nine-month period a year before.

Travel by rail, road and river became much safer and for the first time in years it was possible to operate inter-city public transportation facilities by night. The derailing of trains, the dynamiting of bridges, the mining of roads and attacks on river craft virtually ceased. Within the towns, too, law and order improved markedly.

These measures were not due solely to operations against insurgents and dacoits. They reflected improved organization, communications, equipment and material, better coordination of the law-enforcement bodies in the countryside, improved intelligence and better coordination with the villagers, vigorous action against the insurgents' above-ground sympathizers and poli-

4. *The Nine Months after Ten Years, The Caretaker Government* (Nov. 1958–July 1959), Ministry of Information, Rangoon, March 11, 1959. The failure of casualty and surrender data to tally with the indicated strength of the insurgents at the end of the period is attributed to new accretions to their ranks, chiefly in the Shan States.

5. *Is Trust Vindicated?*, Director of Information, Rangoon, 1960, pp. 31 *et seq.*

ticians who had been allied with criminal elements, expedited judicial procedures, stiffer punishments for law-breakers and, in general, improved discipline throughout the national community. Thus, of the approximately 57,000 firearm pieces recovered during Gen. Ne Win's first fifteen months in office, nearly 52,000 were recovered from unauthorized persons other than insurgents and surrendered personnel. The material and equipment obtained from the U. S. Government under the police loan and the surplus military equipment purchased through the 1957 agreement improved the law enforcement capabilities of the military and the police. Divisional and district security councils were established throughout the Union, in which local military commanders for the first time were given clear responsibility for coordinating the law-enforcing activities of the police and civil authorities. Villagers were encouraged and even pressured to inform on insurgents and dacoits, and were afforded a larger measure of protection than heretofore when they cooperated with law-enforcement bodies. Left wing above-ground sympathizers with the insurgents were harried and, in many cases, arrested. Strict controls were set up at strategic points to stop illegal movements of arms, ammunition and supplies to the insurgents. Expressions of sympathy in the left-wing press were controlled with the aid of new legislation which interpreted the nature of sedition broadly. A number of additional judges and magistrates were appointed to quicken the sluggish judicial process. In the first nine months, the number of offenses tried by sessions judges tripled and the number of offenses tried by ordinary magistrates doubled, as against the comparable figures a year earlier. Finally, the national registration, which had been in process since 1952 in a desultory way only, was vastly speeded up. The number of persons enumerated and photographed was more than double the total enumeration and photography identification in the six years preceding the Ne Win regime. In combination with the steps taken to build morale and instill a spirit of responsibility and discipline in the civil service and to develop a greater sense of social responsibility in community life, these measures made a great contribution toward a more orderly and responsible society.

POLICIES

Apart from the primary objectives and the central measures already discussed, there was relatively little in the way of new policy in the course pursued by the Ne Win Government. While it avowedly favored public economy and expressed horror at what it considered the wasteful and senseless development projects undertaken by the A.F.P.F.L. Government, it did not, in fact, reduce public capital expenditures for development. Not only did it accept without challenge the capital budget for 1958–59 prepared by the outgoing "Clean" A.F.P.F.L. Government; its own capital program for fiscal year 1959–60 was roughly the same size. The departure in investment policy was that the Ne Win Government would no longer borrow abroad for capital development projects, but would, however, accept foreign grants for such purposes, which the previous Government had refused to do.

Despite the reluctance of the Ne Win Government to embark on new development projects, and despite its avowed emphasis on the assignment of greater responsibility for development investment to the private sector, the army itself, through its Defense Services Institute, embarked on an ambitious investment program. The Defense Services Institute had been charged only with the operation of staff shops for the provision of essential commodities to its own personnel. Within a period of a few months after the Ne Win Government took power it had gone into the banking business, the department store business, the construction business, the ocean shipping business and the fishing business. It also operated an automobile service station, a bookstore, a bus line, a radio assembly plant, a motor workshop and a boot and shoe factory, conducted the country's coal and coke import trade, operated restaurants and held agencies for foreign automobiles. Thus it had become the largest and the most powerful business organization in the country.

In developing this large economic complex, the military were opportunistic. Scott & Co., a private English banking firm, had run afoul of the foreign exchange regulations and had had its license revoked. The military seized this opportunity to buy out the enterprise. Rowe & Co., a long-established English firm which had operated Rangoon's largest department store, was facing bankruptcy because for a long time it had been unable to obtain an adequate volume of import licenses. This firm, too, was looking for a purchaser, and the army moved in swiftly. Israel had long before proposed joint ventures or management arrangements in the fields of construction and ocean shipping. Previous governments had hesitated to go forward with these proposals. The army's relations with the Israelis had always been close, and it now went ahead on these projects with Israeli assistance. Other ventures were taken over because of the failure of other Government agencies to handle adequately the responsibilities previously assigned to them.

The army's readiness to move forward with these ventures and responsibilities arose out of more than sheer opportunism. Brigadier Aung Gyi, Colonel Maung Maung and other top officers in the army were, like the A.F.P.F.L. leaders, Socialists by conviction and desirous of economic development. They did not want development activity to slow down, even though General Ne Win was far more reluctant to undertake new ventures than they were. They could make a case, however, that army operation of such enterprises would be more efficient than operation by civilian agencies. Finally, the military men perhaps viewed these ventures as a means of providing for their own future. Retirement in the military services comes early. Here, in this complex of ventures controlled by the army, was the promise of a vast reservoir of future well-paid jobs for military personnel, their relatives and their friends.

There was one other significant development field in which General Ne

Win was anxious to move forward — namely, border settlements. Troubled by security problems near the Chinese border, by indigenous insurgents and by the problem of jobs for discharged military personnel, and impressed with Israel's success with agricultural settlements in border areas, he sent a sizable group of army families to Israel to live and work in settlements of various types, preparatory to the establishment of similar settlements in Burma. In the fall of 1960 the first group thus trained was already building settlements near the Chinese border, and a second group of army trainees was already in Israel.

With respect to the development program inherited from the previous Government, General Ne Win stalled for time on several U. S. loan projects on which agreement had already been reached, apparently because of his reluctance to undertake new commitments and his aversion to the use of foreign loans for such purposes, perhaps even more because of his suspicion that some of his own officers would administer the projects in such a way as to favor relatives and friends. Of the Russian "gift projects," he permitted the three already under construction to be continued — the hotel and technological institute in Rangoon, and the hospital in Taunggyi. But whereas the former Government had declared that the three additional projects included in the original agreement — the agricultural and industrial fairgrounds and the sports stadium complex — would be indefinitely deferred, the Ne Win Government stated that they would be abandoned altogether.

Policy with respect to the private sector was liberalized. Private trade was encouraged to play a larger supporting role than heretofore in rice and teak exports. The state export monopolies established for rubber and cotton were liquidated. Private exports could be rewarded by the issue of highly prized import licenses, up to 10 per cent of the value of the exports. Private investment was encouraged by enactment of the long-pending investment legislation. Approval was expressed, and some budget provided, for the long-considered establishment of an industrial development bank to help finance investment in the private sector.

Development projects in progress were closely reviewed with an eye to tightening up administrative and operating efficiency. In a few minor instances, operations were terminated. Also, presumably for reasons of economy, contract arrangements with the American economic and engineering consulting firms which had served the Government since 1951 were terminated as of February 1959, some seven months before their expiration date. While economy was undoubtedly a factor in these dismissals, they were motivated also by an apparent anti-foreignism which grew out of the military's confidence that they could deal unilaterally with the country's problems on a common-sense basis, and by their identification of the consultants with the previous regime, with which the military wished to make a clean break.

In the case of the economic consultants, there was also some confusion about the function they had served. General Ne Win, at least, was under the impression that their major function had been to seek out new development projects. The American consulting firms were not the only foreign technicians dismissed. The Government also dispensed abruptly with the services of many other paid foreign technicians and firms at the same time, notably the Evans medical firm, which was managing the state-owned pharmaceuticals mill under contract with the Government. The wave of dismissals extended even to the revered J. S. Furnivall, who, though he still retained the honorary title of Planning Advisor to the Government, had been engaged for years on an economic history of Burma, and on whom the Government had previously bestowed its highest honorary title, that of *Thado Thiri Thudhamma*. The dismissal of Furnivall, who had devoted virtually all his long adult life to the welfare of Burma, was perhaps the most unhappy example of the haste and ruthlessness with which the military regime on occasion acted.

The Ne Win regime left its mark on virtually every sector of the economy. For the most part, its achievements were constructive.

It emphasized more intensive farming methods and improved yields; it suspended further land nationalization and distribution pending inquiry into the efficacy of these operations; it terminated the ban on cattle slaughter and revived hides exports; it increased fisheries activities and supplies; it enlarged the capital of the State Agricultural Bank; it took strict measures to enforce repayment of agricultural loans; and it reduced the uneconomic price which had been paid for sugar cane at the mills.

To improve the quality of rice and rice export marketing, the Ne Win Government introduced price premiums for paddy of improved quality; it increased the differential toll payments made to millers for the milling of paddy of better grades; it sought to effect substantial improvements in rice milling facilities; and, in the 1959–60 fiscal year, having learned a lesson the preceding year, it emphasized the early sale of the new rice crop, established attractive prices, and gave price discounts for quantity purchases.

In the field of timber the Ne Win Government initiated the harvesting and export of green teak, a departure in teak marketing, and arranged for some improvement in sawmilling facilities. In the minerals field the Government's contract prerogative was exercised to increase its share in the joint oil venture from one third to 51 per cent, and the pace of exploration was stepped up. The highly inefficient Mineral Resources Development Corporation was merged with the Industrial Development Corporation and put under the management of the latter institution. Completion of the Balu Chaung Hydro-Electric Project was expedited and hydro power was brought onto the transmission line in April 1960. In the field of state-owned manufacturing industry, improved management and higher rates of production were achieved at the pharmaceuticals, steel, jute, cotton and sugar plants and at the brick and tile factory. Improved accounting was of major assistance in highlighting managerial and operating inefficiencies and in pointing the way to remedial action.[6]

While the achievements of the Ne Win regime were clearly visible to all, there is no doubt that the military aroused a considerable amount of resentment throughout the country. Naturally, not all the measures adopted were well-considered or successful. Many of the decisions were made in haste or without the necessary experience and judgment, and proved to be faulty. More important in this regard was that many basically sound decisions were carried out in a peremptory and ruthless manner. This disregard for the feelings of others is so alien to the Burmese cultural pattern that many people developed strong resentment against the military, even though they did not dare to express it. In the civil service, in the trading community, and among cultivators the feeling grew that they were being pushed around and lorded over.

This resentment found its outlet in the elections of March 1960. The Swe–Nyein group, which had hoped to gain votes by the favor of the military and by identification with it in the minds of the public, experienced a bitter disappointment. The overwhelming victory won at the polls by U Nu and his new Pyidaungsu (Union) Party[7] was due not only to the immense popularity of U Nu throughout the country and to his promise to make Buddhism the state religion, but also to his veiled references to fascism and to the popular identification of the Swe–Nyein group with the military authorities. In fact, U Ba Swe, when he became aware late in the campaign that this identification was damaging rather than helpful, attempted to disavow the connection by announcing that, if elected, he would send the colonels back to the barracks. His disclaimer, however, came too late.

6. Ironically, many of the constructive actions taken by the Ne Win Government followed recommendations previously made by the same economic consultants the military had abruptly dismissed, recommendations not accepted or acted upon by the previous Government. Among these were the early sale and shipment of the rice export crop with price discounts for quantity purchases, the payment of incentive prices for improved paddy, a rice mill improvement program and an expanded program for agricultural loans; a saw mill renovation and expansion program and an invigorated highway construction program; liquidation of the industrial joint venture trading corporations specializing in industrial goods imports and award of only part of the import licenses for the commodities they had handled to the remaining joint venture corporations; a severe reduction in the lists of registered importers; removal of the ban on cattle slaughter, accompanied by a revival of hides exports, and emphasis on an increased fish supply; the enactment of investment legislation, establishment of an industrial development bank and the allocation of a more important role to the private trade in rice exports; a greater delegation of authority to and within the public enterprises, emphasis on more timely commercial-type accounting in the boards and corporations; the enforcement of higher standards of qualification and performance in the public services, improved tax collections and enforcement of repayment of agricultural and other loans; and the resumption of night runs by the railways and discontinuation of international flights by the new Viscount aircraft.

7. Pyidaungsu (or Union), it should be clear, was the new name adopted by the "Clean" A.F.P.F.L. Party. The "Stable" A.F.P.F.L., headed by U Ba Swe and U Kyaw Nyein, dropped the adjective, and became the A.F.P.F.L.

There is good reason to believe that some of the military strongly favored the victory of the Swe–Nyein group, perhaps because they felt that U Ba Swe, as Prime Minister, would lend himself to continued control by the military from behind the scenes, while U Nu and his party would not. In fact, there is more than a little reason to believe that, even after U Nu's March 1960 victory at the polls, some of the top military men were in favor of finding some pretext for declining to transfer power to the newly-elected Government, and that this sentiment had to be overruled resolutely by General Ne Win himself. In any event, the transfer of power took place in April 1960. It was perhaps just as well for the military that this was so.

The country had badly needed the emphasis on law and order, improved efficiency, tighter administration, delegation of authority and responsibility, discipline and the national interest which the military regime had provided. Even if the emphasis was exaggerated in some instances, and even if, in execution, the military sometimes went too far, this did correct the most serious weaknesses evident under the previous governments, and pointed clearly to the new directions necessary. But during its 18 months in power, the military had contributed to the country substantially all that it had to contribute. Its thinking was not broad, flexible and statesmanlike enough to deal constructively with the problems of Burma's further development. When U Nu returned to office in April 1960 the real question was what he and his colleagues had learned from the mistakes of the past and from the accomplishments of the military Government. Would U Nu be able to retain and institutionalize in a democratic way the reforms introduced by the military, eliminate the weaknesses and political abuses of previous A.F.P.F.L. Governments and at the same time go forward resolutely to achieve the objectives of economic and social development? These were the questions which confronted U Nu and his colleagues in the Pyidaungsu Party as they once more took up the reins of government.

STATISTICAL HIGHLIGHTS OF THE NE WIN REGIME

General Ne Win's Government spanned the full fiscal year 1958–59 and the first half only of 1959–60. Because the budget for 1958–59 was prepared by the outgoing U Nu Government, and because basic economic developments — such as the size of the rice harvest — cannot be attributed to the Ne Win Government, only some of the highlights described below can be taken as measures of its performance.

Gross domestic product, in real terms, rose in 1958–59 by some 7 per cent over the year before, which had, however, been affected adversely by a poor rice crop and which was itself down 4 per cent from the previous year. Compared with 1956–57, the real product in 1958–59 was higher by only 2 per cent. Initial estimates for 1959–60 suggest another increase of 5 per cent over 1958–59. More than half of the 1958–59 increase was contributed by the agricultural sector, chiefly through the record-breaking post-war rice harvest. In 1959–60, agriculture was expected to account for only one third of the anticipated increase, with substantial assistance from the rice marketing, government, public utilities, forestry and "other industries" sectors.

Although performance in marketing the 1958–59 rice crop was poor — out of availabilities of well over 2.5 million tons, only 1.6 million tons with a value of K 71.6 crores were shipped — other exports increased, and the rice lesson was taken to heart in 1959–60, when the harvest was even larger. Export shipments in the first six months were close to 1.1 million tons, as compared with a little more than 600,000 tons during the first six months of 1958–59, and shipments were expected to reach 2 million tons for the year as a whole. After a slow start, imports in 1958–59 recovered swiftly and, for consumer goods especially, reached a high level in the first half of 1959–60. In March 1960, the foreign exchange reserves, at K 71 crores, were some K 3 crores higher than they had been when the Ne Win Government assumed office. The course of consumer prices during the period has been described. The net increase in the internal public debt for 1958–59, at approximately K 31 crores, was the largest recorded since 1955–56, as was the increase of K 28 crores in the privately held money supply. Further debt and money supply increases were held in check during the first half of 1959–60, but the money inflation of 1958–59 obviously contributed to the whittling away of the substantial price declines achieved during the first half of that year.

Part IV

IMPLEMENTATION BY MAJOR SECTORS AND PROJECTS

CHAPTER 16

Implementation of the

Agriculture and Irrigation

Program

The Five-Year Agricultural Plan adopted by the Pyidawtha Conference was aimed at self-sufficiency through the restoration of pre-war paddy production and rice exports and increased output in a number of other food and fiber crops. These objectives were to be achieved with the aid of irrigation, land reclamation, fertilizer and mechanization programs, and complemented by a land nationalization and distribution program. The American consultants, while precluded by their terms of reference from recommending a comprehensive program for agricultural development, did present a great many recommendations bearing on implementation of the agricultural program in their Comprehensive Report. Their program also provided for the investment of some K 45 crores in irrigation projects. In adopting these recommendations, the Implementation Conference of February 1954 called also for the preparation of a comprehensive plan for agricultural development. Late in 1954 a Land and Agricultural Planning Commission (L.A.P.C.) was set up to prepare such a program. Its draft report, submitted in the spring of 1956, was never formally considered by the Government. The L.A.P.C. Report did, however, provide the basic framework for the agricultural sector of the Four-Year Plan of 1957, and contributed to the emphasis which this plan placed on the need for expanded paddy production and on the role of the agricultural sector in economic development.

Table 31

PUBLIC CAPITAL EXPENDITURES
FOR AGRICULTURE AND IRRIGATION,
1952–53 TO 1959–60

(*K Crores*)

Year	Agriculture	Irrigation	Total
Total	33.50	3.25[c]	36.75
1952–53	.46	[a]	.46
1953–54	6.76	1.24	8.00
1954–55	3.23	.37	3.60
1955–56	4.35	.20	4.55
1956–57	3.25	.68	3.93
1957–58[b]	5.47	.76	6.23
1958–59[b]	6.09	[a]	6.09
1959–60[b]	3.89	[a]	3.89

Source: *Economic Survey of Burma,* various years through 1960, for 1953–54 to 1958–59 data; 1959–60 data from "Capital Expenditures for 1959–60," C.S.E.D., New Secretariat, Rangoon; 1952–53 data from "A Review of Economic Planning in Burma," U Thet Tun, Ministry of National Planning, Oct. 1959.

a. Included in agriculture figure and not separately available.
b. Revised budget estimates.
c. Incomplete.

Public capital expenditures for agriculture and irrigation amounted to nearly K 37 crores from 1952–53 through 1959–60 (Table 31), excluding the cost of the land nationalized (K 9 crores) and the capital provided for the State Agricultural Bank (K 5 crores). While agricultural investment amounted to only some 9.4 per cent of total public capital expenditures for the eight-year period, from 1955–56 to 1959–60 capital outlays for agriculture were 21 per cent greater than in the previous four years.

Details of agricultural capital expenditures are not available for the entire period. They are, however, available by major program component for the first four years of the program. These figures are shown in Table 32.

About seven tenths of the agricultural capital expenditures during the four years ending 1955–56 were for rice storage and related facilities. The next largest expenditures were for irrigation and crop improvement and expansion projects. Within the relatively small sums spent for irrigation, equipment expenditures far exceeded those for irrigation works proper. While detailed data on the distribution of agricultural capital expenditures for the years 1956–57 through 1959–60 are not available, the lion's share was for the land reclamation and paddy expansion project and companion programs for rice storage, milling and handling facilities.

The small share of total public investment devoted to agriculture and irrigation may appear to have been seriously inadequate in an economy which was so heavily based on agriculture, and in which opportunities and need for

Table 32

CAPITAL EXPENDITURES FOR AGRICULTURE AND IRRIGATION,
BY MAJOR PROGRAM COMPONENT, 1952–53 TO 1955–56

(K Lakhs)

	1952–53	1953–54	1954–55	1955–56
Total	103.51	644.43	358.79	361.92
Crops improvement project	51.32	29.26	52.96	32.54
Paddy (expanded production)	44.00	—	—	—
Groundnuts	—	—	.06	—
Tobacco	—	7.37	13.64	22.56
Jute	1.35	5.45	11.55	2.27
Cotton	2.38	3.41	4.83	5.81
Coconut and betel nuts	3.59	13.01	22.86	1.61
Others (onion, coffee, etc.)	—	.02	.02	.29
Rice milling and related facilities	11.22	458.71	215.48	248.45
Farm mechanization scheme	1.63	3.77	.78	42.83
Animal husbandry project	5.69	12.19	13.05	6.69
Construction of buildings, offices, staff quarters for agriculture	.24	7.78	5.23	1.31
Irrigation and soil conservation projects	33.18	124.32	38.11	18.56
Irrigation works				
Irrigation works proper	32.17	24.80	13.06	13.25
Construction of staff quarters and facilities	—	2.36	.01	—
Tools and plant, etc.	1.01	97.16	24.05	5.15
Afforestation and soil conservation schemes	—	—	.99	.16
Land surveys and reforms	—	—	1.12	.76
Aerial survey	—	—	.06	.32
Land nationalization and re-distribution, including colonization	—	—	1.06	.44
Research	—	7.23	29.33	8.95
Agricultural research	—	7.09	22.95	4.94
Veterinary research	—	.14	6.38	4.01
Miscellaneous projects and expenditures	.23	1.17	2.73	1.83

Source: Program Reporting Section, Economic and Social Board, undated (prepared some time during 1956–57).

Note: These detailed tabulations were prepared at an earlier date than were the data shown in the preceding table, and the totals are somewhat disparate. Nevertheless, the details shown in this table reflect with reasonable accuracy the distribution of expenditures within the program.

development of agriculture were so great. This disparate relationship between the possibilities of the sector and the share of public investment devoted to it is not so serious as might be supposed at first glance. In the first place, primary responsibility for investment in agriculture rested with the cultivators and landowners. They were to maintain and build dikes and bunds, increase and improve their livestock and farm buildings, add to and improve their tools and implements, and so on. Secondly, achievement of the agricultural goals required less the investment of huge sums for dams and irrigation works than it did the restoration of civil order and relatively low-cost schemes for land clearance, the building of earth embankments to prevent flooding and erosion, the use of improved seeds and insecticides, the development of extension programs, and similar measures. Deficiencies in the implementation of the agricultural program, as will be seen, were due far more to ineffective planning and execution than to the failure to allot the capital required.

The most important agricultural programs were: (1) crop expansion and improvement in the production of paddy, cotton, groundnuts, jute, sugar cane, coconuts, Virginia tobacco and rubber; (2) rice storage, milling, cleaning and grading, and mechanical loading and handling; (3) irrigation; (4) mechanization; (5) agricultural credit; (6) land nationalization; and (7) extension and research.

CROP EXPANSION AND IMPROVEMENT

PADDY PRODUCTION

The Government adopted as specific targets the restoration of pre-war levels of paddy production and rice exports without formulating specific means by which these objectives were to be achieved. It was, of course, assumed that pacification of the insurgency in and of itself would make a tremendous contribution to increased paddy output. It was also assumed, apparently, that the land nationalization program would result in increased and improved land use. In 1952–53, when the larger concentrations of insurgent bands had been broken up, the Government offered a subsidy of K 10 per acre for additional paddy acreage put under the plow. It also offered a set of prizes to cultivators who produced substantial increases in yields. In that year, the Government paid out K 38 lakhs in subsidies and K 6 lakhs in prizes, and some 600,000 additional acres of land were sown to paddy. Subsidies were, however, paid on only 380,000 of the additional acres. More than one third of the additional acreage was thus not dependent on subsidy payment at all. How much the 380,000-acre increase which received subsidy payment was due to this factor, and how much it was due to improved security conditions in the countryside, is impossible to determine.

In any event, Government support of the paddy expansion scheme was not a factor in the next three years. Improved seed was distributed and agricultural loans were extended, as for most crops. Subsidy payments were, however, discontinued as rice surpluses mounted, export prices declined and stocks spoiled. For a time there was even a growing disposition within the Government to curtail paddy production in favor of other crops so as to prevent further surpluses. This tendency was checked in 1954–55, when rice exports on barter account raised the level of shipments some 400,000 tons over the total of the preceding year and emergency storage facilities were built. The arrangement with India in May 1956 of a five-year, 2-million-ton rice sales agreement, and the findings presented in the L.A.P.C. Report, finally liquidated this negative sentiment. But three years of potential progress had been lost.

As it became clear that close to 2 million tons of rice would be exported in 1955–56 and that a substantial cut would be made in the level of carry-over stocks, the economic consultants pointed out that a determined attack on the problem of increased paddy output could no longer safely be deferred. With annual shipments already at a level in excess of current surplus production, and with stocks declining, it would not be long before export shipments would be limited by the size of the new crop surpluses. A new paddy expansion program was thereupon approved by the Government for the four-year period beginning 1956–57.

The objective of the new paddy expansion scheme was to increase the land under paddy production by some 1.2 million acres. This, it was anticipated, would increase the production of rice and rice products by some 700,000 tons and raise new rice export availabilities to the level of 2.5 million tons annually. It was anticipated that still further substantial production increases would occur on lands adjacent to those reclaimed by the project because of increased flood protection, and that higher yields generally would result from the use of improved seeds and practices. The major techniques to be employed were repairs to embankments, bunds and drainage channels; jungle clearing; loans for purchases of cattle and equipment; and increased use of improved seeds and fertilizers. Pest control, minor irrigation works, emergency seed beds, extension work and some resettlement were lesser components in the program. Budgeted capital costs for the four years 1956–57 to 1959-60 were more than K 13 crores, supplemented by approximately K 9 crores for which provision would be made in current rather than capital budgets. Of the K 13 crores of capital costs, K 5.6 crores were for cattle and equipment purchase loans, K 4.1 crores for embankments and drainage work, K 2.2 crores for jungle clearing and about K 1 crore for fertilizers. Relatively minor sums were provided for other elements in the program.

Responsibility for execution of this second-phase paddy expansion program was given to the Land and Rural Development Corporation (L.R.D.C.). Since adoption of the program coincided with a change in the management of this important organization which brought to it the highly competent and energetic U Ko Gyi as Director-General and the equally competent and energetic U Hpu as Chief Executive Officer, the program was in excellent hands. It was also well conceived and planned. The areas to be brought under cultivation were carefully delineated, and specific measures appropriate to each area were prepared. In addition, both acreage targets and the bringing of new areas into cultivation were phased. Because of the lead time involved in machinery and equipment procurement and in the engineering work necessary to reclaim more difficult areas, the program selected for initial implementation those areas which could be tackled with the least engineering preparation and the least equipment. Care was exercised in the selection of component projects and district officers; the necessary liaison with other Government agencies, including the military, was provided; and the job was attacked with real energy.

In 1956–57, the first year, performance was ahead of schedule. The reclamation target of 200,000 acres was exceeded by 35 per cent. Some 18,000 families were resettled. New embankments and drainage canals improved flood protection and drainage on some 200,000 acres over and above the 270,000 acres reclaimed. This resulted in increased production of some 60,000 tons of rice and rice products in addition to the more than 100,000 tons grown on the newly reclaimed acreage. Still another 30,000 tons of rice and rice products resulted from other program efforts, including tractor plowing and the distribution of almost 1 million baskets of improved paddy seed, 2,500 tons of fertilizer and 200 pumps. Minor irrigation projects, pest control measures and improved storage practices further augmented first-year gains. In combination, these measures increased export availabilities by some 250,000 tons in 1957–58, and provided a vitally important offset to the serious crop losses which occurred elsewhere in the paddy economy because of adverse weather conditions that year. Not the least of the initial benefits was the marked improvement in security which occurred in the project areas. This was due not only to the elimination of insurgent hideouts through jungle clearing, but also to the enthusiastic support of the villagers. Insurgents hesitated to incur their displeasure by sabotaging a project which meant so much to them, and many former insurgents accepted employment with the project.

The program had entered upon its second year when it became, in December 1957, the first project approved under the $25 million U. S. development loan. This loan provided $5.4 million to finance the purchase of needed equipment, including brush cutters, crawler tractors, wheeled tractors, dredgers, earth-moving equipment and spare parts, and work shop equipment for repair and maintenance work. Procurement and delivery were swift. All equipment ordered under the U. S. loan was delivered and placed in operation within the year.

A shortage of skilled tractor operators and mechanics limited the use of much of this equipment to one shift a day, and the shortage of experienced master mechanics made it necessary to carry out all but minor repairs at Rangoon, which made for delays and higher costs. But these bottlenecks were soon broken by the establishment of twelve district workshops, each under the supervision of a master mechanic, and by a training program for tractor drivers and mechanics.

In 1957–58, some 350,000 acres — 50,000 acres more than the target for the year — were reclaimed. Of this total, 270,000 acres were actually placed under cultivation. By the end of 1959, with one year left to go, some 1.15 million acres had been reclaimed, of which 900,000 had been placed under cultivation, and some 60,000 families had been resettled on the reclaimed lands. Mobile workshop units had been introduced to supplement the equipment maintenance provided by the district workshops. Nearly 23,000 tons of fertilizer and more than 8,000 plow cattle were distributed in 1958–59 and 1959–60 alone. Improved seed was introduced on hundreds of thousands of acres.

The project, clearly outstanding among all Burma's development projects, was appraised by Richard McCaffery, Chief of I.C.A.'s informal mission[1] in Burma, as one of the most successful of I.C.A.'s assistance projects anywhere. The success appears to have been due, for the most part, to the following factors:

(1) The project was concerned with something the Burmese knew very well how to do and had already achieved before;

(2) It had the leadership of two of Burma's most capable civil servants, U Ko Gyi and U Hpu;

(3) Special arrangements were made for decentralization of financial authority, which permitted the L.R.D.C. Director-General to make decisions involving up to 2 lakhs on his own authority, and to delegate authority to spend lesser amounts to subordinates and district committees;

(4) L.R.D.C. leadership was given support and a relatively free hand by U Kyaw Nyein, the Deputy Prime Minister and, after 1956, Chairman of the Board;

(5) The program had the cooperation of the military;

(6) It had the enthusiastic support of the villagers because they appreciated the immediate benefits that would accrue to them;

(7) L.R.D.C. leadership readily utilized the suggestions made by the agricultural economist on the staff of the economic consultants because of an association of some five years' standing and the mutual trust and respect which had developed in that time;

(8) New graduates of the Ford Foundation-assisted Agricultural Institute at Pyinmina were available for executive jobs in the field; and

(9) The I.C.A. cooperated not only in the selection of equipment but in insuring prompt procurement and delivery. The careful programing required in connection with the loan application was also beneficial.

1. Although I.C.A. established a staff in Burma to administer the U. S. Development Loan, this group — at the request of the Burmese Government — was not designated a mission, but was formally considered part of the U. S. Embassy staff.

COTTON

The objective of the cotton improvement program was to convert the 400,000 acres already planted to cotton from the short and medium staple Wagale and Mahlaing-3 varieties to a $\frac{7}{8}$-inch staple Mahlaing-5 variety which would provide the necessary raw material for the Government textile mill then in operation and for the additional textile mill capacity contemplated. The 20,000-spindle textile mill required some 15,000 bales of M5 cotton annually and, when expanded, would require some 25,000 to 30,000 bales. Since it was anticipated that enough additional textile mill capacity would be built to utilize 75,000 bales of cotton per year, this was the target adopted for the M5 conversion program.

The basic step was the provision of pure seed to some 12,000 private seed farms. This was to be followed by supervision of their production, grading of cotton in the field, purchase from the seed farms of all cotton with a lint of $\frac{3}{4}$ inch or better, ginning of the cotton in state-owned or state-leased ginneries, resale of the lint to the state cotton mill, and retention of all improved seed for the following year's planting.

Implementation of the cotton improvement program was very poor. Although the reported figures showed an increase in M5 acreage from some 7,000 in 1952–53 to almost 92,000 in 1957–58, the supply of M5 cotton to the mill increased only from 1.8 thousand to 6.8 thousand bales, less than half the amount required and less than 10 per cent of the original five-year target.

The negligible increase in M5 cotton supplied to the mill was due in part to purchases made by the cooperative societies for export. Nevertheless, the increase in M5 production was not commensurate with reported acreage increases. This disparity is a significant clue to the failure of the program. The chief reasons for it were a careless mixing of cotton varieties in the field and poor grading at the purchasing centers. It was necessary to classify longer-staple cotton accurately in the field, keep it separate at the gin, return the pure seed to the cultivators, see that it was planted where cross pollination would not occur and cull out undesirable plants before they could fertilize others. These things were not done successfully. The fault lay chiefly in poor leadership and poor organization at the L.D.R.C. during the first four years of the program, prior to the management change in 1956.

GROUNDNUTS

The groundnuts (peanuts) program called for an increase in acreage from approximately 750,000 in 1952–53 to 1.1 million. This, it was estimated, would increase production of edible oils by some 42,000 tons, make Burma self-sufficient in this important commodity, and so reduce foreign exchange expenditures by some K 4 crores annually. In addition, the program was expected to increase the value of oil-cake exports by approximately K 1 crore annually.

The program relied on the distribution of improved seed, on tractor plowing, which would make possible the production of groundnuts as a second crop after paddy, and on the introduction of groundnuts as a new crop in the Hill States. In its first four years, it brought about a production increase of only some 10,000 tons of additional groundnut oil, or 25 per cent of the five-year target. A start was made, however, toward the growing of groundnuts as a second crop after paddy.

Ineffective implementation of the groundnut project during the first four years was due in large part to the L.R.D.C.'s reliance on the Agriculture Department for the actual job, even though it should have been clear that that department lacked the necessary staff. Poor leadership characterized both agencies. This was especially reflected in seed procurement and distribution. Inferior seeds were distributed, perhaps because of a desire to be economical. Subsequent checks disclosed that in many cases the cultivators did not plant the seeds at all but used them for food and fodder instead. Whether cultivators would have put the seed to such uses if it had been of superior quality is doubtful. In any event, it is clear that the program failed to make adequate provision for liaison with and supervision of the cultivators, on whom it relied for increased production. Poor leadership was also reflected in the rivalry and lack of cooperation which developed between the L.D.R.C. and the Agriculture Department.

With the change in management at the L.R.D.C. in 1956, steps were taken to achieve more effective implementation of this program. Seed procurement and distribution were improved. Responsibility was more clearly assigned, the L.R.D.C. taking responsibility in Burma proper, and the Agriculture Department in the Hill States. The program was also augmented to include the growing of groundnuts as a winter crop on kaing land.[2] Tractor pools, crop loans and arrangements for oil pressing were added to the program for the Hill States. By 1959–60 these measures brought some 250,000 additional acres under groundnut production and the total to very near the target of 1.1 million acres. The increase was more than double that achieved during the four years ending 1955–56.

JUTE

The goal of the jute project was to bring under cultivation 150,000 acres of this crop, which was new to Burma. This goal, it was anticipated, would result in the production of 50,000 tons of jute. Of this amount, some 24,000 tons

2. Kaing land is highly fertile land which is submerged during the monsoon but on which crops can be grown during the dry season.

would be required to enable the new jute mill to produce 24 million bags annually on a two-shift basis. The surplus would be available for export. The techniques to be employed were the operation of jute seed improvement farms for seed distribution to the cultivators, cash loans, the rental of small irrigation pumps for use during the dry season to make possible early plowing, and provision of tractor pools on a credit basis to prepare seed beds. The L.R.D.C. would buy the crop, sell part of the fibre to the Government mill and export the remainder. To facilitate this work it would operate baling presses and storage facilities and help build retting tanks.

The project was initiated in 1952–53, and for the first five years it was almost a complete failure. By 1956–57, when the target of 150,000 acres was to have been reached, only some 7,500 acres were sown to jute. As against the tonnage target of 50,000 tons of fibre for that year, the L.D.R.C. obtained less than 1,000 tons.

Since jute was a crop new to Burma, it was only to be expected that the difficulties would be more serious than those encountered in other crop expansion programs. But this cannot justify the abysmal initial failure of the program. Previous experiments had demonstrated that good-quality jute could be grown in Burma with satisfactory yields. Perhaps the greatest of the problems was difficulty in developing a field staff knowledgeable in jute production. The same weaknesses of leadership, planning and management which plagued other crop production programs from 1952–53 to 1955–56 were also the prime cause of failure in the case of jute. Excessive reliance was placed on cash loans, while other techniques were neglected.

With the change in management of the L.R.D.C. in 1956, a marked acceleration in the jute program soon became evident. Field personnel from the paddy expansion project helped during their off season. The use of small pumps and imported fertilizers was added to the earlier techniques, and improved staff training and supervision, as well as better planning, brought quick results. Acreage sown and fibre produced tripled from 1956–57 to 1957–58, with 22,000 acres sown and some 2,700 tons of fibre produced. Acreage increased to 30,000 in 1958–59, and to 34,000 in 1959–60.

SUGAR CANE

The objective of the sugar cane program was not to increase total acreage and production, but rather to insure an adequate supply of cane for the three Government-owned sugar factories — the nationalized Zeyawaddy plant and the new factories at Pyinmina and Namti. Sugar cane was a long-established crop, in the growing of which the cultivators had a considerable experience, and was used chiefly in the manufacture of jaggery (molasses). Because sugar cane yields a far greater amount of sugar if it is crushed when less than

24 hours old, and because delivery from the fields to the sugar factories is by slow oxcart, sugar cane for factory use should not be grown beyond, say, a 50-mile radius of a sugar factory, and preferably it should be grown within a smaller radius.[3] An assured supply for the three mills required the cultivation of 50,000 acres within such radii to produce 600,000 tons of cane. With an average recovery of 10 per cent, the mills operating at capacity could produce about 60,000 tons of white sugar a year — providing for the then consumption level of 45,000 tons, with something to spare for increased consumption.

No problem was encountered in getting the necessary acreage planted to sugar cane in the vicinity of the mills. The difficulties were of quite another kind. Because the competitive price paid for sugar cane by the jaggery-makers, the only alternative users, was approximately K 20 per ton, and the buying price established at the mills was placed at K 40 per ton arbitrarily and uneconomically, the problem quickly became one of oversupply. This was aggravated by management and mechanical difficulties at the mills — especially the Pyinmina Mill — which kept them operating at considerably below capacity. On more than one occasion the inability of the mills to use the cane resulted in widespread hardship among nearby cultivators and led to acreage cutbacks the following crop season.

A number of other serious problems also arose. The most important of these were low cane yields per acre and poor quality cane. Whereas cane yields on the Pyinmina State Experimental Farms in pre-war years had averaged 38 tons per acre, yield on the same farms had now declined to about 20 tons per acre. Clearly the cane sets were running out, and new strains were required. Even these lower yields were not matched by the producing farmers. As compared with average anticipated yields of 12 tons per acre, yields in the Myitkyina district ranged from 6 to 10 tons per acre, because of poor land clearing, inferior cultivation methods and field spoilages. Substantial portions of the crop were lost to smut and red rot, and insect pest damage was considerable. The impact of the uneconomic buying price established for sugar cane on the economics of the sugar mills will be described elsewhere. As far as the cultivator was concerned, the excessive price paid for his cane lessened his incentive to increase yields and improve quality.

If the establishment of an excessive price for sugar cane and the failure of the mills to operate at capacity were major defects in the implementation of the sugar cane program, the division of responsibility among a number of governmental agencies also contributed to the disappointing results. It was

3. A recovery of some 12 per cent of sugar may be extracted from the cane if milling takes place within the first 24 hours after cutting. The yield, however, will drop as low as 6 per cent from the same cane by the fourth day.

never quite clear just how responsibility was divided among the State Sugar Board, the Agriculture Department, the L.R.D.C. and the Industrial Development Corporation responsible for sugar mill operations. Certainly these agencies failed to coordinate their work effectively.

There existed also a powerful vested interest committed to a continuation of the confusion in sugar cane production and in sales to the sugar mills. Because sugar cane production in the mill areas was in excess of mill requirements, a quota or allotment system was developed which assigned each cultivator the tonnage he might sell to the mills at the windfall prices established. These quotas were established, not by the mill management, which had in effect no control over procurement, but by local representatives of the All Burma Peasants' Organization, the A.F.P.F.L. and the Cooperatives, as the case might be. Because the windfall element in the established price amounted to virtually a 100 per cent premium in excess of that paid by the jaggery-makers, the cultivators paid officials heavily for allotment "tickets." The officials, and perhaps the organizations they represented, had therefore a strong vested interest in the continuation of the windfall price and in its application to all suppliers irrespective of their distance from the mills or the quality and freshness of their cane. They were not interested in pressing for the introduction of the better cane sets, insecticides, and improved production practices which would increase yields and make it possible for cultivators to earn the same net income at lower prices. Thus little was done on this score. Only relatively late in the program was action initiated by the Department of Agriculture and the L.R.D.C. to introduce improved sugar cane strains.

COCONUTS

The original aim of the coconut program was to increase the area under coconut from some 7,000 to approximately 40,000 acres. This, it was estimated, would make the country self-sufficient in coconuts and coconut oil.

In 1954 the L.R.D.C. laid out a program of planting 2 million coconut trees over a ten-year period. By 1956 it had established state-owned plantations covering 14,000 acres with 450,000 trees. These plantations, it was believed, would make Burma self-sufficient in nuts for eating when they came into full production after 1964. After 1956, the L.R.D.C. consolidated its existing acreage. It replanted casualties but did not undertake further expansion.

The coconut program was the only one on which the L.R.D.C. appeared to make significant progress during its first four years of operation. However, because the new management of the organization decided in 1956 to consolidate the position, and because the trees planted will not be due to bear for some years, no further evaluation of this program is possible at the present time. The economics of the coconut plantations appear, however, to be very promising for fresh fruit, if not for oil.

VIRGINIA TOBACCO

As of 1952, Burma was importing some 10 million pounds of cigarette and pipe tobacco annually. By 1956, the Department of Agriculture, with the aid of the rapidly growing domestic cigarette industry, had spurred the planting of some 4,000 acres to Virginia tobacco. Under new management, the L.R.D.C. undertook to expand production still further, to 6,000 acres by 1959. This program was successful; the 6,000-acre target was achieved in 1958. The chief techniques used were establishment of seed nurseries and financing construction of curing barns. The L.R.D.C. also built an air-conditioned storage plant at Mandalay. By 1958, 1,000 curing barns had been established. Since flue curing of tobacco requires skills on the part of the cultivator not previously available in Burma, the L.R.D.C. trained hundreds of private producers at four training centers. The training program is continuing. By the early part of 1959, some 9,000 acres were under Virginia tobacco cultivation.

The success of this program must be ascribed primarily to the effectiveness of the new management at the L.R.D.C. after 1956 and to the imposition of high duties on imported cigarettes. These duties encouraged cigarette manufacture within Burma, thus insuring a profitable market for home-grown tobacco.

RUBBER

No provision for rubber was made in the Five-Year Agricultural Plan. In 1957, however, a report presented by a U. N. technical expert led to consideration of it. Burma had 113,000 acres of rubber trees, nearly all of which had been planted between 1910 and 1930. It now appeared that these trees were approaching the age when tapping would no longer be economic, and that unless a vigorous planting program was undertaken, production would steadily decline and exports of some 11,000 tons of rubber a year would be lost. Also, the Government had created its own monopoly over rubber exports, with a fixed buying price for crude rubber that captured most of the profit from the trade, thus reducing the incentive to private investment in the plantations.

The L.R.D.C. formulated a replanting scheme to replace the existing rubber trees over a ten-year period with seedlings, and to expand acreage to 160,000. It proposed to implement this plan by large cash subsidies to planters, the money to come partly from the public treasury. By the end of the period under review, because of certain questions raised by the consultants about the long-term prospects for natural rubber and the financing of the plan, no program determination had been made. However, the L.D.R.C. did make excellent progress in establishing four nurseries for seedlings to be sold on a subsidized basis. It also established a 500-acre rubber plantation for the production of budwood for grafting.

RICE STORAGE AND RELATED PROGRAMS

RICE STORAGE

No provision had been made for a rice storage program in the comprehensive plan. An emergency program, however, was developed on an *ad hoc* basis because of unsold stocks, which reached 1.5 million tons during 1953–54. Before the war, Burma had shipped out her entire surplus of more than 3 million tons of rice and rice products in the few months following the harvest and before the onset of the rainy season. Thus she had not required storage facilities to protect export rice during the rains, either upcountry or at the ports. In 1953, with surpluses mounting rapidly, an emergency construction program was undertaken by the State Agricultural Marketing Board, providing 1,500 temporary thatched huts for 300,000 tons of paddy. During the next two years, 480 semi-permanent sheds with bamboo sides were built, providing storage for 475,000 tons. In the same period, private millers and brokers built space for 400,000 tons of storage with the assistance of loans from the S.A.M.B. The cost of this storage capacity of under 1.2 million tons was K 8.5 crores. The entire program was conceived and carried through without competent technical advice. The S.A.M.B., when urged to hire rice storage experts, requested technical assistance from the Food and Agriculture Organization of the United Nations instead. The F.A.O. did supply a competent expert. In the interim, however, nearly two years had elapsed, a number of poor facilities had been built, and considerable tonnage had been spoiled by exposure to the elements.

Beginning in 1956–57, a program for the construction of permanent-type facilities was undertaken with competent advice. During the next two years, 380 permanent-type godowns (warehouses) were completed at a cost of slightly more than K 1 crore. These gave the S.A.M.B. permanent paddy storage facilities outside the port cities for some 750,000 tons. These facilities, together with the millers' private storage capacity of 700,000 tons, were adequate for paddy storage, but did not meet the need for rice transit storage capacity in the port cities. Only capacity for 250,000 tons was considered in adequate condition in 1958. The Four-Year Plan of 1957 provided for the construction of an additional 300,000 tons of rice transit storage capacity by 1959–60, and a substantial part was completed.

The need for a large-scale rice storage program developed only because of weaknesses in the marketing and handling of export rice. Realistic pricing policies would have resulted in adequate sales early in each crop year to clear the market. Then effective handling would have made it possible, as in prewar days, for most of the shipments to be made before the rains. Under such circumstances, there would have been no rice storage problem. The key factor in the situation was the socialization of rice export marketing. Had responsibility for rice marketing been left with the private sector and a competitive price been set, the situation would have been quite different. As it was, in addition to the monopoly pricing which kept downward price adjustments too little and too late from 1952–53 to 1957–58, there were equally serious problems of organization, staffing and management, which were inadequate for the purchasing, milling and marketing of the surplus rice crop. With a weak staff and poor procedures and communications, the S.A.M.B. was never in control of the situation. Purchasing as it did from one half to two thirds of the surplus paddy crop and turning it over to private millers for processing, its records were never sufficient to show what quantities of which grades of rice it had at specific stations at any given time. The S.A.M.B. was therefore not in a position to provide effective scheduling of transport to ports and of loadings and shipments. For this reason extra large transit storage facilities were required in port cities, so that loadings and shipments could be made from stocks on hand there. It is against this broader background of nationalization policy and its concomitants that the rice storage program and its implementation must be appraised.

RICE MILLING

Of all the programs which could have contributed to the rapid economic development of Burma, one to improve rice milling facilities should have been of first priority. Burma had some 850 rice mills, most of them small, obsolete, in poor repair and lacking in equipment to mill superior grades of rice. Before the war Burma's largest rice customer was India. Since the grade of rice preferred in India, by virtue of its low price, was Small Mills Special (42 per cent broken), no compelling reason existed, in those pre-war years, for improving capacity to produce superior rice grades. In the 1950s, however, India was herself engaged in a massive food grain production program. Furthermore, she was consuming much more wheat and other food grains relative to rice than previously, and was obtaining huge quantities of these grains from the United States under P.L. 480. While there was a reasonable prospect that India would continue to purchase an average of nearly half a million tons of rice from Burma annually, it was clear that Burma would not be able to make substantial strides toward her pre-war export goal of 3 million tons a year, unless she could find new customers or expand markets already established with buyers other than India. Japan especially constituted such a potential market. While she was buying some 200,000 tons of Burmese rice each year, she was also, by preference, buying much larger amounts from other countries, including the United States, at far higher prices because she preferred their superior grades. A program for improvement of rice quality was therefore an urgent necessity for Burma. Such a program would require not only the growing of superior paddy but also more careful grading and much improved milling.

Attempts were indeed made in these directions. The economic consultants, early in the program period, had urged, and the government had approved, a program which extended all the way from the growing of improved paddy to improved marketing practices. Better paddy quality was achieved both by the distribution of better seed and by the beginnings of a program under which S.A.M.B. purchasing centers paid cultivators premium prices for improved paddy. In the absence of improvements in rice milling, however, these efforts went largely to waste. The sole contributions made by the S.A.M.B. to improved milling were in the form of a few small loans to millers and, much later, the building of three small pilot mills and the establishment of a small rice milling research laboratory. The loans to the millers did not produce much improvement. Indeed, it was subsequently ascertained that many millers did not even use them for the purpose intended. Of the three small pilot mills constructed in 1957–58, one, an American rice mill, had been provided under T.C.A. auspices some five years before and had remained unassembled in a warehouse. When the economic consultants urged the reactivation of at least two large foreign-owned mills (The Ellerman-Arakan and the A.B.C. rice mills near Rangoon) idle since the war, because these could be quickly put into production at only moderate cost, and mill superior grades of rice, it was impossible to get the Government to act.

But the nub of the problem lay in the fact that the Government had some time before enunciated as basic policy its intention to nationalize all the rice mills, and to turn them over to the cooperatives for operation. Although it did not proceed to implement this policy in the program period, the threat of nationalization hung over the mill owners. Under these circumstances, the millers were reluctant, not only to invest in improving their mills, but even to keep them in reasonable repair. Clearly, what was required was a group of policy decisions that rice millers might proceed to modernize their mills without fear of nationalization; that the Government would extend secured loans to millers to facilitate the modernization; that incentives for modernization would be extended by granting S.A.M.B. rice purchase and milling priorities to such millers; that the Government would liberalize the issue of import licenses for rice-milling machinery and equipment; and that S.A.M.B. would install cleaning and grading equipment for paddy at its own procurement and storage centers, in order to improve the paddy going to the millers. Such measures were repeatedly urged by the economic consultants, quite apart from their more basic recommendation that responsibility for export marketing be returned to the private sector. There were indications that these arguments were finding increasing acceptance, but the Government apparently found it too difficult to renounce its previously stated nationalization policy in this area, even though it was no longer determined to proceed with it.

Burma still urgently needs a program which will encourage her rice millers to acquire machines for cleaning and grading paddy, more efficient shellers, polishing cones and machines for classifying and blending rice. This would place her rice mills in a position to provide rice to exact specifications and make it possible to expand existing markets and to capture new markets for quality grades. The beginnings of a rice milling modernization were under way in 1960, when fourteen small but modern rice mills, having a combined daily capacity of 1,250 tons, were under construction.

RELATED RICE PROGRAMS

In 1956–57 and 1957–58, ten power barges and thirty non-powered barges were procured abroad; and, in addition, forty wooden barges were built in Burma for lighterage at Rangoon and other ports. Repeated recommendations that the S.A.M.B. procure a number of low-cost rice cleaning and grading plants did not result in any action. Because of its inability to clean and grade paddy, the S.A.M.B. continued to buy, store and handle, along with paddy, about 40,000 tons of dirt each year. However, S.A.M.B. did arrange with the Port of Rangoon Authority in 1957–58 to improve Ahlone Wharf No. 1 for rice handling and to survey, design and build a second rice wharf.

The procurement of additional lighterage was necessitated, in part at least, by the inefficient use of the existing lighterage. For example, quality inspection was held at shipside rather than at dockside before the lighters were loaded; thus, when quality disputes arose and surveyors refused to accept rice for loading onto the ships, the lighters became floating storage space for rejected rice, and were not available for dock-to-ship loading until the dispute was settled. After this situation had prevailed for a year or more, the S.A.M.B. was persuaded that it was possible to have rice surveyed at dockside before it was loaded onto the lighters. The need for improvement of the Ahlone Wharf No. 1 and the planned construction of a second rice wharf reflected the inefficiency of lighterage handling and the previously mentioned inability of the S.A.M.B. properly to schedule arrivals from upcountry mills.

The S.A.M.B. finally agreed, early in 1958, to order new cleaning and grading machines, as well as a few mechanical loaders, for experimental use. Informal reports indicate that initial experience with this equipment has been most successful.

Capital expenditures for the rice storage and related programs for the years 1952–53 through 1957–58 were as follows:[4]

4. Data from the Economic and Social Board.

(K Lakhs)

	1952-53 to 1955-56	1956-57	1957-58 (Budget Esti- mates)	Total
Totals	934.0	107.5	162.5	1,194.0
Storage and pest control	851.2	46.5	59.5	957.2
Milling	10.8	1.5	1.0	13.3
Transport and lighters	41.7	48.6	37.0	117.3
Ahlone rice wharf	—	10.0	50.0	60.0
Miscellaneous	30.3	.9	15.0	46.2

IRRIGATION

The Five-Year Agricultural Plan made no specific commitments to an irrigation program. It stated only that of the 1.5 million acres of new lands to be put under cultivation, about half would require irrigation. The Irrigation Department, it was stated, would work out plans for a number of projects, including a system in the Yamethin District, the construction of a reservoir at Taungpalu and a project for power pump irrigation in the Dry Zone. The K.T.A. Comprehensive Report envisaged four irrigation projects, two of them major, which would service nearly 1.7 million acres at an estimated cost of K 45 crores. These were approved in principle at the Implementation Conference of 1954. Yet for the first six years of the development program, through 1957-58, total expenditures for irrigation were well below K 5 crores.[5] Of this total approximately K 3 crores were spent for irrigation works proper, the remainder for tools and plant.

During this period only two new irrigation projects of any size were completed. These were the Taungpalu Dam and the Alaungsithu Dam. Both were earth-fill dams and were built by the Irrigation Department without outside assistance. In both instances, construction methods were faulty — the outlet pipes collapsed and parts of the structures had to be rebuilt at substantial additional cost. The acreages serviced by these dams were 6,000 and 4,000, respectively. In addition, the Department constructed a number of small tanks, sluice gates and irrigation canals, and improved a number of previously existing facilities.

The largest single expenditure in the irrigation field was for the reconstruction of the Kabo Dam, which collapsed because of unprecedentedly heavy rains early in 1956. Its collapse threatened the loss of rice cultivation on 300,000 acres. Planning and supervisory responsibility for reconstruction of

5. Actual expenditures for 1957-58 are not yet available, but they were almost certainly lower than the budget figures.

the Kabo Dam was given to Tippetts-Abbett-McCarthy-Stratton (formerly K.T.A. and K.T.A.M.), the Government's consulting engineers. Messrs. E. D. Zublin, A.G., another foreign firm, was awarded the contract for the actual reconstruction. An emergency authority was set up to cut through red tape so that a weir dam could be completed on a forced draft basis before the onset of the next rainy season and save the acreage from flooding while further construction proceeded. Under these special conditions, the job was admirably executed, under the immediate supervision of Mr. John Alexander, within the very short time allotted.

The next largest project was the restoration of the earth embankments along the east side of the Irrawaddy River. This was a long-range project designed to protect some 500,000 acres of Delta paddy land from flooding. By the end of 1957–58, the work was approximately 60 per cent complete and provided protection for some 300,000 acres, bringing assured yields on lands previously subject to annual flood.

There were a number of reasons for the relatively puny accomplishment in the irrigation sector. The Mu River Valley project recommended by T.A.M.S. was large and costly and intensive engineering was required before it could be undertaken. When it was initially discussed, the most serious obstacle to it appeared to be the problem of the many pagodas which would be inundated. This question was raised at the Implementation Conference early in 1954 and the project was taken under further advisement, from which it never again seriously emerged for active consideration. Its potential was tremendous. The I.C.A. and the several World Bank missions showed considerable interest in it and it is quite probable that financing for it could have been found. But the religious scruples of the Prime Minister and his associates were sincere and remained controlling.

This religious concern did not seem to be present in the case of the Yamethin District project conceived by the consulting engineers to service some 600,000 acres at an estimated cost of K 26 crores. This actually was not one project but a complex of projects which did not have to be executed simultaneously. In 1957–58, Soviet technicians surveyed the possibilities for the Thitson Dam, part of the original complex. Unlike the Kyetmauktaung Project, also surveyed and recommended by the Soviet technicians, the Thitson appeared to be an economic project and funds were budgeted for it in 1958–59.

An important reason for the relatively small accomplishment in the irrigation sector is to be found in the Irrigation Department itself. It lacked dynamic direction and enough engineers and skilled construction workers, a difficulty aggravated after 1956 by the transfer of some of its personnel to the L.R.D.C. for work on the land reclamation project. The collapse of the two earth-fill dams reflected its lack of experience in planning and designing large projects and dampened its desire to tackle additional projects. The lack of adequate hydrological data was another retarding factor. Important also was the poor quality of ministerial leadership. Both U Tin Maung and U Kyaw Dun, who served as ministers for Agriculture and Forests during the program period and who as such were responsible for the irrigation sector, were primarily politicians. They appeared to contribute little in the way of inspiration and leadership to the services under them. But perhaps most important was the basic fact that the real priorities in agriculture at that time lay elsewhere. With more than 2 million acres of former paddy land waiting to be reclaimed by earth embankments and jungle clearing at an average cost of perhaps K 50 per acre, and with tremendous production increases possible through the use of improved seeds and other simple techniques on lands already adequately watered, irrigation projects which would insure water supply only at a per-acre cost six and seven times as great were certainly of secondary importance. It was for these reasons that the economic consultants made no serious effort to press the irrigation program.

MECHANIZATION

The Five-Year Agricultural Plan contemplated the introduction of mechanized farming, wherever feasible, to overcome the shortage of plow cattle prevailing in 1952. It saw greater possibilities for mechanized farming in the Dry Zone than in the small paddy fields of the Delta, and contemplated that the provision of tractors to Upper Burma would make possible the diversion of scarce working cattle to Lower Burma. The consulting engineers, in their Comprehensive Report, strongly favored farm mechanization. Early in 1956 the Department of Agriculture had 130 tractors, of which about 100 were in operating condition. It had been using these for custom plowing work for sugar cane, for second-crop groundnut after paddy and for jute cultivation. Plowing was, however, the only agricultural operation which had been mechanized and tractor use had been excessively hampered by inadequate maintenance, breakdowns and a lack of spare parts. The record showed that the average use per tractor was about 500 hours per year, far lower than required for economic operation. With conditions in the country unsettled, with tractor use limited to plowing, with inadequate provision for tractor maintenance and with poor management within the Department of Agriculture, a higher level of utilization seemed unlikely.

However, cultivators displayed a great interest in tractor use, and many of them found custom plowing at the established rates more economic than bullock plowing. Operation of the tractors was on a partly subsidized basis under the direction of the agricultural engineering section of the Department of Agriculture. The purchase of 200 tractors scheduled for delivery in mid-1956 provided the necessary stimulus to establishment of a central workshop for mechanized equipment and a complementary training center for tractor operators and mechanics. Several foreign technicians, one from Israel and others provided under U. N. auspices, were of great help in establishing these much-needed institutions. The next major step came in connection with the paddy and land reclamation scheme, under which not only tractors but earth-moving equipment, jungle-clearing equipment and brush-cutters were procured and effectively utilized. These measures have so far barely scratched the surface of the mechanization potential.

While the value of tractor plowing has been demonstrated in a number of crop applications, the usefulness of tractors for jobs other than plowing — harrowing, harvesting, and so on — cannot be judged without more experiment. The widespread use of tractors in the Delta, even for plowing, would seem to be extremely dubious because of small-scale land holdings. Combining a number of ten-acre farms into large management units suitable for mechanized cultivation would require contouring, which does not always follow property lines. A redistribution of lands in suitable units would be necessary to make possible mechanized paddy cultivation on a large scale. The more immediate possibilities for further mechanization lie, rather, in the Dry Zone and in the Shan States, particularly because of the abundance of land in relation to population there. Finally, it is doubtful whether labor costs in Burma will for some time reach a level in relation to capital costs that will make widespread farm mechanization advantageous.

The emphasis given to mechanization possibilities in recent years has had one undesirable effect. It has made for neglect of husbandry practices to improve the working cattle. Until now little has been accomplished, other than some routine disease prevention. Other practices, particularly proper feeding, offer great possibilities for improving animal power and thus improving farm efficiency. Improvement of animal-drawn equipment, such as rakes, mowers and binders, has also been neglected. Even should mechanization proceed far more rapidly than it has, the bullock will still be necessary, for many decades to come, on a majority of Burmese farms. Improvement of this animal is, therefore, of considerable importance.

It is quite likely that, after the Agriculture Department had taken the lead in procuring tractors and demonstrating their usefulness, mechanization would have proceeded more swiftly and more efficiently through private channels than it did under Government organization and operation. Tractors could have been sold on time purchase to cooperatives and to individuals who would hire them out for custom work and be responsible for their maintenance. These or similar approaches are yet to be tested.

AGRICULTURAL CREDIT

The objective of the agricultural credit program was to enable the cultivators to satisfy their needs for credit at reasonable rates of interest. Until 1953 most of the agricultural loans extended by the Government were the so-called direct agricultural loans issued through township officers directly to the cultivators at 6½ per cent interest. The cooperatives also played an important role in loan issue. However, the total of Government-sponsored loans was less than K 5 crores out of a total of some K 30 to K 40 crores estimated to be necessary. The cultivators still relied on private moneylenders for the bulk of their credit requirements, paying anywhere from 40 to 400 per cent for the money they borrowed from these sources. In 1953–54 the Government set up a State Agricultural Bank with an initial capital of K 5 crores; and up to April 1959, the Bank had established 1,290 village banks in twenty-three districts. No substantial increase in the total volume of Government-sponsored agricultural credit resulted, however. The average total of loans extended remained, as before, in the neighborhood of K 5 crores per year.

The chief accomplishment of the State Agricultural Bank was to reduce the proportion of administrative loans extended through township officers, on which repayment performance has been very poor, dropping from more than 70 per cent in 1952–53 to something less than 50 per cent in 1957–58. These unsupervised administrative loans made under the Agriculturalists Loans Act were progressively replaced by supervised loans issued under the auspices of the State Agricultural Bank and the cooperatives and village banks associated with it. Under these auspices, loan repayments improved considerably. Township officers had little contact with the villagers and could not visit their farms prior to loan issue, maintain contact with them during the life of the loans or follow through effectively in collections. There were undoubtedly other reasons for poor repayment performance as well. Administrative agricultural loans were heavily influenced by political considerations, as local A.F.P.F.L. or peasant organization officials interceded with township officers on behalf of loan applicants, both to obtain loans for them and to request leniency in cases of non-repayment. There can be little doubt that such abuses were widespread on behalf of loyal party adherents. The same cultivators who forfeited on low-interest direct Government loans made every effort to meet the exorbitant interest requirements imposed by private money-lenders and to repay the principal of these loans as well. The reason for this is not difficult to understand. Since cultivators typically obtained only one quarter or one fifth of the credit they needed from the Government and its agencies, they were dependent on private moneylenders for the balance of their credit needs and could not afford to ruin their credit standing with them.

In contrast to unsupervised administrative loans, those issued under the auspices of the State Agricultural Bank were administered by field workers who studied each applicant, visited the farms during the growing season and made the collections. The security of these loans rested primarily on the personal relationships established between the supervisors and the cultivators.

Such supervisors could not be effective without some experience or training in agricultural production.

Thus, the expansion of State Agricultural Bank operations was limited primarily by lack of competent loan supervisors. State Agricultural Bank loans, through both cooperatives and village banks, grew from K 5.3 million in 1953–54 to K 22.5 million in 1957–58. At this rate it will be many years before a major part of the total credit needs of Burma's cultivators can be met at reasonable rates of interest.

The State Agricultural Bank charged an interest rate of 12 per cent on loans to the cultivators, and the village banks subordinate to it were permitted to retain 6 per cent. This arrangement was designed to enable the village banks to build up their own capital and to issue loans independently within their own village communities. Up to 1958 the village banks had not been able to build up reserves to any great extent, since most of their "profit" was utilized to make good on defaults and to cover administrative costs. The chief deficiency of the State Agricultural Bank and its affiliated village banks, apart from their inability to expand the volume of agricultural credit more rapidly, has been that they have done very little to meet longer-term credit needs for cattle, equipment and consolidation of old debts.

In view of the important role played by interest costs in determining the net income of the agriculturalists, the agricultural credit program did not receive the emphasis it merited. As has previously been pointed out,[6] the average net farm income of Burmese cultivators could be increased by one third if their total credit needs could be met at reasonable rates of interest. Surely this potential warranted extraordinary efforts on the part of the Government to train field staff for the State Agricultural Bank, so as to make possible a more rapid increase in the extension of credit by this institution.

Data on state-sponsored agricultural Government loans and repayments for the years 1952–53 to 1959–60 are shown in Table 33.

LAND NATIONALIZATION

The land nationalization program was ambiguously outlined by the Pyidawtha Conference. The Land Nationalization Act, subsequently legislated in 1954, required the Government to examine the tenure arrangements for some 9 million acres of tenant-operated farm land, to nationalize and redistribute the holding rights for as much of this land as was held by absentee landlords and to reduce the holding rights of any cultivator with more than 50 acres, redistributing any acreage above that. The implementation of this program through 1957–58 is shown in Table 34.

6. Chapter 4, p. 43.

Table 33

Government Loans to Agriculturists, 1952–53 to 1959–60

(K Million)

Year	Agriculturists Loans Act		Land Improvement Act		Tenants of Government Estates		Cooperative Loans		State Agricultural Bank				Total	
									Cooperatives		Village Banks			
	Loans	Returns	Loans	Returns	Loans	Returns	Loans	Returns	Loans	Returns	Loans	Returns	Loans	Returns
1952–53	40.4	26.1[a]	0.1	0.1	0.7	0.1	13.9	12.6[a]	Nil	Nil	Nil	Nil	55.1	38.9
1953–54	34.0	20.5[a]	…	…	1.0	1.0	14.0	11.7[a]	4.0	3.9	1.3	1.3	54.3	38.4
1954–55	26.9	16.5[a]	0.0	0.0	0.9	0.7	11.9	10.7[a]	8.7	7.4[a]	3.8	3.5[a]	52.2	38.8
1955–56	16.1	11.2[a]	0.1	0.1	0.3	0.8	13.3	9.8[a]	9.4	8.4[a]	5.6	5.1	44.8	35.4
1956–57	18.1	11.7[a]	…	…	0.3	0.0	11.0	7.4[a]	10.4	10.1[a]	8.5	8.5	48.3	37.7
1957–58	22.7	16.6[a]	0.0	0.0	0.4	0.4	0.6	0.4[a]	10.6	9.9[a]	11.9	11.8[a]	46.2	39.1
1958–59	26.9	8.9	…	…	0.0	0.2	…	…	Nil	Nil	29.0	27.9[a]	55.9	37.0
1959–60[b]	4.2	[c]	…	…	n.a.	n.a.	…	…	Nil	Nil	42.7	36.5	46.9	36.5

Source: Economic Survey of Burma 1960, Table 51, p. 79.

a. Revised.   b. Total up to April 1960.   c. Less than K 50,000.

Table 34

LAND NATIONALIZATION AND REDISTRIBUTION, 1953–54 TO 1957–58

(Thousands of Acres)

Year	Resumed	Exempted	Available for Redistribution	Redistributed	Remaining to be Redistributed
Total	3,357	1,627	1,636	1,456	180
1953–54	281	124	150	142	8
1954–55	1,046	517	511	434	77
1955–56	753	348	379	345	34
1956–57	576	276	283	263[a]	20
1957–58	701[a]	362[a]	313[a]	272	41[a]

Source: *Economic Survey of Burma 1959,* Table 51, p. 79.
a. Revised figures.

In its first five years of operation, something less than 1.5 million acres were distributed out of some 3.4 million acres nationalized. At this rate about twenty years would be required to finish the job. The limiting factor on the pace of the program has been a shortage of personnel for examining land records. Through 1956–57, approximately 141,000 families had been awarded one-yoke farms averaging 8.4 acres in size. Also through 1956–57, less than K .5 crores had been paid out in compensation for nationalized land with an estimated value of K 6.5 crores. There were two principal reasons for this lag in compensation payments. One was the difficulty of establishing the legal ownership of much Chettyar-owned land. Many of the former owners had died or left Burma during the war and legal records of succession were not available. Second, valuation of the land proved difficult because of a requirement in the law that payment per acre would vary with the number of acres nationalized in the case of the individual landowner. Since most large landowners owned farms in many different village tracts, the total size of their holdings and hence the appropriate compensation for individual farms could not be determined until the nationalization process had been completed.

The slow implementation of the land nationalization program was probably more beneficial than harmful. Under previous legislation, land rents had been set at ridiculously low levels, and where absentee landlords were concerned most, tenants were not paying rent at all. Thus the delay involved little hardship for tenant farmers.

Meanwhile, land nationalization adversely affected two important classes of tenants. Those who had been cultivating more than one yoke of land (about 10 acres) were obliged to surrender that part of their holdings in excess of the yoke size determined for their area. According to the 1954 census, more than

50 per cent of tenant holdings in the important Pegu, Irrawaddy and Tenasserim Divisions were in excess of 10 acres. For such tenants nationalization proved a hardship, not a help. The second group adversely affected were tenants who worked on large farms owned by agriculturalists. Under the law, such an agriculturalist could not retain up to 50 acres of land unless he undertook to cultivate it with assistance only from his family or hired help. He was not permitted to continue to rent part of it. Tenants on such larger-sized farms therefore had to become hired hands to stay on the land. As agricultural laborers they no longer enjoyed the tenure which had been their right as tenants.

Quite apart from these defects, which not only imposed inequities on many tenants but also disrupted established production patterns, the administration of land nationalization was subject to many abuses. Local committees established to implement the land distribution were too often peopled or influenced by local A.F.P.F.L. and A.B.P.O. officials. These often caused the better land to be reserved for their friends or falsified registrations to permit manipulation. Another deficiency of the law was that, in determining the appropriate size of a one-yoke farm in any area, it failed to make adequate provision for large families. In any event, there were many instances in which a one-yoke farm was not economic in size.

Finally, the land nationalization as implemented contributed to the deterioration of agricultural capital and thereby retarded production growth. With ownership and tenure unclear, there was little incentive for either owners or tenants to maintain bunds and dikes properly or to invest money or labor in farm improvements. The program is an excellent illustration of the fact that good intentions alone — in this case, welfare and equity objectives — do not insure beneficial results.

EXTENSION AND RESEARCH

The Five-Year Agricultural Plan stated in a general way that arrangements would be made to conduct continuous research and planning in the agricultural sector. The comprehensive development program made provision for the construction of agricultural and veterinarian research institutes, and responsibility for construction was assigned to the Special Projects Implementation Board, which was also responsible for the construction of the pharmaceuticals plant, the new engineering college and the technical high school. Lack of readiness and determination on the part of the Agriculture and Veterinary Departments to staff the research institutes and to prepare meaningful research programs for them made these projects particularly vulnerable to budget slashes or rephasing in the annual budget competition for limited resources. By 1958, the Agricultural Research Institute had 60 per cent of its planned buildings and one third of its planned staff. It did not yet have, however, a dynamic and practical research program geared to the national crop expansion programs. Little progress had been made on the Veterinary Research Institute.

The major activities in the fields of extension service and research were conducted by the Department of Agriculture within its current budget rather than as part of the capital development program. In the pre-war days, the agricultural services were divided into eight so-called "circles," each headed by a regional Deputy Director of Agriculture, and each equipped with an experimental farm. Activities at these farms were generally limited to varietal tests geared to the problems of the region served. Each "circle" also had its own farm school where nine-month training courses were conducted for future extension field workers. Strengthening of the extension service was hampered in the early years of the program by repeated slashes made by the Ministry of Finance and Revenue in the current budget requests submitted by the Department of Agriculture for this purpose. Such cuts would not have been imposed had the requests been subject to review by the Ministry of National Planning, which reviewed capital budget requests only. This pointed up the need for closer coordination between the capital and current budget review processes and closer liaison between the Ministry of Finance and the Ministry of National Planning on complementary budget requests of the two types. More adequate budgetary provision was made for agricultural extension in the latter part of the program.

By 1958, training courses at the eight circle farm schools were producing 400 to 500 village level extension workers per year, 1,700 of whom were already assigned to the villages. Their chief operating difficulty was the lack of transport equipment. In the Irrawaddy Circle, for example, the Deputy Director of Agriculture in charge, with a staff of one agricultural officer, five field inspectors and 105 village level workers, had available only one vehicle — a pickup truck used mostly to haul seed, fertilizers and other supplies. District agricultural officers responsible for supervision, training and inspection over an area of 1,250 square miles were not even provided with bicycles. An extension field man assigned to cover four or five village tracts could travel only on foot or by slow and irregular public conveyance. This lack of transport seriously limited the effectiveness of extension operations.

Despite these handicaps, and with pressure and assistance from the economic consultants, the extension program was beginning to show some results by 1958. A publications program, which included easy-to-read illustrated booklets for cultivators and guidance material for extension workers, had been initiated. Arrangements had also been made to double the number of trainees in the eight circle farm schools as graduates of the Pyinmina Agricultural Training School,[7] who would conduct these training courses, increased in number.

7. A group sponsored by the Ford Foundation and headed by William Gamble did an excellent job in staffing and vitalizing this school.

SUMMARY

The implementation of the agricultural program really breaks down into two phases: from 1952–53 to 1955–56 and from 1956–57 onwards. The demarcation in 1956 came when U Ko Gyi replaced U Tin U as Director-General of the Land Resources Development Corporation. This agency's responsibility was extended to embrace virtually all agricultural projects when, because of inadequate leadership and staffing and lack of initiative at the Departments of Agriculture, Irrigation and Veterinary, many activities originally assigned to these departments were transferred to or assumed by the L.R.D.C. Thus, with the exception of the rice storage and related programs, for which the State Agricultural Marketing Board had responsibility, the L.R.D.C. was in effect responsible for program implementation in the agricultural sector.

Not much could have been expected from the L.R.D.C. in the first year or so of operations, which of necessity had to be devoted to organizing, staffing, programing and housekeeping operations. But the first Director-General of this organization was totally unequipped for the job. He had been hand-picked by Prime Minister U Nu for his devoutness as a Buddhist and for his honesty. As U Nu once expressed his policy:

> However perfect a plan may be, it will be of no avail if the right type of man is not obtainable to implement it. In selecting the right type of man, it will be ideal if we can get one who is both able and honest. Failing to get a person with both these qualifications, we should at least insist on getting one who is honest. If our plans for the good of the masses are entrusted to those who are able but lacking in honesty, these plans will serve as a means of enriching them instead of benefiting the masses. An honest person though deficient in ability can be trained by well-wishers to become efficient.[8]

This officer was a poor executive. He was unfamiliar with agricultural problems. And he lacked the firmness to tell Prime Minister U Nu, who served as Chairman of the L.R.D.C. Board of Directors during the first phase of its operations, that some of the latter's impulsive project suggestions were impractical, either because of their nature or because of the unreadiness of the L.R.D.C. to add additional work to its already heavy load. Staffing, planning and direction were weak and inept, supervision was lacking and the organization was smothered with a multitude of projects to which no priorities were assigned. As a result, the organization failed almost completely to implement any of its programs effectively.

With the change in direction in 1956, the tempo and quality of L.R.D.C.

---

8. "Unity First," speech at the Peace Rally on Sept. 17, 1949, in U Nu, *From Peace to Stability* (a collection of speeches), Ministry of Information, Rangoon, 1951, p. 9.

implementation improved remarkably. The major weaknesses of the agricultural program after 1956 rested for the most part outside that agency.

1. The agricultural program did not appraise and clearly define priorities in program objectives and implementation. Until 1956 it neglected the need to concentrate effectively on the expansion of paddy production. Throughout the entire program period it neglected the crucial need to improve rice milling and related facilities. It failed to place sufficient emphasis on rapid expansion of effectively supervised agricultural credit under Government auspices at reasonable rates of interest. The land distribution program neglected the need to assign priority to uninterrupted agricultural production and the need for stability of tenure, which would have encouraged more private investment in agriculture by landowners and cultivators. The program also affected adversely the ability of the L.R.D.C. successfully to cope with its major crop expansion programs by imposing on it a multitude of lesser projects and programs at the same time. The lack of priority was reflected finally in the failure to assign the agriculture portfolio to an outstandingly capable minister, or to improve the direction of the several departments concerned.

2. Implementation of the program was adversely affected by poor coordination. This was evidenced chiefly in the lack of coordination between the Ministry of Finance and the Ministry of Planning in their reviews of complementary aspects of current and capital budget requests and in jurisdictional confusions and rivalries between L.R.D.C. and the Department of Agriculture. It was evidenced also in the lack of proper coordination between the agricultural authorities and those responsible for the industry program, particularly in relation to cotton mill and sugar mill operations and pricing problems.

3. The program was adversely affected by political pressures exerted by local A.F.P.F.L. and A.B.P.O. authorities. Most clearly evident in the land distribution program, in the extension and collection of agricultural loans, and in the pricing and sale of sugar cane to the mills, the pressures pervaded the entire program.

4. Finally, the lack of civil order in the countryside constituted a persistent and omnipresent limitation on program implementation, not only because it hampered agricultural production and programs but also because it was possible for ineffective officers to use insecurity as an excuse for failure in performance.

Despite these factors, and particularly in the last half of the program period, considerable progress was made and a foundation was laid for further achievements in the future. Lands gone to jungle were being reclaimed, new crops were being introduced, acreage under cultivation had been increased and yields improved. Crop expansion programs, particularly those for paddy, were making headway. That part of agricultural credit which was soundly organized and supervised had been enlarged. The pace of irrigation work was increasing. The foundations had been laid for an extension service and for improved research activities. Farm income was increasing. And, despite increases in paddy production, the agricultural economy was becoming more diversified and better balanced. The major criticism must be not that little was accomplished, but that so much more could and should have been done. But perhaps the major achievement was the change which had come about in the attitude of the political leadership toward the role of agriculture in the future economic development of Burma. Whereas at the outset the leaders had envisaged industrialization and electrification as the major avenues to development, they had now come to appreciate more realistically the major role agricultural development would have to play.

CHAPTER 17

Implementation of the

Program for

State Manufacturing Industry

The manufacturing industry program was central in the thinking which underlay the Burmese approach to their development program. Industrialization was considered the high road to economic development, a view bolstered by Burma's World War II experience with critical shortages of basic consumer goods and the consequent desire to achieve economic self-sufficiency. Long-term strategic considerations also influenced the emphasis on industrial development. In U Kyaw Nyein, the Industries Minister, who was second only to U Ba Swe in the powerful Socialist bloc within the A.F.P.F.L. Government, the manufacturing industries program had a leadership which combined an imaginative, dynamic approach with political prestige and power to a greater degree than existed in any other sector of the development program. U Kyaw Nyein was able to obtain a relatively free hand in conducting the major portion of the program and sufficient allotments to enable him to initiate a substantial part of it at the very outset. These were not enough, unfortunately, to make for success.

The K.T.A. industrial program (Chapter 9) had recommended for the eight-year plan period a group of basic industrial projects at a total cost of some K 23 crores. The American consultants had also stressed the need to modernize and expand existing private industry (particularly the nation's rice-milling facilities), and to encourage the establishment of new industries

Table 35

PUBLIC CAPITAL OUTLAYS IN THE INDUSTRIAL SECTOR,
1952–53 TO 1959–60

(*K Crores*)

Year	Total Capital Outlays	Industry Capital Outlays	Industry as Per Cent of Total
Total	389.3	34.8	9.0
1952–53 to 1955–56	195.8	20.1	10.3
1952–53	32.7	.4	1.2
1953–54	53.8	3.8	7.1
1954–55	60.9	9.0	14.8
1955–56	48.3	6.9	14.2
1956–57 to 1959–60	193.5	14.7	7.6
1956–57	53.8	5.5	10.2
1957–58	52.3	4.1	7.9
1958–59	51.7	3.1	6.0
1959–60	35.6	2.0	5.6

Sources: Tables 55 and 56.

in the private sector as well. They had recommended, particularly, that an Industrial Development Corporation be created and given responsibility to assist private industry to accomplish these objectives. The Implementation Conference of February 1954 (Chapter 10) assumed that the Industrial Development Corporation, by now in existence, would do this job. It concentrated, therefore, on the state manufacturing industries program presented to it by U Kyaw Nyein. That conference approved "in principle" some sixty-five industrial projects, on many of which preliminary economic and engineering studies had not been completed, the total cost of which had not been estimated,[1] and among which no priorities were assigned. Apart from approval of this list, the only significant decision made by the Implementation Conference on the industries program was to prepare a list of industries suitable for development by the private sector.

Responsibility for execution of the state manufacturing industries program was vested for the most part, but not exclusively, in the Industrial Development Corporation. Responsibility for the pharmaceuticals plant, on which positive decision had already been made by the Prime Minister independently, was assigned to a Special Projects Implementation Board, which also had responsibility for the construction of the new engineering college, the new technical high school and one or two lesser projects. Responsibility for completing the already started brick and tile factory, and for a pulp and paper factory, remained with state boards already established for those purposes. Finally, responsibility for the construction of a number of small pilot manu-

1. As of September 1954, total costs, with a few projects still missing, were estimated at K 60.9 crores (Summary of Industrial Development Program, September 30, 1954).

Table 36

PUBLIC CAPITAL OUTLAYS IN THE INDUSTRIAL SECTOR,
BY MAJOR CATEGORY, 1952–53 TO 1959–60

	K Crores	Per Cent of Total
Total	34.8	100.0
1. Major manufacturing projects[a]	24.7	72.1
2. Industrial and cottage industry loans to private sector (gross)	2.8	8.0
3. Other[b]	7.3	19.9

Sources: Item 1 from Table 37; item 2 from "Evaluation of Capital Programme," Robert R. Nathan Associates, Inc., July 22, 1958, p. 31; item 3, by difference from total shown in Table 37.

a. Includes plants for pharmaceuticals, steel, jute, sugar (2 plants), cotton (extension), cement (extension), silk, brick and tile, and tea.

b. Includes minor industrial projects, small-scale and pilot industries program, preparation of industrial sites, establishment of industrial construction equipment pool, industrial research institute, administration, etc.

facturing plants, also previously authorized, remained with the Directorate of Industries.

The manufacturing industries program started off with a bang. The major components in the initial program were the pharmaceuticals plant, a steel mill, a jute mill and two sugar mills. Of lesser importance were the brick and tile factory on which work had started in 1951, a silk-spinning project and a tea-packing plant. The only important additions made to this list during the entire program period were two sizable expansions of existing mills. One called for doubling the capacity of the cotton-spinning and weaving mill completed in 1951. The second called for doubling the capacity of the recently nationalized cement mill at Thayetmyo.

By the time the first group of new state industrial enterprises was under construction, foreign exchange and resource limitations precluded for a while any significant additional industrial starts. U Kyaw Nyein fought vainly to overcome this obstacle, first by joint ventures under the Japanese Economic Cooperation Agreement and with U. S. firms, and then by obtaining medium-term industrial credits in West Germany. But by this time it had already become apparent that the first wave of manufacturing projects was rapidly heading into serious trouble. The emerging difficulties, stressed by the economic consultants, made the Prime Minister increasingly apprehensive concerning the Government's ability to manage its new undertakings, and led finally, in June 1957, to his decision that no new state industrial enterprises would be undertaken. This, in effect, remained the position throughout the remaining life of the A.F.P.F.L. Government. The Ne Win Government confined its efforts in this sector to attempts to consolidate the position by

Table 37

INVESTMENT IN MAJOR STATE MANUFACTURING PLANTS
(EXCLUSIVE OF WORKING CAPITAL), 1952–53 TO 1959–60

(K Crores)

Total	24.7
Pharmaceuticals	6.7
Steel	4.4
Jute	3.6
Cotton (extension)	1.7
Sugar (2 plants)	3.5
Cement (extension)	3.0
Brick and tile	.8
Silk	.7
Tea	.3

Sources: Data for steel, jute and cotton from C.S.E.D. staff papers, 1959; other data from "Evaluation of the Capital Programme," Robert R. Nathan Associates, Inc., July 22, 1958, p. 81.

improving the management and operation of the now completed new enterprises.

Outlays in the industrial sector comprised 9 per cent of total public capital outlays for the period 1952–53 through 1959–60. They reached their peak early in the period and tapered off sharply thereafter, as Table 35 shows. A detailed breakdown of the K 34.8 crores invested is, unfortunately, not available, but a broad approximate breakdown is given in Table 36. More than 70 per cent was for a group of major state manufacturing plants. How investment was distributed among these plants may be seen from Table 37.

A large part of the implementation story in the manufacturing industries sector is, therefore, the story of these plants.

THE PHARMACEUTICALS PLANT

The pharmaceuticals plant was known to be a pet project of Prime Minister U Nu. Motivated by widespread ill-health and undernourishment among the Burmese people and by the recollection of serious World War II shortages of drugs and medical supplies, he was determined that Burma should have a large, modern pharmaceuticals factory which would be capable of supplying the country's needs. Impressed also with what he understood to be the efficacy of yeast as a remedy for prevailing dietary deficiencies, he was determined that the factory should be capable of producing as much yeast as was needed for diet supplements.

Because neither the Health Ministry nor the Industries Ministry showed enthusiasm for the project, the Prime Minister created the previously mentioned Special Projects Implementing Board. He also sent abroad a mission composed of the venerable J. S. Furnivall as Chairman, Secretary of Health

Dillon and Planning Secretary U Tin Pe, with instructions to contract with a reputable pharmaceuticals producer for design of the plant, supervision of its construction and management of it for seven years. Rumor had it that he instructed members of the mission not to return until they had concluded such a contract.

The mission made a contract with a large British pharmaceuticals manufacturing firm. It provided for the design and construction of a plant capable of turning out almost any kind of pharmaceuticals except antibiotics — biologicals, galenicals, sera, vitamins, and yeast and alcohol as well. The economics of a project of this size had not been considered.[2] The contracting firm was not asked, apparently, whether a plant of the kind desired by the Prime Minister would be practical. The contractual arrangements, subsequently much criticized, left implementation of the project completely to the foreign firm, assured it of handsome supervisory and management fees for a period of seven years after completion of construction, and gave it exclusive agency for procuring the raw materials the new plant would require. The contract also assured the managing firm additional royalty payments if any part of the output were exported.

The complex of plants which comprised the pharmaceuticals factory, located at Gyogan, just outside Rangoon, was efficiently and expeditiously constructed. The buildings were beautiful, and the equipment was clearly of the best. But the plant was not economic. At K 6.7 crores, its cost was far out of proportion to the value of the output that could be produced and distributed. Further, it was designed primarily to mix and package drugs and pharmaceuticals imported in bulk from abroad. Raw materials and foreign exchange costs were unusually high in relation to product value, and the percentage of value added in the "manufacturing" process was extremely low.

The pharmaceuticals plant was the earliest of the new plants to come into production. From the outset it was beset with serious problems. The Ministry of Health should have been the largest customer, since it procured drugs and medicines not only for its hospitals and clinics but also for subsidized distribution to people who could not afford to buy commercially the medicines they needed. But the Ministry failed to seek adequate budgets for these purposes. The army, another large buyer, was reluctant to purchase from the new Government factory at higher prices than it was able to obtain from its traditional suppliers abroad. (The plant, in this respect, was somewhat handicapped because it had to procure bottles and other packaging materials from abroad, and the duty on these was as high as that paid on finished pharmaceuticals products.) The volume of operation was, therefore, pitifully low.

Almost ludicrous difficulties were encountered in the distribution of yeast

2. The consulting engineers had prepared a project report for a plant of much smaller size and scope.

tablets. It transpired that an individual consumption of ten or more tablets per day would be required to correct the vitamin deficiencies. There were complaints from those who attempted to participate in the initial distribution that the consumption of so many tablets led to flatulence and other undesirable results. This problem was solved by fortifying the tablets so that a daily intake of only one would suffice. The production cost of the fortified tablet, however, was almost equal to the cost of imported and much-preferred vitamins (and mostly in foreign exchange). But worse was yet to come. The plant turned out a million tablets a day and shipped them out to a list of Government agencies which were supposed to distribute them free — especially in the schools. The distribution "scheme," however, failed to move the tablets beyond their initial distribution points. Tablets soon backed up at the pharmaceuticals plant until they numbered 120 to 150 million — and still no satisfactory distribution plan had been introduced.

Still another difficulty arose in connection with the plant's alcohol production. The sugar mills at Namti and Pyinmina had been designed to recover alcohol from a by-product, molasses. This was an important element in their economic rationale. So obviously weak, however, was the economic position of the pharmaceuticals plant that the decision was made to concentrate all alcohol making in it. This, of course, reduced the profit potential of the sugar mills. In addition, the State Civil Supplies Board, which had procured large quantities of alcohol from a number of small, privately owned distilleries, was now ordered to procure all its alcohol requirements from the pharmaceuticals factory. These measures only partly solved the problem.

Apart from the question of what response the foreign managing firm should have made to the Government of Burma's highly unsophisticated request, the firm efficiently superintended the construction of the plant, the installation of its equipment, the training of its labor force and the production process itself. It showed, however, little consciousness of costs, and failed to make vigorous or imaginative efforts to expand production volume by creating new product lines or developing markets. If the firm had had a substantial financial stake in the enterprise, it would undoubtedly have made greater efforts in these directions.

The steps taken by the Ne Win Government demonstrated that the operating efficiency of this plant could be increased and its losses reduced. Canceling the management contract with the British firm and engaging Israeli technical advisors in their place, the Ne Win Government eliminated a number of unprofitable product lines, stopped yeast tablet production, required the army to purchase its supplies from the plant, introduced a number of supplementary and more profitable product lines, banned the importation of a long list of drugs and pharmaceuticals that the mill was capable of producing, and made the factory management, in effect, the sole importing and distributing agency for the drugs and pharmaceuticals which continued to be imported. Obviously, not all these measures reflected sound economic policy. Their apparent effect, however, was to put the plant in the black for the first time.

THE STEEL MILL

The K 4.4 crores steel mill was reluctantly included in the K.T.A. program because the Government insisted upon it. The Government wanted the mill because it believed that domestically produced steel was basic to an industrialization program, because such a mill seemed to have symbolic and prestige value, and because it wished to develop small-arms manufacturing independent of imported materials. The plant, equipped with electric furnace and rolling facilities, was designed to produce about 20,000 tons of light steel shapes, bars, sheets and wire products per year. Its primary raw material was to be an estimated 170,000 tons of scrap, chiefly of World War II origin.

A turn-key contract was concluded with De Mag, a German firm, to build the mill, which was to be located in Rangoon's industrial suburb, Insein. Six young Burmese engineers were sent to Germany for training, and seventeen additional personnel were sent to India for training for supervisory posts. There were indications, during construction, that the Burmese were trying to "save" money by modifying the design, and that these modifications downgraded the mill's quality. On the whole, however, construction went reasonably well, if one ignores delays caused by the use of Russian cement which failed to set and had to be taken up. Far more important was the "discovery," as the plant neared completion at the end of 1956, that no spare parts had been provided for in the original contract. By June 1957, with production due to begin, less than half the spare parts considered essential for continuous operation had been ordered. Many of the raw materials required — zinc and zinc chloride, acids, electrodes, ferroalloys, and so on — had not been ordered. Some 45,000 tons of crude scrap had been purchased and brought to collection points, but needed to be sorted and sheared. Most serious of all was that, apart from De Mag's test crew, the mill had only one U. N. advisor and had recruited only one of the ninety-two specialized foreign personnel considered necessary in the first period of operations.

The mill finally got into production during the second half of 1957, but to date it has not achieved a satisfactory level of output. The Ne Win Government shut down the sheet section in order to bring pressure on De Mag to modify the equipment. This the firm agreed to do, but the section remained shut down for alterations throughout 1959–60 and only some 6,000 product tons were turned out. It was still shut down early in 1961. The mill was then pouring ingot and slab, but the furnace which fed the re-rolling section was also shut down, and the wire section had been stopped because the mill's product could not compete with imported nails. In consequence, it was turning out no final product at all.

The sheet section, as well as the re-rolling section, would, of course, be brought back into production. The wire section would also be brought back into production, whether by imposing import quotas or higher import duties on foreign nails or by other means. But whether the management would be sufficiently strengthened, the excessive labor reduced and the necessary volume of operations achieved, remained another story. Beyond these factors, still another remained. The scrap supply had not fulfilled the earlier estimates. It would last only a few years at high volume operations. After that, the mill would be able to operate only on imported scrap or billets, which would increase its costs and make it even less economic.

THE JUTE MILL

The jute mill was designed to produce 24 million gunnies annually on a two-shift basis for an assured market — the State Agricultural Marketing Board, which required an even larger supply to bag its annual rice exports. Experiments had demonstrated that jute of good quality could be grown economically in Burma. Given good management, the project promised to be a highly successful one.

The mill was built by the supplying firm as a turn-key job, and no serious problems arose during construction. A competent production manager was engaged, a work force was recruited and trained, and production started. Since the domestic jute production program was lagging badly, imported jute was used for the most part. An excellent product was turned out. Within a few months, a full one-shift level of production was achieved.

The Industrial Development Corporation, however, was far behind in its accounting, and did not know how much the mill had cost. The management therefore could not "cost" depreciation into its own accounting. The jute procured from the A.R.D.C. had not been priced. The jute mill delivered its product to the S.A.M.B. without establishing a price for it. So, for a time, the operation muddled along. As these questions became clarified, others arose. Had the mill, in introducing an incentive wage plan, set the work norms too low? Was it producing a bag of better quality than required, and so reducing its margins unnecessarily? Should its price be set at the "plus duty" cost of imported gunnies, or should it be set somewhat lower than this, to bring pressure on the management to increase efficiency? Should the mill be satisfied to aim at two-shift operation, or should it seek to achieve a highly profitable three-shift operation?

There was no effective means of resolving such questions, which were, in fact, beyond the capacity of the policy-makers to comprehend. The foreign production manager, plagued by inexperienced policy superiors who questioned his every move and refused to hire the specialized assistants he needed, simply could not cope with the job, and eventually resigned. As of early 1961, under still inexperienced Burmese management and with only one foreign advisor, the mill was operating two full shifts and getting little more than one-shift production. Few of the basic management and policy problems had been solved.

THE SUGAR MILLS

The new sugar mills at Namti and Pyinmina were designed to have a daily crushing capacity of 2,500 tons of sugar cane and an annual output of some 37,000 to 39,000 tons of sugar. Together with the output of the nationalized sugar factory at Zeyawaddy, annual sugar capacity would be some 60,000 tons — enough to supply the total national requirement of some 45,000 tons and provide for both increased per capita consumption and population growth.

No construction problems seem to have arisen with the Namti mill, which was supplied by an experienced Dutch firm. The Pyinmina mill, however, encountered serious difficulties. This mill was procured, on a "bargain" basis, from a Japanese supplier which had never before produced sugar mill equipment. Further, the Burmese repeatedly negotiated price reductions during construction — and obtained them at the cost of design, equipment and quality changes which downgraded the mill. Either because the plant was poorly situated or poorly protected or because it encountered bad luck, it suffered serious flood damage during its first producing season, and later had difficulties with its water supply. It also had serious trouble with its production machinery.

But again, as in the case of the other mills, the more serious difficulties were those of management and policy. High-quality management personnel were not engaged. And serious errors were made in the all-important sugar cane procurement. Briefly, the Government arbitrarily set the price of cane to the growers at K 42 per ton. With a sugar recovery of 10 per cent (which the mills did not achieve), this was equivalent to K 420 per ton, or 4.5¢ per lb., for sugar content yet to be recovered. It was also some 50 per cent higher than the cane growers were able to get from non-mill buyers.

A second error in cane procurement was to pay the same price for the cane irrespective of its distance from the mill. This involved far more than transport costs. Cane deteriorates swiftly within hours after cutting. Cane coming from some distance is less fresh and yields a lesser sugar recovery. It was essential, therefore, that the price for cane be uniform only at the mill door, to encourage the greatest production close by. But politics played a large part in the decision. The local farm and cooperative organization officials, who were responsible for determining which farmers would supply how much to the mill at the excessive prices established by the Government, reaped their own "harvest." Farmers were forced to reward these officials with a sizable share of the uneconomic price differential they received.

This situation would not have arisen had the managements of the mills been permitted to arrange for their own cane supplies. Their interest in greater mill returns would have given them incentive to assist farmers with improved cane sets and fertilizers. Then, with increased cane yields per acre, farmers in the vicinity of the mill could have supplied cane at, say, K 30 per ton, and have made more money than they did under the political dispensation. But still other reasons must be sought for the subsequent failure of the new sugar mills to reach satisfactory production levels. In 1959–60 they still produced only about 22,000 tons, or 58 per cent of their rated production capacity.

THE BRICK AND TILE PLANT

Unlike the turn-key arrangements made for the construction of the projects previously described, construction of the brick and tile plant was the responsibility of the Government-owned Brick and Tile Factory Board. Brick had been manufactured in Burma for hundreds of years. The ancient temples of Pagan were built with very fine hand-made bricks. But the Government had never built a brick plant before. The plant — a rather simple one — was begun in 1951, three years after the decision to build it had been reached. Nearly seven years more went by before the plant was completed and in commercial production. The story behind this prolonged delay is an interesting one.

The brick and tile factory was conceived of as an early-phase development project which would turn out some 6 million roofing tiles and some 8 million bricks per year to help meet the building needs of the development program. The estimated cost was K 60 lakhs. Operations began in 1951 with the purchase of clay lands opposite the Rangoon Golf Club and the ordering of the necessary machinery and equipment from abroad. As it happened, the ship bringing the machinery the following year sank, and the equipment had to be re-ordered. Despite this loss of time, building construction had not even begun when the second set of machinery and equipment arrived in Rangoon in July 1953. Building construction started only in March 1954, eight months later.

As of November 1954, the economic consultants submitted a report calling attention to the very slow progress being made and urging remedial action. It was already evident that the completion date of September 1955 could not be met, and that completion would be deferred for at least another year. Meanwhile the site selected for the construction of the factory, kilns, residential and auxiliary buildings was the clay hill which constituted the most accessible raw material source, and it was necessary to lay a road for almost two miles across low-lying paddy fields to reach an alternative source.

As of October 1955, a second report presented to the Economic and Social Board showed highly uneven and unsatisfactory progress. The main factory building had been completed except for its tile presses, which had to be taken out and reset because the foundations were not strong enough to take the load. Contracts for the electrical work had not been let. Although a pilot kiln had been completed, the major brick and tile kilns had not. Foundation work on the tile kiln had been started, but not even a start had been made on the brick kiln. Work on staff quarters and recreation buildings was, however, well under way. Construction of the main kilns was held up because of the lack of a skilled technician to supervise them. No provision had yet been made for the necessary transport, and the seasoning of clay had not been initiated. Although four years had gone by since the initiation of the project and completion still seemed to be some distance off, it was not possible to arouse genuine concern on the part of the Government. More than a year later the major kilns had still not been built and the access road to the clay had not yet been completed. Elaborate housing for the staff, completed some time before, was already beginning to deteriorate.

Progress on the project was finally spurred in 1957 as a result of a report made by the Standing Committee for Supervision and Coordination. The kilns were soon completed, but on first use the brick linings cracked and had to be replaced. It transpired that, in the desire to "save" money again, ordinary brick had been used for the linings instead of the more costly firebrick. New firebrick had to be ordered abroad and nearly another year went by before the plant came into production, early in 1958, at a cost of some K 92 lakhs.

In its first year the plant turned out more than 6 million bricks. These were apparently of good quality and competitively priced. They sold briskly. It developed, however, that there was little market for the roofing tile. Tile production in the first year was about one fifth of the 6 million tile capacity, and very little of this restricted output was sold. Tile prices were apparently too high compared with prices of alternative domestic and imported roofing materials. The factory lacked a sales department, and had made no analysis of the market. The nine distributors authorized were allowed only a 5 per cent discount and were making, naturally, little effort to promote tile sales. An aggressive effort to develop a market for the tiles at a more competitive and still profitable price might have brought results; instead, the decision was to abandon tile production, more or less, and concentrate on the less profitable brick.

The Government was not inclined to take this experience to heart, or to draw from it the obvious lessons. The bumbling and inexperienced management, the lack of the necessary technical help, the poor judgment, timing and coordination which had been so apparent during the life of the project and which had added unnecessarily to its cost registered only lightly, if at all, despite repeated attempts on the part of the consultants to use the case as a vivid example. So long as no glaring dishonesty was involved, and so long as some progress was being made, the time and production loss did not seem to matter much. In fact, early in 1961 the general attitude within the Government seemed to be one of general satisfaction with the project!

THE COTTON SPINNING AND WEAVING MILL

Completed late in 1951 at a cost of more than K 2 crores, this 20,000-spindle, 196-loom mill had by far the longest operating experience of any Government-built manufacturing enterprise. Its record, which could and should have been one of profitable operation and constructive contribution to the nation's economy, is one of poor management and lost opportunities.

There is little doubt that the profitability of the cotton spinning and weaving mill was adversely affected by its relative lack of weaving capacity and its absolute lack of bleaching and dyeing capacity. The decision to concentrate on yarn production was undoubtedly due to the desire to protect the home weaving industry. Another factor which adversely affected the mill's efficiency was the poor quality of the domestic cotton, which made it unsuitable for yarns of higher than 16 count. These factors, plus lack of autonomy for plant management and the poor discipline and morale of the labor force, led to the early resignation of the foreign technician engaged as general manager. The mill never thereafter had a qualified manager.

Heavy losses were incurred in the early years of operation. Although the labor force learned the manual and mechanical skills readily, discipline was poor, supervision and management were weak, and the plant's product mix was not adapted to the raw material available or to the price competition of imported yarns. Current losses and interest arrears soon brought the accumulated cost of the plant to over K 3 crores. As foreign exchange shortages forced a curtailment of imports, high textile prices beginning late in 1955 made it possible for the mill to compete with imported goods for a time. By 1957, however, it was again in serious trouble as the bazaar price of imported yarns declined and the Civil Supplies Management Board, which had been the mill's major distributor, could no longer sell its yarns to the weavers at a price which would enable the mill to break even. For a time the mill was protected by the Government's order that Civil Supplies tie sales of higher-priced mill yarns to its sales of lower-priced imported yarns. This, however, could not be continued long. At the end of the decade the mill was again accumulating heavy inventories of cotton yarns, and its accounts, which carried the inventory at cost, were deceptive.

As late as the fall of 1958, when a special task force of foreign technicians studied the operating problems of the mill, it was still in need of a capable general manager. The Cotton Spinning and Weaving Board lacked the authority to make the necessary policy decisions and failed to delegate to its operating officials enough of the operational authority it did have. Management responsibilities were diffused between the Board Chairman, its Secretary and the so-called General Manager. The mill had by this time been merged with the new Chinese-built mill, doubling its production capacity. It needed at least nineteen specialized production personnel below the level of general manager, but only three of its staff had ever worked in any other textile mill and only four had had any engineering education. Most of the supervisory personnel had had little general education, no technical training and no previous industrial experience at all. Despite serious labor problems, the mill lacked a qualified personnel manager to assist in selecting, recruiting and hiring workers, setting pay rates, establishing incentive systems, handling grievances, negotiating with unions, handling welfare and morale problems, keeping necessary personnel records. Although it was operating two full shifts, it was realizing only about 70 per cent of two-shift yarn production and little more than 50 per cent of three-shift yarn capacity.

Because of large losses in the early years of operation and accrued interest charges, the mill was capitalized far in excess of replacement costs. Combined with low-level production, this produced excessive unit costs which made it impossible for the mill's output to be sold competitively, even at cost. Better supervision, improved maintenance, improved raw material control and a higher level of operations, combined with a more practicable production mix, could have resulted in highly profitable operations. These results could not be achieved, however, in the absence of capable management and management autonomy.

Although it appeared at the outset that the Chinese-built addition to the mill, completed in 1957, would improve the operating efficiency, here, also, unexpected difficulties were encountered before long. It transpired that many of the Chinese-supplied machines had defective ball bearings, which resulted in frequent breakdowns. Needed spare parts were not forthcoming in time or in the quantity required. As of early 1961, five sixths of the looms in the new mill were shut down for want of spare parts, other breakdowns were frequent, and heavy unsalable inventories had again been accumulated.

EARLY-PERIOD OPERATIONS

It is difficult to get a clear, reliable and current view of the financial results of the Government's manufacturing enterprises from the existing data. As of February 1961, commercial-type profit and loss statements and balance sheets had been prepared only through 1957–58 in most cases, and in a few others through 1958–59. Selected investment, operational and profit and loss data derived from these statements are presented in Table 38.

Of the Government-built plants, only the pharmaceuticals plant seemed, in the year shown last, to have earned a profit, and its cumulative position was still one of loss. The jute mill experienced the largest current loss, while the accumulated loss of the "old" cotton mill, in operation since late 1951, had eaten up a considerable piece of the original investment. The largest loss, relative to the scale of current operations, was in the silk project. Here too a sizable portion of the original investment had been lost.

In striking contrast to the Government-built mills, the previously private but now nationalized sugar, cement and brewery plants showed substantial profits which were due, in part, to heavy accumulated depreciation on their original cost.

More recent data on the more important of the Government-built factories are available only on a cash basis, exclusive of depreciation charges, in accordance with their budget submissions.

The net current surpluses or deficits reflected by these budget submissions for the enterprises which were examined here are shown in Table 39. The figures show the pharmaceuticals plant and the cotton mills coming into profitable positions, the others in borderline or losing positions. A rough deduction for depreciation in each case would put the pharmaceuticals plant and the cotton mills on the borderline, and all the others substantially into the red. The cotton mill figures, moreover, conceal potentially heavy losses on accumulated inventory, and the pharmaceuticals factory, as was indicated, depends heavily on state aid through control of imports and in other forms.

A FEW GENERALIZATIONS

In view of the experiences described, a few broad generalizations may be offered at this point. First, while the pharmaceuticals plant was over-sized and excessively costly, and the steel mill, from an economic point of view, should not have been built at all, the cotton, jute, sugar and brick and tile factories were soundly conceived and, given effective implementation and management, would have been highly economic and profitable. Second, plant construction proceeded far more expeditiously when experienced suppliers were responsible for turning over completed projects. Third, the steel, sugar and brick and tile projects suffered because of naïve desire on the part of the Burmese to "save" money during the construction process. Fourth, the really difficult problems were encountered only when the state factories began production. Arrangements for timely and economic procurement of raw materials and other supplies had not been made; skilled staff and technicians needed from abroad had not been hired; accounts had not been kept properly,

Table 38

Selected Financial Data for Government Manufacturing Enterprises

(K Lakhs)

Industry	Capital Cost or Financial Advances from Government	Year of Latest Commercial-Type Accounts	Outside or Self Audit	Current		Profit or Loss	Accumulated Profits or Losses, Inclusive of Current Year
				Revenues	Costs		
Government-built							
Pharmaceuticals	665.8	1958-59	Outside	128.0	117.2	+ 10.8	— 13.3
Namti sugar	181	1957-58 Prov.	Self	101.8	110.3	— 8.5	— 13.2
Pyinmina sugar	446	1957-58	Self	69.2	84.1	— 14.9	— 31.1
Jute	446	1957-58	Outside	167.7	206.2	—38.5	— 58.1
Cotton #1	278.3	1957-58	Self	97.6	98.4	— 0.8	—117.5
Steel	554.8	1959-60	Self	85.4	104.3	—18.9	n.a.
Silk	108.3	1958-59	Self	5.3	16.8	—11.5	— 47.7
Tea	48.6	1958-59	Self	26.9	29.2	— 2.3	— 14.4
Cottage and Small-Scale Industry Board	71.9	1957-58	Self				— 24.0
Nationalized							
Zeyawaddy sugar		1957-58	Self	214.5	211.8	+ 2.7	+ 19.5
Cement		1957-58	Self	61.5	50.4	+11.1	+ 35.5
State brewery		1958-59	Self	170.7	127.8[a]	+42.9	+ 62.8

Source: Financial statements prepared by the several plant managements, Data for the pharmaceuticals and jute plants were audited by Allan Charlesworth Ltd., Chartered Accountants. The statements were made available by the Ministry of Industries.

a. Mostly taxes.

Table 39

CURRENT OPERATING SURPLUS OR DEFICIT,
SELECTED STATE MANUFACTURING INDUSTRIES,
1957–58 TO 1960–61

(*K Lakhs*)

	1957–58 Actual	1958–59 Actual	1959–60 Revised Estimates	1960–61 Projected
Pharmaceuticals	—13.8	31.5	26.4	44.6
Steel	—89.8	—16.4	— 9.8	— 6.0
Jute	—25.9	7.3	2.5	1.7
Sugar				
Pyinmina	—11.9	— 4.2	1.8	5.3
Namti	— 6.7	—16.4	9.4	— 1.6
Brick and tile	— 1.0	3.2	— .1	5.6
Cotton	—40.6	59.2	25.8	28.3

Source: *Budget Estimates of the Government of the Union of Burma 1960–61*, Book III.

Note: Budget figures are on a cash, not an accrual, basis. Interest charges are included in costs, but depreciation is not.

which meant that costs could not be determined intelligently; and, most important of all, appropriate management arrangements designed to fix authority and responsibility, and to permit businesslike conduct of operations, had not yet been made. Finally, the Government had not formulated economic policies on capitalization, pricing, marketing, employment and wage standards, tariffs, and so on, which even able operating managements, had they existed, would have needed for guidance.

One additional comment should be made here in partial explanation of the failure of the Industrial Development Corporation and the Industries Ministry to prepare adequately for emerging management problems as the new industrial plants approached completion. The consultants had recommended that, as soon as a given industrial project had been determined upon, a separate and autonomous sub-board be set up to supervise the execution of the project and to plan and supervise its operations later on. This would have permitted the I.D.C. to supervise, coordinate and provide policy direction for the projects and to perform its other functions as well.

Unfortunately, the I.D.C. did not follow this procedure. Up to the point of project completion it retained for itself responsibilities which should have been delegated. Yet so occupied was the I.D.C. top management with proposals, plans, programs and negotiations for new ventures that it was unable to devote the time and attention necessary to insure success of the ventures already undertaken.

THE PROPOSED JOINT VENTURES

It has already been mentioned, in passing, that Industries Minister U Kyaw Nyein sought to keep the industries program growing, despite resource and management limitations, by arranging for joint ventures with private firms abroad, chiefly further development of the cotton textiles industry in co-operation with Japanese partners, and the building of a pulp and paper mill in cooperation with American or French firms. Invariably, the foreign firm was not itself a textile or paper producer, but rather a supplier of textile or papermaking machinery interested primarily in making an equipment sale. The investments which these would-be partners proposed to make were in no case larger than the profits they could expect to earn on the sale, and they were assured of additional returns in the form of lucrative management fees. What they proposed, therefore, were joint ventures from which the "venture" element had been removed so far as they were concerned. Their proposals could not be regarded as evidence of their confidence in the soundness of the enterprises under consideration. In addition, so anxious was the Industries Ministry to expand its joint venture program that it was prepared to make all sorts of collateral and frequently unwarranted concessions to its partners. For these and other reasons, the economic consultants remained highly critical throughout of the several joint ventures proposed, and, as it happened, none of them was approved.

ATTEMPTS TO IMPROVE IMPLEMENTATION

Industrial engineers and management specialists supplied by the consulting engineers and U. N. economists, cost accountants and production technicians tried their best to help the I.D.C. from within. The economic consultants tried to help at the ministry and central planning and supervisory levels. Their efforts were concentrated chiefly on getting the Government to rely more heavily on the private sector for industrial development; on moderating the exaggerated emphasis the Government was placing on industrial development, as against agricultural development; and on bringing out the need to forego new industrial starts until consolidation of projects already under way had been achieved. The repeated attempts of the Industries Ministry to obtain approval for new projects provided ample opportunity to emphasize these views.

In addition, the economic consultants attempted in three separate yet more or less concurrent ways to cope with the implementation problem in the manufacturing industries field. First, they tried to persuade the Government to set up autonomous corporations for the new industrial enterprises and invite private participation in and management of them through the sale of shares.

U Kyaw Nyein looked with favor on this idea — perhaps because it offered the prospect of reclaiming some of the outlays already made, thus providing resources for additional projects. Specific proposals of this kind were worked out, with his cooperation, for the jute mill and referred to the Attorney General for approval. That was the last that was ever heard of them. The second approach was a more general attempt to get the Government to grant a greater degree of autonomy to all Government boards and corporations. The third was the attempt, through the creation of a special task force composed of foreign specialists, to cope with the specific problems confronting the several industrial plants. These later efforts were lost sight of in the emerging political crisis, and had at the time an educational value only. They did, however, provide orientation and guidance for the military officers who took charge of the state industries during the Ne Win regime, and who adopted many of the recommendations made.

ASSISTANCE TO THE PRIVATE SECTOR

From 1954 on, the logic of events and the advice and assistance the Government received from a variety of quarters combined to bring about a considerable change in its attitude toward private industrial expansion. In 1953–54 and 1954–55, a cash loan program conducted by the I.D.C. extended to private industrialists some twenty-eight loans totaling K 5 million. In June 1955, the cabinet issued an Investment Policy Statement designed to encourage both foreign and domestic private investment in industry. In 1955–56, spurred by the need to utilize reparations and barter credits, a hire-purchase scheme was introduced by the I.D.C., which granted 195 loans to private industrialists for the purchase of industrial equipment in the total value of K 13.4 million. The increasingly liberal issue of import licenses for machinery and industrial raw materials, tariff and import quota aids, the slowdown in new state industrial investment, the completion of the Industrial Research Institute, the introduction of business management courses at the university, and the advent of U. N. and other technicians who, under the auspices of the Directorate of Industries, advised private producers on improved production and marketing methods, all contributed to an improving climate for private industrial development. So, in another way, did the Government's increasing pressure to drive Indian and Pakistani business men out of the import trade, and its action in taking the pawnshop business away from the Chinese. Both moves caused a shift in investment by these groups into industrial activity.

The total effect of all these measures was to contribute importantly to a remarkable expansion in private industrial activity in Burma — a growth which will be examined in detail in Chapter 19. Unfortunately, the Government failed during this period to establish a much needed industrial development bank, which would undoubtedly have contributed to an even greater growth.

The idea of an industrial development bank was seriously considered in 1956. A study mission sent to India, Pakistan and Ceylon offered specific proposals early in 1957, and the World Bank was requested to provide loan and technical assistance. Burma insisted, however, that the Government should have at least a 50 per cent equity interest in the proposed development bank. The World Bank, on the other hand, took the view that the Government's equity interest should be a minor one only. The negotiations bogged down over this point.[3] I.C.A. was also interested in assisting the project under the $25 million U. S. development loan, but could not very well act so long as the World Bank remained in the picture. The Ne Win Government made budgetary provision for an industrial development bank in 1959–60, but took no implementing action. Early in 1961 the proposed bank was still awaiting such action by the Ministry of Finance.

3. The World Bank believed that private management was essential to efficient management. The Government — or U Kyaw Nyein, at least — wished to retain control over the direction of private industrial development and to have continued opportunity to favor Burmese, as against Indian and Pakistani, business men and firms.

CHAPTER 18

Implementation of

Other Public Sector Programs

FISHERIES

The original fisheries program was not clearly defined. Looking to the development of both fresh water and sea fish resources, it allocated responsibility for general planning and management to the Fisheries Bureau of the Department of Agriculture and responsibility for extraction and processing operation to the Ministry of Industries. It anticipated that the latter would not only stimulate extraction operations but also see to the establishment of storage and processing facilities and to the distribution of the catch. No specific projects were programed.

Little was accomplished in the fresh water field, although the Agricultural and Rural Development Corporation moved into the vacuum to some extent to encourage the stocking of fish in paddy fields and streams. The sole constructive step toward encouraging seafood extraction and related activities made by the Industries Ministry was to help finance, through a loan extended by the Industrial Development Corporation, a private joint venture of a Burmese and a Japanese firm. This was the Martaban Company, formed by Bo Let Ya, one of the outstanding freedom fighters and a former Minister of Defense and Deputy Prime Minister. The Martaban Company bought one trawler and leased two others from the Japanese partner. Its operations were, however, hampered by a shortage of working capital, by a heavy burden of short-term debt, by the lack of ready consumer acceptance of sea fish (to which the Burmese were not accustomed) and by the monopolistic practices of the cooperative which controlled the fresh water catch and fish market in Rangoon. Lack of adequate refrigeration, storage and processing facilities was another serious handicap, as was the unwillingness of the Burma Railways to provide refrigerated cars, which would have permitted Martaban to penetrate up-river markets in Mandalay and intermediate points. The rentals paid to the Japanese partner for the lease of the two trawlers kept the Martaban Company in a state of continual financial difficulty.

Despite these handicaps, Martaban's operations expanded and made a significant contribution to Rangoon fish supplies, until the Ne Win Government put pressure on the firm to catch up on overdue interest payments. Then the Company was forced to suspend activities. Adequate long-term capitalization and working funds, combined with good management and adequate transport facilities, would have made possible a much greater and almost certainly highly profitable development of the fisheries industry.

FORESTRY

The Pyidawtha Conference made no recommendations for a forestry program. The K.T.A. Comprehensive Report had emphasized the need to step up teak girdling in the forests, to make possible future increases in teak extraction. It had also emphasized the need for mechanized extraction units to compensate for wartime losses in elephant power, and in general stressed the need to utilize Burma's vast forest resources more fully. The K.T.A.'s specific recommendations in this field, however, were concerned chiefly with the development of six factories at a total cost of K 7.7 crores. Of these, the largest was a bamboo pulp and paper mill, estimated to cost nearly K 6 crores. Other recommended plants were a sawmill, a wallboard plant, a plywood plant, a joinery plant and a furniture factory.

The Implementation Conference of 1954 accepted these recommendations. It deferred decision, however, on the new sawmill, accepting for the time being the proposal of the State Timber Board that two foreign-owned and then inoperative sawmills — those owned by the Bombay-Burmah Trading Company and by Steel Brothers — be acquired and placed in operation. Other recommended projects approved and included in the comprehensive development plan were an experimental mechanical timber extraction unit, access roads and a light rail access system, the development of minor forest products such as turpentine, resin and lac, expanded extraction of non-teak woods and construction of a forest research and training institute. The conference accepted a report prepared under United Nations auspices by Dr. Von Monroy, which emphasized the desirability of an integrated industry for the processing of Burma's forest products and the utilization of waste products. This coincided rather closely with the processing recommendations made by K.T.A. Unfortunately, the girdling program recommended in the K.T.A. Comprehensive Report[1] was not included among those presented to the Implementation Conference and was not specifically approved at that

1. Vol. II, p. 815.

time. The report had stated that "a marked and immediate step-up in the amount of trees girdled is vital not only to the achievement of output targets in the teak industry, but even toward the sustaining of current output levels." Even more important, no recommendation was submitted to the Implementation Conference emphasizing the need to restore pre-war levels of teak production and exports. This should of course have been the first priority target in the forestry program.

Capital expenditures in the forestry field from 1952–53 through 1959–60 amounted to something less than K 5.3 crores, or approximately 1.4 per cent of all public capital expenditures during this period. Accomplishment in the initial program was partial only. The State Timber Board acquired the Bombay-Burmah and Steel Brothers mills and put them in operation. It set up two additional sawmills in Rangoon and one in Moulmein, each with a throughput capacity of 30,000 tons per year, by assembling in each case three semi-portable mills which had been imported as far back as 1948. After successfully experimenting with one mechanical extraction unit obtained in March 1955, the Board acquired two others in 1957–58 with the help of a $690,000 loan under the $25 million U. S. development loan. A few launches and cargo boats were acquired, and a little work was done on the rehabilitation of access roads. Earlier, an experimental kiln drying oven and an experimental timber impregnation unit had been acquired and a small plant had been constructed at the State Timber Board Depot in Rangoon, to build furniture for government departments. Designs for the proposed Forest Research Institute were completed only in 1958–59. The pulp and paper mill and the wallboard, joinery and plywood factories were never built at all.

But the more significant part of the forestry story is not the results of the program approved early in 1954. It was only early in 1955, when heavy foreign exchange losses had depleted the reserves, that emphasis was placed on achieving pre-war levels of teak production and export. Teak arrivals at milling stations at that time were at the level of approximately 80,000 round tons, equal in processed tonnage to the then exports of some 40,000 tons of teak annually, and only one fifth of the pre-war level. Because of the six-year cycle involved in teak exports (three years girdling, one year extraction and two years floating to the mills), it was necessary that the supply of girdled teak at all times be equal to six times the rate of saw-milling throughput desired. The economic consultants had repeatedly called attention to the fact that the stock of girdled trees was only half that required and, worse, that the prevailing rate of girdling was inadequate even to sustain the badly depressed production levels which then obtained.

This low rate of girdling, for which the Forest Department was responsible, was due primarily to the state of insecurity in the forests. The security

Table 40

THE TEAK PRODUCTION CYCLE,
1953–54 TO 1956–57

	1953–54 (*Thousands*)	1956–57 (*Thousands*)	Percentage Increase
Trees girdled (units)	34.3	270.4	688
Trees felled (units)	38.7	114.3	185
Outturn to main river depot (logs)	111.2	182.4	64
Arrival at milling stations (round tons)	77.9	135.9	74
Teak production (cubic tons)	118.3	178.1	51
Teak exports (cubic tons)	36.0	87.0	142

Source: Economic Survey of Burma 1959, Tables 11, 12, 13 and 30.

Note: The average teak tree, trimmed, is equivalent to 1.8 round tons. One round ton mills down to approximately one half cubic ton in teak squares and other dimensions.

forces available to protect girdling and extraction operations were even smaller than those maintained before the war, when no insurrection existed. Requests of the State Timber Board for armed guards had been made through normal channels — from the Board to the Ministry of Agriculture and Forests and thence to the Defense Ministry — and had met with no response. One reason for this may have been a fear on the part of the military that newly hired armed forest guards might desert their posts to join the insurgents. In any event, having made their request, the State Timber Board officials felt they had done their part of the job, and pressed no further. It was only after the foreign exchange crisis had developed, when urgent representations were made directly to the Prime Minister, that budgetary allowances and armed guards were provided. The rate of girdling stepped up markedly in the last half of 1954–55, bringing the total number of trees girdled that year to some 96,000, nearly three times the number girdled in the previous year. In 1955–56 and 1956–57 this rate increased to 229,000. The impact of this increase on fellings, arrival at milling stations, production and exports for the three years ending in 1956–57 is shown in Table 40. The declining rate of increase in the several operations reflects the long lead-time involved in the teak production cycle.

Various estimates placed the elephant force in the possession of the State Timber Board at less than 2,000, as compared with a pre-war elephant force of some 6,000. Another 1,500 elephants were said to be held by insurgents, who used them in part for illicit timber operations. This loss in elephant power was partially offset by the increased use of buffaloes — but mechanical extraction units were needed as well. The three mechanical timber extraction units acquired by the State Timber Board could add only 20,000 tons each to the volume of extraction. Successful experimental operations with the first unit warranted earlier action to provide more units to supplement elephant and buffalo power.

The lag in the teak production cycle provided the State Timber Board with ample time to augment its sawmilling facilities to handle the larger volume of logs arriving at milling stations. As of 1956–57, the six sawmills operated by the State Timber Board had a throughput capacity of approximately 150,000 round tons on a one-shift basis. Only an additional 50,000 tons of capacity would be required to handle the optimum throughput of 400,000 round tons, provided the mills were in good working order and worked two shifts to produce 200,000 cubic tons of milled teak for export. The mills, however, were for the most part old and obsolete, and a number of them were not in condition to work on a two-shift basis. New milling capacity was needed.

There was yet another reason for new capacity. The existing mills were analogous to the rice mills in that they were not capable of producing a high proportion of the higher quality "Europe" grades. Since India began to impose limitations on teak imports from Burma in 1957 to conserve foreign exchange, an increasing level of teak exports could be achieved only if a higher proportion of "Europe" grades could be produced for markets other than India. The State Timber Board, however, was fearful that it might not be able to penetrate new markets or enlarge sales to markets other than India. It preferred to slow down extraction and production rather than risk improvement of sawmill capacity. Proposals to seek U. S. or World Bank financing for new sawmill capacity did not receive the active support of the operating agency. Since the Prime Minister by this time (mid-1957) had already determined to slow down on new state ventures, the proposals were without effect.

After a decline in 1957–58 due to a reduction in purchases by India, production increased substantially in the two years following. Preliminary estimates for 1959–60 indicate teak production exceeded 300,000 round tons, or three quarters of the pre-war level. Sawmill output was only 75,000 cubic tons, and exports were at about the same level. Clearly, sawmill quality and capacity were beginning to operate as bottlenecks to further export recovery.

The chief defects in the implementation of the forestry program have already been noted. Perhaps more important was a basic weakness in the program itself in that it failed to assign priority to the achievement of pre-war levels of teak production and exports. This, more than anything else, contributed to the slow progress, in the early years of the program, of girdling, extraction, sawmilling and exports. The fact that teak extraction, processing and export marketing had been nationalized undoubtedly made for lack of imagination and boldness in program implementation, and the state of insecurity and the lengthy production cycle were of course important contributing factors in the delays. Perhaps more important than these was the leadership at the State Timber Board, which was composed of old-line civil servants, conservative in their outlook and fearful of taking aggressive action for which they might later be held to account. The two ministers for Agriculture and Forests during the program period, as has already been pointed out, were primarily politicians who provided little or no leadership or encouragement to the civil servants immediately responsible. The lack of a clear priority for teak production and exports was accented, especially in the early years of the program, by the emphasis initially placed on the development of an integrated forest industries project. The demands of this project from on high required the few competent people available to the State Timber Board to occupy themselves with engineering studies, plans, designs and prospectuses for the integrated industry and its several factories, and effectively diverted them from the recovery of teak production and export, which should have been their chief concern.

In contrast to teak, the production of non-teak timbers, which remained the responsibility of the private sector, substantially exceeded pre-war output.

MINING

The major job needed in the mining sector was rehabilitation of production and restoration of pre-war levels of exports, which had played so important a part in the country's trade before the war. The Chauk oil fields had been brought back into production, but the refineries at Chauk and Syriam had not been restored. The pipeline had been badly damaged, and either it or some alternative means of transporting the crude oil from Chauk was needed. The lead-zinc-silver mines at Bawdwin were operating at perhaps one-third capacity, and the proved reserves would not last many years at a substantial level of production. Additional ore reserves would have to be proved out before the building of a new ore reduction mill would be economic. The tin-tungsten mines at Mawchi in the Karenni State were still in insurgent hands. The numerous small tin-tungsten mines in the Tenasserim area, which had contributed substantially to the total production of these minerals before the war, were producing far below capacity. Effective action was needed to bring all these producers back to normal. Beyond these restoration jobs lay another task — the exploration and appraisal of additional mineral resources and development of them where warranted.

The K.T.A. program had taken into account the Government's decision to delegate responsibility for the rehabilitation of the oil industry and the Bawdwin Mines to the former owners, with whom the Government proposed to enter into joint ventures. Presumably, the same would apply to the Mawchi Mines when they had once again been brought into the sphere of law and order. The K.T.A. therefore concerned itself with new projects only. It recom-

mended three projects — development of the Kalewa coal fields at an estimated cost of K 7.3 crores; a zinc smelter and refinery at Myingyan, at an
estimated cost of K 3.7 crores and development of the Lough Keng zinc
deposits, at an estimated cost of K .5 crores. The latter two projects were
dependent on successful implementation of the Kalewa project, which was to
provide the fuel required for the smelter.

The Implementation Conference of 1954 was silent on the proposed mineral program. This may have been because U Ba Swe, the then Minister of
Mines, was not inclined to participate in a review of the program within his
province, or because the Prime Minister's office did not venture to invite him
to submit to such a review. In any event, the post-Korea decline in the price
of zinc soon caused postponement of the zinc smelter to an indefinite date.
The Government did, however, enter into joint ventures with the oil consortium and the Burma Mines Ltd., forming the Burmah Oil Company and
the Burma Corporation. The Mineral Resources Development Corporation,
which was entrusted with implementing the Government's own program in
the minerals area, developed a two-pronged program. The major part of this
program was directed toward extraction and development. The second and
minor component was a program of investigation and exploration of minerals
resources.

Among the extraction and development projects, that for Kalewa coal was
by far the largest. Here the M.R.D.C. employed first an American mining
engineering firm and, later, a British firm of mining engineers. Of the other
projects, the tin-tungsten mine at Yadanabon (near Mergui in the Tenasserim area) and the Lough Keng zinc deposits were most prominent. Yugoslav, Japanese and West German engineering teams were used to investigate
and explore copper, coal, iron ore and other mineral deposits.

The Government's investment figures show something less than K 5 crores
of investment in the mining field for the eight years 1952–53 through 1959–60.
This accounted for approximately 1.3 per cent of total capital expenditures
during the same period. These figures, however, do not reflect additional
outlays of more than K 5 crores, which represented the one-third interest
originally purchased in the Burmah Oil Company, the 50 per cent interest
purchased in the Burma Corporation and the 50 per cent interest purchased in
still a third joint venture, the Anglo-Burma Tin Company. Actually, of the
K 5 crores shown as Government outlays, something more than K 2 crores
also represent joint venture investment (presumably the payment required to
increase the original one-third interest in the Burmah Oil Company to a 51
per cent interest). Thus, of the K 10 crores the Government invested in the
mining field, something over K 7 crores represented investments in joint
ventures and something less than K 3 crores expenditures by the Government
itself. In addition, of course, the Government also invested substantially in

push barges for the inland waterways fleet to transport crude oil to the Syriam refinery.

The big success of the mining program was in oil. Crude petroleum production increased from 30 million gallons in 1951 to 187 million gallons in 1959–60, reaching more than two thirds of the pre-war level. Production of gasoline, kerosene and fuel oils quadrupled from less than 25 million gallons in 1952–53 to 101 million gallons in 1959–60. The Government's contribution here was chiefly in the capital it supplied to the joint venture and the river transport facilities it provided. It failed, however, to press the Burmah Oil Company to undertake a vigorous exploration program to develop new reserves. Only toward the end of the decade did the B.O.C., somewhat pressed by impending competition from other foreign companies also interested in joint ventures with the Government, initiate an exploration program.

At the Bawdwin lead-zinc-silver mines, operated by the Burma Corporation, recovery was less complete. Zinc output reached pre-war levels, but lead and silver, limited by declining reserves and the consequent failure to rebuild the ore reduction mill, approximated only about one fourth the pre-war output. Governmental red tape for a long time held up the issue of the prospecting licenses necessary to establish additional reserves. But the company showed no great drive in carrying out an exploration program once this obstacle was overcome.

The greatest weakness, however, was in the tin-tungsten field. Pending reactivation of the once great Mawchi Mines, the real job needed in the early years was in the Tenasserim region, chiefly in the Tavoy District. Numerous producers, small but with substantial output potential, were handicapped by the lack of security, communications and supplies, antiquated methods and illegal workings of their claims. Smuggling resulted in heavy losses of foreign exchange. A determined government could have restored law and order and developed a constructive assistance program that would have brought about sizable production increases. It was apparent, however, that vested interests of a political nature were involved. Too many politicians and officers in the area were benefiting in one way or another from the situation, and their ties to Rangoon were such that little or nothing was done to change it. Of the political leaders in Rangoon, it was U Ba Swe himself, then Minister of Mines and of Defense as well, who had the closest political ties to the area.

Later in the decade, when the Mawchi Mines were reclaimed from insurgent control, protracted negotiations with the former operators resulted finally in an additional major joint venture. Continued lack of security, labor problems, depressed tin-tungsten prices and frictions of various kinds, however, caused its early dissolution.

We come now to that part of the mining program for which the Government itself, chiefly through the Mineral Resources Development Corporation, was responsible. The fumbling, ineptness, disorder and mismanagement evident here were not exceeded in any other development sector. They centered mostly around the Kalewa coal project, which was designed to produce first 400,000, and later 300,000, tons of coal per year.

Kalewa coal was a low-grade, highly friable and, when piled, combustible sub-bituminous coal. Apart from the soon abandoned Myingyan zinc smelter project, Burma Railways and the Rangoon Electricity Supply Board were expected to be the major users. Both consumed large quantities of Indian coal. Development work at the mine proceeded in the expectation that the technical problems posed by the coal's peculiar characteristics would be overcome, and in advance of a firm solution to the transport problem, which greatly affected the economics of the venture.[2] Only in 1958, when U Raschid had become Minister of Mines and Balwant Singh had replaced the irresponsible U Ba Tun as Secretary to the Ministry, was serious study made of transport possibilities and the economics of the venture. The results indicated that the project, as originally conceived, should be abandoned. Fortunately, financial stringency in the mid-fifties had caused severe curtailment of the appropriations, and the monetary losses involved were not great.

Implementation of the Yadanabon, Lough Keng and other M.R.D.C. projects followed a not dissimilar pattern. Basically, the M.R.D.C. was doing mining investigation, exploration and testing by actual extraction and development — a highly speculative and costly procedure. Meanwhile, the Government failed to explore its minerals resources systematically, to overhaul its complicated and restrictive mining laws and regulations and to provide incentives and assistance to domestic miners and potential foreign investors.

While recovery in the mining sector was undoubtedly retarded by the post-Korea price decline, nationalization policy, poor leadership, the continued civil disorder and hopelessly inept management were responsible in far greater degree for the relative lack of progress in the Government's share of this important sector.

ELECTRIC POWER

The K.T.A. K 96 crores power program (Chapter 9) centered around the Pegu, Panglaung, Saingdin Falls, Myingyan, Mu River and Lampha Chaung projects, and incorporated provision for the installation of diesel generating plants in thirty-six towns as well. The program approved by the Implementation Conference of 1954 was substantially the K.T.A. program. Responsibility for its execution was vested in the Electricity Supply Board.

The program actually implemented was, however, a substantially different

2. The K.T.A. Report had assumed that the coal would be transported by barge down the Chindwin River. The question was now raised whether the dry season draft of the undredged river would be adequate to take the traffic.

one. Although designs were prepared for the Saingdin Falls and Pegu Hydro-electric projects, both of these were dropped — Saingdin Falls because it relied on the proposed, but not constructed, paper mill as its major customer, and Pegu because of the decision to upgrade the Balu Chaung project from the minor scale contemplated by the K.T.A. engineers into a major project capable in its first stage of development of generating 84,000 KW. The My-ingyan steam plant was dropped because of the failure to develop Kalewa coal and the zinc smelter on which it depended. The Mu River project was left dangling, first because of religious problems (the inundation of many pagodas was involved), and later because the program already initiated promised to supply all the power likely to be required well into the next decade.

The electric power program brought into being had three major compo-nents. The first of these was the Balu Chaung project, designed to supply a major part of Lower Burma and, later, to reach into the Dry Zone as well. The second, designed to provide the major towns with their own diesel-powered generating units, overlapped the first. The theory — inspired by the general elections due in 1956 — was to bring power to these towns some time before the Balu Chaung hydroelectric project could be completed, and, of course, before the elections too. Once hydroelectric power became available, towns connected to the transmission grid would place their diesel plants on a stand-by basis. Alternatively, the units might be shifted to other towns not on the transmission grid. The third major component of the program was sizable expansion of thermal generating capacity in Rangoon itself.

This last component was developed by the Rangoon Electricity Supply Board, which, although now nationalized and under the jurisdiction of the Electricity Supply Board, retained some of its pre-war British staff and had, in general, far more competent management and staff than did its newer parent organization. Coordination — and perhaps even communication — between the two organizations were at a minimum. For example, there was no serious joint consideration of why costly additional generating facilities should be built in Rangoon if cheaper hydroelectric power from the Balu Chaung would soon become available. The planners and budget authorities hesitated to hold up the Rangoon expansion for fear of protracted delays in the Balu Chaung construction and of possible interruptions in the transmis-sion of hydroelectric power to Rangoon by insurrectionist sabotage.

Construction of the Balu Chaung project was turned over to Japanese engi-neering firms, and was financed in large part by Japanese reparations funds. The Electricity Supply Board took responsibility for the diesel generation program in the towns. The Rangoon Electricity Supply Board managed its own expansion program.

Management at the Electricity Supply Board left much to be desired. It

Table 41

GROWTH OF POWER CAPACITY,
GENERATION AND CONSUMPTION, 1951–52, 1957–58 AND 1959–60

	1951–52	1957–58	1959–60	Percentage Increase, 1951–52 to 1959–60
Installed capacity (thousand KW)	29.6	92.6	106.7[a]	260.5
Units generated (million KWH)	52.5	178.6	235.5	348.6
Consumption (million KWH)	41.6	136.3	183.1	340.1

Source: Economic Survey of Burma, 1958 and 1960, Tables 25, 26 and 27.

a. Exclusive of Balu Chaung hydroelectric plant, completed in April 1960, with 84,000 KW generating capacity.

was, of course, tremendously difficult to build a large organization and engage in large-scale activities at the same time. U Ba Sein, the first Director-General of the E.S.B., was an experienced civil servant who enjoyed the confidence of U Kyaw Nyein, his minister. All things considered, U Ba Sein did as good a job as could have been expected. Unfortunately, and perhaps in the attempt to seek speedier performance, he violated certain administrative regulations and was jailed.[3] U Hlaing Bwa, his nominal successor, was a weak man. His deputy, U Tun Tin, who actually ran the organization, was a totally inexperienced guerilla fighter, zealous to the point of fanaticism. Under his management things went badly indeed.

Payrolls were padded with a large number of unnecessary and unqualified personnel. The budgets submitted were completely unreliable. Accounts were in hopeless disorder. Diesel units were installed in places where revenues failed even to cover the cost of fuel used in generation. Creditors were unpaid and, as funds were sometimes held up by the Ministry of Finance and the Union Bank, there were times when even the payroll could not be met. The staff supplied by the consulting engineers, the management specialist supplied by the Ford Foundation and the rate specialist supplied by the United Nations were unable to contribute their services effectively. This was also the experience, later on, of a Canadian team supplied under Colombo Plan auspices.

In violation of budgetary and program discipline, U Tun Tin inaugurated a "one-a-day" lighting scheme for a number of smaller towns and larger villages, which called, in each case, for the complete installation of street

3. U Ba Sein was held in jail, without bail and without being brought to trial, for approximately two years. When his case was called, he was acquitted.

Table 42

POWER GENERATION AND CONSUMPTION IN
THE RANGOON ELECTRICITY SUPPLY AREA, 1952, 1957–58 AND 1959–60

	1952	1957–58	1959–60	Percentage Increase, 1952 to 1959–60
Total consumers (thousands)	26.8	62.6	81.4	203.7
Installed capacity (thousand KW)	25.0	50.0	60.0	140.0
Units generated (million KWH)	46.5	126.6	165.5	255.9
Consumption (million KWH)	36.9	101.3	138.1	274.3
General	12.1	26.1	35.5	193.4
Street lighting	1.0	4.1	5.6	460.0
All-purpose bulk	7.4	19.0	25.9	250.0
Power	5.4	17.1	23.3	331.5
Bulk power	10.5	34.5	47.1	348.6
Departmental	.4	.5	.6	50.0

Source: Economic Survey of Burma, 1958 and 1960, Table 25.

Table 43

POWER GENERATION AND CONSUMPTION
IN THE REST OF BURMA, 1951–52, 1957–58 AND 1959–60

	1951–52	1957–58	1959–60	Percentage Increase, 1951–52 to 1959–60
Electrified by end of year				
Towns	26	313	309	1,088.5
Villages	—	361	364	—
Installed capacity (thousand KW)	4.6	42.6	46.7[a]	915.2
Units generated (million KWH)	6.0	52.0	70.0	1,061.7
Units sold (million KWH)	4.7	35.0	45.0	857.4
Public lighting	.6	5.8	9.0	1,400.0
Domestic use and power	4.1	29.2	36.0	678.0

Source: Economic Survey of Burma, 1958 (Table 27) and 1960 (Table 26).

a. Exclusive of Balu Chaung hydroelectric plant, completed in April 1960, with 84,000 KW generating capacity.

lighting in one day. A number of fatalities resulted from high voltage wires which soon came down and from short-circuited metal supporting poles.

More fundamental than any of these was the failure to clarify the cost structure, so that power rates could be set on a reasonable basis, and to develop the market for the huge increase in power that would soon be generated. The economic consultants urged the need for clarification of costs. Part of the program's cost, they pointed out, could justifiably be treated as a subsidy to rural electrification, or else as equity investment, rather than as an interest-bearing loan. If, in addition, a decision were made on how much of the total borrowing would be supplied by the Government and how much by the Union Bank (one charged 3 per cent, the other 5 per cent), future costs could be estimated, and rational rates established. (Household consumers in Rangoon were then paying 45 pyas, or about 9.5 cents, per kilowatt-hour!) Two separate attempts to reach such determinations failed, and the E.S.B. continued to muddle along in the dark in regard to the basic economics of the system it was building.

In spite of all this bungling, and considerable delays in project completion, the electric power program did achieve rather striking results. From 1952–53 through 1959–60, investment in it totalled some K 42.3 crores, or nearly 11 per cent of total public capital expenditures. Electric power capacity, generation and use grew as shown in Tables 41–43.

For Burma as a whole, installed capacity (exclusive of Balu Chaung, which was completed only in the final year of the program) more than tripled. With Balu Chaung, capacity was more than six times the 1951–52 figure. Generation was some 4.5 times, and consumption some 4.4 times, the base figures. Absolute growth was greatest in the Rangoon area. Relative growth, however, was far greater in the rest of Burma, where capacity (exclusive of Balu Chaung), generation and use were all approximately ten times as great in 1959–60 as they had been in 1951–52. The number of towns electrified had grown from 26 to 313, and whereas no villages had been electrified before, 361 now enjoyed the use of electricity.

TRANSPORT AND COMMUNICATIONS

The transport and communications program was essentially a rehabilitation program, though it provided for modernization as well. Except for the air-ways, the operating agencies responsible for its execution were (or had taken over) long-established organizations with records of achievement. They had fared disparately, however, in the number of qualified and experienced management personnel they had managed to retain. In this respect, the Burma railways and the Board of Management for the port of Rangoon had fared best, while the Inland Water Transport Board — the nationalized version of the old Irrawaddy Flotilla Company — had fared but poorly. The nature of the programs and organizations involved, however, made for important initial advantages in program implementation compared with areas like electric power and manufacturing, where new projects had to be carried out for the most part by new organizations.

The transport sector enjoyed two additional important advantages. Since it, better than most other program sectors, was able to utilize Japanese reparations credits, and later to obtain sizable World Bank loans, it was not affected as sharply as were most other sectors by the foreign exchange and domestic resource stringencies which developed, and the agencies concerned were able to carry out their programs relatively free of financial problems. And since two of the largest agency programs — the railways and the inland waterways — were concerned in large part with procurement abroad, rather than with construction at home, they were not so difficult to implement as were many other programs.

The K.T.A. program (Chapter 9) had contemplated some K 176 crores of investment in transport and communications. Of this, nearly half (K 82 crores) was to be spent for highways, nearly one third (K 57 crores) for ports and waterways, and about one seventh (K 27 crores) for railways. The Implementation Conference of 1954 approved this program more or less as presented. With the notable exception of the highways program, where very little was done, implementation was substantial. Total outlays exceeded K 86 crores, and comprised more than 22 per cent of all public capital expenditures during the 1952–53 to 1959–60 period.

The railways. The railways program involved chiefly the acquisition of rolling stock, track re-laying, bridge repair and other engineering works. Because trains and bridges were favorite targets of the insurrectionists, who dynamited them frequently, the railroad operated only by daylight until 1959. Full 24-hour operation would undoubtedly have reduced the requirements for motive power and other rolling stock. Improved discipline and better work performance in the modern railway shops would have cut down repair time and contributed to the same result. This factor, however, was beyond the control of the railway management — the unions relied heavily on their political friends in the A.F.P.F.L. leadership — as was perhaps the common failure of train conductors to collect passenger fares, particularly on the Rangoon commuter trains. Also important was the failure to re-lay the second track between Rangoon and Pegu, which had been taken up by the Japanese during the war. And centralized procurement, for a time, constituted an obstacle.

The railways program accounted for some K 33 crores of capital expenditures from 1952–53 to 1959–60. Considering the obstacles and dangers which confronted the railways organization, on the whole it did a good job. This is confirmed by the railways' actual performance, as indicated in the figures below:

	1951–52	1959–60
Freight carried		
(million ton-miles)	159.9	463.3
Passengers carried		
(million passenger-miles)	252.0	983.6

Inland water transport. The I.W.T.B. program involved mostly enlargement of the river flotilla. Expenditures for quarter and stern wheelers, tugs, passenger launches, buoying vessels and non-powered barges accounted for some 85 per cent of the K 16 crores invested. By 1958, the gross tonnage of the flotilla had increased to 104,000, as compared with some 40,000 tons in 1952.

The major deficiency was the failure to improve the company's dockyards at Dalla and elsewhere, so that adequate maintenance and repair could be provided for the flotilla. Freight carried showed relatively little increase during the program period, despite substantial additions to the fleet. I.W.T.B. officials claimed that this was because older vessels became unserviceable as fast as new ones were acquired. But the agency itself showed little desire to improve its maintenance. When in 1958 a loan was negotiated with the United States, primarily for dockyard improvement, the initiative did not come from the I.W.T.B. Shortages of trained personnel and service limited to daylight hours were also serious problems, as was the failure of the Government properly to dredge the rivers.

Underlying these was inept, political management at the top levels of the organization and a lethargic indifference on the part of the minister responsible. Morale in the organization was at a low ebb, and corruption was widespread.

Ocean and coastal shipping. Under the Union of Burma Shipping Board program two ocean-going cargo ships of 8,000 tons each, two coastal vessels of 1,056 tons each, and various smaller coastal vessels for the Arakan fleet were acquired, at a total cost of something under K 4 crores.

The ocean-going vessels were employed in delivering coal from Calcutta to Rangoon. So tight was the schedule necessary to maintain the inward coal traffic that the Board could seldom take the time to load outward-bound freight — even when the State Timber Board urgently required freight accommodation to Calcutta. The time squeeze was partly due to inefficient loading in both Calcutta and Rangoon ports. One or two additional vessels would have relieved the pressure, and made for much more economic two-way freight operations. These came only after the Military Government took over late in 1958 and, with Israeli management assistance, organized the 5-Star Shipping Line.

The new coastal vessels were evidently not well selected; their draft was excessive for most of the small coastal ports. In consequence, they were not fully utilized, and operated at sizable loss. The small Arakan fleet, on the other hand, operated at a profit, and should have been further expanded.

The port of Rangoon. Reconstruction of the badly war-damaged port of Rangoon involved mostly wharf reconstruction and additions to the harbor flotilla, but also pontoons, jetties, bridge and building construction and a number of fixed moorings. Total outlays, in part financed by a World Bank loan, accounted for approximately K 13 crores through 1959–60.

In general, implementation of the port program was good. Recurrent difficulties in port operations were almost always due to conditions beyond the control of the port's Board of Management. During the rice glut of 1953–54 and 1954–55, buyers rejected much rice at shipside. Lighters loaded with rice became floating godowns, choked up the harbor, and slowed down other loading and unloading operations. Lack of labor discipline and slow loading-unloading frequently made it necessary for ships to wait an inordinate time for and at berths. Delays on the part of Government agencies and the joint venture trading companies in clearing their goods from the docks often clogged the transit sheds, and slowed port operations almost to a standstill. Despite such difficulties, traffic handled at the port of Rangoon increased from 2.1 million tons in 1952–53 to 3.3 million tons in 1959–60, as compared with 5.4 million tons in 1939–40. The converted rice wharf, supplied with mechanical loading equipment under the U. S. development loan, was particularly successful.

The airways. The largest single airways project — the splendid Mingaladon Airport outside Rangoon — is not properly part of this story, since it was already nearing completion when the long-term development program was adopted. It was, however, much criticized as a "white elephant" project, and its total cost has never been made known.

The airways investment program contemplated gradual replacement of the antiquated DC-3 (Dakota) fleet and improvement of domestic airports. For the rest, the program was designed to achieve improved management and operations. Disregarding the very real potential for improved and expanded domestic operations, the Government decided instead to buy three Viscount aircraft and broaden its activities in the international travel field (The Union of Burma Airways already flew to Chittagong and Calcutta on the west and to Bangkok on the east).

While the new craft were being procured, there was little study of the proposed expanded routes or preparation for operating them. On the contrary, domestic service deteriorated badly because of the loss of foreign pilots, the shortage of trained Burmese pilots and the deterioration of ground maintenance staff and services. Lack of autonomy made it difficult for the U.B.A. to take remedial action.

A few abortive efforts were made to operate the Viscounts, when they were delivered in 1959, on the route originally planned, but it was obvious that the U.B.A. was not up to the job. Reported attempts to sell the craft were evidently not productive of sufficiently interesting offers. Two of the craft were employed, early in 1961, on the Rangoon-Calcutta and Rangoon-Bangkok flights previously serviced by Dakotas.

Highways. Perhaps no other sector was as poorly dealt with, both in appropriations and execution, as the highways program. Burma's 14,000 miles of roadway had been badly damaged during World War II, and had been permitted to deteriorate further thereafter. Perhaps even the K 82 crores recommended by K.T.A. would not have sufficed to pay for the necessary repair and upgrading and the new roads needed.

As it happened, next to nothing was done. The Highways Department was short-staffed, poorly organized and badly managed and supervised. Unaccountably, district highway engineers were quartered in Rangoon. In addition, the department was lethargic, and was not disposed to compete vigorously with other agencies for a larger share of the funds available. The policy-makers were not concerned about the lag in the highways program. And the World Bank, normally favorably disposed toward highway loans, insisted that reorganization and a training program were necessary preliminaries to loan action.

Some K 3.5 crores of the K 10 to 12 crores of the capital funds spent for highways during the development period were for the purchase of construction equipment — some of it too large to be used in the construction of any road Burma might build. A sizable share of the remainder was spent on the construction of a road between Prome and Taungup, on the Arakan side. This road, which could have had only a political rationale, passes through an almost uninhabited area. Taungup, its western terminus, has a population of only 4,000 or so. It had been estimated that the average daily traffic might be ten vehicles. This would have brought the road's maintenance costs to about K 100 per vehicle trip. Yet the policy-makers approved funds for continuing work, while cutting off the essential work already begun on widening the inadequate roadway from Rangoon to the industrial suburb of Insein, along which the Government's pharmaceuticals plant and its jute, cotton and steel mills, as well as hundreds of smaller private enterprises, had been located, and which was already incapable of handling existing traffic. The Insein road improvement was subsequently completed by the Ne Win Government.

Undoubtedly, the fact that roads could be permitted to deteriorate indefinitely and still be usable, and the fear of domestic inflation, contributed to the Government's disinclination to allot more funds for highway maintenance and improvement. It was, nevertheless, here, more than in any other sector, that much could have been accomplished with relatively small outlays, by invoking voluntary labor by farmers during agricultural off-seasons. This, however, would have required a government more interested in performance than in votes, and one whose posture was such that it could call upon its citizens to do what they could for their country, rather than seek always to have their country do more and more for them.

Telecommunications. The telecommunications program involved chiefly the installation of a new automatic telephone system in Rangoon. It included also the rehabilitation of trunk lines and internal and international radio telephone networks. Total expenditures for these projects approximated K 6 crores.

The automatic telephone project in Rangoon attracted the most attention, partly because the old system worked so badly that much impatience was generated and partly because Rangoon's most influential daily, the *Nation,* chose to make an issue of the decision to select the Ericcson cross-bar dial system rather than its major competitor. The telephone system, as well as the remainder of the program, was badly retarded because of intolerable de-lays in the construction of buildings. It was difficult to ascertain whether the fault for these delays lay with the Telecommunications Department or with the National Housing Board, which was constructing the building for it. There is little doubt that the Telecommunications Department was poorly staffed and directed. It also appears to have been badly hampered by its own ministry, and by the Ministry of Finance, in getting appropriations and financial sanc-tions. Delays in the granting of financial sanctions needed to utilize budgeted funds resulted more than once in the lapsing of spending authority at the end of a given financial year, and required that the process of asking for that authority be repeated the year following.

The telephone system came partly into operation in 1958, and was com-pletely in operation by the following year. Complaints that the underground cables had been inadequately insulated against the heavy monsoon rains caused the contractor to take up and replace some of the cables laid. It may be that the long period of storage to which many of the materials were subjected contributed to their deterioration prior to installation.

The telecommunications program had the advantage of the continuous advisory services of a capable and dedicated communications engineer sup-plied by the Government's engineering consultants. There is little doubt that if he had been used in an executive-administrative rather than in an advisory capacity, program implementation would have proceeded in a much more efficient and expeditious manner.

CHAPTER 19

Implementation by the

Private Sector

It remains to examine the contributions made to the implementation of the development program by the private sector. This will involve a review, first of the contribution made by private capital formation to total investment, and next of the contributions of private individuals and firms in agriculture, forestry, mining, trade, banking and insurance, construction and transportation and in cottage and manufacturing industry. Since any attempt fully to examine private activities in the several economic sectors would overlap with the study of governmental programs just presented, the presentation here will be complementary only.

PRIVATE CAPITAL FORMATION

The target for total gross capital formation during the development period was K 1,067 crores, of which the share assigned to the private sector was K 545 crores. From something less than K 30 crores in 1949–50 and 1950–51, private gross capital formation stepped up sharply in the succeeding years. For the four years beginning 1952–53 it averaged more than K 41 crores per year. And for the next four years, beginning 1956–57, the average annual figure rose to over K 55 crores. For the adjusted program period of something less than nine years, January 1952 through 1959–60, total gross private capital formation was some K 418 crores, or 71 per cent of the target figure.[1] This was a very substantial accomplishment.[2]

1. Accomplishment is compared with target only in the case of the gross capital formation because data on net capital formation are not available separately for public and private sectors. The target for net private capital formation was K 240 crores, within a total target of K 750 crores.

2. The step-up was even more significant than the data indicate. Because the preponderance of housing in Burma consists of bamboo huts with thatched roofs which must be replaced every

This growth in private capital formation was achieved in the face of a climate not basically conducive to private investment. The Government, as we saw in Chapter 5, had dedicated itself to the creation of a socialist state in which the major means of production would be owned and operated by the Government and by producers' cooperatives. Widespread civil unrest and disorder, excessive and even punitive Government controls, the lack of skills, technology and managerial experience and the high rate of interest which prevailed in personal and agricultural lending were other serious depressants to productive private investment. In the face of such obstacles, why and how did this very substantial increase in private investment take place?

In 1950–51 and 1951–52, with the worst of the insurrection over, there existed widespread and severe shortages of almost every kind of commodity desired by consumers. These shortages, combined with the Korean wartime boom — which raised prices of imports and even more the export prices commanded by Burmese rice, timber, minerals and other commodities — provided a great stimulus to domestic production for both home use and export. At the same time, the stepped-up level of Government spending, on both current and capital account, gave a considerable boost to domestic buying power. These factors were bolstered by pragmatic modifications in basic Government policy. Late in 1953 Prime Minister U Nu stated in his National Day address: "The achievement of the programme as a whole, therefore, requires that we institute measures which will enable the people in the private sector to carry out their part of the development programme. It is necessary that we encourage them to make this investment and to equip themselves for carrying out this programme. Government must give them full assistance in carrying it out in an orderly manner."[3]

In accordance with the Prime Minister's directive, the Economic and Social Board at its fourth meeting adopted a resolution which envisaged in broad terms the aid to be extended to domestic commerce and industry. It promised a liberal loan program, the formulation of a list of industries in which private enterprise would be welcomed, provision of tariff aids, tax relief and the assurance of adequate imports of raw materials. This forward step in Government policy, combined with the economic factors mentioned, accounted for the first sharp step-up in private investment.

Still other factors contributed to the second step-up in the four years beginning 1956–57. The first of these was the Investment Policy Statement issued by the Cabinet in June 1955, which in effect implemented the earlier promises. After reiterating that the Government recognized the contribution

---

two or three years, a substantial part of private capital formation each year is accounted for by such replacement. The rate of expansion in private gross capital formation of outlays other than these was greater than is indicated by the total figures. For more details on the data themselves, see Table 59.

3. "Our Goal and Our Interim Programme," reproduced in Appendix II.

which private investment, both domestic and foreign, could make to the economic and social progress of the country, the statement declared that the Government would guarantee new private enterprises against nationalization for an appropriate period; pay equitable compensation in the event of nationalization; make foreign exchange available for the import of raw materials, repair and replacement parts, other operational requirements and interest on foreign loans; protect new industry by tariff and other means; grant loans in suitable cases; and, in the case of foreign investment, permit the remittance of current earnings or dividends and allow for the repatriation of investment over a reasonable period of time. It also listed some forty-seven industrial fields, ten mining fields and two service industries where private investment would be welcomed either on its own or in joint venture with the Government. In addition, the Government declared, it had under consideration special incentives for new investment, such as allowances for accelerated amortization of plant and equipment.

The Investment Policy Statement of 1955[4] marked an important advance over the National Day Statement of 1953 in that it not only broadened considerably the area in which the Government would render assistance to private industry, and made specific commitments, but also in that it no longer stressed, as had the earlier statement, that the contribution of the private sector would be welcomed for an interim period only. Other important stimuli were the "hire-purchase" loan scheme of 1955–56, the Government's changing attitude toward its own program for state manufacturing industries, which virtually precluded new starts from June 1957, the continuing though slow improvement in security conditions, increasing skill and experience, the expanded loan activities of the State Agricultural Bank, continued increases in domestic money supply and purchasing power, the sharp curtailment of imports in 1955 and 1956 and the subsequent squeeze, within a declining private share of total imports, on non-Burmese traders.

AGRICULTURE

The broad story of agricultural production is told in Table 44. By 1959–60 total output was estimated to have reached the pre-war level and to have increased 41 per cent over 1951–52. Of the major crops, groundnut, sesamum and sugar cane had exceeded pre-war production levels. Groundnut, sesamum and paddy, in that order, had achieved the largest production increases over 1951–52. Of these, the output of paddy was of course by far the most important. Production increases here were not accompanied by a commensurate increase in paddy acreage. Part of the increase was due to an increase in yields per acre, as shown in Table 45. By 1959–60 the average yield per acre had increased to 1,452 pounds, or 12 per cent higher than the pre-war average.

4. Reproduced in Appendix III.

Table 44

AGRICULTURAL PRODUCTION, PREWAR, 1951–52 AND 1959–60

(*Thousands of Tons*)

	1936–37 to 1950–51 Average	1951–52	1959–60 (Estimated)	1959–60 as Per Cent of Pre-war	Percentage Increase, 1951–52 to 1959–60
Index, total	100	71		100	40.8
Paddy	7,426	5,250	6,916	93	31.7
Groundnuts	181	176	275	152	56.3
Sesamum	45	48	66	147	37.5
Cotton	21	16	12	57	—25.0
Pulses	250	177	211	84	19.2
Sugar cane	1,000	1,059[a]	1,100	110	3.9
Tobacco	44	45	38	86	—15.6
Millet and wheat	78	71	73	94	2.8

Source: *Economic Survey of Burma*, pre-war and 1959–60 data from 1960 issue, Table 9; 1951–52 data from 1954 issue, except for sugar cane, which comes from 1955 issue.

a. 1952–53; figure for 1951–52 is not available on a tonnage basis.

Table 45

PADDY YIELDS PER ACRE, 1936–41 AND 1951–52 TO 1959–60

	Baskets	Pounds	Per Cent of Pre-war Average
1936–41 average	28.17	1,296	100
1951–52	27.1	1,245	97
1952–53	25.9	1,192	92
1953–54	25.9	1,192	92
1954–55	27.4	1,259	97
1955–56	27.4	1,261	97
1956–57	29.8	1,372	106
1957–58	26.3	1,210	93
1958–59	30.4	1,397	108
1959–60	31.6	1,452	112

Source: *Economic Survey of Burma*, 1960 issue, Table 8, for the last three years, and various issues for preceding years.

Many factors contributed to this performance. First, there was the persistent influence of the basic measures taken shortly after independence to relieve the burdens of the cultivators. These measures included the remission of debts, prohibition against the alienation of land, the limitation on rents charged to tenants and security of tenure for them, and the continuation of land revenue taxation on the pre-inflation valuation basis, which in effect eliminated the land tax burden. In addition, the Government provided loans at low interest rates, distributed improved seed and fertilizer, expanded extension services, price supports and import controls in certain cases, supplied tractors for custom plowing, and did a certain amount of flood control, drainage and irrigation work. There was also a slow but positive improvement in security conditions in the countryside.

However, agricultural production continued to be plagued by continuing though diminished insecurity, by the high interest rates paid for the greater part of the working capital required, by some shortages of plow cattle and, importantly, by the fixed paddy purchase price established by the Government. Even after the sharp downturn in rice prices which began in 1953, there remained a substantial though diminishing margin which would have gone to the paddy farmer under free market conditions but was captured by the Government instead. It seems reasonable also to assume that continued uncertainties, due to changing patterns in land ownership, about the locus of responsibility for the maintenance of bund and dykes adversely affected paddy production. The land nationalization and distribution program had at best a mixed effect on agricultural production. Because it displaced many tenant farmers and established many farm units of uneconomic size, it may be that the net effect of the program was a negative one.

In broad, the rate of recovery in agricultural output was the major determinant of the increases which could be achieved in gross domestic production. The failure of agricultural output to reach the established goals measured the shortfall in achievement against total development plan goals.

FORESTRY

The chief criterion of private performance in the forestry sector is the production of non-teak timbers. As compared with average production from 1936-37 to 1939-40 of 502,000 cubic tons of round logs, and production in 1951-52 of 348.5 thousand tons, output had reached 611,000 tons by 1959-60, an increase of 75 per cent over 1951-52 and of 12 per cent over the pre-war average. This was a far better performance than that achieved by the Government, which had reserved to itself responsibility for teak timbers.

Since a major cause of retarded recovery in Government teak production was the insurrection, a natural question is why this same factor did not equally retard private non-teak timber production. This may have been due in part to the location of the various timber stands, but a more important reason, undoubtedly, was that private timber operators could pay tribute to insurrectionist bands and so buy protection, while the Government obviously could not do so. Another important difference was the fact that the six-year cycle in teak production made its recovery of necessity much slower than that of non-teak timbers.

MINING

Because most private activity in the mining sector was conducted in joint venture with the Government, this part of the story was told in Chapter 18 in

Table 46

CRUDE PETROLEUM PRODUCTION, 1939 AND 1951 TO 1959–60

(Million Gallons)

1939	275.7
1951	30.1
1952	29.3
1958–59	135.6
1959–60[a]	187.1
Percentage Increase	
1951 to 1959–60	522
1939 to 1959–60	−32

Source: Economic Survey of Burma. Pre-war, 1951 and 1952 from 1953 issue, Table 13. More recent data from 1960 issue, Table 14.

a. First half year, at annual rate.

Table 47

PRODUCTION OF PETROLEUM PRODUCTS, 1951–52 TO 1959–60

(Million Gallons)

	Total	Motor Spirit	Kerosene	Other Fuel Oil
1951–52	n.a.	n.a.	n.a.	n.a.
1952–53	24.8	6.9	11.1	6.8
1958–59	89.9	40.2	25.3	24.4
1959–60[a]	100.6	44.1	29.2	27.3
Percentage Increase				
1952–53 to 1959–60	305.6	539.1	263.1	301.5

Source: Economic Survey of Burma, 1960 issue, Table 14, except for 1952–53 data, which come from 1955 issue, Table 14.

a. First half year, at annual rate.

Table 48

PRODUCTION OF SELECTED MINERALS, 1939 AND 1952 TO 1959–60

(Thousand Tons)

	1939	1952	1958–59	1959–60[a]	Percentage Increase, 1952 to 1959–60
Tin ores and concentrates	5.4	1.3	1.0	.9	−55.6
Tungsten ores and concentrates	4.3	.8	.4	.4	−50.0
Mixed tin and tungsten	5.6	2.0	1.5	1.6	−25.0
Lead ores and concentrates	77.2	9.1	35.8	31.4	245.1
Zinc concentrates	59.3	4.3	20.8	18.0	318.6
Silver (million oz.)	6.2	.8[b]	1.8	1.4	75.0

Source: Economic Survey of Burma, 1960 issue, Table 16; 1952 data from 1956 issue, Table 17; 1953–54 silver figure from 1957 issue, Table 17.

a. First half year, at annual rate.

b. 1953–54; earlier figures not available.

connection with implementation of the Government's mining program. It is necessary to add only a few supplementary details here.

By far the best performance was posted in oil production, the essential details of which are shown in Table 46. By 1959–60 crude oil production reached 187 million gallons, more than six times the 1951 production and approximately two thirds of the pre-war output. Production of petroleum products increased from less than 25 million gallons in 1952–53 to over 100 million gallons in 1959–60, as shown in Table 47. Output of gasoline, kerosene, and other fuel oils all increased very substantially. Domestic requirements for kerosene were completely met, and those for gasoline and other fuel oils very nearly so. In addition, paraffin wax production exceeded domestic requirements and made possible a substantial export of this by-product.

The production of selected minerals is shown in Table 48. In 1959 tin and tungsten output was substantially below the levels recorded in 1952, when production in the Tenasserim area was sparked by the high prices prevailing as a result of the Korean War boom and purchases for the U. S. stockpile. The even more unfavorable comparison with pre-war production reflects of course the non-operation of the once great Mawchi tin-tungsten mines.

Lead, zinc and silver production, on the other hand, show substantial recovery from 1952. The unfavorable comparison with pre-war production reflects the limited operations at the Bawdwin Mines by the Burma Corporation joint venture.

TRADE

Although the volume of domestic trade increased during the development period with higher volumes of production and consumption, expanding Government employment, industrial production and agricultural activity drew personnel away from petty trading, where a considerable amount of concealed unemployment existed. At the same time, the substantially expanded operations of the Government's Civil Supplies Management Board and the co-operative societies that were its major outlets encroached on the trade activities of the private sector.

Most of the export trade was in Government hands. During the development period the Government added to its previously established monopolies of rice and teak exports a similar control over cotton and rubber exports. The private export of such agricultural commodities as beans and pulses and oil cakes and of non-teak timber was hampered by controls designed to prevent foreign exchange smuggling.[5]

On the import side, two simultaneous major trends, illustrated in Table 49,

---

5. Commodity smuggling — chiefly of rice to East Pakistan, ores to Penang, opium to Thailand and drugs, medicines and rubber products to China — was persistent and perhaps reached large volumes.

Table 49

PERCENTAGE DISTRIBUTION OF PUBLIC AND PRIVATE IMPORTS,
1954–55 TO 1959–60

	Total	Government	Private Total	Private O.G.L.	Private Licensed
1954–55	100	24.9	75.1	50.1	25.0
1955–56	100	44.0	56.0	27.4	28.6
1956–57	100	43.4	56.6	25.4	31.2
1957–58	100	48.0	52.0	20.9	31.1
1958–59	100	51.1	48.9	14.6	34.3
1959–60	100	35.5	64.5	4.7	59.8

Source: Selected Economic Indicators, C.S.E.D., Rangoon, November 1960, Table 7.

hampered private traders. First, the share of total imports pre-empted by the Government doubled, rising from 25 per cent in 1954–55 to over 50 per cent in 1958–59. Second, the share which could be imported on open general license — in other words, imports open to all traders — was progressively whittled away. While in 1954–55 imports under open general license comprised two thirds of total private imports, by the end of the period they accounted for only 7 per cent. The squeeze created by the Government's growing share thus fell with particular severity on non-Burmese importers, since these were permitted only a relatively small share of the import licenses issued. In 1959–60, however, as the figures show, there was a reversal of the trend as between Government and private imports. This squeeze on non-Burmese importers contributed to increased investment in private manufacturing production.

Within the vastly larger share of private imports under tight control, still another structural factor was at work. Here, beginning with 1957–58, a significant share of the licenses issued was allotted to the new joint venture trading companies, in which private Burmese traders shared with the Government the monopolies established for such major import categories as textiles (other than those monopolized by the Civil Supplies Management Board), general hardware and food and provisions items. Under the Ne Win Government, fortunately, these monopolies were limited in that the joint venture companies were issued licenses for only half the value of the commodities they handled.

BANKING AND INSURANCE

Private firms in banking and insurance had always been branches of foreign companies or predominantly foreign-owned. During the development period the Government cut very seriously into the volume of business done by these firms by establishing the State Commercial Bank and the

Table 50

Estimated Industrial Production, Employment and Number of Establishments, by Type of Industry and Product, 1953–54 and 1956–57

	Total	Foods	Tobacco	Textiles	Footwear and Apparel	Wood Bamboo and Cane	Chemicals Soap and Oils	Machinery and Metals	All Other
Value of Production and Receipts (*Thousand Kyats*)									
1953–54	676,087	294,383	49,440	99,541	45,351	33,934	66,757	16,004	70,677
Industry	463,178	260,399	32,519	56,057	15,434	19,854	39,358	5,645	33,912
Cottage industry	212,909	33,984	16,921	43,484	29,917	14,080	27,399	10,359	36,765
1956–57	1,731,472	510,556	99,750	330,267	132,453	96,188	220,082	52,888	289,288
Industry	1,052,572	405,556	82,850	86,767	70,953	77,888	161,582	36,688	130,288
Cottage industry	678,900	105,000	16,900	243,500	61,500	18,300	58,500	16,200	159,000
Number of Persons Engaged									
1953–54	287,987	74,541	31,916	44,600	23,434	39,872	19,776	9,973	43,875
Industry	113,967	46,398	18,434	12,572	4,170	7,311	5,627	1,603	17,852
Cottage industry	174,020	28,143	13,482	32,028	19,264	32,561	14,149	8,370	26,023
1956–57	407,156	101,228	30,872	70,590	32,183	58,726	24,012	15,390	74,155
Industry	168,356	64,228	15,472	21,890	11,583	16,326	7,612	3,990	27,255
Cottage industry	238,800	37,000	15,400	48,700	20,600	42,400	16,400	11,400	46,900
Number of Establishments									
1953–54	65,369	9,212	3,888	13,370	7,865	13,178	5,150	3,121	9,585
Industry	2,468	839	550	302	199	211	79	66	222
Cottage industry	62,901	8,373	3,338	13,068	7,666	12,967	5,071	3,055	9,363
1956–57	97,550	13,010	5,633	22,027	11,174	16,735	5,578	4,023	19,370
Industry	3,950	1,410	433	527	474	335	178	123	470
Cottage industry	93,600	11,600	5,200	21,500	10,700	16,400	5,400	3,900	18,900

Source: Estimates based on census data, from "Growth in Industrial Production in Burma, 1953–1957," Robert R. Nathan Associates, Inc., Jan. 12, 1959.

State Insurance Board and by nationalization of the pawnshops, which had been operated for the most part by resident Chinese.

CONSTRUCTION AND TRANSPORT

Despite the volume of construction performed by the Government's own agencies and by the Rehabilitation Brigade, private construction, chiefly of buildings, flourished under the impetus of the development program. Private residential construction in Rangoon, for example, had a remarkable growth. Private intra- and inter-city transport activities, by bus, truck and taxi and by river and coastal vessels, also increased substantially. The relatively high freight rates charged by the Railways and Inland Water Transport Boards contributed to the development of private carriers. Bus services were organized largely on a producer cooperative basis, but other transport activities were privately owned and operated.

COTTAGE AND HOME INDUSTRY

The best source of information on the increases in cottage and home industry during the development period is a study made by the economic consultants early in 1959, which covered the entire field of industrial production. So far as cottage and home industry only were concerned, the study, which covered the period 1953 to 1957, was based on the 1953 Census of Cottage Industries and the 1957 Survey of Manufactures. Since the 1953 Census covered 252 towns and a fair sample of villages and the 1957 Survey of Manufactures covered the towns only, the 1957 figures for village production are estimates based on the assumption that cottage and home industry in the villages grew at the same rate over the four-year period as did production in the towns. Under the circumstances the assumption is a reasonable one and the results may be considered fairly reliable.

For this four-year period, the study shows a remarkable growth; witness the following figures:

	1953	1957	Percentage Increase
Number of establishments	62,900	93,600	49
Employment (thousands)	174	239	37
Value of output (K crores)	21.2	67.9	220

The details underlying these figures are shown in Table 50, and the percentage increases in the number of establishments, employment and output by individual cottage industries from 1953 to 1957 are shown in Table 51.

While the data speak for themselves, at least two questions must be asked about them. First, with the number of establishments increasing by 49 per cent, why did employment increase only by 37 per cent? Second, what was

Table 51

COTTAGE INDUSTRY: PERCENTAGE INCREASE
FROM 1953–54 TO 1956–57 IN NUMBER OF ESTABLISHMENTS,
EMPLOYMENT AND OUTPUT, BY TYPE OF PRODUCT

	Establishments	Employment	Output
Total	49.0	37.0	219.0
Foods	38.6	31.5	209.0
Tobacco	55.8	42.4	no change
Textiles	64.5	52.0	460.0
Footwear and apparel	39.6	7.0	105.5
Wood, bamboo and cane	26.5	30.2	30.0
Chemicals, soap and oils	6.5	15.9	113.5
Machinery and metals	27.7	36.2	56.4
All other	101.8	80.4	332.4

Source: Table 50.

behind the tremendous increase in per capita output suggested by the figures? An increase in the number of weeks worked per year and the fact that the employment data do not cover unpaid family workers are part of the answer to both questions. The very substantial increase in per capita output was also influenced to an important degree by price increases and by the use of improved equipment. This was particularly true in the textile field, where the introduction of power looms was made possible by increasing electrification.

MANUFACTURING PRODUCTION

The data on manufacturing production are also derived from the study just cited. The results, however, did not involve a sizable amount of estimating. Growth of production in manufacturing establishments — defined as those employing ten or more persons — is shown in Table 52. The number of manufacturing enterprises increased by 60 per cent, employment by 47 per cent, and the value of output by 127 per cent. It should be noted that many of the additional manufacturing establishments were "new" only by definition. They had previously been classified as cottage industries and were now reclassified because they now had ten or more employees.

In 1953, as shown by Table 53, food production was much the most significant in value of output, with textiles, chemicals and tobacco far behind contending for second position. By 1957 food had declined substantially in rank. Textiles production also declined in rank, although, like food production, it enjoyed a substantial increase in output value. Chemical production had moved up very strongly, quadrupling in value and reducing substantially the leadership margin which food production had earlier enjoyed in relative contribution to total manufacturing value product. The production of foot-

Table 52

PRODUCTION AND EMPLOYMENT IN MANUFACTURING ESTABLISHMENTS
EMPLOYING TEN OR MORE PERSONS, 1953 AND 1957

	1953	1957	Percentage Increase
Number of establishments	2,470	3,950	60
Persons engaged (thousands)	114	168	47
Value of output (K crores)	46.3	105.2	127
Less, government production	2.3	14.3	
Private only	44.0	90.9	107

Sources: Table 50 and "Growth in Industrial Production in Burma, 1953–1957," Robert R. Nathan Associates, Inc., Jan. 12, 1959.

Note: Government manufacturing establishments, including railway shops and sawmills, numbered about 20 and employed some 14,000–15,000 persons in 1957. In 1953, the number of such establishments was much smaller, but employment in them was not much less than in 1957, when the state factories were just starting operations.

wear and apparel, tobacco and wood products also increased their relative contributions to the total, as did the "all other products" category.

The elements which contributed to these notable gains in private manufacturing activity have already been reviewed in Chapter 18 (as regards manufacturing activity specifically) and in a more general way earlier in this chapter.

TOTAL PRIVATE INDUSTRIAL PRODUCTION

The data previously cited are combined in Table 54 to show the growth of total private industrial production. Adjusted to delete Government-owned enterprises, the number of establishments increased by nearly half, paid employment by more than two fifths, and the value of output by nearly one and one half times.

In 1957, cottage and home industry accounted for 96 per cent of the establishments, 60 per cent of the employment and 43 per cent of the value of output. In terms of output value, cottage industry was most significant in textiles production, where it contributed nearly three quarters of the total; in footwear and apparel, to which it contributed nearly half; and in food and wood products production, in each of which it accounted for about one fifth of output value.

In terms of value added, industrial production in 1957 amounted to some K 67.5 crores — about 12.5 per cent of the gross domestic product and double the contribution industry had made to the nation's total output only four years before. To this spectacular result Government manufacturing activity had, at that time, made only a minor contribution. In the next few years, the Government's new manufacturing enterprises stepped up their rate of pro-

Table 53

VALUE OF MANUFACTURING OUTPUT, BY PRODUCT, 1953 AND 1957

	Percentage Increase in Output Value, 1953–57	Percentage Distribution of Output Value	
		1953	1957
Total	107	100	100
1. Food	45	59.2	41.6
2. Textiles	47	11.8	8.4
3. Chemicals	302	8.9	17.4
4. Tobacco	155	7.4	9.1
5. Footwear and apparel	360	3.5	7.8
6. Wood products	283	2.2	4.2
Total, 1–6	—	93.0	88.5
7. All other	242	7.0	11.5

Sources: Table 50 and "Growth in Industrial Production in Burma, 1953–1957," Robert R. Nathan Associates, Jan. 12, 1959.

Table 54

GROWTH OF PRIVATE INDUSTRIAL PRODUCTION, 1953–57

	1953	1957	Percentage Increase
Number of establishments	65,365	97,530	49.2
Cottage and home industries	62,900	93,600	48.8
Manufacturing	2,465	3,930	59.4
Employment (thousands)	276	393	42.4
Cottage and home industries	174	239	37
Manufacturing	102	154	51
Value of output (K crores)	65.2	158.8	143.6
Cottage and home industries	21.2	67.9	220.3
Manufacturing	44	90.9	107

Sources: Tables 51 and 52, crudely adjusted, as per note to Table 52, to deduct Government establishments and employment.

duction and contributed more substantially to total industrial output, but they did not become a major element in it.

According to preliminary data prepared by the Central Statistical and Economics Department early in 1961,[6] the value of industrial production appeared to have increased by another 20 per cent since 1957, the largest relative gains being recorded by textiles, petroleum refining, metal industries, foods and tobacco products. Of these, the increase of two thirds in the value of textile production was by far the most significant.

6. The data are included in "Production Targets, Four Year Plan, 1961–65," Form 1, undated.

SIGNIFICANCE OF THE INDUSTRIAL GROWTH EXPERIENCE

It seems clear that the swift and sizable expansion of private industrial production in Burma has a significant bearing on some widely accepted generalizations concerning entrepreneurial abilities and motivations and the potentials for private savings and investment in underdeveloped countries, as well as for public policies based upon them. It is rather generally held that, in underdeveloped countries, only very limited private savings can be accumulated, and that the scarcity of entrepreneurial ability limits productive investment by the private sector. These views are not supported by the experience in Burma. The policy of state investment in manufacturing enterprises, which in Burma was based at least in part on the belief that the private sector could not be relied upon to develop manufacturing industry, is also demonstrated to have been erroneous.

FOREIGN INVESTMENT IN MANUFACTURING INDUSTRY

As far back as 1949, the Government had made known the country's desire for private foreign investment. But statements to this effect not backed up by specific action of the kind required were scarcely to be taken seriously. They were, in fact, completely unproductive of the desired result.

The first evidences of investment interest on the part of foreign firms developed in connection with the Government's joint ventures. Japanese firms engaged in the sale of textile manufacturing machinery were only too willing to take a 10 or 15 per cent interest in joint venture textile mills, on condition that they provided the equipment for them and were paid fees for management. A U. S. firm was willing to participate in a joint venture paper mill, on a similar basis. This was "venture" without risk, and the proposals were not accepted.

After the Investment Policy Statement of June 1955 was issued, there were a few other expressions of interest, and some of these resulted in actual investment. Unilever proposed a joint venture in soap manufacture in which the company would provide most of the capital required. This proposal was accepted and, after some time, implemented. Glaxo, another British firm, proposed to set up a small plant in Burma to "manufacture" — in reality, to package bulk imports of — infant foods. This too was approved and implemented. The decisions of the investing firms in these cases did not rest solely on the new assurances given by the Government. They appeared to be motivated even more strongly by a natural desire of these firms to retain their traditional share of the Burmese market — a share which was increasingly threatened by the combination of foreign exchange shortages, restricted import licensing, protectionist tariffs, and a rapidly developing home industry. Other firms made additional proposals, similarly motivated, involving chiefly assembly or packaging operations, but the conditions they stipulated were inconsistent with sound policy.[7]

Of all the British firms that had operated on a large scale in Burma before World War II and that still maintained offices and continued to operate, though on a much reduced scale, in the 1950s, only one — the Bombay–Burmah Trading Company — ventured to bring in new capital for productive investment. This firm, which had once dominated teak extraction, sawmilling and exports, invested first in a small boatyard across the river from Rangoon, next in a new concrete pipe plant, and then in a cement-asbestos sheet factory. Though its total new investment was quite modest, the enterprises were efficient, useful and successful. This naturally raises the question: Why did not Steel Brothers and other firms, which had resident staffs and a wealth of experience in Burma, do the same thing?

There were several reasons why they did not. For one thing, the Government was not disposed to treat "captive" investors who were already "locked in" as liberally as new investors who had not earned fortunes in Burma during the colonial days. Steel Brothers, for example, was far more concerned with obtaining fair compensation for its nationalized cement factory at Thayetmyo, and with the future of the monies invested in its Strand Hotel and other properties, than with new investment opportunities. Second, the operation of foreign-owned enterprises in Burma was difficult. It was hard to obtain entry and stay permits for foreign employees, import licenses for materials, operating supplies and replacement parts, remittance privileges for foreign staff, profit remittances, and so on. Foreign firms were required to employ Burmans in given proportions at various wage or salary levels, whether or not adequately qualified local help was available. In their dealings with labor unions, the firms were wrong until they had proved themselves "right" — and this was very difficult to do. And always there was the fear that success would bring nationalization and the same old treadmill of compensation adjudication, collection and remittance privilege would have to be plodded once again. Lastly, and of more than minor importance in this connection, the resident managers and staffs of these firms were essentially "caretaker" types rather than venturesome innovators. With a lengthy experience dating back to "the good old days," it would in any case have been difficult for most of them to appraise the new scene on the basis of a completely different set of premises.

The question, then, is not why only Bombay-Burmah, of the older companies, undertook new ventures. It is rather, why Bombay-Burmah did so. At least one of the reasons was that this company was represented in Rangoon by successive resident managers — Paul Isserlis and Christopher McDowell

---

7. A common condition was assurance of Government protection, in the form of import bans or quotas, from external competition.

— who were somewhat younger (certainly younger-minded) and more dynamic than were most of their peers in the British commercial community. Also, while they were objective and critical enough, they seemed to have a fundamental sympathy for Burmese aspirations, ability to communicate and a confidence that, over the longer run, conditions would improve. Their investigations, reports and recommendations undoubtedy influenced their company's investment decisions.

In 1959, the Parliament enacted a "Union of Burma Investment Act"[8] which went substantially beyond even the Investment Policy Statement of 1955 in the aids offered to new investors, subject to approval by an Investment Committee created by the Act. Among the incentives not previously offered were accelerated depreciation, complete income tax exemption for three years (and possible partial exemption for an additional period), exemption of machinery and raw materials imports from customs duties for a period of three years and income tax exemption for profits re-invested within a year after being set aside for such a purpose. As of January 1961, the Investment Committee had under consideration some fifteen to twenty investment proposals, almost all involving joint ventures with foreign firms, but no definitive action had yet been taken.

8. The text of the Act is given in Appendix IV.

CHAPTER 20

Outcomes and Impact of the

Development Program

This chapter will be concerned with the over-all results of the development program and its effects on the Burmese economy. After viewing the capital expenditure program as a whole, it will examine the impact on gross domestic product, other general measures, capital formation, use of resources, production in selected target areas, economic stability, the structure of the economy and economic welfare. Where appropriate, achievements will be measured against the original goals of the eight-year development program.

Total public capital expenditures from 1952–53 through 1959–60 amounted to some K 389 crores, as shown in Table 55. Of this, defense and law and order expenditures were the largest single component, accounting for nearly one fifth of the total. Transportation followed close behind and, with communications, exceeded the defense total. Social services and miscellaneous programs made up the next largest category, followed by electric power, agriculture and irrigation, construction and industry. Since construction expenditures went for the most part for schools, hospitals, bazaars and office buildings, they would, if properly distributed, substantially augment social services outlays. The percentage distribution of capital expenditures among the various sectors year by year is shown in Table 56.

THE GROSS DOMESTIC PRODUCT

The broad sweep of the gross domestic product, in constant prices, is shown in Table 57 beginning with 1951–52, when the G.D.P. was still less than three quarters of the pre-war figure. The sharp rise in capital outlays which began at that time brought about an increase of some 45 per cent in the next eight

Table 55

PUBLIC CAPITAL EXPENDITURES BY ECONOMIC SECTOR, 1952–53 TO 1959–60

(K Crores)

	1952–53	1953–54	1954–55	1955–56	1952–53 to 1955–56 Total	1956–57	R.E. 1957–58	R.E. 1958–59	P.A. 1959–60	1956–57 to 1959–60 Total	1952–53 to 1959–60 Total
Total	32.74	53.80[b]	60.91[c]	48.33	195.78	53.76	52.33	51.73	35.66	193.48	389.26
Agriculture and irrigation	.46	8.00	3.60	4.55	16.61	3.93	6.23	6.09	3.89	20.14	36.75
Forestry	1.22	.79	.28	.38	2.67	.92	.60	.75	.34	2.61	5.28
Mining	.03	.21	.32	.40	.96	.70	.57	.55	2.20	4.02	4.98
Industry	.40	3.82	9.01	6.85	20.08	5.47	4.13	3.08	2.00	14.68	34.76
Power	.20	3.63	7.97	6.08	17.88	7.35	7.96	6.05	3.04	24.40	42.28
Transportation	6.37	13.12	6.63	7.42	33.54	7.69	10.31	10.47	8.73	37.20	70.74
Communications	.50	.81	3.74	1.86	6.91	1.86	2.18	2.08	2.55	8.67	15.58
Construction	3.52	7.57	7.33	4.46	22.88	4.90	1.53	2.62	3.18	12.23	35.11
Social services	2.89	{1.58	{2.59	{2.14	{18.91	1.81	3.12	4.34	.90	10.17 }	{43.88
Misc. programs	9.71					2.48	6.44	5.10	.78	14.80 }	
Pyidawtha grants	.92	.98	.94	.19	3.03						3.03
Defense, law and order	6.52	12.00	9.10	10.00	37.62	11.05	9.26	10.60	8.05	38.96	76.58
Undistributed Japanese reparations	—	—	—	—	—	5.60	—	—	—	5.60	5.60
Unallocable[a]	—	1.29	9.40	4.00	14.69	—	—	—	—	—	14.69

Sources: *Economic Survey of Burma*, various years through 1960 for 1953–54 to 1958–59 data; 1959–60 data from "Capital Expenditures for 1959–60," C.S.E.D., Jan. 21, 1961; 1952–56 defense, law and order expenditures from C.S.E.D.; 1952–53 data from "A Review of Economic Planning in Burma," U Thet Tun, Ministry of National Planning, Oct. 1959, Table 18.

a. Published data do not account for these sums within the total reported expenditures.

b. Excludes debt repayment of K 14.8 crores to the U.K. (K 9.6 crores) and to India (K 5.2 crores).

c. Excludes debt repayment of K 10.4 crores to India.

R.E. Revised estimates.

P.A. Preliminary actuals.

Note: Construction outlays are largely for schools, hospitals, bazaars and office buildings. If properly distributed, they would augment substantially the expenditures shown in the social services category.

Table 56

PERCENTAGE DISTRIBUTION OF PUBLIC CAPITAL EXPENDITURES BY ECONOMIC SECTOR, 1952–53 TO 1959–60

	1952–53	1953–54	1954–55	1955–56	1952–53 to 1955–56 Total	1956–57	1957–58	1958–59	1959–60	1956–57 to 1959–60 Total	1952–53 to 1959–60 Total
Total	100	100	100	100	100	100	100	100	100	100	100
Agriculture and irrigation	1.4	14.9	5.9	9.4	8.5	7.3	11.9	11.8	10.9	10.4	9.4
Forestry	3.7	1.5	.5	.8	1.4	1.7	1.1	1.4	1.0	1.4	1.4
Mining	.3	.4	.5	.8	.5	1.3	1.1	1.1	6.2	2.1	1.3
Industry	1.2	7.1	14.8	14.2	10.3	10.2	7.9	6.0	5.6	7.6	8.9
Power	.6	6.7	13.1	12.6	9.1	13.7	15.2	11.7	8.5	12.6	10.9
Transportation	19.4	24.4	10.9	15.4	17.1	14.3	19.7	20.2	24.5	19.2	18.2
Communications	1.5	1.5	6.1	3.8	3.5	3.5	4.2	4.0	7.2	4.5	4.0
Construction	10.8	14.1	12.0	9.2	11.7	9.1	2.9	5.1	8.9	6.3	9.0
Social services	8.8	2.9	4.2	4.4	9.7	3.4	6.0	8.4	2.5	5.3	11.3
Misc. programs	29.7					4.6	12.3	9.9	2.2	7.7	
Pyidawtha grants	2.8	1.8	1.5	.4	1.5	—	—	—	—	—	.8
Defense, law and order	19.9	22.3	14.9	20.7	19.2	20.6	17.7	20.5	22.6	20.1	19.7
Undistributed Japanese reparations	—	—	—	—	—	10.4	—	—	—	2.9	1.4
Unallocable	—	2.4	15.4	8.3	7.5	—	—	—	—	—	3.8

Source: Table 55.

Table 57

Gross Domestic Product in 1947–48 Prices, 1938–39 to 1959–60

(K Million)

Industry	1938–39	1947–48	1951–52	1952–53	1953–54	1954–55	1955–56	1956–57	1957–58	1958–59	1959–60
1. Agriculture and fisheries	1,907	1,451	1,440	1,537	1,521	1,577	1,617	1,753	1,620	1,797	1,833
2. Forestry	360	273	266	276	289	303	314	344	347	347	376
3. Mining and quarrying	273	29	34	36	49	60	66	84	101	115	120
4. Rice processing	182	125	119	129	125	125	131	144	124	147	156
5. State marketing	633	286	248	258	278	371	460	482	413	429	486
6. State transport	117	63	48	56	68	79	78	76	74	82	85
7. State banking	...	1	1	1	2	2	9	12	14	13	15
8. Other public utilities	31	14	10	11	22	26	28	31	37	31	55
9. General Government	153	229	314	376	412	435	461	487	535	570	600
10. Rental value of housing	165	151	162	170	177	185	194	203	210	215	220
11. Other industries and services	1,124	935	994	1,049	1,103	1,127	1,092	1,292	1,223	1,274	1,312
12. Gross domestic product	4,945	3,557	3,636	3,899	4,046	4,294	4,450	4,908	4,698	5,020	5,308
Index (1938–39 = 100)	100	72	74	79	82	87	90	99	95	102	107
Percentage increase from preceding year	—	—	—	6.8	3.8	6.1	3.4	10	−4.0	7.8	4.9

Source: Economic Survey of Burma, 1960 issue, Table 2; 1951–52 and 1952–53 data from 1957 issue, Table 2.

years. But the rate of growth was not consistent, and in one year, 1957–58, there was actually a sharp decline due to a short rice harvest. The cumulative growth rate of 5 per cent per year, combined with a population growth of about 1.5 per cent per year, meant a per capita output growth rate of 3.5 per cent per year. In almost any other setting, this would have been remarkable. In a war-torn economy recovering from a badly reduced level of output it was a performance something less than spectacular. But it represented no mean achievement. It did, however, fall substantially short of the ambitious major goals of the eight-year development program, as shown in Table 58.[1]

The actual increase in gross domestic product from 1951–52 to 1959–60 was substantially short of the 78 per cent envisaged in the long-term development plan.[2] The 29 per cent growth in per capita output and 20 per cent growth in per capita consumption were less than half the plan's targets, but the increases were substantial and perceptible to the population.

CAPITAL FORMATION

Gross capital formation totaled some K 886 crores from January 1952 through 1959–60, the plan period, as shown in Table 59. Of this, K 468 crores, or nearly 53 per cent, was public, and some K 418 crores was private capital formation. Stock accumulation, mostly in the public sector, accounted for nearly 10 per cent of the total. The year-by-year pattern corresponds naturally to that of capital expenditures shown in Table 55. The levels, beginning with 1951–52, represent a very sharp increase over those in preceding years. The rate and degree of increase were greater in the public sector. But private capital formation also increased substantially, under the impact of public spending.[3] After a sharp rise in 1954–55, the break in rice prices and earnings caused investment flow to decline in 1955–56. The new flow of supplementary foreign resources that began in 1956–57 permitted another step up to a somewhat higher plateau for the next few years.

Actual gross and net capital formation are compared with the targets adopted in the eight-year development plan, year by year and in total, in Tables 61 and 62. Actual gross capital formation was 83 per cent of that envisaged in the original plan. Public capital formation was nearly 90 per cent,

1. In order to facilitate comparison with the eight-year plan targets, which were stated in 1950–51 prices, the actual data have been adjusted to 1950–51 prices. They are, however, consistent with the data shown in Table 57, which are in 1947–48 prices.

2. Because of faulty statistical techniques in converting from one price series to another, the 43 per cent growth shown here does not coincide with the 45 per cent increase shown in Table 57 from 1951–52.

3. Gross public capital formation, at K 468 crores, is substantially in excess of the K 389 crores of public capital expenditures shown in Table 55, for three reasons: The capital formation figure includes depreciation expenditures; it covers the last nine months of 1951–52; and the 1959–60 figure is still based on revised estimates, whereas the capital expenditure figures are preliminary actuals which have been revised sharply downward.

Table 58

EIGHT-YEAR DEVELOPMENT PLAN,
MAJOR ECONOMIC TARGETS AND ACHIEVEMENTS

| | | | 1959–60 | | Percentage Increase | | | |
| | | | | | 1938–39 to 1959–60 | | 1951–52 to 1959–60 | |
	1938–39	1951–52	Target	Achievement	Target	Achievement	Target	Achievement
Gross domestic product (in K crores, 1950–51 prices)	533.8	392.7	700	560.4	31	5	78	43
Per capita output (in kyats, 1950–51 prices)	326	210	340	270	4	—17	62	29
Per capita consumption (in kyats, 1950–51 prices)	206	147	224	177	9	—14	52	20

Sources: For 1938–39 and 1951–52 data, *Economic Survey of Burma 1954*, p. 115; for 1959–60 data, *Burma's Experience in Economic Planning*, U Thet Tun, Govt. Printing Office, Rangoon, 1960, Table 8, p. 14.

357

Table 59

Gross Capital Formation, Public and Private, 1949–50 to 1959–60

(K Crores)

	Public			Private			Total		
	Fixed	Stocks	Sub-total	Fixed	Stocks	Sub-total	Fixed	Stocks	Sub-total
1949–50	9.1	—6.3	2.8	23.9	5.2	29.1	33.0	—1.1	31.9
1950–51	13.3	4.4	17.7	29.8	.1	29.9	43.1	4.5	47.6
1951–52	22.6	7.2	29.8	38.4	6.1	44.5	61.0	13.3	74.3
1952, Jan.–Sept.[a]	17.0	5.4	22.4	28.8	4.6	33.4	45.8	10.0	55.8
1952–53	25.9	22.3	48.2	39.3	.1	39.4	65.2	22.4	87.6
1953–54	43.5	17.2	60.7	39.8	.6	40.4	83.3	17.8	101.1
1954–55	56.2	3.7	59.9	34.4	6.6	41.0	90.6	10.3	100.9
1955–56	51.9	—1.8	50.1	43.3	—.4	42.9	95.2	—2.2	93.0
1956–57	50.9	.2	51.1	50.9	6.5	57.4	101.8	6.7	108.5
1957–58	53.5	1.9	55.4	60.0	2.9	62.9	113.5	4.8	118.3
1958–59	55.9	9.7	65.6	45.6	1.3	46.9	101.5	11.0	112.5
1959–60	58.0	—3.4	54.6	45.4	8.5	53.9	103.4	5.1	108.5
Total, Jan. 1952 to 1959–60	412.8	55.2	468.0	387.5	30.7	418.2	800.3	85.9	886.2

Source: Economic Survey of Burma. For 1953–54 to 1959–60 data, 1960 issue, Table 5. Earlier data from 1956 issue, Table 5.

a. Taken at three fourths of annual figures for 1951–52.

Table 60

GROSS AND NET CAPITAL FORMATION, 1949–50 TO 1959–60

(*K Crores*)

	Gross Domestic Capital Formation	Estimated Depreciation	Net Capital Formation	Estimated Stock Increases	Net Fixed Capital Formation
1949–50	31.9	21.3	10.6	—1.1	11.7
1950–51	47.6	22.8	24.8	4.5	20.3
1951–52	74.3	24.5	49.8	13.3	36.5
1952–53	87.6	25.5	62.1	22.4	39.7
1953–54	101.1	26.9	74.2	17.8	56.4
1954–55	100.9	28.0	72.9	10.3	62.6
1955–56	93.0	29.0	64.0	—2.2	66.2
1956–57	108.5	30.2	78.3	6.7	71.6
1957–58	118.3	31.8	86.7	4.8	82.9
1958–59	112.5	32.5	80.0	11.0	69.0
1959–60	108.5	34.4	74.1	5.1	69.0

Source: Economic Survey of Burma. For 1953–54 to 1959–60 data, 1960, Table 5. Earlier data from 1956 issue, Table 5.

Table 61

PROGRAMED AND ACTUAL CAPITAL FORMATION, JANUARY 1952 TO 1959–60

(*K Crores*)

	Gross Capital Formation		Net Capital Formation	
	Original Program	Actual	Original Program	Actual
Totals	1,067.5	886.2	750.0	629.7
1952, Jan.–Sept.	62.5	55.8[a]	41.5	37.4[a]
1952–53	83.5	87.6	48.5	62.1
1953–54	103.5	101.1	65.5	74.2
1954–55	119.0	100.9	83.0	72.9
1955–56	131.5	93.0	95.0	64.0
1956–57	138.5	108.5	101.5	78.3
1957–58	140.5	118.3	103.0	86.7
1958–59	143.0	112.5	105.0	80.0
1959–60	145.5	108.5	107.0	74.1

Sources: Original program figures from K.T.A. Comprehensive Report, p. 41. Actual data from *Economic Survey of Burma,* 1956 and 1960 issues.

a. Taken at three quarters of annual figure for 1951–52.

and private capital formation nearly 77 per cent, of the original targets. Net capital formation, public and private, was 84 per cent of that originally scheduled. (The actual figures, to be sure, are stated in current prices, while the plan targets were in constant prices. But even if one were to deflate the actual figures by 15 per cent — certainly a greater than necessary allowance — they would still amount to 72 per cent of the target figures.) In relation to the gross domestic product, gross capital formation averaged something more than 20 per cent during the plan period. This corresponded even more closely to plan expectations, as shown in Table 63.

THE USE OF RESOURCES

The changing pattern in the broad use of resources illustrated in Table 64 is of course due not only to the investment aspects of the development program but to the complex of objectives and policies built into and reflected by it. Before the war, nearly 6 per cent of Burma's production was paid out abroad as income, and another 11 per cent built up balances abroad, leaving only 83 per cent of total output for domestic use. By 1951–52, income paid abroad was no longer a factor, but balances were still being built abroad, and only 94 per cent of production was available for domestic use. In the later years Burma became a net importer, and used more domestically than she produced.

This was important, because it made possible sizable increases in the proportion of total output used by all categories of domestic expenditure — current Government expenditures, capital formation and consumer expenditures — at a time when the size of the pie to be divided was increasing sharply. Capital formation accounted for one fifth of the gross domestic product, as against one eighth before the war and in 1951–52. Direct consumption took only a slightly larger share than before the war, and its share even declined somewhat from 1951–52 to 1959–60. But current Government expenditures, at one sixth the total in 1959–60, took roughly double their pre-war and pre-development shares. Since increased current governmental outlays for health, education and welfare services supplemented direct consumer expenditures, the true share of consumers in the domestic product in the later years was significantly larger than is indicated by the figures shown, and substantially larger also than it was before the war and in 1951–52.

PERFORMANCE AGAINST SELECTED TARGETS

In addition to the gross domestic production, per capita production and consumption and capital formation targets, the comprehensive development plan established a number of specific targets for output in selected areas. Some of these goals, and the results actually achieved, are shown in Table 65. Here, too, the earlier pattern was repeated. Gains, while substantial, were considerably short of the earlier expectations.

Only in crude oil production, railway passenger traffic and the acreage sown to sesamum were the plan targets significantly exceeded. Of the rest, the paddy acreage and rice export targets were crucial to the program; the failure to achieve these goals could not be compensated for by the achievement of any other goal or goals.

Table 62

PUBLIC AND PRIVATE CAPITAL FORMATION, PROGRAMED AND ACTUAL,
JANUARY 1952 TO 1959–60

(*K Crores*)

	Original K.T.A. Program	Actual	Actual as Per Cent of Programed
Gross capital formation	1,067.5	886.2	83
Public	522.5	468.0	89.6
Private	545.0	418.0	76.7
Net capital formation	750.0	629.7	84

Sources: Original program figures from K.T.A. Comprehensive Report, Table III–7, p. 50. Actual data from Tables 59 and 61.

Table 63

GROSS CAPITAL FORMATION
AS PER CENT OF GROSS DOMESTIC PRODUCT, PROGRAMED AND ACTUAL,
1952–53 TO 1959–60

	K.T.A. Plan	Actual
1952–53	18.0	19.0
1953–54	19.9	22.0
1954–55	21.4	21.0
1955–56	22.1	18.1
1956–57	21.9	20.0
1957–58	21.3	22.3
1958–59	21.1	20.5
1959–60	20.8	18.5

Sources: K.T.A. Comprehensive Report, Table III–7, p. 50; *Economic Survey of Burma*, 1957 and 1960 issues, Table 3.

Table 64

THE USE OF RESOURCES, PRE-WAR AND 1950S, A PERCENTAGE DISTRIBUTION

	1938–39	1951–52	1956–57	1959–60
Gross domestic product	100	100	100	100
Less: net exports of goods and services	17.2[a]	6.2	—4.9	—3.2
Goods and services used in Burma	82.8	93.8	104.9	103.2
Expenditures in Burma				
Current Government expenditure	7.8	8.6	13.7	16.6
Capital formation (public and private)	12.2	12.9	20	18.5
Consumer expenditure	62.8	72.3	71.2	68.1

Source: Economic Survey of Burma. For 1956–57 data and 1959–60 estimates, 1960 issue, Table 3. Other data from 1954 issue, Table 2.

a. 11.4 was surplus abroad on current account and 5.8 was income paid abroad.

Table 65

COMPARISON OF SELECTED PROGRAM GOALS AND ACHIEVEMENTS

	1938–39	1951–52	1959–60 Goal	1959–60 Actual or Est.	Percentage Increase 1951–52 to: Goal	Percentage Increase 1951–52 to: Actual or Est.
Acreage sown (million acres):						
Total	19.0	15.4	19.5	17.5	27	14
Paddy	12.8	9.7	13.3	10.7	37	10
Groundnuts	.84	.72	1.45	1.09	101	15
Sesamum	1.36	1.33	1.45	1.55	9	17
Cotton	.41	.26	.48	.37	89	42
Pulses	1.35	.97	1.33	1.25	37	29
Rice exports (million tons)	3.2	1.2	2.6	2.1	117	75
Timber production (thousand tons):						
Total	940	490	1,400	944	186	92
Teak	440	141	500	333	255	136
Hardwoods	500	349	900	611	158	75
Electric power (thousand KW)	93	n.a.	319	190.7	243[a]	105[a]
Electric power sales (million KWH)	233	n.a.	792	235.5	240[a]	1[a]
Coal production (thousand tons)	0	0	400	negl.	—	—
Crude oil production (million gallons)	276	29	98	143	235	390
Railway freight (thousand ton-miles)	579	152	n.a.	406	n.a.	167
Railway passenger-miles (million)	437	250	421	984	68	294

Sources: *Economic Survey of Burma*, 1954 issue, Appendix, p. 116, for goal data, and 1960 issue for actual data or estimates, except for railway passenger-miles data, which are from *Selected Economic Indicators*, C.S.E.D., Rangoon, Nov. 1960, Table 15.

a. In absence of 1951–52 data, percentage is calculated from 1938–39 base.

ECONOMIC STABILITY

In view of the extensive treatment of economic stability in Part III, it is necessary here only to recall the essential facts. Failure to implement the import program effectively in 1955–56 resulted in widespread shortages, excessive increases in the domestic money supply and a quick, sharp increase of about 18 per cent in average living costs. (Prices of many imported commodities rose far more than that, of course, and it may be that living costs rose substantially more for higher income groups than for the low and middle income groups covered by the index.) Prices then leveled off and, under the Ne Win Government, declined again in 1959. Although they rose subsequently after the revocation of price controls in April 1960, they were only 12 per cent higher in September 1960 than they had been in 1954. For the six years beginning with the 1954 low, the rise in living costs averaged only 2 per cent per year (see Table 29, p. 215). This must be considered a remarkable performance.

Something less than stability, however, characterized the balance of payments. From K 96 crores at the end of 1951–52 and K 119 crores at the end of 1952–53, foreign exchange reserves declined to less than K 52 crores at the end of 1954–55, recovered to nearly K 75 crores a year later, declined once again to K 56 crores by the end of 1956–57, and stabilized between K 75 and K 80 crores in 1958–59 and 1959–60, as was shown in Table 17, p. 165. Taking, somewhat arbitrarily, K 60 crores as the safety point (equal roughly to six months' imports), Burma experienced two serious and rather prolonged "scares" with respect to foreign exchange. These were extremely unsettling. Not only did they cause abrupt changes and dislocations in capital budgeting, import programing and money supply; they inspired traders to hoard, speculate and raise prices. They also inspired the Government to meddle increasingly with the structure of the import trade in the directions of Burmanization and joint venture monopoly. Both these efforts — the first inefficient, the second outrageous — were inimical to the interests of the consumers.

STRUCTURE OF THE ECONOMY

The development program did not bring about revolutionary changes in the structure of the economy, either in the composition of the nation's output or in the ownership and control of its wealth and productive processes. There had indeed been a significant takeover of productive properties and enterprises in the period immediately following independence, and a vast expansion in the areas of Government intervention. By 1952–53, however, both these processes had been, to all intents and purposes, completed. The land nationalization and distribution subsequently undertaken do not appear to have been significant in this respect. The economic effects had been for the most part anticipated by the earlier measures prohibiting land alienation and the limiting of land rentals to nominal amounts.

The relatively minor structural changes which occurred in the composition of output may be perceived in Table 57. The relative role of agriculture decreased slightly. That of state marketing, banking and public utilities increased. But the most significant change appears to be the increasingly important role played by general governmental activities. It is likely, however, that the national income data do not adequately reflect the actual increase in "other industries and services," in which manufacturing activities are included. This would certainly appear to be indicated by the evidence presented in Chapter 19 on the growth of manufacturing and cottage industry. Even granted such an understatement in the national income data, it appears that the impact of the development program was not such as to bring about serious structural changes in the composition of total output. It did, however, initiate trends which were bound, in time, to effect such changes.

As regards the agents of economic processes, the state played of course an expanding role during the development period in both import and export, and increasingly in manufacturing as well. Perhaps its most injurious step was the introduction of monopoly into new commodity areas of the import trade, in which private traders were permitted to share. And perhaps the most beneficial were the increased state activities in health, education and other areas of welfare.

WELFARE

The scope and size — if not the quality — of the welfare facilities and services provided during the development period were nothing short of remarkable. The Government made strenuous efforts to improve welfare in both the towns and the villages. Understandably, the greatest contribution was that made to the cultivators in the form of debt remissions, rent limitations, land distribution, agricultural loans, seed and fertilizer distributions, price supports, tractor hire, drainage and flood control, and so on. These have already been reviewed in Chapter 16. Other welfare efforts embraced health, education, housing and local community projects.

The core of the health program was the construction of twenty-eight hospitals with 1,160 beds, and the establishment of over 400 rural health centers, 345 maternity-child health clinics, numerous dispensaries and specialized tuberculosis, leprosy and other facilities. Vigorous anti-malaria spraying campaigns (which reached 10 million persons in 1959–60), B.C.G. tests for T.B. and V.D. testing and treatment, with U. N. technical assistance, produced valuable results. Large-scale training programs were conducted to staff the new facilities, not only with doctors and nurses, but also with health assistants, midwives, women health visitors, vaccinators, malaria inspectors,

Table 66

HEALTH FACILITIES AND PERSONNEL, 1938–39, 1952 AND 1959–60

	1938–39	1952	1959–60
Hospitals and dispensaries	308	294	n.a.
Government	268	n.a.	332
Private	40	n.a.	n.a.
Hospital beds	8,154	8,546	n.a.
Government	5,662	n.a.	9,644
Private	2,492	n.a.	n.a.
Doctors	1,600	1,252	1,221
Government	n.a.	552	513
Private	n.a.	700	708
Nurses	1,000	1,054	n.a.
Government	n.a.	404	513
Private	n.a.	650	n.a.
Maternity and child health centers			345
Rural health centers			409

Sources: For 1938–39, Robert R. Nathan working papers. For 1952, *The Pyidawtha Conference, August 4–17, 1952, Resolutions and Speeches,* Ministry of Information, Rangoon, Dec. 18, 1952, p. 102. For 1959–60, *Economic Survey of Burma 1960* and *Case Study of Planning for Balanced Social and Economic Development in Burma,* C.S.E.D., New Secretariat, Rangoon, Jan. 30, 1960.

laboratory technicians, and so on. From 1952 to 1956, for example, the number of Government-employed midwives had increased from 200 to 1,487, health visitors from 140 to 218 and health assistants from 209 to 297. From 1956 to 1959, the number of Government-employed nurses increased from 196 to 513, health visitors from 218 to 320, public health assistants from 297 to 411, and vaccinators from 226 to 289. Government health expenditures (current and capital) more than tripled over the decade.

The impact of all these programs was considerable. The incidence of malaria, for example, was greatly reduced. And most notably, the rate of infant mortality declined from 221 per 1,000 live births earlier in the decade to 150 in 1957–58–59.

The great expansion in public education can best be seen in the enrollment figures. From 666,000 enrolled in state-provided primary, middle and high schools, enrollments nearly tripled by 1959–60, increasing to 1,764,000, as shown in Table 67. The number of primary schools increased by over 8,000, rising to some 11,557 in 1959–60 (Table 68). Growth in the number of middle and high schools was also significant. A new development was the introduction of technical and agricultural high schools, of which there were fifty-two and thirty-seven respectively at the end of the decade. In the four years from 1955 to 1959, the percentage of eligible children in the primary schools increased from 31 to 51; in the middle schools, from 5 to 9; and in the high schools, from 1 to 3.

Table 67

ENROLLMENT IN STATE SCHOOLS, 1952 TO 1959–60

(Thousand Pupils)

	Primary	Middle	High	Total
1952	468	n.a.	n.a.	n.a.
1953	595	54	17	666
1954	737	80	23	840
1955–56	1,003	105	30	1,138
1956–57	1,282	144	55	1,480
1957–58	1,390	176	52	1,618
1958–59	1,466	201	56	1,723
1959–60	1,544	173	48	1,764

Sources: Economic Survey of Burma, 1956 issue, Table 47, and 1960 issue, Table 59; and *Four Year Plan,* Ministry of National Planning, June 14, 1957, p. K 15–16.

Table 68

NUMBER OF STATE SCHOOLS, 1952 TO 1959–60

	Primary	Middle	High	Technical High Schools	Agricultural High Schools
1952	3,335	180		—	—
1956–57	10,226	415	220	33	11
1957–58	10,978	452	235	40	26
1958–59	11,157	507	271	48	33
1959–60	11,557	520	273	52	37

Sources: Economic Survey of Burma 1960, Table 60, and *Four Year Plan,* Ministry of National Planning, June 14, 1957, p. K 15–16.

The University of Rangoon was greatly expanded and strengthened, and a number of intermediate (two-year) colleges were established in major towns. Mandalay College was expanded, made autonomous and given university status. College enrollments more than doubled, rising from less than 6,000 to over 12,000. Teachers' training courses were hastily organized and conducted on an accelerated basis. Technical training beyond the high school level was also strengthened, chiefly at the Technical Institute at Insein. Scholarship programs were broadened at all levels. Adult education was not neglected, even at the university level. And mass education programs reached many thousands. As in the case of health, combined current and capital expenditures for education tripled over the decade.

Housing programs naturally were not able to reach as many people. A handful of "model" villages were constructed, township development programs were conducted in a few places, some thousands of burned-out squatters were benefited by emergency "fire-housing" projects, and some thousands of apartment type units were built and made available, on a subsidized rental basis, mostly to Government employees and people with political connections. Many more benefited by loan programs which permitted them to replace the thatched roofing of their huts with corrugated galvanized sheets. The building and modernization of bazaars in many towns was a useful adjunct to the housing program. But the greatest single contribution to it was made by the Ne Win Government, in constructing the three satellite towns of Okkalapa North and South and Thaketa outside Rangoon, and in removing to them the scores of thousands of squatter families who had lived for so many years in unsightly, unsanitary hut colonies along the roadsides and back alleys of the capital city.

Other welfare programs embraced supporting grants to special institutions for the aged, the blind, wayward girls and waifs and strays; environmental sanitation (tube wells, latrines, and so on); and a sizable pilot community development project at Payagyi, near Pegu. None of these matched in importance the grant-in-aid support scheme for locally sponsored community development projects which, like the development program as a whole, was called "Pyidawtha" — the welfare land. This program was conducted for only four years, beginning in 1952-53. A maximum of K 50,000 ($10,500) was provided for each township, to be used for self-selected projects and supplemented by local contributions in money, materials or labor. During the short life of the program, nearly 27,000 projects were executed at a total cost of some K 5.2 crores.[4] Of this sum, nearly half was contributed locally. The most popular projects were schools, roads and bridges, wells, tanks and ponds, irrigation and drainage and sanitary projects. Their average cost was a pitifully small K 1,900 ($400) each. Even the schools cost, on the average, only K 3,500 to K 4,000 (say, $800) each. They were really only large bamboo and thatch huts, earth-floored, without glass, sanitary facilities or running water — places where the children could meet their teachers, and not much more. But in the circumstances they marked an advance.

The Pyidawtha program had great potentials. The local political bosses, however, dominated the local councils, and reports of graft and chicanery became so rife that in 1955-56 it was decided to abandon the scheme altogether. This was unfortunate. It would have been far better to reorganize the local councils, eliminating the political members and turning the program over to the people themselves on a far larger scale than before.

SOME GENERAL WELFARE MEASURES

A few scattered population, employment and income comparisons between 1953 and 1957 are afforded by the 1957 sample census of 252 towns in Burma.

4. *Economic Survey of Burma*, 1957 issue, Table 5, and 1954 issue, Table 39.

These shed a few rays of light on the improvement achieved in general welfare:

(1) Whereas in 1953, 34 per cent of the urban population was under fifteen years of age, by 1957 the proportion had increased to 36 per cent. The change reflects chiefly the decline in infant mortality previously noted.

(2) The percentage of children between the ages of eleven and fifteen who were members of the labor force declined from 13 to 11. Conversely, the percentage of children in this age group not working because they were attending school increased from 59 to 84.

(3) The percentage of males over the age of eleven who were married increased from 56 to 60.

(4) The percentage of those gainfully employed engaged in manufacturing increased from 19 to 24, while the percentage of those engaged in commerce (petty trade, chiefly) declined from 33 to 27.

(5) The median individual income increased from K 696 to K 938 per year, or 34 per cent.

(6) The average annual earnings of workers in cottage industries for eight to nine months' work increased from K 420 to K 739.

(7) The percentage of households with annual incomes of K 2,500 and over increased from 15 to 18.

CULTURAL IMPACT

The development program did not bring about great, easily recognizable changes in Burmese society. Superficially, little was changed. But the impact of the program went deep to the core of the culture, where it registered with a certain degree of shock and initiated at least the beginnings of a change which was bound to have a profound effect on the society and its culture ultimately.

Industrialization, urbanization and technology brought a changing tempo and a new emphasis on energy and drive, on skill, on management, on accounting for time and costs, on the necessity and dignity of work, on the need for social discipline and responsibility. The society became more sober as it became clear, first, that independence alone would not guarantee abundance, and next, that socialism alone would not suffice to usher in the era of plenty. Burma had for a long time counted on the Indian coolie to do the hard and dirty work. Now it became apparent to the Burmans that there would be no fruits without work, and that they would have to do the work themselves if they wished to enjoy the fruits. These were the chief elements of the development program's impact, together with an increasing awareness of the need to rely, for technology, resources and markets, on the greater world outside.

If not all Burmans had yet been affected by the beginnings of the change, and if not all those who had were reconciled to the wave of the future, neither could the clock be turned back, or even stopped. A transformation had begun.

Part V

MAJOR PROBLEMS IN PROGRAM IMPLEMENTATION

The Problem of Defects

in the Basic Plan

In discussing the difficulties encountered in the implementation of Burma's economic development effort, it is appropriate to consider first those arising out of the basic plan itself. Now, it is only to be expected that experience in carrying out a major plan will disclose a number of flaws in it — at least from the implementers' point of view. These flaws may have been due to careless work or poor judgment on the part of the planners. They may, on the other hand, have reflected the best judgments possible at the time, involving in some cases closely calculated risks or a choice between almost equally persuasive alternatives. The discussion which follows treats all these cases as defects in the program if they affected the implementation process or its objectives adversely. Whether some of these "defects" (so considered) were avoidable will be controversial.

THE RICE ASSUMPTIONS

Outstanding among the defects was the assumption that the export price of rice would decline only moderately to no less than £50 sterling per ton by 1959–60. Corollary to this was the expectation that rice production would increase progressively and make possible export shipments of no less than 2.3 million tons per year by the end of the decade. These twin assumptions, only the latter of which it was within Burma's power to insure, led to the conclusion that Burma could finance the K 750 crores of net investment called for by the plan entirely with her own resources. The assumptions about the export price and sales of rice did not of course hold, as may be seen in Table 69. The price of standard grade SMS rice dropped from £60 sterling in 1952–53 to

Table 69

RICE PRODUCTION, EXPORTS, PROCEEDS AND PRICES, SELECTED DATA, 1952–53 TO 1959–60

	1952–53	1953–54	1954–55	1955–56	1956–57	1957–58	1958–59	1959–60
Paddy output (million long tons)	5.74	5.53	5.71	5.78	6.36	5.49	6.49	6.92
Exports (million long tons)	1.22	1.27	1.63	1.93	2.0	1.46	1.61	2.08
Value (K crores)	102	84	84.5	87.7	89.5	66.3	71.6	83.7
Proceeds (K crores)	99.2	75.3	66.0	88.9	83.9	71.3	68.0	80.1
S.M.S. price[a] (£ sterling)	60	50	42	36	34	32[b]	33+	32/10s
Average price per ton, rice and rice products (£ sterling)	62/9s	49/14s	39/18s	34/2s	33/14s	34/2s	33/8s	30/4s

Sources: Economic Survey of Burma, 1951 through 1960 issues, and *Selected Economic Indicators*, C.S.E.D., Rangoon, Nov. 1960.

a. Government-to-government price for standard grade. Small Mills Special, 42% broken.

b. To India and one or two other countries; to others, somewhat more.

£50, £42, £36, £34 and £32 successively by 1957–58, rising only slightly thereafter. The size of the export surplus did not increase to more than 1.8 million tons during the program period.

The initial impact of these price declines, and the attempts made on both the investment and resource sides to cope with the situations they created, are traced in considerable detail in Part III. It is not, however, correct to conclude from this, as some have done, that a more conservative assumption about the price of export rice would have resulted in adoption of a more conservative program. The best evidence of this is that the consultants recommended an investment program of no lesser size in their Preliminary Report when, because of the less favorable rice price prevailing in 1951, it was anticipated that approximately one third of the program's cost would have to be borrowed from abroad. The Pyidawtha Conference in 1952 approved this investment program on the basis of that expectation. Key planning officials had been made well aware of the possibility that the rice price assumption might not hold, as is evident from the following excerpt from a memorandum of March 28, 1953 written by U Hla Maung, the then Secretary for National Planning:

In considering these [foreign exchange earnings] estimates, however, it must be remembered that the price of rice over the years plays a dominating part and should there be a sudden drop due to a change in the world production of rice these estimates and many of the assumptions made thereon will become vitiated and our problems will become extremely acute. From information now available, both from international sources such as the FAO and from the United States Agriculture Department (who have made a careful study of the subject), it appears however that rice prices will be fairly firm during the decade, and it is therefore not unrealistic to base our thinking on the assumption that it will not fall below £55 per ton by 1959–60. Further, the estimates are prepared on the assumption that our maximum export of rice will be 2.55 million tons and to the extent that we can grow more and find the market for exporting it, any overestimate in regard to price that may now be made will be balanced by increased quantity. However, as soon as there is any indication that the price will fall below this figure and the gap will not be closed by our earnings from other sources (minerals, timber, etc.) the estimates will have to be revised and our programme and thinking adjusted accordingly.

The consultants' final report had also allowed for this possibility. If the rice price assumptions did not hold, they pointed out, the financing could be made up by a drawdown of excessive foreign exchange reserves, restrictions on consumer goods imports and borrowing from abroad. The difficulty with the price assumption was not that it led to an investment program larger than would otherwise have been the case. It was that it delayed efforts to obtain foreign financing. Emergency program cutbacks and delays in implementation, some of them uneconomic and costly, resulted. Unfortunately, also, the incorrect assumption had a number of other consequences, the combined impact of which was even more profound.

The first and perhaps most damaging of these was that, instead of stimulating even greater efforts to increase rice production and export surpluses, the price drop had precisely the opposite effect. Fearful of rapidly mounting surpluses and declining prices which it was not yet psychologically adjusted to accept, the Government discontinued the production subsidies which had contributed to an increase in paddy acreage of some 600,000 tons in 1952–53, and undertook no further real effort to increase paddy production until 1956–57. There can be no doubt that substantial increases in production and exports, even at prices lower than actually developed, would have mitigated the difficulties encountered.

Second, the easy-financing estimates derived from the higher rice price assumption during the planning stage led naturally to a lack of concern with foreign exchange in other aspects of planning. The foreign exchange component of the programed investments was computed only in a general way and was more than a little underestimated. Further, no particular attention was paid to the varying proportions of this component over the eight-year period, even though it might have been quite clear that a substantially higher proportion of the foreign exchange would be required in the early years of the investment program. The easy-financing psychology contributed also to the undertaking of an excessively large annual program in 1954–55. (U Thet Tun has argued[1] that the faulty rice price assumption was responsible also for the planners' neglect to stress projects with a low import content and those which would be labor-intensive rather than capital-intensive in character. This argument is not cogent. Since a more conservative assumption about rice prices would have resulted in plans for borrowing from abroad at the very outset of the program, it would not have been necessary to place undue weight on foreign exchange saving. More important, because of the long-run outlook for a favorable balance of trade beyond the eight-year program period, it would not have been economic to overemphasize these foreign exchange criteria in relation to others.)

Third, the easy-financing outlook led to less than needed emphasis on greater increases in domestic output, particularly in the agricultural, timber and mining sectors, and especially to failure clearly to formulate specific programs to achieve pre-war export levels in these basic areas. It led also to an inclination to use the excess foreign exchange reserves anticipated to finance large imports of goods for private use as an offset to inflationary pressures in

1. "A Review of Economic Planning in Burma," U Thet Tun, Central Statistical and Economics Department (Ministry of National Planning), Rangoon, Oct. 7, 1959 (mimeo.), pp. 22 and 35.

the domestic economy, and hence to less emphasis on problems of domestic finance than was required.

Fourth, the break in rice prices, when it came, was a serious blow to the Government's confidence — in its plans, in its ability to carry them out, in the planning process, in the planners and even in economic development itself. There was, of course, some recovery from this shock, as barter deals were made, foreign loans were obtained, and the volume of cash sales of rice at lower prices increased. But the recovery was never quite complete, and the Government henceforth displayed more timidity in making decisions than it had previously.

Fifth, the failure of the rice price assumption required the Government to divert a major part of its energy to the so-called foreign exchange crisis over a long period of time. It had to reprogram and rephase the basic plan, negotiate for foreign loans and assistance, and devote attention to other related activities, all at the cost of administrative and supervisory efforts sorely needed in the implementation of the program.

Finally, the break in rice prices, and the rapid accumulation of stocks which could not be adequately protected from spoilage, set the stage for barter deals with the Iron Curtain countries. The import, supply and price problems aggravated by these transactions have already been examined.

Was the rice price assumption well founded, in view of the conditions and foreseeable trends prevailing at the time? Forecasts of international supply-demand conditions and prices for any major international commodity are of necessity hazardous. In essence, the assumption was based on the expectation that the most favorable production increases possible would not suffice to support pre-war per capita consumption levels because population levels in rice-eating countries were increasing rapidly. The actual course taken by international rice prices was so far below the modest decline assumed in the plan as to suggest that, despite the views held at the time by experts of the U. S. Department of Agriculture and the Food and Agriculture Organization of the United Nations, which confirmed the independent analysis of the economic consultants, better judgment would have arrived at a more conservative assumption. Such a conclusion, however, would not take into account at least two important factors which contributed to the break in rice prices in 1953 and thereafter — the highly uncommon succession of three bumper crops in India and the large-scale disposals of food grains by the U. S. Government under P.L. 480, which began at about that time. Neither of these developments was predictable. If they had not occurred, the break in rice prices would undoubtedly have been far more moderate.

OTHER FINANCIAL JUDGMENTS

Another quite serious defect in the plan was the expectation that it would be possible to hold the Government's current budget at the then prevailing level of some K 70 crores throughout the eight-year program period. Clearly, this conclusion was not well founded and it is doubtful whether it would have been reached if the excessive foreign exchange earnings then confidently anticipated had not offered an escape hatch, in the form of counter-inflationary imports, in case of possible error. Even though it was anticipated that military budgets would decline with improving security, it was almost inevitable that current budgetary requirements for health, education and a number of other activities would expand considerably as more schools, hospitals, roads and other facilities were built and additional staff was placed on the public payrolls. Even though it might be expected that greater efficiency would permit improvement in services without proportionate increases in expenditures, there should have been little doubt that the trend of current budgetary expenditures would be upward, and that over the eight years of the program a sizable increase in such expenditures would take place. Actually, current budgetary expenditures exceeded K 90 crores by 1957–58 despite intensive efforts to control their rise, and revised estimates for 1959–60 indicate that current expenditures exceeded K 100 crores in that year.[2]

The size of the current budget was of course of great importance to the domestic financing of the development effort since any excess of revenues over expenditures would be available for financing development. The judgment that current expenditures could be held at the K 70 crores level while current revenues rose had two important negative effects on the program. First, it led to a lack of emphasis on the need for revision of the tax structure so as to produce greater domestic revenues, and this was most difficult to overcome later. Second, it led to an even more serious lack of initial emphasis on the need to improve the efficiency of Government board and corporation operations so as to increase their profits or reduce their losses, as the case might be. Improvement in efficiency, particularly, could have made a tremendous contribution to the domestic financing of development. It would have been well had the improvement been posited as a prerequisite of the development effort.

Finally, the plan treated proposed capital expenditures as though they were synonymous with fixed capital formation, and therefore underestimated them. Capital expenditure requirements were considerably larger than were financing requirements for fixed capital formation. In substantial amounts, capital expenditures took the form of increases in stocks of and transfer payments for the acquisition of existing assets, for the servicing of debt and for the repayment of foreign loans. Still other capital "expenditures" were required to create working capital. To this extent, therefore, the capital input-income response ratio built into the plan was more optimistic than was realized at the time.

2. Current budgetary expenditures in excess of K 70 crores per year were approximately 30 per cent of capital outlays for the seven years 1953–54 to 1959–60.

THE INSURRECTION ASSUMPTION

Another "defect" in the plan was its assumption that to all intents and purposes the civil insurrection would be over by 1954, and that after that time insecurity would no longer constitute a serious obstacle to program implementation. This of course did not prove to be the case. The retarding effects of the
insurrection have already been mentioned, and will be examined in greater detail in the chapter which follows. Even with hindsight, however, it cannot be
said that poor judgment was exercised in adopting this assumption. The importance of security to the successful implementation of the program was
clearly and repeatedly stressed by the planners and recognized by the Government. There can be little doubt that vigorous action by the Government could
have achieved the results required, and the planners had been given reason to
expect that the Government would pursue such a program.

In this connection, the following incident may be of interest. When, early
in 1952, the consultants presented the essence of their preliminary recommendations to a high-level Government conference, presided over by Prime
Minister U Nu, one of the lesser officials questioned the validity of the security
assumption, the importance of which had been strongly emphasized by Mr.
Nathan.

"How can we know," he asked, "that security will have been effectively
established by 1954?"

U Nu rested his chin on his hand and characteristically meditated for a few
moments before replying. "It is true," he said, "that we cannot know. But, on
the other hand, how can we know that it will not be so? We will proceed on
this basis." This terminated the discussion.

THE ASSUMPTION OF ADMINISTRATIVE EFFICIENCY

Another major assumption — this one unstated — was that the Government would implement the development program with a reasonable degree of
administrative and supervisory efficiency. The planners were naturally aware
of the great importance of organization and administration, and the plan
provided for many organizational and administrative steps designed to promote efficiency. These included provision for the reorganization and strengthening of the Ministry of National Planning; for the creation of the Economic
and Social Board to supervise and coordinate program execution; for the
development of a progress reporting operation to assist the Economic and
Social Board in performing these functions; and for the creation of development corporations in industry, mining and agriculture which would be free
from the bureaucratic controls that hampered the operation of the traditional
Government departments. The consultants repeatedly stressed the need for
delegation of authority, the importance of experienced and responsible man-

agement and the necessity for creating conditions under which responsible management could operate effectively. Numerous recommendations for improved organization, administration and procedures were also made in the several sector programs with respect to the Government departments and other agencies concerned.

It transpired, however, that these recommendations, cautions and exhortations were not enough. Action in the key operating agencies, even if carried through, would not have sufficed. The planners had not adequately appreciated the need for a thorough overhaul of the entire Government administrative apparatus and a similar overhaul of its operating procedures to permit effective administration at intermediate and lower levels as well as at the very top, with which they had been more concerned. They assumed, incorrectly, that recognition by a few top leaders of the need for greater delegation of authority and creation of conditions conducive to effective management would result in action which would percolate down through the administrative and executive arms. Because of the lack of full awareness of this problem, it may be said that the plan placed too much reliance on investment as such — almost as though the thrust of investment alone would force performance and insure the desired income response.

Closely related to this problem was the problem of specialized manpower, particularly the shortage of administrative, managerial and technical experience and skills. This potential bottleneck was indeed recognized, stressed and warned against in the plan, and numerous measures were proposed for dealing with it. Some observers — notably the first World Bank Mission to Burma in 1953[3] and Frank Trager[4] — have criticized the plan for failing to evaluate adequately the importance of this factor, and hence for a lack of realism. Since the problem of lack of skills will be discussed in a later section, it may suffice here to assert that the obvious deficiencies in trained manpower did not impose serious limitations at the levels of implementation achieved. The limitations imposed by administration, organization and procedures prevented the personnel available from operating as effectively as they could have under a better setup.

THE SECTOR PROGRAMS

The weaknesses in the sector programs have already been discussed in earlier chapters. Notably, there was a lack of discipline and priorities in the manufacturing industries program and a similar lack of discipline and poor coordination in the electric power program. The program adopted did not place sufficiently great emphasis on the primary agricultural, forestry and

3. Memorandum, "The Economy of Burma," International Bank for Reconstruction and Development, Nov. 4, 1953.
4. Frank N. Trager, *Building a Welfare State in Burma 1948–1956,* Institute of Pacific Relations, New York, 1958, Chapter 4.

mining sectors. Specifically, the land nationalization program was cloudy and ineffective; rice milling improvement was left to the private sector under conditions which precluded effort; recovery targets for teak production and exports were not set; the Kalewa mining project was clearly not economic; the steel and pharmaceuticals industry projects lacked adequate economic justification; the acquisition of Viscount aircraft for international air travel was hasty and unwise; the housing program was poorly conceived; the superimposition of the Soviet gift projects on the original eight-year program was impromptu and political in character and out of accord with any reasonable set of priorities.

Schumacher has criticized the investment program[5] for placing too much emphasis on transport, communications and electric power, which he calls "secondary productive capital," at the cost of agricultural, forestry, mining and manufacturing investment, or "primary productive capital." Whatever might be the merit of this argument under more normal circumstances, it is effectively negated by several facts: Burma's pre-war transport and communications facilities had been virtually destroyed and the plan provided for little more than their rehabilitation. Agricultural recovery did not require heavy investment, and the Government had already undertaken more than it could handle in the manufacturing field.

NATIONALIZED INDUSTRY

Serious though they were, the major weaknesses in the plan were not specific project weaknesses. Far more important, for example, than the weak economic justification for the steel mill or the uneconomic size and scale of the pharmaceuticals plant was the basic Government policy that significant industrial development should be in the public sector — a policy which constituted a parameter for the planners. It was in the state manufacturing sector that implementation, both construction and subsequent operation, was weakest. The difficulties were fourfold in character — first, administrative, organizational and procedural handicaps to efficient construction and operation; second, managerial deficiencies; third, lack, at the policy-making level, of the understanding and flexibility necessary to the timely formulation of appropriate price, wage, managerial and other policies; and fourth, unnecessary and insupportable demands on the talent and leadership available. Thus, while the decision to place industrial development in the public sector was not a decision of the planners, it built into the plan an important element of weakness, so far as implementation was concerned. This weakness was aggravated by a nationalization policy in other areas, notably in rice and teak export marketing, where it failed to mobilize potential resources effectively.

---

5. E. F. Schumacher, "Some Notes on Burma's Economic Development," a memorandum submitted to the Economic and Social Board, Feb. 18, 1955.

CONCLUSION

These considerations lead naturally to the question: Was Burma's development plan too optimistic? Certainly it was optimistic as to rice export earnings and financing, as to the prospects for achieving an early state of civil order, as to the ability of the Government's administrative apparatus to cope with the heavy additional tasks imposed upon it, as to the availability of executive and managerial talent, and as to the determination of Government to do what was necessary to carry it out effectively. Whether it is to be adjudged overoptimistic, and unreasonably so, must depend in part at least on the view taken of alternative strategies of development.

Clearly, ambitious targets can be conducive to maximization of effort. If this is accepted, the question then becomes: Were the targets set so far ahead of any possible achievement as to condemn the plan in advance to substantial failure? To this question, three responses are suggested. First, as compared with the pre-war accomplishment, the targets were exceedingly modest, and it is doubtful whether more conservative goals would have inspired the Government to effort at all. Second, in a very real sense, no underdeveloped country can be "ready" for a major development effort. It cannot wait to "prepare" itself. The "readiness" or ability to cope with development problems must be developed in the course of the development effort itself. Third, experience demonstrated that the plan as formulated was within the power of the Government to achieve in reasonable degree. This is evidenced not only by what was accomplished through 1957–58 but even more strikingly by the results achieved under the Ne Win Government when more effective administration was brought about by clear delegation of authority and determined action on the security front, with notable results. The planning consultants did not err in advising the Government that the recommended program could be accomplished, if it made the necessary effort. (This does not mean, of course, that the advisors were fully confident the Government would do so.)

It must be recognized, however, that a different strategy of development — one that placed considerably more reliance on the private sector — could have been much more successful. For example, if the Government had concentrated its own activities on the rehabilitation of transport and communications, on the development (in more reasonable measure) of electric power, on land reclamation and irrigation, on schools, hospitals and other essential social services, and encouraged private sector investment in rice milling, timber, mining, manufacturing and trade, the results achieved might have been far greater. A narrower delineation of the spheres of public investment would have made it possible to plan for lesser Government income and would have permitted a substantial increase in the price paid to the cultivator for his paddy. Higher paddy prices would have provided increased impetus to recovery in rice production and exports and augmented private incomes throughout the economy, increasing the potentials for private saving and investment. The policy recommendations of the consultants, if followed, would have steered the Government in the direction of this strategy. But the Government was firmly wedded to its own. It listened politely to other ideas, but it did not really hear them.

The final comment which needs to be made here deals not with a weakness in the plan itself but rather with the way in which the plan was presented to the policy-makers — the tactics of presentation. Incorporated as it was in a number of bulky documents, not the least of which was the two-volume report of the American consultants, the presentation did not sufficiently impress the leaders with the key needs: civil order; administrative and procedural overhaul; improved management in the public enterprises; specific programs and action to insure the recovery of primary production and exports; policies which would stimulate private investment, especially in the improvement of rice milling facilities; and, above all, real determination on the part of the leaders and their full-time attention to what of necessity would be a tremendously difficult task. A serious weakness was that the top leadership did not realize how severe would be the demands that implementation of the plan would make upon the leadership itself.

Under the circumstances, development might have been much more effective had the planners presented two alternative plans to the policy-makers — the first, modest and limited in scope, feasible on the basis of the then prevailing conditions and psychology; the second, a plan of the magnitude actually presented, which could be achieved only if a number of basic preliminary conditions were met. Such a choice would have offered the prospect of substantial development, but would have brought more clearly into focus the "price" involved in its achievement.

CHAPTER 22

The Problem of Internal Security

It would be difficult to overestimate the extent to which insurrection and civil disorder retarded Burma's economic development. Never numbering more than perhaps 30,000 and substantially reduced in numbers after 1951, operating spasmodically and for the most part in small bands that did their marauding in the hinterlands or at night, the insurgents and the numerous dacoits masquerading under political banners retarded production, inflicted great physical damage, deterred investment, forced the Government to divert a large portion of its resources to defense and police activities, stimulated graft and corruption, provided excuses for inefficiency and contributed generally to instability and indiscipline in the Burmese society and economy.

The negative effect of insurrection on production was most clearly visible in the extractive industries — agriculture, mining and timber. Its direct effects on these were augmented by its effect on transportation and communications. Trains and inland water transport did not run at night. Passenger and truck traffic between cities was limited, especially after dark, by security considerations. Telephone lines were destroyed. Even town water supplies were frequently interrupted, and the oil pipeline from Chauk to Rangoon was rendered completely inoperative. Thus, even in the towns, production and commerce were adversely affected.

Cultivators hesitated to venture into outlying fields or to camp during the busy season in the fields they did cultivate. Fields were plowed only once or twice instead of a half-dozen times as was customary. Seed was broadcast directly, and the traditional transplanting forgone. These and similar effects reduced both acreages and yields. Incentives to produce were further diminished by the levies imposed by insurgent bands, who would frequently tax the villagers' produce and transport their crops or burn them in the fields — and burn their houses as well — if they did not meet demands. In the forests insurgents interfered with Government girdling, felling and extraction operations, imposed taxes on private operators, stole elephants and logs in transit, and interfered with up-country sawmilling operations. Until 1956 or 1957 the valuable Mawchi Mines were completely under insurgent control. Mining in the Tenasserim district was badly depressed by insurgent operations and related developments.

The capital facilities most subject to damage by insurgents were — in addition to water and oil pipelines and telephone lines — bridges and railway rolling stock, which were almost impossible to protect from dynamiting operations, and the economic losses resulting from the damage were augmented by uneconomic investments forced upon the Government because of the insurgency. Since trains and river boats could not run after dark, locomotives, freight cars and river craft had to be procured in numbers considerably in excess of what would have been required if 24-hour operation had been possible. Another example of uneconomic investment was the procurement of barges for water transport of crude petroleum in place of the pipeline, which could not be protected. Much extractive and transportation activity was conducted at excessive current cost because of the need to provide armed guards. The unsettled political outlook led many individuals to concentrate on the accumulation of gold and jewelry, rather than invest in property which could not be concealed.

The impact of the insurgency on social and political behavior was serious also. It fostered, even among the law-abiding, a pervading feeling of instability and lurking danger and a lack of moral tone. Workers were reluctant to accept discipline on the job or to put forth their best efforts. Students repudiated discipline, and were inclined to demonstrate and even to strike against examinations and standards which could not be met without ability or effort. Business men sought quick, easy rewards through political manipulation, and were unwilling to build soundly toward an uncertain future. Most civil servants regarded transfer to the districts as something to be avoided at all costs, and were thus even more than usually disposed to seek the favor of their superiors, even when this course was inimical to the job to be done. The Government itself, faced by open insurrection, hesitated to require full discipline and compliance with the law and the national interest for fear of alienating special interest groups. Thus, the threat of latent force within the pale of organized society aggravated the more direct effects of the insurgents outside.

Unsettled conditions, the plethora of controls and regulations designed to deal with them, the opportunities which beckoned by way of special favor or protection and the low morale both outside and inside the Government service comprised a set of circumstances in which graft and corruption could and did increasingly flourish. Equally important, perhaps, was the excuse which the civil disorder furnished for poor performance — even to the Government itself. Rare was the district official, high or low, who could not cite the difficulties imposed by the insurrection to cover up his own shiftlessness, incompetence or sheer neglect of duty. Lastly, as civil disorder continued over the years people tended to accept it as a norm. Thus it contributed to a public psychology which increasingly accepted as inevitable the continuation of things as they were. This attitude sapped confidence in, and the desire for, social and economic progress.

Under the circumstances, it may be wondered why the Government permitted the insurrection to continue for so long — why it did not exert extraordinary efforts to suppress civil disorder. It must be recognized, of course, that some of the problems involved were exceedingly difficult. Once the larger bands of insurgents had been broken up into relatively small groups, these were able to conceal themselves in the jungle and in the hills, fading away by day and appearing only at night. Villagers feared to report known insurgents to the authorities because of the dreadful reprisals to which they might be subjected. Many of the auxiliaries armed to assist the law enforcement bodies were themselves notoriously unreliable. Some were former insurgents and "bad hats," and were not above abusing their new-found legal cover to prey on the countryside. Others utilized the opportunity afforded them by the issue of scarce and highly prized arms to slip away and join up with insurgent bands; adventure, violence and loot beckoned attractively. Difficulties of terrain and communication hampered the army and the police. Their tactics were not well adjusted to the situation, their equipment was unsuitable and it may even be that they were somewhat lacking in determination. The existence of powerful above-ground sympathizers afforded aid and comfort to the insurgents in material as well as moral terms. The long-established traditions of violence and lack of discipline in Burmese society, and the admiration which many simple folk felt for the insurgents' daring exploits, also contributed to the difficulty. The very administrative setup in the districts of government itself made the task more difficult. In each district the deputy commissioner and the police and army heads were co-equal in authority and responsibility. These three power elements were responsible for coordinating their anti-insurgent activities, and the coordination was of necessity cumbersome and hampered by the personal interests of the people involved and sometimes by their economic interests. Not until the advent of the Ne Win Government late in 1958 was clear responsibility in any district delegated to one person, in this case the army commander.

Finally, the problem of internal security was made more difficult by the presence of People's China on Burma's northern borders. K.M.T. troop operations within or near Chinese territory might at any time provide China with a pretext for invasion. The situation was all the more delicate because the border was not clearly defined and China did not accept the so-called McMahon line inherited from the British time. Chinese maps, indeed, showed as Chinese sizable areas which the Burmese considered their own. And over the years, considerable numbers of Chinese had filtered across the borders into Burma, most of them no doubt to escape from hunger and terror, but some of them probably to serve their country's designs for expansion or control. The deployment of Burma's military forces had to take these conditions into account, and the forces could not at any time be concentrated.

These difficulties could have been overcome if the Government had been determined to do whatever was necessary to bring an end to the insurrection. What was chiefly necessary was toughness and determination. It was necessary to be tough with the above-ground sympathizers who encouraged the insurgents and provided logistic and other support for them. It was necessary to be tough with the insurgents themselves, both in action against them in the field and in punishment when they surrendered or were caught. It was necessary also to be firm with the villagers who could inform on them but hesitated to do so for fear of reprisal.

The Government, however, was reluctant to be tough. Perhaps four factors were chiefly responsible for this reluctance. The Government leaders, and especially Prime Minister U Nu, were devoted Buddhists who abhorred the taking of life even to protect society from the depredations of outlaws. Some of the insurgent leaders were old comrades, companions-in-arms and even relatives of the A.F.P.F.L. leaders themselves. They had fought alongside the Government leaders against the Japanese and against the British in the fight for independence; and still others, while neither friends nor comrades-in-arms, had been of assistance in these fights. The memory of indebtedness or association was still fresh. Furthermore, the Government hoped for a peaceful resolution of the insurrection if it continued to hold out the olive branch and to promise generous treatment of insurrectionists who surrendered their arms. Finally, many officials in the districts had developed a vested interest in continuation of the state of disorder. In the Tavoy district, for example, mine operators would get protection for visits to their mines more readily if they greased the palm of an appropriate officer. They would more readily be assisted in obtaining protection for ore convoys, or against poachers working their claims, or against bandits who sought to extract tribute from them, under the same conditions. Undoubtedly, this sort of thing was widespread. It is impossible to know how far up the official ladder such gains were distributed, or the extent to which the situation sapped determination in Rangoon. Since only determination and toughness could have succeeded, and since the Government lacked both, the insurrection continued.

The best evidence that determination and toughness could have achieved results is in the notable accomplishments of the Ne Win Government when it took office late in 1958. Announcing at the outset its lack of sympathy and patience with the insurrection, and its intention to make the punishment fit the crime, the Ne Win Government went after the insurgents with unrelenting determination. Within the space of a few months, many insurgents were killed, wounded and captured, many others surrendered, and a great deal of arms and ammunition was seized. Trains and boats began to operate at night. Security conditions were vastly improved, even within the towns. Morale and behavior within the law-abiding society similarly improved. Indeed, so great was the accomplishment, in contrast with the previous state of affairs, that one is inclined to wonder why the army itself had not done the job before.

It may be that in addition to the factors which have already been mentioned there existed beneath the surface a cross-current of conflicting interest between the Government and the military. At least some of the political leaders may have hesitated to build up the power and prestige of the army for fear of the political influence it might come to wield. They may also have been reluctant to divert to the army the resources necessary to equip it to cope effectively with the insurrection. And, looking further ahead, they may have feared that some disorder might attend the future demobilization of a military force so augmented. So far as the military were concerned, some of them may have been quite content with the status the army enjoyed when the Government was under such attack. Army budget requests were seldom questioned. Its establishment was being progressively developed, not so much in arms and equipment for fighting insurgents as in improved officer housing and facilities, in hospital facilities, in conditions of service and in various other perquisites. It may well be that at least some elements in the military establishment were more interested in these benefits than in a pacification of the countryside, which might endanger the liberal treatment accorded them.

The problem of security went beyond the omnipresent threat of the insurgents to life and property. In particular, civil servants, business men and firms were insecure on other counts as well. Civil servants feared the politicians who sought favorable decisions from them in administrative matters; they feared transfer to less desirable posts or lack of promotion if they failed to please their political superiors; and they feared especially action by the Bureau of Special Investigation (B.S.I.), should any of their decisions on the job, no matter how well intended, prove faulty. Under the law, results rather than intentions were taken as criteria of wrong conduct; and a civil servant could be jailed and held without bail pending a trial which might not take place for years, without the right to habeas corpus. This happened to enough civil servants — notably U Ba Sein, Director-General of the Electricity Supply Board — to terrorize all civil servants at decision-making levels. Even ministers of Government felt the threat, as indeed Prime Minister U Nu intended they should in his determination to root out graft and corruption. Undoubtedly the fears held in check the amount of corruption at higher levels of Government. But the situation also aggravated the already existing tendency of officials to seek approval or clearance in writing before taking even obvious action they were perfectly competent to take. This resulted in an ever-increasing sluggishness in the public administration — not only in the traditional Government departments, but also in the commercial-type boards and corporations, where crisp decision-making was essential to even a modicum of operating efficiency. Ironically, the officer who feared to make the decisions necessary to get his job done could be assured that he would not be criticized or punished for his hesitancy. Since action was dangerous, and inaction was safe, only a handful of venturesome and dedicated individuals, to whom performance was more important than safety, took the risks of action. And there were a few others, sufficiently confident of protection from their powerful ministers, who took what they considered lesser risks. U Ba Sein was one of these, but when the time came his minister could not protect him.

Business men and firms also had reason to fear the B.S.I., particularly if they were Indians, Pakistanis or Chinese and if they were engaged in import or export trade. Many of these, uncertain about their future in Burma, actually falsified invoices, by arrangement with foreign suppliers or customers, to minimize their tax liabilities or to transfer assets in violation of strict foreign exchange regulations. This made all of them suspect, and they were frequently harried by the B.S.I., as well as by Customs, Finance and Foreign Exchange officials. Even English firms lived in uncertainty; they did not know whether the nationalization axe would fall, whether necessary permits would be renewed or issued, or when profit remittances might be approved. And indigenous business men were subject to similar uncertainties, as in the case of the rice-millers, who never knew when their mills might be expropriated. Finally, law enforcement by the courts, particularly at lower levels, was political and capricious, which meant that the law itself contributed to insecurity rather than to stability in the social and economic order.

CHAPTER 23

Problems of Cultural Adaptation

Burma's economic development program was aimed essentially at utilizing Western technology to increase output and to enhance living standards and welfare. A reasonably effective implementation of this program required not only the utilization of Western techniques but also some accommodation of Burmese culture to Western values and practices. The Burmese leaders had already, as we have seen, borrowed heavily from the West. Both democratic thought and the ideas of Marxist socialism were embodied in their desire for independence, in their attitudes toward colonialism, imperialism and capitalism, in their desire for economic development and welfare and in their industrialization and nationalization policies. These ideas had been communicated through the A.F.P.F.L. leadership to the younger officers in the civil service and the army and to the leadership of the trade unions and the peasants' organizations. They were of course solidly entrenched in the left-wing political parties. Among the citizenry they were reflected chiefly in the cultivators' desire for freedom from foreign landlordism and usury. But the aspirations and attitudes implicit in these ideas had not come into substantial or direct conflict with the attitudes, values, beliefs and mores deeply rooted in the traditional Burmese culture.

The implementation of economic development, on the other hand, did impinge on Burmese culture in many significant ways, and the accommodation could not be a ready one. Long-established cultural traits do not quickly yield when confronted with challenge. Where implementation of the development effort encountered obstacles of this sort, it was the implementation, not the culture, which yielded to the pressure, though the culture received a shock which probably prepared the way for some accommodation later on.

It is not intended to appraise broadly all the elements in Burmese culture which exerted a retarding influence on economic development and change.

The attempt will be, rather, to consider briefly the effect of a few selected aspects on economic development or functions necessary to it.

CONSUMPTION, SAVINGS AND INVESTMENT

Apart from attitudes toward resident aliens — the *kalah,* or foreigner — and sometimes toward indigenous minority groups, there is virtually no caste or class in Burmese society. It is status that is important, and status seems always to have derived mostly from position in or association with government. The important structure is the power structure, which resides in the government and in its auxiliary institutions. Since the political leaders are committed to both socialism and Buddhism, they strive to be visibly of the people and humble in demeanor. Their dress is simple, their way of life is unostentatious and their personal habits are, with few exceptions, abstemious. The leaders thus set an example of modest living.

Basic wants in Burmese society are few and can be satisfied with relatively little effort. The occasional Indian or Chinese trader builds a fine house, or buys a Chevrolet car. Burmese ministers are provided with rather good housing. They, and a handful of top officials of the Railways, Port, Union Bank and a few other agencies of the Government, are almost the only Burmans who enjoy such a privilege. Ministers are also provided with official cars.[1] But in dress, food habits, housing and in most other ways, there is practically no conspicuous consumption among Burmans. The dress of the clerk out visiting with his wife on a holiday is not readily distinguishable from that of the well-to-do merchant or the senior government official. Even where incomes are markedly disparate, the house of the well-to-do merchant will not be very different in size or furnishing from the sparsely furnished home of the man with only half or one quarter of his income. The fewness of the basic wants and the ease with which they can be satisfied, the absence of caste or class and Socialist and Buddhist moderation all contribute to the absence of ostentatious consumption and thus serve as checks on personal accumulation and investment. And they are reinforced by other aspects of the culture.

The Buddhist religion places great value on giving and deprecates accumulation. Rich and poor alike give daily alms to the monks. No title in the Burmese society is so revered as that of "Pagoda Builder," which accrues to those who finance the building of a pagoda. Even the poor may aspire in a humble way to this honor, although the pagoda they build may be only three feet high. Throughout Burma one finds rest houses for the traveler and roadside stands containing offerings of two earthen bowls, one of rice and one of water, where the passer-by may refresh himself. Indeed, the common greet-

---

1. Some of their wives, to be sure, will on occasion wear costly jewelry. This is generally credited to family inheritance, or sometimes to the woman's independent business activity.

ing in Burma is not "How are you?" but literally "Have you eaten rice to-day?" The religion teaches that giving is blessed. There is no place in Burmese culture, and no expression in the Burmese language, for "Thank you." It is not the donor who confers a benefit. It is, rather, the recipient, since he enables the donor to acquire merit. Ideally, the devout Buddhist divests himself of material things to acquire merit and live a more spiritual life. Thus, giving rather than accumulation is built into the Burmese culture, and is characteristic even among families of the lowest income.[2] There can be little doubt that giving and the building and maintenance of pagodas (especially the periodic replenishment of gold leaf on their domes) channel off a substantial portion of the resources which would otherwise go into consumption, savings and investment.

The Burman is typically improvident, by Western standards. He displays little concern for his future security, but spends freely to enjoy life to the fullest possible degree. Food, finery, gambling, entertainment (especially the cinema and pwes), ceremonies (the shin pyu at which a boy or man is initiated into monkhood, the ear-boring ceremony which marks a girl's coming of age, marriages and the like), and good-will feasts for friends and neighbors — these commonly are the avenues for spending whatever he may have after paying for the necessities of life and giving alms. They may indeed use up whatever he is able to borrow as well. For the Burman is far more likely to be substantially in debt — and not for durable goods the use of which he would continue to enjoy — than he is to have even small savings. Such improvidence is not strange in a land where life has always been short, where basic needs can be met rather easily, and where no relative, no matter how distant the relationship, will refuse temporary or even permanent hospitality to the uninvited guest.

Such savings as may accrue will generally be spent for gold and jewelry. Rare is the man, no matter how low his income, who will not manage to buy some piece of gold jewelry for his wife — a ring, a bracelet, earrings, a gold comb for her hair, or even five small sapphires or rubies to serve as buttons for her blouse (*aingyi*). As for himself, when he dresses up in a collarless neckband shirt (a fashion acquired from the British), he is poor indeed if he lacks a set of linked gold studs to use in place of buttons. And even poorer is the man who does not buy gold earrings, however small, for his daughter when her ears are bored. The incentives here go beyond the desire of the male to please his womenfolk or to enjoy personal finery. The Burman

2. A household expenditure survey conducted in Rangoon in the first half of 1958 among households with an average monthly income of K 338 kyats disclosed that these families spent more for gifts and ceremonials — mostly gifts — than they did for recreation, personal care or house furnishings. The percentage of household income thus devoted was only 1.2 per cent, to be sure, but these were families who had practically nothing left after meeting their basic wants for food, clothing and shelter. It is highly probable that villagers give relatively far more in support of their monks and pagodas than do city folk in Rangoon.

frequently borrows, and he can borrow at substantially lower rates of interest when he can put up gold or jewelry as collateral for his loan. Further, he realizes that money as such will not be safe with him, but will otherwise be spent with nothing left to show for it. If he pledges his studs or his wife's earrings, however, he will make every effort to redeem them. And, of course, these stores of wealth are more readily concealed from thieves and tax collectors than are most others.

Because life typically is short, because of the long tradition of robbery, violence and uncertainty and because improvidence results in a great need for personal loans at high rates of interest, the Burman with money to invest tends to look to the loan market for quick and sizable returns. In the colonial period, loans to agriculturalists provided, through foreclosure, an easy road to land acquisition, landlordism and high rents. After independence, laws against foreclosure and land alienation closed off this ready avenue to wealth. But agricultural loans at high rates of interest, and personal loans at 5 per cent per month against collateral worth double the loan, continue to be a highly attractive way to employ savings. So does the import trade where, under the Burmanization policy, import licenses could be obtained, especially if one had the right contacts in government, and quickly sold for a sizable profit. Export trade, domestic merchandising and government construction or road-building contracts rank after these in relative appeal. All these investments are considered more advantageous, by virtue of their relatively limited capital requirements, limited risk[3] and early and sizable returns, than are investments in manufacturing enterprise. In any event, few Burmans could afford to set up anything but the smallest of production units with their own capital. And the corporate form of enterprise, although operative in the case of the large foreign firms, is still alien and suspect.[4]

WORK, PRODUCTIVITY AND PROFIT

Under British rule, as under the Burmese kings, education beyond the primary level was valued chiefly as an avenue to employment in Government service. This continued to be the case in independent Burma. Next in terms of attraction for the educated youth came the professions, with law and medicine perhaps the most appealing, although more recently engineering, the sciences and public administration have become increasingly popular. Government contracting and trade offered inducements to the more practical-minded. But the great majority of the male youth who enjoyed education through the middle school and beyond aspired to enter Government service.

3. There are, to be sure, considerable risks in the case of agricultural loans, but these are amply covered by the high interest rates.
4. The first real experience the Burmese had with the corporate form of enterprise was with the trading corporations set up in joint venture with the Government in 1956.

This was primarily because of the prestige, status and security conferred by such employment, but also because Government service at higher levels was well rewarded, because it was widely considered to be something of a sinecure and a reward to the educated, and perhaps because it offered opportunities to those of easy conscience to supplement their incomes. This choice reflected also the paucity of advantageous alternatives. Since the Government required more educated and trained people than were available, the channels of employment were always open.

This broad appraisal has taken no account of monkhood as a career. As far back as 1931 the census tallied more than 100,000 Buddhist clergy. The sample censuses of the 1950s are not informative on this point. In any event, a tabulation of those wearing the robe at any given time would have to distinguish between those engaged only in a temporary novitiate and those for whom monkhood is a career. Even this distinction would be somewhat cloudy because monks take the vows for specified and sometimes limited periods of time and are thereafter free to withdraw. What is more significantly unclear is the potential of those who have entered the clergy for achievement in other fields. There can be little doubt that the monkhood as a way of life makes greater appeal to the pious, the selfless, the gentle and the philosophic souls. Whether it also draws off from other careers men with considerable potential for leadership, innovation and management is not known. To the extent that it does, religion may be said to exert a significant influence on manpower as well as on material resources.

It has already been pointed out that climate, the relative simplicity of wants, the beneficence of nature and the seasonal nature of the agriculture in which most Burmese are engaged have permeated the culture and have resulted in a disinclination to work hard over sustained periods of time. Farm work, though intensive and taxing during certain periods of the year, is relieved for weeks on end between peak seasons. But even on the farms the most exacting physical tasks were historically performed in the Delta by immigrant seasonal Indian labor. In the towns, the dirty and menial work was also performed by Indians, and in Burmese eyes such work lost status. The Burman dislikes work which soils the hands, even if it requires skill. Thus, a Burman would rather be a chauffeur than earn much higher pay as an automobile mechanic, because the latter occupation involves "dirty" work. And even a young engineer is disinclined to put on rough clothes and do field work. He much prefers "clean" work in the office. The low regard for physical labor is evident when a government official arrives at his office and his peon or messenger is waiting at the door to carry upstairs the files he has taken home to study. To carry the papers himself is not considered compatible with his status. Similarly, such an official would ring his desk bell and call his peon to move his desk or chair, rather than perform this "menial" task himself.

Both the disinclination to work hard and concepts of work status are evident in domestic employment. If a given household employs a bearer (butler), a sweeper and a cook, none of them working more than a few hours a day, it would be difficult to persuade one servant to take on two of these functions, even at a wage substantially higher than he is paid for his own job; he prefers to work less hard at lower pay. Work responsibilities are clearly divided, and a different status attaches to each. The bearer will consider himself above picking up a broken dish and its contents, even if the sweeper is not there.

Even in the towns, work is not commonly sustained. There is considerable job turnover, and sometimes a considerable interval between jobs. Office hours are not long, and the work routine is broken by a plethora of holidays. What with weekends, earned leave, casual leave, sick leave and many *ad hoc* holidays added to the established ones, it is doubtful whether working days exceed 150 in the year. And work itself usually proceeds at a leisurely pace. This applies to common labor as well as to office and shop occupations. In Government service, office hours are 9:30 to 4:00, but the effective working day is considerably shorter because of lateness in arrival and early departure. And much of the working day is devoted to lounging, gossip, newspaper reading and tea.

Finally, there prevails in Burmese culture a relationship between employer and employee in which the employer is regarded as a protector of the employee, with implied responsibility for his continuing security and welfare. The employee feels an attachment, or even devotion, to his employer in return for this paternalism. Faults on the part of the employee are expected to bring scoldings such as a father might give his child, rather than termination of employment.

In this cultural setting, in which the educated look to a paternal government for employment and other workers look to private employers in much the same way, there is little spur to initiative or innovation. Time is of little consequence. Since overhead costs are slight and labor is cheap, cost-saving devices are not sought. Even obvious ways of improving productivity are ignored. For example, workers in a construction labor gang may be seen carrying six, eight or ten bricks on their heads in an endless chain from the roadside to the construction site as though the wheelbarrow had never been invented.

Because the Indians and, to a lesser extent, the Chinese find it difficult to win acceptance and status in Burmese society, their motivation to achievement in the economic world is far stronger than that of the Burmese, and has spurred them to innovation and enterprise as well as to hard work. These resident alien groups have made contributions to Burma's economic development out of all proportion to their numbers, and they possess the potential for even greater contributions. This potential they have not been permitted

to realize. Indians, particularly, have been discriminated against, even har-
assed, at every turn, whether in citizenship, in government employment, in
the application of regulations, in the issue of licenses, in the extension of
loans, in permission to make remittances abroad and in the repatriation of
capital assets. Despite these limitations, which reflect fear, suspicion, dislike
and insecurity on the part of the Burmese, the Indian contribution has been
a substantial one. It seems quite clear that the pace of development in Burma
will quicken to its fullest only when this resident alien minority is admitted
into first-class economic citizenship.

The Buddhist repugnance to the taking of life has a number of important
effects on production and productivity, and these go far beyond its influence
on Government policy toward the insurrection. The most obvious effect is
the ban on cattle slaughter in Burma Proper (an exception is made for the
Shan and other Hill States). This ban, imposed after World War II, was applied to cattle only. It was not applied, for example, to sheep or goats. At the
time there was indeed a need to replenish as quickly as possible the badly
depleted supply of draft animals, but the ban also reflected the ancient Indian
origins of Buddhism and the associated Hindu taboo on cattle slaughter. Despite shortages of meat which forced up the prices of mutton, poultry and fish,
and despite the loss of export proceeds from hides — proceeds that had been
quite sizable before the war — U Nu's government persisted in maintaining
the ban on cattle slaughter even after the supply of draft animals had been
replenished (despite the obvious argument that slaughter, by increasing the
market for cattle products, would tend to result in larger and improved
herds). And the first act of U Nu's government when he resumed office early
in 1960 was to reinstate the ban, which General Ne Win's government had
terminated to help bring down food prices.

Repugnance to the taking of life extends also to flies, mosquitoes and other
insects, rodents, pariah dogs and even snakes and scorpions. In a land in
which so many people have suffered from malaria it is truly remarkable that
the Burmese persist in their personal tolerance of mosquitoes. They have
permitted United Nations anti-malaria teams to conduct effective spray campaigns against them, but a Burman usually will brush away a mosquito or
fly which is annoying him rather than slap at it. He will pick up a huge
cockroach and release it unharmed outside the door rather than kill it. Poi-
sonous snakes and scorpions will be permitted to go their way, even when
they could be dispatched. Pariah dogs are allowed to roam the streets of the
towns even when they are injured or diseased, and even though, in semi-wild
packs, they howl through the night and offer the ever-present threat of rabies.
(They do, of course, serve as scavengers to supplement inadequate garbage
removal and help to keep down the rat plague. But it is not for this reason
that the Burmese tolerate them.)

The Socialist view of profits as the evil result of exploitation and the feeling that time is of little consequence and hence not costly — an attitude reinforced by the relative unimportance of overhead costs in the Burmese economy — contribute greatly to the Government's lack of concern about the widespread inefficiency in the state-owned enterprises. Obviously, if profits are evil in the private economy, they cannot be very desirable in public activities; therefore the inefficiency which makes profits impossible cannot be viewed as damaging. An absence of understanding of fundamental economic processes is involved here also, of course, a lack of appreciation that unfavorable accounting results in a public enterprise show a social cost greater than the social benefit, and hence a social loss.

PUBLIC ADMINISTRATION, DECISION-MAKING AND MANAGEMENT

Burmese culture has always inculcated in the youth a profound respect for parents, teachers, community elders and all persons of superior *awza,* or station. This reverence is deeply implanted and is manifest in personal relationships throughout the society, whether in home, school, monastery, factory or office. Those lower in age or status will hesitate to question or contradict in the presence of their seniors or superiors. Indeed, when a Burman has hesitated to express himself to an elder or superior, he will sometimes tell a comrade later, "I had anahdeh," meaning, "I feared to offend."

Lucian Pye has developed an interesting theory tracing this behavior to the typical mother-child relationship in Burmese society, and he has also related it to several other Burmese personal and political behavior characteristics.[5] Whatever the cause, such behavior is clearly an important factor in public administration, decision-making and management. Inferiors in age and status, at whatever level and in whatever activity, will seldom question a position taken by a superior or elder even when it is obviously capricious, unreasonable or based on ignorance. On their part, superiors in age or status generally refrain from discussing contemplated decisions with their juniors. Their position requires them to instruct or order rather than seek advice. Indeed, it may be that the widely prevalent custom of consulting the woman of the household before making a business or political decision is due not only to the practical wisdom displayed by the Burmese women-folk but also to the reluctance of their husbands to compromise their status by consulting with their assistants.

Status or *awza* affects the decision-making process in still another way. The person with *awza* is reluctant to endanger his status by decisions or actions which may expose him to criticism or hostility. This attitude, combined with the prevalent view that time is of little consequence, makes for repeated post-

ponement of decisions important to others. Sometimes it encourages delegation of decision-making responsibility to cover up the failure to make decisions at the level where responsibility properly rests. But because power is
precious, delegation of responsibility is seldom accompanied by delegation of
commensurate authority.

Astrologers, of whom there are many in Burmese society, play an important
role in decision-making today just as they did in the time of the kings. It was
astrologers who recommended the precise date, hour and place on which
Burma's independence should be proclaimed in 1948; it was astrologers who
selected the site for the Kaba Aye (Peace Pagoda) and the Great Rock Cave
which housed the Sixth Buddhist Synod; and it is, frequently, astrologers
whose advice is sought on propitious dates and circumstances for important
family or business decisions — on marriage, home purchase, investment, career selection and the like. Even the signing of a contract between a Government agency and a foreign firm of consultants has been delayed for some
time to await the day the astrologer indicates will be propitious.

Nats (spirits) also influence many decisions; in many cases, it is considered
necessary to propitiate them before acting. For example, tree-felling (nats are
supposed most frequently to inhabit trees) obviously calls for propitiation.
Irrigation, land-clearance and dam construction projects require due consideration and propitiation of the spirits. Many Rangoon families would not
consummate a car purchase without propitiating a particularly powerful nat
considered to be especially interested in transport. The advice of spiritualists,
persons considered to be in rapport with the nats and capable of communicating with them, is eagerly sought by many and religiously followed. Burmans are continually on the lookout for omens, and regard them most seriously.
Astrologers, nats and omens add interesting dimensions to the decision-making
process in Burma.

CIVIL ORDER

Certain Burmese character and culture traits seem to be closely related to
civil order, or rather to the relative lack of it. While the typical Burman is
scrupulously clean in his person, frequently bathing three and four times a
day, he is seemingly unconcerned about lack of cleanliness and order in his
surroundings, whether in the bazaars, the streets or the yard behind his house.
The shopper at the bazaar will delicately pick up his *longyi* (skirt) while
making his way through the refuse which the stallkeepers have uncon-
cernedly thrown to the ground and which frequently stinks abominably.
Garbage and waste are carelessly tossed out by the road or into the yard with
little regard for health considerations, the neighbors or passers-by. A common practice in the towns is to toss one's refuse over the fence into the yard
of one's neighbor, whence it is frequently returned with interest. Radios

blare so that they can be heard two and three blocks away, and sometimes in the middle of the night. Trucks and buses, heavily loaded, rumble at high speed along the roads and streets with tires worn to the casing, defective brakes and steering, and shattered windshields — highly dangerous to their own cargo as well as to other vehicles and pedestrians. These are only a few instances of a general social indiscipline.

The Burman combines, oddly, an unusual gentleness with an equally unusual capacity for sudden violence. (Pye's theory, previously cited, suggests an explanation for this also.) This characteristic accounts not only for the high incidence of acts of violence in Burmese society, but also for the tolerance with which they are regarded. It is almost as though people thought, "There, but for the grace of the Buddha, go I." This tolerance for a widespread weakness no doubt contributes to the sympathy and even admiration which the Burmese sometimes display for social outlaws — in recent years, for the insurgents. While the villagers' lack of cooperation with the authorities in their efforts to deal with the insurgents was due in large part to fear of reprisals, it reflected also a concealed admiration on the part of many for the boldness and daring of the rebels, and a vicarious sharing of thrills in their exploits.

ATTITUDES TOWARD THE REST OF THE WORLD

Burmese culture developed over a period of more than eight centuries in relative isolation. Of all foreign influences, Buddhism, which was adopted in the eleventh century, had the greatest impact. There were afterwards, to be sure, wars with the Thais and contacts with the Indians, the Chinese and others. Despite these, the Burmese developed their way of life with little awareness of the rest of the world until the country was occupied by the British during the nineteenth century.

The British introduced the rule of law and a number of basic democratic institutions and ideas. The nature of the relationship was such that the Burmese came to identify the white man as a master and expert who combined in one person both authority and knowledge. The shocking experience of the Japanese occupation during World War II taught them that imperialism was not practiced solely by the white man, and that the foreigner could be cruel and tyrannical as well as paternally masterful. By war's end, the Burmese wanted nothing so much as to be rid of old and new masters alike, and to reassert their cultural heritage as well as their sovereignty. The amalgam of Marxist and democratic ideas which motivated the A.F.P.F.L. leadership in setting up independent Burma were superimposed on this even more basic desire. In a deep sense, this involved disengagement from the rest of the world. The post-war division of most of the rest of the world into two great power blocs accentuated Burma's fear of involvement.

If sovereignty and cultural integrity suggested disengagement, the desire for development required ever closer relations with the rest of the world, for trade and technology if not for aid. These relations could be developed with greatest relative safety with international bodies, with countries that shared similar problems and aspirations, and, among the more advanced countries, with those so small and distant as to represent no possible threat — especially if they too shared some problems and aspirations with the Burmese. Thus, the United Nations exerted great appeal, because it made possible relations without involvement with specific countries or blocs. Close relations with the other Colombo Powers — India, Ceylon, Pakistan and Indonesia — were attractive, not because these countries were all rice importers, but because they too had a new-found independence to consolidate and economic development to achieve. Among the more advanced nations, Yugoslavia and Israel were both small and Socialist. If not completely neutral, neither were they clearly aligned in the great power struggle. Moreover, they were relatively advanced and could assist with technology and personnel without threat to Burma's sovereignty. Participation in the Asian Socialist Congress, and leadership in cementing Buddhist ties with Eastern countries through the Sixth Buddhist Synod, rounded out this pattern.

In practice, it was of course not possible to develop relationships with the world outside only on these comfortable bases. Development seemed to require first technical and then, as the World Bank declined to finance in the hoped-for measure so ambitious and undisciplined a program, financial assistance from the great committed powers. In these relations, the Burmese were always careful to balance arrangements made with one side by similar arrangements with the other. The Government's objective was to protect its internal political position as well as to avoid the appearance of partisanship in the power struggle. And its representatives were always on the lookout for any aspect of proposed arrangements which might be considered to impose strings on Burma's sovereignty or to involve her in the affairs of others.

But fears of the loss of sovereignty or of Burma's neutral position were not the only influences governing her relations with the world outside. Whether with committed or uncommitted nations or their nationals, there was always present also a fear of being outsmarted by others more knowledgeable and cunning. This made for an attitude of wariness, suspicion and hesitation in such relationships. If U Nu himself was less subject to these fears than were most of his colleagues, he obviously had to cater to them. For example, while U Nu's friendship with Nehru would have made for much freer and more open relations with India, most of his colleagues did not share this understanding and indeed never ceased to view India with fear and suspicion — an attitude which applied equally to the sizable Indian minority within Burma. Attitudes toward alien resident business men and firms and toward prospective foreign investors were similarly colored by fears and suspicions. And although the question of promoting tourism frequently arose in connection with foreign exchange, there was little real disposition to relax the many restrictions which discouraged tourists, let alone to take positive action to encourage them.

In general, foreign governments and their nationals who sought cooperation with the Burmese — whether these were diplomats, business men or firms, technicians, tourists or even advisors — had first to overcome basic attitudes of withdrawal, suspicion and insecurity. In this atmosphere, cooperation developed only with difficulty and in limited degree.

CHAPTER 24

Problems of

Specialized Manpower

The problems of specialized manpower encountered in the implementation of Burma's development program were not solely shortages of personnel — managerial, administrative, professional, technical, sub-technical and skilled workers of all types — serious though these shortages were. The poor morale of these personnel and their inability under the prevailing circumstances to function effectively were also problems of major importance, perhaps equal in their effect to the shortages themselves.

SPECIALIZED MANPOWER SHORTAGES

It had of course been evident from the very outset of the program that meeting emergent demands for specialized manpower was one of the key problems the Government would have to solve. In appraising the tasks which lay ahead, the consultants had warned: "Indeed, it would not be overstating the case to say that the success of the development program hinges more on this than on any other single factor."[1] The consultants' initial estimates of the additional skilled manpower requirements of the development program in both the public and the private sectors have already been presented in Table 14 (p. 130). These estimates did not pretend to any degree of precision. They sought only to approximate roughly the magnitudes of the manpower requirements which might develop. While they included several categories — drivers, for example — in which the indicated deficiencies could be met without too great cost in time or money by training programs of various kinds, they did not cover the needs for programs outside the scope of the K.T.A.

1. K.T.A. Comprehensive Report, p. 35.

Report — for example, for doctors, nurses, teachers or agricultural extension workers. However calculated, the requirements would of necessity have been sizable and difficult to meet. But, dangerous though it might be to underestimate these difficulties, they should not be exaggerated. A useful perspective on the problem may be obtained by viewing the development programs of the various economic sectors separately.

In the agricultural sector, the big job had to be done in the first instance by the cultivators themselves and by the cooperative societies in which they were enrolled. The specialized needs in this sector were chiefly in the field of agricultural engineering and mechanics, where relatively few specialized personnel were required, and in agricultural extension and credit work, where well-formulated training programs could develop large cadres of trained workers within a fairly short period of time. In the very important transport and communications field, by far the largest expenditures were for rolling stock and equipment, ships and other items to be procured abroad. Because the organizations concerned had a long operating experience before the war, there existed a relatively large carry-over of qualified engineers, technicians and managers. In manufacturing industry, the need for production supervisors and technicians was rather limited, and could be met by the employment of foreign specialists. Foreign suppliers would supervise the installation of equipment and provide technical assistance and supervisory services during the break-in period. The training of workers was no difficult task, as was demonstrated in the cotton-spinning, pharmaceuticals, jute and other plants. The engineering, construction and installation components of the electricity program were handled by Japanese and other foreign contracting firms, and again no particular labor problems of a technical kind were involved. In the field of mining and oil extraction, experienced foreign firms with which the Government had entered into joint ventures provided specialized personnel. The K.T.A. Report contemplated that these operational and administrative shortages, while serious and even acute, could in time be met through a combination of techniques — by education and training programs, by the use of foreign specialists, by increased productivity and by a variety of special arrangements, particularly with respect to management needs. By and large, these expectations were fulfilled. Thus, the manpower deficiencies were more difficult to meet on the administrative and supervision and coordination fronts — in the civil service and in the central top-level direction itself.

The Government had lost many top-flight British and Indian civil servants during and after World War II. These losses were incurred not only in the administrative services but also in the specialized forest, medical and other services as well. Many Burmese civil servants had, however, already achieved senior rank. To augment their number, experienced high-ranking officers were recalled from retirement. There was in addition a considerable amount of upgrading through accelerated promotion from the lower and middle ranks. Thus, in spite of the rapid expansion of the Government's activities and organizations, it was possible, by spreading the available people thin, to staff the more important civil service jobs, particularly the administrative posts, with experienced officers. It was for the most part in supporting jobs — the Number Two and Number Three men in the various offices — that personnel deficiencies were more evident.

To augment and assist the civil service, foreign specialists were obtained in considerable number under U. N. and Colombo Plan auspices, under various bilateral arrangements with People's China, the U.S.S.R., Israel and Yugoslavia, under Ford and other foundation auspices, and by the direct hire of foreign individuals, mostly from India, and of English and American firms. As of September 1957, 395 foreign specialists were assisting in the development program. Of these, 116 were directly employed, 90 were provided by foreign governments and their quasi-public organizations, 82 were provided by foreign firms, 66 were provided under U. N. and Colombo Plan auspices and 41 by foundations. Of this total, 140 were engaged in the industrialization program, 66 in agriculture and irrigation, 30 in mining, 70 in health, education and housing and 25 in central economic and engineering planning and advisory work.[2] In-service and on-the-job training programs were also utilized to upgrade existing personnel and train new employees. These essentially temporary arrangements were buttressed by a major long-term education and training program.

The Government first stepped up sharply the number of university graduates sent abroad as state scholars to pursue graduate studies in various fields of specialization. By the end of 1956, there were 343 state scholars studying abroad, of whom 80 per cent were studying engineering and the physical sciences. These scholars were committed, under bond, to spend a given number of years in the Government service on completion of their studies. Simultaneously, the Government embarked on a many-faceted program of educational expansion and training, both formal and informal, general and specialized, from the university down through the primary school. The University of Rangoon was much expanded, with emphasis on engineering, medicine, economics, statistics and public administration. Mandalay College, formerly a subsidiary of Rangoon University, was expanded greatly and elevated to university status. Several intermediate colleges were established in lesser towns. The number of Government-supported middle and high schools was increased from 180, with a registration of some 62,000, in 1952 to 793, with a registration in excess of 220,000, in 1959. Within this total there were

2. D. P. Barnes, "Status and Activities of Foreign Specialists in Burma" (memorandum), Ministry of National Planning, Sept. 29, 1958, Table I.

established 52 technical high schools, 37 agricultural high schools, 12 agricultural middle schools and two commercial schools. At the primary school level, from some 3,300 primary schools with a registration of less than half a million in 1952, the number grew to more than 11,500 with a registration of 1.5 million by 1959. Concurrent with these tremendous increases in schools and enrollments was the introduction of a new curriculum, particularly at the middle and high school levels, more closely attuned to the needs of a developing society.

Specialized education and training outside the formal educational system were also greatly expanded, with the guidance of a special commission headed by the outstandingly capable Director of Education, U Kaung. The Technical Institute at Insein, staffed and financially assisted by the Ford Foundation, experienced a ninefold expansion in enrollment from 150 in 1953 to 1,368 in 1959. The Agricultural Training Institute at Pyinmina, again with Ford Foundation staff and financial assistance, was firmly established and expanded. The Rehabilitation Brigade enlisted many thousands of former insurgents, trained them and their wives in metal-working, woodworking and other skills, and organized them into a large building and road construction force. Mass education courses achieved substantial enrollments. Government agencies such as the Union of Burma Railways and the Inland Water Transport Board conducted training and in-service programs and thus met many of their own needs for specialized skills. With the help of the United Nations, Government in-service training courses were established in public administration and later in accounting. Thousands of teachers were trained in new institutes hastily set up for the purpose. All in all, the education and training effort was a major one. Within a few short years it had already made a substantial contribution to provision of specialized manpower.

The specialists from abroad obtained under the variety of arrangements previously mentioned were utilized in almost every field of Government activity. U. N. and Colombo Plan personnel were perhaps most active in the field of health. They also provided specialists in agriculture, mining, industry, cooperatives, labor, social security, public administration, marketing and many other fields. While the United States had until 1953 supplied a number of technicians under the Point IV Program, Burma's abrupt termination of further grant assistance from the United States in that year closed out further U. S. technical assistance under Government auspices. Israeli technicians provided assistance in agriculture, mechanization, medical and architectural services, water resource development and management. Yugoslav technicians were utilized chiefly for mineral surveys and electric power planning. Chinese technicians installed the second unit of the cotton spinning and weaving mill in Rangoon. U.S.S.R. technicians, apart from the special U.S.S.R. "gift" projects, assisted chiefly in the agricultural field. The Ford Foundation, as has already been indicated, contributed mostly to agricultural and technical train-ing. It also assisted in business administration work at the university and in the training overseas of planning personnel. American consulting firms pro-vided the central Government with engineering and economic advice.

Under contract arrangement, an English firm built and managed the pharmaceuticals factory. Other English firms provided architectural services and supervision of construction for the technical high school, the new engi-neering college, and other projects. Foreign firms built the new Rangoon air-port, did reconstruction work on the wharves, installed the new Rangoon telephone system, repaired the Kabo Dam, designed and built the hydro-electric project at Balu Chaung and assisted in the design, construction and initial operation of most other large development projects. In all these cases, Burmese nationals were associated with the foreign contractors and gained valuable training and experience. Finally, the Government employed more than a hundred individual foreign specialists, most of them from India, in various professional and technical capacities.

While the Government utilized foreign specialists both to advise and to assist in the execution of major development projects and programs, the Gov-ernment administration itself was run exclusively by Burmese. Meanwhile, educational and training programs were being expanded and improved to prepare young people for the responsibilities initially assigned to foreign specialists.

These hastily organized measures were of necessity uneven in quality and in effect. The foreign specialists who came to help were not in all cases well selected or motivated, and did not always meet the needs satisfactorily; nor, of course, were all the training programs highly successful. For example, in doubling the number of teachers in state schools from less than 22,000 in 1953 to more than 41,000 in 1959, it was obviously not possible to produce a high proportion of adequately trained new teachers. Many of the new primary school teachers had gone no further than the seventh standard, and their in-structors were as poorly trained. Similarly, many of the trainees in other fields — nurses, vaccinators, draftsmen, accountants, agricultural equipment operators, extension workers, and so on — were far from well prepared. De-spite these deficiencies, significant progress was made. It may indeed be that Burma's achievement in meeting the shortages of specialized manpower was as great as that in dealing with any other major development problem. Taken all in all, it was a remarkable performance.

MORALE

Three important factors underlay the poor morale widely prevalent throughout the Government service and relatively more intense and serious in the upper echelons. The first of these was the relationship between the political leaders, both in and out of Government, and the pre-war administrators. In general, the more senior civil servants who had served before World War II were better educated and more experienced in practical affairs than were the politicians who, even when university-educated, had devoted themselves more to political agitation than to scholarship. The insecurity felt by many ministers in the face of their better-educated and more experienced subordinates was frequently reflected in the antagonism and contempt they displayed toward these senior civil servants on the grounds that they had been "lackeys" of the British. Second, after independence senior civil servants, and particularly those at the secretary's level, experienced severe cuts in living standards, status and prestige as a result of pay slashes, price increases and interference by the politicians. Third, they resented the appointment to senior posts ranking with their own of political camp-followers and personal lackeys of powerful political leaders, appointees who were completely lacking in qualifications and who demonstrated, once they were on the job, that their interest was self or party aggrandizement rather than service.

Looking back, U Nu himself stated part of the case in his initial address to the Parliament on April 5, 1960, when he assumed the Prime Minister's office for the third time:

Mr. Speaker, a parliamentary democracy therefore requires an independent and disciplined civil service of the character described above. During the ten years that we were in power, we failed to recognize this essential characteristic. True, we maintained the civil service intact and did not attempt to substitute it by a party civil service. But we did not meticulously respect the principle that the loyalty of a civil servant must be to his service and its traditions, not to any political party or leader. Many of our acts created a confusion in the minds of the civil service as to where its loyalty lay, and favour was often shown to those who changed their loyalty from their service to individual leaders. Without actually changing it into a party civil service, we introduced tendencies which had a disruptive effect on the independence of the civil service, and consequently on its efficiency and integrity. It prevented the growth of service ideals possessed by an independent and disciplined civil service.

We went even further than above.

We appointed party adherents as civil servants in many government boards and projects. There is, of course, nothing wrong in recruiting persons of ability and integrity to such services, even though they may be or have been members of the party. Our mistake was in recruiting them to the service without obliging them to sever their connection with the Party completely and transferring their loyalty to the service to which they were recruited. This had a most serious effect on the morale, efficiency, integrity and discipline of the service. By these acts, we came dangerously close to creating a party civil service of the kind that exists in totalitarian states.[3]

3. *Burma Weekly Bulletin,* April 7, 1960, p. 458.

In addition to these background factors, a number of other circumstances contributed to poor morale. Offices were dark, dirty and unsanitary. Nepotism had crowded the Government offices with a host of unqualified, inessential and lazy hangers-on whom, because of their connections, it was hazardous to discipline. Files were lost, cases accumulated and the pace of organizational activity became increasingly sluggish. In the secretariat, and even more so in the districts, politicians interfered with the administrative process, and civil servants feared reprisals if they resisted. Lack of effective leadership and policy direction from the top frequently made for frustration. Where latitude for decision existed, fear of the Bureau of Special Investigation and of future punishment for decisions made in good faith, the outcome of which might not please the politicians, were effective deterrents to action. Since commendation was seldom forthcoming for achievement and punishment might follow error and since censure seldom followed inaction, public officials were increasingly disposed to do as little as possible. This was the course of safety, especially since insurrection provided a ready excuse in most cases for failure to accomplish given objectives. Finally, the organization and procedures of the public administration itself were effective deterrents to action and contributors to poor morale.

THE PUBLIC ADMINISTRATION AND MORALE

Despite cost of living allowances, pay scales at the lower levels of the civil service were really inadequate for minimal living standards, and corruption became widespread. In relatively few cases was graft accepted at higher levels. More frequent, and in the end more damaging, was the petty graft paid to persuade Government employees to do what it was their duty to do, because they would not do it in time without the payments. Thus, an applicant for a telephone installation would pay a gratuity to get it. A business man calling on a customs official would give the latter's peon "tea money" to obtain access. The official himself might have to be given somewhat more substantial "tea money" before he would bestir himself and locate the necessary papers. A business man seeking to book a railway freight car might be told that there were no cars available. Once the required gratuity was paid, it would become clear that the car had been available all along. A contractor who had performed services for a Government department and whose invoices had been approved for payment would not be able to get the clerk to prepare his payment check without a gratuity. Clerks at the post office would bestir themselves and hunt through dusty piles of accumulated mail and parcels to find long-undelivered items only when their palms were appropriately crossed. The entire apparatus of Government had thus become afflicted with a massive dose of constipation and functioned at the intermediate and lower levels only by the application of laxatives of the kind described.

Administrators and specialists at higher levels were thus beset with problems from below as well as from above, problems with which they could not effectively cope. The result was, in a great many cases, dull and spiritless performance and a developing cynicism about the integrity and idealism of the political leadership and the Government's stated objectives. Lacking suitable alternatives, and with accumulated pension rights to protect, there was for most officials no place else to go. The loss of morale even went so far as to subvert professional standards and ethics. Thus, many doctors in state hospitals neglected their hospital duties and engaged in private practice to augment their incomes. And they often used the hospitals' meager supplies of scarce drugs and medicines to meet the needs of their private patients.

In many cases the morale of the foreign specialists was not much better. Arriving to do a job, they were often confounded by the confusion they encountered. Questions of office space, secretarial help, transport and housing arrangements were sometimes not worked out for months. The officers to whom they were assigned as advisors or counterparts were frequently uninterested or even hostile. What many foreign specialists found most difficult of all was the general atmosphere of aimlessness and indecision, akin sometimes to chaos, which made it impossible for them to come to grips with the jobs they had come to do. Often they found it difficult even to find someone responsible to talk to, let alone to participate in or speed the decision-making process. In the face of such difficulties, many foreign technicians developed an indifference to their tasks and merely marked time until the expiration of their contracts.

There were, of course, notable exceptions among both the Burmese civil servants and the foreign specialists. In both groups there were men who had idealism and professional pride and who were basically fighters unwilling to accept defeat, who patiently and persistently gave of their best to accomplish what they could. There were still others, close enough to a powerful political leader to be imbued with his drives and confident of his support, who took initiative and assumed responsibility. Such cases were exceptions to the rule. In general, the specialized personnel, both native and foreign, performed at levels far below their potential, and the development program suffered seriously on this account.

THE PRIVATE SECTOR

The private sector had its shortages of specialized manpower as well, and again, chiefly in managerial, administrative, technical and professional personnel. But the needs in the private sector were not so great.

For the most part — aside from the larger British firms who provided their own specialized personnel — local forestry, mining, construction, manufacturing and trading firms were small in scale, employed antiquated methods and did not require highly specialized personnel. Members of minority groups here encountered fewer obstacles and less discrimination in employment and professional practice than they did in the Government service, and resident Indians, Pakistanis and Chinese made a sizable contribution toward meeting the manpower needs.

Since students of economic development frequently assess the shortage of entrepreneurial talent as the most serious of the manpower deficiencies in underdeveloped societies, the relative availability of such talent may be mentioned here. In broad, it appears that there was an abundance of entrepreneurial-minded people, rather than a pronounced lack of them. Some evidence to this effect has already been presented in Chapter 21, in connection with implementation of industrial development in the private sector. Additional evidence may be found in the numerous small enterprises in the mining field, in the many small rubber, tea and coffee plantations, in construction, in foreign and domestic trade, in river and motor transport, in services and, of course, in basic agriculture itself. If enterprise was not even more pronounced and larger in scale in manufacture than it was, this was due not to a dearth of the entrepreneurial spirit or even to the shortage of capital. It was due, rather, to the hostility of Government to large-scale private enterprise, the resulting fears of nationalization, and the structure of profit-making opportunities, which made small-scale money-lending, trade, construction and other activities more attractive to those with limited capital than pooling their funds in larger ventures.

CHAPTER 25

Problems of Finance

The key weaknesses in finance which emerged during the course of the economic development program were the same weaknesses which hampered every other aspect of the program. They boiled down, essentially, to lack of determination to make the effort necessary. The same determination which was needed to mobilize material and manpower resources more effectively, to invigorate public administration and to coordinate, supervise and expedite the total effort would have sufficed also to mobilize the financial resources required. Neither in finance, nor in the many-faceted effort required to mobilize it, were the Burmese ready and willing to pay the "price" of development. This reluctance, rather than inability to provide the necessary finance, was the major problem.

BASIC ATTITUDES AND BACKGROUND

Despite their Socialist convictions, the basic attitude of the Burmese leaders toward finance was at the outset essentially conservative. The years of high rice prices and budgetary surpluses confirmed their adherence to the concept of balanced budgets and the repugnance they felt for deficit financing. Much serious soul-searching and internal debate went on within the Government when it was confronted by a crisis situation in 1954–55. Cuts in the capital program could contribute only partly to solution of the difficulty. The Government was definitely unwilling to impose a substantially heavier tax load on the masses of the people, and substantial increases in tax revenue could be achieved in no other way. Its inclination was to resort to deficit financing and to cut consumer imports to the bone. This expedient, with its threat of serious inflation, the economic consultants opposed. The Government, they felt, could in time be persuaded to pursue a more productive tax policy. Meanwhile, foreign loans could fill the gap. The Government's reluctance to borrow abroad was overcome, finally, only by its even greater reluctance to tax the masses or to incur large-scale domestic inflation, to the dangers of which it had been made sensitive. It therefore decided in favor of foreign borrowing.

The size of the financial problem, once the situation had more or less stabilized in the middle of the development period, may be simply presented. The Government needed some K 140 crores per year — approximately K 90 crores for current expenditures and about K 50 crores for capital expenditures. Income varied from K 80 to K 120 crores per year, depending mostly on the size of S.A.M.B. earnings, which in turn depended on the volume of rice exports and the level of rice prices. With a substantial contribution from the S.A.M.B., the additional financing needed might be as little as K 20 crores — a problem of quite modest proportions. A poor year for S.A.M.B. might swell the deficit to K 60 crores — an almost insuperable problem. There could thus be no effective solution to the finance problem apart from a rice export volume of, say, 2 million tons per year and S.A.M.B. earnings of, say, K 25 to K 30 crores. The rice export problem was central to the finance problem as well as to the foreign exchange problem. S.A.M.B. earnings of K 30 crores would mean Government revenues of about K 110 crores, and pose the problem of financing a deficit of some K 30 crores. It was, as we shall see, well within the capacity of the Government to solve a finance problem of this magnitude.

It was perhaps unfortunate that in 1952 and the early part of 1953, when the basic plan was taking shape, the outlook for financing the development program appeared so bright. The high price of export rice and the prospects for rapid increases in production and export surpluses led to the conclusion that Burma could finance her development with her own resources, and also to the impression that no great effort would be required to mobilize those resources, so far as domestic finance was concerned. The consultants cautioned, to be sure, that the problem of domestic finance might very well be difficult. However, as has already been pointed out, their appraisal of the difficulty was softened by the unfounded expectation that the Government's current budgetary expenditures could be held at the then prevailing annual level of some K 70 crores and by their realization that excess foreign exchange earnings from rice could be converted into domestic finance, in significant degree, by imports for sale to the private sector. Their warning about domestic finance was therefore not taken seriously, and the Government embarked on its large-scale development program without any real appreciation of the possible need for sacrifices.

THE CHANGING NATURE OF THE PROBLEM

The sharp break in the rice export market which began in 1953 diverted the attention of both the Government and the economic consultants to the foreign exchange problem. To the consultants, the dangerous decline in the foreign exchange reserves required, primarily, four steps — first, a sharp cutback in the overambitious 1954–55 capital program; second, a major effort to spur lagging rice production and export tonnages; third, a complementary effort to mobilize loans and assistance from abroad in order to hold the line until adequate export earnings were achieved; and fourth, a serious effort to strengthen domestic finance, to enable it to provide the major part of the financing for the development effort in the future. Indeed, early in 1954, before the foreign exchange "crisis," they had arranged for a special study of this problem. Dr. Richard Musgrave made the study in the summer of 1954, and it was presented to the Government in the fall.[1] His analysis strongly pointed up the prospective insufficiency of domestic finance and recommended a comprehensive program for broadening and strengthening the tax structure. By this time the Government was already becoming immersed in the developing foreign exchange "crisis," but did not appear to perceive its relation to domestic finance.[2] The Musgrave report made little impact.

During 1954–55, the capital program was cut back sharply from its impossible initial level of K 98 crores. By 1955–56, it had been reduced to a minimum essential level of roughly K 50 crores (a level around which it would thereafter continue narrowly to fluctuate), and substantial foreign resources had been mobilized for early use: a $19 million World Bank loan, a $15 million draw from the International Monetary Fund, an Indian loan of K 20 crores, a P.L. 480 purchase of nearly $20 million worth of surplus commodities from the United States for local currency, indeterminate though sizable U.S.S.R. credits and a $25 million U. S. development loan. These supplemented the ten-year $200 million reparations agreement previously concluded with Japan, on which payments were now to begin. Meanwhile, deficit financing and foreign exchange drawdowns were used in large amounts to cover the sizable deficiencies of current domestic finance.

The picture then changed markedly. Rice export tonnages increased substantially in 1955–56. But though volume rose, prices continued to drop, and the deficiency in domestic finance was even greater than it had been in the previous four years. Beginning in 1956–57 and continuing through 1959–60, foreign loans and credits made up the greater part of the deficiency previously met by deficit financing and foreign exchange drawdowns. The efforts of the economic consultants to convince the Government that reliance on foreign loans could be temporary only, and that it was essential to utilize the opportunity they provided to develop a sound program for the mobilization of domestic finance, were for the most part ineffective. In June 1957 U Nu apparently intended to take action, but his intention dissolved with the A.F.P.F.L. split. One of the final efforts made by the consultants, a second

---

1. "Tax Policy for Economic Development in Burma," Robert R. Nathan Associates, Inc., Rangoon, Jan. 1955.

2. The failure to strengthen domestic finance imposed a choice between domestic inflation and large-scale import programs, which would aggravate the foreign exchange problem.

report by Dr. Musgrave (in the fall of 1958),[3] was submerged by the incoming military tide. While the Ne Win Government took some of the steps necessary in 1958–59, these were only partial and preliminary steps. As of the end of 1960, the real job remained to be done.

THE STRUCTURE OF THE GOVERNMENT'S FINANCIAL OPERATIONS

With this overview, the several aspects of the finance problem may now be examined more precisely. The first step is to view the key elements in the Government's financial operations, beginning with the Union Government Budget for the years 1952–53 through 1959–60. These figures are presented in Table 70.

Over the eight-year period, it will be noted, budgetary receipts ranged roughly from K 80 crores to K 120 crores, with current receipts accounting for about five sixths of the total. Budgetary expenditures ranged roughly from K 95 crores to K 140 crores. Current expenditures rose in four steps from some K 65 crores in 1952–53 to about K 100 crores at the end of the period. The capital expenditures shown in the budget do not include capital expenditures made by the Government boards and corporations with funds from sources other than the formal budget. These additional capital outlays, as will be seen, were substantial.

During the eight-year period, a budgetary surplus was experienced only in 1956–57. In all other years, the excess of expenditures ranged roughly from K 15 crores to K 30 crores — anywhere from one seventh to one third in excess of the receipts as shown, and even larger in relation to receipts net of domestic borrowings. Neither the receipts nor the expenditures shown reflect the operations of the state-owned boards and corporations on current account, which are entirely outside the Union Government Budget. For an understanding of the problem, the Government's financial operations must be viewed as a whole. This comprehensive budget of the public sector is provided in Table 71.

The startling fact immediately apparent is that the total financial operations of the Government and its agencies were approximately 2.5 times the size reported in the official Government budget. The major differences, on both the receipts and the expenditures sides, are in the current operations of the state-owned boards and corporations. Loans from abroad are also an important factor on the receipts side in the later years. Another important fact is that, with the exception of 1953–54 and 1954–55, deficits in the comprehensive budget were held to relatively modest proportions, by virtue to be sure, of substantial loans and assistance from abroad. The figures on the deficits in

3. "The Finance of Capital Formation and the Contribution of Tax Policy in Burma," Robert R. Nathan Associates, Inc., Rangoon, Sept. 5, 1958. This report, more than the one of 1953, stressed the need for improved tax enforcement, broader sales taxation, revitalized land revenue, and improved efficiency in the public boards and corporations.

Table 70

THE UNION GOVERNMENT BUDGET, 1952–53 TO 1959–60

(K Crores)

	1952–53	1953–54	1954–55	1955–56	1956–57	1957–58	1958–59	1959–60 Revised Estimates
1. Receipts	81.9	99.6	110.6	76.0	120.9	112.9	104.5	120.9
a. Current	—	84.5	94.0	73.8	96.2	101.9	91.7	105.4
b. Capital	—	15.1	16.6	2.2	24.7	11.0	12.8	15.5
2. Expenditures	96.4	130.0	126.8	102.7	115.7	129.8	132.6	139.5
a. Current	64.6	75.7	73.1	74.5	81.5	93.7	96.5	103.9
b. Capital	31.8	54.3	53.7	28.2	34.2	36.1	36.1	35.6
i. Ordinary	23.8	32.7	20.8	16.0	16.9	18.1	17.3	21.0
ii. Loans and advances to bds. and corps.	8.0	6.8	22.5	12.2	17.3	18.0	18.8	14.6
iii. Loan repayment	—	14.8	10.4	—	—	—	—	—
3. Excess of expenditures	15.3	30.4	16.2	26.7	—5.2	16.9	28.1	18.6
4. Deficit as shown in budget	—2.4	—29.5	12.0	3.4	n.a.	—2.4	—2.7	.7
5. Excess of expenditures financed by:								
a. Borrowing	17.7	15.8	14.6	22.0	4.1	11.4	30.8	19.9
b. Change in cash balances	2.4	—42.2ᵃ	—1.6	—4.7	—1.1	.5	2.7	1.3

Source: Economic Survey of Burma, various years through 1960, except for lines 5a and 5b, 1957–58, which are based on *Selected Economic Indicators*, C.S.E.D., New Secretariat, Rangoon, March 1960, Table 4.

a. Covers also repayment of K 12.7 crores for miscellaneous internal debts.

Note: The deficit as shown in the budget (line 4) differs from the excess of expenditures over receipts (line 3) because domestic borrowing is included in the budget as a receipts item. Capital expenditures do not include all capital outlays made by the boards and corporations. Their self-financed expenditures and expenditures financed by borrowing from banks are excluded.

Table 71

COMPREHENSIVE BUDGET OF THE PUBLIC SECTOR, 1952–53 TO 1959–60

(K Crores)

	1952–53	1953–54	1954–55	1955–56	1956–57	1957–58	1958–59	1959–60 Revised Estimates
Receipts								
1. Revenue receipts	224.5	211.3	252.7	265.1	336.4	306.5	317.7	339.6
2. Loan receipts	81.2	84.5	94.0	73.8	96.3	95.0	95.5	102.4
a. Foreign	13.0	20.8	16.4	25.5	22.5	15.1	27.0	17.5
b. Domestic	—				20.4	13.0	25.9	15.6
3. Other receipts, incl. reparations	13.0				2.1	2.1	1.1	1.9
(reparations)	1.7				27.7	17.8	14.0	12.6
4. Boards and corporations	129.1	106.0	142.3	165.8	189.9	178.6	181.2	207.1
Expenditures								
5. Current, mins. and deptmts.	215.3	263.4	298.3	276.5	328.4	314.7	324.1	348.4
6. Current, bds. and corps.	64.6	75.6	73.1	74.5	81.5	91.4	93.5	103.9
7. Capital, mins. and deptmts.	118.0	119.2	153.9	153.7	193.2	171.0	178.9	190.7
8. Capital, bds. and corps.	24.1	54.6[a]	32.0[b]	16.1	17.0	19.0	18.7	20.6
	8.6	14.0	39.3	32.2	31.1	33.3	33.0	33.2
					5.6[c]			
Surplus or deficit	8.2	—52.1	—45.6	—11.4	8.0	—8.2	—6.4	—8.8

Sources: Economic Survey of Burma, various years through 1960; and, for 1952–53 data, *Case Study of Planning for Balanced Social and Economic Development in Burma,* C.S.E.D, New Secretariat, Rangoon, Jan. 30, 1960, Table 1, p. 20.

a. Includes foreign debt, repayment of K 14.8 crores to the United Kingdom and India.

b. Includes India's debt settlement of K 10.4 crores.

c. Unclassified Japanese reparations.

Note: Capital expenditures as shown in the tables in this chapter differ somewhat from those shown in Table 55 in Chapter 20 for two reasons. They include, of necessity, foreign debt repayments in 1953–54 and 1954–55, whereas the earlier table appropriately does not. Table 55 also includes preliminary actual figures for capital expenditures in 1959–60, whereas earlier "revised estimates," because of their relation to the other data, are retained here. The subsequent analysis is not affected, although some of the computations would be modified to a trifling degree.

414

the comprehensive budget conceal, however, a significant difference between the Government's financial transactions at home and its dealings abroad, and thus conceal also the effect of these operations on the privately held money supply — a most important factor. This effect is revealed in the cash-consolidated budget of the Union Government presented in Table 72.

This table shows, in each year, varying but substantial surpluses on foreign account and varying but substantial cash deficits on transactions with the private sector at home. It was the excess of private foreign payments over receipts, varying with the volume of imports for private use, which reduced this domestic cash deficit and thus held the private money supply in check. The privately held money supply rose swiftly in 1954–55 and 1955–56, was reduced by virtue of a huge import program in 1956–57, was stabilized in 1957–58 and rose sharply again, because of a reduced import program, in 1958– 59. These interrelations, of far greater importance in the Burmese economy than in one less dependent on foreign trade, have profound implications for the financial problems to be examined, and for fiscal, monetary, import and foreign exchange policies.

HOW PUBLIC CAPITAL EXPENDITURES WERE FINANCED

With these data available for reference, we may examine the non-inflationary sources of financing, or actual resources, which were available for the public capital program. These are derived, though not in all their detail, from Table 71, and are shown in Table 73. The domestic resources are the current surpluses of the ministries and departments and of the boards and corporations, the rehabilitation contribution made by the State Agricultural Marketing Board,[4] the miscellaneous capital receipts of the boards and corporations, and "other receipts." Unfortunately, the S.A.M.B. "rehabilitation contribution" — which represents the transfer to the Government treasury of after-tax profits made by that organization — was not treated in a uniform way in Government accounting in the early years of the program. S.A.M.B. profits are reflected in the table partly in the income taxes paid by that organization, which enter into the current surpluses of the ministries and departments. In the early years of the series, additional profits were used to convert current deficits of all boards and corporations other than the S.A.M.B. into the current surpluses shown. Still other S.A.M.B. profits are reflected in "other receipts." This splintered and non-comparable bookkeeping, employed to conceal from Burma's rice customers the size of S.A.M.B. profits during years of high rice prices, makes it somewhat difficult to portray precisely the contribution made to Burma's domestic finance by the organization. It may be

4. Conceptually, the Civil Supplies Management Board was also included here. It was, however, only a negligible factor in the "rehabilitation contribution."

Table 72

Cash Consolidated Budget of the Union Government and Its Effect on the Privately Held Money Supply, 1953–54 to 1959–60

(K Crores)

	1953–54	1954–55	1955–56	1956–57	1957–58	1958–59	1959–60 Revised Estimates
1. Receipts of Union Government	211.3	252.7	265.1	336.4	306.5	317.7	339.6
2. Less receipts from abroad	73.4	90.3	109.0	129.8	109.5	122.9	124.6
3. Equal: Domestic receipts	137.9	162.4	156.1	206.6	197.0	194.8	215.0
4. Expenditure of Union Government	263.4	298.3	276.5	328.4	314.7	324.1	348.4
5. Less payments abroad	61.8	56.0	48.7	56.5	56.6	63.9	59.7
6. Equal: Domestic payments	201.6	242.3	227.8	271.9	258.1	260.2	288.7
7. Cash deficit with private sector	63.7	79.9	71.7	65.3	61.1	65.4	73.7
8. Less: Excess of private foreign payments over receipts	55.1	55.9	47.3	86.9	54.9	46.5	61.9
9. Adjustment for other factors[a]	1.4	4.7	2.5	7.0	−1.5	2.0	−10.0
10. Increase in private money supply	7.2	19.3	26.9	−14.6	7.7	20.9	1.8

Source: Economic Survey of Burma, 1954 through 1960 issues.

a. Net changes in bank credit, private savings, errors and omissions.

Table 73

RESOURCES AVAILABLE FOR PUBLIC CAPITAL EXPENDITURES, 1952–53 TO 1959–60

(K Crores)

	1952–53	1953–54	1954–55	1955–56	1956–57	1957–58	1958–59	1959–60 Revised Estimates
Public capital expenditures	32.7	68.6	71.3	48.3	53.7	52.3	51.7	53.8
Current surpluses, mins. and depts.	16.6	8.9	20.9	–.7	14.8	3.6	2.0	–1.5
Current surpluses, bds. and corps.	10.8	–13.2	–11.6	12.1	–3.3	7.6	2.3	16.4
Rehabilitation contribution, S.A.M.B.					10.0		1.0	
Capital receipts, bds. and corps.	.5				3.0	2.0	1.4	1.0
Other receipts	13.0	20.8	16.4	15.1	2.0	2.9	1.8	6.4
Subtotal, domestic finance	39.1	16.5	25.7	26.5	26.5	16.1	8.5	22.3
Japanese reparations				2.9	14.0	10.0	10.9	9.5
P.L. 480					10.0		9.1	
U.S. loan						3.2	6.8	5.3
India loan					10.0	5.0		5.0
I.B.R.D.					1.2	3.7	2.8	2.7
I.M.F.				7.1				
U.S.S.R. credit						1.1	2.2	2.5
Less, loan repayments and debt servicing								–2.4
Subtotal, foreign finance				10.0	35.2	23.0	31.8	22.7
Total finance	39.1	16.5	25.7	36.5	61.7	39.1	40.3	45.0
Surplus or deficit	6.4	–52.1	–45.6	–11.8	8.0	–13.2	–11.4	–8.8

Sources: Economic Survey of Burma, various years through 1960; and, for 1952–53 data, *Case Study of Planning for Balanced Social and Economic Development in Burma*, C.S.E.D., New Secretariat, Rangoon, Jan. 30, 1960, Table 2.

Note: Corrections made in the Japanese reparations for 1957–58 and in the India loan for 1958–59 provide deficits in those years which are not consistent with the comprehensive budget deficits shown in Table 71. The official foreign finance data cited above are marred by certain omissions and errors. The U. S. technical assistance program was still functioning in 1952–53. Outlays during that year and additional "close-out" payments during the following two years amounted to some K 4.5 crores. The U. S. loan figures for 1957–58, 1958–59 and 1959–60 are not accurately revised. They add up to K 15.3 crores ($22.1 million) against a total availability of about K 12 crores ($25 million). I.C.A. figures put the actual expenditures through Sept. 30, 1960 at K 4.3 crores ($8.9 million). Since this U. S. aid shortfall is partly offset by the earlier omission, of some K 2.4 crores of U. S. aid under P.L. 480 (1041) in 1958–59 and various other aid items, and since the over-all magnitudes in the table are not seriously distorted by these errors, the official figures have been permitted here to stand. I.B.R.D. figures are also overstated. These should total K 8.5 crores, rather than the K 10.4 crores shown.

said, however, that during 1952–53, 1953–54 and 1954–55[5] S.A.M.B.'s contribution to Government finance averaged some K 40 crores per year — about 80 per cent of average annual capital expenditures during the life of the eight-year capital program.

The foreign finance items shown in the table reflect, of course, not the loans and credits available to Burma but rather the portions of these actually used each year. The surplus or deficit data correspond naturally with the surplus or deficit figures shown in the comprehensive budget.

It is clear from an examination of Table 73 how the finance problem varied during the program period. In 1952–53 large S.A.M.B. earnings bolstered domestic finance and, since public capital expenditures were then at their lowest level, sufficed to produce a surplus of resources over capital requirements. In the next two years very substantial deficits were incurred, particularly in 1953–54 and 1954–55. These were the years when capital expenditures (including repayment of pre-war debts) were at their highest, and when the volume of rice exports did not rise sufficiently to compensate for rapidly falling prices. Conditions were already stabilizing in 1955–56, when rice exports increased sharply to nearly 2 million tons and the collection of invoices unpaid during the previous year in large part offset further price declines. By this time the capital program had been reduced to less than K 50 crores, and the deficit was much lower than those of the two previous years. In the following four years, 1956–57 through 1959–60, a substantial inflow of foreign aid and credits bolstered a progressively weaker domestic financial position, and made it possible to meet the requirements of a stable capital expenditure program without further substantial domestic deficit financing.

The total finance picture may be viewed more clearly, if we ignore the internal differences during the first four years of the program, and compare the financing of public capital expenditure during that period with the financing in the second four-year period. This comparison is made in Table 74. Almost half the public capital expenditures of K 221 crores during the first four years was financed by domestic resources, and 5 per cent was financed by foreign aid. The remaining 46 per cent was financed largely by an inflationary expansion of the privately held money supply, though there was a drawdown of past national savings in the form of the foreign exchange reserves.[6]

In the next four years, domestic finance contributed an even smaller portion — one third as against the previous one half — of the cost of public capital expenditure. More than half the cost during this period was met by repara-

5. Cash profits in 1954–55 were bolstered, despite lower prices, not only by an increase in export volume but also by the sale of considerable tonnage purchased the year before.

6. Money supply expansion and foreign exchange drawdowns as shown in the table only roughly approximate the resource deficits indicated. This may be due to the use of unadjusted money supply figures.

Table 74

FINANCING OF PUBLIC CAPITAL EXPENDITURE, 1952–53 TO 1959–60

	1952–53 to 1955–56		1956–57 to 1959–60		1952–53 to 1959–60	
	K Crores	Per Cent	K Crores	Per Cent	K Crores	Per Cent
1. Public capital expenditure	220.9ᵃ	100.0	206.0	100.0	426.9	100.0
2. Current surplus, ministries and departments	45.8	20.7	18.9	9.2	64.7	15.2
3. Current surplus, boards and corporations	–1.4	–.6	23.0	11.2	21.6	5.1
4. Other receipts	65.3	29.6	24.8	12.0	90.1	21.1
5. Domestic resources (lines 2+3+4)	109.7	49.7	66.7	32.4	176.4	41.3
6. Japanese reparations	2.9	1.3	44.4	21.5	47.3	11.1
7. Foreign loans and P.L. 480	7.1	3.2	67.3	32.7	74.4	17.4
8. Foreign resources (lines 6 + 7)	10.0	4.5	111.7	54.2	121.7	28.5
9. Total resources (lines 5 + 8)	119.7	54.2	178.4	86.6	298.1	69.8
10. Indicated deficit	101.2	45.8	27.6	13.4	128.8	30.2
11. Deficit financed by:						
a. Expansion in privately held money supplyᵇ	73.8		24.1ᶜ		97.9ᶜ	
b. Drawn of foreign exchange reserves	21.2		3.6ᶜ		24.8ᶜ	

Sources: Selected Economic Indicators, C.S.E.D., New Secretariat, Rangoon, March 1960; *Economic Survey of Burma 1960* for data on money supply and foreign exchange; other data from Table 73.

a. Includes repayment of K 25.2 crores of pre-war debt, K 15.6 crores to India and K 9.6 crores to the United Kingdom.
b. Unadjusted for changes in private savings and bank credit.
c. Through March 1960 only.

Note: For corrections to data shown in lines 7 and 8, see note to Table 73.

tions, borrowing and other aid[7] from abroad. Reparations contributed about one fifth of total requirements, while foreign loans, credits and P.L. 480 contributed approximately one third. Combined with domestic finance, these resources sufficed to meet 87 per cent of the requirements. The deficit of some 13 per cent was again met by monetary expansion and by a further drawdown of foreign exchange reserves. But the amounts involved were far less than in the previous four years, and constituted neither inflationary pressure nor a serious weakening of the balance of payments and monetary reserve positions.

Tables 73 and 74 make quite plain how Burma met the major financial problems raised by her development program. In the first place, the program was cut back to what was, in effect, a minimum level of average annual capital expenditure of about K 50 crores. Second, national dissaving and monetary expansion and foreign finance were relied upon to fill the substantial gap between this minimum capital expenditure and the negligible contribution made by current domestic resources. And throughout the period the Government walked, as it were, on a tightrope, with domestic inflation looming on one side and foreign exchange loss yawning on the other.

It is possible now, with the aid of the data already cited, to review what the possibilities for a sounder financing of the program actually were — first on the expenditure side and then on the revenue side.

THE POTENTIALS FOR A STURDIER DOMESTIC FINANCE

Concerning capital expenditures, not much needs to be said. An initial and serious error was indeed made in adopting an over-large program for 1954–55. This mistake was subsequently rectified as rapidly as was possible in view of the very large level of commitments. The repayment of the pre-war debt to India was not an ill-timed action and did not weaken the foreign exchange reserve position. It was only the difference between the cash price India was willing to pay for rice (£35 per ton) and the "prevailing" market price of £48 per ton. By 1955–56, the level of the capital program had been reduced to an average of roughly K 50 crores per year, which was virtually an irreducible level if provision was to be made for defense needs, the minimum rehabilitation requirements for agriculture, forestry, mining and transport and communications, the pressing social needs and the amounts required to carry through the electric power and manufacturing industry improvements on which commitments had already been made.

Although current budgetary expenditures of the Union Government, as shown in Table 70, rose more than 50 per cent from the K 65 crores spent in 1952–53, there was not much possibility of holding these in check, either.

7. P.L. 480 assistance, in the form of commodity sales for local currency, brings in real resources but is not borrowing. On the other hand, the borrowing of P.L. 480-generated local currencies which follows from the sale of P.L. 480 goods is borrowing but does not add real resources.

Expenditures for the defense services accounted for roughly one third of the total. Essential administrative services, including the costs of tax collection, police and general administration accounted for nearly one third more. Social services, chiefly those for education and health, accounted for less than one fifth of current Governmental expenditures at the outset of the program. These needs were pressing and grew through the years. The same may be said for the productive services, such as agriculture, forestry, transport, communications and others, which accounted for about one eighth of current Governmental expenditures. Many of these outlays, as in the case of agricultural extension, were essential to complement the expenditures of the capital program itself. Finally, transfer payments, including interest charges, pension payments and contributions to the various state governments, provided little or no room for curtailment. The problem of domestic finance therefore had to be met on the revenue rather than the expenditure side. Some of the possibilities here can be explored by reference to the Union Government's budgetary receipts in detail, shown in Table 75.

It may first be noted that after 1952–53 the total of budgetary receipts varied relatively little, apart from the sharp dip in 1955–56. For the eight-year period as a whole, tax receipts accounted for approximately five eighths of the total. Income taxes provided only about one fifth of total receipts, while indirect taxes, mostly on commodities — customs, excise duties, sales and commercial taxes — accounted for roughly three eighths. Taxes other than these made only a negligible contribution. Reparations made a significant contribution to non-tax receipts only in the second half of the period. Non-tax receipts from ministries and departments and contributions from boards and corporations each accounted for about three sevenths of this non-tax total. However, while the contributions of the ministries and departments increased substantially during the period, the contributions from boards and corporations fell.

It is clear that non-tax receipts, particularly those in the form of contributions from the boards and corporations, depended heavily on rice export sales and profits. It is not equally clear, but important to understand, that tax receipts themselves depended heavily on this same factor, not only because a substantial part of the income taxes shown were taxes on S.A.M.B. income, but also because customs and excise duty revenues depended heavily on the volume of import goods, which in turn was determined largely by foreign exchange earnings from the sale of rice. With this in mind, we may examine more closely the possibilities of more substantial contributions to domestic finance from the various types of taxation.

Customs rates and excise duties on imports were broadly progressive taxes, and rates were set partly with a view to protecting burgeoning local industry. In general, rates were lowest on essential goods bought by low-income groups and highest on luxury goods. Revenues from these taxes were strengthened

Table 75

UNION GOVERNMENT BUDGETARY RECEIPTS, 1952–53 TO 1959–60

(K Crores)

	1952–53	1953–54	1954–55	1955–56	1956–57	1957–58	1958–59	1959–60 Revised Estimates
Total receipts	81.1	99.6	110.6	76.0	121.1	112.9	104.5	120.9
1. Tax receipts	37.7	71.8	63.9	59.1	75.1	72.6	65.0	79.0
Customs	20.0	25.5	25.5	21.4	29.8	27.9	23.0	30.5
Excise duties	3.8	1.9	2.3	3.9	4.6	8.1	8.5	9.6
Taxes on income	5.4	33.3	24.3	22.4	26.4	22.8	19.3	22.8
Land revenue	1.9	1.8	2.4	2.2	2.5	3.0	4.2	3.5
Excise		2.3	3.0	3.3	3.8	4.0	4.0	3.9
Stamps	.4	.5	.5	.7	.5	.7	.8	.8
Commercial taxes	6.2	5.8	5.1	4.3	6.3	5.0	4.6	7.8
Other taxes		.7	.8	.9	1.2	1.1	.6	.1
2. Non-tax receipts	43.4	27.8	46.7	16.9	46.0	40.3	39.5	41.9
Ministries and departments	9.3	9.4	10.3	10.0	17.0	20.3	23.1	24.4
Contribution from boards	34.1	18.4	36.4	5.3	15.0	10.0	5.5	7.0
Reparations	—	—	—	1.6	14.0	10.0	10.9	10.5[a]

Source: Economic Survey of Burma, various years.

a. To be consistent with Table 73, this figure should be K 9.5 crores. Discrepancy is due to inconsistency in source.

during the period by selective rate increases. Their capacity to contribute to domestic finance was, however, more heavily dependent on the total volume and value of imports than on the rates themselves. Thus in 1955–56 and again in 1958–59, revenues from these sources declined significantly in spite of higher rates because the volume of imports for the private sector was curtailed. In any event, it may be said that the Government acted in reasonably effective fashion to exploit the possibilities for added customs and sales tax revenues through selective rate increases, even though it did not accept Musgrave's recommendation that the base of sales taxation rates be broadened.

Musgrave's recommendations in 1954 also stressed the desirability of broadening the income tax base by lowering the personal exemption level, although he did not anticipate that this would make a sizable early contribution to domestic finance. Substantially, company income taxes were paid only by the Government boards and corporations and by the larger (mostly foreign) firms. Personal income taxes were paid mostly by civil servants and employees of the larger firms. The share contributed by personal income taxes, as compared with company income taxes, was rather small. Since firms and government organizations paid income taxes at the rate of 50 per cent and private firms paid business taxes of 8 per cent in addition, these rates could not very well be increased. The collection of income taxes from firms and individuals other than those mentioned was administratively difficult. Nevertheless, more effective enforcement of existing income taxation, chiefly vis-à-vis small business firms and traders, offered far greater possibilities for revenue gains than did either rate increases or lowering of exemption levels.

The problem here was that so few of the firms kept proper books, and that the Government did not require them to do so. Essentially, the tax obligation of the smaller firms was set by a process of adjudication or negotiation between the firm and an income tax officer; if the firm's tax return seemed questionable, the officer reviewed it and, in effect, negotiated an amended return with the taxpayer. Many firms made no returns at all. Musgrave recommended registration of all firms and a system of penalities that would discourage fraudulent reporting. Persistent underreporting, he suggested, should be taken as *prima facie* evidence of an intent to defraud, and minimal bookkeeping rquirements for all reporting taxpayers should be imposed. Such measures could have made a welcome contribution to increased revenues, particularly for 1954–55 and 1955–56, when sharp increases in the market prices of imported commodities made for substantial windfall profits for the importing and trading communities. Unfortunately, the Government did not follow the recommendations.

Before World War II, the land revenue tax had been the Government's largest single source of income, contributing approximately 40 per cent of all tax revenue. The negligible role played by land revenue during the development period naturally raises the question why this once important source was permitted to lapse into insignificance. The chief justification lies in the fact that the nation's paddy farmers were already paying a large indirect tax in the form of the difference between the fixed price paid by the Government for their paddy and its export value. This amounted to as much as, or more than, what they had paid in land revenue taxation in pre-war days. The difference was that, in the post-war period, their contribution was accumulated by the State Agricultural Marketing Board and found various ways into the Government treasury. Thus the adjustment of land revenue assessments to make allowance for the price increases which had meanwhile occurred would have imposed a heavy and inequitable double burden on the paddy farmer. At the same time, however, failure to act on land revenue taxation permitted the non-paddy farmer to escape payment of his fair share. Obviously, action on this front was in order. Musgrave proposed to restore land revenue taxation to an important position in the tax structure. His suggestions would have expedited the reassessment process, placed the tax on farm income rather than on the economic rent basis which prevailed before World War II, and provided differential treatment for paddy and non-paddy farmers. Here, too, the Government failed to take effective action, although it appeared for a time in 1957 that it might do so.

Since the estimated gains from all Musgrave's tax recommendations would have amounted, by the end of the decade, to about K 16 crores per year, it is clear that, even if they had all been adopted, action on the tax front at best could have gone only part of the way toward meeting the resource requirements of the minimum public capital expenditure program actually carried out. Additional contributions to domestic finance would have been needed.

The chief possibility resided in the Government-owned boards and corporations. As we have seen in Table 71, by 1956–57 their scale of operations on current account approached K 200 crores, on both the receipts and the expenditures sides, yet their net surpluses on current account, as shown in Table 73, were negligible, even after bolstering by S.A.M.B. profits. Of all these, by far the most important was of course the State Agricultural Marketing Board itself.

Note has already been taken of the various ways in which the earnings of this important engine for resource mobilization found their way into the public treasury, and of the fact that for 1952–53 and the following two years this contribution averaged about K 40 crores per year. S.A.M.B. earnings, as we have seen, fell away sharply in the years following. These declines could have been checked by larger export sales based on the rice surpluses actually available, by the prevention of spoilage, and by reductions in S.A.M.B.'s costs of operation. Sufficient comment has already been made on why S.A.M.B. failed to achieve higher export volumes. This failure resulted in substantial revenue losses when spoiled rice was sold in later years for feed and industrial purposes at far lower prices than it would have brought as food. Excessive costs and loss of revenues were due also to inefficient procurement, poor milling, extra transport, storage and handling charges, pilferage and poor controls generally. A broad gauge of the additional income potentials from the rice trade is the fact that while export rice cost S.A.M.B. £28 or £29 sterling per ton in port cities, it was estimated that private millers, operating far more efficiently, could supply export rice in port cities for about £22 per ton. This difference in cost of £6 to £7 per ton, applied to exports of 2 million tons, indicates a loss of £12 to £14 million, or K 16 to K 19 crores per year. Of course, such additional revenue could have been obtained only if the rice export trade had been entrusted to the private sector, and if the entire increment in earnings had been recaptured by a matching tax on rice exports. If exporters had been permitted to retain one quarter of the increased earnings, government revenues could have been increased by about K 12 to K 15 crores per year. Such a difference would nearly have matched Musgrave's estimate of the potential of increased tax revenues.

The economic consultants recommended denationalization of the rice export trade on two separate occasions. The Government was not willing, however, to acknowledge the failure of nationalization, even for the greater efficiency and revenues in prospect. Efforts were made to spur export volumes and to achieve greater efficiency. The latter attempt was hampered by prevailing administrative limitations and the lack of experienced management. One Israeli technician, Dr. Lieber, made a substantial contribution here, but the situation required many more such people, with real authority. If the Government had been able to reduce S.A.M.B.'s excessive costs and losses by only £3 per ton, annual exports of 2 million tons would have yielded an additional £6 million or K 8 crores per year.

Substantial opportunities for increased surpluses existed also in the current operations of other state-owned enterprises, and could have been achieved by increasing sales and revenues, by effecting cost reductions or by adjustments in pricing policy. Consideration of these possibilities will require reference to data on the current income and expenditures of the larger state-owned boards other than S.A.M.B. with significant operations on current account. These data are shown for 1956–57, a good year, in Table 76.

Of these boards, by far the largest was the Civil Supplies Management Board, engaged in the supply of essential commodities to the public. The commodities handled were both foreign and domestic in origin, and comprised chiefly low-grade textiles, tinned milk and baby foods, cotton and silk yarns, rubber tires and building materials, including cement. For considerable periods of time, the C.S.M.B. had a complete monopoly on the import and distribution of the foreign commodities it handled. Its markups were rela-

Table 76

CURRENT INCOME AND EXPENDITURES OF
LARGER STATE-OWNED BOARDS, 1956–57[a]

(*K Crores*)

	Income	Expenditure	Surplus (+) or Deficit (—)
1. Civil Supplies Management Board	47.0	46.3	+ .7
2. Union of Burma Purchase Board	11.1	11.6	— .5
3. Union of Burma Railways	8.7	8.5	+ .2
4. State Timber Board	6.9	5.8	+1.1
5. Commerce Development Corporation	5.5	5.3	+ .2
6. Inland Water Transport Board	4.0	3.1	+ .9
7. Electricity Supply Board	1.2	2.3	—1.1
8. Rangoon Electricity Supply Board	1.9	1.3	+ .6
9. Port of Rangoon	3.2	2.6	+ .6
10. National Housing Board	.6	1.3	— .7
11. Union of Burma Airways Board	1.1	1.2	— .1
12. Union of Burma Shipping Board	1.1	1.1	—

Source: Budget Estimates of the Government of the Union of Burma, 1958–59, Book III.

a. This listing does not include the largest organization of all — the S.A.M.B. — whose finances are unpublished. It also excludes many large organizations whose activities are capital expenditure, and which did not have, at that time, significant operations on current account.

tively modest and barely sufficed to cover administrative and other costs. While the distribution side of the operation was far from efficient, the more significant possibility of savings probably lay on the procurement side. C.S.M.B. had no agents of its own abroad to report favorable purchase opportunities. Hampered by strict regulation and controls, it could not operate as would a private concern to negotiate favorable arrangements with captive suppliers, undertake forward commitments when this was advantageous, act quickly to buy up distress merchandise, or concentrate its purchasing in various lines to obtain favorable prices during off seasons. Apart from the tremendous savings possible on the procurement side, a more rational pricing policy — selling essential items like baby foods at only a little above cost and using higher markups on less essential commodities — would have produced additional earnings. The failure to employ such pricing merely provided opportunities for C.S.M.B. distributors — chiefly the cooperatives — to sell their supplies to the black market, or for the C.S.M.B. staff to do the same directly and pocket the difference. When individual consumers were able to buy at standard C.S.M.B. prices, they frequently resold the goods at higher prices. Additional revenues of K 3 to K 5 crores would have been feasible, without exploiting fully the distortions in local market conditions.

Much of the foregoing applies equally to the Union of Burma Purchase Board, which was responsible for some time for all procurement for Government organizations, and responsible throughout the period for purchasing all common user items for Government agencies. Although this organization added 10 or 12 per cent to the landed cost of purchased goods through its charges to the organizations it serviced, inefficient operations resulted in deficits rather than profits.[8] It might well have delivered a revenue of K 1 crore rather than a loss.

The potentials of the State Timber Board lay chiefly in higher levels of sales and shipments and in better milling to reduce waste and upgrade output. These potentials were considerable. The Commerce Development Corporation, with exclusive monopolies for the export marketing of rubber and cotton, should have delivered K 1 crore of surplus on the volume of goods handled, rather than a virtual break-even. The Inland Water Tranpsort Board, operating for much of this period at excessive freight rates because of the comparative safety of water as against road transport, should have delivered at least double the surplus shown. Its failure to do so was due to excessive staffing, inadequate maintenance and widespread graft and corruption. The addition of new craft did not result in greater reported volumes of traffic carried. Periodic checks showed many passengers and much freight traveling on the Board's river craft without payment. Widespread pilferage and damage were also costly. The Union of Burma Railways Board, also operating at high freight and passenger tariffs, delivered practically no surplus, for similar reasons. Lack of discipline in the railway shops kept much rolling stock out of service and increased turn-around time. The organization was overstaffed. Passengers and shippers both avoided payment for transport services by paying petty graft to a corrupt staff. And a more rational rate structure undoubtedly would have increased the volume of operations and revenues in sizable degree.

The operations of the Electricity Supply Board were particularly inefficient; its expenditures were more than double its income. This was due in many cases to the generation and distribution of power in areas where revenues did not suffice to pay even the cost of the fuel used to generate the power. Management was virtually non-existent. The organization was badly overstaffed. Collections were poor. The huge deficit was due also to the previously mentioned failure to solve the subsidy and interest rate questions essential to the development of a rational rate structure which would promote more power use. If the operations of the E.S.B. could not have been put on a profitable basis, surely the deficit could have been eliminated.

The current operations of the National Housing Board also showed a deficit larger than total current income. This was due chiefly to a mistaken policy of subsidizing public housing in a country where subsidies for the urban poor could come only from even poorer rural citizenry. The Union of

---

8. This accounting loss does not reflect fully the true loss to the Government from the operations of this Board. Its inefficiency often resulted in costly supply delays to the organizations serviced, and in the supply of goods of incorrect specifications as well.

Burma Airways Board, plagued by Government controls which prevented its operation on a business-like basis, could not produce a profit even though it had a high load factor, operated fully depreciated equipment, and charged a tariff equivalent to 6 cents per mile in a country where average per capita income was little over $50 per year. This was due chiefly to pilot shortages and poor maintenance, which prevented the line from keeping its Dakotas in the air enough of the time.

This brief review has suggested that a determined effort on the part of the Government could have been productive, in the case of boards other than S.A.M.B., of an additional K 10 crores or more per year, through the reduction of deficits or increases in earnings. With the S.A.M.B. operating as a state venture, but more efficiently, combined additional annual revenues could have approached K 20 crores. With the S.A.M.B. liquidated and rice returned to the private trade, additional annual revenues could have been even larger. These possibilities, together with those in the tax field outlined by Musgrave, could have yielded additional revenues approaching K 40 crores per year. These were the major, but by no means the only, possibilities available to the Government for strengthening domestic finance.

Still other important possibilities — some non-recurring in nature — were the reduction of waste in capital expenditure, the sale of public housing, the sale of shares in the Government's industrial enterprises to the public, the improved collection of outstanding loans to agriculturists and others, the assumption by local governmental bodies of some financial responsibility for schools, water supply and other local functions, more effective savings campaigns, greater encouragement to private enterprise in order to enlarge the tax base and, above all, the re-establishment of civil order to permit the economy as a whole to recover more swiftly. It was the failure of the Government to move vigorously forward on all these fronts which constituted its failure in domestic financing.

WHY THE POTENTIALS WERE NOT REALIZED

This failure was not for want of vigorous and often pressing proposals for action. The economic consultants urged all these measures at one time or another as the occasion served, and particularly at the annual budget-making time. The failure of the Government to act on most of them, and then only in minor degree, was due to a variety of reasons. First, it must be conceded that the Government did demonstrate a fair measure of self-discipline on the expenditure side in resisting strong pressures for increased current and capital expenditures. Second, it had overcome a strong initial repugnance to borrowing, especially from abroad. Third, it had made what it felt was an extraordinary effort to increase rice sales and shipments by lowering prices and by negotiating barter sales. The Government therefore felt it had already made substantial sacrifices on behalf of the capital program.

So far as taxation was concerned, the Government was perfectly willing to tax foreigners, luxury and sin. It imposed a heavy per capita burden on its resident aliens by sharply increasing entry and renewal of registration permit fees. It increased, without reluctance, duties on goods bought by higher income groups, and since liquor and tobacco were repugnant to the Buddhist scale of values, it was perfectly willing to tax these to the point of diminishing returns. But it was not willing to tax in ways that might pinch substantial numbers of voters or, for that matter, to reduce or eliminate costly subsidies or favors which insured continued political support for the A.F.P.F.L. It should be acknowledged that these political considerations had a meritorious aspect. There was a serious regard for the welfare of the common man — the *ludu* — and a disinclination to impose additional burdens on him. But without taxation which reached the masses of the people, there could be no vigorous effort at domestic finance. As regards the more effective enforcement of existing taxes, the chief opportunity here ran counter to the cherished Burmanization policy. The Government was reluctant to enforce tax collections more effectively against Burmese traders whose economic position it was trying to strengthen. And in many cases, it was these very traders who were relied upon for contributions to A.F.P.F.L. party funds.

So far as improving the efficiency of the major boards and corporations was concerned, the magnitude of this opportunity never really struck home. This was partly because the leaders were simply too inexperienced in practical affairs to appreciate the potentials, and the lack of proper accounting made it difficult to demonstrate them clearly. The ideological position that profits in the private sphere equated with exploitation probably affected the leaders' views on profit-making in public enterprises as well. In any case, the staffing and operation of public enterprises were so intimately connected with the total administrative process and so affected by political considerations that the mounting of an effective attack on their inefficiency would have required almost a political and administrative revolution. Indeed, the leadership may well have felt its position was so insecure as to make exceedingly dangerous any program that would alienate the followers, hangers-on and parasites to whom it looked for support.

The Government could not very well sell public housing, tenanted largely by underpaid civil servants and political favorites, without taking a huge and difficult-to-conceal loss or opening the way for substantial rent increases. While there was for a time some disposition to consider the sale of shares in the Government's new industrial enterprises, the leaders did not know how to go about disposing of them, and they suspected that implementation of this policy would require large and again difficult-to-conceal capital writedowns — an embarrassing prospect. The more vigorous collection of outstanding loans, and insistence on the assumption by local government bodies of increasing financial responsibility for local services, also threatened the loss of political support. Encouragement to the private sector went against the ideological grain of most of the leaders, and such steps as were taken were halting, grudging or the accidental by-product of still other situations — as in the case of the loans extended to the private sector for the purchase of machinery from barter account countries whose credits could not be used otherwise. The reasons which underlay failure of the Government vigorously to attack the problem of civil disorder have already been explored.

It may be concluded from the foregoing that Burma could, after a period of preparation, have financed a public capital program of K 50 crores per year out of current domestic resources, given the determination to do so. With foreign aid as well, she could have financed a substantially larger program. Indeed, the economic consultants for a time favored a step-up in the rate of public capital investment to K 60 crores, K 65 crores and K 70 crores for the three years beginning 1957–58. This position, incorporated in the Four-Year Plan of 1957, was based, however, on several conditions, including effective efforts to strengthen domestic finance. When it became clear that the Government was not prepared to meet the conditions, the position was abandoned. It may also be concluded that the additional resources required for the K 50 crores program could have come largely through greater increases in national income, the elimination of waste and inefficiency in the public enterprises and improved tax enforcement rather than out of the standard of living of actual producers; and that commitment to the continued nationalization of rice exports, to existing administrative and political behavior patterns, to the Burmanization policy and to a congeries of outmoded Socialist ideas and attitudes, as well as continued laxness with respect to civil disorder, effectively deterred such resource mobilization. It may further be concluded that foreign aid not only helped Burma to sustain her program, but helped to postpone the day when she would have to face up to the realities of financing her development. So long as this easier road was available, the Government was under no immediate pressure to take the more difficult, though sounder, way. In this sense foreign aid was debilitating as well as helpful.

THE PROBLEM OF DEVALUATION

Perhaps one other problem of finance should be discussed — the problem of devaluation. As of 1955–56 and 1956–57 there were many elements in the situation which seemed to favor devaluation of the kyat to help meet the problem of domestic finance. In the first place, since S.A.M.B.'s sales were for foreign exchange, the conversion of its sales proceeds into local currency at a devalued rate would increase its earnings and hence its ability to contribute to Government revenues. Secondly, part of the additional revenues could be paid to the paddy cultivator in the form of a higher purchase price for domestic paddy. This would not only reduce the inequity under which the paddy farmer labored as compared with non-paddy farmers, but might also act as a spur to increased paddy output. Third, since most imported goods were then selling for prices 50 to 100 per cent higher than landed cost, devaluation would not necessarily raise prices to the consumer, but would tend to come out of the windfall profits then being enjoyed by importers and distributors, who were, for the most part, evading taxation. Devaluation would also spur export of minerals, timber and other products, as well as that of rice, stimulate domestic production, reduce the propensity to import and the temptation to capital flight, and cut down the need for import and foreign exchange controls as well. Finally, since the kyat was being sold on the black market at some 40 per cent of its value by people who wanted to get money out of the country, and traded at such rates in the free Bangkok and Hong Kong markets, it could be argued that most of the effects of devaluation had already been registered.

These considerations were seriously debated within the economic consultants' group, although they were at no time presented to the Government for consideration. Major reasons for doubting the advisability of devaluation were, first, a conviction that it should be only a last resort after all other possible corrective measures had failed; second, the belief that supply deficiencies, due primarily to administrative bungling and the temporary necessity to rely on restrictive barter credits, would soon be corrected, with a substantial easing of prices for imported goods; third, the expectation that with rice export prices stabilizing and volumes increasing, foreign exchange availabilities would permit the inflow in the future of an adequate volume of imports; and, finally, serious doubt whether an increase in the domestic price of paddy would, in the face of continued civil disorder, actually result in a sizable increase in paddy production. The weakness of the kyat in illegal domestic and free foreign markets reflected the stringency of the Government's transfer and remittance controls vis-à-vis its large resident alien groups as much as it did a basic weakness in the currency itself, and in any case, the volume of such trading was limited.

These negative considerations seemed at the time to make advisable the postponement of a decision on devaluation. When the Government in 1956–57 introduced further distortions in the structure of the import trade in the form of the Joint Venture Trading Companies and domestic prices stabilized at levels near their swollen peaks instead of declining, the case for devaluation in the fall of 1957 seemed stronger than it had been before. But in the last analysis there was continued doubt whether a devaluation of the currency and a higher domestic price for paddy would indeed result in a substantial increase in paddy production. It was this, combined with the conviction that dynamic action to strengthen the tax structure and to improve the efficiency of board and corporation operations could solve the finance problem, which influenced the economic consultants against recommending devaluation.

CHAPTER 26

Problems of Annual Budgeting

and Programing

The annual budget and program set targets for development spending each year, adapting the long-term program as required, and attempted at the same time to insure economic stability. Severe fluctuations in the Government's financial fortunes, sharp swings in the international balance of payments and disparate rates of progress in the various economic sectors gave the annual budget-making and programing processes an even greater importance than they otherwise would have had. Because of these factors, the processes presented novel and major challenges each year. Those responsible for meeting the challenges required steady nerves, flexibility, technical grasp and incisive judgment.

THE INTEGRATED PROCESS

The budgeting and programing processes, while not identical, had of necessity to be coordinated. The Union Government Budget, as we have seen, accounted for only some 40 per cent of the Government's total financial activities and had to be set within the broader framework of the comprehensive budget for the public sector as a whole. Program decisions had to take account of probable impact on the domestic money supply and the international balance of payments. These were projected, tested and shown, as reconciled, in the cash-consolidated and foreign exchange budgets. It was also necessary, for practical reasons, to coordinate these program elements with an import program.[1] And in many cases, capital expenditure programs required comple-

1. In the earlier years, all these program elements were set within the even broader framework of an explicit economic budget for the nation, which projected the national output by the eco-

mentary provisions in the current expenditure budget. The testing of proposed programs against the comprehensive and cash-consolidated budgets frequently called for adjustments in the Union Government Budget, in the form of either curtailments of proposed expenditures or action to augment revenues. Finally, the budget review afforded the planners their best opportunity to judge how effectively capital projects and programs were being implemented, to probe for soft spots in the program and to put pressure on the implementing agencies to take remedial action.

The integrated budgeting and programing operation began in March and was timed so that the completed product could be presented to the budget session of the Parliament late in August. The budget call went out, ordinarily, in February. Submissions were made in duplicate to the Ministry of Finance and Revenue, which forwarded copies to the Ministry of National Planning. The Finance Ministry was primarily responsible for estimates of tax and non-tax budget receipts, while the Planning Ministry developed the total resource picture, which included estimates of board and corporation surpluses and foreign resources. The Finance Ministry reviewed the current expenditure submissions of the ministries and departments, and determined the total. The Planning Ministry was responsible for review of the current operating budgets of the boards and corporations and for the capital budget review. Actually, the Finance Ministry reconciled its estimates of budgetary revenues and current budgetary expenditure needs with the Planning Ministry, while that Ministry reached agreement with the Ministry of Finance on the estimates for which it took prime responsibility. Usually, Finance estimated receipts low and current expenditure needs high, so as to show less available for capital spending. But it generally recognized the criticisms made by the Planning Ministry of its initial figures, and revised them accordingly.

The review of current and capital budgets took place concurrently within a framework of tentative, comprehensive, cash-consolidated and foreign exchange budgets worked out by the Planning Ministry on the basis of the broad initial agreements. Thus if the broad program projections indicated that current budgetary expenditures of, say, K 90 crores and a capital expenditure program of, say, K 50 crores would be feasible, and that foreign exchange available for public capital expenditures would be, say, K 30 crores, the Finance and Planning Ministry reviews would proceed with these indicated over-all limitations in mind. During the process, budget and program would be adjusted to each other and, finally, to such changes as might be made in

nomic sectors and the major uses of the resources so generated. For reasons which will by now be apparent, the outcomes for 1954–55 were so wide of the projections in the economic budget for that year that this broadest of programing devices was discontinued as a formal exercise and was thereafter utilized only informally within the Planning Ministry.

the key figures. Meanwhile, the Minister of Finance, the Minister for National Planning and the Chairman of the Economic and Social Board (in the latter two instances the Prime Minister was for most of the period the effective, if not the nominal, minister in charge) would be advised by their secretaries of the way budget and program were shaping up, and their views would be obtained on the major policy questions involved. Upon completion of the work at the staff and secretaries' level, the proposed budget and program were submitted to the Economic and Social Board, and then to the Cabinet for approval.

Presentation to the Parliament, under the circumstances, was a formality only. It was made by the Finance Minister, who submitted not only the proposed Union Government Budget and, separately, the proposed current and capital expenditure budgets of the boards and corporations, but also the annual Economic Survey prepared for him by the Ministry of National Planning, which included the comprehensive and cash-consolidated budgets as well. The foreign exchange budget remained an internal executive document and was neither presented to the Parliament nor made available to the public.

In this process, the economic consultants served not only as advisors but also as the programing and budget review staff of the Planning Ministry. Fortunately, the Central Statistical and Economics Staff of the Planning Ministry were able, over the years, to play an increasingly important role. Toward the latter part of the period, the C.S.E.D. prepared independent estimates of resources, requirements and the like, and also independent analyses of capital budget submissions for consideration by the capital budget review group. By this time the consultants were able to take the quite capable C.S.E.D. estimates as a point of departure, rather than carry through the programing exercise from the beginning on their own.

If the Finance Ministry had had stronger leadership and staff, it would probably have played a much more important role. As it was, the Ministry of National Planning had the services of the economic consultants and of its own rapidly developing economic staff, while the Finance Ministry lacked the staff and know-how necessary to cope with programing and fiscal problems. Only toward the end of the period, when Bo Khin Maung Gale became Minister, did the Finance Ministry show signs of dissatisfaction with its relatively unimportant role. It thereupon made arrangements, through the International Monetary Fund, to obtain on loan the services of a competent professional, Mark Wycelkowski, to assist it in developing its own policy positions and in organizing a stronger budget review staff. Wycelkowski promptly proceeded to organize the equivalent of a bureau of the budget within the Ministry, and despite his relatively short tenure, succeeded in getting the Ministry to take the initial training steps.

COORDINATION

This description of the annual budgeting and programing process suggests that one of the major problems was coordination between the Ministries of Planning and Finance. Actually, with one quite important exception, this proved to be practically no problem at all. The Planning Ministry was careful not to usurp any of the traditional responsibilities of the Ministry of Finance, particularly with respect to estimates of tax revenues and the review of current budget requests. The Ministry of Finance, on the other hand, not only lacked the staff, the technical competence and the inclination to tackle the programing job; it had no desire to take responsibility for the formulation of fiscal policy or the review of capital programs. Even when it mistrusted or disapproved the way the development program was going, it was generally not inclined to dispute the proposals of the Planning Ministry, provided only that it was clear to all concerned that the Ministry of Finance took no responsibility for the proposed programs.

The two ministries found little difficulty in reaching agreement on the key figures — the total resources and foreign exchange likely to be available, and the limitations which should be imposed on total current Government expenditure, total capital spending, foreign exchange payments and imports for private use. The Ministry of National Planning did not question the Finance Ministry's distribution of the total amount agreed upon for current expenditure, and the Finance Ministry was not much concerned with the way the total agreed upon for capital expenditures was allotted. In any event, the so-called Committee of Deputies (later called the Committee of Experts) set up early in 1955 to review and reduce the 1954-55 capital program was, during the remainder of the program period, an effective instrument for coordination of the work of the two ministries. The Secretary of the Ministry of Finance was one of the most influential members of that Committee, which not only reviewed the capital budget submissions of all ministries, departments, boards and corporations and determined the allotments to be recommended to the Economic and Social Board and the Cabinet, but also reviewed and approved all other elements in the program—resource appraisals, the comprehensive, cash-consolidated and foreign exchange budgets, the complementary policy recommendations, and the import program as well. In effect, then, the Planning Ministry did the staff work for an inter-ministry coordinating group in which the Finance Ministry played a leading role. Both Planning and Finance were committed to the program so developed.

Coordination was seriously lacking only in reviews of the current and capital budgets of individual agencies or activities. Thus, the capital program approved for the Department of Agriculture might require a substantial expansion of the agricultural extension staff, and provision for this would be needed in the current budget. Or the capital expenditure programs of the Irrigation and Highways Departments might require provision in their current budgets for expanded engineering staffs. Since the Secretary of the Ministry of Finance was the only person in that Ministry familiar with the capital expenditure program, and since he did not personally participate in the review of its current budgets, the current budget frequently, and sometimes seriously, failed to make provision for essential expenditures complementary to the capital programs.

DEFENSE SPENDING

Another important problem, that of defense budgets, was deliberately bypassed by the planning officials. Defense accounted for approximately one third of all current Government spending, and about one fifth of all capital outlays. These requirements were handled separately from the rest of the budgeting and programing, and the programers took them as priority claims on the available resources. The review of military budgets by civilian officials is always a somewhat delicate matter. Since the foreign economic consultants played so important a role in the budgeting process, they realized that such a review would, in their case, have been intolerable, and they made their awareness of this clear at the outset of the development period. The separate mechanism established elsewhere in the Prime Minister's office for consideration of the military budget contributed importantly to the ability of the Planning Ministry and the consultants to function effectively on all other aspects of the budgeting and programing jobs. And since any increase in law and order resulting from higher military expenditures would almost certainly contribute more to economic output than would any other investment, there was little reason for the planners to be concerned about them.

PROBLEMS OF RESOURCE APPRAISAL

Difficult problems were, however, encountered in connection with the appraisal of resources. These centered for the most part around estimates of the rice surplus, the volume of shipments, the prices at which export rice could be sold and the profits and foreign exchange earnings of the State Agricultural Marketing Board. Estimates were especially difficult because the budget and program had to be whipped into shape during June and July for the fiscal year beginning October 1, while the first official estimates of the new rice crop did not become available until November, and it was only in December and January that reports from abroad indicated the probable size of export surpluses or crop deficiencies in importing countries. Old crop carryovers provided some margin for error in new crop estimates, and long-term sales agreements helped in formulating estimates of shipments, but estimates of average price were something else again. In view of the importance of rice in the resource picture, a fiscal year beginning January 1 or April 1 would have been much more suitable for planning and programing purposes than the October 1–September 30 fiscal year. The 1953–54 and 1954–55 budgets and programs were thrown off badly because of unanticipated developments in rice. Again in 1957–58, a short crop, due to bad weather, threw the budget and program calculations out quite seriously and necessitated substantial adjustments in the approved import and other programs.

The problem of forecasting rice revenues and foreign exchange earnings had another interesting facet. The estimates of probable surplus, sales, shipments, prices and earnings were prepared in the first instance by the State Agricultural Marketing Board and by the Ministry of Trade Development, to which it was administratively responsible, on the basis of crop forecasts prepared by the office of the Commissioner for Land Revenue and Settlements. Estimates of export surpluses prepared by S.A.M.B. on the basis of the total crop estimates were hampered by lack of reliable data on domestic consumption requirements, which that agency tended to overestimate. The S.A.M.B. and the Ministry of Trade Development were, moreover, inclined to be extremely conservative in their estimates of probable sales and shipments. The Ministry of National Planning and its consultants, on the other hand, were always under the necessity of putting pressure on these operating agencies to maximize forward sales and shipments, since accomplishment here was vital to the economic objectives of the Government. Yet, when the Ministry of Planning forced upon these agencies the higher export targets which it regarded as not only feasible but mandatory, and these estimates were accepted by the Economic and Social Board, it became difficult to resist demands for total and foreign exchange spending allotments at levels lower than realization of these incentive figures would have made possible. Ideally, higher estimates of earnings would have been utilized to provide incentive for the operating agencies, while more conservative figures were used for expenditure authorizations. So great, however, were the pressures for maximum allotments for current and capital expenditures and for import purposes that it was not possible to make this separation. As we have seen, S.A.M.B. sales and earnings entered into the Government revenues not only through income taxes and rehabilitation contributions but also through the customs and sales tax revenues, which varied directly with the amount of foreign exchange allocated to imports. The S.A.M.B. operation was therefore crucial, and constituted the greatest single variable in the over-all resource appraisal.

The timing of foreign resources was sometimes a problem. Thus, when the first P.L. 480 arrangement was made with the United States early in 1956, the import program had already taken into account the inflow of cotton textiles to be financed by this program in 1955–56. Actually, agreements with the processing countries which were to convert the cotton into fabrics were not concluded until July of 1956, and the first P.L. 480 cotton goods began to arrive only toward the end of the fiscal year. Similar difficulties in the timing of availabilities were encountered also in using barter credits and, until the flow started, in utilization of reparations as well. Some of these difficulties were obviated by tying specific expenditure allotments to various loan, reparations or other resources. This was intended to insure that the programs would not go forward unless the specific resources to which they were tied actually became available in time. While this prevented greater than planned deficits, it sometimes slowed down the programs so tied, and held up related programs dependent on them. In any case, such delays disrupted the desired balance in program implementation.

Another awkwardness was that such resources could not be used freely and economically. Thus, reparations credits were not freely allocable to meet any and all needs of the Government but could be used only for capital purposes, and then only for such capital requirements as could be supplied in Japan. Barter credits, not nominally restricted to capital requirements, were in practice strictly limited by availabilities and delivery prospects. In the case of both reparations and the barter countries, prices were often substantially higher than in other markets, choice was far more limited and qualities were frequently inferior. These considerations often made it uneconomic, though necessary, to utilize these restricted resources. The outcome was sometimes ludicrous, as when the Rangoon Electricity Supply Board, having been required to procure copper wire it needed under reparations from Japan, paid approximately 2.5 times the U. K. price. In the case of the U. S., tinned milk procured under P.L. 480 cost 17 per cent more than that available from Scandinavian suppliers. Such conditions made it difficult to get the operating agencies to accept allotments so restricted, and provided them with ample incentive to evade the restrictions when they could. Thus the allotment and control processes were made far more difficult than they would normally have been.

PROBLEMS OF CURRENT BUDGET REVIEW

The problems involved in the current budget review arose largely out of limitations within the Ministry of Finance and Revenue itself and in the public administration. In its review of current budget submissions, this Ministry was interested chiefly in reducing the total of current spending requests to the limit established. In making such reductions, it did not care particularly which ministries and departments were cut, or how. It was not interested in examining the submissions carefully with an eye to selective cuts. In fact, the Ministry had no staff sufficiently familiar with the duties and functions of the various ministries and departments to make selective cuts on a rational basis.

The manner in which financial sanctions were exercised by the Finance Ministry was also conducive to casual and even sloppy budget review. Approval of an agency's budget, and enactment of that budget into legislation by the Parliament, did not mean that the agency was thereupon free to spend the money, except for the pay of existing staff and routine expenditures. Items which involved additions to the staff, procurement of supplies in excess of minimum values and most other expenditures had to be submitted first to the department's own ministry for administrative approval, and then to the Ministry of Finance for financial sanction. This meant that a large part of an agency's budget, even when legislated, was still tentative and subject to two further reviews before the "authorized" monies could be spent. The Finance Ministry was therefore not very concerned at budget time with either the adequacy of budget submissions or its own review of them. It relied on the opportunity it would have later to review specific expenditures more carefully. And when requests to spend money were made, the tendency in the Finance Ministry was to let them pile up and wait. The reasoning behind this was that if a proposed expenditure were really important, the department and the administrative ministry concerned would prod the Finance Ministry for action. If these agencies did not do so, the request remained part of an ever-growing pile of "pending" requests.

Obviously, if the Finance Ministry was not concerned with the quality of current budget submissions, the agencies were not going to take great care to make their presentations as effective as possible. Weak submissions contributed even further to the disrespect shown by the Ministry of Finance for budget submissions. Where a department head or a secretary to the administrative ministry concerned was vigorous and determined, the Finance Ministry might be pressed to expedite sanctions. But in many cases this was not done, and many important activities — such as agricultural extension — were hampered by delays in getting the financial sanctions necessary. The practice of passing a supplemental budget each February — that is, toward the middle of each financial year — also contributed to careless initial current budget submissions and review. If mistakes or deficiencies in the regular governmental budget could be corrected at mid-year, it did not seem so important to get the budget right the first time.

Finally, some ministries and departments occasionally relied on the Prime Minister's known interest in their activities, and on their own ministers' ability, to get budget cuts made by Finance restored at cabinet level. This too contributed to careless budget presentation and review. Fortunately, such changes were seldom of a magnitude to throw the prepared program seriously out of balance.

PROBLEMS OF CAPITAL BUDGET REVIEW

Although the comprehensive program, and later the Four-Year Plan, provided the framework for annual capital budget proposals, agency budget proposals frequently included new projects not previously considered, for which the justifications were completely inadequate. Time pressures at budget time did not permit sufficient examination to determine whether or not such requests were justified or practical, and many hasty decisions were made. This situation was corrected, after some time, by the ruling that new project proposals needed scrutiny and approval by the Planning Ministry before they could be included in a budget submission. This proved to be an excellent control device.

Another deficiency, particularly on the part of capital spending agencies which were also engaged in significant current operations, was poor accounting and poor estimates of their net capital requirements, which were based in turn on their unrealistic projections of current income, expenditures and surpluses or deficits on current account. Some, like the Electricity Supply Board, repeatedly forecast sizable current operating surpluses, only to end up with substantial operating deficits. This made it extremely difficult to determine the net additional financing they required.

Also difficult was appraisal of the extent to which proposed annual capital programs could actually be implemented within the budget year, and of the expenditure shortfall which might occur if the requested allotments were granted. There were many programs which it was desirable to expedite. On the other hand, if the desired allotments were granted in full, limitations of total resources would require other agency programs to be cut back. If it turned out that the favored agency was unable to carry out as much of its program as had been approved, this meant that some other program had been retarded unnecessarily.

More important than any of these was the fact that, for most of the period, foreign exchange imposed limits on the capital budget. The foreign exchange component of an agency's total proposed capital spending had, therefore, to be taken seriously into account, especially because it soon became clear that foreign exchange allotments could be spent far more quickly than the local currency allotments which complemented them. An agency might pay out quickly for machinery from abroad, and then delay interminably construction of the buildings necessary to house and utilize it. Such imbalanced spending tied up scarce foreign exchange. In still other cases, the ability of an agency to utilize reparations or barter credits for a given program sometimes made it necessary to give the program priority over another which required free foreign exchange, even though the latter might merit higher priority on other grounds. Still other factors which entered into the decision might be the special interest taken in some program by a powerful minister, the extent to which contractual obligations had already been undertaken and the relative readiness of some agencies to move ahead more effectively. Thus the criteria imposed by practical and political necessities were often far removed from the ideal.

The lack of discipline frequently shown by the operating agencies was still another difficulty. For example, while allotments might be made to the Union of Burma Railways on the basis of budget submissions for specific uses, that agency might divert substantial sums intended for the acquisition of rolling stock to build staff housing instead. The National Housing Board would divert funds from one project to another it favored more, frequently holding up work in progress for other agencies in favor of its own. The telecommunications program, in particular, was held up by N.H.B. in this way. The Electricity Supply Board would divert funds authorized for thermal generating facilities in larger towns to its own unauthorized "one-a-day" lighting program in smaller communities. Agencies would sometimes attempt to spend not only the sum authorized for a given year but also the unexpended carryover from their budgets of the previous year, even though they knew very well that unutilized authorizations might not be carried over from one year to the next. During the 1955–56 fiscal year, both the Electricity Supply Board and the Industrial Development Corporation came in for large supplemental budget authorizations which created a serious strain on resources because they had concealed anticipated carryovers in their budget presentations. Finally, in a number of cases, operating agencies ignored the fact that the reparations and barter credits allotted to them were part of the financing provided for their approved budgets and attempted to spend such sums over and above their authorized allotments. As such abuses came to light, controls were devised to eliminate them. Meanwhile, however, they weakened the program.

But perhaps the most serious of all the problems connected with the capital budget review was the disorderly way in which the agencies were again and again called upon to revise and resubmit their budgetary requirements outside the budgetary process. Much of this, to be sure, was unavoidable. Thus, in February 1955 all agencies were called upon to resubmit their requirements for the 1954–55 fiscal year, so that substantial cuts could be made in the programs previously approved. In April and May of 1955 the agencies were again required to submit their requirements, showing for the first time a detailed breakdown of the foreign exchange components of their spending needs, so that a control system for Governmental foreign exchange payments could be instituted. These early 1955 exercises were necessary to adjust spending to the radically changed resource picture.

During June, July and August, the 1955–56 budget submissions were reviewed. Again, this was essential. But from September through November 1955, the agencies were once again required to submit proposals, this time on a three-year basis through 1958–59, so that an austerity capital program could be fashioned. In April, May and June of 1956, new submissions through 1959–60 were called for and reviewed so that the four-year program requested by the Economic and Social Board could be prepared. In June and July 1956 the agencies were again involved in the 1956–57 budget review. In January, February and March 1957 they were involved in still another review to enable the just completed four-year program to be converted into a completely articulated plan. And in June 1957 the directives issued by Prime Minister U Nu called for the submission of a set of expenditure proposals further to the 1957–58 budget requests just submitted by the agencies. Some of these later exercises were not necessary. They also tended to confuse long-term planning with annual programing, though the planners fought hard to keep these processes separate.

These incessant demands upon the agencies for almost continual reformulation of their programs, and the rounds of hearings which followed the resubmissions, required the chief operating officials to devote an inordinate amount of their time to the budget and program adjustment process, when they should have been concerning themselves with implementation of the programs under way. In ordering these reviews, the policy-makers had no idea of the amount of time, work and effort required for the preparation of submissions and subsequent review. Both U Nu and U Ba Swe, in ordering total long-term program reconsideration at different times, expected this task to be accomplished in a matter of a few weeks. One unhappy by-product of this kind of exercise was that many of the operating officials and, it may be added, many of the planning officials as well, lost respect for the programing exercise. They came to feel that the higher authorities were captious, unrealistic and unsteady in purpose, that they were more interested in paper work than in solid achievement and that they had little regard for the operating people who had to devote endless hours to carrying out instructions so lightly given. The failure of the policy-makers to consider seriously the product of all this work was the final blow. It was difficult under these circumstances to expect serious budgeting and programing performance within the operating agencies. Another by-product, also serious, was that the key economic secretaries and staff charged with review and program adjustment had to neglect other and equally important functions — review of program implementation, further analysis of weak projects, supervision and coordination and policy formulation and adaptation, as well as their individual job responsibilities.

THE IMPORT PROGRAM

Perhaps the most vexing, if not the most difficult, of the programing exercises was the preparation of the import program, so important to the cash-consolidated and foreign exchange budgets. From the planning point of view, the initial difficulty was to get the fashioning of the import program made part of the over-all programing process rather than a private affair conducted within the Ministry of Trade Development. However, the need to allot at least some portion of the country's barter credits to the financing of imports for the private sector and the role of various public agencies, chiefly the Civil Supplies Management Board, in the importation of such goods, provided the planning authorities with a valid claim to supervision of the import programing process. The administrative deficiencies of the Trade Development Ministry, which so badly retarded import license issue and imports during 1955–56 and which contributed so greatly to the rapid run-up in domestic price levels, emphasized the importance of the import program to the economic stability for which the Planning Ministry was responsible. Finally, questions of high policy were involved in the distribution of import responsibilities among the private sector, the Civil Supplies Management Board, the cooperatives and later the joint venture trading companies, and such questions could not be entrusted to the Trade Ministry alone. Who should be given responsibility for given imports was as important as how much and what kind of imports should be authorized. As has already been indicated, these problems were among the most vexing encountered during the life of the eight-year development program, and the manner in which they were resolved was about as unsatisfactory as any of the high-level determinations made.

PROBLEMS OF STATISTICS

The weakness and tardiness of essential statistical data were serious handicaps to the annual budgeting and programing process. At various times the tardiness or lack of data on foreign exchange reserves, imports, tax revenues, expenditures, rice shipments, outstanding rice receivables, project commitments, current barter balances, domestic price levels, consumer expenditures and similar matters made it necessary for budget and program decisions to be made on the basis of inadequate or obsolete data adjusted by broad "guesstimates." One serious instance of this has already been described in Chapter 10 in connection with the preparation of the 1954–55 program. This deficiency was gradually remedied over the years by the strengthening of the Central Statistical and Economics Department, which made possible both the development of new data and more up-to-date reporting across the statistical board, but the deficiency persisted though on a diminishing scale.

POLITICAL DECISIONS AND COMMITMENTS

The final, though by no means the least, of the budgetary and programing problems, was the disposition to make capital program decisions and commitments at the very highest level without the possibility of considered re-

Table 77

THE UNION GOVERNMENT BUDGET, 1954–55 TO 1959–60, PROGRAM AND ACTUAL

(K Crores)

	1954–55		1955–56		1956–57		1957–58		1958–59		1959–60	
	Program	Actual	Program	Actual	Program	Actual	Program	Actual	Program	Actual	Program	Rev. Est.
Receipts	109.5	110.6	87.1	76.0	116.7	121.1	113.7	112.9	116.5	104.5	108.8	120.9
Current	92.6	94.0	73.8	73.8	89.0	96.4	98.0	101.9	99.8	91.7	96.5	105.4
Capital	19.2	16.6	13.3	2.2	27.7	24.7	15.7	11.0	16.7	12.8	12.3	15.5
Expenditures	144.2	126.8	107.1	102.7	125.6	115.6	135.8	129.8	133.7	132.6	121.7	139.5
Current	77.5	73.1	76.0	74.5	87.7	81.9	94.1	93.7	94.4	96.5	94.3	103.9
Capital	66.7	53.7	31.1	28.2	37.9	33.7	41.7	36.1	39.3	36.1	37.4	35.6
Ordinary	33.2	20.8	19.9	16.0	19.9	16.4	22.9	18.1	19.4	17.3	19.8	21.0
Net loans to boards, etc.	33.5	32.9	11.2	12.2	18.0	17.3	18.8	18.0	19.9	18.8	17.6	14.6
Operating Surplus or deficit	−34.7	−16.2	−20.0	−26.7	− 8.9	+ 5.5	−22.1	−16.9	−17.2	−28.1	−22.9	−18.6
Net change in national debt	+ 2.3	+14.6	+ .9	+22.0	+ 9.0	− 4.1	+21.5	+19.3	+16.6	+30.8	−22.9	−19.9
Receipts by Source												
Total receipts	109.5	110.6	87.1	76.0	116.7	121.1	113.7	112.9	116.5	104.5	108.8	120.9
Tax receipts	45.9	63.9	61.6	59.1	69.1	75.1	73.1	72.6	74.6	65.0	70.5	79.0
Customs	24.2	25.5	23.0	21.4	25.5	29.8	30.0	27.9	28.3	25.0	25.6	30.5
Income taxes	7.0	24.3	22.5	22.4	26.5	26.4	24.0	22.8	25.5	23.5	22.2	22.8
Other	14.7	14.1	16.1	15.3	17.1	18.9	19.1	21.8	20.8	22.0	22.7	25.7
Non-tax receipts	57.0	46.7	25.5	16.9	47.6	46.0	40.6	40.3	41.9	39.5	38.3	41.9
Ministries and depts.	11.6	10.3	12.5	10.0	15.6	17.0	19.6	20.3	19.9	23.1	21.8	24.4
Contributions from boards	45.4	36.4	13.0	5.3	15.0	15.0	6.0	10.0	10.0	5.5	7.0	7.0
Reparations				1.6	17.0	14.0	15.0	10.0	12.0	10.9	9.5	10.5

Source: Economic Survey of Burma, various years through 1960.

444

Table 78

Comprehensive Budget of the Public Sector, 1954–55 to 1959–60, Program and Actual

(K Crores)

	1954–55		1955–56		1956–57		1957–58		1958–59		1959–60	
	Rev. Est.	Actual	Program	Actual	Program	Actual	Program	Actual	Program	Actual	Program	Rev. Est.
Receipts	246.7	252.7	257.7	265.1	313.0	336.4	337.5	306.5	359.0	317.7	328.9	339.6
1. Revenue receipts	86.5	94.0	73.8	73.8	99.1	96.3	98.0	95.0	99.8	95.5	96.4	102.4
2. Loan receipts	28.3	16.4	15.7	25.5	35.2	22.5	37.1	15.1	28.8	27.0	23.3	17.5
a. Foreign						20.4		13.0	26.8	25.9	20.9	15.6
b. Domestic						2.1		2.1	2.0	1.1	2.4	1.9
3. Other receipts, incl. reparations						27.7		17.8	17.2	14.0	14.5	12.6
4. Boards and corps.	131.9	142.3	168.2	165.8	178.7	189.9	202.4	178.6	213.2	181.2	194.7	207.1
Expenditures	311.8	298.3	279.8	276.5	319.9	328.4	342.4	314.7	355.4	324.1	335.9	348.4
5. Current, mins. and depts.	75.3	73.1	76.0	74.5	87.7	81.5	94.0	91.4	94.4	93.5	94.3	103.9
6. Current, bds. and corps.	152.9	153.9	148.8	153.7	173.2	193.2	191.7	171.0	205.2	178.9	187.4	190.7
7. Capital—Total	83.6	71.3	55.0	48.3	59.0	53.7	56.7	52.3	55.8	51.7	54.2	53.8
a. Mins. and depts.	38.9	32.0	19.0	16.1	19.9	17.0	22.9	19.0	20.1	18.7	18.3	20.6
b. Bds. and corps.	44.7	39.3	36.0	32.2	39.1	31.1	33.8	33.3	35.7	33.0	35.9	33.2
						5.6[a]						
8. Surplus or deficit	—65.1	—45.6	—22.1	—11.4	—6.9	+8.0	—4.9	—8.2	+3.6	—6.4	—7.0	—8.8

Source: Economic Survey of Burma, various years through 1960.

a. Unclassified Japanese reparations.

Note: The program for 1954–55 was completely disrupted by the post-budget decision to increase capital spending to K 98 crores. No comprehensive budget was prepared on the basis of this figure. The authorized capital program was, however, reduced during the course of that year. Revised estimates are therefore shown in place of the original program.

Table 79

Cash-Consolidated Budget of the Union Government and Its Effect on the Privately Held Money Supply, 1954-55 to 1959-60, Program and Actual

(K Crores)

	1954-55		1955-56		1956-57		1957-58		1958-59		1959-60	
	Program	Actual	Program	Actual	Program	Actual	Program	Actual	Program	Rev. Est.	Program	Rev. Est.
1. Receipts of Union Govt.	427.5	252.7	257.7	265.1	313.0	336.4	337.5	306.5	359.0	317.7	328.9	339.6
2. Less: receipts from abroad	120.0	90.3	103.5	109.0	129.0	129.8	134.9	109.5	137.3	122.9	127.9	124.6
3. Equal: Domestic receipts	307.5	162.4	154.2	156.1	184.0	206.6	202.6	197.0	221.7	194.8	201.0	215.0
4. Expenditure of Union Govt.	462.5	298.3	279.8	276.5	319.9	328.4	342.4	314.7	355.4	324.1	335.9	348.4
5. Less: Payments abroad	62.5	56.0	53.0	48.7	62.6	56.5	57.5	56.6	63.9	63.9	62.8	59.7
6. Equal: Domestic payments	400.0	242.3	226.8	227.8	257.3	271.9	284.9	258.1	291.5	260.2	273.1	288.7
7. Cash deficit with private sector	92.5	79.9	72.6	71.7	73.3	65.3	82.3	61.1	69.8	65.4	72.1	73.7
8. Less: Excess of private foreign payments over receipts	70.0	55.9	50.5	47.3	71.0	86.9	80.6	54.9	66.2	46.5	66.3	61.9
9. Adjustment for other factors[a]	− 2.5	+ 4.7	+ 2.6	+ 2.5	—	+ 7.0	− 1.0	− 1.5	− .3	+ 2.0	+ 2.0	−10.0
10. Increase in private money supply	+25.0	+19.3	+19.5	+26.9	+ 2.3	−14.6	+ 2.7	+ 7.7	+ 3.9	+20.9	+ 7.8	+ 1.8

Source: Economic Survey of Burma, 1954 through 1960.

a. Net changes in bank credit, private savings, errors and omissions.

view or the opportunity to fit such decisions into the total program in an orderly way. The oustanding example of this was, of course, the Soviet "gift project" arrangement. Others were the abortive nation-wide reroofing scheme of June 1957 and the new Rangoon-Mandalay Highway proposed by the Ne Win Government in 1959. Still another was the repeated reinstatement of the Viscount purchase program at cabinet level, after the program-makers had recommended its termination. On the resource side, the barter arrangements concluded with the U.S.S.R., People's China and the several countries of the Soviet bloc were also made outside the regular planning and programing process and caused, as has been seen, endless disruption and confusion.

Despite these problems, it was possible, though only with great strain and difficulty, to keep the annual budgeting and programing process on a fairly orderly basis. While, on occasion, individual components in the total annual program were thrown rather badly out of gear, it was possible for the most part to make compensating adjustments and, after 1954–55, to keep final outcomes within hailing distance of the original programs. Divergencies between the annual programs and their final outcomes may be examined in Tables 77–79, which compare, for the years for which they are available, the Union Government budgets, the comprehensive budgets of the public sector and the cash-consolidated budgets with actual outcomes for these years. The largest deviations toward the deficit side came in 1958–59 as a result of shortfalls in rice exports and curtailments in the import program. These were reflected chiefly in the far larger than programed increase in the privately held money supply in that year.

CHAPTER 27

Problems of Management

in the Public Enterprises

Burma's public enterprises were responsible for providing the essential public utility services on which the entire economy depended, for earning most of its needed foreign exchange, for procurement and distribution of a substantial portion of all imports, for the execution of most of the public development program, for the operation of the new manufacturing facilities and for stimulating and assisting private development in agriculture, mining and industry. We have already examined (in Chapter 25) their great potential contribution to resource mobilization. Clearly, the satisfactory management of these enterprises was of tremendous importance to the country's economy and to development efforts.

THE PUBLIC ENTERPRISES

The public enterprises were of six distinct functional types. First, there were the public utility enterprises engaged in supplying transport, communications and electric power services to the public. Most of the transport agencies had functioned before World War II as private organizations, and had since been nationalized. They included the Union of Burma Railways Board, the Inland Water Transport Board, the Union of Burma Airways Board, the Union of Burma Shipping Board, the Civil Aviation Board and the Port of Rangoon Authority. In addition, postal and telecommunications services were operated under departmental auspices. Electric power was generated and supplied in Rangoon by the Rangoon Electricity Supply Board, also a private enterprise in the pre-war days, while power up-country was supplied by the new Electricity Supply Board, of which the Rangoon Board had been made a subsidiary.

The second group of public enterprises were those engaged in trading activities. Of these, the State Agricultural Marketing Board and the State Timber Board were responsible respectively for rice and teak procurement, processing and exports. The Civil Supplies Management Board was responsible for the procurement at home and abroad of essential commodities for consumer use. The Commerce Development Corporation was responsible for rubber and cotton exports and for supervising the Government's interest in the joint venture trading companies engaged in major import activities. While the S.A.M.B., the S.T.B. and the C.S.M.B. came into being early in the postwar period, the Commerce Development Corporation was organized only in 1954.

The third major functional group were the development corporations for industry, minerals and agriculture organized in 1952–53. The Industrial Development Corporation, the Mineral Resources Development Corporation and the Agricultural Resources Development Corporation (later the Land Resources Development Corporation) were responsible not only for public developmental activities but for the stimulation of private developmental activities as well.

The fourth functional group was concerned with state manufacturing. For the most part — as in the case of the steel, jute, sugar, sericulture, cement, tea and a number of smaller pilot plants of various kinds — the enterprises were conducted under the aegis of the Industrial Development Corporation. There were, however, three important exceptions to the I.D.C.'s responsibility. The pharmaceuticals plant fell under the Special Projects Implementation Board, and the brick and tile factory and the first cotton mill were built and operated by autonomous boards. As it approached completion, each of the manufacturing enterprises developed by the Industrial Development Corporation was placed under the supervision of a sub-board responsible to the I.D.C.

The fifth group, which may be called the service group, was made up primarily of two organizations — the National Housing Board and the Union of Burma Purchase Board — whose major function was to service other governmental organizations. The Union of Burma Purchase Board existed solely to procure supplies for other Government organizations. The National Housing Board, on the other hand, was responsible for urban and rural housing and community development activities of its own, as well as for acting as agent or contractor for other Government organizations with construction programs — mostly in the fields of education, health and welfare. In addition, the Rehabilitation Brigade, which also performed construction activities for Government organizations, may be included in this service category.

Finally, there existed a miscellaneous or catch-all group engaged variously in banking and insurance activities, as in the case of the State Commercial Bank, the Pawnshop Board and the Insurance Board, and few others of lesser importance.[1]

Since the public enterprises were of highly disparate types, since they had been established at various times and had very different experience records and since they were somewhat differently organized, the management problems they encountered varied widely. There was, nevertheless, a very important group of problems common to all of them, which adversely affected their operation. It is with these that we shall, for the most part, be concerned.

ORGANIZATION OF THE PUBLIC ENTERPRISES

It is necessary first to understand the organizational setup of the public enterprises and the way in which they were related to the Government. The Government boards and corporations were created sometimes by executive order, sometimes by legislation. The ruling body in each case was a board of directors headed by a chairman. The development corporations were creatures of the legislature, and they were headed for some years by the country's three foremost political leaders. Prime Minister U Nu was the first Chairman of the Agricultural Resources Development Corporation. U Ba Swe, the then Defense Minister and Minister for Mines, was Chairman of the Mineral Resources Development Corporation. U Kyaw Nyein, the then Minister for Industries, was Chairman of the Industrial Development Corporation. The boards, generally created by executive order, frequently had ministers as chairmen, as in the case of the National Housing Board when U Raschid was Housing Minister. Senior and trusted civil servants also served in some cases as board chairmen, as in the case of U Ko Gyi and later U Ba Khin at the State Agricultural Marketing Board. The boards of directors were made up exclusively of Government officials — parliamentary secretaries, secretaries to the ministries responsible for the boards, secretaries to central or related ministries and senior civil servants of somewhat lesser rank. In the development corporations where the top leaders served as chairmen, ministers sometimes served as board members.

A chief executive officer served under the board of directors. In the case of the development corporations his title was director-general. In other cases, he might be called chief executive officer, chief engineer or general manager. This office was sometimes filled by the secretary to the ministry most concerned, as in the case of U Ba Tun, Secretary of the Mines Ministry, who served also as Director-General of the M.R.D.C. The chief executive officer

1. This grouping intentionally excludes organizations in which the Government engaged in joint ventures with private capital, notably in the mining and import fields. Since in such cases management responsibility was entrusted to the private partners, their management problems do not fall within the scope of this chapter.

might also be a retired civil servant recalled to duty, as in the case of U Zin, the former Income Tax Commissioner, who served as Director-General of the I.D.C.

Theoretically, each of the public enterprises was autonomous. It was, as in the British system, administratively attached to the appropriate Government ministry through which it was to receive Government policy direction, and through which it was responsible to the Government. Such policy direction and supervision by the Government were obviously essential. The existence of the boards and corporations was, however, a recognition that the functions assigned to them did not lend themselves to the regular departmental form of governmental organization, and, in fact, could not be performed effectively under the rules and procedures to which the traditional Government departments were subject. The very purpose of their creation was to free them to the maximum degree possible from such controls, and allow them enough autonomy to achieve efficiency. The major problem of the managers of these enterprises was that they did not, in fact, enjoy such autonomy.

THE LACK OF AUTONOMY

In practice, the public enterprises could not determine independently the personnel they required or establish the pay scales necessary to attract and hold competent personnel. They could not procure independently the supplies and equipment they needed, award contracts, determine their product mix and prices, dispose of assets or arrange for short-term financing, without approval by their administrative ministries and the Ministry of Finance. Even when, as in some cases, their terms of reference permitted them independent decision on some of these matters, they could not exercise the authority in practice.

Over and above the restrictions imposed by the need for administrative and financial sanctions and central procurement, the boards and corporations were dominated — more negatively than positively — by the ministers who served as their chairmen or to whom their board chairmen reported. (The minister himself, in turn, might take no position until he had consulted the senior political leader whose satellite he was.) Very few of the ministers were capable or interested.[2] Virtually none of them devoted to the affairs of the public enterprises the time and attention they required. When they did, their interests — with few exceptions — were more political than objective. In any case, they shied away from taking positions on matters unfamiliar to them and the importance of which they did not really appreciate — which meant, in effect, most of the important questions.

The negative domination resulted in a sluggish or almost non-existent deci-

2. Among these, U Raschid and U Kyaw Nyein were outstanding, and Thakin Chit Maung and U Tun Win were far above average.

sion-making process, and the virtual stagnation of management. The political domination resulted in favoritism and nepotism in staffing at higher levels and in excessive employment and payrolls further down the line.

A TYPICAL CASE — THE UNION OF BURMA AIRWAYS

The application of some of these factors may be illustrated from the operating experience of the Union of Burma Airways Board. The political overloading of staff at the U.B.A. is apparent from the following figures:

	1950–51	*1956–57*	*Percentage Increase*
Flight revenues (lakhs)	130	156	20
Expenditures (lakhs)	99	146	47.5
Employees	431	970	125.1
Operations	24	39	62.5
Traffic	97	258	166
Managerial and accounts	79	235	197.5
Other	231	438	89.6

Over a six-year period, flight revenues increased by only 20 per cent, yet employment more than doubled. Operating personnel increased "only" by three fifths, while the number of people engaged in managerial and accounts work and in traffic nearly tripled.[3]

In 1956–57, however, the U.B.A. had a total of eleven pilots only, as compared with twenty pilots in 1952. Foreign pilots, who had made up half of the earlier pilot force, had quit *en masse* in a dispute which involved complaints of excessive flying hours and inadequate pay scales. The U.B.A. had been unable to replace them because the Ministry of Finance refused to sanction adequate pay scales. The consequence was that the limited national pilot force had even more excessive flying hours and yet aircraft utilization declined to less than five hours per day.

Another handicap was the inability of the U.B.A. to dispose independently of surplus non-operating aircraft, which had cost it almost as much as its operating Dakotas. In its early years, the U.B.A. had purchased four Doves, three Marathons and one Catalina aircraft. These had never operated, and it had become clear that they were unsuitable for Burmese conditions. Several times the U.B.A. had attempted to dispose of them. On receiving tenders, it had submitted them to its own Ministry and the Ministry of Finance for approval. On each occasion the lengthy time interval which elapsed before the approvals came through had resulted in withdrawal of the bids. In conse-

3. In the course of the 1958–59 budget review, the Rangoon Electricity Supply Board — one of the better-managed enterprises — admitted that at least 40 per cent of its manpower was redundant and indicated that it was powerless, because of government tolerance of feather-bedding and lack of discipline, to do anything about it.

quence, the redundant aircraft continued to deteriorate, and the U.B.A. was unable to liquidate these unproductive assets.

Another U.B.A. operating problem was that the Government had "requested" it to cut its fares during school vacations and national festivals, despite the fact that these coincided with periods of peak traffic from December to May. Further, U.B.A. planes were frequently commandeered on the shortest of notice for ministers' tours, even though this involved abrupt cancellations of scheduled commercial flights.

It is not suggested that these limitations on the operational autonomy of the Union of Burma Airways accounted for all the managerial deficiencies of that organization. The U.B.A. had many other weaknesses, of course, for which lack of autonomy was not responsible. The fact remains, however, that U.B.A.'s lack of autonomy contributed heavily to its operational deficiencies. Under such restrictions, management could not be expected to function effectively, even on matters where it was not so restricted. Since U.B.A.'s Board Chairman, U Chit, had the confidence of Prime Minister U Nu and personal access to him, the U.B.A. was, if anything, in a relatively better position than most other boards. The very nature of the service it rendered imposed minimum standards of performance on it. It did, in fact, function relatively better than did most other public enterprises. Yet compared to the potential, its management and performance were very poor indeed.

THE LACK OF EXPERIENCE

Except for the personnel engaged in the older transport and communications organizations and the pre-war staff retained by the R.E.S.B., civil servants, and certainly the ministers concerned, lacked experience in commercial-type operations. The ministers had little appreciation of the problems involved in public enterprise operation or of the skills, effort and policies required to manage them effectively. The staffing of the boards of directors of these enterprises was entirely without relation to the abilities and experience needed. In designating civil servants to act as members of such boards, no attention was paid to the load imposed on senior civil servants who had full-time responsibilities elsewhere. Thus, key secretaries, such as those in the Planning, Finance, Industries and other ministries, were made members of five, ten or more boards, even though — in addition to the full-time duties of their positions — they had very heavy responsibilities as members of the Advisory Committee of Experts to the Economic and Social Board, the Anti-Inflation Committee, the Foreign Exchange Control Committee and many others. Under the circumstances, it was impossible for these officials to give the time required to their board duties. Nor did the ministers appreciate the desirability of appointing qualified individuals from private life to the boards. Yet representative lawyers, bankers, accountants, engineers and business men would have made a substantial contribution to better enterprise management.

Lack of experience was also reflected, significantly, in the choice of chief executive officers of the various enterprises, and in the failure to delegate internal responsibility and operational authority to them in necessary degree. So far as U Nu himself was concerned, he regarded it as far more important that the executives be honest than that they be capable. By and large, political and personal loyalty was the main criterion used by most of the ministers in selecting their executive officers. But on whatever basis the chief executive officer was chosen, in no case did his board of directors delegate to him the authority he needed to do his job successfully. Countless day-to-day operating decisions had to be put before the boards of directors; and, since many of these boards met infrequently, they were often unable to cope with the questions which had accumulated since their last sitting. Agenda were interminable, and most of the agenda items dealt with matters which should never come before a board of directors at all. These included such questions as whether one or two additional clerks should be hired, whether a telephone should be installed, whether a truck should be repaired and similar trivia which should not have reached even the general manager, let alone his board of directors. Overwhelmed as they were with such matters, most boards of directors never even considered, or called for consideration of, the far more important questions.

The lack of experience at policy and executive levels was reflected in other deficiencies as well. There was an almost complete lack of appreciation of the number of technically qualified people needed in supervisory and executive posts, of the importance to cost reduction of near-capacity operations, of the role of pricing in achieving greater volume, of the importance of cost accounting in rational management decisions, of the importance of incentives and, in general, of how much planning and hard work were required for good performance. Lacking an appreciation of what constituted efficient operation, the enterprise managers were also not aware of their own limitations, and frequently undertook far more than they were capable of executing effectively. This was especially evident in the case of the Industrial Development Corporation. Having initiated the first wave of manufacturing enterprises — the steel, sugar, jute and other mills — it continued to concern itself with plans and negotiations for still other manufacturing enterprises, without any awareness that, while these plants were under construction, a host of organizational, staffing, procurement, pricing, production and other problems had to be anticipated and prepared for.

This inexperience also meant that, even in the few organizations where competent foreign technicians were available, those responsible for direction did not know how to make use of their services effectively, and in fact seldom did so. Thus, the specialized management personnel available to the Industrial Development Corporation through the consulting engineers and to the

Electricity Supply Board through the Ford Foundation were seldom heard and seldom used.

THE LACK OF INITIATIVE

For a variety of reasons board chairmen, boards of directors and executive officers in the boards and corporations failed almost uniformly to display initiative or self-reliance. Some of the reasons for this have already been discussed. The individuals concerned were, in fact, little more than clerks, messengers or observation posts for the politicians responsible for their appointment. Most of them were uninterested or lethargic. Others feared censure or action by the Bureau of Special Investigation, which might follow mistakes or unpopular decisions. In any event, there was little incentive to exercise initiative, or to assume the risks involved in some decisions. Blame for mistakes had to be feared; rewards for good performance could not be expected. Not only did officials refer to their superiors questions they should have handled themselves; they also failed to bring to their superiors questions or problems that required action at high levels. Thus, if existing regulations or policy stood in the way of effective performance and required action at a higher level, officials were unwilling, even when aware of the problems, to submit them for consideration.

POOR COORDINATION

Coordination with other Government agencies was also a serious problem for most of the public enterprises. One reason for this, undoubtedly, was that public enterprises made contact with other agencies of Government not directly, but only through their ministries. But inexperience and lack of initiative contributed even more to this result. Thus, it was found in 1955 that lagging timber exports were due not to declining production and sales but to the inability of the State Timber Board to arrange for commercial shipping space, and its failure to arrange with the Union of Burma Shipping Board to carry timber on Government-owned vessels. (This failure was especially difficult to understand because the timber was to be shipped to India, and Shipping Board vessels were traveling in ballast to Calcutta to pick up coal.) Thus, also, the state-owned cotton mill was unable to reach an understanding with the Civil Supplies Management Board on the yarn counts it should produce, or the prices at which its yarn should be sold. Similarly, the state-owned pharmaceuticals plant quarreled with the Civil Supplies Management Board over the price the latter should pay for its alcohol, and over how much inventory the marketing agency should carry for it.

Such situations could, and frequently did, persist for many months at a time. The instances mentioned came to the attention of the higher authorities only by chance, as when the Economic and Social Board inquired into the reasons for lagging timber exports, or in the course of the capital budget review. Left to themselves, the public enterprises might never have solved such problems of coordination at all, or brought them forward for solution by a higher authority. But problems involving only two organizations were far less complicated than were others which involved high-level coordination among a number of agencies and related policy action as well. Thus, the pharmaceuticals plant was confronted with a number of problems which required, variously, an increase in the budget of the State Medical Stores Board so that it could buy more supplies from the pharmaceuticals plant; a reduction in tariffs on bottles and other packaging materials which, illogically, were at a higher rate than was paid on competitive imported pharmaceuticals; a practical inter-agency program that would insure the effective distribution of the yeast tablets which the plant was producing at the rate of one million per day, stocks of which already exceeded the 100 million mark; a decision to use the molasses by-product of the sugar mills rather than broken rice for the manufacture of alcohol. Problems such as these could not be solved by the pharmaceuticals plant management by direct negotiation with the Government agencies concerned. But the management should have been capable of presenting to the Government at the highest policy and coordinating level a comprehensive program for action along the lines required.

THE LACK OF CLEAR-CUT AND APPROPRIATE GOVERNMENT POLICIES

Without question, the lack of clear-cut or appropriate economic policies imposed problems on the public enterprises with which they could not cope by themselves. These involved, chiefly, capitalization, depreciation, interest, wage, price and profit policies.

The Government had not formulated an appropriate policy for the capitalization of the new enterprises. In the construction of the steel and pharmaceuticals plants, for example, heavy costs had been incurred for site clearance and fill, for laying electrical, water and sewer lines and for other development costs, including access roads. These were charged to the enterprises, even though a strong case existed for charging them to general development instead. The enterprises paid interest from the date the financial advances were made, even though in some cases it would have been more appropriate to defer such charges until construction was completed and a reasonable level of operation achieved. In some cases it would have been reasonable to consider part of the governmental financial advance a subsidy, as in the case of part of the Electricity Supply Board's rural electrification cost. In other cases it would have been appropriate to consider all or part of the Government's financial advance an equity investment rather than an interest-bearing loan. In still others, it would have made sense to write down the capitalization because of excessive costs due to both inexperience and delays beyond the agency's control. But in none of these cases could policy be amended or formulated to make possible the desired results.

Some questions involving pricing and profit policy were more problematical. For example, the output of the jute mill was bought *in toto* by the State Agricultural Marketing Board, and the question arose whether the product should be priced at the duty-paid cost of the gunnies previously imported or at a lower price which, while still potentially profitable, would impose the need for more economical two-shift operation on the jute mill. In the case of the inefficient cotton spinning and weaving mill, which could not supply cotton yarns to Civil Supplies at a price competitive with imported yarns, the Government determined to protect the cotton mill by requiring Civil Supplies to tie in its sales of scarce but cheaper imported yarns with the compulsory purchase of higher-priced cotton mill products. This decision, of course, relieved the cotton mill management of the onus of achieving a higher volume and reducing its excessive costs. So far as profit policy was concerned, only the S.A.M.B. and the S.T.B., of all the Government boards, understood clearly that they should maximize their profits to the degree possible. Other boards lacked clear-cut directives to guide costing, pricing and profit policies.

These were not the only policies lacking appropriateness or clarity. Another problem of significance was in employee housing. The vested interest in public enterprise operation lay in providing housing for their top officials, if not for all their employees. The older transport organizations had historically provided such facilities for their higher officers, chiefly because in prewar days these officials were Englishmen who brought their living standards with them. The disposition of the I.D.C. in setting up the state manufacturing enterprises was to do the same. Housing was also provided, at considerable cost, by the pharmaceuticals and the brick and tile factories for both executives and workers. The provision of such facilities meant, in effect, that these enterprises were engaged simultaneously in commercial operations and in programs of subsidized public housing at the expense of the general public. Though this problem was quite important, the Government never once consented to take it under advisement and to formulate a clear-cut policy on it. The only control by the Government was that exercised on an *ad hoc* basis by the budget-makers in allotting capital funds.

Nor had the Government formulated a clear wage policy for the public enterprises, although it was expected that, in general, wages would conform to the pay scales prevailing in the regular Government departments. Departmental scales were, however, scarcely useful as a guide to wage policy in the new manufacturing enterprises. The jute mill provided the unique instance in which a public enterprise, in the absence of clearly defined Government policy, took the bull by the horns and established a policy satisfactory to itself. This it did under instructions from the Industrial Development Corporation, probably at the urging of the powerful then Deputy Prime Minister U Kyaw Nyein, to achieve full production as rapidly as possible. The incentive wage system introduced, however, set production norms at an abnormally low level and, in effect, paid overtime incentive rates for all production in excess of these very low norms. This created a wage structure which was not only uneconomic but far out of line with that prevailing in private manufacturing employment and that in the comparable state-owned cotton mill as well. Efforts made in 1958 to obtain high-level consideration of this enterprise-determined wage policy met with no success.

THE LACK OF ADEQUATE ACCOUNTING

If the best management in the world had been put in charge of the public enterprises, its first major task, of necessity, would have been to put the accounts in order. With few exceptions the accounts of the public enterprises were in a hopeless condition. They could not be used as management tools.

Basically, the accounts of the public enterprises were on a cash basis. They recorded receipts and payments, as did the departmental accounts, and were designed primarily to insure that no money was paid out without proper authorization or voucher, or stolen. Moneys advanced to field officers, contractors, and so on, were carried as suspense accounts, and the final accounts for any given year were held open until detailed statements had been received. Partly because of this, enterprise accounts for any given year were seldom closed for three, four or five years after the fact. Even on a purely cash basis, therefore, it was difficult to get an accurate current picture of the financial affairs of any of the public enterprises.

Profit and loss positions were even more difficult to establish. Some agencies showed depreciation charges; others did not. Loans, advances and other capital items were frequently treated as current costs. Inventory accounts were especially bad. The S.A.M.B. could not establish its holdings within a couple of hundred thousand tons, and took its first physical check of stocks only in 1958. In September 1960, the inventory position of the Civil Supplies Management Board, a merchandising agency, was available only as of September 30, 1958.[4]

The Union of Burma Airways is another example. As of September 1956, its accounts for fiscal year 1952–53 were reported as final but not yet verified. The accounts for 1953–54 were still provisional. Operating and traffic statistics were on an actual basis only through the first nine months of 1953–54, and were estimated for the fifteen months thereafter. Even estimated data were not available for 1955–56. Costs by major expenditure categories (flight operations, ground operations, services and general administration) had been ana-

---

4. *Selected Economic Indicators,* C.S.E.D., Rangoon, July 1960, p. 27.

lyzed only through the year 1952–53, and were unavailable for the three years following. Aircraft utilization data had been computed through 1952–53. Data on load factors on domestic flights were available only through January 1956.[5]

In the absence of reliable and current accounting which would show not only cash receipts and payments but also profit and loss and balance sheet positions, and provide internal cost accounting as well, it was simply impossible to make rational management decisions. Nor could intelligent supervision of and control over the public enterprises be exercised without the figures.

These deficiencies in the public enterprise accounts reflected far more than mere weaknesses in accounting personnel. They reflected also the managements' lack of appreciation that accounting data are essential to good management, and a lack of appreciation on the part of the Government that they are essential as a check on management performance and as a guide to resource allocation. The Auditor-General was satisfied if he could, in due course, check whether expenditures made had been duly authorized, and whether proper vouchers existed to cover all outlays. He was not particularly concerned because the audit process was three, four or five years behind the fact, or because enterprise accounts were useless for management purposes. Accounts meant little to the ministers and to most of the board chairmen who reported to them. In many cases managements conducted their affairs in such a way as to make it almost impossible for their accountants to keep effective records. In consequence, it was almost impossible for the managements themselves to know whether they were making or losing money and how much; how earnings or losses compared with those of previous years; which elements of their operations were more profitable or more costly than others; or to make any of the other analyses relevant to decisions on employment, wages, procurement, pricing, inventory and similar matters.

THE LACK OF EFFECTIVE SUPERVISION AND CONTROL

If the boards of directors of the public enterprises failed to manage them with a reasonable degree of efficiency, the deficiencies could be corrected only by action from above. But the ministries to which they were responsible had already collaborated, through their ministers, in the failure. The Cabinet, in which these ministers sat, was equally incompetent and indisposed to act. And the Economic and Social Board, to which the economic consultants were attached and where they repeatedly urged the necessity for remedial action, was, after all, not much better in this respect. Nor could public opinion — the ultimate arbiter in a political democracy — make known, through the ballot, the parliamentary opposition, or the press, its dissatisfaction with this

---

5. These data, and the U.B.A. data earlier cited, are taken from a memorandum, "U.B.A. Status and Prospects," prepared by Robert R. Nathan Associates, Inc., Sept. 20, 1956.

state of affairs. Public, press and parliamentary opposition all lacked the facts necessary to appraise the situation.[6] If the Government and the enterprises themselves could not know the position, neither could the potential critics. Underlying the entire situation was the apparent belief that Burma, as a welfare state, could afford waste, inefficiency, nepotism, lack of discipline and mismanagement in her public enterprises.

ATTEMPTS TO COPE WITH THE MANAGEMENT PROBLEM

In their Comprehensive Report, the consultants had laid great stress on the crucial importance of good management in the public enterprises to the success of the development program. They had cautioned against the management weaknesses which would result from lack of adequate autonomy, the staffing of boards of directors with civil servants only, and the failure of boards of directors to delegate adequate operating responsibility to their chief executive officers. They had also suggested a number of ways in which organizational problems and shortages of managerial personnel could be met.[7]

Upon completion of the planning period toward the end of 1953, the economic consultants were more and more impressed with the compelling nature of these problems. Beginning with fiscal year 1953–54, they were confronted almost weekly with new challenges arising out of deficient management, and they attempted to cope with them in one way or another.

The attempts were of various kinds and were made at various levels. In some cases they were attempts to be of direct assistance to the public enterprises in dealing with broad or specific management problems. In other cases, the consultants tried to persuade the Ministry of National Planning or the Economic and Social Board to take action or to establish policies designed to improve management in all the public enterprises. In still other cases, they attempted through direct communication with the Prime Minister or the Deputy Prime Minister for National Economy to modify existing Government policies and practices, or to formulate new Government policies which might result in improved management.

Thus, in the first category, the economic consultants tried to help the Industrial Development Corporation and the Electricity Supply Board by suggesting plans for more effective organization and staffing. The I.D.C. was advised also of the criteria that might properly govern the extension of loans to private industry. The Rangoon Electricity Supply Board was offered sug-

6. The public enterprises reported their finances, to be sure, in the budget document each year. What they presented were revised estimates of current income and expenditure for the year then ending, proposals for the new financial year, and "actual" — though still not final — income and expenditures for the period ended two years before. All these were purely on a cash basis, not profit and loss statements. There were no balance sheets. The budget accounts were not a substitute for commercial accounting, and did not lend themselves to an appraisal of enterprise affairs and management performance.

7. K.T.A. Comprehensive Report, Chapter VI.

gestions on pricing and profit policy. Suggestions on pricing were made at the newly nationalized cement mill. The S.A.M.B. was urged to establish a rice marketing intelligence unit. Attempts were made, through the Ministry of Industries, to set up a reasonable financial structure for the Electricity Supply Board, and thus make possible the development of a rational set of electric power tariffs.

Working through the Ministry of National Planning and the Economic and Social Board, the economic consultants urged broad governmental action to improve public administration in all its aspects, and suggested the major steps which should be taken toward this end. They tried to get these central agencies to spur the public enterprises into developing and maintaining improved accounts. Through the report of a special consultant, Dr. Locklin, they tried to help the railway and inland water transport enterprises to rationalize their rate structures. They recommended that the assistance of the Ford Foundation be sought to obtain the services of a management and cost accounting team, which they hoped would contribute in major degree to improved enterprise accounts and management. They urged the Government to obtain the services of special management teams for the S.A.M.B. and for the Electricity Supply Board. They urged persistently and repeatedly that the Government create the basic conditions essential to improved management in the public enterprises by placing them on a truly autonomous basis; by strengthening their boards of directors through appointment to them of private engineers, accountants, bankers, lawyers, business men and others with appropriate experience; by insisting that these boards of directors delegate to their chief executive officers appropriate authority and responsibility for dealing with day-to-day operational problems; by turning over to the private sector enterprises not appropriate to Government ownership and management, the management responsibility of which hopelessly overburdened the Government apparatus; and, where appropriate, by selling shares in the public enterprises to private individuals, firms and institutions, so that private participation in management and appropriate incentives for better management might be introduced.

Finally, in direct conversations with and memoranda to the Prime Minister and Deputy Prime Minister, the economic consultants never gave up trying to bring home the deficiencies in public enterprise management and the necessity of taking determined steps to correct them. They pressed repeatedly for the formulation of Government policies where such policies were lacking, and for the modification of policies which were not appropriate. They also pressed upon these leaders the desirability of a "go-slow" policy on new ventures, pending constructive action on the management problems which demanded solution.

During the latter part of the development plan period, members of the economic consultants' staff were spending all or a good deal of their time attempting to improve management in specific situations, or to assist management in coping with major problems. Personnel had been detailed on a full-time basis to the State Agricultural Marketing Board and to the Civil Supplies Management Board. Others were working full-time on the Task Force effort initiated by the consultants to cope with the broad array of management problems at the jute, pharmaceuticals and cotton textile plants. Management assistance of specific kinds was also being given to the Mines Ministry and the Mineral Resources Development Corporation, the Industrial Development Corporation and the Land Resources Development Corporation. In fact, from 1955–56 on, the attempt to achieve improved management in public enterprises and in public administration generally became, other than the annual budgeting and programing effort, the major activity of the economic consultants.

The economic consultants were of course not alone in these efforts. The engineering consultants provided specialized personnel who worked toward improving management at the Industrial Development Corporation, the Electricity Supply Board, the Telecommunications Department, the S.A.M.B. and other agencies. The United Nations provided specialized help in public administration, in accounting, in mining and in industrial management. Israel provided two management specialists who helped at the S.A.M.B. and at the Ministry of Trade Development. The Ford Foundation provided the Ministry of National Planning with a Public Administration Service cost accounting and management team and, through the University of Utah, assisted the University in establishing courses in business administration. Two specialized Canadian teams, one in electricity and one in highway management, were provided under Colombo Plan auspices through the good offices of the World Bank. The Ford Foundation also provided a management specialist for the Electricity Supply Board.

By and large, the experience of all these foreign technicians was similar, in that they were never able to bring existing management face to face with its basic management problems, or to get effective consideration of their recommendations at higher levels. They were given opportunities to observe and to present recommendations, but without much result. In cases where the advisors were able to win the confidence and attention of the chief executive officers or the chairmen of the boards of the enterprises, the officers and chairmen were individuals who had already made a reasonable effort to improve conditions within their own organizations, and who were effectively stymied by circumstances over which they could exert little control. Such reports and recommendations as came before the central authorities — for the most part, the Economic and Social Board and the National Planning Commission, its successor agency after 1957 — failed to elicit favorable action.

A special comment on the P.A.S. cost accounting team may be in order. Attached to the Ministry of National Planning, which wanted to win acceptance of its services by the various enterprises, the accountants were instructed to offer assistance only when the agencies themselves requested it. They thus found themselves engaged in particularized efforts — such as the improvement of inventory records and controls — rather than in the introduction of new accounting systems. While these narrower services were useful as far as they went, they did not meet the needs.

Nevertheless, the persistent efforts of the economic consultants and others over the years, combined with experience and the hard facts of developing conditions, did exert some influence. The Government was persuaded to make some effort to improve management in the public enterprises. Disturbed in the early years of the development program by persistent reports of weak and ineffective management in the public enterprises, the Government established a high-level board of inquiry into their operations — the so-called "Board of Boards." This Board's inquiry, a "hush-hush" affair, resulted in a voluminous report never made public and never translated into English. Although it called upon the various enterprises to undertake certain corrective measures, it certainly failed to bring about any basic, or even important, remedial measures by the Government itself. However, the report of the Board of Boards may have influenced Prime Minister U Nu to establish, early in 1956, just prior to his withdrawal from office, the Standing Committee for Supervision and Coordination previously mentioned. One of the activities of the S.C.S.C. was to follow up the recommendations made by the Board of Boards, and to report to the Economic and Social Board on the steps taken by the various enterprises to conform with the recommendations.

More important perhaps than these efforts was their effect on Prime Minister U Nu, bringing him finally, in 1957, to the determination that the state should undertake no new ventures and that, in general, a "go-slow" policy should henceforth be pursued while a determined effort was made on a broad front to achieve improved management in the public enterprises. Ironically, in view of their growing political conflict, Deputy Prime Minister U Kyaw Nyein was arriving at very much the same general position at about the same time. U Kyaw Nyein, as well as U Nu, welcomed the economic consultants' suggestion that task forces be established to help improve management in the various boards and corporations. But for the cleavage in the A.F.P.F.L. which ensued shortly thereafter, some positive action on the part of the Government would undoubtedly have followed. As it happened, it was the colonels under General Ne Win who tackled the problem of public enterprise management most directly. What enabled them to do so was the clear delegation of authority and the clear orders to accomplish this mission.

With the return to civil authority in April 1960, management in the public enterprises essentially reverted to its former state, but the situation was, at least temporarily, somewhat improved. Because of the emphasis that the Ne Win Government had placed on improved accounting, the new civilian managers were in a better position than before to appraise the problems confronting them. Whether they also inherited from the military regime a disposition on the part of the Government to permit them a greater degree of operating autonomy than before remained to be established.

In only one case did the Government turn over full responsibility for management of a public enterprise to a foreign management firm. This was the Evans Medical Ltd., which built the pharmaceuticals factory, and undertook to manage it for a seven-year period. Its management was, within its own jurisdiction, quite efficient — and outstandingly so in relation to other public enterprises. Even internally, however, it suffered from some conflict of interest, and it lacked the incentive of private enterprise to maximize returns — as when it packaged imported pharmaceuticals without cost advantage, or maintained many unprofitable product lines. The chief deficiencies of the plant were due, however, not to faulty management but to excessive initial investment, and to the failure of the Government to deal effectively with many problems outside the management's area of authority. Despite the limitations of the particular experience, it certainly appears that management contracts with experienced foreign firms could have contributed greatly to the improved management of Burma's public enterprises.

Problems of Supervision

and Coordination

Responsibility for supervision and coordination of the development program was vested in the Economic and Social Board. Created by executive order on October 21, 1952,[1] the Board was empowered to determine priorities of development and other projects and supervise execution of them and to act on broad problems of economic and social policy. The executive order also called for establishment of a system of progress reporting and project inspection.

The functions of the Economic and Social Board went beyond these. It reviewed and approved or modified the plans and programs brought before it by the Ministry of National Planning. It resolved such major disputes as arose between development agencies or ministries. It supervised economic cooperation with other countries and international institutions and made final decisions in this area. While Board action on broad problems of social and economic policy was "subject to the control of the Cabinet," the composition of the Board made it, in effect, a super-cabinet agency.

The Economic and Social Board was, initially, composed of the Prime Minister as Chairman, the Minister for National Planning as Vice Chairman, the Ministers for Industry, Mines, Agriculture and Finance, the Chairman of the Union Bank of Burma and the Executive Secretary. After the cabinet changes of 1956, it comprised the Prime Minister as Chairman, the Deputy Prime Minister for Economic Affairs as Vice Chairman, the Deputy Prime

1. This order was superseded by the "Union of Burma Economic and Social Board Order, 1953" (Annual Report of the Union of Burma Economic and Social Board for the year 1955–1956, Appendix III).

Minister for Social Affairs, the Ministers for Industry, Mines, and Finance, the Chairman of the Union Bank and the Executive Secretary.

Since the membership included the chief political leaders and senior ministers, the Board's decisions were seldom questioned by the Cabinet. More important from the point of view of policy control was the Central Executive Committee of the A.F.P.F.L. This Executive Committee met every Saturday to consider not only party but also Government affairs and problems. It included the leaders who were most influential in the Cabinet, and previewed the agenda to be covered by the Cabinet the following Monday. Since it determined basic policy positions the Economic and Social Board tended to defer its own basic policy decisions until the party committee had acted.

The Board had no established meeting times. It met at the call of the Prime Minister, and the frequency of its meetings depended largely on the pressures on his schedule. During the first year or two of its existence, it met infrequently. Officials of the ministries and agencies most concerned with the problems before it were invited to attend, and the Executive Secretary presented the agenda, outlining the salient facts and considerations bearing on each item. From 1955 onward, members of the "Committee of Experts," who had been charged with screening the agenda and preparing recommendations, were invited to participate in all the meetings. This group included not only the key economic secretaries to the Government and a few other officials but also the chief technical and economic advisors to the Government.[2]

Over the years, the Economic and Social Board used the Committee of Experts in a number of ways. Its leading members served as a sub-committee on control of foreign exchange spending by Government agencies, as a sub-committee on inflation problems, as a standing committee supervising the activities of the Government's boards and corporations, and as prime movers in the annual budgeting and programing process. They also handled liaison and negotiations with foreign governments and international institutions on loans, credits and economic cooperation and served in various *ad hoc* capacities. The Executive Secretary of the Board acted as Chairman of all these working sub-committees, and the Secretaries for National Planning and Finance, the Executive Secretary of the Foreign Office concerned with reparations and foreign exchange, and the Secretaries to the two Deputy Prime Ministers concerned with economic and social affairs were members of most of them. It was in this substructure of the Board that the real work, up to the point of decision, was done.[3]

The Economic and Social Board was indispensable to the management of Burma's development program and economy. It is inconceivable that Burma

2. The resident chiefs of the T.A.M.S. and Robert R. Nathan Associates engineering and economic consulting firms held these titles.

3. The membership of these important working sub-committees of the Board is listed in Appendix V.

could have accomplished what she did without it. Only the Cabinet could have attempted to perform its functions, but the Cabinet was far too unwieldy and uninformed to do the job. It could not have opened its doors informally to the key secretaries and the foreign advisors, or enjoyed the same degree of informal exchange with them. The Board was virtually the only power locus where informed decisions could be made on economic programs and policy because it was the central source of information on the programs and had the facilities for solid staff work, and because the operating agencies knew that it was the authority to which they were responsible.

While the Economic and Social Board made a tremendously important contribution to what was actually accomplished, its performance was weak in many important respects, and the weaknesses were responsible in major degree for Burma's failure to achieve the development possible. The Board's deficiencies lay largely in its decision-making process, rather than in the decisions themselves.

GETTING IMPORTANT ISSUES BEFORE THE BOARD

A major weakness of the Economic and Social Board throughout its life was its neglect even to consider many basic problems which its staff and advisors attempted to bring before it. This deficiency was of course due in large part to its members' inability to appreciate the importance of some of the questions or to their reluctance to come to grips with them. It was also due, however, to the infrequency of the Board's meetings, since a host of questions which demanded early action accumulated in the intervals between them. Questions of basic policy, organization, procedures and management had no deadlines. Most questions of far less importance did.

Among the agenda items which pressed for immediate or early decision were many of a trivial nature. Many of these came before the Board because agencies or ministers refused to take responsibility for dealing with them and sought the sanction of the highest authority. In many other cases, however, the Board's agenda was clogged because it had itself insisted that certain matters come before it for approval.

In its six years of life from 1952 to 1958, the Economic and Social Board[4] and its successor agency, the National Planning Commission, averaged perhaps six meetings a year, fewer in the first three years and somewhat more later on. One reason for the infrequency of its meetings in the earlier years was the frequent absence of the Prime Minister and Chairman from Rangoon and from the country. During the fiscal year 1954–55, for example, he was in China most of December, went abroad to the Colombo Powers Conference later that month, traveled to both Bangkok and New Delhi during March 1955, was again away a good part of April for the Bandung Conference, de-

4. The Ne Win Government suspended further activities by this organization.

parted toward the end of May for an extensive trip to Israel, Yugoslavia, the United Kingdom, the United States and Japan and left again about the middle of October, not long after his return, on another lengthy trip to the U.S.S.R., India, Afghanistan, Finland, Sweden, Norway, Denmark and Poland. During his absences, meetings of the Economic and Social Board were not called by the Vice Chairman, and months sometimes elapsed between meetings.

The infrequency of the Board's meetings was also due to other factors. An event like the completion of the Kaba Aye Peace Pagoda and the sessions of the Fifth Buddhist Congress could preoccupy the Prime Minister for months. Frequent visits to Rangoon by heads of state, prime ministers and important delegations from abroad, important party conferences and periods of meditation and rest also prevented him from convening the Board more frequently. Thus, even in 1955–56, when the Board's performance in holding nine meetings was better than average, only one meeting was held between February 13 and July 2, a period of almost five months.

As to the nature of the Board's agenda, its Annual Report for the year 1955–56[5] is of considerable interest. During that year, the Board dealt in the course of its nine meetings with 97 agenda items, of which nine or ten were repeat items. "More than half of these involved review and approval of the employment of foreign technicians and firms, and administrative matters."[6] Few of these items were of any importance. For the most part they concerned the hiring of individual technicians by Government boards and corporations and came before the Board for review only because it refused to delegate authority to act to the operating agencies. While the Board seldom devoted much time to reviewing these matters, they did take time which could far more usefully have been devoted to questions of greater importance.

The nature of the matters with which the Board concerned itself, exclusive of the trivia mentioned above, is illustrated in Appendix VI, which lists the agenda items for its 1955–56 meetings. Two full meetings toward the end of the fiscal year were devoted to consideration of the four-year program then before the Government. Most of the other items concerned joint venture proposals made by foreign firms, proposals for economic cooperation with foreign governments and institutions, new contracts, budget revisions and new projects proposed by development agencies. In only a few cases were questions of economic policy considered. These concerned the Government's purchase price for paddy and the milling rates paid to rice millers, arrangements with foreign firms on oil exploration, U. S. surplus commodity disposal, internal freight rates, participation in the International Finance Corporation and a bi-lateral investment guarantee agreement with the U. S.

---

5. The only annual report ever prepared within the Board.
6. Annual Report of the Union of Burma Economic and Social Board for the Year 1955–1956, p. 7.

Government. Notably absent from the Board's agenda were questions of resource mobilization, of management in the public enterprises, of wage, price, profit, capitalization, tariff, nationalization and other basic economic policies and review of program implementation and project problems.

THE PROBLEM OF GETTING FIRM AND CLEAR DECISIONS

The mere fact that questions were brought before the Board was no guarantee that they would receive adequate consideration or that consideration would result in firm, clear decisions. In most cases, the matters had been documented and the salient facts presented in a staff paper, often in the form of comments offered by the economic and technical advisors, who actually originated many of the agenda items. Frequently, however, the Board's deliberations raised questions which were political in nature or were neither pertinent nor valid.[7] These often resulted in deferral of final decision, pending further deliberation, staff action or reconsideration by the Committee of Experts.

Generally speaking, the Prime Minister would make a decision if none of his colleagues raised questions or objections. But if even one firm objection or serious question was raised, there was a marked reluctance to decide. For example, decision was deferred several times on the proposed investment guarantee agreement with the United States, on various joint venture proposals with foreign firms and on proposed P.L. 480 arrangements. Because of this propensity to seek unanimity, the economic consultants were remarkably effective in their opposition to various proposals, whether these concerned programs, projects, joint ventures or policies. When they took a negative position, the Board almost always upheld them. When they sought affirmative action, they were much less successful.

Difficulties in getting the Board to make a decision were accompanied by difficulties in getting a clear decision. Discussions were often terminated inconclusively. The Chairman might abruptly turn to the next agenda item, leaving the Executive Secretary at a complete loss as to whether a decision had indeed been reached. Thus, after one meeting at which the proposed investment guarantee agreement with the United States was considered, the Secretary believed that a favorable decision had been reached. Only some time later did he discover that this was not the case. Apparently the Chairman himself had not really reached a decision at the time, had reflected on the matter afterwards, and decided to bring it back to the Board for further consideration.

---

7. On one occasion, Trade Minister U Tin proposed to amend the approved import program by deleting the provisions made for liquor imports. The discussion revealed that his motive was not the stated one — which lacked logic — but rather his reluctance as a devout Buddhist to take moral responsibility for the license issue. When it was pointed out to him that he would be absolved of this responsibility by the Board's refusal to accept his proposal, the good man was quite happy.

WEAK IMPLEMENTATION OF BOARD DECISIONS

Another of the Board's major weaknesses was its failure to follow through to insure that its decisions were effectively implemented. The members tended to believe that once a decision had been made and the necessary orders signed, implementation followed automatically.

This tendency is illustrated in an amusing incident in which U Raschid, then Housing Minister, was concerned. The Board had decided to have hostels for medical students built on the Prome Road in Rangoon directly opposite the buildings of the Union of Burma Purchase Board, which stored much of its heavy equipment and supplies on the lot in question. A short time after the order had been signed, the Prime Minister, who was very interested in the project, asked U Raschid whether the National Housing Board had begun work on the foundations. U Raschid replied that he had not been able to start because the lot was still occupied by heavy pipe, wire fencing and other Purchase Board supplies. The Prime Minister insisted that this could not be so. When U Raschid reiterated that it was, the Prime Minister became upset. "You must be wrong," he declared, "I signed the orders for this several days ago." Only when U Raschid persuaded the Prime Minister to ride with him to the lot was the latter convinced.

Another instance of the failure of the Board to follow through on a decision may be cited. This was quite an important decision because of its bearing on the operating autonomy and efficiency of the public enterprises. Early in the development period, the economic consultants had utilized the occasion presented by the Board's review of the proposed employment of a foreign technician to urge that, in general, the boards and corporations be given a far greater measure of operating autonomy than they enjoyed, and, specifically, that they be empowered to engage the personnel they required, subject only to such general policies as the Government might lay down to guide them. The outcome of the discussion was seemingly very satisfactory. The Ministry of Finance was directed to lay down the general policies. But it never did so, and the Board never checked to find out why. Boards and corporations continued, through all the years following, to bring the proposed employment of foreign technicians before the Economic and Social Board. Everyone concerned had completely forgotten the earlier decision.[8]

This identification of word with deed, of order with execution, was quite pervasive. The executive function was considered synonymous with the giving of orders. The decision-makers unfortunately lacked the experience to

8. In this matter, the present writer is perhaps as guilty as anyone else. Although he presented the original recommendation to the Economic and Social Board, in time he too forgot about the decision and failed to note the Finance Ministry's neglect to do its part. He recalled this only when he came across the pertinent papers in the course of the present study.

appreciate the time and energy required to carry out their decisions and — an important factor — the need to check periodically to see whether the decisions had been carried out. Thus U Ba Swe, when he was Prime Minister, could call upon the Committee of Experts to complete a thorough review and present a new four-year program within a period of three weeks; and U Nu, on approving the task force approach to improved management in the public enterprises, could expect the entire job to be completed within a period of six weeks.

The weakness in follow-through was due sometimes to the fact that the Board delegated responsibility for implementation without conferring the necessary authority. Thus the Board frequently referred to the Committee of Experts, the Anti-Inflation Committee or the Standing Committee for Supervision and Coordination responsibility for taking action on certain problems when it should have been clear that these bodies were completely without authority to take the necessary steps, or could take them only by invading the prerogatives of the several ministers. Under such circumstances, the civil servants could at best only flounder along or bring their recommendations back once again to the Board itself. The case of the Standing Committee for Supervision and Coordination is especially pertinent in this connection.

The Standing Committee for Supervision and Coordination was created by Prime Minister U Nu in June 1956, just prior to his demission from office, to insure that boards, corporations and other Government agencies were functioning in accordance with their directives; that their policies and procedures were appropriate to the purposes for which they were established; that their properties and stocks were properly maintained and accounted for; that their accounts and accounting systems were adequate; that they were free of corruption and mismanagement; and that their development projects were properly run. The S.C.S.C. was to report its findings directly to the Prime Minister.

It was obvious, however, from the beginning that the already heavily burdened secretaries and officials who comprised the S.C.S.C. could not possibly do this enormous job or carry out such instructions as the Prime Minister might give as a result of the findings they brought to him. Each of the enterprises into which they were directed to inquire was under the administrative supervision of a minister. No group of civil servants could presume to make a frank evaluation of the performance of a minister and take corrective steps without inviting reprisals. In its functioning, the S.C.S.C. was innocuous. It reported to the Prime Minister on its inspections of a number of industrial projects, presented some observations on the organization of the rice improvement scheme and some recommendations for modification of the procurement system. It also issued a questionnaire in September 1956 to all boards and corporations "as a first step toward action" to improve efficiency. More than a year later, when the A.F.P.F.L. was on the verge of splitting up, replies to this questionnaire were still being analyzed.

FAILURE TO CHECK ON PROGRAM PROGRESS AND PERFORMANCE

Pursuant to strong recommendations by the economic consultants, the original charter of the Economic and Social Board specifically stipulated that the Board should establish a system of progress reporting and project inspection. A progress reporting unit and system were indeed established in 1953–54 under the direction of a specialist provided by the economic consultants for the purpose, and the engineering consultants provided personnel for project inspection. In practice, it did not prove feasible to obtain useful monthly reports on project progress from the operating agencies. It did, however, prove feasible to develop comprehensive quarterly reports on project and program progress on both a financial and a physical basis and to prepare selective reports that made bottleneck-breaking possible.

The quarterly reports were presented to the Board, as were a number of special progress reports on situations which required special attention. But the Economic and Social Board never reviewed any of them. The economic consultants brought a few of the more glaring cases to the personal attention of the Prime Minister or the Deputy Prime Minister for National Economy. In a somewhat more circumspect manner, the Standing Committee for Supervision and Coordination also presented such situations to the Prime Minister, but with little effect.

The economic consultants made a special effort quite early to impress upon the Prime Minister the usefulness of the progress reporting function and the need for close supervision of program progress. In the case of the brick and tile factory — with its unconscionable delays in construction, its failure to schedule different phases of the work concurrently and its use of ordinary rather than fire brick in the kilns (see Chapter 20), they found what they considered a dramatic case in point. They anticipated that the Prime Minister would be extremely perturbed, and would try to apply the lessons of this experience to other projects as well. The failure of these reports to make a strong impression can be explained only by his failure to realize that the undue loss of time on this project was synonymous with a loss of money and a real waste of social resources.

WEAKNESS IN THE SECRETARIAT

To function effectively the Economic and Social Board needed either a strong, capable executive vice chairman or a strong, capable executive secretary. U Nu did not of course delegate executive authority to his vice chairmen. Failing this, he needed an executive secretary who could be relied upon to bring important issues forcefully to his attention, to keep trivia off the Board's agenda, to dispose of many of the matters brought before the Board himself and to see to it that the Board's decisions were effectively implemented. The Board's first Executive Secretary, U Hla Maung, was indeed such a man. He had a keen sense for the strategic and the important, he had the self-reliance to act responsibly on his own authority when this was appropriate and to take the action necessary to insure effective implementation. These very qualities, however, combined with the confidence that the Prime Minister was known to repose in him, soon made him *persona non grata* to several powerful ministers and organizations. Because of this, he became a political liability to the Prime Minister and before long was shifted to a diplomatic post. U Thant, his immediate successor, remained at the Economic and Social Board only for a very brief time before he was designated Burmese Ambassador to the United Nations. The late U Tin Maung, who succeeded U Thant, was an intelligent, conscientious and devoted officer. He strove manfully to carry an impossibly heavy load; but, perhaps mindful of U Hla Maung's experience, he was careful to avoid any semblance of real initiative and personal responsibility and seldom attempted to deal with the minor questions himself so as to reduce the work burden of the Board. Nor was he willing to bring forcefully to its attention problems in which the Board itself had expressed no interest, or to present firm recommendations on the issues that he did bring before it. U Mo Myit, the Planning Secretary who succeeded him, was energetic, forceful and quick. Unlike U Tin Maung, he was ready to assume considerable personal responsibility, was appreciative of some of the major problems with which the Board had dealt with inadequately if at all, and was willing to press for action upon them. By this time, however, the political situation had deteriorated to such an extent that the kind of action needed was no longer feasible.

CONFUSION IN THE SUPERVISORY RESPONSIBILITY

While the responsibility of the Economic and Social Board for supervision and coordination of the development program was clear until 1956, the situation became somewhat confused thereafter, when U Kyaw Nyein was named Deputy Prime Minister for National Economy. Clearly this designation meant something. But what it meant was unclear. As Minister for National Economy, U Kyaw Nyein was presumably responsible for supervising ministries concerned with economic affairs and coordinating their activities — specifically, the Ministries of Agriculture, Industry, Mines and Transport and Communications, and the departments, boards and corporations responsible to them. His responsibility did not, however, extend to the Ministries of Finance or National Planning. Lacking responsibility for these central ministries, he obviously could not coordinate the national economy. His authority over even the ministries specifically assigned to his office was also unclear. He himself could not figure out where his responsibility for them ended and that of the Economic and Social Board began.

If U Kyaw Nyein had been designated Executive Vice Chairman of the Board as well, this problem would have disappeared. As it was, the economic secretaries and staff never knew quite where to bring certain of their problems. Fortunately U Tun Thaung, Secretary to the Deputy Prime Minister, and U Mo Myit, as Executive Secretary to the Economic and Social Board, respected and understood each other and had worked together effectively on the Committee of Experts and other sub-committees of the Board. Their ability to resolve the procedural questions which inevitably arose out of the confused jurisdictional situation undoubtedly prevented an extremely awkward situation from developing.

The most deleterious effect of the confusion of responsibility between the Board and the Office of the Deputy Prime Minister for National Economy was the stifling of the task force effort in the winter of 1957–58. The work of the task forces in industrial enterprises was originally welcomed by U Nu, and U Kyaw Nyein later welcomed the idea of assigning them the broader task of dealing with public enterprise in all fields. But their efforts were blocked because it was simply impossible to locate the proper forum for consideration of their findings. U Kyaw Nyein's Economic Committee, operating pursuant to U Nu's June 1957 directives, had recommended that the Deputy Prime Minister's office act on task force recommendations, and the Prime Minister had publicly confirmed in his September 1957 speech that the task force effort would be made. Because of the emerging political split, which took place only the following May, U Kyaw Nyein was reluctant personally to act on the initial task force findings and recommendations or to give his Secretary, U Tun Thaung, clear instructions on what to do. U Mo Myit, on the other hand, could not very well act on his own responsibility to take jurisdiction on behalf of the National Planning Commission, which had by then succeeded the Economic and Social Board. Nor was the Prime Minister disposed to give him clear instructions in this matter. In consequence, the task force effort fell between the two offices.

A lesser confusion developed when the Economic and Social Board was succeeded by the National Planning Commission late in 1957, and U Raschid was designated Executive Member. Again, the responsibilities of the Executive Member were not clearly defined. It was presumed he would act on behalf of the Chairman on the matters which required attention between meetings or during the Chairman's absence, but whether he would act only on routine and administrative questions or on more important and substantive questions as well was not indicated in the order. If, as Executive Member, U Raschid had attempted to act, in effect, as would an executive vice chairman — an

authority which had been withheld from Vice Chairman U Kyaw Nyein —
an open conflict between them would undoubtedly have developed. And U
Raschid was far too intelligent to invade what would ordinarily have been the
Vice Chairman's prerogatives in the absence of a clear mandate. While the
benefits that could have accrued from the functioning of a capable Executive
Vice Chairman were lost, the civil servants on whom so much depended were
spared the unpleasant necessity of being forced to take sides in a jurisdictional
and power conflict.

CONFUSION BETWEEN THE PLANNING AND SUPERVISORY AGENCIES

A final element of confusion arose out of the Board's sometimes ambiguous
relationships with the Planning Ministry, a relationship which changed over
the years as the personnel changed. In the early years when the Planning
Secretary, the late U Tin Pe, had become involved through the Special Projects Implementing Board in the implementation of a number of important
projects, the Board's Secretary U Hla Maung stepped into the planning
vacuum and had a good part of the planning activity performed by the economic consultants under the aegis of the Economic and Social Board itself.
Upon Hla Maung's departure and the advent of U Mo Myit as Planning
Secretary, this situation was reversed. Not only did U Mo Myit take up the
planning load which had moved over to the Board — because he was more
enterprising and willing to take on personal responsibilities than was Board
Secretary U Tin Maung, the Planning Ministry found ways, within the conventions of the planning and programing processes, to exercise a number of
supervisory and coordinating functions which might, more properly, have
been undertaken by the Board. In the final stage, of course, the liquidation of
the Board, the location of its successor agency (the National Planning Commission) within the Planning Ministry and the appointment of U Mo Myit
as Executive Secretary to the Commission, as well as Planning Secretary, resolved the question of the relationship between the planning and the supervisory bodies. In any event, the shifting of responsibility and function between the two agencies did not seriously affect their combined performance.

SUMMARY

The weaknesses of supervision and coordination in Burma's development
program were primarily weaknesses on the part of the Economic and Social
Board. These arose out of: the Board's failure to appreciate the full nature of
its responsibilities and to devote to them the time and energy they required;
the Chairman's failure to delegate authority to the Vice Chairman; a number
of weaknesses in the decision-making process; inconclusive delegations of
responsibility without accompanying authority; the failure to create and support a strong secretariat; and the failure to follow through on decisions made

to insure that they were effectively implemented. Because of the Board's failure to discriminate between important and unimportant matters and its inadequate attention to its duties, it failed completely to meet its responsibility for periodical review of program and project progress. And more important than any of these was the Board's failure to come to grips with fundamental problems of economic policy, management and efficiency which were at the heart of the implementation problem.

CHAPTER 29

Problems of

Public Administration

If public administration is conceived broadly as embracing the organization and conduct of governmental affairs at all levels, it is to weaknesses in the public administration that the chief deficiencies in the implementation of Burma's development program must be attributed. These deficiencies had their origin in the colonial administration inherited from the British. They were compounded by the loss of a qualified staff and the enlarged tasks undertaken by the newly independent nation. But, serious as these factors were, they were overshadowed by the colossal abuses to which the public administration was subjected by monolithic political control, and by the failure of the political leadership to recognize and live up to its responsibilities. Political abuses subverted, frustrated and corrupted the executive apparatus. In failing to reform and invigorate that apparatus, the leadership failed to meet the demands of the hour, and in this respect failed the country.

Various aspects of the public administration problem have already been discussed, and in some detail, in earlier chapters — especially in Chapters 7 and 23–28 and (historically) Chapters 10–15. This treatment has covered, among other matters, the organization of central and district administration (Chapter 7); the administration of import policy and implementation (Chapter 12), attitudes toward the public service and decision-making (Chapter 23), morale in the public service (Chapter 24), the administration of financial sanctions (Chapter 26), management in the public services (Chapter 27), and top-level supervision and coordination (Chapter 28). The ensuing discussion will rely upon the reader's recall of these earlier references.[1]

1. A rounded treatment of Burma's public administration would require examination of the central Government administration, of district and local administration under it, and of the special

THE COLONIAL INHERITANCE

The colonial Government had been concerned chiefly with law and order, revenues and the interests of the business community. Since its business was mainly to administer and only a small number of foreign officers could be assigned to run the country, it was wary of new policies or activities which might disturb the placid surface and the orderly flow of events. The procedures it developed were designed to enable the few at the top to exercise complete control over the public administration. Anything that smacked of policy or threatened to establish new precedent was naturally reviewed at the highest level.

The supervision, however, extended beyond the area of policy. To insure correct performance, the details of all operations were scrutinized and checked at successively higher levels all the way to the top echelons. There was little delegation of authority and responsibility below this top layer of officialdom. Routines and procedures were minutely prescribed in bulky manuals designed to minimize the exercise of judgment at lower levels and to isolate and question the novel at successive levels of review. Tight control by a handful of foreign officers required also that detailed registers be kept of all paper movements, that documents be translated and summarized by clerks, and that all matters before the Government be presented in a manner which facilitated spot decisions. These took the form of a brief instruction or note on the file. Instructions or decisions pursuant to such a process served the purpose so far as budgetary approvals, judicial appeals, tax assessments and the like were concerned. They were not conducive to constructive performance across the broad spectrum of activities carried on by a welfare state. They did not make for the exercise of leadership in performance, supervision or review.

In fact, the colonial administrative system was negative in its design and quality. It is difficult to conceive of a system better calculated to suppress initiative and constructive performance. Yet, when the Burmese inherited it, they were so happy to have gained the direction of it that they saw little reason to question or modify the system itself.

PROBLEMS OF OVERLAPPING ORGANIZATION

The organization of the central Government of Burma as of July 1953 is shown in the chart at the back of the book. This shows twenty-six ministries under the Prime Minister (twenty-one of them functional, five represent-

---

case of the several state (Hill People's) governments. Elaboration of the earlier discussion of district and local government and treatment of the special case of the several state governments are not essential to this analysis. The comments which follow will concentrate, therefore, on the central Government administration. For a fuller account of state, district and local administration, the reader is referred to Daw Mya Sein's *The Administration of Burma;* F. S. V. Donnison's *Public Administration in Burma;* and J. S. Furnivall's *The Governance of Modern Burma.*

ing state governments) and the departments, boards, commissions, and so on, responsible to each of them. Even casual inspection reveals a number of instances in which ministries overlap one another, and where consolidation would be in order. Thus, the Ministry of Land Nationalization clearly belongs with the Ministry of Agriculture; the Ministry of Democratization of Local Administration with the Home Ministry; the Ministry of Cooperation and Commodity Distribution with the Ministry of Commerce (later called Trade Development); and the Ministry of Relief and Resettlement with the Ministry of Social Services. The Ministry of Religious Affairs obviously would fit better into the Ministry of Culture than into the Ministry of National Planning. This proliferation of overlapping ministries was of course influenced more by the desire to give pride of place to influential politicians than by organizational and functional requirements.

Another kind of organizational overlapping is not evident in the chart. Each ministry had a number of clerical branches, headed by branch superintendents, to handle the flow of paper work. These branches were duplicated by similar branches within each of the departments under the several ministries.

These overlapping organizational and staffing arrangements, while wasteful and inefficient, need not by themselves have had serious effects. Their effects were, however, terribly aggravated by the personnel and procedural weaknesses later described.

STAFFING AND PERSONNEL MANAGEMENT

The key officials in the central Government administration were the secretaries to Government, in executive charge of the ministries, who were comparable to the Permanent Under-Secretaries in the British governmental system. Next in importance came the department directors and the top officials in the specialized services — police, engineers, health, and so on. With the attainment of independence, the ranks of top administrative personnel had been badly depleted. Furnivall, comparing the quarterly Civil Lists of October 1947, immediately prior to independence, and of April 1948, immediately following independence, found the following:

In the October list, there were 99 members of the Superior Civil Service, the mainspring of the administrative machinery; by April, 71 of these had retired or were on leave preparatory to retirement. Out of the top 50 in the list 33, two thirds, had gone; and of the top 25 only 4 remained. In the Police Service, so essential for the maintenance of order, out of 37 officers with the rank of District Superintendent or higher, 31 had gone. In the October list there were 23 permanent officers with the rank of Executive Engineer and upwards, but in April there remained only five, of whom two were non-Burmans. The situation in the Civil Medical Service was not quite so deplorable; of 36 doctors with the rank of Civil Surgeon upwards, 18 still remained, though only 6 of these were Burmans. In the Frontier Service, responsible for administration in the tribal hills, there was almost a clean sweep; out of 62 officials only 9 were left.[2]

Not only had the ranks of top administrative personnel been depleted — the new tasks and much broader functions undertaken by an independent Burma greatly increased the requirements. According to one skilled observer, Burma had left "not much more than one-tenth" of the higher administrative and technical officers "required for the efficient organization of a democratic country."[3] The gaps were of course filled by promotion and outside appointment, but those chosen for the jobs were substantially less qualified than their predecessors. The situation was aggravated by compulsory retirement at age 55.

Secretaries to Government were sometimes assisted by additional, joint, deputy and assistant secretaries. All these personnel, including the secretaries, came from the administrative service and lacked technical background in the work done by the departments under their control. In the British days, the broader general training of the secretaries, the paucity of specialized activities in the Government and the qualifications of the department directors minimized the dangers inherent in this situation. With all these circumstances changed, the lack of technical background had extremely serious results. And the situation was not helped by frequent transfers which kept the innocence of incumbents practically intact.

Another serious weakness was that ministries and departments were staffed to an excessive degree by clerks and lacked executive and administrative officers in proper ratio. Staff management and supervision were consequently highly inadequate and unsystematic. Indeed, officers frequently did not know their authorized staff strength or the number of posts unfilled. As Jackson points out, "In many Departments and Ministries senior and responsible officers have no clear idea of their authorized quota of staff at any given moment or at any previous date; they have not the necessary information to hand and to provide it would require research. This arises from a lack of modern establishment and staff records, readily available and understandable."[4]

At lower as well as higher levels, personnel were too frequently shifted to learn their jobs thoroughly; they went from ministry to ministry, from Rangoon to the field or from the field to Rangoon. Transfers were not only fre-

2. J. S. Furnivall, *The Governance of Modern Burma*, 2nd ed., International Secretariat, Institute of Pacific Relations, New York, 1960, p. 28.
3. George T. Jackson, *Report of a Survey of Public Administration in Burma*, Supt., Govt. Printing and Stationery, Rangoon, 1954, p. 9.
4. *Ibid.*, p. 14.

quent but arbitrary. Only a small proportion of jobs in the civil service were controlled by Public Service Commission appointment, and promotion was based on seniority. All promotions above a junior rank required approval by the Cabinet.

A visitor to a typical Government office would find it situated in an old, dirty, dark and poorly ventilated building. On entering, he would observe a multitude of clerks lounging at tottery desks, which were jammed one against the other and heaped high with dusty files that appeared not to have been moved for months. Even higher piles of older and dustier files would be stacked against the walls, on top of crowded cupboards and sometimes in the corridors. More clerks would be reading newspapers, sipping tea or chatting with their neighbors than would be working. If the official sought by the visitor was in his office, he too would be surrounded by files, and was not likely to be found working on them. The prevailing atmosphere was a compound of indifference, indolence and lethargy. The typical office gave the impression of a badly kept archive which was being used temporarily as a hiring-hall.

In this desultory setting, lateness, frequent absences during the working day and departure before the day's end did not much matter, and one scarcely noticed the broken-down typewriters, the telephones and mimeograph machines that functioned so poorly, or the absence of business machines of all kinds. One could not, however, fail to observe, in any office which dealt directly with the public — the postal and telegraph offices, the customs, the foreigners' registration office, for example — the inevitable crowds waiting, waiting, while the wheels of Government imperceptibly ground, waiting for someone to attend to them.

PAY SCALES

The poor quality of the public administration is more easily understood in the light of the government's pay scales. These were clearly inadequate to attract or retain qualified personnel, to sustain morale, or to prevent widespread petty corruption. An idea of these pay scales is afforded in Table 80.

With independence, the salaries of the all-important secretaries to Government were reduced from K 3,500 to K 1,600 per month, and living costs increased about five times. The secretaries' real income had thus been reduced to about one tenth of the pre-war level. The remaining wage levels also speak for themselves. At the bottom of the scale, they help to explain why letters destined for abroad often failed to reach their destination — the clerks simply removed the stamps and threw the letters away — and why almost all employees at lower levels were under pressure to find ways to augment their meager incomes.

Table 80

Selected Pay Scales in the Public Service, 1954

	Monthly Pay (*Kyats*)
Chief Justice	3,000
Puisne Judges	2,500
Auditor-General, Chief Secretary, Finance Commissioner	1,800
Secretary to Government, Joint Secretary, Divisional Commissioner, Senior Directors, Directors of Agriculture, Directors General of Telegraphs, of Posts, of Police, of Public Instruction, Inspector General of Hospitals, Collector of Customs, and Chief Conservator of Forests, Commissioner of Income-Tax, Chief Engineer (Irrigation), Accountant-General	1,600
Additional Secretary, Junior Directors, Directors of Posts, of Veterinary Services, of Geological Survey, of Public Relations, of Labour, of Civil Aviation, Inspector-General of Prisons, Excise Commissioner, Commissioner of National Revenue, of Land Settlement and of Land Records	1,400
Deputy Secretary, Deputy Commissioner, District and Sessional Judges, Assistant Collector of Customs	1,000 to 1,400
Deputy Director in Departments, Deputy Inspector, District Superintendents, Forest Conservators and Principal and Superintending Engineer	1,300
Controller of Immigration, Executive Engineer, Divisional Forester, Hospital Superintendent, Controller and Assistant Director, District Representative of Co-operatives, Chief Superintendent of Excise, Chief Aircraft Inspector, Director of Meteorological Services, Senior Geologist	800 to 1,200
Assistant Secretary	600 to 800
Senior District Officer, Subdivision Officer, Treasury Officer, Assistant Engineer, Head Appraiser of Customs, Deputy Controller of Immigration	350 to 700
Chief Superintendent and Superintendent of branches in large offices	350 to 450 plus cost of living bonus of 55 to 92
Senior Upper Division Assistant (Clerk), Head Clerk, Inspector, District Treasury Representative, Veterinarian	200 to 300 plus cost of living bonus of 97
Upper Division Assistant (Clerk), Sub-Inspector of Police, Treasury Accountant, Stenographer, Examiner, Revenue and Settlement Inspector, Settlement Inspector	110 to 200 plus cost of living bonus of 75 to 97
Lower Division Clerk, Typist, Machine Operator, Revenue Surveyor, Record Keeper, Weather Observer	70 to 110 plus cost of living bonus of 56 to 75
Draftsman, Record Supplier (file keeper), Head Constable, Laboratory Assistant, Driver, Assistant and Untrained Teacher	50 to 60 plus cost of living bonus of 47 to 51
Constable, Office Boy, Messenger, Peon	40 to 50 plus cost of living bonus of 42 to 47

Source: George T. Jackson, *Report of a Survey of Public Administration in Burma,* Supt., Govt. Printing and Stationery, Rangoon, 1954, pp. 18–19.

PROCEDURES

Before the first attempts to introduce self-government in 1923, the day-to-day flow of work in Government operations was naturally simple and restricted, and the responsibility for decisions was limited and drastically centralized. Manuals and directives were all written and published with this practice and policy in mind. There was apparently no time, or at least no attempt was made, to change these between 1923 and the outbreak of World War II, and certainly since then events have moved too quickly for anything definitive to be done. Therefore manuals of procedures for the Township and District officers, Departmental Headquarters and the Secretariat were written under a form of administration when Burma was still a Province of India. The Secretariat Manual is of a later date, but still was compiled before the war and before the achievement of independence.

These manuals have become the cause of great delays, misunderstandings, bottlenecks in procedure and operations, and limit the granting of authority or assumption of responsibility.[5]

One may well hesitate to accept the statement that there was no time, between 1923 and World War II, to change the manuals. But there is no reason to question the final statement in the quotation. If anything, it understates the fact. The effect of these outmoded manuals of procedure is vividly illustrated by the manner in which correspondence was handled by the several ministries and departments. No less than thirty-nine separate steps were involved. The temptation to cite them in full is irresistible.

In most Ministries and Departments correspondence follows 39 steps. These are laid down in old, out-of-date Manuals and directives or, in some cases, are followed because of lack of directives:

(i) Mail is delivered by Postman or Peon.

(ii) It is registered or recorded.

(iii) It is received by a Lower Division Clerk.

(iv) It is delivered to the Chief Superintendent or the Senior Superintendent once or twice a day, and he retains all except personal, secret and confidential mail.

(v) He opens the mail, or it is opened for him by a Peon, and is date stamped.

(vi) He allocates mail to branches. Then it is registered; this usually involves entering the date, subject in detail, name of sender, allocation by Superintendent, and file number.

(vii) He places all mail on a flapboard and it is sent, sometimes once and sometimes twice a day, to the Assistant Secretary for his information.

(viii) The Assistant Secretary notes and passes the in-coming mail (usually called the "dak") to the Deputy Secretary.

(ix) The Deputy Secretary notes and passes the "dak" to the Joint Secretary or Secretary.

5. Jackson, *op. cit.*, p. 9.

(x) The Secretary notes it and may indicate action to be taken.

(xi) The "dak" is passed back from the Secretary to the Senior or Chief Superintendent, often through the Deputy Secretary and Assistant Secretary.

(xii) The Chief Superintendent receives the "dak," usually at least twenty-four hours after it was received initially at the office, provided all the officers were in their offices. If they were absent, then the "dak" may arrive several hours later. Sometimes, and too often, it is days later.

(xiii) The Chief Superintendent sends it to the Branch Superintendent.

(xiv) The Superintendent reads it and allocates to Clerk or Diarist.

(xv) The Diarist or Clerk registers it in daybook, file register and loose leaf register.

(xvi) The Clerk assigned by the Superintendent to deal with the case may, or not, draw the file and prepare a summary and notes.

(xvii) The letter, papers, files or documents are passed to a Senior Clerk to "note" (that is, make notes on the file).

(xviii) Actions are recorded in the diary.

(xix) The Superintendent notes.

(xx) The Chief Superintendent notes.

(xxi) The Assistant Secretary notes or expresses an opinion.

(xxii) The Deputy Secretary notes and may give instructions.

(xxiii) If passed to the Secretary, he notes and gives directions.

(xxiv) The Assistant Secretary notes the decision.

(xxv) The Chief Superintendent sees and passes to the Branch Superintendent.

(xxvi) The Superintendent sees and passes to the Clerk.

(xxvii) The Clerk prepares a draft letter or reply and the Diarist records.

(xxviii) The draft is checked by a Senior Clerk, who may amend it.

(xxix) The draft is checked by the Superintendent, who may amend it.

(xxx) The draft is checked by the Chief Superintendent, who may amend it.

(xxxi) The draft is checked by the Assistant Secretary, who may approve or amend it, or it may require the approval of the Deputy Secretary or Secretary.

(xxxii) The Superintendent sees the decision and corrections and sends it through the Diarist, who records it, to the Examiner in charge of the Copyists.

(xxxiii) The Examiner records it and gives it to the Copyist to prepare a fair copy.

(xxxiv) The Branch Clerk checks the fair copy against the final draft.

(xxxv) The Superintendent checks it; perhaps also the Chief Superintendent checks it.

(xxxvi) The Assistant Secretary may sign for the Deputy Secretary or the Secretary, or he may sign his own name.

(xxxvii) It is forwarded to the despatch section to send out the letter by post or by Peon. It is recorded in a register by Branch number, file number, date, subject, in some cases, and by the name of the recipient.

(xxxviii) The file is returned to the Branch Superintendent to check to determine any other action before directing that it be put away.

(xxxix) The Lower Division Clerk puts it away or places it in the pending file or the pile of pending files.[6]

Jackson also describes a number of variations from the above procedure, the net effect of which is further to complicate and lengthen the process. This methodology reduced output per employee to negligible proportions. "In one ministry examined, which had seven Branches and thirty employees, there was an average of 120 pieces of incoming correspondence a month."[7] This meant five pieces of correspondence per employee per month.

The same observer found also that:

It is at present not at all unusual to find correspondence seven or more days old on the desks of responsible clerks, without any action having been taken. In one instance under examination a request from one Ministry to another for routine information which could have been given within 48 hours was found still outstanding after forty days had elapsed. Investigation of incoming mail, reaching Assistant Secretaries on the flapboard after all the recording processes had been completed, showed that it was already ten to twenty days old. This often applied to quite routine reports.[8]

It does not take much exercise of the imagination to envisage the effect of the situations described on the operation of the administrative apparatus. Yet procedures for the handling of correspondence were matched by equally complicated and time-consuming procedures in other administrative functions.

The stultifying effects of the financial sanctions exercised by the Ministry of Finance have been mentioned elsewhere, but the limited financial authority given to executive officials needs to be taken into account here also. Two examples of this may suffice. Departmental directors could sanction only expenditures of 200 kyats or less. An irrigation assistant in charge of the construction of a section of canal could sanction the expenditure only of 10 kyats or less.[9] Because of this limited financial authority, Jackson inquired into the specifics of the financial controls exercised by the Finance Ministry. Three of his random findings are listed below.

(ii) A position required on a permanent basis was, after a three-month review in Finance, approved for six months. An extension had to be obtained at once and after one year an appointment was obtained . . . .

(iii) A Department of a Ministry requested the establishment of a post in October, and the Ministry sent the request forward to Finance who first asked for more information in February; this was sent by the Department to the

6. Jackson, *op. cit.*, pp. 54–55.
7. *Ibid.*, p. 57.
8. *Ibid.*, p. 64.
9. *Ibid.*, p. 47.

Ministry late in February, and in March was forwarded by the latter to Finance. In April Finance rejected the application and in May the Department was advised of the rejection.

*   *   *   *

(v) The Director of a technical Department spent some time with his technical staff developing a programme and a project that was necessary to carry out the wishes of the Government in reference to a certain policy. After careful study and planning the needs were submitted to the Ministry concerned. Here it was examined by clerical staffs and correspondence between Ministerial non-technical staffs followed. The request may not yet have reached Finance, but after two years there was still no decision and no action.[10]

The last example in particular explains a good deal of the inefficiency which attended the implementation of the development program.

OTHER FACTORS

If the weaknesses of public administration described above were inherent in the structure of government organization, practice and procedures, they were infinitely compounded by a number of other factors. Reference has already been made to civil disorder, Burmanization, bad accounting, poor morale, nepotism, attitudes toward public employment and decision-making and the widespread fear of the Bureau of Special Investigation. These were discussed in other connections; while it would be interesting to pursue their application to the present problem, considerations of space suggest that this be left to the imagination of the reader. It will perhaps be accepted that all these factors seriously hampered officials at higher levels in the exercise of their duties and in the decision-making process. The Government's tolerance of inefficiency and lack of discipline also contributed to poor performance. The assumption by the Government of a number of responsibilities which might better have been left to the private sector further strained the administrative apparatus. But more important than all these was the colossal abuse of the administrative apparatus by the political party in power.

POLITICAL ABUSES

To the A.F.P.F.L. leadership and their followers, public administration was an instrument to be used for their own purposes. Motivated as they were primarily by the desire to retain power and, next, by individual and group power conflicts within the party coalition, they were — in a collective sense — blind to the country's needs for efficient administration. They clogged the Government apparatus with their retainers, and directed the Government's services and benefits in such a way as to favor their supporters outside. Loans, tax collections, import licenses and even judicial decisions were politically in-

10. *Ibid.,* p. 36.

fluenced and controlled. In the districts, every local A.F.P.F.L. boss felt free to tell the district commissioner and other local officials how to conduct their affairs, and in whose favor. Thus, through a party domination not unlike that of Tammany Hall in its heyday, public administration was corrupted, subverted and misused.

This political manipulation and abuse of the administrative apparatus, and the terribly inept public administration to which it so greatly contributed, would not have been possible if a responsible and critical opposition had existed in the Parliament. Unfortunately, even for itself — from the long-run point of view — the A.F.P.F.L. dominated the Parliament too. Until the 1956 elections, the Parliamentary opposition was both weak and irresponsible. Although the National United Front returned a highly vocal minority at that time, it was neither well-informed nor responsible, and its criticisms could be brushed aside as not worthy of serious consideration. Thus, until the split in May 1958, the legislative branch, like the executive branch, of government, was essentially a party creature. The Parliament met only for four to six weeks in August and for two to three weeks in February, and it concerned itself chiefly with enactment of the annual and supplementary budgets. The party hacks in Parliament, with rare exceptions, displayed no initiative or independent judgment. They followed unquestioningly the orders of the Party Whip. Within the Party itself, there was little democracy. Congresses were not called, and the Supreme Council met infrequently. The small Executive Committee ruled Party and country, and within it the leadership resolved their differences, occasionally by compromise, more often by postponing the real issues.

Within the Parliament, U Kyaw Min, of the small Arakanese bloc, was an isolated voice in the wilderness who tried manfully each year, on the shortest of notice, to analyze and criticize the Budget. Other critics, like U Ba Nyein, spoke for the Communists, and had no constructive contribution to make. Neither did the press, aside from U Law Yone's independent and courageous English-language *Nation,* truly attempt to play a constructive critical role. Thus the Government was in a real sense irresponsible, except when it went to the country for general elections every four years. And even then it counted on the party bosses, the party-controlled mass organizations and the faithful followers, in whose favor it had discriminated, to provide it with recurrent majorities. This political irresponsibility resulted inevitably in irresponsible government and administration.

DECISION-MAKING AT THE TOP

Having thus described the role and effect of the Party and Government leadership, it remains to convey some understanding of how decisions were made within this leadership. Although it was widely believed, at one time, that U Nu, U Ba Swe, U Kyaw Nyein and Thakin Tin had divided among themselves the several areas of governmental power, this was not the case. The Prime Minister, with rare exceptions, consulted his colleagues, or afforded them the opportunity to express their views, when important decisions were to be made. But it was truly remarkable how seldom even one of these senior ministers and powerful politicians would take it upon himself to make a decision of consequence, even when the matter clearly fell within his area of ministerial responsibility, when the basic policy governing the matter had already been decided, when the case was clear and the timing urgent. Almost invariably the disposition was to wait and see what the Prime Minister would say.

This disposition undoubtedly arose out of a keen respect for U Nu's sagacity and was colored by relationships going back to university days, when the entire group looked up to him as an "elder brother." It also reflected, however, some fear that he might find good reason to criticize an action independently taken, and that this criticism might be sharply or even scornfully expressed. The quality of most of the ministers was such that this was entirely possible. Such a prospect none of the group was willing to face. In any case, such were U Nu's qualities of imagination, insight, energy and leadership that he frequently anticipated problems, issues and situations, and took positions long before most of his ministers had become aware of the questions. When questions came *de novo* before the ministers in the council, it was U Nu who was best able to place them in perspective, to probe most effectively for the less obvious factors involved and sense their implications. His ministers waited for him to voice his reactions, and generally had little to say thereafter.

These factors contributed greatly to making government very much a one-man show, with the merits, and the failings, of that man reflected in it. And naturally, the burden was far too great for any one man, however able, to carry.

SUMMARY

If any factor was more important than the abuse of political power in the weakness of public administration in Burma, that factor was the failure, so strongly emphasized throughout this study, adequately to delegate authority and responsibility. The Prime Minister did not delegate enough authority to his ministers. They did not delegate enough authority to their secretaries. The secretaries did not delegate enough authority to their deputies and assistants. In the departments, from the directors down it was the same story. The same was true, as we have seen, in the public enterprises.

Because of this failure to delegate authority and responsibility, matters of all kinds floated inevitably to the top. These comprised not only the important but also the trivial. The resulting necessity for so much decision-making at the top led to overcentralization, to intolerable delays followed by hasty decisions, to a lack of perspective and to the pre-empting of a disproportionate amount of the time of the top policy-makers by the unimportant, the procedural and the irrelevant, while many matters of great moment never got considered or decided at all. It led finally to an irritation on the part of the leadership with the decision-making process itself. Attendance at the Economic and Social Board, for example, was almost invariably poor. Worse still, the weight of this decision-making responsibility made it impossible for the leaders to find time for supervision, review and appraisal of the Government's far-flung activities, or even to consider the actions necessary to expedite or improve them. A general slackness and eventually an indifference to waste and inefficiency were the inevitable result.[11]

The weaknesses in Burma's public administration, and the necessity for corrective action, had not gone unnoticed. Several Burmese Commissions, in the early post-war years, had rendered constructive reports. The American consultants had stressed these points in their final report. The economic consultants, as has been amply noted, continued to do so, both in general and specific terms, and with increasing emphasis, over the years. The Jackson report, in 1953, made over eighty specific suggestions for corrective action, many of them valuable. These were augmented by Divers and other United Nations specialists in public administration, and by foreign technicians in other fields. U Chit Pe, for the Home Ministry, proposed an action program in 1957, at a time when Prime Minister U Nu had become receptive to the idea. The *Nation* and later the *Guardian* called attention periodically to the same need. The more intelligent members of the public were also aware of it, as is evidenced by the following excerpt from an "Open Letter to U Nu," from the *Guardian* of June 11, 1958, written by a retired civil servant:

Dear Sir:

May I, one of the humble *ludu* [masses] submit this to you now that God has granted you a fresh lease as head of the Government of our adolescent country. I say NOW because this is the time for many members of your AFPFL group to turn over a new leaf.

From my personal knowledge of your good self, you have not been a very realistic Executive and you were given to tall talks of doing things like a third rate politician. There are many examples of this, but only two will be mentioned here. They are — (1) a house, a motor car and a monthly income of K 800/- for every Maung Tin, Maung Yin and Ma Khin in the country and (ii) your silly reception with flowers and garlands of Pakistani cows at the Sule Pagoda Wharf.

Now in an effort to get out of the mess stemming from 10 years of A.F.P.F.L. mis-rule, let first thing be done first. As no projects or programmes can be properly

11. An excellent analysis of this same fatal weakness in another country may be found in Paul Appleby's "Re-examination of India's Administrative System," almost all of which applies equally to Burma.

implemented without a good administration, I request that you start only with the following, leaving the spectacular things well alone for the moment.

HERE ARE SOME TO BEGIN WITH:
1. Trim down the Administrative Machinery. It is overcrowded.
2. For God's sake, do not overcrowd the Cabinet AGAIN. What is needed is quality and not quantity. There are still a few third rate men in your Cabinet.
3. Weed out educationally unqualified persons from the services irrespective of connections and KILL NEPOTISM AT ALL LEVELS.
4. Make the Heads of Departments, Boards and Corporations realize that Govt. desires clean and good administration within 3 months and allow them to run their own show. If any Head fails after the time-limit spare him no more and give the responsibility to the next man. And let service men see that Government means business and that only hard work, honesty and solid results count for their advancements.

*   *   *   *

11. Give the poor *ludu* a good Government this time, for there can be no greater prosperity and liberty than under a good government. Whether an appeal to the country is to be made or not at the end of the Budget Session, please begin with the above MUSTS for the sake of the suffering *ludu* and you will be remembered for that at the time of next General Election.

This is by no means a complete list of THE MUSTS you ought to do.
Good luck,

Yours faithfully,
U Lay

U Lay (whoever he might be) was no expert in public administration, but he had put his finger on the sore spot, and prescribed the remedy. More uncommon, however, than his good sense was his boldness in speaking out publicly when so many others equally appreciative of the problem did not.

Of the leaders, it was Prime Minister U Nu who was most aware of the need to improve the public administration and who was most receptive to suggestions for improvement. But receptivity to the idea of action and taking vigorous action were two different things. The Prime Minister spoke his mind, vigorously and forthrightly, on this question, many times. But he did not seem to know how to set about getting the job done. Most of the time he did not appear to realize that concrete action programs were necessary to achieve the desired result, but rather to believe that the mere statement that action was needed was enough. Alas, it was not. In the end, it was the accumulated and almost desperate need for such action which provided much of the impetus and motivation for the assumption of power by General Ne Win and the military in September 1958.

CHAPTER 30

Problems of

Central Economic Policy

In the period immediately following independence, the strongest and most clearly defined central economic policies were nationalization, Burmanization and industrialization. Over the years, other important central economic policies were formulated as circumstances required. Still other policy areas became important in a negative kind of way because, despite the need, the Government shied away from clearly defining its attitude on them. These central economic policies, whether clear or ambiguous, had an important effect on the implementation of Burma's economic development program. The nature and effect of these policies is the subject of the discussion that follows.[1]

NATIONALIZATION POLICY

The initial wave of nationalization rolled over, at varying depths, virtually every sector of the economy — the land, the forests, transport and communications, electric power and the few existing large manufacturing enterprises. It engulfed most of the export trade and a substantial part of the import trade as well. Even the pawnshops were nationalized, and the field of commercial banking was invaded. Only in the mining sector did the Government exercise relative restraint. Here joint venture companies were formed with the largest of the foreign mining firms and successfully operated. In al-

1. This discussion is not entirely self-contained. It will not repeat, or even necessarily recall, discussions in earlier chapters in which various economic policies were covered. Among policies earlier discussed were those concerning paddy production, finance and taxes, devaluation, central procurement, private investment and pricing, and capitalization and financial advances, in the new state manufacturing enterprises. Foreign aid policy will be treated separately in the following chapter.

most every other case, the results of nationalization ranged from disappointing to calamitous.

Land distribution was inefficient, corrupt, disruptive of orderly production and — because of confusion about title and tenure — inimical to good maintenance, especially of dikes and bunds. Unsatisfactory procurement, processing, handling, marketing and pricing badly retarded rice exports and foreign exchange earnings. The extraction, milling and marketing of teak timber also suffered in Government hands. Transport, communications and electric power services were poor and costly, and their deficiencies acted as a depressant upon the entire economy. Nationalization of the Thayetmyo cement and Zeyawaddy sugar mills resulted in poor management, sharp reductions in output and higher costs. The monopoly import of essential consumer goods by the Civil Supplies Management Board resulted in less efficient distribution and higher prices to consumers.

Losses in output, sales and earnings, particularly in foreign exchange, hurt badly but were not the only adverse results of nationalization. The threat of nationalization effectively deterred the nation's private rice millers from maintaining and modernizing their plants, with great loss to the economy. The same threat deterred other new investment, whether by the remaining foreign "captive" firms or by new domestic and foreign investors. By vastly expanding opportunities for corruption for persons both within and outside the Government, nationalization accounted in substantial measure for its spread. Finally, by adding enormously to the Government's administrative and management burdens and by spreading the limited specialized managerial and executive manpower too thin, nationalization contributed greatly to inefficiency throughout the entire range of the Government's normal activities.

Implementation of the Government's compensation policy did little to mitigate the ill effects of nationalization. Apart from the land nationalization, it was the Government's general policy to pay compensation for nationalized facilities on the basis of investment less depreciation. This in itself was reasonable enough, although some of the firms concerned argued vainly for compensation on the basis of replacement cost or capitalization of potential earning power. The investment-less-depreciation formula, however, was complicated in many cases by questions of how the commonly experienced war damage was to be treated or what allowance, if any, should be made for compensation payments already received from the United Kingdom Government on account of such damages. Even after these questions had been decided, there remained questions about the arithmetic employed by the Government's accountants. More important than all these was the interminable process of getting the compensation determination made and the subsequent and equally interminable delays in payment and permission to transfer the funds. From the point of view of the firms expropriated, and of potential foreign investors as well, the implementation of compensation policy was highly unsatisfactory and an additional deterrent to investment.

By 1955–56 the impetus to nationalization had just about run out. This was not entirely because the most obvious of the private enterprises had already been nationalized. There still remained, for example, two large foreign-owned though non-operating rice mills, a number of fair-sized sawmills, mines, manufacturing plants, and other enterprises, including a large department store, in private hands. Indeed a few new and quite promising enterprises had been started, including a boat yard and a concrete pipe plant built by the Bombay-Burmah Trading Co. But the confidence of the early 1950s that nationalization was the high road to development and welfare had by this time been largely dissipated. Increasing difficulties with the public enterprises — the nationalized, the new and those still under construction — had dampened the Socialists' ardor. Even so confirmed a Socialist as U Kyaw Nyein began to doubt the wisdom of some of the decisions already made. By 1956–57 the Government was ready to agree that it should reverse the nationalization trend by selling shares in the new industrial enterprises to the general public. While financial stringency provided a ready excuse for this decision, the underlying cause was the leaders' loss of confidence in their capacity to operate the new enterprises effectively. Indeed, only a reluctance publicly to confess the failure of nationalization policy prevented serious consideration of a proposal to return rice exports to the private trade.

The decision to divest the Government of ownership of the new manufacturing enterprises was not, however, followed by action. When the Government's economic consultants explained the necessary preliminaries to such a divestment — the separate incorporations, the clarification of financial structures and capitalizations, the prospectuses, the subsequent management arrangements, and so on — the Government simply shied away from this complicated task which it did not understand and for which it had no stomach. In this moment of truth, the Government might have learned that it was easier to get into business than to get out of it.

BURMANIZATION POLICY

Second only to nationalization policy in its debilitating effects on the economy, and more pernicious in its social effects, was the Burmanization policy.

Of all the policies pursued by the Burmese Government, Burmanization was, historically and psychologically, the most deeply rooted and the most powerfully motivated. In view of the colonial experience, this was not strange. It was only to be expected that the Burmese people would wish to remove all vestiges of foreign domination. With independence, political domination was ended. The Burmese set out to complete the job by ousting the foreigners from positions of control in their economic life. With the larger British enterprises nationalized and with the Chinese ousted from the pawnshops, Burmanization policy tended to direct itself against the Indian. Whatever satisfactions this policy may have yielded to national pride were more than offset by its pernicious economic effects.

In the first place, Burmanization provided a high-octane fuel for nationalization policy. To the Burman, nationalization had two complementary aspects — the ousting of the foreigner and his replacement by a Burmese national were just as important as the socialization of the major means of production. It is doubtful whether the scope of nationalization would have been as broad, or its pace as rapid, in the absence of the Burmanization urge.

We have already noted how Burmanization policy in the import field impeded the free flow of imports and disrupted distribution, resulting in high prices to consumers. Other forms of discrimination through which Burmanization policy expressed itself — the denial of loans and foreign exchange remittances, and the non-issuance of entry permits for technicians, for example — discouraged investment and encouraged capital flight. Discrimination at the University, in the Government service and in business occupations lessened Burmans' incentives to improve their skills and exert their best efforts. Aliens who had lived all their lives in Burma found it difficult to obtain re-entry permits for sons they had sent abroad for advanced professional and technical study. But the sapping effects of such discrimination on the development of a trained manpower force were far outweighed by the slackness which Burmanization policy encouraged among Burmese youth. Because Burmanization policy most clearly favored Burmans in the field of import trade, it tended to attract to this occupation talents and energies which would otherwise have been directed into more productive activities. The broad result of all these measures was to depress the contribution which the deviant minority groups were capable of making to every aspect of the nation's economy and social life.

A policy so strongly rooted in the frustrations and hates of the past could not be expected to be moderate, logical, or even consistent with other basic policies. In the import field, for example, the supply of goods to the consuming public at the lowest prices possible was presumably a clear Government objective. When Burmanization policy came into conflict with this objective, it was the Burmanization policy which conquered. As to the logic of the policy, a discussion with U Kyaw Nyein, the then Deputy Prime Minister for National Economy, was illuminating. He had stated frankly his intention to drive the Indians out of the import trade. When asked where he wanted to drive them, he replied, "Into manufacturing production." Yet when he was asked whether resident Indians and Pakistanis would receive equal treatment in the matter of Government industrial loans, he admitted that they would not.

Burmanization policy not only reflected a basic insecurity on the part of the Burman vis-à-vis the foreigner; it confirmed and strengthened that insecurity. It therefore contributed greatly to indecisiveness throughout social life. The repressive and discriminatory measures in which this insecurity found its expression led in turn to the need for ever more stringent controls, which affected not only those at whom they were primarily aimed but society at large as well. Worst of all, by providing a scapegoat on whom almost every conceivable economic and social ill could be blamed, Burmanization enabled the Burmese to blind their eyes to their own defects, and to avoid facing up to the real issues.

If the case against Burmanization is stressed, it is partly because this aspect of the Burma experience provides a lesson that many of the emerging countries in Africa need to take to heart. "Africanization," it is already clear, seems destined to be an equally powerful policy.

INDUSTRIALIZATION POLICY

Together with nationalization and Burmanization, industrialization was one of the three strongest and most clearly defined central economic policies of the young Government. Industrialization was considered, if not equivalent to, at least the high road to, socialism, modernity and development. Industry, it was thought, was more productive than agriculture, would create employment opportunities for surplus agricultural labor, help to diversify and stabilize the economy and, by making Burma self-sufficient, provide insurance against a recurrence of severe wartime shortages and bolster the newly won political independence with its economic counterpart. In addition, by developing an economic base for at least small arms production, industrialization would help make the country more secure. These beliefs were complemented by two related ideas. Industrialization could not be confined to light industries; it needed basic support in heavy industry — i.e., a steel factory — as well. And, of course, industrialization would have to be carried out by the state — whether because the private sector could not, or should not, be permitted to do the job was not altogether clear.

The industrialization policy caused the Government to commit itself in principle, at the outset of the development program, to some sixty-five industrial projects the total cost of which was never calculated. The initial wave of projects — the steel, pharmaceuticals, jute, sugar, brick and tile and other plants — far exceeded in cost the eight-year allotment recommended by the consultants. Even when financial stringency developed in 1954–55 and precluded further state-financed industrial starts, the industries people, headed by U Kyaw Nyein, continued to try by all possible means to broaden the industrialization program with additional cotton textile and steel capacity and with new pulp and paper, fertilizer, rubber, glass and other plants. When confidence in nationalization policy weakened, the emphasis in industrialization policy was directed to joint venture arrangements.

The weaknesses in the industrialization policy arose in large part out of weaknesses in the logic on which it was predicated. Industrialization is not necessarily equivalent to development in any setting and at any given time. Industry may, to be sure, yield a greater output per capita than, say, agriculture, but the same amount of capital invested in agriculture may yield a far greater total return to the economy. With much previously cultivated land waiting for reclamation, with vast cultivable areas still available, and with great potentials for increased yields from relatively simple, low-cost improvements in seeds, fertilizers, insecticides, and so on, Burmese agriculture was not yet burdened by a true labor surplus, and was not likely to be for a considerable period of time. In any case, the Burmese notion of the contribution industrialization could make to the nation's gross product and to direct employment was vastly exaggerated. (U Kyaw Nyein was startled to learn that less than one fourth of the U. S. labor force was currently employed in manufacturing.)

Diversification within agriculture would help stabilize the economy even more than would the modest amount of industrialization which could be expected in the short run, and economic self-sufficiency, if pursued far enough, was the road to poverty rather than to economic independence, autarchy being no less fallacious in the Burmese setting than in any other. Textile mills, using domestic cotton, could prevent the recurrence of wartime shortages (but could be justified on better grounds). The pharmaceuticals plant, dependent on the import of bulk drugs and packaging components, could not. And a 20,000-ton steel mill, designed to produce chiefly light steel shapes, bar, sheet and wire products, could not, of course, support significant arms production and thus serve a strategic purpose. In any event, it was unrealistic to think that Burma, even as a neutral, could isolate herself from the economic effects of possible future war. Light industry in Burma would indeed require a heavy industry base. That base existed — elsewhere — and it made no sense to try to create it, less efficiently, less reliably and at much higher cost, in Burma.

Finally, the capacities of the private sector were far greater, both in talent and in capital, than the A.F.P.F.L. leaders realized, or than could be translated into action under the Government's excessive controls and in the face of its general hostility. In any case, state ownership and operation were not the only means of insuring industrialization — certainly not in the case of small and even medium-sized plants, and not necessarily even in the case of the larger ones. The Government could have exercised the necessary initiative, and provided capital — as loan capital, or as equity capital in partnership with private investors (domestic, foreign, or both) — without itself acting as sole entrepreneur. Burma determined on state-owned industrial enterprise, not because this was the sole alternative, but because her leaders, at least at the outset, were hostile to private ownership and were intent on building a Socialist state.

Overemphasis on industrialization, and the related ideas which entered into the complex of industrialization policy, weakened Burma's development effort in many ways. It led to poor judgment in project selection, as in the case of steel, and in the determination of project size, as in the case of pharmaceuticals. It diverted to industrialization resources which would have been more productively employed in other sectors. These included leadership and administrative resources as well as manpower, materials and the finances which command them. If, for example, the dynamic U Kyaw Nyein had been named Minister for Agriculture, rather than Industries, at the very outset of the program, there is no question that Burma's recovery and development would have proceeded at a steadier and more rapid pace. Industrialization policy also hurt by diverting attention from the need to improve internal security and public administration and other priority requirements.

Enthusiasm for industrialization under state auspices also blinded the leaders to the practical problems of management. Not only did it lead them to disregard these problems at the outset of the program; so intent were they on seeking ways to implement new plants that they continued to ignore management problems even as the first wave of industries commenced operations in an atmosphere of near chaos. This disregard of management problems was terribly costly in money, in public confidence and, ultimately, in political consequences.

FISCAL, MONETARY AND CREDIT POLICY

In view of the extensive discussion in Chapter 27, only a few brief comments on finance are required here. The 1954–55 consequences of the disregard for sound fiscal and monetary policy in the 1953–54 capital program registered deeply. The Government was thereafter sufficiently concerned with inflationary threats to comply in a general way with the advice it received on policy in these areas. It refused, however, as we have seen, to place adequate emphasis on a strengthening domestic finance to achieve a soundly based economic stability, and chose instead to take the easier road of borrowing from abroad. It relied heavily on imports and foreign exchange as instruments of monetary policy. The structure and nature of the economy did not afford much opportunity to use credit policy as a tool for achieving stabilization objectives. Central bank rates, rediscounts, open market operations and reserve requirements could not be utilized effectively, as in the case of more developed economies, to contribute in major degree to economic stability.

On the whole, the fiscal, monetary and credit policies were better than their implementation. This was due in an important degree to the reliance placed on import policy for anti-inflation control and to the administrative and structural weaknesses in the implementation of import programs. It was due also to the inability, already noted, of the State Agricultural Bank to assume responsibility for an ever-increasing portion of the credit needs of the cultivators. This failure not only prevented the living levels of the cultivators from rising; it also continued to channel into agricultural credit the savings that would otherwise have found their way into more desirable productive uses.

FOREIGN TRADE AND EXCHANGE POLICY

Burma abandoned her adherence to the old British Imperial Preference System in 1953. She displayed few preferences thereafter either in making foreign purchases or in seeking markets for her goods abroad.

On the export side, policy was opportunistic both in direction and in payments. Barter was resorted to as a technique for rice disposal to the Soviet bloc countries. This reflected the desire to maximize export earnings, and was not politically motivated. Less publicized were other barter arrangements periodically proposed by Free World countries like Indonesia and the Philippines, which the Government was always ready to consider. The Government was even inclined to consider barter deals offered by private firms, such as the East Asiatic Company, but fortunately was dissuaded from accepting them. As late as 1958 a large-scale open-account arrangement was concluded with India, involving on Burma's side timber and a number of additional commodities other than rice (which was governed by a separate cash agreement).

On the import side, Burma's purchase of dollar goods was strictly limited by a rather Spartan, self-imposed interpretation of her obligations as a member of the Sterling bloc. Quotas and licensing, rather than tariffs, were used for control purposes, and the volume of imports was used as a variable to safeguard foreign exchange reserves or to curb domestic money supply, as the case might be. Policy and practice with respect to the structure of the import trade — the applications of nationalization and Burmanization policy — have already been described, as have the problems resulting from them.

The barter arrangements for rice reflected the mistaken notion that excessive carry-over stocks of rice could be sold only in this way. Actually, at any time, Burma could have sold all her rice for cash, had she been willing to adjust her prices realistically early enough in the season to make larger shipments possible. When she sold rice to Soviet bloc countries on barter account for the "price" paid by cash buyers, she sold in reality for a far lower price, because the goods she obtained in exchange were, with the exception of Chinese and Czech goods, priced far above competitive goods elsewhere. In fact, rice sold to the Soviet Union constituted, in effect, a non-interest-bearing credit to that country, for desired goods could not be obtained in payment.

These credits were reduced periodically, chiefly by subsequently negotiated tripartite arrangements which permitted their use in Czechoslovakia. Of all the Soviet bloc countries, only China and Czechoslovakia proved satisfactory trading partners. Hungary, Poland, Rumania and Bulgaria, as well as the U.S.S.R., were highly unsatisfactory from the point of view of availabilities, qualities, prices and deliveries. Fortunately, successive decreases in export rice prices increased cash purchases virtually to the level of available supplies by 1957, and barter sales were thereafter reduced to relatively minor amounts. One might say, therefore, that rice barter sales were used — though not by design — as a substitute for effective rice marketing and pricing.

Burma's policy on U. S. disposals of surplus rice, wheat and other food grains under P.L. 480 to countries which were traditional markets for Burmese rice was noteworthy. Although much criticism was voiced in the press at the time, early P.L. 480 disposals to such countries in 1953, 1954 and 1955 evoked no official protest by the Burmese Government. Once Burma herself became the recipient of P.L. 480 assistance, chiefly in cotton, her leaders felt it would be illogical to complain about the P.L. 480 assistance others received. The economic consultants had several times suggested that Burma at least communicate her concern to the United States, and request that she be consulted before new P.L. 480 food grain arrangements were undertaken with countries which were traditional markets for Burma's rice. This Prime Minister U Nu refused to do. His reasons were that he would not prevent food from reaching hungry people, that the United States was perfectly capable of managing her own affairs and that any complaint Burma might make would in any case be ignored. On more than one occasion when the United States sought informally to ascertain Burma's reactions to P.L. 480 disposals then under contemplation, Burmese officials declined to express them.

Tariff policy was moderate, and geared increasingly to revenue and to protection for new home industry. The tariff schedules still retained many vestiges of the colonial structure, with raw materials and components dutiable at rates equal to those imposed on finished products, and without special consideration for capital goods.

Foreign exchange policy aimed broadly at maintaining reserves at a level double that required for currency cover and equal to approximately six months' import requirements. It was heavily relied upon, as has been noted, to implement domestic stabilization policy.

PRICING POLICY

Only with respect to the Government-established domestic purchase price for paddy was pricing policy clear, purposeful and determined. In most other applications it was fuzzy, timid and weak, and not attuned to development objectives.

Maintenance of the fixed purchase price for paddy provided the Government with huge profits as rice export prices rose to their peak in 1952, and with increasingly narrow and ever more needed profit margins as export prices dropped thereafter. The profit margin built up the huge cash and foreign exchange reserves with which the Government so confidently embarked on its large-scale development program, and on which it counted so heavily to finance the program. Objections from the paddy cultivators to the fixed purchase price were strangely lacking. They did not realize, perhaps, how great was the Government's profit margin and how disproportionately they were contributing to the cost of the development effort.[2] The organizations which supposedly represented them — the A.B.P.O. and the cooperatives — were political arms of the A.F.P.F.L., and did not speak up for their interest in this matter. What was more surprising was the failure of the Communists to exploit this issue, on which the Government was so vulnerable. It is difficult to believe the Communists were not aware of the realities and the political potentials. Were they silent because, always hopeful of early success in winning control of the Government, they too wished to use this same powerful engine for resource mobilization? Whatever the reason, the issue was never strongly pressed.

The pricing of export rice illustrates the classic difficulty of determining that monopoly price which, over time, best combines with volume to yield maximum profit. This problem would have been difficult even for sophisticated managers, which the S.A.M.B. and the Cabinet (the power to make price decisions was never delegated to the S.A.M.B.) were not. Furthermore, the ministers did not trust one another. (One of the key issues on which U Nu and U Kyaw Nyein had fallen out was the former's charge that Kyaw Nyein, on one occasion when U Nu was out of the country, had gone beyond the bounds of propriety in approving a certain rice sale.) Lacking confidence in their own judgment, and fearful of error — though unwilling to liquidate their monopoly — the ministers hesitated to attempt boldly, in 1953 and the following years, to price the rice surplus at a level which would clear the market. Under pressure from the market and their own consultants, they accommodated prices, step by step, to the market decline. But until 1956 this accommodation was always too little and too late.

By 1956–57, U Nu and his chief colleagues had accepted the proposition that Burma's increasing rice supplies could be sold only if priced competitively with wheat, in terms of historic wheat-rice price ratios (broadly adjusted for remaining post-war distortions). When this idea finally "took," it took hard, and was inflexibly applied. Thus, it proved extremely difficult to persuade the Government to mark up the price of rice in 1958, when bad weather resulted

---

2. Even under private trade, before the war, the traders' margins appear to have been more than competitive. In addition, rents and land revenue taxes were relatively far less burdensome than before. The cultivators' net income, therefore, was not far different.

in a short crop and buyers' demands for S.M.S., at £32 per ton (the price previously established only in the Indian contract for that year) far exceeded the available supply.

Civil Supplies pricing of imported essential consumer goods has been mentioned. Although the Government's stated purpose was to supply such goods to consumers at the lowest possible prices, inefficient procurement and management made the Civil Supplies Board incapable of competing with private trade, and the Government yielded to demands for a monopoly over the goods handled by it so that higher than competitive prices could be maintained. Attempts to eliminate the monopoly privilege were only partly successful, despite the Government's desire, especially after its shock by the 1956 election results, to insure lower prices. Thus, nationalization policy, like Burmanization policy, triumphed over basic pricing policy.

When shortages in 1955 and 1956 resulted in a tremendous increase in the prices of imported goods, and rationed Civil Supplies goods were being resold by buyers at large profits, the economic consultants recommended that these windfall profits be recaptured by the Government through higher Civil Supplies prices. These, they suggested, should be set just below the market, and adjusted to lead market prices step by step back toward normal as import volumes increased. The first part of the recommendation was followed. The second, which required flexibility, judgment and initiative, was not, and much criticism rightly ensued.

Pricing in other fields was equally faulty. The railways and the waterways did not adjust their rates downward as security improved and capacity and freight volume grew. In many cases, inland traffic hauls of 400 miles cost more than a 4,000-mile ocean haul to Rangoon from suppliers' ports. Electric power, at 45 pyas (9.5¢) per KWH for domestic use, was extremely expensive. Yet even when sizable new generating capacity was installed, power rates were not modified. The Thayetmyo cement mill, when privately owned, had sold cement at Thayetmyo (upriver on the Irrawaddy from Rangoon) at a monopoly price based on the cost of imported cement at Rangoon, plus freight to Thayetmyo — in other words, as though the cement had actually been imported. The Government, after nationalization, continued the same pricing policy, despite criticism by the economic consultants. It is doubtful whether the Government understood the principles involved, or recognized that they were discriminating, as the former private monopoly owners had done, against construction and development in the hinterland.[3] Subscription to the Rangoon telephone system, at K 600 per year, was costly, and very difficult to obtain. This charge did not vary with the number of calls made, nor was extra charge made for long-distance calls. (Of course, there were not many

3. Some of the pricing policy problems of the new state manufacturing enterprises have been mentioned in Chapter 27.

destinations to which such calls could be attempted, and still fewer to which they could intelligibly be completed!) This pricing scale was a carry-over from the pre-war days when only privileged English officials and traders had telephones. But no one thought to change the tariff.

Thus, for the most part, pricing was determined by timidity, by politics and by inertia. Policy itself was lacking for the most part. While a forum existed for its formulation, appreciation of the necessity and function of pricing policy was wanting, and too many questions of far less importance preoccupied the policy-makers in such time as they found to devote to development affairs.

PRIVATE SECTOR AND INVESTMENT POLICY

In the early days of independence, even the moderate elements in the A.F.P.F.L. had joined with the Socialists in denouncing capitalism and profit-seekers as exploitative, mercenary and evil. By 1949 the desperate fortunes of the insurrection-torn state had led to a plea for private investment from abroad, and the strong passions of Burmanization had somewhat softened the Government's animus toward Burmese business men. Indeed, by 1953, when Burmese traders who had overstocked themselves with imported textiles during the Korean War boom were caught badly by a sudden sharp drop in prices, they were able to demand that the Government — just because it called itself a socialist government — bail them out by buying their goods at cost, and actually got consideration of this request! Surely it was a strange kind of socialism that could seriously entertain such a demand! The economic consultants pointed out (with some pleasure) that even a capitalist government dedicated to a free enterprise profit (and loss) economy would give short shrift to such requests.

By the end of 1953, the Government affirmed its readiness — for an interim period — to assist Burmese producers and traders, financially and otherwise. Priority in import licenses for traders and industrial loans for producers soon followed. In 1955 the Government issued a statement concerning private investment policy designed to encourage both domestic and foreign investors. This was formalized in legislation in 1959.

While the thinking of some of the leaders, and the Government's public statements and announced policies, did turn in the direction of private investment, they did not turn far enough, and Government practices did not turn with them. Security remained a problem. Taxes continued to be burdensome. Labor policies and legislation were unrealistic. Import licenses for raw materials, spare parts and operating supplies remained uncertain. Too many unnecessary production and distribution controls were still in effect. Essential services (water, transport, communications, and so on) were no more reliable than before. Too many Government employees and party adherents still needed to be paid off. The duration of the official "interim period" during which private enterprise would be tolerated was as uncertain as were most other factors pertinent to investment decisions. In general, the climate for investment remained unfavorable. Thus, although the initial animus against private enterprise and investment was modified, and some Government policies were developed which were relatively favorable, the total attitude was at best ambivalent, and the Government's actual practices were discouraging. It is remarkable that the private sector responded to the degree that it did. This response, under so many adverse circumstances, is strong evidence of the challenging profit opportunities offered by the economy and the inherent capacity and inclination of the private sector to realize them.

PLANNING PRIORITIES

Since priorities inevitably reflect policies as well as strategies, some discussion of priorities would seem to be called for in the present context of economic policy.

In their development planning, the American consultants had assigned high priority to internal security, to the restoration of pre-war levels of production and exports in the primary sectors, to manpower training, to maximum participation by the private sector, to improved organization, administration and management, and to supervision and coordination to insure satisfactory implementation of a balanced development program. These emphases, as we have seen, did not register effectively with the Government. The Government's program assigned high priorities to nationalization, Burmanization and industrialization and, so far as the physical program was concerned, seemingly gave priority to doing everything possible at once — which meant, in practice, that it really assigned no program priorities at all.

With financial and foreign exchange stringency in 1954–55–56, and the need for program cutbacks, priority was given to projects already committed and under way, to the basic rehabilitation of transport and communications, to projects which promised to earn or save foreign exchange, to projects which could readily use reparations or barter credits and to emergency projects such as restoration of the destroyed Kabo dam, as well as to projects basically more essential. The relative readiness of the various operating agencies was also an important factor, as were political considerations in a number of cases. This state of affairs makes any discussion of basic priorities somewhat academic and even irrelevant to the actual situation. Indeed, when the World Bank Mission asked, early in 1955, for a statement of the priorities in the Government's development plans, those responsible for framing the reply approached the task with a feeling of some awkwardness and even unreality.

More and more, as experience accumulated, the consultants felt that the basic priorities were not so much those involved in the allocation of resources as those they had stressed at the very outset — the absolute primacy of internal law and order, restoration of primary production, encouragement of the private sector, improvement of the public administration and the essential services, improvement of management in the public enterprises, expansion or creation of essential institutions like the State Agricultural Bank and an Industrial Development Bank, improved supervision and coordination of program implementation and formulation of the policies required to facilitate achievement of development goals. These emphases, which, to be sure, involved resource allocations to some extent, were of far greater practical importance than were the more conventional priorities usually discussed in the context of resource allocation.

HOUSING POLICY

The general welfare objectives of the Government, combined with practical and political considerations, had led to a public housing policy which subsidized certain groups — chiefly higher level Government employees and political workers and favorites.[4] This policy resulted in the construction, until 1956, of several thousand urban housing units at an average cost of K 10,000–K 15,000. These involved a substantial subsidy to the favored few to whom the units were made available at a rental far below cost. This policy made little sense in an economy in which the cost of subsidies could be borne only by the less favored urban poor and by the even poorer agricultural segments of the population. When this point was made to U Nu and, separately, to U Kyaw Nyein, both grasped it at once, and the construction of relatively high-cost housing units requiring subsidy rentals was abandoned.

What the Government failed to do was to sponsor a low-cost housing program, of units appropriate to the environment, and at a cost which would be covered by the low rentals people could afford to pay. Such a program, with housing units and communities of approved designs and specifications, could have been carried out by private builders with simple incentives like ten-year tax exemptions and low-interest loan capital, and would have served a highly useful purpose. Even after the nationalization drive lost its initial impetus and doubts of its further value had set in, the Government was not yet ready seriously to consider such an approach.

LAND ALIENATION POLICY

One of the earliest policies for agricultural relief was the prohibition of land alienation, designed to prevent the foreclosure of mortgages on agricultural land and further increases in tenancy. The law implementing this policy also prohibited the acquisition of land ownership by foreigners. Whether by

4. Families dispossessed by fire from their hutments were either assisted in rebuilding them or housed in low-cost, publicly built, non-subsidized "emergency" units.

accident or design, this prohibition applied to urban properties as well as farm lands. In terms of development objectives, this latter prohibition was extremely undesirable. Since most of the banks were owned by foreigners, it prevented Burmese owners of urban land and improved properties from using these assets as collateral to raise capital for investment. U Kyaw Nyein appreciated this point, when it was presented to him, but never got around to doing anything about it. Thus an unanticipated application of a well-motivated policy exerted a retarding influence on development and, as in many other instances, inertia proved too powerful to permit its correction.

Incidentally, even the protection the policy gave to cultivators had its negative aspect. The farmer could no longer be foreclosed off his land for nonpayment of debt or interest. By the same token, however, the diminished security meant that the borrower had to pay higher rates of interest for money from private lenders. Under the circumstances the protection afforded the cultivator came at high cost, and its value may have become debatable. Interest rates might have been reduced by a Government-guaranteed loan repayment insurance program, under which all borrowers would pay a premium to cover defaulters, but such a possibility was not explored.

SUMMARY

This consideration of central economic policy should have made it quite obvious that Burma's economic policies were not geared to her development objectives. Nationalization, Burmanization, industrialization, private investment, fiscal and other policies operated in many ways to retard and distort, rather than to support, the development process. This of course was not clear to the Burmese leaders at the outset of the program. In their eyes, these policies were more than reconcilable with the central development objective; they were viewed as highly essential and complementary to it — as policies which would spur development and make it healthier by strengthening the social and economic structure, by building more equitable relationships into it and by establishing a sounder basis for continued growth in the future.

In Burmese eyes, each of these major economic policies was a different aspect of the welfare goal that development was designed to serve. Nationalization, they believed, would protect the *ludu* — the "masses" — from exploitation. Burmanization would similarly protect them from the greedy and untrustworthy foreigner. Industrialization would provide them with the good things of life and make for a stronger independence. And light taxation, easy loan collection, subsidized housing, spread-the-work employment policy and easy standards of performance were but obvious applications of the welfare principle. If the goal of development was welfare, it seemed perfectly logical to have some of the welfare now.

Insofar as the goal of welfare called, in the present, for relatively greater shares to consumption and relatively fewer shares to savings and investment, this was a choice which any society is entitled to make for itself. The Burmese, however, were not consciously choosing more today at the price of less tomorrow. They thought they were so conducting their affairs as to achieve the more tomorrow as well. But the fact was that their economic policies, instead of helping to achieve that greater economic growth which alone could make possible the increased welfare they desired, actually retarded and distorted that growth.

If, at the time of independence, the Burmese believed that welfare would easily and quickly be attained, the experience of the 1950s taught them otherwise. They later realized the validity and wisdom of what Furnivall had told them many years before: "Independence is a condition of, but not a guarantor of, welfare." They questioned whether nationalization and industrialization would indeed contribute to progress. They had begun even to realize that hard work, efficiency, management and improved administration might be necessary, difficult though these were to reconcile with popular notions of welfare. But Burmanization policy did not seem to have been affected.

CHAPTER 31

Problems of Foreign Aid

Foreign aid[1] accounted for more than 50 per cent of public capital expenditures in the second half of the eight-year program, and for nearly one third of such expenditures for the eight-year period as a whole. While the amount of foreign aid actually delivered in the first four years was minor and the real aid harvest was garnered only in the second half, consideration of the need for foreign aid began early in 1954, and considerable time and attention were devoted to it in the next two years.

With foreign aid playing so large a role in the financing of the development effort, the many problems which arose in connection with it were obviously of considerable importance. The basic policy problems arose out of the possible impact of foreign aid on Burma's sovereignty and neutrality and the extent to which Burma and the various sources of aid had common objectives in the matter.[2] The remaining problems were, for the most part, the availability and timing of aid, its nature and flexibility, the conditions under which it was offered and methods of utilization. The nature and seriousness of these problems, and their effect on the implementation of the development program, may perhaps best be examined by reference to Burma's experiences with her major aid sources — Japan, the United States, the U.S.S.R., India, the World Bank and the International Monetary Fund. It will be useful to provide here the chronological highlights of the foreign aid experience (Table 81) and to tabulate the aid commitments and deliveries actually received (Table 82).

Aid commitments, and deliveries through September 30, 1960, are shown

1. Problems of foreign investment have been separately treated in Chapter 19. Problems of technical assistance will be separately treated in Chapter 32.

2. The question whether Burma should resort to foreign aid at all and the question of the appropriate distribution of the resource burden between foreign and domestic finance are discussed in Chapter 25.

Table 81

CHRONOLOGICAL HIGHLIGHTS OF THE FOREIGN AID EXPERIENCE

March 1953	Burma served notice on the United States that she desired the special technical and economic assistance program to end as of June 30, 1953.
November 1954	The Japanese Reparations Agreement was concluded. Burma also submitted to the World Bank a list of projects totaling $163 million to serve as a basis for selective World Bank loan consideration.
March 1955	The foreign exchange situation and outlook having become quite grave, the economic consultants recommended that the Government seriously consider loans from the United States, the International Monetary Fund and the World Bank.
May 1955	The Foreign Affairs Subcommittee of the Cabinet recommended to the Government that such loans be sought. The United States Government indicated informally that it would entertain favorably a loan request from the Burmese Government.
August 1955	Negotiations were initiated with India which resulted the following month in an agreement on the part of that country to lend Burma K 20 crores. Before these negotiations were concluded, a request was made to the United States Government for a loan of $50 million, primarily for balance of payments purposes.
September 1955	Agreement was reached in Washington in principle on a $20-million sale to Burma of surplus agricultural commodities under P.L. 480, to be paid for in domestic currency.
December 1955	Messrs. Khrushchev and Bulganin visited Burma, and preliminary understandings were reached with respect to a U.S.S.R. aid program.
February 1956	A $21.7-million P.L. 480 agreement was concluded with the United States. Intermittent discussions concerning a development loan were continued.
March 1956	The International Monetary Fund permitted Burma to draw $15 million.
	The United States Government offered to purchase 10,000 tons of Burmese rice in exchange for roughly $1 million, to be used for the employment of U. S. technicians.
	Mr. Mikoyan, on behalf of the U.S.S.R., negotiated separate agreements providing for the annual purchase over a five-year period of up to 400,000 tons of rice in exchange for Russian goods and services, and for six gift projects in the value of K 21 crores which would be matched by a gift of Burmese rice to the U.S.S.R.
April 1956	The United States offered a $25-million development loan to Burma.
May 1956	Burma accepted the rice for the technicians exchange offer extended by the United States. The World Bank extended two loans to the Burma Railways and Rangoon Port Authority totaling $19.35 million.
July 1956	The United States agreed to amend the conditions attached to its previous $25-million development loan offer along the lines requested by Burma.

Table 81 (Continued)

November 1956	Burma indicated its acceptance of the $25-million U. S. loan offer.
December 1956	Burma requested a second P.L. 480 program of three years' duration.
January–March 1957	The United States offered "interim" P.L. 480 assistance in the form of a $1 million tobacco agreement and $5 million in Indian rupees for textile purchases under Section 104d, both for local currency.
March 1957	The $25 million U. S. Development Loan Agreement was signed.
July–August 1957	Understanding was quickly reached between Burma and the United States for a $10 million loan for police equipment and supplies and for the purchase by Burma, for $2 million of local currency, of U. S. surplus military equipment and supplies at bargain rates.
October 1957	Parliament approved the $25 million U. S. loan.
January 1958	Arrangements for the U. S. police loan and military supplies purchase were consummated.
May 1958	A second P.L. 480 agreement, for $18 million, was concluded with the United States.
September 1958	Burma accepted the $5 million Indian textiles offer under P.L. 480, Section 104d.
July 1959	The United States agreed to grant Burma $31 million and $6 million in local currency toward the cost of a new highway between Rangoon and Mandalay, and for additional facilities at the University of Rangoon.

Source: Robert R. Nathan Associates files, and *Survey of Burma's Foreign Economic Relations, 1948–58*, Rangoon-Hopkins Center for Southeast Asia Studies, Rangoon University.

in Table 83. The Japanese commitment accounted for almost half the total; the U. S. commitment for slightly more than one quarter; and the Indian and U.S.S.R. commitments for approximately one twelfth each. The World Bank and International Monetary Fund commitments accounted for 4 and 3 per cent, respectively. The actual delivery picture was quite different. Japan contributed about three eighths of total deliveries; the United States about three tenths; India about one sixth; and the U.S.S.R., the World Bank and the International Monetary Fund about one twentieth each. But neither the commitment nor the delivery schedule accurately measures the relative importance the Burmese attributed to the several sources of aid or the intensity of the problems encountered in connection with them.

Japanese reparations did not register very strongly. Once negotiated, they were taken for granted, and they involved neither repayment nor a sense of obligation. In addition, problems of implementation were relatively minor. The Indian and the International Monetary Fund loans were easily and quickly negotiated, and involved no problems of use at all. The World Bank

Table 82

MAJOR FOREIGN AID AGREEMENTS, 1951–60

(K Crores)

	Japan	India	United States	U.S.S.R.	I.B.R.D. (World Bank)	I.M.F.
1951–53			Special economic and technical assistance, K 9.3 crores.			
Nov. 1954	$200 million reparations program — K 9.5 crores annually for 10 years.					
Sept. 1955		Loan K 20 crores.				
Feb. 1956			P.L. 480 sale, K 10.3 crores.			
March 1956						Dollar draw, K 7.1 crores.
April 1956				"Gift" of 6 projects costing K 21 crores.		
May 1956					Loan, K 8.5 crores.	
March 1957			Development loan, K 12 crores.			
May 1958			P.L. 480 sale, K 8.6 crores. Police loan, K 4.8 crores.			
June 1958			Military goods sale for local currency, K 1 crore.			
Oct. 1958			P.L. 480(104d) aid, K 2.4 crores.			
July 1959			Special assistance grant, K 14.3 crores.			

Source: Robert R. Nathan Associates files, and *Survey of Burma's Foreign Economic Relations, 1948–58*, Rangoon-Hopkins Center for Southeast Asia Studies, Rangoon University.

510

Table 83

AID COMMITMENTS AND DELIVERIES
THROUGH SEPTEMBER 30, 1960

	Commitments		Deliveries	
	K Crores	As Per Cent of Total	K Crores	As Per Cent of Total
Total	239.6	100	125.1	100
Japan	119.0[a]	49.7	47.3	37.8
Reparations	95.2	39.7	47.3	37.8
Economic cooperation	23.8	9.3	—	—
United States	63.2	26.3	37.3	29.8
T.C.A. program	9.3[b]	3.9	9.3	7.4
P.L. 480 (Title I)	19.4[c]	8.0	19.1	15.3
Development loan	12.0	5.0	4.3	3.4
P.L. 480(104d)	2.4	1.0	2.4	1.9
Police loan	4.8	2.0	.9	.7
Sale of military goods	1.0[d]	.4	1.0[e]	.8
Special assistance grant	14.3[f]	6.0	.3	.2
India	20.0	8.3	20.0	16.0
U.S.S.R.	21.0[g]	8.8	5.8	4.6
I.B.R.D.	9.3	3.9	7.6	6.1
I.M.F.	7.1	3.0	7.1	5.7

Source: Table 73, corrected for omissions and adjusted for more recent information from I.C.A. and I.B.R.D.

a. Distributed equally over 10 years beginning Japanese fiscal year 1955–56. Commitments through September 1960 only would be K 52.8 crores.

b. This program was initiated in September 1950 and terminated in June 1953. Deliveries are here taken as commitments.

c. Includes shipping cost. In addition, nearly K 1 crore was separately supplied to voluntary-aid societies in Burma.

d. This sale was for local currency, hence qualifies as aid.

e. It was anticipated that the real value of surplus military goods to be delivered, because of their bargain prices, would be far in excess of actual purchase cost to Burma.

f. Excludes grant of K 2.9 crores in local currency as not additive of real resources.

g. This was the roughly estimated total cost of the six "gift" projects originally agreed upon. Burma subsequently deferred, then canceled, three of the projects.

Note: The U. S. programs omit a loan of $17 million in local currency, and a $1 million exchange of rice for technicians, which are not aid within our definition.

loans were not easily obtained; they required much documentation and negotiation over a considerable period of time, and use of them was carefully supervised. Also, the Bank's sharp differences with program and policy came as something of a shock to the Burmese. The Bank's impact was thus out of all proportion to the size of its loans. The U.S.S.R. contribution was augmented, in Burmese thinking, by the Soviet commitment to purchase up to 400,000 tons of Burmese rice per year for a five-year period. (Actual purchases amounted to 383,000 tons at a cost of K 18.5 crores, mostly in 1955–57.) Since the Burmese originally considered these purchases effective aid, Soviet commitments for quite some time bulked far larger in their eyes than those of the United States, most of which developed later.[3] But there is no question whose aid involved by far the most serious problems for the Burmese, from the point of view both of policy and utilization. On both these counts, it was the U. S. aid.

Treatment of the several aid experiences which follows is extremely disparate. The relative fullness or brevity of treatment is related to the importance attributed to each by the Burmese, rather than to the volume of aid committed or delivered. The treatment of U. S. aid is out of all proportion, even on this basis, because it seems here appropriate to provide a factual basis for the judgments about U. S. foreign aid policies and practice which are formed in Chapter 35.

THE JAPANESE REPARATIONS EXPERIENCE

The negotiation of a reparations agreement with Japan was no mean task. Intermittently over the years after the war, the two governments had exchanged views on the question of reparations. While the Japanese openly acknowledged an obligation, the rather extravagant claims made by the Burmese precluded any serious negotiations. The position, for the Burmese Government, was not an easy one. Indonesia, the Philippines and the new countries of the Indo-Chinese peninsula also had large reparations claims against Japan, and none had as yet reached a settlement. Whichever country settled first faced the possibility that the others might obtain more favorable terms. To offset this, Japan had let it be known that she was determined to limit reparations to $100 million for Burma, $200 million for Indonesia and $400 million for the Philippines. This stand could not, however, eliminate competitive risks for the claimant that settled first.

Nevertheless, early in 1954 Burma decided to seek a settlement with the Japanese. Fortunately the Government was thinking now in more realistic terms. It had already considered a memorandum by U Hla Maung which examined Burma's capacity to absorb capital goods from Japan. It now took into consideration studies made by its economic consultants of Japan's ability to produce and transfer reparations goods and services. When, late in the summer of 1954, Minister of Industries U Kyaw Nyein led a reparations negotiating team to Tokyo, he was prepared to take a realistic approach that

3. If the criterion of foreign aid is whether or not a net addition in goods and services requiring foreign exchange has actually resulted, over and above that which could have been obtained if the host country had employed its own current or previously accumulated resources, the question whether U.S.S.R. barter purchases of Burmese rice did constitute aid turns on whether the rice could have been sold otherwise. It could not have been sold for cash at the price sought by the Burmese. It could undoubtedly have been sold for cash at some lower price. Our judgment is that even the lower cash price which the rice would have brought in world markets would have provided at least the equivalent of the goods and services received from the U.S.S.R. and by the use of U.S.S.R. credits elsewhere. We do not, therefore, classify U.S.S.R. rice purchases from Burma as aid. The point is that the Burmese, at least for a time, did so consider them.

would make possible an expeditious settlement. This was accomplished, and the two parties ratified in Rangoon early in November the agreement reached in Tokyo some weeks before.

The Reparations and Economic Cooperation Agreement had two major features. Japan undertook to supply, as reparations, goods and services averaging in yen the equivalent of $20 million a year over a ten-year period, or $200 million in all. She undertook also to facilitate additional availability of Japanese goods and services, in an amount equivalent to $5 million per year over a ten-year period, for joint enterprises between Japanese firms and either the Burmese Government or individuals. Of this $5 million per year, $2 million might be made available as loans to the Government of Burma for investment in such joint enterprises. While the reparations goods and services were to be supplied for "economic rehabilitation and development and the advancement of social welfare" and the list of items did not include consumer goods, it was agreed that consumer goods required for the stated purposes might be included when both countries consented. The peace treaty signed at the same time also committed Japan to re-examine Burma's reparation claims at some future time in the light of settlements ultimately made with other countries.

After the basic agreement was concluded, the two countries had still to agree on the mechanics of its implementation. This proved more difficult and time-consuming than the negotiation of the basic agreement itself. The Japanese proposed a series of arrangements which were in many ways awkward or undesirable. The most important of these was the proposal that the Burmese Government be required to submit contracts with Japanese suppliers to the Japanese Government for approval. Meanwhile, Burma, with the assistance of her economic consultants, had studied the West German–Israeli reparations agreement and the procedures employed in its implementation. U Soe Tin, the extremely capable officer in charge of the Economics and Reparations Divisions at the Foreign Office, negotiated skillfully to arrive at a practicable and equitable implementation agreement with the Japanese which would not permit them to play the role of "Big Brother." The delay in reaching this implementation agreement, and the difference in the Burmese and Japanese fiscal years (the Burmese fiscal year began October 1, the Japanese fiscal year six months later) made for an additional one-time delay. The Burmese fiscal year 1955–56 saw deliveries of less than K 3 crores of reparations. Only with the 1956–57 fiscal year did reparations begin to flow in the contractual amount.

Burma did not find the necessity of procuring reparations goods and services only in Japan unduly restrictive. The range of goods available was considerable, and it was possible to lay out procurement schedules for the full amount of the capital goods the reparations would provide for the development program. The large hydroelectric project at Balu Chaung was placed

almost entirely on Japanese reparations, the largest single use of these resources. Other large procurement items were railway rolling stock, electrical
goods and appliances, industrial machinery and equipment, construction
materials and trucks and buses. The lack of flexibility in the use of reparations was, however, felt quite keenly when the Burmese sought, as part of the
fight against inflation, to utilize reparations in some substantial measure for
consumer goods — which they could do only with the consent of the Japanese.
Japan's response to the request was that the procurement would be acceptable
only to the extent that it was in excess of normal procurement of such goods
from Japan. Under the circumstances, it was impossible to meet this condition.

The difficulties encountered in programing the use of Japanese resources
with the operating agencies have been described in Chapter 28, and require
no further mention here. However, the difficulties met in the pricing of Japanese goods and services do warrant description.

In spite of the precautions taken in the implementation agreement to
specify commercial practices and to assure competitive pricing, most of the
goods procured under Japanese reparations were priced from 5 to 15 per cent
above competitive Japanese prices. These discrepancies were caused by the
failure of the Government of Japan to allow to reparations suppliers the tax
abatements and favored rates of interest that applied when these suppliers engaged in commercial export transactions. There was little the Burmese could
do about it.

But it was in Japanese technical services that price discrepancies were most
marked. Burma would have been willing to employ the services of many Japanese technicians in agriculture and other fields. Preliminary negotiations revealed, however, that the Japanese wanted these personnel to be paid two and
three times the salary rates prevalent within Japan itself. The Burmese naturally balked at this, and obtained their technical personnel elsewhere. The
Japanese thereby lost a major opportunity. Widespread use of their technical
personnel in Burma would undoubtedly have led to the increased use of
Japanese equipment, processes and services over and above the reparations
flow, and have built a solid foundation for increased purchases of spare parts
and operating supplies in the future.

Implementation of the economic cooperation aspect of the reparations agreement would perhaps fall more appropriately under a discussion of foreign
private investment. In view of its incorporation within the reparations agreement, it will be discussed here.

As of February 1961, not one joint venture involving the use of Japanese
economic cooperation funds had been concluded. This failure was not due to
lack of effort on the part of the Burmese Government or Burmese business
men. It was due rather to the fact that not one of the Japanese proposals

evidenced the slightest willingness to assume a risk. While many Japanese firms were interested in joint business arrangements, their objective was to eliminate the risk, or venture, element.

In almost every case, the joint venture proposals originated with Japanese suppliers of equipment. Although it had initially been agreed that the Burmese side would take a 60 per cent interest in such ventures, and the Japanese side 40 per cent, the proposals limited Japanese financial participation to 10 to 20 per cent of the equity capital required. Since this 10 to 20 per cent investment would be provided by the profits on the plant and equipment they supplied to the venture, the Japanese suppliers were not proposing to put up any capital of their own. Further, since the proposals uniformly envisaged that the Japanese suppliers would manage the enterprise in return for a handsome fee, the Japanese side was assured of a return even though the venture incurred substantial losses.

Proposals of this kind were made by Ishikawa and other textile machinery manufacturers, by manufacturers of pulp- and paper-making machinery and by others. While the Ministry of Industries was eager to conclude joint venture arrangements, particularly in the textiles field, the criticisms made by the economic consultants, and U Nu's increasing reluctance to have the state engage in new manufacturing enterprises, resulted in rejection of the proposals. Here, even more than in the reparations implementation itself, the Japanese lost a potentially rewarding opportunity to strengthen their economic relations with Burma.

THE UNITED STATES AID EXPERIENCE

THE SPECIAL TECHNICAL AND ECONOMIC ASSISTANCE PROGRAM

The first U. S. aid program to Burma — a grant program of technical and economic assistance — was begun in September 1950 and was terminated abruptly by Burma as of June 1953, although projects still under way were permitted to run for more than a year thereafter. Costing about K 9.3 crores, or $19.6 million, the program included aid in port rehabilitation, environmental sanitation, public health, agriculture, education, housing, transport, economic and engineering planning, and industrial research. Although technical assistance weighed heavily in the program, there was also a substantial degree of capital assistance, particularly in port rehabilitation. The project most significant in its effect on Burma's development effort was the engineering and economic survey conducted by K.T.A.

The occasion for the termination of the T.C.A. program, as already noted, was Burma's feeling that she should not be accepting U. S. assistance when she charged before the United Nations — as she planned to do shortly — that the Kuomintang Government of Formosa was responsible for acts of aggression in Burma. While making no charge, the Burmese plainly felt that the United States could have brought pressure on the Kuomintang Government and effected the liquidation of K.M.T. activities within Burmese borders.

Quite apart from the K.M.T. issue, a considerable amount of dissatisfaction had already developed in Burma with this U. S. aid program. It had been charged by the press and in the Parliament that the United States had dominated the composition of the program; that the U. S. mission leadership had exploited differences of opinion among the Burmese leadership and officials; that "white elephant" projects were being supported; that some of the new projects were not well selected; that some of the technicians provided by the United States were not properly qualified; and that the basic aid agreement, under the Mutual Security Act, tended to make Burma a satellite of the United States. Some local newspapers had taken a strong dislike to the U. S. mission and to U Hla Maung, the planning official responsible for liaison with it. They were influenced not only by the above considerations, but by the fact that a project they had mutually espoused — a clubhouse for Burmese journalists, to be paid for out of U. S. aid funds — was rejected. In fact, the Burma Journalists Association considered in 1951 (though it did not adopt) a resolution to boycott all U. S. aid news. Undoubtedly the failure of the U. S. aid program to satisfy unrealistic and even extravagant expectations was a major factor in the widespread criticism. U Hla Maung's identification with the program, and the hostility to him which was already developing among certain powerful ministers, also hurt.

THE FIRST P.L. 480 PROGRAM

The idea of further U. S. aid in the form of a loan was proposed by the economic consultants during the foreign exchange crisis early in 1955.[4] Prime Minister U Nu responded to this suggestion with diffidence. At the time the Government was involved in a tripartite arrangement with Ceylon and People's China under which additional rice exports were made by Burma to Ceylon on China's account in exchange for shipments of Ceylon rubber to China. The Prime Minister feared that this arrangement or similar transactions in the future would be viewed unfavorably by the United States and would lead to friction were the United States to extend a loan to Burma. The fact that the Government of India was relying heavily on U. S. assistance without compromising her independent role in international affairs did not suggest to him that Burma might do the same. In any event, the Prime Minister was already preparing for his forthcoming trip to the United States, where he hoped to contribute to an easing of tensions with People's China, and he did not wish to confuse the matter by loan discussions. He also intended to

---

4. The Prime Minister had previously explored with the U. S. Ambassador whether or not the United States would buy some of Burma's surplus rice.

test again whether the United States would help by purchasing surplus Burmese rice for distribution to hungry Asia.

Meanwhile, informal exploration with the U. S. Embassy, some time earlier, of the prospects for a loan had brought indications from Washington that the United States would entertain a Burmese loan request favorably. The foreign affairs subcommittee of the Burmese Cabinet, to which the question had been referred, recommended in May that a foreign loan be sought. But the Prime Minister, by now familiar with the provisions of the Battle Act,[5] was even more wary of the possible political implications than he had been before. He refused to act, even though the United States had responded coolly to his suggestion, made both before and during his visit, that she buy some Burmese rice. And when, in August 1955, early foreign aid seemed more essential than ever, U Nu determined to seek a substantial loan from India in preference to one from the United States, and sent U Raschid to India for that purpose. We have already described how U Raschid's initial report on his negotiations in India led the Government to believe that India was prepared to make only K 5 crores available. Negotiations looking toward a U. S. loan were thereupon immediately begun, before clarification of the misunderstanding showed that Burma would be able to borrow some K 15 crores to K 20 crores from India. But for this fortuitous circumstance, negotiations for a U. S. loan might not have been initiated at all.

What Burma suggested to the United States in August 1955 was a loan of about $50 million to be used primarily for balance of payments purposes. The plan was not to expend the dollars at all, but to use them to defend and strengthen the foreign exchange reserve position while £ sterling, barter and reparations resources were drawn down as required. Ambassador Barrington, who conducted the negotiations in Washington, was soon apprised of the initial U. S. reaction. While the United States was sympathetic and indicated that all possible means of complying with the request were being explored, the prospects were not bright. It was, however, suggested that the United States might be able to make a substantial contribution toward Burma's early needs through sale of surplus agricultural commodities for Burmese currency. Continuing discussions led to the conclusion that a P.L. 480 surplus agricultural commodities sales program was the only way in which the United States could be helpful to Burma at that time; and in September it was agreed in principle that such a program, in the approximate amount of $20 million — chiefly in the form of raw cotton — would be initiated.

This was a disappointing conclusion. The Government of Burma had been

---

5. Mutual Defense Assistance Control Act of 1951 (22 U.S.C. § 1611 note). This was an act to provide for the control, by the United States and cooperating foreign nations, of exports to any nation or combination of nations threatening the security of the United States, including the U.S.S.R. and all countries under its domination, and for other purposes.

debating for months whether to seek such a loan — both before and after the United States had informally indicated that assistance would probably be made available. One significant reaction to the P.L. 480 arrangement, expressed at the time by one highly placed Burmese minister, was: "I appreciate that this sale to us of U. S. cotton and other commodities for kyats will be very helpful to us in our present foreign exchange situation. But I wonder whether the United States did this to help us, or to find a market for her surplus commodities."

Although the general magnitude and basic commodity composition of the first P.L. 480 assistance program were established by September 1955, the agreement itself was not concluded until February 1956. A number of factors were responsible for this delay. The Burmese were concerned at the outset that there should be no Battle Act type restrictions on Burma's trade arrangements with other countries. This concern, arising from Burma's fear of possible infringement of her sovereignty, and her neutrality between the major power blocs, was allayed by a special arrangement which, by deferring agreement on the use of the local currency proceeds for loan purposes, deferred application of the Act. A number of practical questions also arose. P.L. 480 required that assistance rendered under it avoid disruption of normal international trade patterns and that private channels of trade be used. It was not easy for Burma to interpret the concept of normal trade patterns, since her trade patterns had recently been disrupted, not only by foreign exchange difficulties and barter arrangements, but also by the fairly recent abandonment of the British imperial preference trading system and by the reparations agreement with Japan. This concept, therefore, needed clarification. Burma was willing to observe the private trade channels requirement as far as procurement within the United States was concerned, but not for activities within Burma, where the Civil Supplies Management Board was to import and distribute a considerable part of the cotton textiles to be procured through the agreement. Another important question was how the United States might in the future dispose of the local currency that would accrue to her in payment for P.L. 480 commodities. A major share would be reserved for future development loans to the Government of Burma, but Burma wanted assurances that kyats reserved to the United States, over and above embassy and other minor requirements, would not be used to purchase Burmese goods that could otherwise be sold for foreign exchange.

Still other questions were whether Burma would have to buy all the U. S. cotton provided for, even if she were unable to arrange the necessary processing agreements with third countries, and whether Burma would be able to continue to export her own lower-grade cotton, which was not suitable for textiles manufacture. All these questions were finally resolved in a manner satisfactory to Burma, but valuable months were consumed in the process.

More important, conclusion of the sales agreement in February did not mean that the program could be implemented immediately.

Of the $20.8 million commodity program, $17.5 million was to go for purchases of raw cotton in the United States.[6] Since Burma required cotton textiles rather than cotton, only about one half of the U. S. cotton was intended to provide the raw cotton content of the textiles; the other half would serve as payment for the processing to be done by third countries. These countries, Burma had already decided, would be West Germany, the United Kingdom, Japan and India. Burma could have saved time by negotiating the processing agreements on a tentative basis while the details of the basic purchase agreement with the United States were being ironed out, but she did not do so. Nor did Burma, once the P.L. 480 purchase agreement was concluded, proceed expeditiously with the processing negotiations. Here, too, questions arose concerning the complicated mechanics, the possibilities of price changes before delivery of the textiles, and, in the case of Japan, the possible effect of the processing arrangements on the P.L. 480 cotton arrangements that Japan had already concluded with the United States.

The processing agreement with West Germany was not concluded until May, those with the United Kingdom and Japan until June and that with India until July. The consequence was that deliveries of the cotton textiles did not begin until nearly the end of fiscal year 1955–56. But Burma's import program, in view of the agreement which had been reached in principle with the United States the previous September, had counted on P.L. 480 to supply the major part of the cotton textiles to be imported during that same fiscal year. Failure to conclude and implement the agreement promptly resulted in severe shortages of cotton textiles, and contributed greatly to price inflation in 1955–56.

THE $25 MILLION DEVELOPMENT LOAN

Meanwhile, in December 1955, the Russians had made their first push on aid to Burma. Messrs. Khrushchev and Bulganin had visited Rangoon and agreed to make Burma gifts of a technological institute and an airplane, and to extend technical assistance in agriculture, irrigation and other fields. Then, early in 1956, the Burmese began another informal exploration of the possibilities for a U. S. loan. Informal talks with State Department officials visiting Rangoon suggested a renewed interest in a general-purpose or program-supporting development loan in the range of $50 to $150 million. But only after Mr. Mikoyan, following up the Khrushchev–Bulganin visit late in March, concluded a two-pronged arrangement early in April whereby Russia undertook to buy 400,000 tons of Burmese rice per year for a five-year period,

---

6. Other commodities were: dairy products, $2 million; tobacco, $1.1 million; and dried fruit, $.2 million. With $.9 million to cover freight costs, the agreement totaled $21.7 million.

and to make Burma a gift of five major development projects in addition to the technological institute, did the United States offer Burma a $25 million development loan later that month.

The U. S. offer was disappointing from several points of view. It was, in the first place, much smaller than the Burmese had hoped for in support of an eight-year program which had been severely cut back because of foreign exchange shortages, and which still had more than four years to run. It was much smaller, also, than the Burmese had perhaps been permitted to expect. Secondly, the offer was made not in general support of the total program, which would have given it flexibility; use of the funds would be restricted to specific new projects to be agreed upon by the two countries. Most of the development program was already under way; large elements in it were already committed to Japanese reparations, World Bank and other specific financing; very few new project starts were contemplated and these might not be of a nature the United States would wish to finance. It was clear, therefore, that utilization of so restrictive a loan would not be easy.

On the positive side, there were indications that the $25 million loan might be merely the first of a series of similar annual loans, and the proposed interest and payments provisions were certainly liberal. The loan would be repayable over a forty-year period, beginning four years after the loan itself, and could be repaid either in dollars at 3 per cent or in domestic currency at 4 per cent. While the loan would be project-tied, the money could be spent anywhere in the Free World.

Burma wished to accept the loan offer, but was still wary of possible misunderstandings arising out of U. S. interpretations of Battle Act requirements as applied to Burma's trade arrangements with Soviet bloc nations. Burma was not only involved in the previously mentioned tripartite arrangement with Ceylon and People's China; she had made arrangements also for the direct sale of small quantities of rubber to People's China at a price 10 per cent in excess of world market prices, and believed that the volume of her rice sales to China might depend, in part, on implementation of this rubber sale. She did not wish to accept the U. S. loan offer only to learn later that the United States expected her to terminate such trade arrangements.

In May, Prime Minister U Nu determined to resolve the question by communicating frankly to President Eisenhower the nature of the dilemma with which Burma felt she was confronted. The Burmese position, in essence, was as follows: Burma was desirous of accepting the generous offer of the United States, but was unwilling to jeopardize the excellent relations which prevailed between the two countries. Burma would not undertake to abandon the trade arrangements she had already made with Soviet bloc countries, or even commit herself not to duplicate them in the future. If the United States was still willing to extend a loan, Burma would accept it — with the clear understanding that if the United States should ever want to terminate the arrangement because of some action Burma might take in the future, Burma would accept the decision without any hard feelings. Such an arrangement, Burma felt, would protect her own sovereignty and neutrality, the interests of the United States and the cordial relations between the two governments. On the other hand, if the United States were not willing to enter into a loan arrangement on the basis of this understanding, Burma would cheerfully accept this decision also.

Fortunately President Eisenhower, in July, responded in a positive manner to this communication. Once again, however, a considerable period of time was to elapse before the two countries reached formal agreement. The chief reasons for the delay were the questions raised within the Burmese Cabinet over the clauses in the loan agreement draft (mandatory under the Mutual Security Act enabling legislation) which provided for U. S. audit and end-use checks of the loan monies spent. These provisions troubled the Burmese greatly. Although the loan arrangements concluded with the World Bank not long before provided for similar checks, the Bank's loans had been extended to the Railways and the Rangoon Port Authority directly, rather than to the Government itself. Further, the Bank, as an international body, was free of the power bloc implications attached to the United States. Therefore, the Bank arrangements had not raised the question of infringement upon sovereignty which some of the ministers were inclined to read into the proposed U. S. loan requirement.

By the time these fears had been allayed, the August-September sitting of the Parliament had already been concluded. Approval by the Cabinet in November did not permit implementation of the loan to go forward. Under Burmese law, foreign loans required approval by the Parliament, which was not scheduled to meet again until February. Even at that session, and undoubtedly for internal political reasons, the loan was not submitted for ratification. The Government did proceed to sign the loan agreement in March 1957, some nineteen months after the first request for U. S. loan assistance, and almost two full years after the United States had first indicated receptivity. But only after ratification the following September did it become legally possible for the Burmese to use the loan funds.

THE SECOND P.L. 480 PROGRAM

Unlike the case of the first P.L. 480 program, when six months elapsed between Burma's loan request of August 1955 and conclusion of the agreement in February 1956, some seventeen months were to elapse between Burma's request for a second P.L. 480 program and the conclusion of negotiations in May 1958.

The economic consultants had begun to explore prospects of a second P.L.

480 agreement in June 1956, while cotton-processing arrangements with third countries incident to the first P.L. 480 program were being concluded. There were two reasons why it was necessary to undertake negotiations for a second agreement at an early date. The inordinate time involved in negotiations required an early start, if an interruption in the continuous flow of P.L. 480 commodities was to be avoided. Second, the $3 billion available for P.L. 480 commodity sales had already been heavily committed and would probably not be supplemented by the U. S. Congress until the summer of 1957. In September 1956, therefore, the economic consultants recommended that the Government of Burma request a three-year P.L. 480 arrangement similar to that the United States had recently concluded with India. Since there was some doubt whether the United States would be willing, as in the first agreement, to supply raw cotton not only for the cotton content of the textiles needed but also to pay for the processing, they recommended that Burma seek annual aid of $20 million to $30 million for the three-year period, the amount to depend on whether cotton was to be provided for cotton content only or for processing costs as well.

Unfortunately, by the time Burma made this request in December 1956, virtually the entire $3 billion availability had been committed — the last $500 million within the preceding month or so. From the U. S. point of view it would not be possible to consider so substantial a request until the Congress had granted new authority. Burma was, however, invited to submit an emergency or interim request, which the United States would do its best to meet out of the very limited authority still available, supplemented by such amounts as might be freed by modifications in commitments already made to other nations. In January, Burma submitted an interim request for a program of some $28 million or K 13.3 crores. The United States reply suggested that it could provide an additional $1 million of tobacco, and that it might be possible also, under Section 104d of P.L. 480, to allow Burma to use about $5 million of U. S.-owned rupees in India for purchases of Indian textiles. Burma accepted the tobacco offer, which was implemented by amendment to the first P.L. 480 agreement, raising this from $21.7 million to $22.7 million in value. However, the offer of rupees under Section 104d raised some very serious questions for Burma.

Burma's first reaction to the Section 104d offer was to wonder whether, if she accepted the U. S.-owned rupees to purchase relatively small amounts of Indian textiles, the United States might not subsequently ask her to permit the use of the U. S.-held kyats in Burma for the purchase of rice for India in far larger amount. When it was pointed out that India had no such intention, and that U. S.-held kyats could be used for purchases in Burma only with the consent of the Burmese Government, the Burmese reaction was that moral as well as legal questions were involved. If Burma accepted the use of Section

104d when it was to her advantage to do so, how could she morally refuse her consent to any future proposal that would favor India? Of lesser importance was the fact that the United States had offered the rupees as a loan rather than as a sale. A loan would require approval by the Parliament, whereas the sale of the U. S.-owned rupees for kyats could not. And still another vexing problem was the U. S. desire for greater flexibility in using the local currency it would acquire than it had under the P.L. 480 agreement itself.

By the time these questions were satisfactorily resolved, difficulties had developed on the Indian side. Because India's foreign exchange position had deteriorated substantially since she agreed to use of the rupees, she wanted assurances from Burma that the textiles purchases would be in excess of Burma's normal textiles procurement in India. Lengthy and sporadic negotiations then ensued on what should properly be considered normal procurement. Burma suggested that her average textiles purchases in India for the last three years be taken as the norm. India was not satisfied with this criterion. And one issue with the United States — use of the resulting kyat payment — still remained. Not until September 1958 — some eighteen months after the United States suggested this use of Indian rupees under Section 104d — were the negotiations concluded.

Meanwhile, in August 1957, when new P.L. 480 authority had been legislated by the Congress, the United States indicated readiness to negotiate a new P.L. 480 program. It was by now clear that she would no longer be willing to provide cotton with which to pay processing costs. Nor would she be willing to agree to a three-year or even a two-year program. Because of the priority given to negotiations with other countries, it was not until November that the United States was actually ready to negotiate.

In December, one year after the Burmese request, the United States proposed a new one-year program amounting to $18.4 million, or nearly K 9 crores, of which $13.6 million would be in cotton. The proposals incorporated provisions substantially different from those in the earlier agreement. Not only would there no longer be cotton to pay processing costs, but, whereas only general assurances with respect to normal marketing had heretofore been acceptable, the United States now proposed that Burma agree that her normal procurement of cotton and wheat from other sources would reach stipulated tonnages, and that these would be procured from countries "friendly to the United States." While the proportion of the local currency generated by the agreement to be set aside for future development loans to Burma was the same as in the earlier agreement, 25 per cent of the proceeds were to be set aside for loans to American business firms and their affiliates in Burma, in accordance with the new Cooley amendment (Section 104e of the new legislation).

The Burmese were prepared for the deletion of cotton-for-processing costs.

They were profoundly shocked by the other new conditions proposed. Their reaction was that the United States was "tightening its grip." Old fears about sinister U. S. motives, which had long been laid to rest, were now revived. The Burmese refused to commit themselves to procure non-P.L. 480 cotton textiles only from "countries friendly to the United States." They declined also to accept the Cooley amendment, and proposed instead that the financing desired by American business firms and their affiliates be met through the same channels (i.e., the proposed new industrial development bank) which would finance domestic investors. They pointed out, also, why the specific tonnage assurances for normal marketing proposed by the United States would be impracticable.

By March, most of these issues had been acceptably negotiated. The chief remaining issue was the Cooley amendment requirement, and both countries remained adamant on this. What disturbed the Burmese about this requirement, it transpired, was not so much the fear of "American economic imperialism" as the possibility that American firms might choose resident Indian business men as their affiliates in Burma, and thus prolong the entrenchment of Indian traders in areas from which the Burmans were intent upon ousting them. In setting aside 25 per cent of the local currency generated for American firms and their affiliates, Section 104e stated that these funds would be available for loans "for economic development and business expansion." The economic consultants now suggested as a compromise that this language be changed to read "for industrial development." Since this would channel potential Indian affiliates into manufacturing industry, where the Burmese were not averse to having them, but would not make loans available for use in fields where Indians were not wanted, the Burmese were willing to accept this language, and a compromise was finally reached.

The second P.L. 480 agreement for about $18 million, or K 8.6 crores, was concluded in May 1958. Because of the many changes (including some highly involved and impractical U. S. requirements for relating the cotton content to the value or weight of the textiles to be imported, which evoked specific and sharp objections by the United Kingdom and Japan), it took even longer this time to negotiate processing arrangements with third countries. These were concluded six months later, in November 1958, nearly two years after the Burmese request of December 1956.

THE POLICE LOAN AND THE SALE OF SURPLUS U. S. MILITARY EQUIPMENT AND SUPPLIES

More expeditious and much more satisfactory to the Burmese were the negotiations for the $10 million (K 4.8 crores) police loan, and the sale of U. S. surplus military goods for $2 million in local currency (K 1 crore) which had been consummated in the meantime. (The reader may recall that these aid arrangements arose out of Prime Minister U Nu's decision, in June 1957, to give top priority to the re-establishment of law and order in the new four-year plan.) Since it was impossible to finance the law and order program and, at the same time, continue development capital expenditures at the minimum essential level, Burma requested the United States to consider additional financial aid.

This approach, made in July 1957, was soon followed by assurances from the United States that the request would be granted. Agreement was reached, in principle, within a few weeks on a loan of $10 million for police equipment and supplies and on the sale, at bargain prices, of surplus U. S. military equipment and supplies. Since the Burmese, for internal political reasons, would not have been willing to accept a U. S. loan for the purchase of military goods, the alternative sales arrangement, which was made at their request and which did not require approval by the Parliament, was a valuable political, as well as economic, accommodation. Although these arrangements were formally concluded only the following May and June, no real loss of time was involved, since the intervening months were devoted to preparations for implementing the agreements.

IMPLEMENTATION OF THE P.L. 480 PROGRAMS

If the laborious process of negotiating agreements for the processing of the cotton supplied are considered part of the P.L. 480 program implementation — as indeed they must be — this part of the implementation story has already been told. The other major difficulty, or rather complex of difficulties, in implementation had to do with the "fitting" of P.L. 480 textile imports into the total textiles import program, and with the implementation of that program. These difficulties, which were particularly pronounced in the case of the first P.L. 480 program, were described at length in Chapters 11 and 12 of this study and do not need to be restated here. It may, however, be affirmed that the problems were not inherent in the P.L. 480 programs themselves, but arose out of the conjunction of the P.L. 480 import arrangements with the necessity to use even more restrictive barter credits in the same import program, complicated by the impractical application of Burmanization and nationalization policies to the import trade at the same time and by the administrative deficiencies of the ministry and agencies responsible for implementation of the import program.

Apart from these major problems, one additional problem of implementation requires mention here: the pricing of some of the P.L. 480 aid goods, particularly milk. When bids were solicited from American suppliers of evaporated and condensed milk, the Burmese discovered that American prices were substantially higher than those quoted by Burma's traditional Scandinavian suppliers. Not only did the acceptance of such bids raise difficulties for the procuring agencies, which were required to purchase at the most competitive prices available — the Burmese were not sophisticated enough to think of P.L. 480 commodities as a gift (on the assumption that the major part of the local currency generated by the commodity sales and turned over to U. S. account would never be transferred to or utilized by the United States); they were genuinely troubled by what seemed to them a highly uneconomic purchase. Further, in selling such milk supplies to the public through the Civil Supplies Management Board, they were faced with the problem of whether or not to raise milk prices. An increase in prices would undoubtedly result in widespread criticism of the P.L. 480 program; a failure to increase prices would involve the Government in bookkeeping losses it was disposed to consider real. After much hesitation and debate, it was decided to procure U. S. milk supplies, despite their substantially higher prices,[7] to maintain the previous selling prices, and absorb the loss.

There remains to be considered the utilization of the domestic currency generated by the P.L. 480 programs. The P.L. 480 agreements thus far described were sales agreements. It was expected that each of these would be complemented by a loan agreement which would provide that the greater part of the local currency generated would be lent to the Burmese Government for development purposes. The first P.L. 480 sales agreement was complemented in March 1957 by a loan agreement covering $17.3 million worth of local currency. The local currency agreement also provided that the funds loaned for development purposes would be paid over a forty-year period beginning four years after the first disbursements were made, with interest at 3 per cent if repaid in dollars and 4 per cent if repaid in kyats. While the second P.L. 480 sales agreement stipulated that $10.25 million of the local currency it generated would be reserved for loan purposes, Burma had not been willing, well into 1960, to conclude the loan agreement.[8]

Neither were the Burmese anxious, upon the conclusion of the first P.L. 480 loan agreement, to avail themselves of this "privilege." They saw clearly that the domestic currency generated by the sale of P.L. 480 commodities did not represent real resources. Having used P.L. 480 procurement and sales to supplement scarce foreign exchange resources and to offset inflationary pressures, they were aware that borrowing and utilizing the domestic currency withdrawn from the private sector would have an inflationary effect. While the use of such funds would result in a better looking budgetary picture —

7. Had Burma been aware of this situation prior to conclusion of the agreements, she might have requested that the United States make her a grant of part of the local currency generated in an amount adequate to cover the difference between U. S. and world market prices. Such arrangements have indeed been incorporated in the P.L. 480 agreements with India.

8. The second loan agreement, for $8.45 million, was concluded in September 1960. In addition, $6 million of local currency, which would otherwise have been available for loan purposes, was donated as a grant conditional on conclusion of the loan agreement.

domestic currency borrowings from the United States would either reduce the deficit or increase the surplus shown in the Union Government budget — the fiscal result would be precisely the same as if there had been deficit financing and borrowing from the central Union Bank. In the latter case, the Government would pay 2 per cent for short-term money instead of 4 per cent and, by virtue of its 50 per cent interest in Union Bank profits, would get back half of this. Utilization of P.L. 480 domestic currency loan availabilities was, therefore, undertaken only with reluctance, when it was made clear to the Government that the utilization of the borrowings would be an important factor in the rationale supporting further P.L. 480 sales agreements.

As of December 31, 1960, some K 7.1 crores of the first (1956) P.L. 480 sale proceeds had been programed for local currency loans to nine development projects. These were, in every case, projects which had also received dollar assistance under the $25 million development loan. Of this total, less than K 1 crore had been disbursed to the Government of Burma. No loans had been agreed upon for the proceeds of the second (1958) P.L. 480 sales agreement.[9]

IMPLEMENTATION OF THE $25 MILLION DEVELOPMENT LOAN

Four simple chronological facts tell a good deal about the implementation of the $25 million U. S. loan. The first project agreement under it came in December 1957, nine months after the signing of the basic loan agreement. It was June 1958, fifteen months after the basic loan agreement, before virtually all the $25 million had been allocated to projects.[10] As of September 30, 1960, three and one half years after the basic loan agreement had been reached, less than $19 million, or three quarters of the loan, had been obligated, and actual loan deliveries, at $9 million, were only a little more than one third of the loan commitment. Delays in allocating the loan were largely on the side of the United States. Delays in the utilization of the loan thereafter were largely on the side of the Burmese.

The chief problem facing the Burmese in booking up the loan was selection of Four-Year Plan projects which would meet the criteria favored by the United States. The sooner the loan could be allocated to projects, and the projects started, the sooner additional loans might be forthcoming. Project selection got under way well before the formal conclusion of the basic loan agreement. Concurrently, informal discussions were held with I.C.A. in Washington to ascertain U. S. thinking about loan implementation.

U. S. reactions made it clear that while new and uncommitted projects were clearly preferred, it might be possible to provide loan funds for new and

9. Office of the Representative, International Cooperation Administration, Rangoon.

10. Actually, loan project agreements totaled only $20.2 million. Because the Parliament had not yet acted to approve the $10 million police loan, some $4 million of the development loan had temporarily been allocated to the police supplies project, and would be released only after ratification of the police loan made possible re-transfer.

distinct phases of some projects already under way, if these could be clearly separated from the old. I.C.A. officials also indicated that their preference would be for projects which promised to have substantial impact on both economic development and public opinion, were clearly feasible both economically and technically, held high priority within Burma's development program and could be completed quickly.

It was also apparent that certain types of projects, otherwise desirable, might have serious disadvantages from the U. S. point of view. Thus, a project which looked to the expansion of rice production would be viewed with some concern, because of the adverse reaction it might generate among U. S. congressmen and senators representing rice-producing states. Thus, also, projects for financing the acquisition of ocean-going vessels or aircraft to fly international routes would be open to question because of possible competition with American carriers.

It was not easy for the Burmese to select new projects, or distinctly separable phases of projects already under way, which met these criteria, and in which procurement procedures would be in accordance with the payments procedures prescribed by the United States. Nevertheless, within a month after the signing of the basic loan agreement, I.C.A. Washington had already been advised informally of many of the projects the Burmese were considering for loan-financing, and I.C.A. had already expressed informal reactions to them. These projects included the emergency reconstruction of the Kabo Dam, special barges and tugs for the river haul of cement, mechanical timber extraction units, replacement of the domestic aircraft fleet, mechanical equipment for land reclamation purposes, municipal water supply projects, highway construction and an industrial development bank. By May, only two months after the signing of the agreement, project summaries and justifications of projects amounting to $28 million in foreign exchange costs had been forwarded to I.C.A. Washington.

Thus, as of May 1957, the Burmese were prepared to negotiate actively for the allocation of the $25 million to specific projects. But the United States was not quite ready. The I.C.A. had determined to send a group of six representatives, functioning as a separate unit within the U. S. Embassy rather than as a separate I.C.A. mission, to negotiate on the spot. The chief of this group did not arrive in Rangoon until May, and although he was shortly joined by his deputy, the remainder of the staff did not arrive in Rangoon until some months later. Housing, office and orientation arrangements for this group took up several months. Unfortunately, the contract periods of the American consulting economists and engineers ended early in August. This meant not only considerable staff turnover but also home leaves for the personnel who would continue to serve in the following contract period, and created new delays in internal coordination and documentation on the Burmese

Table 84

CHRONOLOGY OF

U. S. PROJECT LOAN AGREEMENTS

Agency	Project	Date of Agreement	Amount in Dollars
Total			$20,200,000
1. L.R.D.C.	Land reclamation	12/10/57	5,400,000
2. S.T.B.	Timber extraction equipment	12/17/57	690,000
3. S.A.M.B.	Rice mill parts	4/4/58	56,000
4. Environmental Sanitation and W.S.B.	Village water	5/20/58	577,000
5. N.H.B.	Rangoon water supply	5/20/58	1,400,000
6. U.B.A.R.I. (Applied Research Inst.)	Industrial laboratories and A.R.I. staff	5/20/58	955,000
7. UB Shipping Board	Arakan fleet expansion	5/29/58	1,325,000
8. I.W.T.B.	Fleet, dockyards	5/29/58	5,150,000
9. N.H.B.	Rangoon sewerage	5/29/58	645,000
10. N.H.B.	Town water supply	5/29/58	224,000
11. Telecoms Department	Rangoon-Mandalay carrier line	6/10/58	176,000
12. Civil Aviation Department	Airport equipment	6/20/58	474,000
13. L.R.D.C.	Kabo Dam	6/26/58	1,700,000
14. U.B.A.R.I.	Isotope laboratory and staff	6/26/58	496,000
15. Ministry of Health	Rangoon General Hospital—extension	6/26/58	752,000
16. S.A.M.B.	Rice loading and cleaning equipment	6/27/58	180,000

Source: Office of the Representative, International Cooperation Administration, Rangoon.

side. Only when the foreign advisory staffs were in the field at full strength again late in the year, and the deputy chief of the economic consultants' group was loaned full-time to the Chairman of the U. S. Loan Committee to co-ordinate loan activities on the Burmese side, did the process of loan allocations really get under way.

The sequence of the individual loan agreements signed is shown in Table 84, beginning December 1957 and ending the following June.

It will be observed that an interval of nearly four months elapsed between the signing of the second and third project loan agreements. This time was taken up chiefly by the preparation of supplementary data, detail and analyses requested by the I.C.A. representatives, by I.C.A. Rangoon investigations and preparation of its own analyses and recommendations, by I.C.A. Washington reviews and clearances, and by preparation of the project loan agreements themselves. In the case of two projects — those involving the Research Institute and the Kabo Dam, on which work had already been begun and expenditure commitments assigned — it was necessary for I.C.A. to seek Presidential waivers so that they might be financed under this loan. But by and large, once the requisite state of readiness had been developed on both the U. S. and the Burmese sides, the booking-up of the $25 million proceeded as expeditiously as could have been expected.

Obviously, the heavily committed nature of the Four-Year Plan and the many restrictions imposed by the United States had not made it possible to find many big-impact projects of the kind desired by the United States. Despite fears of adverse reaction in Washington, the land reclamation project — really a rice production expansion project — went through. Rehabilitation of the flood-destroyed Kabo Dam was also an "impact" project, particularly because of the time factor. Its execution, under the able supervision of John Alexander on behalf of T.A.M.S., was splendidly carried out. The Rangoon water and sewerage projects represented the first engineering planning phases of what promised to be tremendous and important twin projects. And the I.W.T.B. dockyard improvement also promised to make a significant contribution. Many of the remaining projects, while soundly justified, represented the kind of "scatteration" I.C.A. had hoped to avoid.

Once the process of booking the initial $25 million loan was well under way, the economic consultants initiated steps looking toward the continuation and expansion of U. S. loan aid. By this time, the United States had already established the Development Loan Fund and made it clear that this would be the major source of economic aid funds, on an individual project basis, in the future. Nevertheless, the consultants urged that Burma request assurance from the United States that she could count, in the three years following, on some $75 million of additional aid from D.L.F. and other sources that might be available. The developing political crisis during the remainder of the year made it impossible, however, to get the Government to take a definite stand on a further proposal of this kind, and the advent of the Military Government, with its very different views about foreign aid, precluded a further loan request.

Not only did the Ne Win Government refuse to go forward with a new loan request to the United States, but, believing as it did that there had been too much borrowing already, and suspicious as it was of the soundness of the projects sponsored by the previous Government, of the procedures employed and even of the propriety of some of the arrangements already made, it refused to pursue many of the projects already agreed upon until it had subjected them to thorough review. In the case of the Rangoon water supply and sewerage projects, General Ne Win himself ordered the cancellation of the arrangements made with an English engineering firm, and no further work was done. Further questions with respect to the Arakan Fleet expansion and the I.W.T.B. Dockyard and Rangoon General Hospital extension projects prevented any substantial progress from being made on them as well. Thus, it was the attitude of the new Burmese Government that was chiefly responsi-

Table 85

IMPLEMENTATION OF THE $25 MILLION U. S. DEVELOPMENT LOAN:
STATUS OF PROJECTS AS OF SEPTEMBER 30, 1960

(Thousands of Dollars)

Project	Obligated	Contracts	Arrivals
Total development assistance—loan	18,894	9,597	9,092
Land reclamation	5,400	4,650	4,600
Mechanical timber extraction	662	662	662
Applied Research Institute	1,008	780	624
Fleet improvement—I.W.T.B.	5,150	198	—
Fleet improvement—Arakan	1,325	170	170
Rangoon water supply	1,035	—	—
Rangoon sewerage system	515	—	—
Village water supply	577	577	570
Rice mill spare parts	55	55	55
Rangoon General Hospital	752	92	2
Telecommunications	153	153	153
Civil aviation	410	410	406
Rice handling and processing	152	152	152
Kabo Diversion Dam	1,700	1,700	1,700

Source: Official data.

ble for slowing down utilization of the $25 million loan, as may be seen in Table 85.

One interesting aspect of the development loan implementation remains to be described. The $20.2 million of projects allocated by June 1958 had left $4.8 million still available. Four million dollars of this had been temporarily allotted for the procurement of police equipment and supplies pending ratification of the separate $10 million loan. The $4.8 million became available for allotment by the Ne Win Government, which planned to utilize the funds for the construction of modern rice and rice bran oil extraction mills, dividing the money almost equally between the two projects. The project agreement covering the rice mills was actually signed. The rice bran oil project, which called for the construction of twelve small plants, was approved by I.C.A. only after a special study of its technical and economic feasibility. When the draft loan agreement came before General Ne Win for approval, he objected to the stipulation that the mills subsequently be sold to the private sector and to the rate of interest to be paid by the buyers. In his view, these provisions were a clear invasion of Burmese sovereignty by the United States. When he was told that a precedent had previously been established in the rice mill project already accepted by his Government, he abruptly canceled that project as well.[11]

11. There is some reason to believe that the question of sovereignty was not the only one involved in Ne Win's rejection of these projects. It appears, on reliable authority, that several high military officers involved in the project's negotiations were already quarreling over whose friends

IMPLEMENTATION OF THE $10 MILLION POLICE LOAN AND
THE $2 MILLION SALE OF SURPLUS MILITARY GOODS

As in the case of the $25 million Development Loan, the Ne Win Government was responsible for slowing implementation of the Police Loan also. As of September 30, 1960, contracts had been let for only $2.1 million of the $10 million available. Of this, $1.8 million had already resulted in deliveries. The Ne Win Government let it be understood that it was not satisfied with the procurement procedures followed by the police. The fact that it put a halt to further implementation soon after coming to power, and for the better part of eighteen months thereafter did nothing to revitalize it, suggests that other considerations were involved. Since the Burmese were given procurement access to U. S. military surplus stockpiles at bargain prices, $2.1 million in contracts may have provided a major part of their requirements. It may also be that the military were hesitant to strengthen the police in relation to the military power. The failure of the Civilian Government, on its return to power under U Nu in April 1960, to press forward once again with this project suggests that it felt it was still necessary to defer to the military's view.

Implementation of the sales agreement covering surplus military equipment and supplies is classified information, both in the United States and in Burma, and it is not possible to provide factual data on it. The nature of the agreement, however, makes possible delivery of such supplies in any quantity and value the two countries may agree upon, and it may be taken that deliveries have been substantial.

THE SPECIAL ASSISTANCE GRANT OF 1959

Whereas A.F.P.F.L. Governments had steadfastly, though somewhat inconsistently,[12] refused to compromise their neutrality by accepting grant aid from any source after the termination of U. S. grant aid in 1953, the Ne Win Government abruptly reversed this policy. Not long after coming to power, it requested capital assistance from the United States, provided it were afforded on a grant basis. The first instance of this came when Colonel Kyi Win, the new head of the L.R.D.C., asked the U. S. Ambassador whether grant funds could not be made available for new agricultural projects in Central Burma. Other requests from officers newly in charge of other development areas followed. Under the circumstances, it was difficult for the Embassy to determine whether these requests represented merely irresponsible attempts

---

and relatives should be given preference in buying the proposed mills from the Government in the future.

12. The inconsistency lay in the fact that, throughout the period, Burma continued to accept Colombo Plan aid on a grant basis. While this was small-scale and, for the most part, technical assistance, it did, nevertheless, violate the general principle.

of ambitious officers to develop support for ever-larger programs or a change in Burmese Government policy. In any event, it was impossible to consider seriously individual requests which did not appear to have been coordinated within, and have the support of, the Burmese Government. The communication of this view to General Ne Win did not appear to improve the harmony or the understanding between the two governments.

Not long afterwards, in the spring of 1959, completely bypassing the U. S. Embassy in Rangoon, General Ne Win sent U Law Yone, the editor of the *Nation,* as a special emissary to the United States with a personal letter to the President. Suggesting a lack of sympathy on the part of and failure of communications with the U. S. Embassy in Rangoon, and positing a favorable response to his request as a test of the friendship which the United States affirmed for Burma, the General asked that the United States finance, on a grant basis, the construction of a new highway from Rangoon to Mandalay. Ambassador McConnaughy, recalled for consultations, supported the request. In July, the United States announced that it would make, and that Burma would accept, a grant of $37 million, largely for this purpose. Of the $37 million, $31 million would be in U. S. dollars and $6 million in U. S.-owned Burmese currency. Of these amounts, $28 million in dollars and $500,000 in local currency were programed for the construction of the highway, and $2 million in dollars and $5.5 million in local currency were earmarked for the university. An additional $1 million would cover the engineering and other feasibility studies required.

In agreeing to make this large grant for the construction of a new highway, the United States was undoubtedly motivated not only by a desire to mollify a new and rather obstreperous government (which nevertheless had strong anti-communism and a passion for administrative order in its favor), but also by the presumed strategic significance of the project. Whether these considerations justified the sharp difference between U. S. reaction to this request and its attitude to those of preceding years is something else again. In any event, U. S. action was unusually expeditious.

Swift agreement was one thing; implementation was quite another. A survey completed after many months by American consulting engineers indicated that the road would cost more than $70 million, the greater part of which would be in foreign exchange. When the Burmese showed a reluctance to finance the part of the cost not covered by the U. S. grant, the United States began to have second thoughts. The State Department and I.C.A. now questioned whether so substantial an outlay was really warranted by the benefits the proposed new road would confer. Negotiations were still continuing when U Nu returned to office in the spring of 1960. He requested the United States to finance the total cost of the road. As of the end of 1960, the United States had replied that the best solution might be to improve and modernize the old road between Rangoon and Mandalay, which might be done largely within the existing grant, rather than to build a new one. This undoubtedly is, and was at the outset, the only sensible thing to do. Meanwhile, as of September 30, 1960, virtually the only outlays under the special grant had been those for the engineering survey. Undoubtedly the same engineers would now do a new survey of the job to be done on the old road — a problem previously worked upon in 1951–53 by the K.T.A., and later by the Canadian engineers brought in through World Bank efforts.

THE U.S.S.R. AID EXPERIENCE

When the U.S.S.R. agreed, in April 1956, to buy 400,000 tons of rice a year from Burma for a period of five years in exchange for Soviet goods and services and to make Burma a gift of six major projects, for which the Burmese insisted on paying with a return gift of rice, Burmese opinion regarded these twin actions as an aid move of tremendous significance. Burma was still burdened with heavy carry-over rice stocks she had been unable to sell at the prevailing S.M.S. price of £36 sterling per ton. Since the U.S.S.R. agreed to take Burma's rice at world market prices, it seemed to the Burmese that these sales would help maintain existing prices, and help dispose of her surpluses at the same time. Burma would obtain the gift projects on credit, deferring her own return "gift" to future years when rice surpluses — so the thinking tended to go — would undoubtedly still be bothersome. Although U Ba Swe and U Kyaw Nyein were startled and displeased by the gift projects arrangement, this was more because Prime Minister U Nu had not consulted his colleagues before expanding and concluding the arrangements than because of the substance of the agreement itself. In general, reaction to the twin arrangements was highly favorable.

So far as the negotiations alone were concerned, nothing could have been simpler, more expeditious or more pleasing to the Burmese Government in every possible way. Messrs. Khrushchev and Bulganin, it will be recalled, had visited Rangoon for a few days in December 1955. At that time, they made Burma gifts of a technological institute and an Ilyushin aircraft for the Prime Minister. They also agreed to provide technical assistance for agriculture and industry. There undoubtedly was some talk of buying rice as well. When Mikoyan followed up their visit at the end of March, the expanded arrangements were concluded in less than a week.

It was agreed that the U.S.S.R. would take the 400,000 tons of rice at world market prices — that is, the price being paid by Burma's cash buyers. Her own goods, again at "world market prices," would be available in return. Significantly, there was no "swing" provision requiring a periodic balancing of trade deficits and payment of any difference in cash. Nor did the Burmese request, or receive, assurances that credits established with the U.S.S.R. could be used elsewhere in the Sino-Soviet bloc, if the goods Burma desired were not available in the Soviet Union. The absence of such provisions reflected both the naïveté of the Burmese and the fact that the Prime Minister had conducted the negotiations without professional staff or advisory assistance.

With regard to the "gift" projects, here, too, all was beautifully simple. All Mr. Mikoyan wanted to know was what Burma desired — the U.S.S.R. was prepared to give it. When U Nu stated that, in addition to the promised technological institute, Burma would like a hospital, a hotel and a cultural and sports complex made up of a stadium, a theater and agricultural and industrial exhibition buildings, the Soviet response was immediate and positive. The U.S.S.R. requested only the most general indications of the size, type and location of these projects. There was no question of essentiality, no question of whether these or other projects would best serve Burma's needs, no attempt by the U.S.S.R. to criticize, advise or suggest. Nor was there any mention of, or even concern over, cost. Whatever the cost might be, the Soviet Union was prepared to meet it, not only the foreign exchange cost, but the local cost in materials and labor as well.

The suggestion that Burma would make a return gift of rice came from U Nu, not from the Russians. When this offer — which, in view of Burma's well-known policy of accepting no grant aid from any source, might very well have been expected — was made, it was accepted as offered. There was no discussion of whether Burma's return gift would be on a token basis only, or whether its value would correspond to the cost of the projects. Nor was there any mention of the time period over which the return gift would be distributed, or of a rate of interest on the credit, or of any other economic or commercial aspect. There was not even a question about how the U.S.S.R. would finance the sizable local costs of the projects undertaken. It would be difficult to envision any aid negotiations and arrangements which would offer the recipient so blank a check, or which would be more unlike those with the United States. As in the case of the rice sale, this arrangement, too, was concluded on the spot, without consultation or advice.

Later discussions at lower levels resulted in refinement of the arrangements. The technological institute, it was decided, would be located at Insein, the industrial suburb of Rangoon, and would accommodate 1,100 students, including 100 graduate students. It would include lecture and laboratory buildings, hostels for 800 students, living quarters (flats, rooms and cottages) for 86 faculty members, and so on. The hospital, situated in the Shan States at Taunggyi, would provide 200 beds, an out-patient department for 100 patients, hostels for nurses, and other facilities. The hotel, in Rangoon, would contain 206 "apartments," including 25 "de luxe" suites. The stadium, in Rangoon, would be of the Olympic type, with a seating capacity of 50,000 and have an arena, a swimming pool area with 10,000 seats and a training area.

The remaining projects would also be located in Rangoon. The industrial fair grounds would provide a major pavilion for the Union of Burma, an industrial show hall, which could be used also for tennis matches, and an open-air theater seating 4,000. The combined cost of these projects was estimated by the Burmese engineers to be about K 16 crores. Subsequent review by the consulting engineers raised this estimate to K 21 crores, of which K 14 crores would be in foreign exchange. The corresponding rice gift would be spread out over twenty years beginning 1962–63.

It was at this point that the cold light of analysis was first thrown on the agreement. The economic consultants, in reappraising resources for the Four-Year Plan, concluded that the 400,000 tons per year rice sale would not add to Burma's resources. The response to successive reductions in the price of rice indicated that Burma would be able to market for cash practically all the export rice she was likely to grow and be able to ship. The real effect of the Soviet rice sale, therefore, would be to divert substantial rice sales from cash to barter. Dr. Tun Thin, Director of the Central Statistical and Economics Department, who had been a key figure in planning, programing and budgeting activities for the preceding year or so, concurred in the consultants' opinion, and ventured to state it to the Prime Minister as his independent opinion. U Nu was so angered by what he considered to be a politically biased judgment that he ordered Dr. Tun Thin to return to his former post at the University.[13]

But other questions, on the programing side, were yet to come. When U Nu left office in June, and his successor, U Ba Swe, called for a reshaping of the Four-Year Program, it was necessary to decide whether the Soviet projects could be superimposed upon the total program or whether they would have to be fitted into a program of the size previously envisioned. The economic consultants took the view that resources had not been augmented by the barter sale. Even if the Government held that foreign resources would be increased, manpower, materials, transportation, administrative and other resources would not permit the superimposition of the Soviet projects upon the program which would otherwise be feasible. But arrangements and negotiations with the Russians were being conducted by an inner group of secretaries from which the American consultants, quite understandably, had been excluded. Only when the implementing agreement worked out by this group came before the Economic and Social Board for review in December 1956 were the consultants invited, at the last moment, to express their views.

The modified Draft Agreement, they pointed out, referred to the various projects to be executed by the Soviet Union as a "gift" to the people of Burma, and referred also to a "gift" by the Government of Burma to the people of

13. Since Dr. Tun Thin was considered to be a protégé of U Kyaw Nyein, the Prime Minister may have considered the alleged bias as one of internal, rather than pro-Western, politics.

the Soviet Union, "of an appropriate quantity of rice and other products of Burmese origin." It was apparent, however, that Burma's "gift" in exchange for the projects would be not a token but a corresponding quantity of rice and other products.

Obviously, the use of the word "gift" was not realistic. It glossed over the fact that the projects would have to be paid for with rice that could otherwise be sold for cash. Financing would have to come ultimately out of the total pool of resources available to the Union Government for its capital development program. Whatever decisions were made on the scope and timing of these projects would have to take that hard fact into account.

The Draft Agreement was notable in that it provided no estimate of the costs of the projects. The covering memorandum of the Executive Secretary, however, cited an estimate of nearly K 16 crores for the "gift" projects. There was no indication of how this would be divided between foreign exchange and domestic costs.

The economic consultants pointed out that not only financial considerations, but also availability of manpower, local materials, transport facilities, and general management and public administration limitations placed effective upper limits on the size of the total capital program the G.U.B. could undertake. This meant that the incorporation of the "gift" projects would require cancellation or deferment for a number of years of many other projects which appeared to be of a much higher order of essentiality, and which would have been given priority in any well-conceived development program. One cost of the so-called "gift" projects would thereby be, they held, a weakening of the total program.

The Draft Agreement made provision for financing the local costs of the projects by stipulating that Burma would allow imports of consumer goods from the U.S.S.R. at world market prices. Proceeds from the sale of these imports to consumers would be credited to a special Soviet account, and the balances in that account would be used exclusively for local expenditures connected with the "gift" projects. However, this provided no assurance that the kinds, quantities and qualities of the consumer goods which Burma might desire would be available in the Soviet Union. Burma's experience with the Soviet Union thus far indicated that such goods would not be readily available, and that the proposed arrangement was likely to add to the very sizable credits already established against the Soviet Union by rice shipments. The consultants held, therefore, that an arrangement of the kind proposed would, in all probability, add considerably to inflationary pressures in Burma, as previous rice shipments to the Soviet Union had already done.

The consultants stated that while the hospital and the hotel could be regarded as being to some degree essential, the theater, the cultural and sports ensemble (including a stadium) and buildings for industrial and agricultural exhibitions seemed to be luxury projects. They noted also that a magnificent set of buildings for engineering students at the University of Rangoon had just been completed, and that the services of first-class engineering professors and technicians for that institution appeared to be of more immediate importance than a new set of buildings for a technological institute.

In view of the foregoing, they recommended: that Burma make firm commitments on as few projects as possible, leaving decisions on the others until later; that the scope and cost of the agreed-upon projects be held down as much as possible; that the initiation of the projects be deferred, and their construction phasing be deferred as long as possible; and that the Soviet Union be requested to do one of three things: give satisfactory assurances of the availability of consumer goods Burma desired, in terms of category, quality, cost, quantity and timing; allow multilateral use of Soviet Union credits in other countries, including China; or cover the local costs of the projects by payments of gold, sterling or other readily convertible currencies.

It is interesting to note that, up to that point, it had not yet been explicitly established that Burma's return "gift" of rice would correspond in value to the cost of the projects; also, cost estimates were still extremely fuzzy. The Board, under the Chairmanship of U Ba Swe, accepted the Chief Technical Advisor's estimate of their cost at K 21 crores, as against the previous estimate of K 16 crores. It also accepted the economic consultants' recommendation that the projects be curtailed and deferred to the extent possible, ruling that three of the projects — other than the technological institute, the hospital and the hotel — would be deferred until the end of the plan period in 1959–60. It also determined, in view of the questions raised, that Burma herself would finance the local costs of the projects. At a later meeting, in July 1957, it was still necessary to point out that the Draft General Contract Agreement then submitted for approval referred somewhat oddly to the U.S.S.R. as the "client" rather than as the "contractor," and made no provision for the Burmese to review and approve the designs and the cost estimates before construction got under way. These changes were thereupon incorporated into the agreement.

Once the projects actually got under way, the Russians went to work in what appeared to be a most efficient manner. The general consensus was that the ample number of technicians they put in the field were capable and hard working, and that the technicians concentrated strictly on their jobs and studiously refrained from political or propaganda activities. There was not much reaction in Rangoon as work went forward on the technological institute and the hotel. A few people asked what the courses of study at the institute would be, or who — other than the Russians themselves — would occupy the hotel. But these questions were asked, for the most part, good-humoredly and without rancor. If any aspect of the gift project implementation proved irksome to the Burmese, it was the Russian assumption —

Table 86

BURMA'S CREDIT POSITION WITH THE U.S.S.R., 1955–56 TO 1959–60

(K Crores)

	Credits on Rice Sales Account	Debits on Gift Project Account	Net Credit
At end of:			
1955–56	10.3	—	10.3
1956–57	5.4	—	5.4
1957–58	2.8	1.1	1.7
1958–59	3.4	2.2	1.2
1959–60	3.9	2.5	1.4
Five-year average	5.16	1.16	4.0

Sources: For debits on gift project account, *Economic Survey of Burma,* 1958, 1959 and 1960. For credits on rice sales account, Union Bank.

openly stated — that the U.S.S.R. would staff and operate the "gift" projects for many years to come.

In the Shan States the reaction was sharp. Many local people resented the location selected by the Russians for the hospital — at the top of the bluff commanding the approach of the road from Kalaw and Yawnghwe on the Inle Lake — as being too far out of town and far less practical than their own suggested site, which the Russians refused to accept. They also questioned how it would be possible to staff and maintain the hospital. In view of the staff shortages at the still fairly new 200-bed hospital they had acquired not many years before, they disliked the impending necessity to do so. When the Russians complained to Sao Pye, the Shan State Home Minister, about the quality of the local sand and water, his unsympathetic reply was: "These are what we use. If you don't like them, bring yours from Russia."

As of September 1960, all three projects were nearing completion. A number of Burmese medical personnel were in training in the Soviet Union preparatory to staffing the new hospital. The facilities of the technological institute would be used only in part for the original purposes. The remainder would house the engineering college, which would vacate its still new buildings on Prome Road. The hotel, for which the Burmese had supplied inferior timber and workmanship, would be turned over to private management for operation. An arrangement concluded with Pan American Airways and Intercontinental Hotels Corporation early in 1961 to operate the hotel was subsequently terminated in favor of Israeli management.

We come now to what is, in some ways, the most interesting aspect of the Soviet aid program in Burma. Despite the substantial impact made by Russian aid measures in 1956, the fact is that for the period ending September 1960, at least, the Soviets extended no aid to Burma at all. The Burmese figures show U.S.S.R. gift project performance in a value of K 5.8 crores as of that date. This performance, on a credit basis, by itself constitutes aid. But, at the same time, the Russians had failed to deliver goods to Burma against the rice they had bought on a barter basis beginning in 1956. Throughout the period thereafter, Burma was a creditor in the barter arrangement in the average amount of K 5 crores. For the period 1955–1960 as a whole, Burma was a net lender to, rather than a receiver of aid from, the U.S.S.R., though she extended no loans as such and received no interest payments. (See Table 86.)

THE WORLD BANK AID EXPERIENCE

When Burma first thought of foreign loans late in 1953, there was no question of turning to any source other than the World Bank. Burma's idea at that time was to seek aid on a token basis, and develop an association that would provide insurance against possible future declines in the price of rice. Even if the aid proved to be unnecessary, it was felt that the experience gained in negotiating and implementing one or two small World Bank loans would provide valuable discipline in programing and implementation, and that the lessons, though learned most directly by the operating agencies immediately concerned, could be made to benefit other agencies and programs as well.

Even as she prepared to approach the Bank, early in 1954, with such objectives in view, fears of rice price declines began to be realized, and it was decided to seek aid on a more substantial basis. Again, but now for quite different reasons, the Bank was the only source of aid considered. It seemed clear that Burma's independence, sovereignty and neutrality could best be safeguarded by resort to a non-governmental, international banking institution affiliated with the United Nations. In 1954, through an aide mémoire presented by U Hla Maung, the Bank was invited to assist substantially in financing Burma's development program. The Government also stated its belief that "close association with the Bank" would be of "great benefit to Burma in the implementation of her programme of development," because of the advice, guidance and intimacy which would be concomitants of a loan relationship.

The Bank, which had previously sent a fact-finding mission to Burma early in 1953, was already familiar with the problems and programs. The Demuth Mission, after careful study, had concluded that perhaps the chief weakness in the long-term program then being developed was a lack of appreciation of the retarding influence which would be exerted by critical shortages of trained administrative and managerial manpower. The Mission feared that the shortages would constitute major bottlenecks to successful execution of the program. When, in response to the new invitation, the Bank sent a second, "credit-worthiness" mission under Dr. Antonin Basch in December 1954, its findings were even more serious. The foreign exchange out-look, which had appeared so bright in 1952, was now radically altered. By this criterion alone, the program seemed overambitious. In addition, the industrial and electric power programs, by now under way, seemed headed for serious managerial troubles, and the failure to move effectively toward rehabilitation in the primary agricultural, timber and minerals sectors was clearly visible.

U Kyaw Nyein, at that time Minister for Industries, supervised the dealings with the Basch Mission. He was profoundly disturbed by its critical reac-tions to the industry and electric power programs, and even more by what he felt was the Bank's ideological bias in viewing with disfavor possible loans for the construction of additional state-owned manufacturing enterprises. Burma proceeded to submit a list of projects for loan consideration in the amount of K 77.5 crores, of which only 10 per cent was to be applied to indus-trial projects, with hydroelectric, railways, highways and shipping projects accounting for most of the total. U Kyaw Nyein, however, had already pretty well written off the Bank in his own mind. It was his impression that, as a capitalist institution, it was completely out of sympathy with Burma's socialist aspirations, and could no longer be considered seriously as a major source of foreign finance. For its part, the Bank seemed disposed to conclude that Burma had much to do to put its house in order before serious loan discus-sions could be held.

U Nu, however, was still unwilling to risk a loan from the U. S. Govern-ment, and continued discussions with the Bank during his subsequent visit to the United States in the summer of 1955. In August, while loan requests were being made to India and the United States, the Bank was advised that Burma had taken a number of steps generally in accord with the Bank's sug-gestions. In the expectation that the Bank would now be favorably disposed to extend some loans, it was asked to send another mission to Burma as soon as possible.

The third Bank mission, again headed by Dr. Basch, arrived in November 1955. This time it was prepared to consider seriously early loan action, at least for the port of Rangoon and the railways. It advised the Government to this effect, and included among its members specialists in these fields. The Mission seemed to be reasonably impressed with the steps taken in the pre-ceding year to curtail the development program, place Government foreign exchange expenditures under strict control, initiate an export drive and en-courage private investment. But it seemed even clearer that the Bank was disinclined to assist in financing state manufacturing industries.

One development which jarred the Mission may be of interest. Because of previous understandings, the Bank was in the process of organizing a special Agricultural Mission to review the Government's programs in this field, and advise on a course of action. To Dr. Basch's consternation, the Khrushchev–

Bulganin visit, which coincided with that of his own, ended with the announcement that Burma had accepted the offer of U.S.S.R. technicians as advisors in this same field. The Prime Minister, when questioned, saw no problem. The U.S.S.R. technicians, he said, would concentrate on special aspects of agriculture, like irrigation, mechanized farming and cotton, and their work would not conflict with that of the Bank. The Bank was not disposed to share responsibilities (or compete) with the U.S.S.R., and abandoned its contemplated mission.

The visit of this mission did result, however, in the only loans the Bank extended to Burma during this period. These were concluded in May 1956, some two years after Burma's original request. The first, a twenty-year loan of $14 million, was for the port of Rangoon. The second, a fifteen-year loan of $5.35 million, was for the Burma Railways. Both loans carried a 4¾ per cent interest charge. Amortization began after four years and three years of the loan extensions, respectively.

The last two missions sent by the Bank did not result in additional loans. The fourth mission, in January 1957, again headed by Dr. Basch, was sent especially to consider a substantial highways loan, and perhaps one for the outports of Moulmein, Bassein and Akyab. It considered that reorganization and training of the Highways Department was an indispensable prerequisite to any substantial highways program or loan. When Burma accepted the Bank's offer to be of service in obtaining a Canadian team of highway engineers to help develop such a reorganization and training program,[14] the Bank proceeded to make the necessary arrangements, and Canada provided the services under the Colombo Plan. The Bank also thought that further studies, and certain legal and organizational measures, were necessary preliminaries to consideration of a loan for the outports. Some steps were taken along the lines indicated, but in the case of neither the highways nor the outports did loans eventuate.

While interested in Burmese proposals for a much needed industrial development bank to help finance private industrial development, the Mission made it quite plain that the Bank would view with disfavor any financing institution in which the Burmese Government planned to hold a substantial equity interest. As in the case of the Bank's earlier position on state manufacturing enterprises, this impressed U Kyaw Nyein as a manifestation of ideological bias.

So far as the Government was concerned, the World Bank no longer played an important part in its plans. At the outset Burma had looked primarily — indeed, exclusively — to the Bank for the foreign loan financing she desired, but the stately and deliberate way in which the Bank moved and the

---

14. The Bank had been of similar service earlier, in arranging for a Canadian team of electric power specialists to help reorganize the Electricity Supply Board.

lack of sympathy it displayed for key projects, programs and policies dear to the Burmese had long since caused Burma to turn elsewhere, and successfully, for the aid she desired. The Bank's help was no longer important to her.

On the Bank's side, there was also a growing dissatisfaction with the way relations had developed — or rather, had failed to develop. The Bank did not wish to continue to operate in Burma in a small way. It wanted to participate more substantially, more meaningfully and more intimately in Burma's development effort. This was apparent when a fifth mission, headed by Mr. Martin Rosen, director of the Bank's newly established Far Eastern Department of Operations, visited Burma early in 1958. This Mission was intent on developing, if possible, a closer relationship and understanding as a basis for a more substantial program of financial assistance. The Bank's view seemed to be that it had been held at arm's length, rather than treated as a trusted friend and advisor. It was troubled, too, by the apparent inconsistency between the development objectives the Government affirmed and the existence of a number of policies, practices and objectives obviously inimical to these objectives.[15]

Unfortunately, the time was inopportune for the success of such a mission. The political leaders were completely absorbed with the aftermath of the A.F.P.F.L. Congress, and with events which were to lead to the A.F.P.F.L. split in May. Mr. Rosen could speak seriously only with U Kyaw Nyein about his major concern — and the latter, of all the Burmese leaders, had been, since 1955, the one most coolly disposed toward the Bank. At staff levels, various new loan possibilities, including further dieselization of the railways and new sawmilling facilities, were discussed. But it seemed clear that additional loans would have to await a resolution of the basic question.

This resolution could not very well be sought with General Ne Win's Government, which was determined to shun additional foreign loans from any source. And U Nu's Pyidaungsu Government, in its first months in office, was concerned with far different questions. Thus, oddly, a relationship which began with Burma looking exclusively to the Bank for massive aid, and not finding it, ended with the Bank seeking the opportunity to render massive aid, and finding Burma, at least for the time being, no longer interested in receiving it.

THE INDIAN AND INTERNATIONAL MONETARY FUND AID EXPERIENCES

Little need be said about Indian and International Monetary Fund aid to Burma, beyond pointing out briefly why these were the most satisfactory by

---

15. The report of this Mission, incidentally, was an unusually sensitive and perceptive one, and defined quite clearly the internal policy inconsistencies and conflicts which were retarding Burma's economic progress.

far of Burma's foreign aid experiences. The reasons in both cases are very similar. In each case the loan desired was granted after only a short period of negotiation. The resources made available to Burma, in each case, were hard currency which could be utilized anywhere in the world and for any purpose. The agreements entailed no supervision, no further agreements, no controls and no conditions of any kind beyond the stipulated repayment and rate-of-interest provisions. The K 20 crores Indian loan, as amended shortly after it was first negotiated, was repayable in twenty-four semiannual installments, beginning three years after the loan drawdown. Interest at 4¾ per cent was charged only for the part of the loan actually drawn. In the case of the I.M.F. $15 million draw of March 1956, repayment was due from December 1958 to February 1961. Since, at the time, Burma believed her foreign exchange stringency would be of relatively short duration, these short and medium-term repayment periods gave her no concern.

CONCLUSION

When, in 1958, Burma permitted her drive for development to slow down, this was because — even before the Military Government took over — the A.F.P.F.L. Government had come to doubt seriously the wisdom and the priorities of the development program, and Burma's capacity to carry it out effectively. It was these doubts, rather than her experiences with foreign aid in the 1950s, which made her disinclined to exploit the additional aid opportunities in prospect from the Development Loan Fund, P.L. 480, the World Bank and other sources.

In the thinking of the Ne Win Government, these doubts became convictions. The military were also convinced Burma was already overborrowed; and while they sought grant aid from the United States, they refused, at the same time, to execute a number of loan projects undertaken by the previous Government. When U Nu's Pyidaungsu Government returned to power in April 1960, it too was not ready to move forward vigorously on the development front, much less to seek a revival of foreign aid. Nevertheless, Burma's experiences with foreign aid undoubtedly contributed to these attitudes and, quite apart from the more fundamental factors, might well have caused her to rethink the entire foreign aid question, and perhaps consider seeking new sources of aid that would be more congenial.

Certainly foreign aid experience had been both trying and unsatisfactory. Japanese reparations, while sizable, had been restrictive (particularly where consumer goods were concerned), patronizing and uneconomic. The economic cooperation which had also been provided for had not eventuated. Negotiation of U. S. aid had been painfully slow, its programing had been exceedingly difficult, and implementation had been delayed. Both the P.L. 480 sales program and the Development Loan, in different ways, had — in the

Burmese view — involved threats to Burma's sovereignty and neutrality, and had tried her patience as well. World Bank aid had also been difficult to enlist and slow in coming. Further, since the Bank had made plain its lack of sympathy with some of Burma's basic policies and programs, a sense of cooperation or partnership was lacking. Soviet aid had proved itself difficult in quite different ways. Though easily obtained, and apparently on the most generous of terms, the Soviet projects had turned out to be costly in terms of the other projects they displaced and in terms of sharpened internal political stresses. And it transpired unexpectedly that the credits extended to Burma on gift project account were exceeded by the credits Burma involuntarily extended on the separate rice barter sales account. On balance, then, Burma was financing the U.S.S.R., rather than being financed by her. If Indian and I.M.F. aid, in contrast, were ideal, the Indian loan could not offset the resentment created when, not long before, Burma had been forced to sell rice to India at a cash price £13 sterling per ton below the prevailing market, and the I.M.F. loan scarcely created a ripple at the time.

Burma's aid experiences, therefore, had not given her the sense of "lift" that might be expected to accompany aid programs. The aid seemed, for the most part, to have been centered on the several donors' needs, policies and objectives, rather than on Burma's. After receiving some K 126 crores in foreign aid through 1959–60 from so many different sources, Burma felt, in spite of it, quite isolated. The aid programs had not brought her significantly closer to any foreign institution, nation, or the world outside. Indeed, it seemed almost as though her experiences were causing her to withdraw, once again, toward her historic isolation.

Burma's hesitation, however, was tied more to a reappraisal of fundamental objectives and methods than to her experience with foreign aid. By the end of 1960, she was formulating a new Four-Year Plan, and was preparing, though more cautiously, to move forward again. On the foreign aid front, a $14 million loan was being negotiated with the World Bank for the further dieselization of the railways. More significant, shortly after the turn of the new year, Premier Chou En Lai's visit to Rangoon to sign the border treaty was climaxed by the announcement that China would extend Burma an $84 million equivalent credit over the period October 1961–September 1967, which would be repayable from 1971 to 1980. Burma's willingness to accept such a loan from a new source was a significant commentary, not only on her desires to move forward again on the economic front and once again to demonstrate her neutral role with regard to the rival power blocs, but on her unsatisfactory aid experiences in the past, particularly with the West.

CHAPTER 32

Problems of Technical Assistance

SOME GENERAL CONSIDERATIONS

For most of the 1950s the belief was prevalent that capital and technical know-how were the two chief needs of the underdeveloped countries, and that supplying them would enable these countries to achieve the economic development to which they aspired. Burma received, as we have just seen, a considerable amount of capital assistance during the 1950s and a fairly considerable amount of technical assistance as well. But the utilization of technical assistance was no more free of problems than was the utilization of foreign capital assistance, or any other aspect of the development process.

Burma's inability to make efficient use of the substantial technical assistance available to her arose initially out of a complex of naïve expectations and views of the uses and limitations of technical assistance. Problems arose also out of her lack of appreciation of her need for such assistance, out of a lack of careful programing to obtain the assistance needed, out of a failure effectively to assign and direct the personnel available, and out of a failure carefully to consider and apply the recommendations made. The deficiencies, however, were not all on the Burmese side. On the foreign side, problems arose chiefly out of shortcomings of the people engaged or supplied, defects in their motivation, orientation and attitudes, out of the working arrangements established and, inevitably, out of cultural and standard-of-living differences.

Early in the 1950s, the rationale of the Burmese attitude toward technicians from abroad ran somewhat as follows. All foreign technicians were experts in their fields. They were, by definition, persons who knew all there was to know about some function. Somewhere there existed predetermined answers to any question or problem which might arise. Experts were capable of reaching back into their prodigious store of knowledge and memory and selecting, on almost a moment's notice, the "right" answer to any question. The ability to solve problems by hard work, while no doubt praiseworthy, was probably not expertise but something else. In a sense, an expert was one who could be expected to perform semi-miracles. As one very senior minister stated on one occasion, "We need experts to help us do the impossible."

This same thought was expressed on another occasion by the Prime Minister in explaining why he liked a certain foreign expert. "The man," he said, "is good because he is not negative. He tells us how we can do what we want to do, when others tell us why we cannot do it." With so naïve a set of initial attitudes, it is not surprising that the Government was inclined to identify the acquisition of experts with problem solution and progress — almost as though, once an expert was engaged, the job was virtually done.

These attitudes did not, of course, persist. In time, the Government learned that experts could not easily and almost automatically solve the problems posed. In fact, instead of solving problems, they frequently brought to light new problems of which the Government had been unaware. All too often, and sometimes to the point of irritation, they stressed that additional time and study were required. They found it necessary even to state, on occasion, that their own expertise was not adequate to cope with some of the specialized problems and to urge the need for additional experts and studies. Many of the specialists engaged on only vague terms of reference demanded to know more specifically what it was they were supposed to do, while the Burmese expected the experts to tell them what the specialists' tasks should be.

Additional irritations developed when experts criticized the accepted or preferred ways of doing things, or when they insisted it was necessary that the Government do things it did not wish to do. The occasional disagreement between experts came as something of a shock, since it placed the Government in the unhappy position of having to decide which of them was right if it did not want to call in a third expert to adjudicate the issue. Still another blow was the occasional discovery that the "expert" was really not expert at all, or was impractical, or insensible of local conditions which made his transplanted expertise inapplicable. There were even those baffling occasions when a Burmese official was able, in open meeting, to refute a position or an analysis offered by one of the foreign experts. And, as time went by, it sometimes became clear in particular cases that the resentment of local officials, or the press or the public, made some foreign experts political liabilities, and therefore expendable.

But what was perhaps the most significant change in the attitude toward the foreign technicians was the growing recognition that they did not necessarily make the work burden of the Burmese, or their consciences, any easier. On the contrary, utilization of foreign experts often necessitated far more work and effort than the Burmese had expended before — they were called

Table 87

SOURCES OF FOREIGN SPECIALISTS ASSISTING
THE GOVERNMENT AS OF SEPTEMBER 1957

Total	395
1. Direct contract with individual specialists	116
2. Foreign governments	90
a. People's China	41
b. U.S.S.R.	19
c. Israel	17
d. Japan	12
e. West Germany	1
3. Foreign firms	82
a. United States	28
b. West Germany	22
c. United Kingdom	20
d. Other	12
4. United Nations	66
a. Technical Assistance Administration	21
b. World Health Organization	16
c. Food and Agriculture Organization	9
d. International Labor Organization	7
e. Other	5
Colombo Plan	8
5. Foundations: United States	41

Source: "Status and Activities of Foreign Specialists in Burma," memorandum by D. P. Barnes, Chief Planning Engineer (T.A.M.S.), Ministry of National Planning, Rangoon, Sept. 29, 1958, Table I.

upon to give more attention to problems and alternatives, to probe more deeply into them, and to make more effort in executing policies.

The initial naïveté thus evaporated over the decade. In its place there developed a quite different and far more realistic attitude, one not entirely free from disillusion, disappointment and even irritation. Some foreign experts might be useful; others might not. But one thing was clear: Even the best of them could work no miracles.

THE SOURCES AND USES OF TECHNICAL ASSISTANCE

Since effective use of the available technical assistance was closely related to the sources from which it was obtained, the kinds of specialization and the fields of activity involved and, finally, the governmental arrangements under which the services were performed, it will be useful to examine the situation with respect to these factors.

As of September 1957, some 395 foreign specialists were assisting the Government of Burma. The sources or auspices for these specialists are shown in Table 87.

Direct contracts with individual specialists, the largest single category, provided chiefly for doctors, engineers and artisans recruited, for the most part, in India, at salary levels not far removed from those prevailing in the Burmese civil services. In the next largest category, specialists provided by foreign governments, the group provided by People's China was engaged on one project only — the installation of a cotton textile mill. The Japanese group was similarly engaged in the construction of a hydroelectric project procured under the reparations settlement. The U.S.S.R. technicians were also concentrated mostly on the Russian "gift" projects. The Israeli technicians were, however, dispersed among a number of activities. Of the specialists provided by foreign firms, the U. S. technicians provided central economic and engineering services to the Government, whereas the others were engaged in specific project execution. Technicians from the United Nations (with the notable exception of those from W.H.O.) and the Colombo Plan were chiefly advisory. The sizable group provided under the auspices of the Ford Foundation and other American foundations were engaged chiefly in training and research activities.

The memorandum on which Table 87 is based classifies 170 of the total group as operating professionals, 134 as advisors and consultants, 49 as specialists and technicians, and 42 as artisans. Most of the advisors and consultants were obtained under United Nations, Colombo Plan and foundation auspices, and from U. S. private firms. Most of those in the other categories were obtained by direct hire and from foreign governments and firms.

The distribution of the group by field of activity is shown in Table 88. By far the largest number were concerned with industrial activities. These were obtained mostly by direct hire. The remainder of the activity distribution is not related significantly to the sources of aid, except in the case of central planning and supervisory activities, where the specialists were provided by the two American advisory firms.

Finally, the placement of foreign specialists by the various types of Government organization to which they were attached is shown in Table 89. About two fifths were engaged by the major development corporations, and another fifth with State Boards and other operating organizations. Ministries and departments accounted for another fifth. The central planning and supervisory agencies utilized about six per cent of the total.

The Government's experience with direct hire arrangements was not good. It was not easy for the agencies to find or select the best-qualified candidates. Pay scales were substantially lower than those for specialists provided by foreign firms, and were not attractive to highly qualified people. On the job, difficulties and dissatisfactions with housing, transport and working conditions tended to develop. If the specialist was dissatisfied with the job or its attendant arrangements, there was little he could do about it. Morale was frequently poor, turnover was undesirably high and many vacancies remained unfilled.

Table 88

FOREIGN SPECIALISTS ASSISTING THE GOVERNMENT
AS OF SEPTEMBER 1957, BY FIELD OF ACTIVITY

Total	395
Industry	140
Agriculture	40
Mining	30
Public health	28
Irrigation	26
Education	25
Housing and public buildings	17
Administration	10
Communications	5
Research	5
Cooperatives	2
Undistributed	42
Central planning and supervision	25

Source: Same as Table 87.

The private firms were in a much better position to select competent people, and to see to it that they were adequately paid. These firms negotiated contracts with clear provisions concerning housing, transport, medical care and other arrangements, and were in a position to manage their own work programs so as to provide more constructive work opportunities and guidance for their personnel. They also had direct access to Government officials at high levels, and could iron out the work difficulties which arose. For these reasons, their personnel manifested higher morale than did direct-hire personnel. Job performance was better and turnover was lower. The firms also provided a desirable continuity of experience. Not the least advantage of the private firm with an established reputation in its field was that the Government was inclined to consider its recommendations carefully, while it tended to ignore those coming from other sources, including its own people.

U. N. technical assistance was subject to a number of weaknesses. Since budgets were on a year-by-year basis, technicians could be supplied only on a one-year basis — although the services of individual specialists were frequently extended. In so short a period of service, a large part of the time was necessarily devoted to job orientation and "settling in," and later on to preparations for departure. Many of the personnel supplied were something less than first rate. Reports were frequently rendered only after the specialists' departure, and it was often many months more before the organization responsible (e.g., T.A.A., F.A.O.) had approved their reports and recommendations and submitted them officially to the Government. Sometimes these reports came only after the need for them had changed or passed, and seldom was the specialist or a successor on the spot to follow through on acceptance and utilization. Significantly, if the specialist's counterpart or the organization

Table 89

GOVERNMENT AGENCIES UTILIZING SERVICES
OF FOREIGN SPECIALISTS,
AS OF SEPTEMBER 1957

Total	395
1. Development corporations	160
a. Industrial Development Corp.	113
b. Agriculture Resources Development Corp.	17
c. Mineral Resources Development Corp.	30
2. State boards and other operating organizations	82
a. Electricity Supply Board	25
b. National Housing Board	17
c. Airways Board	15
d. Other	25
3. Ministries and departments	78
4. Educational and research institutions	32
5. Planning and supervisory agencies	23
a. Ministry of National Planning	16
b. Economic and Social Board	7
6. Other	20

Source: Same as Table 87.

he served was disinclined to consider his views seriously, there was little he could do about it. The U. N. Resident Representative did not coordinate, supervise or take responsibility for the specialists' work, or try to get Government action on their recommendations.

The Israeli technicians, dispersed like the U. N. personnel among a number of activities and projects, were quite outstanding. This was because, among other things, they were hand-picked by their Government, and realized that their success would help cement the cordial relations their Government desired to establish with Burma; because they were sympathetic to Burmese aspirations and problems; because they themselves came from a nation-building operation and brought with them a certain zeal; because they were conditioned to accept hardships; and because their assignments, for the most part, were "do-it" jobs, rather than advisory ones.

This last was very important. Setting up tractor service stations and training their operators, designing military camps and facilities, supplying medical services to the army hospital, running chicken farms and similar "do-it" assignments were simpler to perform satisfactorily than, say, getting effective results by advising on rice marketing or import trade policy. And since they worked mostly with and for the military authorities, who understood administration and who created arrangements under which they could work effectively, the Israelis were able to contribute more than they could have under other circumstances.

The foundations combined the advantages enjoyed by the private firms and those which came with active, self-chosen "do-it" assignments, chiefly in the training field, which enabled them to engage qualified, serious personnel and to retain them on the job with relatively high morale. A favorable Burmese attitude toward the foundations was heightened by their private philanthropic character and, of course, by the fact that they were self-financed.

This quick run-down of the sources of technical assistance available to the Government of Burma needs to be supplemented by mention of the assistance privately and directly extended by hundreds of missionaries serving throughout the country, engaged chiefly in educational and medical activities (as well as in their religious activities, of course). Missionaries in Burma were quiet, self-effacing, dedicated people who remained in Burma year after year, spoke the language, and lived close to the people they served so well. Their schools and hospitals were of the best, and they were held in high regard.

SOME KEY PROBLEMS

There were a number of problems affecting technical assistance which arose quite generally, whatever the sources and uses of the assistance. Language, fortunately, was not much of a problem, since virtually all Burmese officials had at least a passable command of English. (The U.S.S.R. technicians had their own interpreters, of course, while those from other non-English-speaking countries were almost invariably familiar with English.) Unfortunately, not all of the specialized foreign personnel who came to Burma were desirably motivated and oriented. Some, on the verge of retirement, were interested primarily in money. Some were maladjusted persons who could not function satisfactorily at home. Still others were adventurers, innocent "do-gooders," impractical academicians, hypochondriacs, egotists, "milktoasts" overeager to please, or cynical sophisticates scornful of the environment in which they found themselves and of the Burmese. Professional competence, integrity and sense of workmanship, ingenuity, adaptability, imagination, patience, health, energy, realistic optimism, sense of values and tactics, some teacher instinct and a pinch of missionary zeal — all highly desirable in foreign specialists — were rarely combined. And matters were not helped by the highly disparate and, under the circumstances, even ostentatious, living standards of the foreigners, which tended to make them a cultural enclave within the broader community. The wives of the foreign technicians also played a very important role. If they were not healthy, cheerful, adaptable, friendly and constructive in their outlook, it was difficult for their husbands to function with full effectiveness. Generally, a good man at home was a good man abroad — but with an important proviso. Obvious weaknesses blew up to monstrous proportions and weaknesses which might have been only latent at home suddenly erupted seriously in the new cultural and work setting.

The deficiencies naturally were not all on the side of the sources of aid or the foreign personnel. They were even more serious on the Burmese side. We have already mentioned the naïve expectations which characterized, at the outset, the Burmese approach to their foreign "experts." In engaging foreign specialists, especially on direct hire, the Burmese tried to "save" on salaries, even when this could be accomplished only at the expense of quality, morale and performance. They frequently requested, or accepted, U. N. or other technical assistance just because it would not cost anything in foreign exchange, without regard to objective need, intended use or their ability to utilize it. Little attempt was made to orient foreign specialists arriving for tours of duty. Precious time was lost because of delays in providing housing, transport, office space, secretarial or typing assistance, arranging the necessary liaison, and even in clearly laying out the job to be done and the terms of reference. Local counterparts were not always provided to work with, and be trained by, the foreign specialists. The officials to whom foreign technicians were attached were sometimes indifferent to, or even resentful of, them. In any event, many of these officials were usually less than frank in disclosing their work problems — partly because they were comfortable in their established ruts, and partly because they hesitated to reveal their own inadequacies. Nor were they inclined to act upon the recommendations received, when this required them to urge new programs, procedures and additional effort, and perhaps costs, upon their superior officers. Finally, the Burmese made little effort to coordinate the work of foreign specialists provided under different auspices, even when their assignments overlapped.

Generally speaking, foreign technicians were most effective when they were engaged in clear-cut "do-it" jobs — such as conducting anti-malaria spraying or vaccination campaigns, operating experimental farms, conducting technical or agricultural training schools, setting up tractor service stations — where the authority to act was clearly delegated. Performance on management jobs, where the necessary authority was not clearly delegated, and where the necessary supporting staff was not provided, was another story. Technicians in jobs which were essentially advisory encountered serious difficulties in obtaining the required attention, decision and follow-through.

These difficulties and limitations in the uses of foreign technicians had considerable significance for technical assistance "needs." Measured in terms of what needed to be done to reach the development goals, the needs were tremendous, and more than the available personnel could handle. (Of course, if Burma's public administration had utilized the capacities of its own officials more effectively, the need for foreigners would not have appeared to be so great. Similarly, "needs" would have been reduced if policy had called for more participation by the private sector.) However, measured in terms of how ready the Burmese were to accept foreign specialists and utilize them effectively, it sometimes seemed as though the 395 foreign technicians Burma had were already too many.

Quite apart from the criteria of needs, however calculated, and the ability to utilize aid, there seemed to be psychological and political limitations on the amount of technical assistance Burma could accept. Beyond a given point, the number of foreigners with flashy cars, pucka housing and large-scale entertainment would undoubtedly have begun to have social and political repercussions. The number could grow only so far before technical assistance would begin to take on an outward appearance something like that of the colonial regime. For these reasons, as well as those inherent in the limited ability to utilize technical assistance effectively, it was perhaps just as well that the volume of technical assistance did not grow much larger than it did.

SOME CONCLUSIONS

It would appear, from the Burmese experience, that the effectiveness of technical assistance depends heavily on careful selection of the foreign personnel, using standards that combine desirable motivations, orientation and personal characteristics with technical competence. Direct hire of individuals is not a satisfactory method of procurement. Foreign firms offer substantial advantages, both for assistance in the execution of specific projects and in central consulting and advisory capacities. U. N. technical assistance, while welcomed, has a number of weaknesses, and seems to operate most successfully when "do-it," rather than advisory, jobs are concerned. On the governmental side, for a number of special reasons, Israeli technical assistance appears to have outstanding advantages. Foundation-sponsored assistance is also highly advantageous.

The unique and successful aspects of Israeli, foundation and missionary aid suggest another source of technical assistance which might profitably be tapped, and to which countries like Burma might be singularly receptive. Labor, cooperative and progressive farm organizations can draw on large reservoirs of trained and disciplined people who also have some sense of mission — that "pinch of missionary zeal" mentioned earlier. They also represent movements with a built-in sense of sympathy for the aspirations of countries like Burma. The West, and the United States particularly, would do well to encourage, and even to finance, a broad measure of participation by these movements in technical assistance programs.

In quite another vein, there is still one more group that should increasingly get into technical assistance operations. Not all requirements for "technical" assistance are of a professional or technical character. There is a tremendous need for managerial assistance as well. This need is not met by technicians, except insofar as accountants, lawyers, personnel officers and persons of related management skills enter the picture. But the entrepreneurial aspects of management are not, as such, identified with technical skills. They are identified with business men. The business communities of the United States (and other advanced nations) have a great contribution to make in this field. If American business firms provided their Government with countless "dollar-a-year" men during World War II, surely they could duplicate this contribution now, in order to assist their country's efforts on behalf of the underdeveloped countries. And what better preliminary could there be to an increased volume of private foreign investment abroad?

This suggests one final point. Private firms in Burma, as well as the Government, need technical assistance, and frequently seek to employ it. They are unduly hampered in this attempt by unreasonable difficulties imposed by the Government in the granting of the necessary entry and extension-of-stay permits, and by restrictive regulation of remittances abroad. These arise, of course, out of undue provincialism and Burmanization policy. They are not consistent, however, with the Government's own use of technical assistance, or with its development objectives.

THE ROBERT R. NATHAN ASSOCIATES EXPERIENCE
(A Unique Experience in Technical Assistance)

The experience of Robert R. Nathan Associates, the economic consultants to the Government, first, in advising Burma on the formulation of her economic development program, and then, over a period of years, in helping to adapt and carry it out, was unique. A brief review of the major aspects of this experience may be of special interest to those concerned with the role of technical assistance in these fields, and the auspices and arrangements under which such services may be performed.

Robert R. Nathan Associates was chosen by the Government of Burma, not by the U. S. Government. During the first two-year contract period, the U. S. Government paid the dollar cost of the firm's services; in 1953, 1955 and 1957 these contract services were extended by the Government of Burma at its own expense. During the 1951–53 period, the firm was part of a joint economic and engineering planning team. From 1953 on, it was independently engaged to render economic advisory services to the Economic and Social Board and the Ministry of National Planning. Its contractual responsibilities were considerable. They included:

CONSULTING ECONOMIST shall assist the Economic and Social Board in carrying out its responsibilities in relation to the development program, and shall assist the Ministry of National Planning in continued planning studies and program revision. The functions of CONSULTING ECONOMIST in rendering this assistance to the Economic and Social Board and the Ministry of National Planning shall be:

1. To analyze the relationship from year to year between the growing capital equipment of the country and the level of production and national income, and to recommend adjustments or revisions as necessary and desirable in the overall income goals and the overall development expenditure plans for a period of years.

2. To aid in the formulation of each year's development program, by advice concerning:

a. The feasible magnitude of expenditures for each coming year;

b. The economic balance between projects of different types forming parts of the program;

c. The availability of domestic funds for private investment and for governmental development expenditures, and concerning measures which will affect the volume of available funds, such as revenue measures, banking policies, and foreign trade and foreign exchange controls;

d. The availability of foreign exchange and measures affecting it.

3. To advise and consult on the economic aspects of plans, programs, projects, and policies in the fields of manufacturing, power, transportation, communications and construction, and on their relationship to the total development plan. This will include advice as to the timing and priorities of development projects; the balance among them; the availability of productive resources, including manpower and management; and other pertinent economic factors.

4. To advise and consult concerning the relationship between development plans in other fields and the agricultural economy of Burma, and to recommend plans, programs and policies of an economic nature in the field of agricultural development.

5. To make special studies within the limits of staff time available of the markets, prices, costs, and benefits of development programs in specific industries, such as the forest products industry or the textile industry.

6. To make special studies within the limits of staff time available of transport rates and costs, and their effects upon the operation of the economy as a whole.

7. To make studies of world markets for Burmese exports, including price trends, and of other matters affecting prospects for foreign exchange earnings; to make similar studies of sources of supply of necessary imports and of other matters affecting foreign exchange expenditures; and to advise concerning ways of conserving foreign exchange by enlarging domestic expenditures or of economizing on domestic expenditures by enlarging foreign exchange expenditures, as occasion may warrant.

8. To aid in the development of the annual fiscal budget of the Government by advice concerning the relationship of the development program to the budget as a whole.

9. To advise concerning methods and procedures of budgetary control of the development program.

10. To review development plans and priorities and to submit to the Government at regular intervals reports on the economic aspects of the program.

11. To advise concerning a system of statistical and accounting records and charts; to assemble, organize and maintain current information concerning the

progress of the development program; to evaluate and analyze progress, and to make recommendations as to remedial actions necessary to improve the progress of the development program.

12. To advise and consult, and otherwise assist in the development of central and top level implementing and expediting policies and procedures.

13. To advise concerning administrative organization for expediting developmental planning, programming, budgeting, and execution.

14. To advise concerning methods of improving the collection and analysis of data concerning national income and components thereof, including saving, consumption, capital formation, production, and other components and series useful and necessary for most effective planning, programming and control of a development program.

15. To analyze population and labor force data, wage policy and trends, and advise concerning potential shortages and bottlenecks in the supply of special skills and types of labor and methods of meeting or avoiding them.

16. To advise concerning methods of financing individual projects and development corporations handling groups of projects.

17. To advise concerning ways of financing the country's productive activities, including the extension of credit to agriculture, indigenous industry, and cottage industry.

18. To advise concerning the effects on production incentives and on other aspects of economic activity of changes in economic policy measures such as revenue measures, banking policies, and foreign exchange and foreign trade controls.

C. OTHER SERVICES

It is agreed that the CONSULTING ECONOMIST may be called upon to perform duties other than those specifically set forth herein, which may be reasonably within the scope and purpose of this Agreement.[1]

During the latter part of the 1951–53 planning period, the firm's team comprised five professionals — a chief (and fiscal) economist, national income, agricultural and industrial economists, and one junior economist. Beginning with 1953, the firm maintained a staff of seven or eight persons in Rangoon most of the time, and, toward the end, ten staff members. These included, as a constant core, a general manager and chief economist, fiscal, industrial and agricultural economists, a progress reporting analyst and an administrative officer. These were supplemented at the outset by a national income economist, and later on by a deputy chief economist, an economic statistician and specialists in merchandising and rice marketing intelligence. The progress reporting job was changed, toward the end, into a management analysis job. Consultants in taxation and freight rates augmented the work of the field staff on a short-term basis.

1. Agreement between the President of the Union of Burma and Robert R. Nathan Associates, Inc., July 20, 1953, Article I, B, and C.

The field staff had general "back-up" from the firm's home office and the full-time assistance of a special "desk officer" in the home office. The home office support included not only special and major research jobs in such fields as rice marketing and minerals, foreign investment legislation, development institutions, industrial joint ventures, and reparations, but also economic counsel to the Burmese Embassy in Washington, including assistance in loan and P.L. 480 justifications, negotiations and implementation; orientation and assistance to Burmese missions, officials, business leaders, students and others visiting Washington; maintenance of effective liaison with U. S. and international agencies interested in Burmese economic developments; and general assistance to prospective investors in Burma. Robert R. Nathan, the firm's President, made, in addition, two visits of two to four weeks' duration to Rangoon each year.

The team was required contractually to function through its general manager and chief economist, who reported to the Government through the Executive Secretary of the Economic and Social Board. This remained throughout the formal process, but individual staff members were in almost constant contact with secretaries to Government, board chairmen and other officials, and much effective preventive or remedial work was done in this way which never reached the Economic and Social Board at all. Certain activities were basic and repetitive from year to year — chiefly the annual fiscal, capital, import, foreign exchange and related programs, and, in the early years, the annual Economic Survey. Requests from the Economic and Social Board for comments and recommendations on matters referred to it for decision, and for staff assistance in negotiations and other activities, constituted a heavy work load. But more than half the team's time and energy was spent on studies, analyses and action and policy proposals that it initiated itself, and that dealt with problems of which the Government had not yet become aware.

While the firm's function was defined as an advisory one, it was necessary from time to time to use the firm's advisory staff on purely operational matters. These included, notably, the creation and initial direction of foreign exchange control and progress reporting operations, capital budget reviews, and assistance in loan and joint venture negotiations and in the implementation of P.L. 480 agreements. And while the concern of the economic consultants was primarily with economic questions, the firm found it necessary to focus increasingly on problems of implementation, management and public administration. In fact, from 1956–57 on, the team felt that problems of this kind had assumed the greatest importance and most needed positive remedial action.

At the outset, the firm depended for its effectiveness on the confidence of the Executive Secretary to the Economic and Social Board, who in turn enjoyed the confidence of the Prime Minister. The direct confidence of the Prime Minister himself was soon won. In time, direct contacts and, frequently, direct services made for closer relations and greater confidence and acceptance on the part of other ministers, secretaries to Government and other officials and agencies. There was some disposition, in the early months, to regard the team as "belonging" to, and even as being in the exclusive and partisan service of, certain leaders and officials. This view was soon dispelled, as it became evident that the firm was disposed to be critical of weaknesses in plans, projects, programs, policies and errors of whatever kind, no matter which leader, official or agency happened to be identified with them. This objectivity and political disengagement helped to promote the acceptance and effectiveness of the economic consultants.

In housing, transport, office facilities and staff and other working arrangements, the firm encountered no serious difficulties. The salary, living allowances, medical care, import and other arrangements it enjoyed were liberal, and the Government scrupulously observed its contractual obligations in these and other matters within its control. Nor did the firm encounter any serious problems of communication. Officials with whom the team had occasion to work invariably spoke English. It was only at the ministerial level that the consultants encountered, on occasion, a language problem. At meetings of the Economic and Social Board, where the chief economist sat by invitation, documents were often in Burmese, and Burmese was spoken, with lapses into English from time to time. But there had usually been time to translate and abstract the documents, and an interpreter's assistance was available.

The problems encountered by the firm were of a more important nature. In spite of the liberal compensation arrangements made, it was not easy to recruit staff of the caliber required or, in all cases, to find individuals who combined professional competence with ideal personal characteristics, motivations and outlook. There was always more to do than could be done by the limited staff available, and "rush" jobs and "emergency" situations frequently necessitated deferment of more fundamental tasks. It was sometimes difficult to avoid involvement or apparent partisanship in personal or power struggles between Government officials and organizations. It was sometimes difficult also to criticize certain decisions, actions or trends on practical grounds without inviting the suspicion that the firm's views were biased by a "capitalist" preference for free enterprise and a corollary prejudice against socialism. While the firm soon convinced the Government of its loyalty and enjoyed a remarkable degree of confidence, it was nevertheless not invited to submit its views regarding Soviet bloc economic arrangements — the rice barter deals and the U.S.S.R. gift projects — before these were concluded. It is quite possible that this reflected more a desire to spare the consultants the possible awkwardness of divided loyalties than a suspicion that they would lack objectivity on such questions — but the problem was there just the same.

While the Government did little to coordinate the work of the foreign specialists serving it under various auspices, the firm and its staff members were able to effect informal practical working arrangements with U. N., foundation, direct-hire and other specialists. Relationships with the central bank, the private business community and various embassies were also satisfactory. The U. S. Embassy was fully appreciative of the firm's relationship and obligations to the Government of Burma and, although the firm and its staff frequently assisted their clients in discussions and negotiations with U. S. officials and agencies, at no time was a conflict in loyalties involved.

For a time, the firm encountered some difficulties in using the young and inexperienced Burmese economic staff within the Ministry of National Planning. This staff had originally been attached (or "seconded") to it, and worked under the direction of the consultant's staff members. In the next period, which was one of transition to an autonomous functioning for the local staff, the firm recruited and trained a number of young economists, and then turned them over to the local staff. Friction developed when the local staff was placed on an independent work status, and questions arose about how certain work responsibilities should be allocated, and the channels through which the consultants' views should be communicated to the Government. The firm's general manager took the view that the local group could best advance by operating autonomously. This ended the friction and, over the later years, the Central Statistical and Economics Department developed rapidly in experience and competence.

Another problem grew out of the attacks which occasionally appeared in the press, which was singularly uninformed about the role of the economists and, of course, about the nature of the advice they were giving. The services the consultants rendered were direct and confidential, and it did not seem appropriate to respond to the misinformed judgments that were sometimes made — though it would almost invariably have served a useful public purpose to do so.

But undoubtedly the most difficult and important problems the consultants faced were those which arose out of the Government's impractical socialization and Burmanization policies and, once the program was well under way, out of its inept performance in public administration and implementation. The questions here were basically tactical. One major question was: Should these problems be tackled generally and frontally, or on the practical merits of the individual cases in which they manifested themselves? And a second major question was: Should the firm's advice to the Government be, in effect, "You can execute a program of the size and composition you desire, provided that you also take the necessary complementary steps to improve economic policy, public administration, management, and so on," or should it rather be, in effect, "You must abandon all thought of attempting to continue with this program *until* you have taken the necessary complementary measures..."?

On the first of these choices, the strategy changed bit by bit over the years from one which confined itself to the merits of individual cases to one which concentrated more broadly on the fundamental issue. On the second question, which was a major cause for soul-searching within the consultants' group, the decision was to continue to stress the first ("provided") alternative. It may well be that the second ("until") alternative would have jolted the Government harder, and been more productive of results. But perhaps only a refusal by the firm to renew its contract with the Government could have registered with the necessary impact, and even this would probably not have sufficed to bring about substantial improvement.

In terms of results, the advisory firm was far more effective in certain areas of policy and decision than in others. With the exception of the 1954–55 capital program, it was invariably able to win acceptance from the Government of the upper limits it recommended for the annual spending programs and of its views on the size of the capital and current budgets within them. The firm's views on the annual foreign exchange budgets, and the size and commodity composition of the annual import programs, were similarly accepted. The consultants' views were almost invariably respected also when they opposed — as they often did — specific projects and programs, whether on economic, management or administrative feasibility grounds. They were least successful when they opposed decisions motivated by Burmanization policy, or attempted to correct abuses arising out of this policy, and when they tried to persuade the Government to initiate vigorous (and sometimes tough) action in tax policy and enforcement, in project and program implementation and in public administration. Between these extremes they were moderately successful. They gradually exerted a considerable influence on rice marketing and pricing policies and on the mobilization of foreign resources, helped to slow down further public industrial development, were influential in the cutback of the U.S.S.R. "gift" program, in the expansion of agricultural extension services and in the increased priority given to the agricultural and other primary sectors.

I shall not, because of my personal involvement, offer an appraisal of the firm's contributions to economic development in Burma. It is appropriate, however, to comment in general on the usefulness, or advantages, of private consulting firms in central economic planning and advisory relationships to underdeveloped countries, as suggested by the experience of Robert R. Nathan Associates.

There is no question that a private firm, engaged by a government itself (and, preferably, paid by it out of its own resources), is far more likely to enjoy that government's confidence, and to be consulted on intimate and even delicate questions, than an advisory group on the payroll of any assisting government would be. Whether a private firm would enjoy greater intimacy and confidence than a university-sponsored or a foundation-sponsored team might is perhaps debatable. If the university team were financed by another government, the advantage would still be clearly with the private firm. If the university group were financed, on the other hand, by a private foundation, the choice would seem to become moot. The private firm would have no advantage over a U. N. team, except insofar as the government might be more inclined to consider recommendations seriously if it was paying for them.

This question of intimacy and confidence is of more than passing consequence. To see the problems from the "inside," so to speak, is to understand better the motivations and attitudes which so importantly influence the decision-making process; to be in a position to discuss the problems in terms of those factors; to be able to anticipate and "time" emerging problems; and to have that ready access to the policy-makers which is so crucial to effective advisory performance.

The chief disadvantages of the private firm in such a role, it is sometimes suggested, are that its services are costly and that, in order to retain a profitable contract, it will be inclined to seek to please its governmental client, rather than to be objective. Neither of these objections is really valid. The real cost of such advisors lies in the cost of the mistakes which may result from their recommendations. This, of course, could be enormous. Conversely, the real value of such services inheres in the enormous benefits which may accrue. The potential on either side is so great as to make any possible direct costs pale into insignificance. With respect to bias, or vested interest, the governments of underdeveloped countries may be unsophisticated, but they are not as unsophisticated as all that. If anything, they will tend to be suspicious, and, having an ample supply of their own, will not be inclined to pay high salaries and fees to foreign "yes men" for long. Finally, only brief reflection will be required to find in university, foundation and even in foreign government personnel teams, "vested interests" in winning and retaining approbation analogous to those attributed to the private profit-making firm.

Part VI

CONCLUSIONS AND
APPRAISALS

CHAPTER 33

Significance of the Experience

for Burma's Further

Economic Development

After summarizing the highlights and appraising the lessons of Burma's development experience through 1960, this chapter will attempt to apply those lessons to determine the policies, programs and emphases most likely to promote her further economic development.

Burma's experience in the 1950s may best be appraised by considering three separate and distinct phases: the A.F.P.F.L. period ending in the fall of 1958; the Ne Win Caretaker Government period; and the Pyidaungsu, or Union Government, period, which began with U Nu's return to office in April 1960.

THE A.F.P.F.L. PERIOD

The A.F.P.F.L. Government started out with high hopes, and enthusiasm. It had faith that planning was the road to welfare, that investment would automatically result in greater production and productivity and that it had only to formulate plans and engage experts to stake out the path. Industrialization, it believed, was the main avenue to progress, nationalization would hasten progress and insure social justice, and Burmanization would see to it that the fruits of progress were channeled to Burmese nationals and control of the economy was transferred completely to Burmese hands. If these views were not shared universally, or held as strongly by all the social and economic groups within the nation as they were within the A.F.P.F.L. Government itself, they commanded either overt assent or, at least, passive acceptance on the part of the public. The only effective opposition was the challenge of the armed insurrectionists to the Government itself.

Soon after embarking upon its development program, the A.F.P.F.L. Government ran into serious foreign exchange difficulties, domestic inflation, administrative and managerial difficulties, party problems and conflicts and, finally, political crisis. These troubles were aggravated by continued insurrection, the weakness of the civil service, shortages of technically trained personnel, conflicting policies, outmoded, overloaded and overcentralized public administration, the lack of the necessary determination and toughness, the leaders' own inexperience in practical affairs, and many other cultural attitudes and values inimical to the development goal. More serious perhaps than any of these were the absence of effective delegation of authority and responsibility and the pernicious subversion of the public administration by an irresponsible party machine which abused that administration for its own political and personal ends.

In spite of these difficulties and weaknesses, the A.F.P.F.L. Government actually accomplished a great deal. A long-term development program was planned, introduced and, in good part, implemented. Total output was increased on an average of 5 per cent per year, per capita output by some 4 per cent per year. Agricultural acreage and output were substantially increased, forestry and mining partly restored, transportation and communications largely rehabilitated, new electric power and new industries developed and new schools, hospitals and public housing built. The Government survived continued insurrection, drastic declines in the price of rice and damaging mistakes in barter sales and many other fields; it adjusted its program, contained inflation and maintained a reasonable degree of economic stability. These were significant accomplishments. However, in succumbing to anti-foreignism and other pernicious economic policies, in failing to separate the public administration from political bossism and nepotism and to establish discipline, responsibility and standards of hard work and sacrifice among civil servants and the citizenry at large, it failed also to achieve the degree of success which it could and should have reached. It was the failure to achieve what was practicable under the circumstances, rather than the failure to achieve at all, that was the real measure of the failure of the A.F.P.F.L. leadership.

For the essential failure was in the leadership. Even the best among them were too often characterized by indecision, by lack of critical acumen, by the desire for unanimity and the wish to avoid conflict, even when doing so meant knuckling down to undisciplined employee groups, demonstrators, troublemakers or insurgents. The rest of the party leadership was characterized by lack of interest and sloth (so far as their public responsibilities were concerned), by nepotism and self-aggrandizement, by a lack of political and moral courage, by vested interest in continued disorder and corruption and by deals and understandings with bully-boys in the districts. And the entire leadership was guilty of a terrible ineptitude in administration.

Underlying these defects and the basic errors of the leadership in planning, programing, policy and implementation were a number of misconceptions and illusions. These included the beliefs, quite generally held, that independence, throwing off of the imperialists' yoke, would automatically usher in a golden age; that development was an easy process, quickly and painlessly achievable, in which plans, by some miraculous process, became transmuted into actuality; that development was equated with nationalization and industrialization; that the private sector was unreliable, incapable or both; that the Government could and should initiate and carry out all significant economic projects; that sloth, inefficiency, nepotism and graft in government had no connection with development or economic growth; that tenure in office warranted the use of office to perpetuate the tenure; that postponement of decisions neither hurt society nor resulted in significant social costs; that Government orders needed to be related only to their objectives and not to their practicality; that minorities could be discriminated against without damage to the economy; that administrative systems adequate to the limited functions of a colonial government were adequate also to deal with the greatly expanded functions of a welfare society; that avoidable errors could be condoned as "teething troubles"; that civil servants, though entrusted with important tasks, did not need to be adequately paid, and, though technically untrained, could handle highly technical jobs; that bonuses, subsidies and non-repayable loans could be handed out in large amounts to large groups without affecting others or the general welfare; and, even among the most sophisticated, the belief that what was suitable and desirable for Burma by way of equipment or technique was the latest, the best and the most costly which advanced economic societies had developed.

If these were some of the misconceptions which underlay the weaknesses of the A.F.P.F.L. Government, it was the lack of a responsible and critical opposition which permitted these weaknesses to persist without effective check or correction. Neither within the A.F.P.F.L. nor outside it — not in the Parliament, the press or organized groups within the law-abiding society — was criticism expressed forcefully enough to make the A.F.P.F.L. pause and review the fundamentals. Nor could the economic consultants, close to the Government though they were, go far beyond their province and analyze what was at the root of the matter — the incapacity of the leadership that employed them to recognize and discharge its responsibilities. Of the leadership, it was Prime Minister U Nu who came closest to appreciating these realities.[1]

1. This recognition was best stated at the time in his September 1957 "marathon" address to the Parliament, which has been summarized in Chapter 13 and a section of which is reproduced in Appendix I.

THE NE WIN CARETAKER GOVERNMENT

The advent of the Caretaker or Military Government is commonly attributed to the split in the A.F.P.F.L., the threats of widespread civil strife which followed that split and to fears that U Nu's post-split "Clean" A.F.P.F.L. would be swayed by its dependence on N.U.F. support to make dangerous concessions to the Communists. This is a superficial interpretation; it ignores the underlying cause — namely, the increasing recognition within the country of the failure of the A.F.P.F.L. leadership, the increasing impatience with its excuses, and the growing disbelief in its promises that the errors of the past would be corrected. Among members of the military elite, this disillusion and cynicism had gone as far as complete disgust. Their concealed political take-over expressed their refusal to tolerate any longer the "mess" the politicians had created and their determination to clean it up. For the military men this meant primarily the establishment of law and order, the imposition of social discipline and the elimination of inefficiency in public administration and public enterprises. It meant, also, the elimination of profiteering in the private sector. Evasion and temporizing on issues, they were determined, would be replaced by crisp decision; political abuse of the public administration would be liquidated; nepotism and incompetence would be ended; drift would be replaced by drive, lack of interest by zeal. Above all, respect for authority, so sadly lacking under the previous Government, would be impressed upon all individuals and groups in the community.

If the measures taken by the military, and especially the manner in which they were carried out, seemed somewhat extreme, the wonder is perhaps that they were not even more so. The challenge to patriotism and to the sense of responsibility and order was so great that it would have served to explain, if not to justify, actions far more extreme than those actually taken by the Ne Win Government. Indeed, the fact that the Military Government came to power and the nature of its subsequent program and actions constitute in themselves an historical commentary and critique of the A.F.P.F.L. Government.

As the Caretaker Government proceeded to carry out its self-appointed, yet objectively necessary, mission, the initial reactions of the country were almost universally those of satisfaction and relief. There were adverse reactions from individuals and groups whose interests were affected, to be sure — from traders whose warehouses were sealed and whose books of account were seized for inspection; from citizens who were required to open their safe-deposit boxes so that a search might be made for illegally held foreign exchange; from the pony-cart drivers ordered off the streets of Rangoon; from the squatters peremptorily ordered to dismantle their basha huts and move to the new satellite towns outside the capital city; and from civil servants irked by the new discipline imposed by the military officers who had taken charge of the departments and public corporations. Even more significant than these grievances was the fact that the people seemed afraid to voice them, except in close confidence and with furtive looks over their shoulders. Nor did the press venture to criticize the new dispensation. By and large, the country recognized how important and constructive a job the military were doing. But the authority and the discipline went too far, particularly in the districts, where junior officers sadly abused their authority. Certainly it went too far for continued acceptance by the Burmese, whose culture was geared to tolerance rather than to discipline. As the months went by, the country became increasingly restive. Just as an almost perceptible sigh of relief had gone up shortly after the advent of the Caretaker Government, so did a comparable sigh of relief go up when it became clear, late in 1959, that general elections would again be held and that there would soon be a return to civilian government.

THE PYIDAUNGSU GOVERNMENT

When U Nu and his Pyidaungsu Party were returned with an overwhelming majority in the February elections, the important question was what he and his colleagues had learned from the experience of the past. Did U Nu recall those lessons in the same terms he had stated them in September 1957? Had he learned even more from the A.F.P.F.L. crisis and split, the military take-over and the eighteen months of the Caretaker Government? To what extent was his reading of these experiences matched by those of his colleagues and of his party? Would the policies, plans, programs and conduct of the new Government be based squarely on these lessons of the past and shaped to correct the inadequacies?

During the first year of the Caretaker Government's tenure, U Nu pondered deeply over the lessons of the past. In these reflections he went far beyond the economic and administrative errors on which he had concentrated in his September 1957 speech. He had always been given to periods of meditation, particularly when he did not feel the burdens of office were pressing. Now, partly because he was searching for the deeper meanings of the previous experience, partly because the Military Government was being cavalier with civil rights and was relying, in major degree, on fear to carry through its reform program, and perhaps partly because of a brutally frank analysis of the past conduct of the A.F.P.F.L. made to him by a respected advisor,[2] U Nu

2. That analysis, in a letter dated February 13, 1959, had closed with the following words:

"I could go on and on with this — but to what purpose? What this all boils down to, in my mind, is that the Party leadership was inadequate to its responsibilities, and to its opportunities. I raise again the question — what has the Party leadership, of *both* A.F.P.F.L. groups, learned from its debacle in the last few months? What promise can it hold out to the country for better performance in the future?

"As I write this, on February 13, the Parliament is again in session. Perhaps before this letter

now came to the conclusion that the fundamental reason for the failures of the A.F.P.F.L. period had been that the party and the country had neither understood nor effectively practiced democracy.

The essence of U Nu's thinking at this time is expressed in three remarkable statements — "We Must Defend Democracy," a speech delivered on June 5, 1959; "The Pyidaungsu Policy" (the role of the party, the opposition and the civil service), a speech delivered to the Supreme Council of the "Clean" A.F.P.F.L. on September 26, 1959; and his speech to the Parliament on April 5, 1960, when he again assumed leadership of the Government. In these speeches, U Nu strove to educate his party and the country regarding the real nature and meaning of the democratic way of life; to show how the failure to practice democracy within the A.F.P.F.L. and the Parliament and in relation to the civil service had been responsible for the errors of the past; and to lay out a program of corrective action.

The A.F.P.F.L., he declared, had erred grievously in the past by interfering with the operation of the Government's administrative machinery, by stifling the parliamentary opposition and by subverting the independence of the civil service. Moreover, the A.F.P.F.L. had not practiced democracy within its own organization. Instead of a leadership based on free choice from the bottom up, leadership and policy had been imposed on the membership from the top down. In the economic sphere, he held, policies and programs had been undemocratically arrived at on the initiative of a few leaders, without adequate consultation either within or outside the party. Economic policies had been used to entrench the party's position. State participation in economic activity had been undertaken without awareness of the limitations of a democratic government.

On behalf of the new Government, the Prime Minister pledged that these errors would be corrected. The Pyidaungsu Party would be reorganized to insure internal democracy. The party would scrupulously respect the rights of the opposition, and encourage it to make a responsible and constructive contribution. The party would carefully refrain from encroaching upon the administrative machinery and operations of government. Every major problem would be submitted for examination and discussion with everyone concerned. The independent role of the civil service would be respected, so that it could function as an objective and disciplined service and serve as an effective instrument for the promotion of democratic ideals. Full provision would be made for its rights and privileges. Above all, there would be complete adherence to the rule of law.

---

is delivered to you, the decision will already have been made on whether to continue the life of the Caretaker Government, or to hold general elections. If extension of the life of the present Government would help or inspire or even force the major A.F.P.F.L. groups to seek to learn from the lessons of the past, and to reform themselves, in every way, so that they could do a much better job in future, it might prove a blessing to the future of the country."

With regard to economic policy, the Government's principal objective would continue to be promotion of the welfare of the masses. While U Nu affirmed that the Government would still have to participate actively and directly in economic development, he stressed that "We must at the same time recognize that there are definite limitations under which a [democratic] government must operate, and that failure to recognize these limitations inevitably leads to frustration, and to the defeat of the objective itself."[3] He saw these limitations chiefly in the absence of a civil service with the strength and ability needed to run state enterprises on an extensive scale.

Our policy must therefore be [he continued], one of gradual withdrawal of the State from economic activity until its scope becomes narrow enough for our available man-power resources to handle it with efficiency, or, alternatively, to strengthen our civil service to the required extent. In concrete terms, we propose during the next four years that we shall be in power not to embark on any new State enterprise without paying specific attention to the limiting factors I have described above, and, in particular, not to nationalize any existing industry or enterprise which is in private hands. We propose accordingly to hand back to private enterprise such of the existing State enterprises and organizations as after due enquiry appear to be incapable of efficient operation by State agencies.

The new Four-Year Development Plan, U Nu also declared, would give due consideration to such factors as the proper balance between agriculture and industry, the extent of direct Government participation in the economy, protection of the interests of peasants and workers, the ultimate direction of all economic activity to Burmese nationals and the prudent utilization of available resources. The plan would have to provide full economic security for the people, be in full harmony with the resources and talent available and safeguard the people against profiteering. It would have to free national traders and business men from the domination of foreigners, safeguard the economy against all kinds of smuggling (including smuggling of foreign exchange) and also safeguard it against the use of economic activity for the aggrandizement of the party or the personal advantage of politicians. When drawn up, the plan would be submitted for critical appraisal to all groups and interests concerned.

Whereas U Nu, in September 1957, had read the errors of the previous years primarily in economic and administrative terms, he had by now probed to a deeper level of assessment, inquiring not only into *what* the overt errors had been but also into *why* these errors were made, and had come up with a political answer. In stressing the undemocratic nature of the party, both internally and within the Government, and the improper influence exerted by the party upon the machinery of government and the need for an independ-

3. Address to the Parliament, April 5, 1960.

ent, efficient civil service, he had arrived at fundamentals of the greatest importance. In recognizing also that the Government had undertaken economic activities far beyond its management capacities, he had again pointed to one of the major elements responsible for poor implementation and administration in the past. There were, however, certain important weaknesses in his appraisal, in terms both of what he said and what he failed to say.

One major weakness arose out of U Nu's misreading of the essential nature of Western democracy and the democratic process. In U Nu's view this takes on a strangely passive and almost Buddhist complexion. Examine this excerpt from his statement to the Parliament of April 5, 1960: "We shall henceforth base all our decisions and actions in the economic sphere on thorough discussion and consultation with all interests concerned, irrespective of whether they are members of our Party or not. We shall endeavor to be guided as completely as possible by the democratic principles of discussion, consultation and compromise."

The democratic process surely requires thorough discussion and consultation. It requires compromise, however, only to the extent necessary to insure majority support. Granted a majority, there is no democratic requirement which would prevent the majority from making well-considered decisions after a thorough hearing of opposition views, even if the minority is unalterably opposed to the course of action decided on. The only exceptions to this are decisions which would violate the fundamental rights of the individuals or groups concerned. In U Nu's understanding, the democratic process would seem to require virtual unanimity prior to major decision or action. Such an interpretation would emasculate the democratic process of its dynamics and render it impotent.

With respect to economic policy and the new Four-Year Development Plan, there is no need to quibble with most of the generalities stated. If they would not help much, neither would they do much harm. However, the statements about the freeing of national traders and business men from the domination of foreigners, the ultimate direction of all economic activity to Burmese nationals and the safeguarding of the economy against all kinds of smuggling make it clear that U Nu had still not recognized the pernicious effects of Burmanization policy.

Among the notable omissions from this latest appraisal of the lessons of the past was recognition of the need for a cabinet composed of the most able people available and free of party hacks; of the crucial importance of decentralization and delegation of authority and responsibility in public administration; of the need to eliminate substantial waste in the economy; of the need to improve in every reasonable way the climate for private investment and to adopt other constructive economic policies; of the need to eliminate special favors and subsidies to special interest groups, to impose greater financial responsibility on local governmental bodies for meeting local needs in education, water supply, and the like, and to improve tax enforcement; of the need to strengthen domestic finance generally, and to recognize that, in a country comprised mostly of the poor, Government finance could not be adequate unless the poor also contributed; and of the need to energize all forces in the nation to contribute to the fullest extent possible to further development. There was no real recognition of the significant possibilities of guiding and controlling the economy by indirect measures, as against direct controls and intervention. Neither did U Nu call attention to the static rice export surplus which, in the absence of sharp upward growth, would shackle future attempts to promote economic development.

If these distortions and omissions were important, acceptance and future application of the valid points was equally so. More than once in the past, admissions of previous errors had been made. They had, similarly, been accompanied by promises to correct them. These promises had not been fulfilled, because U Nu had turned his attention to other matters, because he left the fulfillment to others or because he simply did not know how to translate intention into actuality. A further question now was whether his colleagues and his party fully understood the positions he had taken and would do more than accept them passively. (On this point it is interesting to note that one of the ablest ministers in the new Pyidaungsu Government, who is also one of U Nu's warmest supporters, displayed unawareness, as of February 1961, of some of the major policy positions taken in the April 1960 address to the Parliament.) The answers to these questions are at least partly discernible in the record of the Pyidaungsu Party's first ten months in office, from April 1960 through January 1961.

THE FIRST TEN MONTHS OF THE PYIDAUNGSU GOVERNMENT

Despite the Pyidaungsu Party's overwhelming victory at the polls — a victory based on U Nu's tremendous personal popularity, on widespread antipathy to the military regime and on certain campaign promises U Nu had made[4] — the Pyidaungsu Government was not entirely free to govern as it wished. The army had made it quite clear that it would watch developments carefully to insure that there was no significant backsliding which would undo its achievements and, in its view, endanger the nation. Moreover, within the military elite, there was a powerful group of men who were convinced it had been a mistake to permit a civilian Government to return, and who hoped for an opportunity to convince their colleagues that this was the case. In this setting, it was necessary for the new Government to move with circumspection.

4. These included pledges to make Buddhism the state religion and to create new Arakan and and Mon States within the Union, if the Arakanese and Mons so desired.

On the positive side, the Pyidaungsu Party proceeded to tackle the internal reform for which U Nu had called. This involved, essentially, a series of party elections beginning at the village level and proceeding upward through the townships and the districts to the party's top governing council. But, although the party had presumably accepted U Nu's demand for reform, this acceptance was far from universal. A basic conflict soon developed within the party. While this was initially described by the press as a conflict between the "Educated" and the "Noneducated" leaders, and later as one between the "U's" and the "Bo's" on the one hand and the "Thakins" on the other,[5] it was, essentially, a fight between those determined to clean up and democratize the party and the Old Guard opposed to reform. U Win, former Ambassador to the United States, Bo Hmu Aung, former Speaker of the House, and Bo Min Gaung, one of the more vigorous ministers in the old A.F.P.F.L. days, led the reform group. Thakin Kyaw Dun, who had been so important an issue in the 1958 A.F.P.F.L. split, was presumably the leader of the Old Guard in this fight. Oddly, though U Nu had spearheaded the demand for reform and had been instrumental in bringing a number of former civil servants into the party to infuse new blood,[6] he now appeared to take a neutral position above the battle. Similarly, U Raschid, who might have been expected to align himself with the reformers, and Thakin Tin, who might have been expected to align himself with the Old Guard, both affected neutrality. As the months went by, the reformers scored a number of notable victories. It appeared that, at best, the Old Guard would succeed only in executing a delaying action.

Also on the constructive side, progress was made in building up the role of the opposition. The leader of the opposition was given salary status to enable him to devote full time to political activity. U Nu re-established personal contacts with U Ba Swe, U Kyaw Nyein and other A.F.P.F.L. and N.U.F. leaders. They were consulted on many problems, both centrally and in the districts. Representation was accorded to opposition leaders on important committees. With respect to the civil service, the strictures laid down by U Nu seemed to have good effect. Politicians were careful to avoid any overt appearance of interference with civil servants in the independent execution of their jobs.

Less positive was a step taken in pursuance of the Prime Minister's new faith in consultation. The Government set up a group of elder statesmen — the so-called "Five Wise Men" — to advise it on important issues. Referred to this body were the questions of Buddhism as a state religion and the creation

5. Based on the honorifics with which they were addressed, "U" simply meant "uncle"; "Bo" meant "officer," and was still used by many former freedom fighters; and "Thakin" meant "master," and was the address assumed in the 1930s by those who wished to declare their determination to be masters in their own land.

6. Among these, the best known were U Chan Tha, former head of the B.S.I.; U Chit Pe, former Secretary of Agriculture; and U Tin U, onetime Director-General of the A.R.D.C.

of the proposed Arakanese and Mon States. Its advice was also sought on other questions, some quite trivial in nature. Indeed, it appeared to some that matters were referred to the "Five Wise Men" so that the Cabinet could avoid responsibility for decision and action.

The Public Administration Commission, set up and sent on a study tour around the world, struck many as another device for avoiding decision. Previous commissions and foreign experts had provided the Government with ample basis for action to improve the public administration, if action were its object. Under the circumstances, the appointment of still another study commission did not appear to be necessary.

Other actions and omissions by the new Government were even more negative in character. While U Nu, following General Ne Win's example, set up a small Cabinet allocating three or more portfolios to most ministers, he did not select outstandingly able people for it. As in the past, party seniority and status seemed to be the governing factor in the selection of ministers and the allocation of posts. The result was disappointing. The Government's first act upon taking office was to reinstitute the ban on cattle slaughter. This promptly forced up the prices of fish, poultry and mutton in the market place. The new Government also undercut efforts to strengthen admission standards at the University (which caused Dr. Hla Myint, the Rector, to resign), deferred execution of an order which would have separated some thousands of unqualified civil servants from public employment, and raised the purchase price of sugar cane paid by the Government sugar mills to an uneconomic level once again. It also permitted the re-registration of a number of bogus importers whose registrations had been revoked by the Ne Win Government, and allowed the recently achieved standards of cleanliness and sanitation in Rangoon to deteriorate. Further, pending formulation of a new Four-Year Plan, the Government imposed a slowdown on the rate of development spending from that provided in the 1960–61 budget enacted by the previous Government.

The lack of a dynamic sense of purpose was evident on a number of other fronts. Work on the Four-Year Plan proceeded at staff level without effective policy guidance from above. While the staff planning envisaged a continuation of approximately the same levels of public capital spending as had prevailed since 1955–56, it continued to place the same degree of overreliance on foreign resources — 60 per cent, inclusive of reparations — as it had before. This also cast doubt on the seriousness of the approach to improvement. Operation of the government-owned factories was still distressingly weak. The jute mill was employing two full shifts to get little more than one-shift production. Maintenance at the cotton mill was poor,[7] and an important part of the mill's output could not be sold because it was not competitively priced.

7. An important factor here was the difficulty in procuring spare parts from China, which had built the extension to the original mill.

The steel mill, with a capacity of 20,000 product tons, had produced only 6,000 product tons the previous year, and, as of February 1961, was pouring slab and ingot but producing (in part for temporary reasons) no finished products at all. The sugar mills were producing at about 50 to 60 per cent of their capacity, and the planners were talking about the need for a new sugar mill to make up this production deficiency. In spite of these continued weaknesses, no steps had yet been taken, in accordance with the policy statement, to turn these industries over to private ownership or management.

Utilization of the major portion of the $25 million U. S. development loan — the implementation of which had been slowed down by the Ne Win Government — still lagged. The Government was seemingly unaware of the vital importance of the failure of the agricultural program to achieve increases in the rice export surplus. Nor did the Government take action to improve rice milling and sawmilling facilities, expedite non-rice agricultural programs, stimulate mining, expand low-cost agricultural credit, establish the long-awaited and badly needed industrial development bank for which budgetary provision had been made, or in any other significant way provide incentives to the private sector. For these and similar reasons it appeared that the economy had entered upon a period of pronounced stagnation.

The most dynamic element in the economy was the Defense Services Institute of the army (the D.S.I.), which, under General Ne Win, had developed, on its own initiative and with virtually no assistance from the Government other than a small initial loan and the services of a number of military officers, enterprises in the fields of banking, ocean shipping, construction, trading, coal and coke purveying, bus and taxi fleet operation, shoe manufacturing and many others, including department store operation. Brigadier Aung Gyi was the driving force behind the D.S.I. activity. While the D.S.I. bank was favored by deposits from army personnel and the department store was liberally treated in the issue of import licenses, the secret of the D.S.I.'s successful commercial operations was simple. The organization simply hired capable managers — in the case of the department store these were the experienced Englishmen who had been in charge of the business before, and in the case of the bank, the shipping line and the construction company, they were experienced Israelis — and clearly delegated to these managers the responsibility for running the enterprises.

It was not clear whether the military wanted to establish bench marks of initiative and efficiency for other Government enterprises and for the private sector, to play a major role in Burma's further economic development, or to provide rewarding post-retirement occupations for its personnel in the future. Nor was it clear whether U Nu was "going along" with the D.S.I. because he wanted to harness the army's drive and energy for economic development and to provide models for other Government agencies and the private sector or because he was trying to insure that this powerful army group, headed by Brigadier Aung Gyi, would oppose Brigadier Maung Maung and others intent on taking over the reins of Government once again. It may be that the motivations on both sides were mixed. As of February 1961, two facts were unmistakably clear, however. First, the delegation of authority and responsibility to experienced managers was working effectively for the D.S.I.; second, the Government had not even recognized the possibility that this same principle might be applied usefully to other public enterprises.

Apparently on the initiative of Brigadier Aung Gyi, negotiations were undertaken with People's China looking toward a substantial credit for economic development. When, early in January 1961, the Government, upon signing the long-awaited border settlement with People's China, simultaneously concluded an agreement for a Chinese credit equivalent to £30 million sterling ($84 million), it seemed to be tacitly understood that the D.S.I. would execute a number of projects under this loan. Among those mentioned were a paper mill, a fertilizer plant, a new cement factory, an additional sugar mill and another cotton textile mill. Shortly thereafter, however, it was indicated that the Government would form a new economic development corporation, which would absorb the existing commercial activities of the D.S.I. and execute any new projects the D.S.I. might have undertaken. The officers who would staff the new corporation would presumably take leave or retire from the army and operate as civilians.

If utilization of the Chinese loan for the construction of new state-owned industries was inconsistent with the statements made in the Pyidaungsu policy speech and in the April 1960 address to the Parliament, this was only what might have been expected — that political considerations, as before, would override economic and administrative considerations. (It could, of course, be argued alternatively that U Nu viewed the military as a special case, to which the questions of competency and administrative ability which he recognized as limiting factors affecting the remainder of the civil service did not apply.)

This brief account of the first ten months of the Pyidaungsu Government in office cannot adequately answer the major problem posed, namely, whether Burma's political leaders had learned enough from the mistakes of the 1950s to lead Burma reasonably well in the development effort. It was very much to be doubted, however, whether their desire for development had ever been strong enough to meet the price that development demanded in tough, determined effort and in the degree to which conflicting desires for Burmanization, for nationalization and for taking the easier rather than the harder road would have to be accommodated to the development goal. It was also doubtful whether the experience of the 1950s had enabled the leaders to appreciate the full price even now. In the absence of that appreciation, they were still unable, consciously and intelligently, to make the necessary choices

—to determine whether they wanted the maximum possible development in the shortest possible time or limited growth combined with the comfort that would come with continued indulgence of their prejudices and less than all-out effort. Some of the important lessons of the past, it appeared, had been learned only too well; others appeared not to have been learned at all.

Yet the margin for error which had existed early in the 1950s had been greatly reduced. The confidence of the citizenry had been seriously shaken. The liquid savings accumulated during the period of high post-war prices were gone. And a new failure might see a new, and this time more permanent, military take over, with unforeseeable consequences for the future of democratic government.

THE ESSENTIALS OF A PROGRAM FOR BURMA'S FURTHER ECONOMIC DEVELOPMENT

The projects most strategic and essential to Burma's further economic development are relatively few in number. They would make up the core of any rational investment program.

The most important single job to be done is to achieve once again the pre-World War II level of rice exports. Since domestic consumption has grown by about one million tons in the interim, this involves considerably more than the restoration of pre-war paddy acreage. It involves also either a substantial addition to pre-war acreage, or an equivalent increase in yields per acre, or a combination of both. The importance of this task cannot be overestimated. In the absence of substantial progress on this front, Burma simply cannot achieve continued economic growth on a self-sustaining basis.

Of almost equal importance is modernization of the country's antiquated and inefficient rice mills, so that the paddy crop can be milled to the grades desired in various markets and command better prices.

The cotton, groundnut, sugar cane, jute, livestock and various other production programs undertaken a decade ago (including plantation crops) still await effective implementation. Basic to these are improved programs for agricultural research, experimental and demonstration farms and farm extension services. A large-scale fisheries program is also needed.

In forestry, renovation and expansion of the teak sawmills is the step most urgently required.

In mining, a comprehensive and definitive resource survey should be carried out.

In industry, the creation of an industrial development bank to help finance modernization, expansion and new investment by the private sector is the key strategic project.

Completion of the rehabilitation of transport and communications, especially of the highways, the construction of farm-to-market and special access roads, additional transmission and distribution facilities for electric power, additional facilities for training doctors, nurses, teachers and for training in various technical, commercial and administrative skills, and a large-scale, low-cost, non-subsidized housing program more or less round out the list of essential projects. The specialized training facilities which exist should be used much more intensively, on at least a two-shift basis.

More important than these or any other investment program, and basic to them, are improvements needed in the processes and functioning of the Government itself, in the quality of the public administration, in the essential services provided to the public, in the management of the public enterprises, in the economic policies, and in the degree of public support accorded the program. In the absence of such improvements, no substantial program for further economic development could be effectively carried out, or have the effect desired. In fact, no program for further economic development could be very significant unless it were specifically aimed at such objectives, and made appropriate provisions for achieving them.

Basic to any attempt to achieve better government must be a general awareness, at all levels of Government and among all social groups, that achievement of the goals of peace, democracy, prosperity and welfare demand of every individual patriotic effort, hard work, a sense of obligation and responsibility, and devotion to a common cause. Such an awareness can be generated only in time, as the Government demonstrably improves itself and inspires confidence, respect and emulation.

Within such a context, the suppression of remaining pockets of insurrection and the final establishment of law and stability throughout the countryside is a first requisite. Reform within the Pyidaungsu Party, full observance of the rights of the opposition, separation of the dominant party from the public administration and the independence of the civil service — the steps stressed by U Nu in April 1960 — are important, but do not go far enough. The Government must also eliminate party hacks and make room at the top for a new order of leaders, including outstanding civil servants and the most able and dedicated of the military elite.[8] The Parliament must be made a much more effective institution, sitting most of the year rather than for a few weeks only. It must expose proposed legislation to criticism at public hearings and challenge the policies and operation of the Government. The colonial-type local administration must be replaced by responsible local and district self-government.

To improve public administration, effective decentralization and delegation of authority and responsibility must be introduced, starting at the very top.

---

8. The Constitution has enough flexibility to provide room in the Cabinet, on a temporary basis, for non-parliamentarians. Their continued participation in the Government could be assured by persuading such men to stand for the Parliament in by-elections.

The post of Deputy Prime Minister for National Economy should be revived, and an outstandingly able man appointed to it, armed with broad authority to supervise program development and execution. Ministers should be made fully responsible for operations within their spheres. The public boards and corporations need to be given full authority and responsibility for conducting their affairs in a businesslike way, subject only to broad Government policy review. Qualified representatives of the public should have at least minority membership on all boards of directors of such enterprises. Delegation of authority should proceed downward from these topmost levels all along the line. In particular, boards of directors should delegate responsibility for day-to-day operations to their chief executive officers. Such delegations, at all levels, must be accompanied by adequate periodic review and appraisal. The maintenance of adequate and timely commercial accounts should be insisted upon as indispensable to improved management in the public enterprises.

The power of financial sanctions by the Ministry of Finance should be curbed drastically, and much higher standards of budget preparation and review substituted for it.

To strengthen the civil service, higher standards of selection and recognition of merit in the promotion process need to be stressed. Adequate pay scales should be established, accompanied by a reorganization of offices and procedures and by a wholesale letting out of the incompetent, the indolent and the unessential, a move which would offset the salary increases.

In combination, improved public administration and a strengthened civil service would improve the essential services rendered to the public and, by reducing costs and increasing revenues in the far-flung public enterprises, mobilize resources for development.

In the field of economic policy, the Government should denationalize all existing activities for which a clear case for continued governmental operation cannot be made on the grounds of high public policy and efficiency. This would insure denationalization of the rice and timber export trade and of the Government-owned industrial enterprises, and result in greater efficiency in these activities and greater output by the economy. In particular, improved margins in the rice export trade would make feasible an increase in the price paid for paddy, and stimulate increased production of this vital crop. By lightening the overload presently hampering public administration, such denationalization would also contribute to more efficient operation in the spheres the Government continued to administer.

Burmanization policy should be modified substantially. It is only natural and right that Burma should insist on equal opportunities and rewards for her own nationals, and that she should make every effort to train her own nationals so that they can progressively take over responsibility for the most important economic posts and functions. This objective can be achieved only by programs appropriate to the purpose, however. It cannot be achieved by discriminating against other groups and individuals in favor of Burmese nationals. Such discrimination has adversely affected the functioning and growth of the economy and the interests of the general public. The joint venture trading corporations should be dissolved. There should be no discrimination in import licensing, the granting of loans or in other matters that involve significant relations between Government and individuals and firms.

The Government should re-examine all existing regulations and practices which have occasioned complaint by private business men and firms, with an eye to revoking or modifying those for which a truly valid case does not exist. The policy should be to encourage and assist the private sector in every way consistent with sound public policy and the general interest, and to convince potential investors that this has indeed become the policy. While the Government has shown that it is aware of the desirability of new foreign investment and has made gestures in this direction, it should now concentrate rather on changing those circumstances — especially in connection with foreign exchange remittances — which have made the pre-war foreign companies still active in Burma reluctant to invest further, and concentrate even more on encouraging private domestic investment. It is clearly in this last category that the greatest near-future foreign investment potential lies.

Agricultural policy should reconcile land-sharing with maximum production objectives. The outmoded land revenue structure should be overhauled, simplified and modernized. With tenants adequately protected as to both tenure and rents, land ownership *per se* is no longer of sufficient importance to warrant the disruptive displacement of tenants or the creation of farm units of uneconomic size. The policy of inefficient Government operation of tractors for custom hire should be replaced by the sale of tractors on hire-purchase (the installment plan) to trained operators, who would themselves conduct a custom-hire operation. Agricultural credit policy should aim at the earliest possible sound expansion of State Agricultural Bank credit at reasonable rates of interest to meet the bulk of the cultivators' credit needs.

Mining policy, controls and programs should be thoroughly revamped to encourage and assist private exploration, development, extraction and export, subject to proper social safeguards and controls.

Industrial policy should give priority to divesting the Government of the industries it owns, through outright sale, through the sale of shares, through lease or through arrangement of management contracts with private firms. The tariff structure should be thoroughly reviewed to eliminate remaining vestiges of colonialism, which favored import of finished goods over import of raw materials and components, and to lighten the duties on production equipment and spare parts. The industrial development bank to be established should have appropriate financial assistance, but the majority of equity finance and management control should be in private hands. Investment legislation should be amended to make most of its benefits automatic, if the investment is in approved industries, rather than available only upon approval by a governmental investment committee. Entry and stay permits for needed technicians should be made easier to obtain. The land alienation law should be amended to permit urban properties to be put up as security for investment loans.[9] This, too, would contribute substantially to new industrial development. The provision of more agricultural credit at low rates of interest, as previously proposed, would also channel to industrial development a considerable amount of savings presently employed in high-interest agricultural lending.

In the field of transport and communications, a thoroughgoing revision of rates, which would bring down costs and promote greater traffic volume, appears to be as important as any other step needed.

Clarification of the financial structure of the electric power system, defining the amount of subsidy to be granted and the interest rates to be paid, is essential for establishment of rational and promotional electric power rates.

Both great needs and opportunities exist in the field of housing. The policy here should be to provide incentives in the form of low-cost loans and tax abatements to private builders who construct private dwellings of approved design, standards and cost which they can profitably sell or rent on a non-subsidized basis.

Whereas the welfare-minded A.F.P.F.L. Government emphasized what it was doing for the people, the Ne Win Government placed more emphasis on what the people should do for themselves and for the country. Such an emphasis is essential. The Government should seek to develop a maximum of public understanding, sympathy, participation and support for the development program. It should establish a nation-wide Youth Corps (in lieu of military service) to engage in such nation-building tasks as land clearance and drainage, construction of irrigation canals, forest conservation, light road building, and work on earth dams and ponds, wells and environmental sanitation, and at the same time to acquire valuable work disciplines, self-respect and skills. The manpower, drive and technological capacities of the military should be utilized to the fullest possible extent, particularly in engineering projects, such as road, bridge and dam construction. Finally, the villagers should be stimulated to contribute their labor in the agricultural off-seasons to community projects of direct benefit to themselves — wells, ponds, drainage and irrigation canals, streets and community buildings and facilities. Any development program which does not promise direct and immediate benefits sufficient to enlist the energies, imagination and support of its people in these ways will be sadly deficient.

9. At present, foreign banks may not take over title to real property of any description. They will not, therefore, make loans to Burmese nationals against such security.

A comprehensive development program built on such foundations — the projects and institutions most strategic for Burma buttressed by improved government, a more effective public administration, a strengthened civil service, constructive economic policies and widespread public participation and support — would produce astounding results. The rate of growth would be out of all proportion to the capital invested, and resemble the growth rates achieved by Japan and West Germany in the post-World War II period, rather than more typical investment-income ratios. With such a program Burma would reduce progressively her need for reliance on foreign aid. At the same time, voluntary participation by her own people would reduce the inflationary potential that would otherwise be generated. She would have shifted to the private sector the responsibility for activities it can handle more efficiently than the Government can. In so doing she would progressively augment the experience and capacity of the private sector, and at the same time improve the attitude of the Government and its capacity to discharge its proper and continuing responsibilities.

CHAPTER 34

Significance of the Burma

Experience for Economic

Development in Other Countries

For other countries that have only recently embarked, or are about to embark, upon economic development efforts, the Burma experience highlights the critical importance of a number of factors, in addition to investment, which are vital to effective development progress — law, order and stability; vigorous, dedicated and responsible leadership; realistic goals and approaches; honest, capable public administration; efficient implementation and management; flexible and appropriate economic policies; full utilization of the potential of the private sector; and widespread popular support and voluntary participation in development projects and programs.

This chapter will address itself to these and to a number of related questions. Because of the interrelation of the topics into which the discussion is organized, a certain amount of repetition will be encountered. This may be regarded as redundancy or as a useful restatement of thematic leitmotif, as the reader may prefer. Much of the discussion should be broadly applicable to most underdeveloped countries. Some of it, while perhaps more limited in application, should be especially significant for those countries — including a number of African countries — that share a heritage and problems similar in many ways to those of Burma. The discussion will have some relevance also for current theories and strategies of economic development.

No attempt will be made at comprehensiveness or originality of statement. It is hoped, however, that at least a few fresh insights will emerge that will be useful to those concerned with development and development assistance in other countries.

DESIRES AND GOALS IN ECONOMIC DEVELOPMENT

Even where, as in the Burma case, landed aristocracies or other powerful groups with vested interests in the status quo no longer exist, not all individuals and groups in underdeveloped countries will participate in or identify themselves with the so-called "revolution of rising expectations." The dominant political majority, the military elite, the civil service, the students, the intellectuals, the merchants, the non-agricultural producers, the artisans, the laborers and the cultivators — these groups will quite naturally have disparate interests and different attitudes toward economic development. Development will not mean the same thing to all of them, and differences will exist within as well as among these groups. The desire for development, even if dominant in the society, will of necessity reflect these differences. Obviously the development goals adopted are not likely to be simple, clearly purposeful or even consistent with each other.

The problem of economic development would be enormously simplified, both for countries seeking to achieve it and for those desirous of assisting them, if economic growth *per se* were accepted as the goal.[1] This, of course, is not possible, or even desirable. It is inevitable that development in such societies should be regarded as synonymous with, or closely related to, such other broad national objectives as greater social and economic justice, minimization of the role of the foreigner in the society, increase in national power and prestige, industrialization, economic diversification, higher consumption standards, autarchy or socialism. Whatever the concepts accepted, the goal will be composite, not monolithic. And, more likely than not, not all of the elements that make up the composite goal will complement each other, or buttress the growth objective. Some will tend to conflict with it, at least in the short run.

These inconsistencies contribute to the enormous complexity of the development process, which requires not only capital, technology and know-how, but basic adaptations and transformations in the social structure and its processes, and in traditional philosophies, ethics, policies, attitudes and conduct. Economic development takes place, therefore, only within a broad context of fundamental social and cultural changes which are essential components of the development process yet add their own peculiar difficulties to it.

THE IMPORTANCE OF GOOD GOVERNMENT

Perhaps the first major conclusion which emerges from the Burma experience is the overwhelming importance of good government to economic development. I mean here, in the first instance, government which is good in

---

1. Even the growth goal is not a simple one. Emphasis might be on the rate of growth to be achieved, on the absolute levels of output and consumption to be achieved, on reaching the point of "take-off," after which self-sustained growth becomes possible, etc.

terms of the law and order it maintains, the social and economic justice it dispenses, the essential services it provides, the policies it adopts, the programs it pursues, the honesty and responsibility it displays and the effort it makes.

It is necessary, however, to go beyond these stipulations. To a far greater extent than in more advanced democratic societies, governments in underdeveloped countries must take major responsibility for initiating and carrying through accelerated economic development. It is the government which must appraise the potentials, set the targets and determine the priorities. It is the government which must marshal the resources, select the appropriate strategies, stimulate and harness the energies (in the private as well as the public sector), clear away major obstacles and bottlenecks, insure the efficient execution of its programs, provide effective supervision and review, and adapt programs, policies and methods to changing circumstances.

In view of the nature of these responsibilities, which cannot be delegated or evaded, it is clear that economic development cannot be successful if the government concerned fails to cope with them seriously.

THE IMPORTANCE OF GOOD LEADERSHIP

It is also clear how enormous is the task which these responsibilities impose on the political leadership. Theirs is the ultimate responsibility for the crucial decisions. And the need to overcome somehow the weaknesses of their inheritance — inadequacies of experience, staff, organization, means, technology and all the rest — is also theirs. How much more difficult, thus regarded, is their task than that of the leadership in more advanced societies!

If the leadership in an underdeveloped country inevitably lacks the experience to surmount such difficulties, it must, at the very least, be sufficiently free from illusion and prejudice, sufficiently dedicated to the development objective and sufficiently determined to do what is necessary to achieve that objective to expose itself to advice from competent sources or staff (whether indigenous or foreign), consider carefully the alternatives set before it, make the indicated decisions and follow through with efficient execution.

Since this is the least that reasonably effective development requires, it will not be surprising that development in most of the underdeveloped countries appears to have achieved thus far something less than success.

THE DANGER OF ONE-PARTY DOMINATION

A third major conclusion to be drawn from the Burma experience is the danger to good government which arises out of a combination of factors common to many underdeveloped countries, chiefly from an electorate new to the ways of democracy (and naïve in its expectations of early and easy plenty), and from a virtual one ("freedom") party domination in the political arena. This last factor is especially dangerous, because it means that for some time to come there will be no political opposition to criticize the Government's plans, programs, policies, ineptitudes, failures and abuses, and to propose alternatives to the electorate. In such circumstances, power tends to corrupt ever more swiftly. Perspective is lost. In the absence of accountability the sense of responsibility is dissipated, nepotism and graft flourish, and party control entwines itself around the public administration like parasitic honeysuckle in an untended garden, slowly sapping and strangling what it feeds upon.

THE IMPORTANCE OF IMPLEMENTATION

A fourth major conclusion is that, in a practical sense, the implementation of economic development plans is far more important than the plans themselves. There are two main reasons why this is so. In the first place, while expert professional assistance may play a major role in the formulation of plans for economic development, such assistance can play only a relatively minor one in the execution of the plans. Implementation must remain, for the most part at least, the task of the country concerned. Second, provided reasonably good judgment is exercised in setting program goals and in estimating and allocating the resources likely to be available, results are bound to be rewarding if the plans are efficiently carried out, even though the targets, priorities, strategies and projects may be considerably less than ideal. On the other hand, no development plan, no matter how well conceived and formulated, can yield satisfactory results if there is serious failure in implementation.

Here too, as in the case of the good-government concept, it is necessary to conceive of implementation in a broad sense. Good implementation is required, of course, at the project level, as in the case of building a dam, or at the program level, as in the execution of a diversified program for the improvement of a country's agriculture or one for industrial modernization and expansion. This is where application of the implementation concept usually tends to stop. The need for effective implementation, however, goes much beyond this. Effective implementation is needed also in the mobilization of resources, in the realization of policies, in the administrative processes of government and in supervision and coordination of the development process at the very highest levels of government. Weakness in these broader aspects of implementation can undermine development even more seriously than can the faulty implementation of projects and programs themselves. In fact, it will be almost impossible to achieve satisfactory implementation on the project and program levels without effective implementation on these other fronts.

SOME ESSENTIALS OF EFFECTIVE IMPLEMENTATION

Good leadership, characterized by determination, integrity and dedication — leadership which provides an inspiring example to the civil service and to the country at large — is a first essential for effective implementation of a development program.

Next in importance perhaps only to this is the need for effective public administration. On the basis of the Burma experience, this is very closely related to the need to delegate authority and responsibility appropriately, from the topmost levels of governmental authority all the way down through the public administration and the civil service. The failure to delegate is responsible for wasteful delays at lower levels, for failure to use the capacities already existing, and for failure to develop those capacities further through use. The failure to delegate is also responsible, at top levels, for a top-heavy decision-making burden on policy-makers, who are too far removed from many of the questions to decide them wisely. If they reserve for themselves decisions that they should delegate, they do not have adequate time for the more important decisions which they alone can make, or time to provide adequate supervision, coordination and review of performance at lower levels.

The practice of financial sanctions by ministries of finance is merely another aspect of the failure to delegate responsibility adequately, in this case for the expenditure of authorized funds by the agencies responsible for the operations. The application of regulations and controls used for regular government departments to government agencies that conduct operations of a commercial nature is not appropriate, and is merely another aspect of this failure to delegate authority and responsibility adequately.

In a broad and non-ideological sense, the determination of many governments to undertake and execute development projects and programs which could more appropriately be carried out by the private sector is still another illustration of the failure to delegate authority adequately. Even where governments believe that activities of this kind are appropriately (by ideological standards) carried out under governmental auspices, practical considerations dictate that they should encourage private individuals and firms to take responsibility for them, if only to relieve excessive strains on the government's limited administrative, technical and managerial manpower as much as possible.

A third essential for effective implementation is a competent civil service with high morale. Objective standards of selection, promotions based on merit as well as on seniority, reasonably adequate working conditions, tools and aids, freedom from political interference, high standards of performance and, above all, pay scales which permit appropriate living standards are prerequisites for such a service. In the absence of adequate pay scales, it is doubtful whether any program designed to improve performance and integrity in public administration can succeed.

Although integrity and morale have already been mentioned in connection with the leadership and the civil service, the question of honesty in government is of such great importance that it should be mentioned separately.

Corruption not only raises the costs of projects; it also subverts the decision-making process and leads to uneconomic projects or to uneconomic designs or locations for projects that could be economic. At lower levels, corruption becomes a cost of doing business with the government, whether this involves the delivery of mail, police protection, clearance through customs, garbage removal, the booking of freight or anything else. It thus constitutes a private and informal system of taxation which increases costs and deters growth in the private sector.

Another essential, often not fully appreciated, is reliable and timely accounting in public enterprises. In the absence of such accounting a society has no way of measuring whether output equals input, whether management is efficient and whether pricing and other policies are appropriate. Where the public sector is large and its accounts are in a deplorable state, good planning, good programing and good budgeting will be very difficult to achieve.

Still another essential element in good implementation is the existence of an informed, responsible and critical opposition. We have already noted some of the consequences which may ensue when a government is not made to feel accountable. Another consequence is that such a government will tend not to take the public into its confidence, and will operate increasingly behind a veil of secrecy. In the absence of information on government activities, the public will have no adequate means of appraising the job the government is doing, and will be unable to exert informed pressures where they are needed most. Governments operate best when they are constantly aware that a challenging political opposition and the public in general are looking over their shoulders. Countries in which one party dominates the political scene, and which do not make a special effort to inform the public fully about their activities, unwittingly surrender by default a very important technique for improving implementation.

Still another technique that can contribute effectively to good implementation is progress reporting. No country engaged in a development program should neglect to install a progress reporting system appropriate to the nature of its activities and designed to enable it to measure and evaluate progress periodically, discern or anticipate bottlenecks and take the necessary remedial measures promptly.

Finally, and of great importance, since a substantial contribution to development must be made by private individuals — if only in the agricultural sector — governments should do everything within reason to provide appropriate incentives for such efforts and, perhaps even more pointedly, should remove or minimize those obstacles which governments themselves create.

If industrial development by the private sector is desired and long-term credit institutions are lacking, industrial development banks are a key strategic institution for fostering private industrial investment. Where governments persist in undertaking industrial enterprises under their own auspices, joint ventures with private partners and appropriate management arrangements with private firms will vastly increase the prospects for efficient construction and operation.

THE IMPORTANCE OF ECONOMIC POLICY

Through the exercise, or lack of exercise, of its powers over economic policy, a government can be positive, negative or neutral regarding consumption, savings, investment, production and trade. It can foster or discourage economic activity, cause it to flow into desired channels, and radically alter the distribution of the resultant product. Through economic policy, governments can, in effect, control the accelerator, the brakes, the distributor and the steering wheel of the economic motor car.

To use economic policy in these ways requires a certain sophistication — both an awareness of the possibilities and an understanding of the techniques of applying economic policy to achieve desired results — and the flexibility to change the policy as circumstances change. Most underdeveloped countries will lack, as Burma did, this awareness and understanding. The tendency will be, therefore, to rely to a greater degree than will be practical on direct governmental intervention in the economy, to overload the government's executive apparatus and to run into all sorts of administrative, managerial and implementation problems.

Given, however, a dedicated and responsible leadership — one that is made responsible to the electorate by virtue of a critical opposition — serious attention will, of necessity, be given to some aspects of economic policy. If land or tax reforms are being considered, a serious government will almost inevitably be compelled to inquire whether the kind of land reform proposed will result in more or less production or whether a given series of tax reform measures will so adversely affect incentives as to bring about a serious loss in total revenues.

Fiscal, monetary, credit and other economic policies may require greater sophistication, and the capacity to make use of them may develop only in time. But none of these policy problems is so abstruse that it precludes an understandable presentation to the policy-makers by competent staff, in terms which will permit decision to be based on choice between the various alternatives and their probable results.

For this process to take place, there must exist a high-level forum within the government where questions of economic policy can be considered regularly by those in a position to decide them, and there must be an opportunity for competent staff to submit policy proposals and problems for consideration. This, of course, will not insure that the necessary decisions will be made, that they will be made on time, or that they will be wise decisions. It is essential, however, that such a forum be created, and that it function. If nothing else, the process will make those concerned increasingly aware of the role of economic policy, and enable them increasingly to make more informed policy judgments. With this greater awareness and capacity will come a growing reliance on indirect, and frequently more effective, means of controlling the economies, and less reliance on direct controls and measures.

The development of these means of economic control by the governments of underdeveloped countries is in itself one of the concomitants, if not a prerequisite, of more effective economic development.

THE LACK OF ENTREPRENEURIAL CAPACITY — A MYTH

It is widely accepted, both in the professional literature and in the policies of many underdeveloped countries, that the relative absence of a middle class with entrepreneurial capacity and talent makes it necessary for governments to initiate and operate enterprises which are generally left to the private sector elsewhere. I do not intend to argue against the proposition that most underdeveloped countries have only the beginnings of a middle class, and that this group cannot mobilize capital and organize production in a degree comparable to the activities of their counterparts in more advanced societies. This does not mean, however, that the private sector cannot contribute significantly to the development process. Substantially, the current view — on the basis of the Burma experience — would appear to be a dangerous myth.

The desire to improve one's material welfare, to increase one's income or to make a profit is, if anything, even stronger in underdeveloped societies than in the more advanced countries. Very little more than a perceived opportunity is necessary to transform this desire into entrepreneurship. The greatest number of potential entrepreneurs exists in the agricultural sector, where landless tenants aspire to land ownership and where landholders and tenants alike will readily hire tractors, or use improved seeds, fertilizers, insecticides and other capital aids if they are shown that these will yield a profit. Entrepreneurship is also significantly, even abundantly, evident in international and domestic trade, in construction, in home and other small-scale industries and, notably, in money lending. It is incorrect and misleading to ignore such evidence.

The presumption that entrepreneurial capacity is lacking in the underdeveloped countries has no doubt been influenced greatly by the scarcity or absence of relatively large-scale private industrial enterprises. This, however, fails to take adequate account of such factors as the hostility to private enterprise frequently found in such countries, the excessive controls applied to it, the fears of nationalization, the lack of credit institutions and money markets, and the prevalent unfamiliarity with and distrust of the corporate form of business organization (because it involves a pooling of resources and effort with people outside the family or the small circle of trusted friends). The judgment appears also to have been influenced by what looks like unbusiness-like management by business men in these countries — for example, their common failure to keep adequate records and accounts. This, in fact, is a widespread phenomenon; it does not reflect a lack of entrepreneurial ability but rather a highly rational, if wily, technique for baffling the tax collector.

It is highly probable that in many underdeveloped countries, as in Burma, entrepreneurs and entrepreneurial abilities are by no means lacking. Despite a superficial appearance of inefficiency, these entrepreneurs are in fact efficient, in that they seek out the investments which produce the largest short-run returns with the least risk. "Considering the special circumstances of many underdeveloped countries, their decisions may constitute a perfectly rational evaluation of the structure of economic opportunities."[2] And if, as Adler has pointed out, "the development process in underdeveloped countries . . . proceeds *in spite* of the strength of the social and cultural forces opposed to it,"[3] surely this must reflect, so far as the private sector is concerned, an entrepreneurial drive of quite remarkable vigor.

Burma's failure to appreciate the capacity for saving, investment and entrepreneurship in the private sector, and the desirability of stimulating and utilizing this capacity to the fullest extent possible, was rooted in an ideological bias: an identification of private enterprise with foreigners and alien minorities, a lack of appreciation of how the economy could be stimulated indirectly and guided by appropriate investment, fiscal, monetary, credit, tax and other economic policies, and a similar lack of appreciation of how private profit could be made compatible, through appropriate safeguards, with broad social welfare objectives. In consequence, her development effort suffered not only to the degree that the private sector failed to make the full contribution of which it was capable, but also to the degree that the Government sector, overburdened with unnecessary tasks it was not equipped to handle, failed to execute properly tasks which only the Government itself could do.

It would seem to follow that efforts to realize the potential of the private sector should be a major component in development strategies and plans. Such efforts, of necessity, would include the elimination of hostile, impractical or merely unnecessary policies and controls, and the introduction of policies, programs and institutions designed to stimulate and assist the private sector to develop its constructive potential progressively. Nationalization policy, punitive taxation and over-close remittance controls are prime examples of the obstacles imposed; investment incentives, research and technical assistance and industrial development financing institutions are good examples of the stimuli that might be applied.

2. Nathan Rosenberg, "Capital Formation in Underdeveloped Countries," *American Economic Review,* Sept. 1960, p. 713.

3. John H. Adler, "Some Policy Problems in Economic Development," *Economic Development and Cultural Change,* Jan. 1961, p. 113.

ECONOMIC THEORY AND STRATEGY IN ECONOMIC DEVELOPMENT

Most economic theorists agree that investment is central to economic growth. The development strategies currently recommended, however, do not agree on the emphasis to be placed on saving and investment. Some emphasize instead the importance of particular skills and attitudes, and, therefore, a strategy aimed at the development of entrepreneurs, investors, decision-makers, technicians and other key groups. Still others emphasize the importance of political structures and psychological motivations, and, therefore, a strategy designed to shape values and political attitudes or to influence particular political groups.[4]

Reacting against overemphasis on these non-investment factors, Adler agrees that capital formation "is not the whole story. But it is at least half of it, and the other half is rather meaningless without it." Capital formation may thus be viewed as "a necessary but not a sufficient condition of economic development."[5]

Evidence can be culled from the Burmese experience to support almost any theory. The experience certainly emphasizes the importance of cultural values and attitudes, political attitudes and psychological factors as well as the need for investment. It also supports the emphasis others place on the importance of entrepreneurial, investor, technical and decision-making skills. Hagen,[6] for example, could find cogent evidence in the case of Burma's Indian, Pakistani and Chinese resident alien minorities for his thesis that innovation and enterprise tend to originate in deviant minority groups. Hirschman,[7] on the other hand, might find it more difficult to support, by reference to the Burmese experience, his thesis that development strategy should be directed at maximizing investment (which he equates with development) decisions. Decision-making was indeed a critical factor in this experience. But the decisions which were most needed and most lacking were not investment decisions, but administrative, managerial and policy decisions.

It would be difficult to use the whole varied Burma experience in support of any one of these major theories or strategies, much less in support of the more specialized theories which logically fall within them. It would be difficult even to select any important aspect of that experience which did not significantly involve, though in varying degree, investment, skills, cultural attitudes and values, and politics. And certainly, if one were to seek support in the Burmese experience for the "big push" investment strategy, or its variant, the "balanced growth" theory, or the theory favoring emphasis on invest-

4. Gustav F. Papanek, "Framing a Development Program," *International Conciliation, Carnegie Endowment for International Peace,* March 1960, p. 312.

5. Adler, *op. cit.,* pp. 118–19.

6. Everett E. Hagen, "How Economic Growth Begins: A General Theory Applied to Japan," *Public Opinion Quarterly,* Fall 1958, pp. 373–83.

7. Albert O. Hirschman, *The Strategy of Economic Development,* Yale University Press, New Haven, 1958.

ment in "social overheads," the selection would have to be forced, even though "big push" and "balanced growth" thinking greatly influenced Burma's planning consultants.

Superficially viewed, the Burmese experience would appear to substantiate, if anything, Hirschman's unbalanced growth development theory. On the basis of his previously cited analysis that the relative absence of the ability to make investment decisions is the key factor limiting development, and that development strategy should concentrate, therefore, on maximizing such decision-making, Hirschman concludes that decisions which create shortages and imbalances in the economy, and thereby induce and even compel further investment decisions to restore that balance, are the most effective route to development. Within this context, he maintains, priority should be given to direct-production activities which compel additional investment decisions rather than to social overheads which merely permit them; to capital-intensive projects which create products new to the economy rather than to labor-intensive projects which compete with and supplant existing handicraft industries; to projects which require high-quality precision or maintenance standards, precisely because failures will be so glaring (e.g, airplane crashes vs. potholes in roads); and to industries where the worker must keep up with the machine rather than set his own pace.

In Hirschman's development lexicon, every economic cloud, it seems, has a silver lining. Inflation, balance of payments difficulties and population pressures all are seen as serving the development goal somehow, so long as imbalance is the most useful and, indeed, the strategic route. But to those not readily enchanted by the paradoxical, the Hirschman strategy may seem to resemble that incorporated in such statements as "The most efficient way to walk a tightrope is to advance, swaying precariously first to one side and then to the other," or "To teach your child to conduct himself safely in traffic, set him off to cross Times Square against the traffic light."

Consider the following statement:

> We have argued that economic development typically follows a path of uneven growth; that balance is restored as a result of pressures, incentives, and compulsions: that the efficient path toward economic development — and therefore the one that will often be instinctively taken if we can rely on the "principle of least effort" — is apt to be somewhat disorderly and that it will be strewn with bottlenecks and shortages of skills, facilities, services and products . . .[8]

However much we may be inclined to accept the general validity of this observation, we cannot but be jarred when Hirschman describes the typical and perhaps inevitable disorderliness of the development process as "efficient."

8. *Ibid.*, p. 158.

It is easier to accept his earlier and less formalized comment on the same phenomenon, before the typical became the "efficient":

> In any event, the underdeveloped countries see only the fruits of economic progress and have little advance knowledge of the road they need to travel to obtain them. If they desire these fruits, they will somehow set out after them. Thus they will find out about the changes required in their own society in the course of the development process as they make false starts and as they meet with, and overcome, successive obstacles. It is in this fashion rather than a priori that they will determine which of their institutions and character traits are backward and must be reformed or given up. The tension of development is therefore not so much between known benefits and costs as between the goal and the ignorance and misconceptions about the road to that goal.[9]

This strikes me as absolutely right and completely substantiated by the Burmese experience. But while this experience might support a historical theory of development in the terms stated, it does not support a strategy of development which would seek (by design?) to teeter on the development tightrope from imbalance to imbalance.

If the Burmese experience has significance for economic development theory and strategy, this would seem to be that no single element or factor is an absolute prerequisite to development, any more than any single factor or simple strategy can alone suffice to insure it. Galbraith perhaps has come as close as anyone to a formulation which stresses all the strategic factors.

Galbraith has stressed the essentiality, together with investment, of education, good government, social and economic justice and a clear sense of purpose.[10] By these he means: education in the sense of both widespread literacy and a rather high degree of learning and training, among the elite groups at least; good government chiefly in the sense of a reliable apparatus of government and public administration; social justice in the sense of an equitable sharing of the gains achieved; and a clear sense of purpose in the sense of a realistic understanding of what development involves. The Burmese experience completely supports the emphasis Galbraith places on good government and clear purpose. While a relatively high degree of literacy was present in Burma, progress in basic education and in the higher education of the elite had been something less than optimum. On the score of social justice, Burma had swung perhaps too far, rather than not far enough, but I do not question the applicability of this criterion in many underdeveloped societies.

Where the Galbraith formulation seems more than a little brash is in affirming that development cannot progress if any of these decisive elements

9. *Ibid.*, pp. 9–10.
10. John K. Galbraith, "A Positive Approach to Foreign Aid," *Foreign Affairs*, April 1961.

is missing. While it may be agreed that all these components are essential to *optimum* development progress, it by no means follows that no significant progress is possible in the absence of one or more of them. Development *is* taking place in many underdeveloped countries of the world in the absence of one or more of these factors, though the progress in many cases is uneven, partial and considerably less than could be achieved under more ideal conditions. This is true in Burma.

The Burmese experience, then, would tend to support a theory of economic development which would view capital formation as "a necessary but not a sufficient condition" and emphasize very strongly the contributory, though not prerequisite, role of the Galbraith factors (which could be interpreted broadly enough to embrace most of the elements we have previously stressed).[11] It would regard these, however, as essential only to *optimum* progress, bearing in mind that even advanced societies achieve far less than optimum results from their own efforts, and recognizing (with Hirschman) that the efforts of the underdeveloped societies, precisely because they are underdeveloped, will inevitably achieve, at best, far less than optimum results.

Such a discussion offers little help in making many basic decisions and choices which are inescapable applications of development strategy. It sheds little light, for example, on such problems of resource allocation as the distribution between consumption and investment, or the choices between public and private investment, between the directly productive and social overheads, between industry and agriculture, or, within a given sector, among various projects and programs. Many of these decisions will inevitably be influenced by ideological considerations, by flair, by "feel," by political sensitivity, by questions of practical readiness and, in general, by rough judgments on the part of the decision-makers (even though the decisions, once made, may look as though Hirschman's strategy had been employed!).

In the light of the Burmese experience, we may regard with suspicion any development strategy which does not emphasize: the desirability of assigning a significant contributory role to the private sector; the priority which should be accorded to improving existing production and distribution as against new production; or the possibilities of using the capacities of military establishments and of youth corps and other forms of widespread voluntary participation in a development effort.

11. Galbraith's theory, by its emphasis on social justice, recognizes the importance of human motivations, but it does so primarily within the context of a more equitable distribution. The individual, he says, will never exert his maximum efforts "if the gains therefrom accrue to feudal landlords or employers, or to tax collectors, merchants and usurers." True, and critically important; but the statement does not go far enough. Social justice may contribute, through land reform, to a revitalized agriculture; but it will not contribute directly to industrial and related investment. Greater incentives will make the worker work harder, and result in greater output from the existing productive plant. But opportunities, incentives and aids to new investment are also required. While these are compatible with greater social justice, they are not provided by it. Recognition of the potential of the private sector, and positive action to realize it, are also essential and of sufficient strategic importance to require special emphasis.

But perhaps the broadest of all strategic choices is whether the attempt should first be made to prepare the way for development by pushing literacy programs, training a key elite, developing key institutions, carrying through basic essential reforms, improving public administration, and thus achieving readiness for effective investment, or whether the strategy should be to plunge, so to speak, into a maximum investment effort and learn by doing, creating at the same time the pressures for carrying through simultaneously what might be regarded alternatively as preparatory measures.

This choice, which might be termed crudely the choice between strategies of preparation and plunge, may be considered by some to be one of those imponderables which can be judged only subjectively, in terms of one's temperament, predilections and biases. In my view the Burma experience, painful though it was, gives a fairly clear answer. It supports the strategy of "plunge" (which Hirschman seems to have rationalized into a theory of imbalanced development). It is difficult to envisage how Burma, in her immediate post-war circumstances, could have chosen the preparation strategy and deferred the investment plunge. She did make a start on many of the "preparatory" steps, however shakily, when she embarked upon her investment program. It was only the plunge itself, however, which created the strains and the pressures and pointed to the necessity for realistic purpose and effort, and for remedial and complementary actions on the governmental, administrative, management and policy fronts, to which she is now beginning to face up squarely, for the first time.

SOME PRACTICAL APPLICATIONS

The discussion in this chapter has, until now, concentrated on the conclusions arising out of the Burma experience which may have significance for economic development in other countries. I shall now venture to suggest a number of specific applications which arise out of these conclusions.

ECONOMIC PLANNING

(1) Plan goals should be both ambitious and feasible — optimistic enough to aim at full use of resources, but still attainable, so that frustration and disappointment may be avoided.

(2) Evaluation of growth potentials should be tempered by advance appraisal of the impact of nationalization and other goals which may exert a negative effect on growth.

(3) Feasibility judgments should be tempered by appraisal of prospects for effective implementation, as these are likely to be affected by weaknesses in leadership, public administration, civil service, management, policy and other areas.

(4) To the extent that such factors threaten to affect the achievement of the goals adversely, specific provisions for making the needed improvements

should be incorporated in the plan itself, and it should be made unmistakably clear that their satisfactory implementation is essential to the attainment of other plan objectives.

(5) It is not possible to determine the composition of a development program, or to allocate resources within one, solely on a rational basis. Many of the facts needed are not known, theoretical concepts are sometimes too difficult to apply, priorities differ within, as well as between, various sectors, the projects of highest priority are not necessarily those requiring the most capital and it is frequently necessary to go ahead with projects of lesser priority because the prospects for more effective implementation favor them.[12]

(6) It is essential that the planning organization — whether a ministry, board or whatever — be headed either by the Prime Minister or by an outstanding leader who is close to him and enjoys his confidence, and that the planning staff have direct and ready access to the head of the planning organization.

(7) The planning staff may be divided effectively, one unit dealing with central economic functions, such as national income, fiscal, monetary, credit, trade, manpower and economic policy, and another dealing with major sectors of the economy — agriculture, industry, transport, and so on. These should be supported by strong statistical and census operations.

(8) The planning organization should work up plans, programs and policies. It should not seek responsibility for final determinations, or for supervising plan execution.

(9) The views of important private economic groups and organizations should be sought in developing and adapting plans.

(10) Long-term development plans, programs and policies need to be kept under continuous review and adjusted periodically to changing circumstances and experience. This can be done most usefully when modifications are coordinated with the annual budget-making process.

CAPITAL FORMATION AND RESOURCE MOBILIZATION

(1) Unlike early capitalism and latter-day communism, underdeveloped countries pledged to early increases in welfare can neither permit ruthless exploitation by private employers nor ruthlessly suppress consumption themselves in order to mobilize resources in a high proportion to current output. Their policy must, therefore, be directed to securing such increases in output as will permit moderate increases in consumption and welfare and, at the same time, mobilize the resources needed for investment (to the extent that these are not available from abroad).

(2) Even at low levels of output, the potential of private saving (as evidenced by luxury consumption, the high price of gold and precious stones,

---

12. See Papanek, *op. cit.*, pp. 310–41, for an interesting discussion of this problem.

and, even among the poor, by religious giving and sharing with relatives) is significant in underdeveloped societies.

(3) In seeking greater output, first emphasis should be placed on existing agricultural and other production, and on the elimination of obvious wastes, both of which tend to be neglected in favor of new projects and products.

(4) In countries where population is growing at a rapid rate and is pressing on resources, the need to control population growth is inescapable, if significant per capita output increases are to be achieved. This was not a factor in Burma, however.

(5) So far as public capital formation is concerned, Burma's experience emphasizes that punitive tax rates do not yield maximum returns; that the relative handful of well-to-do persons, the few foreign companies and the alien minorities cannot be relied upon to produce the bulk of the tax revenues necessary; that, in one way or another, the poor must also contribute (though in small individual measure) to the tax revenues needed; and that the nature and structure of income distribution, and difficulties of tax administration and enforcement in such societies, will frequently require that far greater reliance be placed on indirect taxation than is considered equitable in the more advanced societies. The potential increase in tax yield through improved enforcement of existing direct taxes on personal and company income should not be ignored.

(6) Where tax enforcement is seriously hampered by the failure of business men to keep proper books and accounts, governments can:

(a) lay down the rule that repeated failures of this kind will be taken as intent to defraud;

(b) provide standardized, simple books of account and accounting procedures, and offer free advisory assistance to those requiring it, in order to eliminate excuses for bookkeeping failure;

(c) provide stiff penalties for faulty or inadequate tax reporting thereafter.

(7) The greatest possibilities for additional public revenue or capital formation in such societies lie, perhaps, outside the tax field — in state export monopoly and other trading enterprises (if these can be operated efficiently), in savings programs and loan operations, in improved management and efficiency in the state enterprises dealing with the public, in the pricing policies of these enterprises, in the use of military manpower, equipment and administrative capacity to build roads, dams, bridges, wharves and other essential facilities and, significantly, in mobilizing the youth, villagers and civic groups, on a voluntary basis, to contribute their energies to community and nation-building tasks.

(8) In this connection, savings programs can be bolstered effectively by interest rates appropriate to prevailing conditions, by bond issues of small denomination which incorporate a lottery feature for early redemption and

prizes, and by the introduction of old-age and other social security insurance programs. On the loan side, governments can effectively enter the high-volume small personal loan (pawnshop) field, lending safely and profitably against security at rates of interest substantially lower than those charged by private moneylenders.

EXPANDING AGRICULTURAL OUTPUT

(1) In the search for economic development, the spotlight should focus first not on the factory but on the farm.

(2) Initial emphasis should be placed on improvement of primitive farm practices through better land use, better seeds, manures, composts and fertilizers, better insect and pest controls, better tools and equipment, better grading, storage and marketing practices, and so on.

(3) Low-cost flood control, land clearance and drainage projects may yield greater relative returns than costly irrigation and multi-purpose schemes, and should receive careful attention despite their relative lack of glamour.

(4) A farm extension service appropriate to local conditions and integrated with related research and experimental and demonstration farms should be established and fully supported.

(5) Where farmers can obtain needed working capital only by paying unduly high rates of interest, alternative sources of capital at reasonable rates of interest should be provided.

MODERNIZING AND EXPANDING EXISTING INDUSTRIAL ENTERPRISES

(1) Opportunities for low-cost, high-benefit modernization and expansion of *existing* small production units are frequently overlooked in favor of new high-cost, large-scale industrial production units.

(2) Investment banking facilities should be created to assist such modernization and expansion with long-term loans at moderate interest.

(3) Technical, marketing and other advice should be made available to such producers, and obstacles to their effective operation and growth should be removed.

(4) Used equipment which is already outmoded in advanced industrial economies, and can be bought very cheaply, will sometimes be more economic in relation to labor and other cost factors than more modern equipment. The "latest and best" in advanced industrial societies is not always the most economic for retarded economies.

ELIMINATING OBVIOUS WASTES

(1) Improved storage facilities and storage practices at farms and concentration points may save from 10 to 30 per cent of the agricultural output commonly lost because of weather, pests and spoilage.

(2) Efficient distribution units of the department store, chain store and supermarket type could reduce consumer costs, increase buying power, create more productive employment opportunities for redundant labor engaged in petty trade, and raise living standards generally.

(3) The cost of standardized goods, such as steel and newsprint, which individual buyers in underdeveloped countries import in warehouse lots, could be substantially reduced by cooperative or group buying, since the small orders could then be combined into mill-order sizes at lower prices.

IMPROVING THE SOCIAL SERVICES

1. *Health*

(1) Limited health funds will yield better results if priority is given to preventive measures such as improved sanitation, vaccination and anti-malaria campaigns, and improved nutrition programs.

(2) Improvements in staff, equipment and supplies at existing hospitals and clinics will frequently yield better results than investment in new health facilities.

(3) Accelerated training programs for medical personnel should aim not only at meeting the need for doctors and nurses, but at lessening the need through the training of vaccinators, health assistants, midwives, first-aid specialists and others.

2. *Education*

(1) There is little point in school construction programs which are considerably in advance of the supply of teachers with at least minimum preparation.

(2) Educational programs and curricula should be geared to the needs of the society.

(3) At the high school and university levels, tuition charges, combined with a liberal scholarship program for more able students, will be more effective in promoting higher standards and progress than universal free education at all levels will be.

(4) Special efforts should be made to attract university youth to engineering and scientific fields, public administration, business management, education, agriculture, public health, economics and other fields in which the supply of skills is critically short.

(5) It is important that a major effort be made, throughout the educational process, to inculcate an understanding of the need for hard work, and a respect for the essential dignity of work, including manual labor. It is also important that educational processes geared to learning by rote be converted to processes which develop the ability and disposition to think independently and critically.

(6) Perhaps nothing could do so much to create a widespread awareness of a new atmosphere of change, and at the same time overcome critical educational deficiencies in the underdeveloped societies, as could television used primarily as an educational tool. Quite apart from its possible use in the schools, the installation of only one communal receiver in each village would make possible the dissemination of vitally needed farm, health and other information with greater effectiveness, and at lower cost, than could any other technique.

3. *Housing*

(1) Public housing projects which provide improved housing through substantial subsidies are not appropriate to underdeveloped countries whose economic structure is such that the subsidies can be paid only by the poor. (Usually, it is the rural poor who subsidize the better-circumstanced urban poor).

(2) Public housing projects in such countries should aim, not at emulating costly Western-type housing, but at improving existing local housing conditions and standards. Improvements of this kind can usually be made on a non-subsidy basis, using mostly local materials, with the aid of land grants, tax rebates and cheap credit.

IMPROVING PUBLIC ADMINISTRATION AND MANAGEMENT

(1) Politicians should not be permitted to meddle in administrative matters.

(2) The Government should be kept out of activities it is not equipped to handle.

(3) Civil service positions should pay enough to attract and hold competent people, and to relieve them of any necessity for seeking petty graft.

(4) Civil servants should be selected and promoted on the basis of qualifications and merit, and the incompetent, the indolent and the dishonest should be weeded out.

(5) Outmoded and unwieldy organizational structures and procedures should be revamped, and adequate working quarters, tools and conditions provided.

(6) Authority and responsibility should be delegated to organizations and individuals as appropriate.

(7) Awareness that government servants are truly servants of the public should be instilled, and the public should be encouraged to complain to an office especially created for the purpose if the service is poor.

(8) Where government commercial-type enterprises are concerned,
    (a) They should have the necessary degree of autonomy.
    (b) Private individuals of appropriate background and experience, as well as civil servants, should serve on the boards of directors.

(c) The boards should delegate adequate authority and responsibility to their general managers.

(d) Periodic, adequate and timely commercial-type accounts and public reporting by these enterprises should be insisted upon.

(e) Engaging in joint ventures with private firms, or engaging private management firms to take over complete responsibility for management, will, in many cases, be the only practicable road to improved management.

OFFSETTING THE LACK OF POLITICAL ACCOUNTABILITY

Where one political party enjoys a virtual monopoly over the support of the electorate, there is no good way to insure that government leadership will be responsible, in the sense of accountable. Such governments, if they are aware of the dangers involved, can, however:

(1) encourage and practice democracy within the party organization;

(2) air internal policy differences to the press and public before party positions are decided;

(3) when sharp differences on fundamental policies develop within the party, consciously encourage a party split and the formation of new parties, rather than unsatisfactory compromise or evasion of the basic issues (such a course will be difficult for leaders who have developed close ties as comrades-in-arms in a fight for political freedom, but it will be better for their country, and for them, in the long run);

(4) make a special effort to provide full reports to the Parliament, the press and the public on every aspect of governmental activity, and encourage the various social and economic organizations and groups to express their views on pending government acts and decisions.

ESTABLISHING KEY INSTITUTIONS

In almost every underdeveloped country, the creation of certain key institutions can assist greatly in the development process. Among such institutions are a planning ministry; autonomous development corporations or boards to assist development in specific sectors; a central bank; an industrial development bank; an agricultural bank; applied research institutes for agriculture, industry and other fields important to the economy; central economic, statistical and census organizations and staffs; a tax research unit; and an investment advisory and technical assistance center.

SPECIALIZED MANPOWER TRAINING

(1) Full advantage should be taken of all feasible training opportunities. These should include apprentice and in-service training as well as more formal training in universities, institutes and schools.

(2) While the advantages of overseas training for advanced and special students should not be minimized, it will frequently be more useful to bring the instruction and training to the job site than to send trainees overseas for it. Thus, more people may be trained more effectively at lower cost if medical teams, statisticians and highway engineers are brought to conduct training on the job than if difficult-to-spare personnel are sent overseas.

(3) Such scarce specialized and high-cost training facilities as exist — engineering colleges, technical high schools and vocational schools — should be used intensively, on at least a two-shift basis. Instructional staffs should be supplemented by the part-time use of qualified personnel working at other jobs and by the recall of retired instructors. Paid overtime work by the regular staff and by technicians from abroad will also be helpful.

REALIZING THE POTENTIALS OF THE PRIVATE SECTOR

(1) Basic government policy should be to encourage and assist private sector investment in every reasonable way.

(2) Improved public administration and essential services rendered to the public will help greatly in this regard.

(3) Existing regulations affecting private firms should be overhauled to scrap those that are unnecessary and to modify others so as to make them more practicable.

(4) Legislation should provide assurances against nationalization and unfair government competition, and offer attractive tax and other incentives.

(5) Critically needed are institutions (like industrial development banks) to supply long-term, low-cost investment capital to qualified borrowers for modernization and expansion, as well as for new enterprises.

(6) Organized means of periodic consultation and communications between government and business organizations should be established.

CHAPTER 35

Significance of the Burma

Experience for U.S. and

Western Aid Policy

This chapter will cover the weaknesses of U. S. and Western aid policy and practice in Burma and the corrective measures required. I shall venture to suggest an organizational solution for certain administrative problems that arose in making the aid available and conclude with brief reflections on the aid "competition" of the Sino-Soviet bloc and the relationship between economic development and political and economic stability.

WEAKNESSES IN U. S. AID POLICY AND PRACTICE

The weaknesses in U. S. aid policy and practice in Burma did not differ in any essential way from those which American and foreign critics have found in U. S. aid policy and practice around the world during the 1950s. Objectives, strategy, the kinds of aid provided, the conditions attached to it, and the administration of it, all could have been improved. Another weakness was lack of coordination with other aid sources, and, finally, there was the neglect to integrate our aid with appropriate measures of self-help on the part of the recipient nations. Of these shortcomings, it was the weakness in our aid objectives which was basic, and which was responsible, inevitably, for all the rest.

The criticism is now general that the primary objective of U. S. foreign aid policy during the 1950s was not the economic development of the countries we assisted, but rather the strengthening through "mutual security" of the U. S. position in the Cold War with the Soviet bloc. This the Burmese discovered for themselves without great difficulty a number of years ago. Whether the aid took the form of military aid, defense support or economic assistance, they saw the lion's share of the funds apportioned to countries like Korea, Vietnam, Taiwan, Iran, Thailand and Spain because of their avowed positions in the front line of the Cold War. And both Burma and other un-committed countries took note of U. S. readiness to overlook the actual or near dictatorship, corruption and resistance to social and economic reforms characteristic of these countries. The point here is not directed against security assistance as such. It is rather that security assistance should not have been con-fused with, or been regarded as a substitute for, development assistance.

To the Burmese, our aid policy and programs indicated a lack of sympathy with their development aspirations. They saw U. S. aid motivated chiefly by the desire to do the minimum necessary to avert the Communist danger, in the form of either internal insurrection or growing sympathy with the Soviet bloc. Our P.L. 480 disposals of agricultural commodities — a major aspect of our aid to Burma — appeared to many Burmese to be motivated by the need to get rid of embarrassing surpluses, rather than by a desire to help. In any case, there were many who believed their country was hurt more by U. S. rice disposals in other Asian countries than it was helped by U. S. cotton disposals to Burma. U. S. aid, as Burma saw it, was small, grudging, too little and too late. It came, moreover, rigidly tied to conditions and procedures which, when they did not raise questions of sovereignty and neutrality, left the United States in the dual position of banker and "Big Brother," who would help only if inexperienced and foolish "little brother" accepted his review and super-vision. And, finally, quite apart from its other aspects, the bilateral character of U. S. aid made it difficult, in the context of the international power bloc struggle, to accept it freely.

This one-sided view of U. S. aid, as seen through Burmese eyes, is not com-pletely objective. But it is not, in fact, very wide of the mark. Security was our major objective, in Burma as elsewhere, and Burma's economic develop-ment was not a major or even a serious objective of U. S. policy. We were not enough interested in this objective, for example, to think hard about it, and ask ourselves what reasonable development goals for Burma would be, what programs were necessary to achieve them, what contribution Burma herself could make, how much and what kinds of aid she would need to supplement her own efforts over what period of time, what sources could supply various types of aid and how they could be coordinated. The United States provided Burma with private consultants who tried to work out answers to these ques-tions — answers which soon needed substantial amendment on the aid side — but the United States took no real interest in this program thereafter.

U. S. aid was extended slowly, painfully and inflexibly, on a piecemeal basis. Apart from surplus disposals, it was project-tied and oriented. It bore no necessary relation to broad development goals or to the total development program. It was not coordinated in any significant way with aid from any other source — except as it appeared to be a competitive response to Soviet aid measures. It was not related to, or integrated with, Burma's own self-help efforts in any significant way, and it did not exert any influence on them.

One final element, while totally divorced from the U. S. aid program, nevertheless considerably affected both Burma's development prospects and her receptivity to U. S. aid. This was the economic and social posture of the United States at home. Less-than-full employment and recession in the U. S. economy affected world prosperity and Burmese markets for export commodities. Segregation, civil liberties, less-than-full employment and other unresolved domestic problems distorted the image we wanted democracy to present abroad.

THE WORLD BANK AID PROGRAM

If the World Bank's aid program in Burma resembled that of the United States in that it too was small, took too long to negotiate, was project-tied and conservative in outlook, it had great strengths which more than balanced these weaknesses. From the start, the Bank was interested in Burma's total program, in the feasibility of her goals, in the soundness of her economic policies and in the degree of effort she herself was making to support her program. Further, even though the Burmese believed that the Bank, in effect, was controlled by the United States, they regarded it as an international institution interested primarily in its own business and sufficiently divorced from international politics to insure that acceptance of its loans would not expose Burma to charges of partiality toward the West. This reaction was bolstered by the always correct posture the Bank maintained in its relations with the Burmese and in the way these relations were conducted. Significantly, the Bank considered its relations with Burma important enough to send sizable missions comprised of high-quality personnel to Burma several times, and these missions remained long enough to devote serious and unhurried study to the problems at hand.

THE U. N. AID PROGRAM

U. N. prestige in Burma was such that, despite the organization's inability to provide anything but technical assistance, its aid was both respected and welcomed. The assistance itself left much to be desired. The personnel provided were not always of high caliber, or seriously motivated. They could be provided only for one year at a time, although duty tours were frequently extended on request. The reports and recommendations of U. N. specialists were frequently pigeonholed at lower levels in the organization or ignored higher up. The Resident Representative was apparently not authorized to supervise or coordinate the work of the individual U. N. technicians. He did not attempt to seek a hearing for the specialists' recommendations at high levels, or to insure the necessary follow-through when the recommendations were adopted.

These weaknesses themselves suggest the correctives needed. A permanent international civil service would do much to improve the quality of U. N. technical personnel, to conserve and utilize the experience acquired and to enable the technicians to be posted, not as short-time advisors, but as operating executive and administrative officers in the countries needing their help. The Resident Representative should have more coordinating authority over U. N. staff, and play a more active role at high government levels in promoting implementation of the recommendations made by the technical staff once these have received the necessary internal clearances.

NEEDED CORRECTIVES IN U. S. AID POLICY AND PRACTICE

U. S. policy-makers have recently discovered that if U. S. aid is to be effective in helping underdeveloped countries achieve economic development, it must be seriously directed to that purpose. Though somewhat belated, this is a worthwhile discovery. It may even be fortunate, for the underdeveloped countries as well as for us, that the discovery has come so late. Ten years ago — and more recently, too — we knew far less about the nature and problems of development than even the little we know now.

We saw the problem of aid to these countries in much the same way we saw the problems of Western Europe immediately after World War II. As in the Marshall Plan, we sought primarily to provide capital, which we considered to be the missing link. This and a little technical know-how, we thought, would do the job. We did not — as we now begin to — see the job as a long, laborious, painful and even unsettling process. Had we embarked on large-scale development aid programs in the 1950s with our then more naïve expectations, it is quite possible that we should be dismayed and frustrated by the results, and that the underdeveloped countries would now be saddled with factories they could not manage, transport they could not operate or maintain, graduates they could not employ, current budgets they could not finance without the aid of the printing press, external debts they could not service, and frustrations for which they could find no constructive release.

Economists and foreign aid personnel have learned much in the intervening years. If our policy-makers have now decided that our national heritage, as well as our national purpose, demands that we help the underdeveloped nations of the Free World to achieve the development to which they aspire, it follows quite naturally that we must separate this kind of aid from military and defense support aid, that we must think seriously and hard about development goals which will be adequate and feasible for each country, about the plans and programs (investment *and* non-investment) necessary to achieve them, about the self-help efforts each country can reasonably be expected to undertake, about how much and what kinds of aid each will require to supplement its own efforts, about the sources that can supply such aid, and about how the aid programs can be coordinated and administered most effectively.

Clearly, aid requirements will have to be measured against total long- or medium-term programs, rather than against individual projects. Aid will have to be undertaken as a commitment over a plan period of some years, rather than as a series of annual or spot commitments. If loans are for long terms and at low rates of interest in keeping with the requirements of many of these countries, it will not matter too much if there is only a small proportion of grant assistance, or if the loans made are to be repaid in foreign exchange rather than in local currency. And if we ourselves can achieve a rate of economic growth that will maintain full employment, this alone would afford considerable "aid" to the underdeveloped nations. Finally, a liberal dollar loan policy to private U. S. enterprisers who are willing to invest in underdeveloped countries — say $3 of loan for each dollar of equity investment — might provide a most useful stimulus to this significant form of aid.

Aid, however, cannot be more than aid. It cannot *do* the development job; and there is little point in extending large-scale aid if the country concerned does not show either a reasonable prospect of doing the necessary job itself or a willingness to accept the kind of help which may improve that prospect. Such a country should show evidence of a realistic approach to its goals. It should be willing to prepare, with assistance if required, a practical plan. It should be willing to incorporate in this plan the necessary provisions for improving its public administration, the needed social and economic reforms (or perhaps plans for moderating and making more practical those already introduced), the economic policies needed, measures for providing needed incentives and for mobilizing its own resources and energies, especially in the private sector. It should, in short, show an appreciation of, and a willingness to pay, the price of development.

Given such an attitude, U. S. and Western aid policy should be to assist such countries to the extent required and feasible, and aid programs should be geared accordingly. A unified aid agency in the United States, and an organized means of coordinating Western aid, are requisites to such assistance.

It is easy to see how Western aid may be coordinated in the sense of maximizing, on an equitable basis, contributions to a total aid program. The O.E.C.D. (Organization for Economic Cooperation and Development) has recently been established partly for this purpose. Whether individual Western countries will each undertake to contribute one per cent of their gross national product, as has been widely suggested, or whether some other formula to maximize contributions on an equitable basis is agreed upon, no great difficulty should be involved in the determination, or even in related decisions on the kinds and terms of the aid to be contributed. The tendency, of course, will be for the O.E.C.D. to go much further than this. After asking how much each donor country shall contribute to the total development aid requirement, it is bound to ask, What is the total needed? and Which country needs how much? Will the O.E.C.D. tend to become a central operating organization, with missions in each country appraising needs, allocating funds and evaluating progress? If so, many years would be needed to build up the requisite organization, staff and know-how, all of which would be redundant to existing institutional arrangements. And the O.E.C.D. would be confronted, no doubt, with an increasing clamor from the assisted nations, who would demand full membership privileges in the "club."

The United Nations, regrettably, is not the ideal instrument of coordination. While it has a certain amount of know-how in planning and development and is well accepted by the underdeveloped countries, the United States and other large Western donors are simply not going to channel the major part of their contributions through the United Nations as long as the U.S.S.R. and its satellites do not contribute commensurately, use aid consciously as a Cold War weapon, or harass and sabotage the U. N. executive apparatus.

There is yet another serious aspect to this problem. We have stressed the necessity for the recipient countries to plan realistically, to transform their economies and social orders, to streamline and make more effective their public administrations, to modify their economic policies and to exert the maximum effort of which they are capable. Yet how can the United States, or any other assisting power, induce or compel such steps on the part of proud, newly independent nations jealous of their sovereignty, intent upon preserving their neutrality in the international power struggle and suspicious of any "strings" to development assistance?

There seems to be only one institutional arrangement by means of which Western aid could be effectively coordinated, development plans and programs effectively assisted and appraised and pressure applied to make the recipient countries contribute the maximum practicable to their own development. In the development field, the World Bank has greater combined prestige, know-how and acceptance among the underdeveloped nations than has any other institution. If it placed resident missions in the underdeveloped countries, it could help them develop appropriate plans, assess their own potential contributions and the residual need for external aid, act as the coordinator for all Western aid, assist the countries in executing their programs and periodically evaluate their progress.

Such a dispensation would not preclude supplementary arrangements which individual countries might prefer, or which the Bank itself might wish to arrange to help it shoulder so heavy a load. The Bank arrangement, however, would serve as the general nucleus.

With such an approach to the difficult problems of aid coordination and well-directed self-help by the recipient nations, it would be possible to view more equably the problem of "competitive" aid programs by the Sino-Soviet bloc. In fact, the program and financing framework suggested here would help to forestall non-program projects which might otherwise be financed by the U.S.S.R. or China, and would take the resources they provided into account in calculating the Western aid required. Sino-Soviet aid might thus become complementary, rather than competitive.

There remains the vexing case of aid to dictatorships, to countries notoriously corrupt and to countries in which powerful vested interests block the road to reforms essential to development. The clear separation of military and defense support from development aid, in the administering agency as well as in purpose, would help considerably, but it would not, of course, solve the problem. The marriages of convenience into which we have entered with such countries will continue to plague us because of the compromises they force us to make with our own principles, because of the reactions of the uncommitted nations and because such countries, which themselves provide a culture in which the local Communist virus flourishes, are weak reeds to lean upon. Surely, in such cases, new departures in our aid policy are called for — even if they call specifically and publicly for the necessary changes, and lend aid and comfort to internal reform groups contesting for political power.

One final problem of development aid is again unrealistic thinking — this time on our own part. We have tended to believe that, because the absence of aid and development in the underdeveloped countries would open the door to political and economic instability, aid and development would necessarily strengthen democracy and stability. This, unhappily, is not the case.

On the contrary, the revolutionary nature of the development process inevitably creates problems, tensions, instabilities and dangers of its own. Profound economic and social transformation cannot be effected without a shake-up of the body politic. This is bound to result because of the disparate and often conflicting goals within these societies, because of the grave difficulties which such societies encounter in carrying out their development programs and because of the impact of new modes of production and social organization on traditional values and attitudes. The most favorable outcome it is possible to envisage will not be free of many and serious instabilities. More obvious, and perhaps glaring, failures to go fast enough, slow enough or with enough efficiency may expose such governments to powerful political attacks, either from the Left or the Right, and the obvious dangers of collapse or take-over. "Thus, after having long been a mirage, the quest for development is apt to turn suddenly into a nightmare."[1]

If the West, politically speaking, has now come to recognize the dangers inherent in a failure to provide adequate assistance to underdeveloped countries in their efforts to achieve development, it is time now also to realize the dangers that exist in positive attempts to help them. It would be dangerous not to help the uncommitted underdeveloped world to achieve development. The attempt to do so rephases and alters the nature of, but does not eliminate, the danger. While this is a sobering reflection, it should not discourage us in this effort. As President Black of the World Bank has wisely said, "part of facing the realities of this world is recognizing that economic development, while not sufficient, is necessary for progress towards all of the political, economic, and humanitarian aims which the free peoples believe in and seek beyond their shores. By choosing to make it their special purpose to help find ways out of poverty the free nations are serving the ideal of freedom in the most tangible way open to them."[2]

1. Albert O. Hirschman, *The Strategy of Development,* Yale University Press, New Haven, 1958, p. 210.

2. Eugene R. Black, *The Diplomacy of Economic Development,* Harvard University Press, Cambridge, Mass., 1960, p. 19.

Premier Reports to the People:
The National Economy

(Excerpt from translation of speech delivered by the Hon'ble Prime Minister U Nu in the Chamber of Deputies, September 27, 1957, on Law and Order, National Solidarity, Social Welfare, National Economy and Foreign Affairs)

Mr. Speaker, Sir, having dealt with social welfare, I now come to the National Economy. In this part of my speech I shall discuss the following questions:
1. The progress made in the national economy since Independence;
2. The Eight-Year Pyidawtha Plan for economic and social development;
3. The lessons learned from experience in the last few years;
4. The Four-Year Plan for capital expenditures; and
5. Our revised plans for better implementation and policy.

In the course of this discussion, I shall state my views on the strengths and the weaknesses of our accomplishments thus far; on why and how our plans are being modified; on what we hope to achieve in the next few years; and on what we shall do to ensure better results from our efforts.

I. Progress in the National Economy Since Independence

How shall I sum up for you, without being over-lengthy, the progress which has been made in these years? Books could be written about this question. In describing our progress, I shall apply first the commonly accepted yard-sticks for such a measurement, using only a few key figures for which the detailed substantiation will be found in the Economic Survey which is being separately presented to you by the Hon'ble Finance Minister, and in other official documents.

Progress in Total Production

You are all familiar with the general course of our national economy since the war. At war's end, the national economy was badly damaged and disrupted. Total production in 1946–47 was only three-fifths of the pre-war level. There followed a substantial rise in output in 1947–48 to about seven-tenths of the pre-war level. Due to insurrection, the next two years saw a loss of all that had been gained. Only by 1951–52 did we see a return of total output of the national economy to approximately the level which prevailed at the time of Independence. If therefore I measure the progress which has been made in the national economy since 1951–52, I shall at the same time be measuring in approximate terms the progress made from the time of Independence.

Measuring then from 1951–52, the total output of the economy (what the economists call the Gross Domestic Product) increased by 29 per cent to 1956–57, the fiscal year now ending. This increase, let me stress, is measured in *constant* prices, so that it expresses the real change which has occurred. This increase has brought national output in five years from 74 per cent of the pre-war base to 95 per cent of the pre-war base. However, our population has been increasing during this time, and total output *per capita* is a more important measure of progress than is total output. During this time output *per capita* has increased 20 per cent — an average increase of 4 per cent per year. What does this mean? One authority states that 2.5 per cent of real increase in *per capita* output per year is the dividing line between normal growth and accelerated growth. By this measure, it would seem that our increase during the past five years has been well above the norm. In this connection, however, we must remember that our growth has been not from a normal base, but from a badly depressed base. At the same time, it has been achieved in spite of widespread civil disorder and unrest. Taking all these factors into account, it may be considered that our overall progress has been quite substantial indeed.

Progress in Consumption

While this increase in output was being achieved, what was happening to consumption? According to our figures, there was very little improvement in average consumption *per capita* until this year. This year, with an inflow of imported goods for consumers' use exceeding substantially those of any previously recorded year, real consumption *per capita* is calculated to be some 10 or 11 per cent higher than it was in 1951–52. Whether this figure reflects the availabilities of goods for consumption, rather than actual consumption, will depend in part on how rapidly these imported goods are finding their way through the channels of distribution to the actual consumer.

Progress in Specific Sectors

Let me make a few additional comparisons of progress in the national economy. Output in agriculture, fisheries and forestry rose from approximately three-quarters of the pre-war base in 1951–52 to approximately nine-tenths of pre-war this year. Rice processing rose from approximately two-thirds of pre-war in 1951–52 to approximately three-fourths of this year. State marketing rose from approximately two-fifths of the pre-war base to approximately four-fifths of pre-war this year. State transport rose from approximately two-fifths of the pre-war base to approximately three-fourths of pre-war this year. Mining is the only sector which continues to lag badly behind all the rest. Output in this very important sector rose from about one-tenth of the pre-war base in 1951–52 to approximately one-fourth of pre-war this year.

Sir, let us look at a few other measures. Exports of rice and rice products increased from 11.5 lakhs tons in 1951–52 to close to 20 lakhs tons this year, a rise of about 70 per cent. Teak exports in tons increased about 30 per cent, but the value of minerals exports increased very little over this period. Total agricultural acreage sown increased 8 per cent, paddy acreage 6 per cent and all other agricultural acreage 12 per cent, over this period. The acreage under irrigation increased by about one-third, the tonnage of traffic moving through the port of Rangoon by about one-half, and railway freight ton miles about two-fifths, during this period. Extraction of crude oil more than doubled in these years. These, you will agree, are solid evidence of growth.

The Use of Resources

How have we used the resources which have been available to us? Before the war, about one-sixth of our total output was accumulated abroad, largely for the benefit of foreign investors. About three-fifths was available for consumption, approximately one-twelfth was devoted to current government expenditures, and about one-eighth went into domestic investment for the future. Since that time the use of our resources has changed radically. The accumulation abroad has been virtually eliminated. About two-thirds are available for domestic consumption. About one-seventh, as compared with the previous one-twelfth, goes into current government expenditures, much of it for health, education and social services to the people to supplement their direct consumption. About one-fifth, compared with the previous one-eighth, goes into investment for the future. In recent years, this investment has been divided roughly half and half between public investment and private investment.

The facts I have given do not by any means tell the complete story of the progress made in the national economy since Independence. They provide only a skeleton for that story. Let me try now to add some flesh to the bones, and a little colour in the cheeks.

Development Measures

Let me recall first the progress which has been made in restoring our ravaged physical facilities — our capital wealth. Great strides have been made in rehabilitating the nation's transport — the railways, the waterways and the ports. The oil refineries have been rebuilt. The chief mines have been rehabilitated. Electric generating facilities have been restored. Schools, hospitals and other essential buildings have been rebuilt.

But we have gone far beyond mere rehabilitation. We have made considerable progresss in changing the national economy from the over-specialized and too highly-dependent colonial economy of the pre-war years in the direction of a better balanced, less dependent and more self-reliant national economy. In agriculture we are emphasizing new and expanded crops like jute, sugar cane, higher grade cotton and groundnuts, reclaiming jungle lands, building irrigation projects. We are exploring our mineral wealth. We have developed an air service. We have gone into industry with steel, sugar, cotton spinning, pharmaceuticals, jute and other factories. We have fostered the growth of cottage industries. We are rapidly expanding our electric generating facilities, and building a transmission and distribution network to take this electric power throughout the country. We are building new and better communications systems. We are building new schools, hospitals, dispensaries, new engineering colleges, technical high schools, vocational training facilities, and essential public buildings, of all kinds. We are sending many of our best young people abroad for advanced study.

The Agricultural Sector

I cannot go into detail at this time with respect to all these avenues of activity and progress without writing that book with which I threatened you earlier. But let us take just one sector, the agricultural sector, and review very briefly the progress which has been made in the position and status of the cultivator, and the benefits received by him. Over these years we have taken steps to safeguard the cultivator in his tenure on the land. We have protected him as to the rents he must pay. We are engaged in a land nationalization and distribution scheme which has already given tens of thousands of farm families land which they never had before. We have extended crores of loans to the agriculturalists at moderate rates of interest, far below the extortionate rates they have had to pay to private money lenders. We have expanded the agricultural extension service to teach improved farming practices — to encourage the use of better seed, insect and pest control, fertilizer use, etc. We have brought pump and other irrigation to the countryside; introduced mechanization; sent in mass education teams to help the cultivator in all aspects of his daily and village life; built model villages; assisted him in the establishment of cooperatives; given him price supports when necessary; sunk tube wells; erected schools and clinics; brought medical assistance within his reach; and made grants in which he had a voice in allocating for ponds, tube wells and a variety of other locally-needed projects. The cultivators are the heart and soul of Burma. They and their families constitute perhaps four-fifths of the total population of this country. By bringing all these reforms and benefits to the cultivator and his family, we have been bringing economic progress to Burma.

Other Changes

I have not yet mentioned the many institutional and structural changes we have introduced in the national economy for the benefit of our people. The State has gone into trading, into banking, into insurance, into the import trade, into the export trade, into industry. In each case the object has been to advance the national economy and to increase the benefits which may be brought to the people, in terms of recapturing profits which would otherwise go to middlemen, in providing goods and services at lower prices, and in establishing better balance and increased productivity in the national economy. I shall not deny — indeed I have already affirmed and shall again affirm in this speech — that all this activity has not been without its drawbacks. These attempts have strained our resources. They have not in all cases been carried out with efficiency and adequate management. They have revealed many flaws in our ability to do so many things at once, and to do them effectively. We must not ignore however that they do reflect, at least in some degree, positive achievements and benefits.

International Aspects

The position of our national economy has also been strengthened in its international aspects. This may sound odd to some, in view of the decline in our foreign exchange reserves from the level of some years ago. On the whole, however, I think the statement is a correct one. We have paid off our pre-war debts. We have demonstrated the basic soundness and credit-worthiness of our economy, so that we could borrow substantial sums from the World Bank, from India, and from the United States to contribute to our economic development. We have been able to establish very substantial credits with other countries, such as West Germany, the USSR and China. We have negotiated and are now utilizing effectively a reparations settlement with Japan. We have bolstered our foreign exchange position by arranging to buy for kyats large quantities of agricultural commodities from the United States. We have made trade agreements with many countries which have assisted in disposing of our rice surplus and which have encouraged increased trade in other commodities as well. We have obtained valuable technical assistance from the United Nations, received valuable aid under the Colombo Plan, and utilized the technical services of engineering, economic and other specialists from many countries whether under the auspices of institutions like The Ford Foundation, or of friendly nations like Yugoslavia, Israel, the USSR and China, or in our direct employ.

Policy

Our economic policies have progressed during these years. I would draw particular attention to our private investment policy, as expressed in our statement of 1955, and in the hire-purchase loan scheme carried on by the Industrial Development Corporation for the last two years. But economic policy has not developed as rapidly as has our physical progress in these past years. We shall remedy this in our Four-Year Plan.

Finance

No description of the course of our national economy since Independence would be complete without some reference to the course of our finances, and to prices.

From 1951–52 to 1956–57, Union Government budgetary receipts rose from about 71 crores to about 126 crores. Budgetary expenditures rose at the same time from approximately 65 crores to approximately 126 crores. The receipts include rehabilitation contributions. The expenditures include advances to Boards and Corporations. During this time our domestic debt, exclusive of ways and means advances, grew from 7.7 crores at the end of 1951–52 to 93.4 crores in May, 1957 — an increase of 85.7 crores. This is indeed a large growth in the domestic debt. But this increase was incurred to create capital assets owned by the people which will yield continuing benefits to the national production and welfare. Also, the debt, in relation to the total annual output of the country, is not as large as it is in most other countries, nor is the interest burden a heavy one. If we can keep this debt from growing too rapidly, — and this we propose to do — we shall have nothing to fear on this score. As for our external debt, this at the present time is substantially less than it was at the end of 1951–52.

Prices

In evaluating what has happened to prices, the most significant index which can be used is that which measures the prices of articles and services most commonly purchased by the great mass of consumers. The prices of luxury goods purchased by a relatively small number of people are interesting and significant in many ways. But in all countries of the world, it is recognized that the consumers' price index is the most important yard-stick.

In Burma, after Independence, there was a gradual rise in prices. There are several reasons for this.

In the first place, when a country builds more schools, more hospitals, more roads, and more industrial plants, for the development of the social and economic fabric of the country, there is an inevitable rise in prices. This is an economic law. For instance, Burma exports yearly rice, timber and minerals. The foreign exchange thus brought in by exports has to be used for buying consumer goods. As the materials, such as steel, needed for building a great many schools and hospitals, and the equipment needed for the national transport system have to be brought on a large scale from abroad, not much foreign exchange can be spared for importing consumer goods. And as imports of consumer goods go down, prices rise. At the same time, deficit financing involves increasing the supply of money in the country. Thus prices have risen.

The second factor in the rise of prices here is that world prices themselves have risen. In industrial countries like the USA, Germany and other European countries, prices have gone up four to six times higher than the pre-war figures. There was a slight decline for a time, but since then world prices have risen gradually. Burma has had to buy manufactured goods from these industrial countries, and prices in Burma have kept pace with the rising world prices. This rise in prices has occurred also in the Soviet Union, China, Poland and East Germany since their international trade is also geared to world prices. Recently, in an issue of the American magazine *Newsweek,* there was an interesting comparison which was based on the official cost-of-living indexes of 53 countries, for the period January, 1948, to December, 1956. Only six out of 52 other countries showed cost-of-living increases smaller than Burma's 12 per cent increase for the period. Compared with our 12 per cent increase, the cost of living in the United States increased 15 per cent; that of West Germany, 18 per cent; Canada and Italy, 25 per cent; the United Kingdom, 34 per cent; France, 52 per cent; Japan, 55 per cent; Sweden, 29 per cent; New Zealand, 33 per cent; Australia, 52 per cent.

Let us examine the increase in the cost-of-living of those countries which have recently become independent nations like Burma, or which are striving for progress and are engaged in nation-building tasks in the field of education, social welfare and economic development just as our country is doing. India, which did not suffer the ravages of war like Burma, has an increase in the cost-of-living of 15 per cent;

Malaya, 28 per cent; Thailand, 35 per cent; Indonesia, 59 per cent; Israel, 66 per cent, and Korea, 99 per cent.

Need I say more? Clearly, the entire world has been going through a process of continuing inflation, from which Burma could scarcely expect to remain immune. As regards prices, we may indeed have been more fortunate than we have realized.

Sir, this rise in prices, although we may say that the situation in our country is comparatively better than that in other countries, is in reality neither a desirable nor a welcome phenomenon. Therefore, the Government has already taken measures to combat the rise in prices, and the Government is resolved to take additional measures in the future to cause a decline in prices.

But, let me take this opportunity, Sir, to stress one or two points in connection with this matter.

However hard the Government may endeavour to prevent prices rising and to cause prices to decline, if the commercial circles and the public will not give the Government their whole-hearted support and co-operation, prices will not decline as much and as fast as they should.

If prices are really to become lower effectively, the Government on its part will have to ensure an adequate supply of consumer goods in the country. At the same time, the importers, distributors and traders will have to curb their desire for large profits. The public also will have to exercise the utmost restraint so as not encourage directly or indirectly black-marketing.

If there is this concerted action and whole-hearted co-operation on the part of the Government, the commercial circles and the public, the rise in prices is bound to be halted in the quickest possible time.

Summary

Mr. Speaker, Sir, how then shall we sum up the progress which has been made in the national economy since Independence? We have finally restored production until it is now very close to that of pre-war. We have established a better balance in the economy, so that we shall no longer be as dependent as we were before on the production of a few key commodities for export. We have made great strides toward the restoration of our essential services in transport, electric power, communications, etc. We have raised standards of living and welfare. We have been making large capital investments in transport and communications, electric power, industry, social services, etc., which will contribute greatly to future production and welfare. We have begun to encourage private investment, both domestic and foreign, to contribute to our national output and well-being. We have kept our finances sound. We have kept price increases within reasonable bounds, and have contained them.

In short, considering the conditions from which we began and the difficulties which have plagued us, we do not need to be ashamed of what we have accomplished in these years. In fact, I think that on the whole we can take a considerable amount of pride in our achievements. Please recognize that when I say this I find no room for smug complacency. On the contrary, I think we must be highly self-critical of these accomplishments, because we could and should have achieved even more than we did. But our weaknesses were not the fault of indifference and lack of effort. They resulted for the most part from over-ambitiousness and over-eagerness to do everything at once. Fortunately, we have learned from this experience.

Sir, the lessons of our experience can perhaps best be brought out in connection with consideration of the Eight-Year Pyidawtha Plan.

II. The Eight-Year Pyidawtha Plan

Goals

The Eight-Year Programme envisaged a rise of 78 per cent to 700 crores (in 1950–51 prices) in the total output of the national economy by 1959–60. *Per capita* national output was to increase by 62 per cent. *Per capita* consumption was to increase by 52 per cent. These increases in output and in consumption were to be achieved chiefly by a net capital investment of 750 crores, both public and private. Quite detailed plans were prepared for investment in the various sectors of the economy — agriculture, minerals, timber, transportation, communications, industry, electric power, schools, hospitals, housing, and so on.

Assumptions

This Eight-Year Plan was based, as all plans must be based, on certain major assumptions. The most important of these assumptions had to do with law and order. We assumed for the purpose of the plan that law and order would be substantially restored within three years after the beginning of the plan period. Another major assumption was that the price of rice in international markets would decline only moderately. A third major assumption was that we would succeed by a variety of means in meeting the shortage of managerial, administrative and technical skills that would inevitably be encountered in the execution of the plans.

I do not need to tell you that none of these major assumptions has proved to be completely valid. While very considerable forward strides have been made in achieving law and order, this progress has been far less than we hoped for or needed to have. Our failure to establish the degree of law and order necessary to successful fulfilment of the plan has been the most serious single obstacle limiting the progress of the national economy thus far. So far as the price of rice is concerned, the decline in the price of rice in international markets has been greater than was anticipated. I would point out, however, that this has not been as serious a blow to the success of our plans as some people seem to think. After all, the chief result of this difference in the price of rice has been that instead of being able to finance our development scheme entirely out of our own resources, as we thought we would be able to do, it has been necessary to turn abroad to meet the deficit in our own resources. Thus, while the decline in the price of rice temporarily slowed us down until we could establish loans and credits abroad, such loans and credits have been obtained without undue delay. The price of rice has therefore not been so critical a factor in limiting our development efforts. Far more serious than this have been civil disorder and the shortage of managerial, administrative and technical skills.

Investments

In spite of these and related difficulties, we made very considerable forward strides, as I have just enumerated, in the first half of the Eight-Year Plan. In the four years 1952–53 to 1955–56, the Government made capital investments of just over 170 crores, an average of some 43 crores per year. Of this, some 16 crores, or 9 per cent of the total, went to agriculture, irrigation and forestry. Close to 43 crores, or 25 per cent, went to transportation and communications. About 18.5 crores, or almost 11 per cent, went to electric power. Investment in industry amounted to some 19.5 crores, more than 11 per cent of the total. Building construction, including schools, hospitals, and housing, took 27 crores, or 16 per cent of the total. Some 36.4 crores, or more than 21 per cent of the total, went to defence.

Continuous Planning

I do not want the impression to prevail that we proceeded with the Pyidawtha Plan right up to the present time, only to discover all at once that things were wrong, and that radical changes were necessary. Nothing could be further from the truth. We started to amend and adjust the Pyidawtha Plan almost from the very beginning in the light of new information, additional studies, experience and changing circumstances. Investment schedules were modified from year to year in accordance with the prevailing financial situation and outlook. The plans for some basic sectors — as in the case of electric power — were changed in significant degree almost at the very outset of the plan. With the decline in the price of rice and the stringent foreign exchange position which developed during 1954, an intensive review was made of the entire investment programme, and sharp reductions were effected. Late in 1955 we worked out a three-year investment schedule on a much more austere basis than had hitherto been planned. Again, early in 1956 when we had succeeded in obtaining loans from India and from the World Bank, and in negotiating an agreement for the purchase of surplus agricultural commodities from the United States for domestic currency, and when we could envisage still further loans and credits from abroad, we undertook once again an intensive review in which all agencies of Government participated, and formulated a revised Four-Year Programme of capital expenditure to cover the second half of the Eight-Year Plan period. By July, 1956, the first year of that Four-Year Plan was approved and incorporated into the Budget for 1956–57 — the current financial year.

Since the preparation of the 1956–57 budget, the planning job has continued. By March of this year the forward plans for the next three years, through 1959–60, had been thoroughly reviewed and reformulated. The Four-Year Capital Expenditure Programme is therefore not a hasty improvisation. It is an out-growth rather of a continuing process of modifying and adjusting our basic plans right through the years. What I called for in my June speech and directives was not the formulation of a new Four-Year Plan for capital expenditure — this we already had — but rather a modification of it to ensure better implementation and policy, with greatly increased emphasis on law and order, fire prevention, efficiency, morale, education, investment policy, and the like. This will involve, to be sure, modifications in the Four-Year Capital Programme. But it is aimed primarily at utilizing the lessons learned in recent years in achieving even greater progress in the years immediately ahead.

III. The Lessons of Our Recent Experience

Mr. Speaker, Sir, what were the lessons of our experience these past years?

1. First, we have learned that without the complete restoration of law and order, our efforts at economic and social development cannot fully succeed. However hard we try, our energy and material resources in large part will be wasted, and go down the drain.

2. Second, we have come to appreciate more clearly the importance of the basic sectors of our economy. Agriculture, timber and minerals must be restored to at least their pre-war output before satisfactory gains in other important sectors of the national economy can be made and sustained.

3. Third, we have learned that new industrial ventures require intensive preparation, organization, supervision and management in order to be successful. Technical and economic studies must be made. Manpower must be found. Careful co-ordination must be provided so that the projects may go forward on all fronts in an orderly way. Skilled management must be found for their operation. In many cases domestic raw materials must be developed — cane for sugar factories, jute for the jute mill, scrap for the steel rolling mill, and cotton of proper quality for the spinning and weaving mill. Labour must be trained, efficiency must be achieved, proper accounting systems must be introduced, marketing methods must be developed, distribution must be worked out. Our small group of able and trained people while having to cope with all these tasks in the industries we have already undertaken, have not been able, at the same time, to plan and initiate activities for the further expansion of state-owned and operated industries.

4. A fourth lesson which has come home to us with increasing force in recent years is the fact that the morale of our public servants has deteriorated very considerably, and that until radical steps are taken to improve this morale, all efforts of Government toward economic and social betterment must be badly retarded by this factor.

5. Fifth, for a variety of reasons, efficiency throughout the Government's operations, and particularly in the State-owned Boards and Corporations, is at a very low level. This means that costs are far higher than they should be; that revenues are lower than they should be; that prices to consumers are higher than they ought to be; that where moderate profits should be enjoyed, losses are incurred; and that where large profits might be expected, only very small profits are received. Obviously, strenuous efforts are called for to achieve higher levels of efficiency.

6. Sixth, and closely related to some of the lessons I have already mentioned, is the realization that too much centralization is a bad thing. Over-centralization of authority and responsibility for the Government's far-flung activities mean the hopeless overburdening of a relatively small number of people at the very top who cannot give adequate time and attention to the many problems involved, which range all the way from questions of major policy down to the smallest detail. It has become quite clear that if the Government apparatus is to function smoothly, and if our efforts at development are to go forward unhampered, there must be far more decentralization and delegation of authority and responsibility than has been the case till now. At every level of execution and management, there must be exercised that degree of authority and responsibility which is appropriate to the level concerned. Officers at every level must exercise judgment and initiative. We cannot afford to have officers at any levels fearful of making decisions appropriate to their office, and passing responsibility for such decisions as these up and up for approval by higher authority before acting, until they reach the very highest levels of Government. This is managerial constipation.

7. Seventh, we have learned that Government just cannot undertake responsibility for everything that needs to be done. Ways and means must be found to permit or encourage or assist the private sector to do those things which are necessary, and which the private sector is capable of doing. No Government can do everything. It was our inclination, when we saw a need for something to be done, to think first in terms of having the Government do it. We must change this thinking. We believe the Government should undertake only those tasks which are appropriate to undertake, leaving other tasks to co-operative organizations and the private sector.

8. The eighth lesson is that if we are to invest for economic and social development, and if we are at the same time to avoid inflation, the people of the country must contribute in reasonable degree to the financing of this investment. Only two-fifths of our capital outlays in the four years ending 1955–56 were financed by taxes and other current earnings of Government. Of the remaining three-fifths, one-fifth was financed (a) by a sizable reduction in our foreign exchange reserves; and (b) to a limited extent by reparations, loans from abroad and private savings in Burma; and (c) almost two-fifths of the total by an increase in the domestic money supply — in other words, by deficit financing. For the next few years, as matters have stood till now, we could anticipate an even smaller relative contribution toward planned capital expenditure from taxes and other current earnings of Government. We shall have to rely in very large measure on reparations and on foreign loans. But it is also imperative that we contribute more out of current taxes and earnings of Government if we are to avoid inflation. We can do this by improving the efficiency of our Government enterprises and of our tax collections, and by stimulating private savings. To some extent we shall have to do it also by increasing some tax rates or by introducing some new tax measures.

9. Still another lesson we have learned is the importance of a high level of availability of goods for consumers' use both through increased domestic production and increased imports, to counteract the otherwise inflationary influence of large scale Government expenditures for development, and the need for improved efficiency in the distribution of those goods.

10. Finally, but in a somewhat different category from these lessons I have mentioned, is the recognition that our educational system must be basically improved, that the periodic and costly fire scourge must be eliminated, and that the city of Rangoon must be rehabilitated.

The SAMB

Mr. Speaker, Sir, to illustrate some of the points I have made, let us take the case of the SAMB. Only a few short years ago, the affairs of that vitally important agency of Government were in a terrible mess. Unsold surpluses had accumulated in huge quantity. Adequate storage could not be provided, and large quantities of rice were spoiled or deteriorated. Large scale rejections by buyers at shipside resulted in the inefficient use of lighters, which became in effect floating godowns for rejected rice. Transit sheds were used for permanent storage, and prevented efficient use from being made of Ahlone Wharf. When SAMB stopped storing rice, and stored paddy instead, it had to arrange for milling on SAMB account. This involved extra storage, handling, transport and other costs, as well as an organization SAMB did not have. This was not all. SAMB was not equipped to buy paddy selectively or efficiently, to arrange for prompt payments, to keep track of its stocks, etc., etc. The situation grew quite desperate indeed.

However, early in 1954, with the help of our economic consultants, we prepared a programme for improving rice quality and marketing. Slowly, since that time, we have been correcting the mess, and extricating ourselves from the morass. With lower prices and increased sales, private millers are buying more paddy. Premiums for quality rice have led to more selective buying, and more quality rice. Storage facilities and practices have been notably improved. Transit sheds have been cleared and others constructed. Ahlone Wharf is being used more efficiently. A start has been made on additional wharf facilities, on a market intelligence and research programme, on a mill improvement programme. Operational statistics, internal management organization, invoicing and collections, have all been improved.

Despite all these gains, much yet remains to be done. The Board must be given more authority to make business decisions in a business-like way. Excessive costs must be reduced. Better milling, handling, stock control, cost control and coordination of procurement, sales, stocks and shipments must be achieved.

While the details are different, a somewhat similar story can be told about almost every Government-owned enterprise.

Our Mistakes — In Perspective

In enumerating thus the lessons learned from experience in recent years, it will be clear that this is equivalent to saying, we have made many mistakes. There will be some, no doubt, who will attempt to make political capital out of this admission.

This does not worry me. First, if we have made mistakes, the honest thing to do is to admit them. We will never try to conceal them. Second, it is natural for a young government to make mistakes. Only in this way is it possible to learn. The only way to avoid mistakes is to make no decisions and attempt no improvements. But such a do-nothing policy would be the greatest mistake of all. Third, we are learning from our mistakes, and correcting them. Fourth, we are not the only government which makes mistakes, as can readily be demonstrated.

I would refer, in this connection, to a study recently prepared and issued by the World Bank, based on the reports of twelve economic survey missions sent by the Bank to Colombia, Guatemala, Nicaragua, Cuba, Mexico, Ceylon, Turkey, Iraq, Nigeria, Jamaica, British Guiana and Surinam in recent years. Reading this report, one could readily think it was about Burma. The same basic conditions, problems, mistakes and needs are revealed throughout. Key words and phrases similar to those I have used are also found there: poor management; inefficient public administration; excessive government intervention in the economy; the need for agricultural development; the need to stimulate private investment in industry; the need to develop transport, highways and electric power; the need for better administration of education, for maintenance of financial stability through increased taxation and savings; for encouragement of private enterprise; for favourable treatment of foreign capital; and for the improvement of public administration. Does not all this sound very much like ourselves?

Sir, to take a few other examples, the Soviet Union, as a Government, is much older and more experienced than we. Yet look at the colossal mistakes they have recently admitted: the mistake of the personality cult, the mistake of the over-centralization of control of industry, the mistake of over-collectivization in agriculture, the mistake in their diplomatic relations with Yugoslavia. People's Republic of China admits to having made serious mistakes in failing to recognize and correct the contradictions between the Communist Party and the people, and in its agricultural policies.

Prime Minister Chou En-lai's Report on the Proposals for the Second Five-Year Plan abounds with references to mistakes made during the first Five-Year Plan. He admits to excessive grain collections as a result of which "discontent arose among a section of the peasantry." He says "We erred on the side of setting (individual) targets too high or too low"; he mentions "inappropriate cuts in investments," plans which were "not quite satisfactorily fulfilled," failures "to strike a proper balance," and a tendency to do many things at once and (to) be "impatient for success." There were, he says, "difficulties in finance and waste of manpower and material resources." There were "over-estimates" and "under-estimates" and "one-sidedness." He admits "we still lack experience in planning, and our plans are often incomplete and inaccurate." He mentions "subjectivism and bureaucracy among the leadership" at higher levels, and "commandism at lower levels." He refers to lower organizations "inundated with official documents, telegrams and forms," and to negligence which results in "big mistakes and great losses."

Yugoslavia has admitted the mistake it made in concentrating too much on heavy industry, as compared with light industry.

Turning to a less political type of problem where industrial efficiency is concerned, I should like to remind you that even in a great and efficient industrial economy like the United States, not every industrial investment manages to succeed. It is quite common there for new industrial ventures to lose money for the first three or four years, while their labour is being trained, production volume is being increased, and various difficulties are ironed out. True efficiency and lower costs are achieved only after continued and time-consuming efforts. Even then, many firms are unable to survive the competitive struggle, and fail, or are taken over by other firms.

The American automobile industry, world famous for its size and efficiency, is now made up of three giant firms — General Motors, Chrysler and Ford — and a very few others which are in great financial difficulty. What very few people (including most Americans) realize is, that these few firms are all that remain of several hundred automobile manufacturing companies which survived only a short time, and then disappeared from the scene.

Those who compare the inefficiency of State Enterprise with the efficiency of private enterprise should remember that not all private enterprise is efficient. The so-called profit system is really a profit-and-loss system, and the system is not free of losses. I do not wish to condone our inefficiency, or our other mistakes. I merely wish to place them in proper perspective. Of course we must correct our mistakes. It is unfortunate that they are made. But let us not regard them as unnatural or calamitous. Let us rather be thankful that we can perceive them, and take vigorous and constructive action to correct them.

Sir, how do we propose to remedy the failings I have just described? We propose to do this in two ways — (1) by our modified Four-Year Plan for Capital Expenditure through 1959–60; and (2) by a Revised Plan for Better Implementation and Policy.

IV. The Modified Four-Year-Plan for Capital Expenditure

Mr. Speaker, I have already described the history of the preparation of this modified Four-Year Plan for Capital Expenditure. You have seen that it is not the hasty product of a month's work, but rather the culmination of the work of years. Let me now describe to you some of the key features of this Plan.

1. The plan was related realistically to the financial resources which we have in firm prospect, or on which we can reasonably count.
2. The plan aimed at achieving a balance in our foreign exchange receipts and payments.
3. The plan provided for a large programme of imports for private use to counteract inflationary influences.
4. The plan was based on clearly defined priorities and criteria. Within the resources likely to be available, it aimed at achieving the maximum increases in output consistent with financial stability. It placed a much heavier emphasis than heretofore on the primary sectors of the economy — agriculture, forestry and mining. It gave emphasis to projects which would either save or earn foreign exchange. It limited new industrial enterprise to a few

projects for which capable management is assured. It looked to the further development of a balanced and co-ordinated economy. It struck a sound balance between productive projects, basic services and social welfare projects. It provided for the orderly completion of projects already under way. It made only tentative provisions for projects on which additional technical and economic studies still need to be made. It provided for the geographic dispersion of projects. Wherever possible, considerations of specialized manpower and management requirements were taken into account.

So much for the general aspects of the Plan.

More specifically, the modified Four-Year Plan aimed at a real increase in the total output of the national economy of 28 per cent from 1955–56 to 1959–60. It anticipated a real increase of 21 per cent in output *per capita*. Total consumers' purchases during this period were to increase by 33 per cent. Consumption *per capita,* it was anticipated, would increase by 26 per cent at the same time. The value of agricultural production was to increase by 23 per cent, paddy acreage by 17 per cent, all other agricultural acreage by 15 per cent, and the tonnage of rice exports by 30 per cent. Acreage under irrigation was to rise by 18 per cent, teak extraction by 130 per cent and crude oil extraction by 58 per cent. Railway freight ton miles were to increase by 44 per cent, passenger miles by 25 per cent, tonnage going through the port of Rangoon by 25 per cent.

Why then has this Plan not yet been accepted by the Government, and why are we not yet in a position to present this Plan, in all its details, to the Parliament? This is because, at the same time this Plan was being worked out in detail, it became increasingly clear to us that first priority had to be given to law and order, and that it was absolutely necessary to initiate a major effort to establish law and order throughout the country in the shortest possible time. Obviously, this effort, which we are now organizing and equipping ourselves to make, will make a substantial additional claim on our financial and other resources. So great an additional claim obviously requires a reduction in the funds available for the national economy and for social welfare. This means that the March plan must be vetted and adjusted to make room for the new law and order requirements, if an excessive drain on our foreign exchange reserves and an undue pressure on domestic prices are to be avoided. We have worked very hard to adjust these allotments for the next fiscal year, 1957–58. These adjustments are already incorporated in the Budget for next year. But we have not yet had the time to work out all the details for all the Board and Corporation programmes, or for the remaining two years of the Plan. This work will be continued with all possible speed.

However, I do not believe that the reduction in investment in the national economy which will now be required on account of the intensified law and order campaign will result in less production and economic growth than would have resulted from higher levels of investment. I believe that substantial improvement in the state of law and order will, in and of itself, result in marked increases in agriculture, timber and mineral production, in improved and less costly transport and trade, and in increased manufacturing activities as well. In other words, while we shall add fewer new productive facilities in the next three years, we should be able to obtain improved use of the productive facilities we already have. I expect therefore a very sizeable increase of some 5 or 6 per cent a year in our total national production in each of the next three years, despite a lower level of productive investment, provided that our efforts to improve the state of law and order are successful.

Modification of the Four-Year Plan, while due in major degree to our decision to inaugurate a greatly strengthened law and order campaign, will be affected by other factors as well. New emphasis and priority to achieve fire prevention, improved efficiency in the Government Boards and Corporations, improved rehabilitation of Rangoon town, and other objectives stated in my June speech and directives, will also involve changes in the Plan. But I wish to emphasize that we shall be modifying the Four-Year Plan, not only with respect to capital expenditure, but with respect to implementation and policy as well. It will be not only a Four-Year Plan for Capital Expenditure, but also a plan for better implementation and policy. It will be appropriate therefore if I now describe some of the policies which we shall emphasize. Needless to say, these arise clearly out of the lessons we have learned from experience in recent years, and which I earlier described to you.

V. The Revised Plan for Better Implementation and Policy

It is now time to describe how we plan to rectify our mistakes of recent years in order to achieve better implementation and policy.

1. *Law and Order*

The establishment of law and order will be from now on the first priority task of this Government. Nothing will be permitted to stand in the way of the achievement of this goal. The Law ond Order Committee has recommended more and better guns, ammunition, uniforms, communications equipment, patrol boats, improved staff quarters, better roads, and a variety of other needs, to accomplish this goal. These things may cost a great deal of money — perhaps as much as an additional 20 crores of kyats a year. But I say without the slightest hesitation that, whatever the increase in expenditures necessary to achieve our aims, that money will be provided. If we can obtain special loans from abroad for this purpose, so much the better. But even if it means a drastic reduction in our cherished plans for economic and social development, the money necessary will be provided.

But I also want the Parliament, the country, the military, the police, and everyone else concerned to understand this: what is involved in re-establishing law and order is, in the first instance, not money, but *determination*. We must be determined to stamp out and eradicate this social cancer that is eating away the vitals of our country. The key words must be initiative, intelligence, communications, mobility, imaginative tactics, and above all, determination. I call upon the military, the police, and the civil administration to mark these words. And I call upon the people throughout the country to co-operate with the authorities and the armed forces in eliminating this scourge.

2. *Agriculture, Timber, Minerals Production and Exports*

The modified Four-Year Plan for capital expenditure provides ample funds for the restoration of production and exports in these vital primary sectors. Primary production will also benefit greatly from the restoration of law and order, and from various other measures to be described below.

3. *State Industrial Ventures*

First of all, we shall definitely slow down so far as new State-owned industrial ventures are concerned, until we consolidate the advances made thus far. State-owned industries must be brought to a reasonable state of efficiency. This will be achieved by a combination of measures, including more concentration of time, attention and energy; an improved supply of raw materials; greater autonomy of operation; and the enlistment of private financial and managerial participation in appropriate projects.

New industrial ventures will be undertaken only in partnership with private capital and know-how, or when satisfactory management arrangements can be made in advance. The Industrial Development Corporation, which has supervisory responsibility for the operation of most of the State-owned industries, will be re-organized and supplied with experienced management personnel to enable it to do this job.

4. *Increased Efficiency in the Government Boards and Corporations*

When I refer here to the Government Boards and Corporations, I refer also to the State-owned industrial enterprises.

It is easy to over-simplify the problem of greater efficiency. Nevertheless, I am convinced that a major and perhaps prior step in achieving this objective is the placing of responsibility more squarely on the shoulders of the Boards of Directors responsible for their operation. Especially when the Government enterprises concerned are engaged in operations of a commercial type, they must be given freedom to make the decisions involved in day-to-day operations.

Secondly, such Boards of Directors should not be limited to Government servants, many of whom lack necessary experience and business judgment. Competent laymen — lawyers, accountants, bankers, industrialists, engineers, and the like — should also be asked to serve on these Boards of Directors, and serve their country in this way.

Thirdly, and of prime importance, is the need for improved and more timely accounting in the Government enterprises. We shall now insist on regular and timely accounts and balance sheets.

Each of the Government Boards and Corporations will be studied during the course of the next year by a technical staff composed of economists, engineers, accountants and management specialists, under the aegis of a high level policy Committee. Recommendations will be made to reduce costs and to improve operating efficiency. Where necessary, expert assistance will be brought in from the private sector or from abroad.

5. Encouragement of Investment by the Private Sector

We shall look increasingly to the private sector, and encourage, permit and assist it to do many things which till now have been undertaken by the Government.

In the field of industry, for example, we shall propose legislation to stimulate foreign and domestic private investment in industry, which will go considerably beyond the Investment Policy Statement of 1955.

We shall establish a Development Bank to assist enterprises in appropriate ways.

As soon as appropriate plans can be developed, we aim to encourage and assist private capital to engage in the construction of low-cost or low-rent housing units.

The administration of the Foreign Exchange Control of the Union Bank will be liberalized and speeded up, to permit profit remittances by foreign private limited companies under proper safeguards, in advance of their tax assessments; to speed up procedures; to liberalize salary remittances; etc.

We shall recognize the constructive contribution which resident foreign minority groups can make to the development and operation of our economy, and make it increasingly possible for them to make that contribution.

These policies may lead some to ask — are we abandoning Socialism? My answer is — No. We are however modifying somewhat our ideas of what Socialism is, and how it can work effectively in the modern world — and especially, in an under-developed country like Burma. Socialism has changed, and come of age, in the modern world; and we must change with it. No longer is Socialism necessarily identified with Government ownership and operation of the means of production.

Moreover, in carrying out the aims of Socialism, we have to bear in mind one primary factor, namely, the danger of over-hastiness. I should explain why we cannot afford to ignore this danger. When, for instance, we intend to nationalize an enterprise, or to initiate a State industry or a State project, we will have to consider deeply the following two requirements:

(1) Whether we have qualified and adequate managerial personnel for the enterprise, and

(2) Whether we have qualified and adequate technical staff for the enterprise.

But over and above these two requirements, what is of the highest importance is the need to examine carefully whether or not the staff and the employees concerned with the execution of the enterprise are really imbued with the ideals of Socialism, and whether or not these people are firm believers in Socialism.

A State enterprise is not like a private enterprise. In a private enterprise, because of the profit motive, the owner of the enterprise:

(1) works hard, and does not countenance employees being negligent or idle;

(2) is tactful in personal relations concerning the work, but does not mind being disliked and unpopular in the interest of the enterprise;

(3) is mindful of wastage and loss;

(4) is always endeavouring to acquire more technical or professional knowledge necessary for the enterprise; and

(5) has no need to steal from his own enterprise, nor does he countenance any stealing by employees.

In a State enterprise however, there is no profit motive for the managerial personnel or the employees. Therefore, only when such personnel and employees are firm and convinced believers in Socialism, will they —

(1) work hard themselves, and will not countenance other employees being negligent or idle;

(2) be tactful in personal relations concerning the enterprise without being afraid of being disliked or unpopular in the interest of the enterprise;

(3) prevent wastage and loss;

(4) endeavour continually to acquire technical or professional knowledge for the success or improvement of the enterprise, and

(5) neither be guilty themselves of stealing from the enterprise, nor countenance any stealing by other employees.

If, on the other hand, managerial personnel and employees of a State enterprise are not firm and convinced believers in Socialism, they —

(1) will take every opportunity to be idle and negligent in their work, and even if they themselves are not negligent or idle, will not interfere with other employees being negligent or idle;

(2) will not be tactful in personal relations concerning the enterprise, and will avoid incurring dislike or unpopularity even in the interest of the enterprise;

(3) will ignore wastage and loss;

(4) will have no interest in the work, and thus make no effort to acquire technical or professional knowledge concerning the enterprise; and

(5) will steal at every opportunity from the enterprise, countenancing other employees' stealing too.

Therefore, whenever we embark on an enterprise so as to put Socialism into practice, just as it is necessary to plan and organize a programme for the project, it is equally and vitally necessary to make systematic arrangements and plans for converting the managerial personnel and employees at all levels to become firm and convinced believers in Socialism.

In States where dictatorship prevails, idleness and negligence on the part of employees are drastically dealt with. Wastage and loss are ruthlessly punished. Inefficiency is severely weeded out. And stealing from a State enterprise results in liquidation of the culprits.

In countries where Socialism is put into practice in a democratic way, it is not possible to take such ruthless measures to deal with these offences and shortcomings. This being so, if Socialism is to be successfully put into practice in our country we must give priority to the task of converting managerial personnel and employees at all levels in State enterprises to be firm and convinced believers in Socialism in the same way as we give priority to the planning and organization of the programme of the projects.

If, without doing this vitally essential task, we are over-hasty in embarking on a State or nationalized undertaking, it will be simply putting the cart before the horse. It will be like trying to build a building before any foundations are laid, and moreover, it will be like putting down a deal wood box on a nest of termites. The enterprises will disappear in no time.

Sir, in fact, nationalization is just one method of achieving our Socialist goals, which are:

(1) the greatest welfare of the greatest number of people;

(2) social and economic justice;

(3) maximum output;

(4) maximum welfare and security; and

(5) equal opportunity for every national.

Sir, where and when nationalization can achieve these goals better than other techniques can, we shall have nationalization. But where these goals can be achieved better by other means, we shall employ those other means without fear. Socialism and nationalization in every field are not equivalent terms in our thinking, any longer. I repeat — by taking this stand, we do not abandon Socialism.

6. *Increased Revenues and Savings*

While we should and will use loans from abroad to supplement our own resources in further developing our country, we cannot and will not continue a policy of deficit financing which can only have the effect of pushing prices higher. There is no magic way of obtaining better irrigation, roads, schools, hospitals without paying for them. Inflation is the most unjust, and most disruptive way of paying for them. We simply must find a better way — and we shall. Improved efficiency and lower costs in our public enterprises will help. So will expanded rice, timber, minerals and other exports. So will improved efficiency in our tax enforcement and administration. So will continued expansion of the economy in general. So will increased savings on the part of the public.

Our anti-inflation efforts thus far, as I pointed out earlier, have been reasonably successful. This has been due in large part to the very large volume of imports for private use for which we have made provision in licences and foreign exchange. The lower prices which now prevail for cotton textiles and for a number of other items, including those which have been restored to O.G.L., testify to this. However, recent months have seen sizeable price increases in a number of locally produced items, which must be dealt with by other means. But most important of all, Government's fiscal and monetary policies must be geared to moderate prices. This means that we must avoid unnecessary expenditures and cost, and that we must obtain sufficient revenues and earnings to finance our necessary outlays without resorting to large scale deficit financing.

To some extent, therefore, we shall have to increase certain tax rates, or introduce new tax measures. In doing this, we shall be careful not to impose restraint on, or damage necessary incentives to, investment and useful production.

7. *Hard Work*

One other policy must receive mention here. We have been too easy-going, too leisurely, too lackadaisical in our approach to the task of rehabilitation and development of our country.

There must be an end to this attitude of indifference — of putting off till tomorrow what can and should be done today. These backlogs must be caught up with. Current work must be done currently. Full hours must be put in. Extra time should be put in, if necessary to catch up or keep up with the work load. The Government is here to serve the people. They must be served.

Mr. Speaker, Sir, I therefore, with your permission, call upon all Government offices and departments, officers and clerks alike, to buckle down to hard, serious work. Take pride in your performance, and your achievements. Do not tolerate indifference, sloth, or inefficiency in others, or in yourself. Do your part in making your office or department outstanding for orderliness, efficiency and good reputation. No matter how high or how low your station, no matter how humble your appointed task, you can do your part towards making your Government a more effective servant of the people, and towards building a better, stronger and happier Burma. Let us all work together toward this common goal.

Our Goal and Our Interim Programme

(Published by Superintendent, Government Printing and Stationery, Rangoon, 1953)

Our Goal

The ultimate objective of the Government and the people of the Union of Burma, as embodied in the Constitution, is to create a democratic Socialist State. We must never lose sight of the fact that the Socialist State we wish to establish implies neither Communism nor State Capitalism. The tyranny and oppression inherent in these two systems must not be allowed in the Socialist State that we wish to create. The new era that is our goal must not have a gilded exterior hiding a mass of evils underneath. We must devise a way of life which will combine full political rights, economic security and a high standard of living with spiritual uplift and morality. It must not only guarantee religious freedom but also provide opportunity for each individual to exercise his religious rights and beliefs at the highest possible plane. Socialism in Burma must be fully harmonized with the religious beliefs and cultural background and heritage of the people.

This new era must not be imposed on the people from above. It must be set up by the people themselves and must harmonize with their culture, religious beliefs and traditions.

This new era is none other than the Pyidawtha State to which we have pledged ourselves.

Interim Programme

The measures we must carry out in the interim period while marching towards the above objective must comprise: —

(1) Fundamental Rights;
(2) Democratic Stability;
(3) Social Measures; and
(4) Economic Measures.

(1) *Fundamental Rights*

Chapter II of the Constitution of the Union of Burma guarantees the following fundamental rights: —

(a) Rights of Equality.

(b) Sights of Freedom.

(c) Rights relating to Religion.

(d) Cultural and Educational Rights.

(e) Economic Rights.

(f) Rights in relation to Criminal Law.

(g) Rights to Constitutional Remedies.

The fundamental rights of the citizen of the Union of Burma are thus provided for by the Constitution itself.

(2) *Democratic Stability*

Democracy is our most treasured possession. Hatred of oppression and love of liberty being a human passion, man has always endeavoured to free himself from all forms of repression. On achieving liberty he has attempted to safeguard it by many means. In his struggles, man has ultimately discovered that the best safeguard against repression and slavery is a system of Government where the rulers derive power from the people and not *vice versa*. This is the system known as democracy.

A review of world history will, however, show that after this valued treasure had been acquired, it had often been eclipsed by other political systems. It had not always held sway after its introduction in any particular country. We have learnt that few people realize that democracy cannot get stabilized merely by their accepting it in principle and establishing it as a form of Government. They forget that sustained effort is necessary in order to maintain its sway, and that is why at the end of every periodic election people are inclined to sit back, regard their responsibility to have ended and leave all power and responsibility in the hands of Government. When a Government on its part finds itself exercising the powers and responsibilities entrusted to it without criticism or opposition from the people, its morale declines and it will ultimately betray its trust. When such betrayal takes place, democracy itself comes to an end.

Human history also shows that at times the people themselves have betrayed the trust, and this is of even greater significance. Such betrayal stems from a lack of understanding of the fundamentals of democracy. It occurs when people begin to think that democracy implies the right to do as one wills and without any restraint. When such beliefs creep in and the people forget their own responsibilities, democracy degenerates into mob-rule.

There have also been occasions in history when the very liberties guaranteed by the democratic system have led to the downfall of democracy itself. Thus, for example, though both Spain and Germany were democratic states before Franco and Hitler, the misuse by them of the democratic freedom which they enjoyed ended in the destruction of democracy itself in these two countries and led to the setting up of dictatorships. There are many in this country who are also similarly mad for power and will not hesitate to take advantage of the democratic liberties they enjoy because ours also is a democratic State. We must ever be on our guard against the misuse of democratic freedom by such power-crazy individuals.

Government has taken full cognizance of these dangers facing our democratic system. As a first step towards safeguarding the Union of Burma against such dangers, we have introduced the Democratic Administration Act and are now in the process of implementing it. This act can be of great assistance in stabilizing democracy. Under this Act, power must be delegated right down to the village. By such delegation —

(a) people throughout the Union will be obliged to assume responsibility for administering their own affairs;

(b) with the shouldering of such responsibility, the people themselves will become a fortress against the misuse of power either by Government or by the power-crazy individuals;

(c) all the problems of the *ludu* will be solved more expeditiously and more satisfactorily than if the solution were to depend on the pressing of a button at the centre; and

(d) the exercise of democratic rights and responsibilities in every village unit will lead to the creation of large numbers of people with a firm belief in democracy and with experience and knowledge of the responsibilities of democracy.

While implementing the above measures, in order to prevent the power-crazy individuals from destroying democracy by taking advantage of democratic rights, we must —

(a) make the words "Defend Democracy at All Cost" ring in the ears of the people at all times;

(b) watch closely every movement of the power-crazy individuals;

(c) take action commensurate with its severity against all criminal attempt to destroy our form of democracy; and

(d) ensure that the love of one's own country and a passion for democracy infiltrates into every corner of the country.

(3) *Social Measures*

Throughout the period of our struggle for independence, we had pledged ourselves to creating a new country and a new social order. We must however admit that though six years have passed since we achieved Independence, we have not yet succeeded in creating the new social order to which we had pledged ourselves. No one can deny that six years is too short a period to create such an order. But there are other reasons which had prevented us from achieving our objective in this respect. They are: —

(a) all our attentions have been devoted towards safeguarding the Union against the multi-coloured insurgents rather than to carrying out measures for social advancement;

(b) the administrative machinery which we had inherited at the time of Independence was designed not for promoting welfare but for the preservation of law and order and for the collection of revenue;

(c) the insurgents had destroyed whatever little capital equipment we possessed for promoting welfare; the number of skilled personnel for carrying out the welfare scheme had also been extremely limited;

(d) the gap between our capital and personnel needs for creating the new order that is our dream and their actual availability is tremendous and our efforts had to be concentrated on creating the necessary equipment and personnel.

As soon however as insurgency was brought sufficiently under control, we turned our attention towards welfare activities. The following measures adopted during the Pyidawtha Conference held in August 1952 and which are now in the process of implementation are the results of this effort: —

(a) New Educational Plan.

(b) New Health Plan.

(c) Transport and Communications Plan.

(d) Housing and Rehabilitation Plan.

(e) Discretionary Grants Plan.

But we are not satisfied with just these measures of social welfare. It is for these reasons that we had obtained the assistance of the United Nations for drawing up a Comprehensive Plan of Social Development. This Plan has now been completed and is being implemented through a new Directorate of Social Welfare.

In all our planning for social welfare, our emphasis has been more on the welfare of the villagers than on that of the urban population. Before Independence, almost all measures of social welfare were designed for the benefit of urban communities. Thus measures relating to education, public roads, electric supply, water supply and public health catered for the needs of the 15 per cent who lived in urban areas rather than the needs of the 85 per cent who lived in the villages.

We are now in the process of reversing completely this state of affairs. The Mass Education Plan, Health Plan, Environmental Sanitation Plan, Discretionary Grant, Union Electrification Plan, etc., emphasize the welfare of the rural population. They form the spearhead of our efforts in this direction.

(4) *Economic Measures*

Since the time we have assumed responsibility for the Government of the country, economic measures in two categories, *viz.* (a) for the benefit of the cultivators and (b) for the benefit of traders and commercial interests, have been adopted and put into effect. The following measures for the benefit of the cultivators have already been adopted: —

(i) limiting rent to twice the land revenue;

(ii) transferring to the cultivator the right to let out tenancies;

(iii) fixing the price of paddy at K 285 per 100 baskets and thus preventing profiteers from buying paddy from the cultivators at low prices;

(iv) relief of agricultural indebtedness;

(v) the Land Nationalization Act;

(vi) raising agricultural loans from K 900,000 to K 50 millions; and

(vii) setting up an Agricultural Bank.

These are interim economic measures for the benefit of the cultivators. Because of these measures, the economic conditions of the cultivators have improved very considerably. Thus, while cultivators before Independence had to cultivate their land at a loss of K 1 to 7 per acre, they can now make a profit of up to K 46 per acre.

But we do not propose to rest content with just these measures. Accordingly, a Five-Year Agricultural Plan was adopted during the Pyidawtha Conference, 1952, and an Agricultural and Rural Development Corporation has been set up to carry out the objectives of the Plan. Under this Plan, we propose to achieve within five years: —

(a) economic self-sufficiency;

(b) export of rice up to the pre-war limit; and

(c) irrigation projects which will give great benefit to the *ludu*.

In regard to traders and commercial interests, we have taken the following measures: —

(a) allowing 60 per cent of all import licences to nationals; and

(b) a Five-Year Co-operative Plan adopted and approved at the Co-operative Convention held in January, 1951.

In the field of commerce, however, though we had allowed 60 per cent of all import licences to national interests, they have not derived full benefit therefrom because of —

(a) lack of financial resources;

(b) lack of experience in the field of commerce, due to the extremely short period during which nationals have taken an active part therein; and

(c) lack of direct contacts and connections with suppliers abroad.

In the field of industries also not much success had been achieved because of —

(a) lack of financial resources;

(b) lack of experience both in the administrative and in the technical fields; and

(c) lack of opportunities for acquiring knowledge and experience.

These deficiencies have received our constant attention. Whereas, in the past, we had considered that allowing 60 per cent of all import licences to nationals, and Government taking the initiative in regard to the Co-operative Plan, would remedy all these defects, now we know that these measures are not sufficient. We are now convinced that if we confine our efforts to just these two measures our people will soon degenerate into agents and stooges of foreign commercial interests.

There is one other reason why the above measures are no longer sufficient. The Economic Target Resolution adopted by the Pyidawtha Conference, 1952, provides for a capital formation programme of K 7,50 crores by 1958–59. Of these, K 5,10 crores fall within the public sector, and we have established the Industrial Development Corporation, the Mineral Resources Development Corporation, the Housing Board and other similar organizations by Acts of Parliament for achieving this programme. The balance of K 2,40 crores must be achieved by the private sector. It is the responsibility of the private individual to achieve this part of total capital formation programme.

The achievement of the programme as a whole, therefore, requires that we institute measures which will enable the people in the private sector to carry out their part of the development programme. It is necessary that we encourage them to make this investment and to equip themselves for carrying out this programme. Government must give them full assistance in carrying it out in an orderly manner.

We have accordingly directed the Economic and Social Board to submit detailed recommendations for achieving the above objectives in the fields both of commerce and industry and for overcoming the difficulties and handicaps under which our nationals labour at present. In making its recommendations, the Economic and Social Board shall bear the following guiding principles in mind: —

Guiding Principles. —

(a) In the Socialist State that we shall create, commerce and industry must serve the interest of the *ludu* and the *ludu* must not serve the interest of commerce and industry. It must not be a system which will extract the maximum profit from the *ludu* without any regard for its welfare and interest.

(b) Ultimately, all trade and industry must be organized into public corporations and co-operatives controlled and managed by the representatives of the workers and consumers.

In making its recommendations to Government, the Economic and Social Board will suggest means by which the seed will be planted for the control of all key means of production and distribution to pass ultimately into the hands of the consumers and workers.

Priorities. — The aid and assistance to be granted by Government shall be given in accordance with the following priority: —

(a) In the field or industrial production, to —
   (i) State enterprises;
   (ii) Joint ventures between Government and nationals and/or foreigners;
   (iii) Co-operative Societies;
   (iv) Public limited liability companies owned solely by nationals;
   (v) Public limited liability companies in which nationals own at least 60 per cent of the shares;
   (vi) Private companies;
   (vii) Partnerships; and
   (viii) Individuals.

(b) In the field of commerce and distribution, to —
   (i) State enterprises;
   (ii) Joint ventures between Government and nationals;
   (iii) Co-operative Societies;
   (iv) Public limited liability companies owned wholly by nationals;
   (v) Public limited liability companies of which at least 60 per cent of the shares are owned by nationals;
   (vi) Private companies;
   (vii) Partnerships; and
   (viii) Individuals.

We believe that there are many nationals who have the capacity to make a significant contribution to economic development, but cannot now do so due to lack of opportunities. We are now in a position to help these nationals whose talents have so far lain hidden. The Economic and Social Board will therefore explore means and submit detailed recommendations to Government for rendering maximum assistance to nationals in the fields both of commerce and industry.

Resolution of the Fourth Meeting of Union of Burma Economic and Social Board

THE ECONOMIC AND SOCIAL BOARD, in compliance with the instructions of Government to formulate detailed recommendations for the encouragement of national interest in the fields both of commerce and trade and of industrial production, for overcoming the serious handicaps and other disadvantages under which they labour at present, and for ensuring that ultimately all trade and industry is organized into public corporations controlled and operated by the consumers and workers through their representatives,

RECOMMENDS as follows: —

Commerce and Trade

Internal and External Trade

1. As the first step in carrying out the policies and objectives laid down in the Government Statement on "Our Goal and Our Interim Programme," the goods and commodities produced in Burma and entering into the internal distributive trade and into export should be classified by categories and by agencies which handle them as in Appendix I to this Resolution.

2. A Commerce Development Corporation, on the lines of the Mineral Resources Development Corporation, the Industrial Development Corporation and the Agricultural and Rural Development Corporation, should be set up as the main Agency of Government for carrying out the objectives in the Government Statement.

Import Trade

3. The principal reasons for the present unsatisfactory condition of national importers and their failure to benefit from the majority of all import licences being issued to them are: —

(a) lack of direct contacts with foreign manufacturers and suppliers;
(b) lack of specializations;
(c) lack of adequate organization and knowledge and experience in the fields of commerce and trade;
(d) lack of adequate financial resources.

Direct Contacts and Specialization

4. These defects can be remedied only through the efforts of importers themselves. In order to encourage them to establish direct contacts and specialize in certain selected lines, and discourage the present practice of using licences simply for placing orders with foreign firms acting as local agents of manufacturers and suppliers, *it is recommended* that the categories of importers in respect of whom priorities are established in the Government Statement on "Our Objective and Our Interim Programme" should be further divided into the two following categories: —

(i) those who have established direct contacts with foreign manufacturers and suppliers, and specialize in certain selected lines of commodities; and

(ii) those who rely mainly or entirely on foreign local agents.

Licences to those in category (i) *for commodities in respect of which they have established direct contacts and for commodities in which they specialize* should be issued liberally and under near-OGL conditions. These firms should be allowed to import such commodities even if the total volume is in excess of the limit now set in terms of paid-up capital.

5. There are however certain commodities in respect of which patent and other rights prevent their import except through established Agents, most of whom are foreigners. While licences should be issued in adequate volume during the interim period for such of these commodities as are in high demand, *it is recommended* that the Ministry of Commerce make detailed enquiries in respect of such commodities and Agencies with a view to diverting such goods and commodities to the maximum degree possible into national agency channels. The foreign Agencies concerned should also be encouraged to form themselves into partnerships with national interests.

6. *It is further recommended* that Government strengthen its staff of Commercial Attachés in its foreign embassies and legations, and entrust to them the task of assisting national importers to establish direct contacts with foreign manufacturers and suppliers, and of finding substitutes for commodities covered by patent and other trade rights which are now imported solely by foreign wholesalers, and who do not fall in with Government's policy of entering into partnership with national interests.

Adequate Organization and Methods

7. *It is recommended* that Government institute measures for examining the organization and business methods adopted in firms who are given import licences liberally as recommended above, with the object of advising them on how to improve their organization and put their business on a sound, technical basis. Government should develop a staff of technical inspectors and advisors well versed in business methods and techniques, recruiting qualified personnel from abroad for an initial period.

8. *It is further recommended* that Government establish a Polytechnic for teaching modern business methods and techniques and business accountancy, or at least a

course of instruction at the University of Rangoon following the latest available knowledge and syllabus in these fields.

Financial Assistance

9. *It is recommended* that Government render financial assistance to national importers and business interests in two different ways: —

(i) by setting up joint Corporations with indigenous interests, to which Government will subscribe a large part of the capital, exercising the minimum control consistent with the public interest in the Board of Management. Such Corporations will thus be free from financial handicaps, and share the credit and prestige of Government in establishing foreign contacts and securing adequate business; and

(ii) by issuing straight loans at low rates of interest. The issue of loans should however be subject to the enterprise satisfying certain minimum conditions of efficiency in business organization, and to the contacts it has established being such as to ensure a regular flow of business. The loans must be adequately secured.

Protecting the Interest of the Ludu

10. Government's paramount purpose must be to protect the interest of the *ludu,* and to ensure that the assistance given to individuals and firms does not operate against the welfare and interest of the *ludu. It is recommended* that this purpose be achieved in two stages: —

(i) by ensuring that during the interim period, at the same time as the measures recommended above for encouraging national commercial interests are carried out, the interest of the *ludu* is fully protected; and

(ii) by ensuring that ultimately all industry and trade is organized into public corporations controlled and operated by the producers and consumers through their representatives, and into Co-operative Societies.

11. In order to achieve the objective set out in (i) above, Government must ensure that the goods and commodities which the *ludu* needs are available to them at reasonable prices — prices which do not contain more than a fair share of profit for the middle-man. The most effective means of achieving this is to ensure that the goods and commodities which the *ludu* needs are imported in adequate quantities, and are not controlled and monopolized by a few import houses. The present policy of basing the volume of imports to be licensed on past imports is inadequate, and *it is therefore recommended* that the volume of imports to be licensed in future years be determined in accordance with the following principles: —

Imported commodities can from an economic point of view be divided into (a) commodities the demand for which will increase very little even though total expenditures on consumer goods and services rise substantially, e.g., commodities with an income elasticity of demand less than unity; and (b) commodities with an income elasticity of demand greater than unity. Following this economic principle, all imported goods under licence should further be classified into three groups, according to whether (i) the demand for them will increase by about the same percentage as consumer expenditures as a whole, or (ii) by a somewhat greater percentage, or (iii) by a much greater percentage. The volume of imports to be licensed in each category should then be determined in accordance with these percentages.

Appendix II to this Resolution shows the classification of goods under licence in these three categories, and illustrates the manner in which the volume of imports can be regulated in accordance with the economic principle described above. Thus, the demand for goods in the first category is expected to increase in the same proportion as the increase in consumer expenditures — which during 1953–54 is estimated at 10 per cent. The total value of licences for the import of goods in this category during 1953–54 should therefore be 10 per cent above the 1952–53 level. Similarly, in the case of goods in the second category, the total value of licences to be issued during 1953–54 should be 15 per cent above the 1952–53 level, and 20 per cent in respect of commodities in the third category.

The above is a rough measure, but will, it is hoped achieve the objective of ensuring that the import of goods in each category will bear adequate relation to demand. If goods are available in adequate quantities, prices will also remain at a fair and stable level.

12. In regard to (ii), strict adherence to the priorities laid down in the Statement on "Our Goal and Our Interim Programme" should ensure that gradually all import and commercial houses are organized either as public corporations in which Government and the small shareholder own the major interest, or as cooperatives. This policy thus lays the seed for the ultimate control by the *ludu* and their representatives of all distributive trade.

Industrial Production

13. In the field of production, there are many industries and enterprises which will not be covered by the Government's programme of industrialization, but the setting up of which should prove both profitable to those who set them up and be of benefit to the economy and to the masses. There are many nationals who have the imagination and the technical and managerial ability to set up these enterprises and operate them efficiently and at a profit, but are unable to do so due to lack of adequate finance, and to some extent of precise information as to possible industries which can be set up and operated profitably. *It is therefore recommended* that Government through the Industrial Development Corporation and the Mineral Resources Development Corporation grant liberal loans at low rates of interest to those national interests who are willing to set up industries and give proof of their ability to organize them and run them as profitable enterprises. The amount of loan should be determined in each case by the needs of the industry itself, and must be secured by mortgaging to Government the machinery and other immovable properties acquired for the industry. Other conditions should be discussed with each individual concern and worked out mutually.

14. *It is recommended* that Government should consider joint ventures with individuals or groups of individuals in suitable cases.

15. *It is further recommended* that Government publish at an early date a list of

industries which on the basis of expert studies appear to be feasible and profitable, and make them available to private enterprises. These studies should be developed to the stage of preliminary economic and technical justification, and it should be the duty of the person or persons desirous of setting up the industries to develop detailed plans and specifications with the help of experts. Government should be prepared to assist individuals financially in the preparation of detailed plans, but the grant of loans for establishing the industries should be conditional on the undertaking and completion of such detailed plans and specifications for each industry.

16. *Government should also consider* the following measures for encouraging industries: —

(a) the setting up of a Tariff Board with powers to determine the amount and duration of protection that should be granted to each industry so as to safeguard it against unfair competition from imported goods, recommend variations in export duties to suit changing conditions, and other allied matters;

(b) facilitating the import of raw materials and other goods necessary for the operation of industries; and

(c) granting tax-relief for an initial period.

17. *Government should also be prepared to consider* such other measures of assistance as may be proved to be necessary in respect of particular industries and enterprises.

APPENDIX 1

Interim Economic Measures

PRODUCTION

Industrial Production	Mineral Production	Forest Production	Agricultural Production
Foreign Individual. National Individual. Co-operatives. Joint Ventures with (a) Nationals and (b) Foreigns. Industrial Development Corporation.	Foreign Individual. National Individual. Joint Ventures with (a) Nationals and (b) Foreigns. Mineral Resources Development Corporation.	Other Forest Products — Co-operatives, National, Foreign. Timber Milling — State, Co-operatives, National, Foreign. Forest Rehabilitation.	Land Nationalization. Five-Year Agricultural Development Plan.

DISTRIBUTION

Import	Export	Internal Distribution
Foreign Individual. National Individual. Co-operatives. Joint Ventures with (a) Nationals and (b) Foreigns. State.	Foreign Individual. National Individual. Co-operatives. Joint Ventures with (a) Nationals and (b) Foreigns. State.	Foreign Individual. National Individual. Co-operatives. Joint Ventures with (a) Nationals and (b) Foreigns. State.

APPENDIX·2

Category I. — About the same percentage as consumer expenditures as a whole: —

1. Foodstuffs —
   (1) Wheat flour
   (2) Sago and tapioca.
   (3) Vermicelli.
   (4) Fruits and vegetables, all sorts other than canned or bottled including coconuts, garlics, onions.
   (5) Seeds, all sorts (other than coffee-seeds).
   (6) Betelnuts.
   (7) Spices, all sorts.
   (8) Ghee.
   (9) Gambier.
2. Chinese raw medicines.
3. Black tea.
4. Boots, shoes and sandals.

Category II. — By a somewhat greater percentage than consumer expenditures as a whole: —

1. Textiles.
2. Provisions of all sorts — assessable under BCT items Nos. 2, 4, 5, 10, 13, 18, 19, 27, 28, 39, 40, 68, 305, 306, and coffee-seeds (in case of coffee unroasted from India only and roasted from other countries).
3. Cigarettes and pipe tobacco.
4. Household goods —
   (1) Earthenware, Chinaware and porcelainware, all sorts.
   (2) Enamelled Ironware.
   (3) Glassware including empty glass bottles.
   (4) Lampware and Stove, parts and accessories thereof.
   (5) Cutlery of all sorts.
   (6) Tableware, all sorts (plated).
   (7) Stainless steel utensils.
5. Miscellaneous licences —
   (1) Toys and games, all sorts.
   (2) Plastic goods.
   (3) Glass bangles, glass beads and false pearls.
   (4) Cork and cork manufactures.
   (5) Smokers' requisites (BCT 308).
   (6) Buttons, all sorts.
   (7) Imitation jewellery.
   (8) Imitation gold and silver thread, lametta, spangles and articles of like nature of whatever metal made (BCT 135).
   (9) Polishers for boots and shoes.
   (10) Umbrellas and umbrella fittings.
6. Radio and radiograms —
   (1) Wireless receiving sets
   (2) Radiograms
   (3) Sound equipment all sorts including tape and wire recorders
   (4) Domestic refrigerators
   (5) Air conditioning units

   } and spare parts and accessories thereof.

7. Manufactures of leather and artificial leather and articles of clothing.
8. Paper and stationery not under O.G.L.

Category III. — By a much greater percentage than consumer expenditures as a whole: —

1. Watches and clocks, spare parts and accessories thereof.

2. Musical instruments, spare parts and accessories thereof.
3. Liquor —
   (1) Whiskey.
   (2) Brandy.
   (3) Gin.
   (4) Shamshoo.
   (5) Liqueurs.
   (6) Rum.
   (7) Bitters.
   (8) Wine.
   (9) Beer.
   (10) Ale.
   (11) Porter.
   (12) Cider.
   (13) Stout.
4. Perfumery — Perfumes, spirits and toilet articles.
5. Fountain pens — Spare parts and accessories thereof.

Capital Goods. — In general, capital goods are now under O.G.L. The one class of capital goods which is under licence is that included within import licence group, General Hardware Goods. This group includes the following: —

Hardware and cutlery, all sorts, including imitation jewellery.
Polishes and compositions, all sorts.
Methylated spirit.
Brushes and brooms.
Oil cloth, floor cloth, including linoleum and leather cloth.
Tarpaulins and canvas, all sorts.
Instruments, apparatus and appliances, all sorts.
Pipes and hoses made of rubber, plastic and canvas.
Cotton yarn waste.
Coir yarn, coir fibre.
Rubber goods, excluding rubber toys.
Compounds falling under (BCT 319).
Campcots, holdalls.
Plastic sheets.

The most important of these for the development programme are those in italics. Since ample imports of these items should be assured, licences for the group should be increased by 25 per cent above 1952–53 imports.

Investment Policy Statement
Council of Ministers
Government of the Union of Burma

In response to various enquiries which have been received from potential investors concerning Government's policy with respect to private investment, Government of the Union of Burma clarifies the policy as follows: —

1. Government recognizes the contribution which productive private investment, both domestic and foreign, can make to the economic and social progress of the country, and to the long-term investment programme for increasing output, productivity and raising living standards. The managerial and technical skill which accompany private foreign investment are also welcome.

2. The only economic activities closed to private investors are major public utilities and munitions manufacture. Enterprises for the extraction of natural resources may be conducted by private enterprise in partnership or under contract with the Government.

3. There are many opportunities for profitable private investment in the Union of Burma in a variety of manufacturing activities, in processing, in distributive and service enterprises. Such opportunities will multiply as the nation's development programme proceeds. The country is rich in undeveloped natural resources; its people are quick to learn new skills; transport, electric power, and other facilities are being steadily improved; and the market for goods and services of all types is expanding rapidly.

4. To encourage suitable private investment the Government will —

   (a) Guarantee new enterprises against nationalization for an agreed period which will normally be not less than ten years. In appropriate cases Government may also consider extending similar guarantees in the case of extension or modernization of existing enterprises.

   (b) Pay fair and equitable compensation in the event of nationalization after the agreed period of time. Government is agreeable to discuss with prospective investors the basis on which such compensation shall be computed.

   (c) Make foreign exchange available for the import of necessary raw materials, repair and replacement equipment, other operational requirements, and interest on foreign loans.

   (d) Render protection and support of industry by tariff or other means.

(e) In the case of foreign investment, permit the remittance of current earnings or dividends and allow for the repatriation of investment over a reasonable period of time.

(f) In the case of domestic investors, grant loans in suitable cases through the appropriate Government agencies.

5. In addition to the above, Government has under consideration special incentives for new investment, such as allowance of accelerated amortization of plant and equipment. Suggestions from prospective investors concerning other incentives especially important in individual cases are welcome.

6. In concluding arrangements to encourage private investment along the lines indicated above, Government will be guided by such criteria as: —

(a) Will the enterprise assist in developing Burma's economy on a sound and balanced economic basis?

(b) Will the enterprise contribute towards increasing the productivity of the Burmese economy and towards raising living standards?

(c) Will the enterprise provide essential goods and services for public and private consumption?

(d) Will the enterprise increase Burma's export potential or reduce Burma's needs for imports which can be produced economically within the country?

7. In all cases of foreign investment, it is expected that maximum employment opportunities will be afforded to citizens of the Union and that training programmes will be instituted designed to qualify citizens of the Union for technical, supervisory and executive positions.

8. Further enquiries from prospective investors should be addressed to the Ministry of Industry or Ministry of Mines as appropriate. Government will be glad to make available to prospective investors the information at its disposal concerning investment opportunities in the Union of Burma. These opportunities have been explored by engineering surveys and related economic studies which establish the technical and economic feasibility of ventures in many fields, and provide a valuable basis for detailed planning by private interests contemplating new investment.

9. Appended hereto are some of the fields in which private investment, both domestic and foreign, is especially desired.

By Order,

WIN PE,

Rangoon, 8th June 1955   Secretary to the Council of Ministers

APPENDIX

Industrials

(1) Agricultural Tools.

(2) Aluminium Ware manufacture.

(3) Asbestos and Cement Products manufacture.*

* Denotes industries suitable for joint ventures.

(4) Bricks and Tiles manufacture.*
(5) Carbide Plant.
(6) Compressed and Liquidified gases.
(7) Cooperage.
(8) Cordage, Rope and Twine.
(9) Cotton and other Textiles, Spinning, Weaving, Bleaching, Finishing and Printing.
(10) Dairy Products manufacture.
(11) Deep Sea Fishing.*
(12) Edible Oil extraction and refining.*
(13) Electrical Goods manufacture.*
(14) Fertilizer manufacture.
(15) Fruit and Meat Canning, Packing and Preservation.
(16) Furniture making.
(17) Glass manufacture.*
(18) Gypsum products.
(19) Hardware and Cutlery.
(20) Hosiery manufacture.
(21) Lac and Tung Oil extraction.
(22) Leather tanning and Leather Goods manufacture.
(23) Light Steel Products manufacture.
(24) Limestone quarrying and continuous Lime burning.
(25) Machine shops.
(26) Paints, Varnish and Enamels manufacture.*

(27) Plastic Powders and Plastic Goods manufacture.
(28) Plumbing Accessories.
(29) Pottery and Ceramics.
(30) Pulp and Paper manufacture.*
(31) Rice Milling industry.
(32) Rubber Products manufacture.*
(33) Salt manufacture by solar and vacuum evaporation.
(34) Sand, gravel and aggregate production.
(35) Saw Milling industry.
(36) Sea Food processing industry.
(37) Ship building.*
(38) Silk weaving with power looms.
(39) Small Tools, Screws and Bolts manufacture.
(40) Starch manufacture.
(41) Stationery goods including manufacture of fountains, slates and pencils.
(42) Structural Steel fabrication.
(43) Soap manufacture.
(44) Surgical Cotton and Surgical Goods manufacture.*
(45) Tobacco Products manufacture.
(46) Veneer and Plywood manufacture.
(47) Wood distillation.

Mining Industries (To be developed by partnership or under contract with the Government)

(1) Antimony.
(2) Bauxite.
(3) Chromium.
(4) Coal, Coke and by-products.
(5) Columbite.
(6) Copper.
(7) Gems and precious stones.
(8) Graphite.
(9) Gypsum.
(10) Iron Ores.

(11) Lead and Silver.
(12) Manganese.
(13) Mica.
(14) Petroleum and Natural Gas.
(15) Pyrites.
(16) Radio Active Minerals.
(17) Sulphur.
(18) Tin.
(19) Tungsten.
(20) Zinc.

Service Industries

(1) Hotels and Restaurants.

(2) Tourism.

*Denotes industries suitable for joint ventures.

The Union of Burma
Investment Act, 1959

(*Act No. XLI of 1959*)

It is hereby enacted as follows: —

1. (1) This Act may be called the Union of Burma Investment Act, 1959.

   (2) It shall be extended to the whole of the Union of Burma and shall apply to manufacturing, mining, fishing, tourism, processing of agricultural, forest, mineral or fishery products and such other economic activities as may, by rules, be bought under the Act.

   (3) It shall come into force on such date as the President of the Union may, by notification, appoint.

2. In this Act, unless the context otherwise requires —

   (a) "Committee" means the Union of Burma Investment Committee appointed under section 3;

   (b) "Promotor" means a person whether citizen of the Union of Burma or a foreigner submitting an investment proposal to the Committee;

   (c) "Proposal" means an application submitted by a promotor to the Committee for approval of an intended investment;

   (d) "Permit" means the document by which approval by the Committee of an investment proposal is expressed;

   (e) "Foreign Capital" means property imported into the Union of Burma by a person who is a foreigner for the purpose of investment in business enterprise under the provisions of this Act and the property accrued therefrom which is invested as aforesaid including the following: —

       (i) foreign exchange;

       (ii) machinery, equipment, instruments, machinery components and spare parts and other similar property for investment;

       (iii) intangible rights such as licences, trade marks, patent rights and similar rights;

       (iv) reinvested profits which would have been entitled to be transferred abroad.

   (f) "Investor" means a promotor whose proposal has been approved.

3. A Committee to be called the Union of Burma Investment Committee shall be appointed by the President.

4. (1) The Committee shall consider every proposal submitted to it and may, without prejudice to any law in force, approve such proposal as is in conformity with national economic interests.

(2) The Committee shall, on a proposal being approved, issue to an investor a permit in such Form as the President may, by rule, prescribe.

5. Investors shall be granted all or any of the following: —

(a) facilitated allocation of foreign currency for import of necessary raw and auxiliary materials;

(b) right to bring into the Union of Burma under contract to be approved by the Committee, managers, technicians and skilled workers who are foreigners; provided that such investors have an approved training and promotions programme for the advancement of Burmese nationals;

(c) right to pay income-tax on behalf of foreign employees and such payment to be considered as business expenses for the purposes of income-tax assessment;

(d) right to reserve for reinvestment accrued profits of the business and exemption from income-tax on such profits if they are re-invested within one year after reserve is made;

(e) right to accelerate depreciation at the rate fixed by the Committee to the extent of the original investment for the purpose of taxation;

(f) complete exemption from income-tax for the first three years and partial exemption for an additional period, if any, to be determined by the Committee;

(g) exemption from Customs Duty on machinery for the first three years;

(h) exemption from Customs Duty on raw materials for the first three years' commercial production.

6. (1) No enterprise shall be nationalized for a period of 10 years from the date on which commercial operation commences; provided that the President may, after taking into consideration public interests and the magnitude of investment, extend the aforesaid period up to twenty years.

(2) If an enterprise having foreign capital as a part of its investment is nationalized, compensation for the foreign capital so invested shall be paid accordingly in the foreign currency in which such investment was made.

(3) The following shall be transferable abroad in the foreign currency concerned at the prevailing official rate of exchange: —

(a) profits after taxation accruing to the investors of foreign capital subsequent to the date of commencement of this Act;

(b) the net share of the investor of foreign capital in the proceeds of the sale of assets, in partial or complete liquidation of an enterprise;

(c) the proceeds of the sale of part or all of the foreign capital in a going enterprise; and

(d) the principal and interest on foreign loans.

7. The Committee may, at any time, require a promoter submitting an investment proposal to furnish in the manner specified by the Committee, such evidence or information as the Committee may deem necessary for the purpose of this Act.

8. The Committee shall have powers to take any step as may be deemed necessary or appropriate for the discharge of its functions.

9. The Committee shall supply information, advice and assistance to promoters and other interested persons for planning and implementing investment projects.

10. The Committee shall hear complaints, if any, from investors regarding failure to receive prompt and equitable treatment with reference to the provisions of the Act and take necessary action in respect thereof.

11. The Committee shall, from time to time, recommend to the Government, measures and actions necessary to facilitate and promote private investment, domestic and foreign.

12. (1) The President may, by notification, make rules consistent with this Act for the purpose of carrying out the provisions of this Act.

(2) Without prejudice to the generality of the powers mentioned in sub-section (1), such rules shall prescribe the following matters: —

(a) membership, tenure, rules of procedure and quorum of the Committee;

(b) prescription of form of the Permit under section 4, sub-section (2);

(c) determination of procedure for presentation of evidence or information under section 7;

(d) signing of contracts and other documents on behalf of the Committee;

(e) other matters to be prescribed by rule under this Act.

Membership of Important Working Economic Committees, as of 1955–56

*(From "Annual Report of the Union of Burma Economic and Social Board"
for the year 1955–56)*

EXPERT SUB-COMMITTEE

(1) Executive Secretary, Economic and Social Board (*Chairman*)
(2) Deputy Prime Minister's (National Economy) Secretary
(3) Deputy Prime Minister's (Social Affairs) Secretary
(4) Secretary, Ministry of Finance & Revenue
(5) Secretary, Ministry of National Planning
(6) Secretary, Ministry of Trade Development
(7) Secretary, Ministry of Industry
(8) Secretary, Ministry of Agriculture & Forests
(9) Secretary, Ministry of Mines
(10) Director, Foreign Exchange Control Sub-Committee
(11) Chairman, Union Bank of Burma
(12) General Manager, Union Bank of Burma
(13) Mr. J. S. Furnivall, Planning Adviser to GUB
(14) Chief Technical Adviser to GUB (TAMS)
(15) General Manager, Robert R. Nathan Associates, Inc.,
　　　Consulting Economists to GUB

FOREIGN EXCHANGE CONTROL SUB-COMMITTEE (DEPUTIES)

(1) Executive Secretary, Economic and Social Board (*Chairman*)
(2) Secretary, Ministry of Finance and Revenue
(3) Secretary, Ministry of National Planning
(4) Secretary, Ministry of Trade Development
(5) Secretary, Ministry of Supply
(6) Director, F.E.C. Sub-Committee

EXECUTIVE SUB-COMMITTEE FOR ANTI-INFLATIONARY MEASURES

(1) Sithu U Tin Maung (Executive Secretary, E.&S.Bd.) (*Chairman*)
(2) Thray Sithu U Chan Tha (Chairman, B.S.I. Administration Board)
(3) Thray Sithu U Win Pe (Prime Minister's Secretary)

(4) Sithu U Kyaw Nyun (Secretary, Ministry of Finance & Revenue)
(5) Thiri-pyan-chi U Mo Myit (Secretary, Ministry of National Planning)
(6) Sithu U Ba Khin (Chairman, S.A.M.B.)

STANDING COMMITTEE FOR SUPERVISION AND COORDINATION

(1) Sithu U Tin Maung (Executive Secretary, E&S.Bd.) (*Chairman*)
(2) Thray Sithu U Chan Tha (Chairman, B.S.I. Administration Board)
(3) Thray Sithu U Win Pe (Prime Minister's Secretary)
(4) Sithu U Kyaw Nyun (Secretary, Ministry of Finance & Revenue)
(5) Thiri–pyan-chi U Mo Myit (Secretary, Ministry of National Planning)
(6) Sithu U Ba Khin (Chairman, S.A.M.B.)

Subjects Considered by the Economic and Social Board at Its Meetings Held in the Financial Year 1955–56

(Excluding Review of Proposed Employment of Foreign Experts and Firms, and Administrative Matters)

(From "Annual Report of the Union of Burma Economic and Social Board" for the year 1955–56)

OCTOBER 14, 1955

1. Report on fixation of buying price of rice for 1955–56 crops.
2. Agreement for joint venture for radio assembly plant between E. K. Cole Ltd. of England and I.D.C.
3. Contract for construction of Balu Chaung hydroelectric project.

NOVEMBER 10, 1955

1. Procedure for negotiating with World Bank Mission. (Extraordinary meeting)

JANUARY 5, 1956

1. Election of a new member from amongst the Ministers to the vacancy caused by the resignation of the Hon'ble U Win, Minister for National Planning and Religious Affairs in the Sub-Committee of F.E.C.
2. Procurement of materials required for reconstruction of Sittang Railway Bridge.
3. Securing of approval of the Controller of Foreign Exchange prior to opening of letter of credit for goods ordered under O.G.L.
4. Procurement of Tugs and barges by SAMB under Japanese Reparation Agreement.
5. Issuance of License to B.O.C. (Burma Ltd. 1954) for oil exploration in Delta region.
6. Allotment of K 70 lakhs for construction of Union Central Medical Centre buildings.

7. Economic History Research.
8. Erection of Soap Factory by Unilever Company Limited, in the Union of Burma.
9. Proposed Joint Venture between the GUB and Glaxo Laboratories Limited, for Milk Food Packaging Industry in the Union of Burma.
10. Erection of Paper Factory in the Union of Burma.
11. Setting up of Joint Venture Company between GUB and Mawchi Mines Company Limited.
12. Tourist Development Programme submitted by the Ministry of National Planning.

FEBRUARY 4, 1956

1. B.O.C. license for oil exploration in Delta.
2. 3-Year economic plan.
3. Israeli Economic Mission to Burma.
4. Co-ordination with Research Centre for Southern Asia on the social implications of industrialization.
5. Expansion of cement factory at Thayetmyo.
6. Purchase of machinery for expansion of Spinning and Weaving Factory from Republic of China.
7. Erection of heavy vehicle repair shops at Mandalay by Ministry of Defense.
8. Erection of Electric Motor and electric goods manufacturing plant.
9. Joint Venture between Glaxo Laboratories Ltd. and GUB for milk food packaging industry in Burma.
10. Supplementary Grant of funds for Industrial Development Corporation.
11. Dissolution of 1954 Purchase Mission.
12. Revised budget Estimates for Electricity Supply Board.

FEBRUARY 13, 1956

1. Issuance of license to B.O.C. (Burma Ltd. 1954) for exploration of oil in Delta region.
2. Supplementary Grant of funds for Industrial Development Corporation.
3. Revised Budget Estimates for E.S.B. for 1955–56.
4. Proposed Joint Venture between the GUB and Glaxo Laboratories Limited, Milk Food Packaging Industry in the Union of Burma.
5. Proposed Agreement between U. S. and Union of Burma on U. S. Foreign Investment Guarantee Insurance.
6. Erection of factory for manufacturing Electric Motors and electrical apparatus in the Union of Burma.

MAY 2, 1956

1. Proposed joint venture between the GUB and Glaxo Laboratories Ltd. for Milk Food packaging industry.
2. Erection of factory for manufacturing electric motors and electrical apparatus.
3. Agreement between United States and Burma on U. S. Foreign Investment Insurance Programme.

4. U. S. food surplus donation programme.
5. Purchase of generators, boilers, and other machinery for R.E.S.B. on deferred payment system.
6. Agreement between Yugoslavia and Burma for exchange of Yugoslav textiles for Burmese cotton.
7. Proposed joint venture between Ishikawa and G.U.B. for Spinning and Weaving Factory.
8. Proposed joint venture for construction of a cement silo and packing plant.
9. Extension of functions of Union School Construction Board till the end of financial year 1955–56.
10. Revision of freight rates and formation of Freight Rate Commission.
11. Rice prices and milling rates, Fixation of buying price of rice and milling rate for 1955–56.

JULY 2, 1956

1. Construction of U.C.M.C. buildings.
2. Proposed establishment of a Joint Israel Burmese contracting firm to carry out construction works and also to establish building materials industry.
3. Proposed Joint Venture between Anglo-Burma Tin Co., and G.U.B.
4. Participation of the Union of Burma in the International Finance Corporation as a member.
5. 1955–56 Programme for imports.

AUGUST 16, 1956

1. Four-Year Economic Development Programme.

AUGUST 25, 1956

1. Four-Year Economic Development Programme.

Robert R. Nathan
Associates Field Staff in Burma,
September 1951–February 1959

General Manager–Chief Economist
Everett E. Hagen, 1951–53
Louis J. Walinsky, 1953–59

Deputy General Manager and
Deputy Chief Economist
Irving Swerdlow, 1955–57
Haldore Hanson, 1957–59

Agricultural Economist
Shigeharu Takahashi, 1952–59
Garret Roelofs, 1957–58

Industrial Economist
Donald Wilhelm, 1952–53
Saul Nelson, 1953–55
Vincent Rock, 1955–57
Glen L. Parker, 1957–59

Fiscal Economist
(the late) *Karl Arndt*, 1953–54
Robert Bangs, 1955–56
John Lindeman, 1956–59

Progress Reports Analyst
Irving Swerdlow, 1954–55
John Coppock, 1955–57

Management Economist
Murray Bryce, 1957–59

National Income Economist
Irving Licht, 1952–56

Economic Statistician
Abner Hurwitz, 1957–59

Marketing Consultant
David Chewning, 1958–59

Rice Market Intelligence Advisor
Frank Lowenstein, 1957–59

Economic Analyst
Peter Vukasin, 1951–53

Tax Consultant
Richard Musgrave, 1954,* 1958*

Transportation Rates Consultant
Philip Locklin, 1954*

Chief Secretary and (from 1955)
Administrative Officer
Marie Caudle Chan, 1953–59

Administrative Officer
Alex Tatischeff, 1953–55

Home Office Burma Desk Specialist
A. J. Creshkoff, 1953–59

* Short-term special assignments.

	1938–39	1947–48	1949–50	1951–52
Gross domestic product, K crores, in 1947–48 prices	494.5	355.7	303.8	363.6
Gross domestic product, 1938–39 = 100, in constant prices	100.	72.	61.	74.
Output per capita, 1938–39 = 100, in constant prices	100.	66.	55.	64.
Consumption per capita, 1938–39 = 100, in constant prices	100.	84.	63.	68.
Index of agricultural production, 1937–41 av. = 100	100.	77.	65.	75.
Paddy production, million long tons	8.05	5.54	4.69	5.25
Timber extraction, thousand cubic tons				
Teak	453.	n.a.	37.9	141.3
Non-teak	502.	n.a.	160.8	348.5
Electric power consumption				
Million KWH: Rangoon				
Other				
Railway freight, million ton-miles	579. [a]	238.7	n.a.	151.9
Exports, in K crores, total	47.8	74.4	65.7	110.
Rice	22.3	58.4	57.6	81.
Non-rice agricultural commodities	3.2	7.3	6.5	14.4
Timber	3.3	6.5	1.3	5.6
Minerals	5.7	2.2	1.3	6.9
Other	1.33	[b]	[b]	1.4
Rice and rice products exports, million long tons	3.3			1.16
Imports, in K crores, total	21.6	57.2	43.2	82.
Consumer goods	16.8	45.	36.	67.
Capital goods	4.8	12.2	7.2	14.
Private	n.a.	n.a.	n.a.	68.
Government	n.a.	n.a.	n.a.	14.
Public capital expenditures, K crores[e]	n.a.	n.a.	n.a.	n.a.
Gross capital formation, total, K crores	17.8	60.2	31.9	74.3
Gross capital formation as per cent of G.D.P.	12.2	16.9	10.2	18.2
Internal Government debt, K crores[e]				8.
Privately held money supply, K crores				62.
Foreign exchange reserves, total, K crores				95.8
Monetary reserves, K crores				87.
Consumer price index, Rangoon, 1958 = 100[f]	29.6[g]	89.6	104.5	94.8

Source: Except as noted, all data are from the *Economic Survey of Burma,* 1951–60 inclusive. Data for any given year are revised for latest issue of the Survey in which they appear. Data for private and government imports, internal government debt, monetary reserves and consumer price index are from *Selected Economic Indicators,* Central Statistical and Economics Department, November 1960.

Selected Economic Indicators in Burma, 1938-39 to 1959-60

1952–53	1953–54	1954–55	1955–56	1956–57	1957–58	1958–59	1959–60
389.9	404.6	429.4	445.	490.8	469.8	502.	530.8
79.	82.	87.	90.	99.	95.	102.	107.
68.	70.	73.	75.	81.	77.	81.	85.
72.	72.	72.	72.	86.	79.	80.	85.
84.	79.	79.	81.	93.	82.	95.	100.
5.74	5.53	5.71	5.78	6.36	5.49	6.49	6.92
132.7	118.3	127.1	165.4	178.1	187.1	237.2	332.9
368.9	559.5	598.2	593.6	704.9	689.7	597.7	611.
		54.9	63.2	77.5	101.3	118.8	138.1
		16.0	22.7	30.	35.	37.4	45.
219.	271.8	322.3	324.3	344.3	339.8	389.8	405.5
130.	107.	112.	117.	118.	89.	99.	117.
102.	84.	84.5	87.7	89.5	66.3	71.6	82.7
15.9	14.9	16.8	15.7	15.8	11.7	15.2	17.8
3.2	2.7	3.1	5.6	6.6	5.9	6.4	8.6
6.1	3.6	5.7	6.5	4.9	3.7	4.0	3.6
2.2	1.4	1.5	1.9	1.5	1.6	2.0	3.0
1.22	1.27	1.63	1.93	2.0	1.46	1.61	2.1
88.	95.	91.	87.	132.	111.	96.	125.0
72.	70.	62.	58.	94.	63.	62.	89.0
16.	24.	29.	29.	39.	48.	33.	36.0
70.	78.	68.	49.	75.	58.	47.	80.0
18.	17. [b]	23.	38.	57.	53.	49.	45.0
32.7	63.8	53.9	50.9	46.4[d]	50.	51.3	
87.6	101.1	100.9	93.0	108.5	118.3	112.5	108.5
19.	22.	21.	18.1	20.	22.3	20.	18.5
10.	30.	81.	111.	102.	119.	148.	128.
81.	89.	109.	136.	121.	130.	157.	150.
119.	76.	51.6	74.6	56.	68.2	78.5	76.7
104.	64.	38.	59.	43.	54.	60.8	58.3
92.5	88.3	91.8	97.9	103.9	100.	88.9	100.

a. 1937–41 average.
b. Included in non-rice agricultural commodities.
c. *A Review of Economic Planning in Burma*, C.S.E.D., October 1959, Table 18.
d. Net of K 5.6 crores of Japanese reparations.
e. Includes Government-guaranteed securities.
f. Data are for calendar years; thus, figure shown in 1947–48 column is for 1948.
g. 1941.

INDEX

A

A.B.C. rice mill, 284
A.B.P.O. *See* All Burma Peasants'
  Organization
A.F.P.F.L. *See* Anti-Fascist People's
  Freedom League
A.F.P.F.L. Government, 565–68
Accountability, political, 603
Adler, John H., 592, 592n
Administration. *See* Public administration
Administrative divisions, 107
Ady, Peter, 57, 77n
Agricultural and Rural Development
  Corporation, 217, 318; *see also* Agricultural
  Resources Development Corporation
  (former name) and Land Resources
  Development Corporation *(later name)*
Agricultural and Rural Development Five-
  Year Plan. *See* Five-Year Agricultural Plan
Agricultural Bank. *See* State Agricultural Bank
Agricultural Marketing Board. *See* State
  Agricultural Marketing Board
Agricultural Research Institute, 294–95
Agricultural Resources Development Corpora-
  tion, 449, 450, 551(t); *see also (later names)*
  Agricultural and Rural Development
  Corporation *and* Land Resources Development Corporation
Agricultural Training Institute (Pyinmina),
  295, 403
Agriculture: acreage, 41(t); agrarian reform,
  76; in British Burma, 18–22; cooperatives,
  52, 53, 280, 292(t); credit program, 289–91;
  farm mechanization, 271(t), 288–89;
  financial data, 221(t), 270–71(t), 352,
  353–55(t); Five-Year Plan, 98–99, 148, 269,
  286, 288, 294; and foreign specialists,
  550(t); future needs, 578, 581; goals and
  achievements, 362(t); and industrialization
  policy, 496; and insurrection, 382; and
  K.T.A. reports, 91, 135–38; labor, 33(t),
  35(t), 392, 401; loans, 42–43, 123, 289–91,
  292(t); and Ne Win Government, 263; pre-
  World War II, 33(t), 35(t), 40–43, 41(t),
  42n, 49(t), 339(t); in private sector, 338–
  40; production statistics, 41(t), 339(t),
  372(t), 660–61(t); products, 5; program
  implementation, 269–98, 338–40; progress report, 616; proposals for expansion, 600; and
  Pyidawtha Conference, 98–99; and taxation,
  423–24; tenant farmers, 20, 35(t), 40–41,
  293–94; and Two-Year Plan, 64–65; *see also
  specific products*

Agriculturists Loans Act, 290, 292(t)
Ahlone rice wharf, 285, 286(t)
Aid. *See* Foreign aid
Air France, 47n
Airways: and K.T.A. reports, 94(t), 135(t),
  141, 141(t); program implementation,
  333–34
Airways Board. *See* Union of Burma Airways
  Board
Akyab, 48, 139, 144
Alaungsithu Dam, 286
Alcohol production, 304
Alexander, John, 287, 530
All Burma Peasants' Organization, 97, 123,
  241, 280, 500
Amber production, 44
American consultants, 76–77, 80, 83–86; dis-
  missal of, 262–63; *see also* K.T.A. Compre-
  hensive Report; K.T.A. Preliminary Report;
  Knappen Tippetts Abbett Engineering Co;
  Pierce Management, Inc.; Robert R.
  Nathan Associates, Inc.
Andrus, J. Russell, 7n, 10n, 18n, 38n, 40,
  41(t), 47, 48n, 50(t), 51, 53
Anglo-Burma Tin Company, 324
Anti-Fascist People's Freedom League
  (A.F.P.F.L.), 58–60, 264n; and A.B.P.O.,
  500; and capitalism, 502; Central Executive
  Committee, 466; and Communists, 75; and
  elections of 1956, 203; and elections of 1960,
  264–65; and public administration,
  486–87; and Pyidaungsu Government, 574;
  and Pyidawtha Conference, 97; split, 224–26,
  236, 237–49, 568; third Congress of, 239–41
Apparel. *See* Footwear and apparel
Appleby, Paul, 489n
Applied Research Institute, 529, 529(t), 531(t)
Arakan area, 3, 4, 5, 17–18; fleet, 332–33;
  proposed Arakanese state, 246, 573n, 575
Arakanese (people), 4, 13, 19
Area, 3, 5
Army: investment program, 261; officers in,
  256n; *see also* Ne Win Government
Athins (political associations), 26
Attlee, Clement, 60
Aung Gyi, Brigadier, 253, 254, 261, 577
Aung San, U, 29, 58, 64, 64n; assassination
  of, 60
Aviation. *See* Airways
Awza (status), 395–96

B

B.S.I. *See* Bureau of Special Investigation
Ba Khin, U, 205n, 250, 450, 654
Ba Nyein, U, 487
Ba San, U, 177n, 195, 212
Ba Sein, U, 328, 328n, 386, 387
Ba Swe, U: and A.F.P.F.L., 241, 245–48, 264n;
  and Burma Revolutionary Party, 29; as
  Chairman of M.R.D.C., 450; differences
  with U Nu, 225; and Economic Planning

Ba Swe, U (*Contd.*)
Board, 178; and Economic and Social Board, 125; and elections of 1960, 264–65; and Finance Subcommittee, 171; and Four-Year Plan, 536; and governmental powers, 488; as Minister of Mines, 181n, 324, 325; prime-ministership, 207n, 210, 217–24, 219n; and Soviet "gift" projects, 534, 538
Ba Tun, U, 326, 450
Bagawta Chaung hydroelectric project, 65–66
Balance of payments, 165, 167, 171, 175, 363; *see also* Foreign exchange
Balu Chaung hydroelectric project, 139(t), 148, 263, 327, 329n, 330, 404, 513–14
Balwant Singh, 326
Bamboo industry: production and labor statistics, 344(t), 346(t); pulp and paper mill, 144, 144(t), 319, 320; uses of bamboo, 43
Banking, 52–53; and agricultural loans, 290–91, 292(t); financial data, 355(t); and Government financial policy, 497; and K.T.A. Comprehensive Report, 124; labor, 33(t), 37; private firms, 343–45; State Commercial Bank, 226, 343, 450; Union Bank, 162, 165, 167–68, 219, 226, 239, 330; village banks, 124, 290–91, 292(t); *see also* Finance; State Agricultural Bank
Barnes, D. P., 402n
Barrington, James, 182, 245, 517
Barter trade, 168, 169–70(t), 174, 176, 179, 181, 186, 187, 188–91(t), 201, 209, 210, 212, 216, 236, 250, 272, 375, 438, 498–99, 534–39
Basch, Dr. Antonin, 169, 540-42
Bassein, 48
Battle Act, 177, 209, 210
Bawdwin Mines, 6, 13, 22, 44n, 45, 142, 323, 325, 342
Birth rate, 38
Black, Eugene R., 612, 612n
Boards, state-owned, 425–28, 629; financial data, 426(t), 444–45(t); and foreign specialists, 549, 551(t); *see also* Public administration; Public enterprises; *and specific boards*
Bombay-Burmah Trading Company, 17, 319, 320, 350, 493
Brewery plants, 312, 313(t)
Brick and Tile Factory Board, 128, 308
Brick and tile plant, 300–01, 302(t), 308–10, 312, 313–14(t)
British Burmah Petroleum Company, 45
British economists, recommendations of (1951), 76–78
British Imperial Preference System, 498
British rule in Burma, 17–30, 56–60, 478; *see also* United Kingdom
British White Paper (1945), 58
Buddhism, 12–13, 13n; in British Burma, 20; Buddhist strengths, 105, 105n; and Burmese

society, 389–90; Fifth Buddhist Synod, 21, 21n; and monarchy, 10–11; proposal to make state religion, 573n, 574; repugnance to taking life, 394
Budget: annual, problems of, 432–47; budget review, 243, 438–42; military, 436; of public sector, 414(t), 445(t); rise of expenditures, 375–76; of Union Government, 412–15, 413(t), 416(t), 422(t), 432–34, 444–46(t); *see also* Capital expenditures
Building construction. *See* Construction industry
Building materials, imports of, 192(t), 212(t)
Bulganin, Nikolai A., 194, 508(t), 519, 534
Bulgaria, 499
"Bullinger Pool," 27–28
Burchardt, F. A., 77n
Bureau of Special Investigation, 219, 225, 386–87, 455
Burma: British rule, 17–30, 57–60; Constitution of 1937, 29; Constitution of 1947, 61–63; during 1950s, 565–78; geography, 3–6; independence, 56–61; insurrection starting 1948, 68–69; Japanese occupation, 56–59; pre-British Burma, 10–16; pre-World War II economy, 31–55; separation from India, 29
Burma Airways. *See* Union of Burma Airways Board
Burma Corporation, 45, 142, 324, 325, 342
Burma Journalists Association, 516
Burma Labour Gazette, 37
Burma Mines Ltd., 324
Burma Railways. *See* Union of Burma Railways Board
Burma Revolutionary Party, 29
Burmah Oil Company, 45, 142, 162, 324, 325
Burmanization policy, 72, 493–95, 560, 573, 580–81
Burmans (people): characteristics, 7–9; in labor force, 35(t); *see also* Burmese society
Burmese society: effects of Eight-Year Program, 368; problems of cultural adaptation, 388–99
Butler, Sir Spencer Harcourt, 24

C

C.S.M.B. *See* Civil Supplies Management Board
Cady, John F., 7n, 10n, 18n, 58n
Canadian experts, 220, 462
Capital budget. *See* Budget; Capital expenditures
Capital expenditures: actual (1938–60), 660–61(t); actual vs. programed (1954–60), 444(t), 445(t); for agriculture, 270, 270–71(t), 286(t); in budget (1952–60), 413(t), 444(t); in budget, public sector (1952–60), 414(t), 445(t); budget demands (1954–55), 158–60; budget review, 440–42; and capital formation, 376; by economic sector, 353–54(t); financial sources, 415–20, 417(t), 419(t); in forestry, 320; for industry, 300–

02(t); for irrigation, 270, 270–71(t); reduction of, 411; *see also* Four-Year Plan

Capital formation: and capital expenditures, 376; economic goals, 111–15, 114(t); financial sources, 117–20; G.D.P. ratio, 361(t), 660–61(t); net, 359(t), 361(t); in other underdeveloped countries, 596, 598–600; pre-World War II, 31–32; private sector, 114(t), 336–38, 356, 358(t), 359, 361(t); public sector, 358(t), 361(t); total, 356, 358–59(t), 359–60, 361(t), 660–61

Capital goods, imports of, 212–13(t), 251, 660–61(t)

Caretaker government. *See* Ne Win Government

Cattle. *See* Livestock

Cement industry, 209, 302(t), 312, 313(t); Thayetmyo mill, 301, 492, 501

Central Purchasing Board, 155n, 206n

Central Statistical and Economics Department, 126, 154, 203, 560

Ceylon: study mission to, 317; trade with, 50(t), 138, 161, 164, 169–70(t), 176, 238–39, 516

Chan Tha, U, 205n, 574n, 653, 654

Chauk oil fields, 142, 323

Chemicals industry: establishments, 344(t), 346(t); fertilizer, 138, 144, 144(t), 145; labor, 33(t), 344(t), 346(t); production statistics, 344(t), 346(t), 348(t)

Chettyars (money lenders), 22, 23, 52–53, 58, 293

Children: health centers, 365(t); in labor force, 368

Chillies, 41(t)

China: border problems with, 262, 384–85, 577; credits in, 204n; loans from, 545, 577; technicians from, 403, 548(t), 549; trade with, 13–14, 50(t), 168, 169(t), 170(t), 176, 188(t), 191(t), 498–99, 516, 520

Chindwin River, 326n

Chinese, in labor force, 35(t), 393

Chins (people), 4, 6n, 13

Chit, U, 453

Chit Maung, Thakin, 245, 451n

Chit Pe, U, 249, 489, 574n

Chou En Lai, 545

Civil Affairs Service, 59

Civil Aviation Board, 448

Civil Aviation Department, 529(t)

Civil disorder. *See* Insurrection

Civil service, in British Burma, 23; *see also* Government service

Civil Supplies Management Board, 449; and cotton mill, 455, financial data, 426(t); and Government finance, 122; and imports, 172, 181n, 186, 187–92, 194, 195, 208, 218, 443, 492, 518; inventory position, 458; and management, 462; monopolies, 204, 205, 206n; and pricing, 197, 232, 310, 426, 501; and retail distribution, 231, 258, 425–26

"Clean" faction (Nu-Tin group), 245–48, 264n

Coal industry: and Eight-Year Program, 362(t); imports, 188(t); Kalewa coal fields, 6, 65, 93, 142, 142(t), 324, 326

Coconuts, 271(t), 280

Coke imports, 188(t)

Cold War, and U. S. foreign aid, 605–06

Collis, Maurice, 57, 57n, 59

Colombo Plan, 402, 403, 462, 532n, 542, 548(t), 549

Colonial Government. *See* British rule in Burma

Commerce Development Corporation, 157, 158, 426(t), 427, 449

Committee of Deputies, 435

Committee of Experts, 178–80, 187, 211, 220, 243n, 453, 466

Communications: financial data, 221(t), 352, 353–54(t); and foreign specialists, 550(t); and K.T.A. reports, 94(t), 135(t), 140–42, 141(t), 331; pre-World War II, 48; program, 330–31, 335; and Pyidawtha Conference, 100–01; and specialized manpower, 401; radio facilities, 48; telegraph system, 48; and Two-Year Plan, 66; *see also* Telephone systems

Communism: in independent Burma, 60–61; and insurrection beginning 1948, 68–69; U Nu on Communists, 75

Constitution: of 1937, 29; of 1947, 61–63

Construction industry: capital expenditures, 221(t), 353–54(t); highways, 334; private, 345; *see also* Housing

Consultants, foreign. *See* American consultants; British economists

Consumer goods: imports, 186ff, 198(t), 212–13(t), 251, 660–61(t); purchases, goals (1938–60), 112(t), 113

Consumer prices. *See* Prices, consumer

Consumption, attitude toward, 389

Cooley amendment, 523–24

Cooperatives: agricultural, 52, 53, 280, 292(t); and foreign specialists, 550(t)

Cost of living. *See* Prices, consumer

Cottage and home industry, 46, 301(t), 344(t), 345–47, 348(t)

Cottage and Small-Scale Industry Board, 313(t)

Cotton industry: financial data, 271(t), 302(t), 313–14(t); improvement program, 276, 362(t); labor, 46(t), 47; production statistics, 41(t), 339(t); spinning and weaving mill, 301, 310–12

Cotton purchase agreement with U. S., 197, 202, 519, 522–24

Cotton Spinning and Weaving Board, 128, 311

Cotton textiles processing agreements, 197n, 202–03, 205, 522–24

Council of Economic Advisors, 166–67, 168

Council of Ministers, 647–49

Credit: agricultural, 289–91; Government policy, 497–98; and K.T.A. Comprehensive

Credit (*Contd.*)
  Report, 124; sources of, 52–53; *see also*
    Loans, domestic
Credits: and China, 204n; and Czechoslovakia,
    204n, 206, 218; and U.S.S.R., 204n, 206,
    218, 411, 417(t), 539(t); and West
    Germany, 218, 301; *see also* Loans to Burma
Crime: and Ne Win Government, 259; *see
    also* Law and order; Security
Culture. *See* Burmese society
Currency. *See* Money
Customs revenue, 51, 51(t), 122(t), 422(t),
    444(t)
Cutch, export of, 43
Czechoslovakia: credits in, 204n, 206, 218;
    trade with, 169–70(t), 186, 188(t), 191(t),
    498–99

D

Dayan, General, 243
De Mag (German firm), 305
Death rate, 9n, 38, 103
Debt: internal Government, 266, 660–61(t);
    net change in national debt, 444(t); repay-
    ments to India, 175, 419(t), 420
Decision making, 395–96, 487–88
Defense expenditures. *See under* Security
Defense Ministry, 321
Defense Services Institute, 261, 576–77
Delta, 3–4, 5, 288–89
Democratization, 107–08; *see also* Public
    administration
Demuth Mission, 540
Dentists, number of, 39
Department of Agriculture, 124, 277, 280, 281,
    288, 294, 297
Development corporations, 111, 449, 450, 549,
    551(t); *see also individual development
    corporations*
Development loan (U. S.). *See under* Loans
    to Burma
Development Program. *See* Eight-Year
    Development Program
Diesel locomotives, 141(t)
Diesel-powered generating plants, 139(t), 140,
    326, 327
Dillon, Secretary, 303
Diseases, 38, 103; *see also* Health
Divers, Brigadier Sydney, 249
Dock strike (1930), 27
Doctors, number of, 39, 103, 365(t)
Domestic currency. *See* Money
Domestic finance: and K.T.A. Comprehensive
    Report, 111–25, 112(t), 114(t), 122(t);
    potentials for sturdier, 420–30; and total
    economic policy, 497; *see also* Finance;
    Gross domestic product
Donnison, F. S. V., 478n
Dorman-Smith, Governor, 58, 59, 59n
Draft General Contract Agreement, 536–38
Drugs. *See* Pharmaceuticals industry

Dry Zone, 4, 5, 40, 286, 288, 289, 327
Dyarchy system, 26

E

East Germany, trade with Burma, 188(t),
    191(t)
Economic and Social Board, 465–76; aid to
    private sector, 337; and brick and tile plant,
    309; and capital program, 171–73, 211n;
    and Council of Economic Advisors, 166n;
    establishment, 154, 377, 465; and foreign
    exchange, 167; and foreign loans, 177; and
    foreign specialists, 551(t); and Four-Year
    Plan, 211n, 221, 226; fourth meeting,
    resolution of, 640–44; and import program,
    187; and "Interim" program, 156–57, 157n;
    and joint ventures, 197; and K.T.A. Com-
    prehensive Report, 125, 126, 155; liquida-
    tion, 237; meetings, attendance at, 489;
    meetings held in 1955–56, 655–57; and
    Ministry of National Planning, 237n, 465,
    475; and planning, 154n; and policy-making,
    220, 223–24; and progress reporting, 158;
    and public enterprises, 455–56, 459, 460–62;
    reorganization, 178; and Robert R. Nathan
    Associates, 126, 555, 558–59; and Soviet
    "gift" projects, 536; and Union of Burma
    Airways, 172n; *see also* National Planning
    Commission
Economic consultants. *See* American con-
    sultants; British economists; Robert R.
    Nathan Associates, Inc.
Economic development: future of Burma,
    565–83; goals, 111–16, 362(t); theoretical
    aspects, 584–604; *see also* Eight-Year
    Development Program
"Economic Indicators" (publication), 203n
Economic planning. *See* Planning
Economic Planning Board, 178, 180
Economic policy: consultants' recommenda-
    tions, 121–25; importance of, 590–91; and
    Ne Win Government, 254–66; problems of,
    491–506
Economists, foreign. *See* American consultants;
    British economists; Robert R. Nathan As-
    sociates, Inc.
Education, 8–9; agricultural, 294–95; in
    British Burma, 20–21, 25; and Burmese
    society, 391–92; and Eight-Year Program,
    365–66, 366(t); expenditures, 52; and
    foreign specialists, 550–51(t); improvement,
    601–02; pre-World War II, 39–40; and
    Pyidawtha Conference, 105–06; specialized,
    402–04, 603–04; teacher training, 403–04
Eight-Year Development Program, 80–149;
    administration of, 125–29, 465–76; budget-
    ing problems, 432–47; and Burma's further
    economic development, 565–83; and
    Burmese culture, 388–99; changes in, 148–
    49; characteristics of, 146–47; cultural
    adaptation problems, 388–99; defects in

basic plan, 371–81; economic policy problems,491–506; finance problems, 409–31; financing of, 117–21; and foreign aid policy, 605–12; foreign aid problems, 507–45; Government influence on, 147; implementation by fiscal years, 153–266; implementation by major sectors and projects, 269–368; implementation problems, 369–562; and insurrection, 377, 382–87; K.T.A. Preliminary Report, 83–95; manpower problems, 129–33, 400–08; Prime Minister's report on, 620–21; priorities, 217–36, 503–04; programing problems, 432–47; public administration problems, 477–90; and public enterprises, 448–64; Pyidawtha Conference, 96–109; results of, 352–68, 357(t), 362(t); Robert R. Nathan Associates, role of, 555–62; significance for other countries, 584–604; technical assistance problems, 546–62; *see also* K.T.A. Comprehensive Report

Eisenhower, Dwight D., 520–21

Elections: of April 1956, 203; of March 1960, 264–65

Electric power: capacity, 328–29(t); consumption, 328–29(t), 660–61(t); financial data, 352, 353(t), 354(t); and K.T.A. reports, 93, 139–40; production, 328–29(t), 362(t); program implementation, 326–30; projects, 65–66, 139, 139(t), 140, 148, 263, 326, 327, 329n, 330, 404, 513–14; and Two-Year Plan, 65–66

Electricity Supply Board, 65, 448–49, 542n; and budget authorization, 441; coke and coal supplies, 181n; and dieselization scheme, 140; and electrical appliances, 187; financial data, 426(t); financing and rate structure, 243; and foreign specialists, 551(t); management, 220, 460, 461, 462; operations, 427; and power program, 326–28; Rangoon Electricity Supply Board, 140, 326, 327, 426(t), 438, 448, 452, 460

Elephants, as motive power, 44, 321

Ellerman-Arakan rice mill, 284

Employment: employer-employee relationship, 393; industrial, 33(t), 46–47, 46(t), 344–48(t); *see also* Labor

Engineering consultants. *See* American consultants; Knappen Tippetts Abbett Engineering Co.

Engineering establishments, 46(t)

England. *See* United Kingdom

Entrepreneurial capacity, 591–92

Establishments, industrial, 46(t), 344–48(t)

Evans Medical Ltd., 263, 464

Exchange rate, of rupee and kyat, 36n

Excises and excise duties, 51(t), 122(t), 123, 422(t)

Executive Subcommittee for the Implementation of Anti-Inflation Measures, 205, 208, 653–54

Expenditures: current, 51(t), 413–14(t), 444–45(t); defense, 51(t), 221(t), 421, 436; farm, 42; Government, 51(t), 52, 413(t), 416(t), 444(t), 446(t); household, 390n; *see also* Capital expenditures

Exports: agricultural, 660–61(t); Government policy, 498; minerals, 44, 660–61(t); petroleum, 44; rice, 660–61(t) (*see also* Rice exports); teak, 5–6, 321(t), 322; timber, 660–61(t); total, 48–51, 49(t), 50(t); *see also* Foreign trade

Extension service, 294–95

F

F.A.O. *See* Food and Agriculture Organization

Factories, number of, 46(t), 344–48(t)

Families: income of urban, 38(t); status of, 12

Farming. *See* Agriculture

Fertilizer, chemical, 138, 144, 144(t), 145

Fifth Buddhist Synod (1871), 21, 21n

Finance: data for 1938–60, 660–61(t); economic policy, 590–91; fiscal, monetary, and credit policy, 497–98; inflation, domestic, 185–216; fiscal year 1953–54, 153–62; fiscal year 1954–55, 163–84; fiscal year 1955–56, 185–216; fiscal year 1956–57, 217–36; fiscal year 1957–58, 237–51; fiscal years 1958–59 and 1959–60, 252–66; and K.T.A. reports, 90–91, 93, 111–25, 112(t), 114(t), 122(t); and Ne Win Government, 252–66, 412; pre-World War II, 31–32, 51–53, 51(t); price policies, 499–502; Prime Minister's report on, 617–18; private sector, 336, 502–03; problems of, 371–76, 409–31; public manufacturing enterprises, 302(t), 311–12, 313–14(t); results of Eight-Year Program, 352–64; *see also* Banking; Budget; Capital expenditures; Capital formation; Debt; Expenditures; Foreign aid; Foreign exchange; Gross domestic product; Investment; Loans; Revenue; Taxes

Firewood, 43

Fishing industry, 5, 43; financial data, 355(t); labor, 33(t); program implementation, 318–19; and Two-Year Plan, 66

"Five Wise Men," 574–75

Five-Year Agricultural Plan, 98–99, 148, 269, 286, 288, 294

Flotilla, 47, 140–41, 332

Food and Agriculture Organization (F.A.O.), 282, 375, 548(t), 550

Foods: crops, 5; labor, 33(t), 344(t), 346(t); imports, 189(t), 191–92(t), 198(t), 212(t); production, 344(t), 346(t), 348(t)

Footwear and apparel, 344(t), 346(t), 348(t)

Ford Foundation, 295n, 403–04, 455, 462, 549

Foreign aid: and Ne Win Government, 262, 530–33, 544, 576; problems, 507–45; weaknesses of policy, 605–12; *see also* Foreign technicians and specialists; International Monetary Fund; Loans to Burma;

Foreign aid (*Contd.*)
P.L. 480 programs; Reparations, Japanese; World Bank; *and under individual countries*
Foreign consultants. *See* American consultants; British economists
Foreign exchange: and capital budget, 440–41; crisis in, 163–84, 363, 411; fiscal year 1953–54, 161–62, 165; fiscal year 1954–55, 163–84, 410–11; fiscal year 1955–56, 212, 226; fiscal year 1956–57, 236; fiscal year 1957–58, 239, 251; fiscal year 1958–59, 266; and Four-Year Plan, 220; and Government economic policy, 498–99; and K.T.A. Comprehensive Report, 119, 124–25; and Ne Win Government, 255; reserves (1938–60), 660–61(t); transactions and reserves (1952–60), 165(t); *see also* Foreign trade
Foreign Exchange Control Subcommittee, 195, 653
Foreign investment in Burma, 53–54, 349–51
Foreign loans. *See* Loans to Burma
Foreign technicians and specialists: morale of, 407; Russian, 538–39, 542; sources, 402, 548–52, 548(t), 607–08; Task Forces, 237, 241–42, 249, 462, 474; utilization of, 263, 402, 403–04, 548–52, 550–51(t); *see also* American Consultants; British economists
Foreign trade: balance of payments, 165, 167, 171, 175, 363; with dollar countries, 188–89(t); and Economic and Social Board, 156, 640; enterprises, 449; by fiscal years, 660–61(t); fiscal year 1953–54, 156, 161–62; fiscal year 1954–55, 163–84; fiscal year 1955–56, 185–216; fiscal year 1956–57, 219–20, 226, 236; fiscal year 1957–58, 238–39, 250–51; fiscal years 1958–59 and 1959–60, 266; and Government economic policy, 498–99; import program, 442–43; joint venture trading companies, 207, 219, 226, 227, 249, 258, 343, 581; and K.T.A. Comprehensive Report, 118–19, 124; and Ne Win Government, 258, 262; pre-World War II, 13–14, 33(t), 48–51, 49–50(t); private, 342–43; tripartite arrangement, 516; *see also* Barter trade; Exports; Foreign exchange; Imports; *and under individual countries*
Forest industries, 144(t), 145; *see also* Wood products
Forestry, 43–44; financial data, 122(t), 221(t), 353–55(t); goals and achievements, 362(t); and insurrection, 340, 382–83; labor, 33(t); and Ne Win Government, 263; in private sector, 340; program implementation, 319–23, 340; and Two-Year Plan, 66; *see also* Teak industry; Timber industry
Four-Year Plan, 204, 210–11, 220–23, 226–29, 232–34, 571–72, 626–28; and anti-inflation subcommittee, 208; and L.A.P.C. report, 269; and projects, 211n, 527–28, 530; and public capital investment, 430; and rice

storage, 282; and Soviet "gift" projects, 536; staff planning, 575
Freight, railway, 332(t), 362(t), 660–61(t)
Fuel oil production, 341(t)
Furniture plants, 144(t), 319, 320
Furnivall, J. S., 10n, 12, 12n, 14n, 18n, 23, 26, 28n, 29, 39n, 55, 68n, 166n, 225n, 262, 302, 478n, 480n, 506, 653

G

Galbraith, John K., 595–96, 596n
Gamble, William, 295n
General Council of Burmese Associations, 25, 26
Germany, trade with, 50(t); *see also* East Germany; West Germany
Glaxo (British firm), 349
Godowns, construction of, 282
Gold: in Burmese society, 390–91; production, 44
Government: in British Burma, 19; under Constitution of 1937, 29; in pre-British Burma, 11–12; relation to economic development, 585–86; *see also* A.F.P.F.L. Government; Government service; Ne Win Government; Parliament of Burma; Pyidaungsu Government; Public administration
Government service: attractions of, 391–92; manpower problems, 400–07; office hours, 393; pay scales, 481, 482(t); personnel management, 479–81; procedures, 483–86; strengthening of, 580
Grain production, 41(t)
Grant, W. J., 7n, 39, 39n
Great Britain. *See* United Kingdom
Gross domestic product: and capital formation, 114(t), 361(t), 660–61(t); data in actual prices (1953–60), 114(t); data in 1938–39 prices (index, 1938–60), 660–61(t); data in 1947–48 prices (1938–60), 355(t), 660–61(t); data in 1950–51 prices (1938–60), 357(t); data by industry (1938–60), 355(t); fiscal year 1953–54, 163; fiscal year 1954–55, 182; fiscal year 1955–56, 215; fiscal year 1956–57, 236; fiscal year 1957–58, 250; fiscal year 1958–59, 265–66; goals and achievements, 114(t), 357(t); and K.T.A. Comprehensive Report, 111, 112(t), 113; results of program, 352–56
Groundnuts (peanuts), 41(t), 271(t), 276–77, 339(t), 362(t)
Guardian (newspaper), 489–90
Gunny production, 306

H

Hacohen, David, 201
Hagen, Everett, 9n, 10n, 40, 40n, 57, 57n, 593, 593n
Hall, D. G. E., 10n
Hall, H. Fielding, 13n
Handicraft industries, 15, 47

Harvey, George E., 6n, 7n, 10n, 17–18, 18n, 32n, 39, 40, 45, 53

Health, 8-9; and foreign specialists, 550(t); improvement, 601; medical expenditures, 52; medical facilities, 38–39, 103, 104, 364–65, 365(t); medical workers, 33(t); pre-World War II, 38–39; and Pyidawtha Conference, 103–05

Highways: and K.T.A. reports, 94(t), 135(t), 141, 141(t), 331; labor, 33(t); pre-World War II, 48; program, 334–35; projects, 111, 334, 533

Highways Department, 334, 542

Hirschman, Albert O., 593–94, 593n, 596–97, 612n

Hla Maung, U, 83–84, 160n; and Council of Economic Advisors, 166n; and Economic and Social Board, 126–27, 164, 166n, 473, 475; and economic policy, 155n; and expenditures program, 172; and Japanese reparations, 512; and K.T.A. Preliminary Report, 95; and manufacturing sector, 143; and rice prices, 373; and U. S. aid program, 516; and World Bank loans, 540

Hla Myint, Dr., 166, 166n, 172, 575

Hlaing Bwa, U, 328

Hlutdaw (council), 11

Hmu Aung, Bo, 574

Home industry. *See* Cottage and home industry

Home Ministry, 107, 479

Hospitals: number, 38, 103, 365(t); program, 104, 364, 365(t); Taunggyi hospital, 535, 539

Household expenditure survey (1958), 390n

Housing: and Eight-Year Program, 366–67; financial data, 355(t); and foreign specialists, 550(t); Government policy, 504; improved, 602; programs, 257, 367; and Pyidawtha Conference, 101–03

Housing Board. *See* National Housing Board

Hpu, U, 273, 275

Hungary, trade with, 188(t), 191(t), 499

Hydroelectric power. *See* Electric power

I

I.C.A. *See* International Cooperation Administration

I.D.C. *See* Industrial Development Corporation

I.M.F. *See* International Monetary Fund

I.W.T.B. *See* Inland Water Transport Board

Immigration, from India, 19

Imperial Airways, 47n

Implementation, of economic development plans, 587–90

Implementation Conference (1954), 157–58, 269, 286, 300, 319, 324, 326, 331

Imports: and Burmanization policy, 494; C.S.M.B. program, 192(t); of capital goods, 212–13(t), 251, 660–61(t); by commodity, 189–92(t), 212(t); of consumer goods, 186ff, 198(t), 212–13(t), 251, 660–61(t); by country, 188(t); fiscal years 1953–54 and 1954–55, 198(t), 212–13(t); fiscal year 1955–56, 186–99, 188–91(t), 198(t), 212–13(t); fiscal year 1956–57, 226, 236; fiscal year 1957–58, 239, 250–51; fiscal years 1958–59 and 1959–60, 266; of food, 189(t), 191–92(t), 198(t), 212(t); and Government policy, 196, 498; licenses, 156, 173, 176, 187, 188(t), 192–94, 193n, 195, 206ff, 219–20, 343; and Ne Win Government, 258, 266; of pharmaceuticals and drugs, 303–05; pre-World War II, 48–51, 49(t); program, 442–43; public and private, 342(t), 660–61(t); total (1938–60), 660–61(t); *see also* Foreign trade; *and under specific products*

Income. *See* Wages

Income, farm, 42–43

Income Tax Department, 219

Income taxes, 51–52, 51(t), 122(t), 123, 123n, 422(t), 423, 444(t)

Independence, attainment of, 56–61; economic goals, 61ff

India: Burma's separation from, 29; debt repayment to, 175, 419(t), 420; emigration from, 19; loans from, 182, 185, 218, 411, 417(t), 508–11(t), 544, 545; processing agreement with, 205; study mission to, 317; technicians from, 404, 549; trade with, 14, 50, 50(t), 161, 164, 169(t), 170(t), 188(t), 191(t), 204, 204n, 227, 238–39, 243, 273, 322, 522–23

Indians, in labor force, 35(t), 392, 393–94

Indo–Burma Petroleum Company, 45

Indonesia, trade with, 169–70(t)

Industrial Development Corporation, 449–51; administration, 127; budget authorizations for, 441; establishment, 93, 300; and foreign specialists, 551(t); hire-purchase scheme, 194; and jute mill, 306; loans by, 157, 318, 460; management assistance to, 462; merger with M.R.D.C., 263; and public enterprises, 314, 454, 457–58; and sugar mill operation, 280

Industrial Research Institute, 102, 316

Industrialization policy, 495–97

Industry: in British Burma, 22; cottage and home industry, 46, 301–02(t), 344(t), 345–46, 345–46(t), 348(t); and Economic and Social Board, 643–44; establishments, 46(t), 344–48(t); expansion, 600; financial data, 221(t), 300–01, 300–01(t), 313–14(t), 352, 353–54(t); fiscal year 1955–56, 211n; and foreign specialists, 550(t); handicrafts, 15, 47; industrialization policy, 495-97; and K.T.A. reports, 91, 93, 94(t), 135(t), 143–46; labor, 33(t), 44n, 46–47, 46(t), 344–48(t); manufacturing program, 299–317; and nationalization, 379, 492–93; and Ne Win Government, 263–64; pre-World War II, 33(t), 45–47, 46(t); in private sector, 315, 345–51, 496; production statistics, 344–

Industry (*Contd.*)
48(t); and Two-Year Plan, 65–66; *see also* Manufacturing
Infant mortality. *See* Death rate
Inflation, domestic, 185–216; anti-inflation program, 205–08; *see also* Finance; Prices
Inland Water Transport Board, 330, 448; financial data, 426(t); and freight rates, 345, 427; operations, 427; program, 332; training, 403; and U. S. loans, 529(t), 531(t)
Inland-water transportation. *See* Waterways transportation
Insurance firms, 343–45
Insurrection (beginning 1948), 68–69; number of insurgents, 69, 259; retarding effects of, 377, 382–87
Interest rates, 53, 291
Interim Programme (1953), 634–40
International Cooperation Administration, 275, 275n, 317, 527–29, 531, 533
International Labor Organization, 548(t)
International Monetary Fund, 185, 199, 200–01, 411, 417(t), 508(t), 510–11(t), 544, 545
Investment: in Burmese society, 391; and economic growth, 593–94; under Eight-Year Program, 621; foreign, 53–54, 349–51; and K.T.A. Comprehensive Report, 113–16; military, 261; in private sector, 113–16, 119, 262, 316–17, 337–38, 502–03, 630–32; public, 113–15, 270–71; in state manufacturing plants, 302(t); *see also* Capital expenditures
Investment Act (1959), 650–52
Investment Policy Statement (1955), 337–38, 349, 647–49
Iran, economic report on, 83–84
Iron ore production, 44
Irrawaddy (river), 6, 287
Irrawaddy–Chindwin River System, 6
Irrawaddy Flotilla Company, 47, 330
Irrigation: financial data, 221(t), 270–71(t), 352, 353–54(t); and foreign specialists, 550(t); and K.T.A. Comprehensive Report, 135(t), 138–39, 286; projects, 139(t), 286–88
Irrigation Department, 139, 286, 287
Ishikawa (Japanese firm), 515
Israel: and agricultural settlements, 262; and 5-Star Shipping Line, 333; joint-venture proposals, 261; technicians from, 403, 462, 548(t), 549, 551, 554; trade with, 169(t), 170(t), 188(t), 191(t), 201
Isserlis, Paul, 350–51

J

Jackson, George T., 480n
Jackson Report, 480n, 489
Jadeite production, 44
Jaggery production, 278–79

Japan: and Balu Chaung project, 327; and joint ventures, 301, 514–15; Martaban Company, 318–19; occupation of Burma, 56–59; processing agreement with, 205; and reparations, 163, 168, 169, 327, 331, 353–54(t), 411, 417(t), 419(t), 422(t), 438, 444–45(t), 508–11(t), 509, 512–15, 544; technicians from, 514, 548(t); trade with, 50, 50(t), 138, 161, 164, 169(t), 170(t), 194
Jewelry, in Burmese society, 389n, 390–91
Joinery plant, proposed, 144(t), 319, 320
Joint Committee on Indian Constitutional Reform, 24–25
Joint ventures: with foreign firms, 301, 315, 349–51, 514–15; in import field, 156, 197; and industrialization, 496; trading companies, 207, 219, 226, 227, 249, 258, 343, 581
Jones, Howard, 200, 200n
Jute industry, 144–45, 271(t), 277–78; mill, 144(t), 278, 301, 302(t), 306–07, 312, 313–14(t), 316, 457–58

K

KLM Royal Dutch Airlines, 47n
K.M.T. *See* Kuomintang
K.N.D.O. *See* Karen National Defense Organization
K.T.A. *See* Knappen Tippetts Abbett Engineering Co.
K.T.A. Comprehensive Report, 3n, 80–82, 110–11; administration of program, 125–29; and agriculture, 135–38; and communications, 135(t), 140–42, 141(t), 331; economic goals, 112–21; economic policies, 121–25; and electric power, 139–40, 326–27; and farm mechanization, 288; financing of program, 117–21; and forestry, 319–20; and irrigation, 135(t), 138–39, 286; and labor, 90, 129–33, 130–31(t), 401; and manufacturing, 143–46; and mining, 135(t), 142–43, 323–24, 326n; and public enterprises, 460–62; and rice export prices, 373–74; sector programs, 134–49; and transportation, 135(t), 140–42, 141(t), 331; *see also* Eight-Year Development Program
K.T.A. Preliminary Report, 80–83, 83–95; findings, 87–92; recommendations, 92–95, 97–98; results, 154; and rice export prices, 373
K.T.A. Program. *See* Eight-Year Development program
Kabo Dam, 286–87, 404, 503, 528–30, 531(t)
Kachins (people), 4, 6n, 13
Kaing land, defined, 277n
Kalewa coal fields, 6, 65; project, 93, 142, 142(t), 324, 326
Kalewa steam plant, 139(t)
Kandaw Village irrigation project, 139(t)

Karen National Defense Organization, 68
Karens (people), 4, 6n, 13, 19, 20; revolt, 68–69
Karma (Buddhist tenet), 10
Kaung, U, 105, 403
Khin Maung Gale, Bo, 224, 243n, 434
Khin Maung Pyu, U, 243, 245
Khrushchev, Nikita S., 194, 508(t), 519, 534
Knappen Tippetts Abbett Engineering Co. (K.T.A.), 80, 83, 85, 86–87, 126; dismissal from Burma, 262–63; *see also* K.T.A. Comprehensive Report; K.T.A. Preliminary Report
Ko Gyi, U, 273, 275, 296, 450
Kuomintang (K.M.T.) troops, 110n, 126n, 384, 515–16
Kyat: devaluation of, 430–31; exchange rate of, 36n
Kyaw Dun, U, 239, 240, 241, 244, 288, 574
Kyaw Min, U, 246, 487
Kyaw Myint, U, 97n
Kyaw Nyein, U: and A.F.P.F.L., 225, 240–41, 244–45, 264n; and Burma Revolutionary Party, 29; and Burmanization policy, 494; capability of, 451n; as Chairman of Executive Committee, 208; as Chairman of I.D.C., 450; as Chairman of National Economy Committee, 229–31; and Civil Supplies, 204; and conflict with U Nu, 500; as Deputy Prime Minister, 208, 211, 224, 241–42, 458, 473; and Economic and Social Board, 125; and Finance Subcommittee, 171; and foreign credits, 244; and governmental powers, 488; and housing policy, 504; and industrial development, 211n, 227, 495–97; and Japanese reparations, 512–13; and L.R.D.C., 275; and land ownership, 505; as Minister of Industries, 140, 143, 197; on nationalization, 493; and parliamentary test, 245–46; and public enterprises, 463; and Soviet "gift" projects, 219n, 225, 534; and Task Force effort, 474; and World Bank, 541–43
Kyaw Nyun, U, 172, 177n, 202, 205, 254, 654
Kyetmauktaung irrigation project, 287
Kyi Win, Colonel, 532

L

L.A.P.C. *See* Land and Agricultural Planning Commission
L.R.D.C. *See* Land and Rural Development Corporation *and* Land Resources Development Corporation
Labor: agricultural, 33(t), 35(t); Burmese attitude toward, 391–95; children in labor force, 368; industrial, 33(t), 44n, 46–47, 46(t), 344–48(t); and K.T.A. reports, 90, 129–33, 130–31(t), 401; manpower problems, 378, 400–08, 540–41; manpower requirements, 129–33, 130–31(t), 401; in pre-British Burma, 15; pre-World War II,

32–36, 33(t), 35(t); specialized, 400–08, 603–04; transportation industry, 33(t), 37, 401; women in labor force, 32–34; *see also* Employment; Wages
Lac, export of, 43
Lampha Chaung hydroelectric project, 139(t), 326
Land: alienation, 28, 504–05; distribution and redistribution, 100, 293, 293(t); nationalization, 99–100, 136–37, 147, 263, 291–94, 293(t), 492; ownership, 20, 35(t); reclamation, 275; revenue, 51, 51(t), 122(t), 123, 422(t), 423–24; surveys and reforms, 271(t); tenure, 15; *see also* Agriculture
Land and Agricultural Planning Commission, 200, 269
Land and Rural Development Corporation (L.R.D.C.), 273–81
Land Improvement Act, 292(t)
Land Nationalization Act of 1948, 99
Land Nationalization Act of 1954, 291
Land Resources Development Corporation, 296–97, 449, 462, 529(t)
Landowners, number of, 35(t)
Languages, 6–7, 6n
Law and order: financial data, 352, 353–54(t); and Ne Win Government, 259–60, 385–86, 568; *see also* Security
Law Yone, U, 487, 533
Lead production, 44, 341(t); *see also* Bawdwin Mines
Leftist Unity program, 70, 74
Let Ya, Bo, 318
Lieber, Dr., 425
Life expectancy, 38
Literacy rates, 39
Livestock, 5, 40, 43, 289; animal husbandry project, 271(t); ban on cattle slaughter, 5n, 263, 394
Loans, domestic: agricultural, 42–43, 123, 289–91, 292(t); to boards, 444(t); to private sector, 301(t), 316; receipts from, 413(t), 445(t); *see also* Credit
Loans to Burma: chronological highlights, 508–09(t); implementation, 511; sources, 507; *see also* Foreign aid
—— China, 545, 577
—— I.M.F. dollar draws, 185, 199, 200–01, 411, 417(t), 508(t), 510–11(t), 544, 545
—— India, 182, 185, 218, 411, 417(t), 508–11(t), 544, 545
—— U. S.: and Burmese public capital expenditures, 417(t); development loan of $25 million, 202, 208–10, 218, 238, 274, 317, 320, 411, 508–11(t), 519–21, 527–31, 529(t), 531(t), 544–45, 576; for dockyard improvement, 332; and Ne Win Government, 262, 530–32, 544, 576; police loan of $10 million, 232, 243–44, 509–11(t), 524–25, 532; proposed $50 million loan, 182,

Loans to Burma—U. S. (*Contd.*)
508(t), 517; proposed $75 million loan, 242
—— World Bank: extended, 200, 208, 331,
333, 411, 508(t), 509–11, 510–11(t), 521,
539–43; sought, 162, 168, 177, 182, 201,
211n, 317, 334, 539–43
Local administration, 107–08; *see also* Public
administration
Locklin, Dr., 461
Loikaw Area irrigation project, 139(t)
Lough Keng zinc development, 142, 142(t),
324, 326
Lower Burma: agriculture, 18–19, 18n, 20, 22,
41; annexation by British, 17; electric power,
327; government, 11; trade, 13

M

M.R.D.C. *See* Mineral Resources Development
Corporation
Machinery industry, 344(t), 346(t)
Maize acreage, 41(t)
Malaria, 394
Malaya, trade with, 59(t), 169–70(t)
Management, in public enterprises, 448–64;
see also Public administration
Mandalay, 21
Mandalay College, 366, 402
Mandalay–Rangoon highway, 533
Manpower. *See* Labor
Manufacturing: cottage and home industry, 46,
301(t), 344(t), 345–46, 345–46(t), 348(t);
establishments, 46(t), 344–48(t); financial
data, 300–01(t), 313–14(t); foreign invest-
ment, 349–51; handicraft industries, 15, 47;
and K.T.A. reports, 93, 94(t), 143–46;
labor, 33(t), 46–47, 46(t), 344–48(t), 401;
and Ne Win Government, 263–64; pre-
World War II, 33(t), 45–47, 46(t); in
private sector, 346–51, 348(t); production
statistics, 344–48(t); program implementa-
tion, 299–317, 346–47; state enterprises,
299–317, 449
"Marathon Speech," 233
Marketing, state, 355(t)
Martaban Company, 318–19
Martin, K., 77n
Maternity centers, 365(t)
Maung Maung, Colonel, Brigadier, 253, 254,
261, 577
Mauritius, trade with, 169–70(t)
Mawchi Mines, 6, 22, 44n, 45, 142, 323, 325,
342, 383
McCaffery, Richard, 275
McConnaughy, Ambassador, 533
McDowell, Christopher, 350–51
McMahon line, 385
Medicine: expenditures, 52; facilities, 38–39,
103, 104, 364–65, 365(t); medical workers,
33(t); and Pyidawtha Conference, 103–05;
see also Health
Messrs. E. D. Zublin, A.G., 287

Metals. *See* Minerals
Midwives, number of, 39
Mikoyan, Anastas I., 201, 508(t), 519, 534,
535
Military equipment, surplus, 524–25, 532
Military regime of 1958–60. *See* Ne Win Gov-
ernment
Military Staff Council, 253, 254, 256
Milk imports, 525–26
Millet production, 41(t), 339(t)
Min Gaung, Bo, 154, 155, 196, 209, 574
Mindon (king), 21
Mineral Resources Development Corporation,
449; establishment, 143; and foreign special-
ists, 551(t); loan policy, 157; management
assistance, 462; merger with I.D.C., 263;
minerals program, 324–26; organization,
450
Minerals, 6, 44–45; exports, 49(t), 660–61(t);
and K.T.A. reports, 91, 93, 94(t), 142–43;
labor, 33(t); and Ne Win Government, 263;
production statistics, 341(t); program implementation, 323–26; *see also* Mining; *and
specific minerals*
Mingaladon Airport, 333
Mingaladon Airport Board, 128
Mining: financial data, 221(t), 353–55(t); and
foreign specialists, 550(t); and insurrection,
383; and K.T.A. Comprehensive Report,
135(t), 142–43, 323–24, 326n; labor, 44n;
pre-World War II, 44–45; in private sector,
340–42; program implementation, 323–26,
340–42; *see also* Coal industry; Minerals
Mining consultants. *See* American consultants;
Pierce Management, Inc.
Ministry of Agriculture and Forests, 321, 479
Ministry of Commerce, 157, 479
Ministry of Cooperation and Commodity Distribution, 479
Ministry of Culture, 479
Ministry of Democratization of Local Adminis-
tration, 479
Ministry of Finance and Revenue: budget role,
433–35, 438–39; and extension service, 295;
and foreign exchange, 165, 169–72; and
K.T.A. reports, 93, 120, 125; and Ministry
of National Planning, 297; and telecom-
munications, 335
Ministry of Health, 302, 303, 529(t)
Ministry of Industries: and Economic and
Social Board, 157; and fisheries, 318; and
industrial projects, 219, 231, 314; and joint
ventures, 315, 515
Ministry of Land Nationalization, 479
Ministry of Mines, 462
Ministry of National Planning: and agriculture,
295, 297; and budget, 433–35, 433n, 437,
440, 443; and Central Statistical and Economics Dept., 203, 434, 443; decision to
retain, 178; and Economic and Social Board,
237n, 465, 475; and foreign specialists,

551(t); and Four-Year Plan, 220, 221(t), 233; and K.T.A. reports, 93, 125–27, 154, 154n; and National Planning Commission, 237; organization, 125–27, 154n, 377; and program implementation, 155, 158; and public enterprises, 460–62; and retrenchment proposal, 171; and Robert R. Nathan Associates, 126–27, 555, 560; and Task Force effort, 249

Ministry of Relief and Resettlement, 479

Ministry of Religious Affairs, 479

Ministry of Social Services, 479

Ministry of Supply, 206

Ministry of Trade Development, 157n; and import licenses, 173, 174, 187, 193, 195, 206, 208; and import program, 443; and Israeli specialists, 462; and retrenchment proposal, 171; and rice exports, 167, 168, 176, 255, 437; and U. S. cotton agreement, 203

Minority groups, 13, 19

Missionaries, 552

Missions: purchasing, 154–55, 155–56n; of World Bank, 168–69, 185, 187, 194n, 242, 244, 378, 503, 540–43

Mo Myit, U, 127, 177n, 202, 203n, 205n, 242, 254, 473–75, 654

Mogok mines, 45

Monarchy, 10–11

Money: currency devaluation, 430–31; domestic currency, 526–27; exchange rate of kyat and rupee, 36n; policy, 497–98; reserves, 660–61(t); *see also* Banking; Finance; Money supply, privately held

Money supply, privately held: in 1951–60, 419(t), 660–61(t); fiscal year 1954–55, 183; fiscal year 1955–56, 199; fiscal year 1956–57, 236; fiscal year 1957–58, 251; fiscal year 1958–59, 266; and Government budget, 415, 416(t), 446(t)

Monkhood: as career, 392; influence of monks, 12

Mons (people), 4, 6n, 13, 19, 20; proposed Mon state, 573n, 575

Morrison–Knudson engineers, 84

Moulmein, 48

Mountbatten, Lord, 59, 60

Mu River projects, 139(t), 287, 326, 327

Musgrave, Dr. Richard, 197, 411, 412, 423, 424, 428

Mutual Defense Assistance Control Act (1951), 517n

Mya, U, 63

Mya Sein, Daw, 478n

Myingyan industrial complex, 139, 140, 142, 144

Myingyan steam plant, 139(t), 140, 148, 326, 327

Myingyan zinc project, 142, 142(t), 324, 326

Myitkyina district, 279

Myosas, system of, 14, 21

Myothugyis (township chiefs), 11–12, 20

Myowuns (provincial governors), 11

N

N.U.F. *See* National United Front

Nagas (people), 4

Namti sugar mill, 278, 304, 307, 313–14(t)

Nathan, Robert R., 84, 159n, 377, 558; *see also* Robert R. Nathan Associates, Inc.

Nation (Rangoon newspaper), 335, 489, 533

National Day, 26

National debt. *See* Debt

National Economy Committee, 229, 230, 231

National Fitness Council, 104

National Housing Board, 101, 449; chairman, 450; financial data, 426(t); and foreign specialists, 551(t); operations, 427; and Rangoon telephone project, 335; and telecommunications program, 441; and U. S. loans, 529(t)

National Planning Board, 93

National Planning Commission, 249, 250, 462, 467, 474; replaces Economic and Social Board, 237

National registration, 260

National United Front, 203, 245–47, 487, 568, 574

Nationalism, in British Burma, 23–30

Nationalization, 65; effect on economy, 491–93; in industry, 379, 492–93; of land, 99–100, 136–37, 147, 263, 291–94, 293(t), 492; and Pyidaungsu Government, 571; *see also* Public enterprises

Nats (spirits), 396

Natural resources, 5–6

Ne Win, General: and Defense Services Institute, 576; as Deputy Prime Minister, 69; elected Prime Minister, 248; and proposed mills, 531, 531n; and Rangoon projects, 530; and U Law Yone visit to U. S., 533; *see also* Ne Win Government

Ne Win Government (1958–60), 252–66, 568–69; and administration, 256–57, 380, 384; and cattle slaughter, 5n, 394; and cost of living, 257–59; and finance, 265–66, 412; and foreign aid, 262, 530–33, 544, 576; and housing, 367; and import registrations, 575; and industrial development bank proposal, 317; and Insein road improvement, 334; and insurrection, 385–86; and joint venture companies, 343; and Martaban Company, 319; and price levels, 363; and private sector, 262; and public enterprises, 463–64; and rice mills, 531; and state industrial enterprises, 301–02; and steel mill, 305–06

Ngapi (fish paste), 43

Nu, U (or Thakin Nu), 28n, 60n, 71n; and A.F.P.F.L., 225, 244–49, 568–69, 569n, 570, 574; A.F.P.F.L. Congress speech, 239–40; and anti-inflation program, 204–05; and brick and tile factory, 472; and Burmaniza-

Nu, U (*Contd.*)
tion policy, 572; and cattle slaughter ban,
5n; and centralized procurement, 206n; as
Chairman of A.R.D.C., 450; as Chairman of
L.R.D.C., 296; on civil service, 405; on
Communists, 75; compromise program (May
1948), 70, 70n; and Constitution of 1947,
62–63, 63n; and Defense Services Institute,
576–77; on democracy, 570–71; and development program, 234–35, 242–43; and Economic and Social Board, 467–68, 469; and
economic programs, 70–75, 75n, 82; economy, review of, 233–36, 613–33; and Eisenhower, 520–21; and finance, 184, 411; and
foreign exchange crisis, 177, 181–82; on
foreign technicians, 547; and Four-Year
Plan, 224–33, 571; and government-
improvement program, 227–29; and governmental powers, 488; and honesty in office-
holders, 296, 296n, 454; and hostels for
medical students, 470; and housing policy,
504; and industrialization, 71, 71n; and
insurrection, 68–69, 69n; and K.T.A. Report,
83–84, 84n; and Kyaw Nyein, U, 244–45,
500; and National Planning Commission,
237; and nationalization, 571; on Ne Win
Government, 252; and pharmaceuticals
plant, 302; on private sector, 156, 337; on
program implementation, 159–60; and
public administration, 490; and public enterprises, 463; and Pyidaungsu Government,
569–77; on Pyidawtha, 96, 96n; and Rangoon–Mandalay highway, 533–34; and Rangoon University, 29; and relations with
outside world, 398; report to people (Sept.
27, 1957), 233–36, 613–33; resignation
(1956), 207n, 210; resignation (1958), 248;
return to prime-ministership (1957), 224;
return to prime-ministership (1960), 264–
65, 569, 573; and rice redistribution, 165–66,
499; and Robert R. Nathan Associates, 559;
and security assumption, 377; and Soviet
"gift" projects, 534, 535; and Soviet rice
sale, 536; and Standing Committee for Supervision and Coordination, 205n, 463, 471;
and Three-Year Plan, 199; trips abroad, 181,
186; and U. S. loans, 177, 181–82, 209, 517;
and World Bank, 541
Nu-Tin group. *See* "Clean" faction
Nurses, 39, 103, 365(t)

O

O.E.C.D. *See* Organization for Economic Co-
operation and Development
O.G.L. *See* Open General License
Ohn, U, 243
Oil. *See* Petroleum
Okkalapa housing program, 257, 367
One-party domination, danger of, 586–87
Open General License (O.G.L.), 173–74, 173n,
176, 186, 187, 188(t), 206, 207, 213(t),
215, 217, 219, 239, 239n

Open letter to U Nu (in *Guardian*), 489–90
Organization. *See* Public administration
Organization for Economic Cooperation and
Development, 609–10
Ottamu, U, 26–27
Output. *See* Production
Overseas Consultants consortium, 84
"Oxford Economists," 77n

P–Q

P.L. 480 programs: financial data, 417(t),
419(t); first (1956), 182, 194, 195, 195n,
202, 212, 437–38, 508(t), 510–11(t), 516–
19; implementation, 525-27; rupee funds,
227; second (1958), 218, 220, 243, 509–
11(t), 521–24; surplus U. S. commodities,
182, 202, 209n, 375, 411, 499, 606; and
textile imports, 186n, 195n, 227, 437–38
P.V.O.'s, 68
Paddy. *See* Rice production
Pagoda building and maintenance, 389–90
Pakistan: study mission to, 317; trade with,
169–70(t), 238–39
Palaung-Was (people), 6n
Pan American Airways, 539
Panglaung hydroelectric project, 139(t), 326
Papanek, Gustav F., 593n
Paper Board, 128
Parliament of Burma: and A.F.P.F.L., 245–46,
487; and General Ne Win, 254; reform of,
579; and Union of Burma Investment Act,
351
Passengers, railway, 332(t), 360, 362(t)
Pawnshop Board, 450
Pawnshops, nationalization of, 345
Pay. *See* Wages
Payagyi community development project, 367
Peanuts. *See* Groundnuts
Pegu, Kingdom of, 4; *see also* Lower Burma
Pegu Division, 294
Pegu hydroelectric plant, 139(t), 140, 148, 326,
327
Pegu Yomas, 3
Pension payments, 52
People's China. *See* China
People's Comrade Party, 247
Peres, Shimon, 243
Petroleum: British firms, 45; Chauk oil fields,
142, 323; and Eight-Year Program, 362(t);
exports, 44, 49(t), 50; labor, 33(t), 46,
46(t); production statistics, 44, 341(t);
program implementation, 325; reserves, 6
Pharmaceuticals industry, 302(t), 313–14(t);
plant, 300–05, 312, 464
Pierce Management, Inc., 80, 85
Planning, 621–22; economic, 597–98; priorities,
503–04; *see also* Eight-Year Development
Program; K.T.A. Comprehensive Report;
K.T.A. Preliminary Report; Ministry of
National Planning; Pyidawtha Conference
Plywood plant, proposed, 144(t), 319, 320
Poland, trade with, 186, 188(t), 191(t), 499

Police expenditures, 52
Police Loan, 509(t), 532
Pongyis (monks), 26–27
Population, 3, 4, 5–6; characteristics, 6–9, 368; growth, 18–19
Port of Rangoon Authority. *See* Rangoon: port program
Ports, 48; and K.T.A. reports, 94(t), 135(t), 140, 141(t), 331
Post offices, number of, 48
Power industry: financial data, 221(t); and K.T.A. reports, 94(t), 135(t); *see also* Electric power
Price policy, Government, 499–502
Prices, consumer: and Eight-Year Program, 363; fiscal year 1953–54, 198(t); fiscal year 1954–55, 183, 198(t); fiscal year 1955–56, 196–99, 196n, 198(t); fiscal year 1956–57, 236; fiscal year 1957–58, 251; indexes, 198(t), 213–15(t), 660–61(t); and Ne Win Government, 255, 257–59; Prime Minister's report on, 618–19
Prices, rice export, 138, 161, 163, 164, 183, 238, 371–75, 372(t), 499–501
Prime Minister, office of, 125–26; *see also* Ba Swe, U; Ne Win, General; Nu, U
Printing establishments, 46(t)
Priorities: and economic policy, 503–04; program, 217–36; *see also* Eight-Year Development Program
Private sector: agriculture, 338–40; banking, 343–45; capital formation, 114(t), 336–38, 356, 358–59(t), 359, 361(t); construction industry, 345; cottage and home industry, 345–46, 348(t); entrepreneurship in, 591–92; foreign trade, 342–43, 343(t), 660–61(t); forestry, 340; industry, 315, 345–51, 496; insurance, 343–45; investment in, 113–16, 119, 262, 316–17, 337–38, 502–03, 630–32; investment, foreign, 349–51; loans to, 301(t), 316; manpower problems, 407–08; manufacturing, 346–51, 348(t); mining, 340–42; and Ne Win Government, 262; program implementation, 156–57, 336–51, 588–90; realizing potentials, 604; transportation, 345
Processing agreements, textile, 197n, 202–03, 205, 522–24
Procurement of supplies, 206, 206n, 426, 449
Production: agriculture, 41(t), 339(t), 372(t), 660–61(t); cottage and home industry, 344–46(t), 348(t); electric power, 328–29(t); goals and achievements, 362(t); indexes (1938–60), 660–61(t); manufacturing, 344–48(t); minerals, 341(t); petroleum and products, 44, 341(t); timber, 321(t), 660–61(t)
Productivity, Burmese attitude toward, 392–94
Profits, Burmese attitude toward, 395
Programing: function of, 125; problems of, 432–47; *see also* Eight-Year Development Program

Progress-reporting function, 125–26
Prome-Taungup road, 334
Public administration: and British rule, 478; and Burmese culture, 395–96; and corruption, 406–07; democratization of local, 107–08; and development corporations, 127–28; improvement of, 218, 460–64, 602–03; and K.T.A. reports, 92–95, 125–29; and Ne Win Government, 256–57; need for, 579–80, 588; and nepotism, 406; practices and procedures in, 483–86; and private sector, 94, 129; shortage of administrative personnel, 480; and state boards, 128; and technical assistance, 546–62; weaknesses in, 228–29, 377–78, 406–07, 453–55, 477–90; workers in, 33(t); *see also* Boards, state-owned; Government service; Public enterprises
Public Administration Commission, 575
Public Administration Services cost accounting team, 462–63
Public enterprises: and K.T.A. reports, 92–94, 460–62; management problems, 448–64; organization, 450–51; types, 448–50; *see also* Boards, state-owned; Development corporations; Public administration
Public health. *See* Health
Public investment. *See* Investment
Public Law 480. *See* P.L. 480 programs
Public utilities: enterprises, 448–49; financial data, 355(t); *see also* Communications; Electric power; Transportation
Pulses, production of, 41(t), 339(t), 362(t)
Purchase missions, 154–55, 155–56n
Pye, Lucian, 395, 395n, 397
Pyidaungsu Government, record of, 569–78
Pyidaungsu (Union) Party, 264–65, 569–70, 574, 579
"Pyidawtha," meaning of, 96
Pyidawtha community development projects, 367
Pyidawtha Conference, 80, 81, 96–109, 291, 319, 373
Pyidawtha grants, 221(t), 353–54(t)
Pyidawtha Plan, 106–07; *see also* Eight-Year Development Program
Pyinmina Agricultural Training School, 295, 403
Pyinmina State Experimental Farms, 279
Pyinmina sugar mill, 278, 304, 307, 313(t), 314(t)
Quarrying industry, 355(t)

R

Racial constitution of population, 6–7
Radio facilities, 48
Railways: freight, 332(t), 362(t), 660–61(t); and K.T.A. reports, 94(t), 135(t), 140, 141(t), 331; labor, 33(t), 37, 46(t); passengers, 332(t), 360, 362(t); pre-war statistics, 47; program implementation,

Railways (*Contd.*)
331–32; and Pyidawtha Conference, 101; workshops, 46(t)
Railways Board. *See* Union of Burma Railways Board
Rangoon, 48, 81; automatic dial telephone system, 101, 141, 141(t), 335; consumer price index (1938–60), 660–61(t); electric power, 327–30, 329(t), 660–61(t); housing, 102, 257; industrial complex, 139, 140, 144; port program, 101, 140, 141(t), 208, 333, 426(t), 448, 542; Soviet "gift" projects, 535–36; water and sewerage projects, 530, 531(t)
Rangoon Electricity Supply Board, 140, 326, 327, 426(t), 438, 448, 452, 460; *see also* Electricity Supply Board
Rangoon-Mandalay highway, 533
Raschid, U, 29; and A.F.P.F.L. reform, 574; capability of, 451n; as Chairman of National Housing Board, 450; and foreign exchange, 178; and foreign trade, 168, 193–95, 204, 206, 209, 210; and Four-Year Plan, 211n, 226; and hostels for medical students, 470; and housing, 101–02; and loan from India, 182, 517; as Minister of Mines, 326; and national planning, 237, 246; and National Planning Commission, 474–75; and rice agreement with India, 204
Receipts. *See* Revenue
Red Flag Communists, 60
Rehabilitation Brigade, 403, 449–50
Rehabilitation Conference (1947), 64
Religion, 12–13; religious workers, 33(t); *see also* Buddhism
Rentiers, number of, 35(t)
Reparations, Japanese, 163, 168, 169, 327, 331, 353–54(t), 411, 417(t), 419(t), 422(t), 438, 444–45(t), 508–11(t), 509, 512–15, 544
Research: agricultural, 271(t), 294–95; and foreign specialists, 550–51(t)
Reserve Bank of India, 52
Resources: appraisal of, 436–38; mobilization of, 598–600; use of, 360, 361(t), 615
Revenue: farm, 42; Government, 51–52, 51(t), 122–23, 122(t), 413(t), 416(t), 422(t), 444(t), 446(t); land, 51, 51(t), 122(t), 123, 422(t), 423–24; in public sector, 414(t), 417(t), 419(t), 445(t); *see also* Taxes
Rice bran oil, 144(t), 145
Rice Control Board (World War I), 26
Rice exports: in British Burma, 19; budget estimates, 436–37; direction of, 169–70(t); fiscal year 1953–54, 161; fiscal year 1954–55, 164–65, 182–83; fiscal year 1955–56, 194, 215–16, 272–73; fiscal year 1956–57, 236; fiscal year 1957–58, 238–39, 250; fiscal year 1958–59, 255; fiscal year 1959–60, 263, 266; future needs, 578; goals and achievements,

362(t); and Government finances, 410, 411, 425; and K.T.A. Comprehensive Report, 119; and Ne Win Government, 255, 263, 266; in pre-British Burma, 14; pre-World War II, 5, 49(t); prices, 138, 161, 163, 164, 183, 238, 371–75, 372(t), 499–501; and S.A.M.B., 91, 118, 122, 138, 162, 167, 176, 238, 255, 424–25; sales agreements, 161, 194; U. S. disposals of rice, 201, 208, 499; volume and value, 169(t), 170(t), 362(t), 372(t), (1938–60) 660–61(t); *see also* Barter trade
Rice Marketing Board, 59
Rice (paddy) production, 272–75; in British Burma, 18–19, 18n; chemical fertilizer in, 138; effects of war on, 136–37; and export price assumption, 371–75; financial data, 271(t), 355(t); goals and achievements, 362(t); and K.T.A. Comprehensive Report, 137; labor, 33(t), 46, 46(t); milling, 143, 271(t), 283–85, 286(t); and Ne Win Government, 263, 266; pre-World War II, 33(t), 37, 41, 41(t), 46(t), 339(t); programs, 282–86, 286(t); and Pyidawtha Conference, 99; short paddy crop (1957–58), 238; storage program, 282–83; volume, 339(t), 362(t), 372(t), (1938–60) 600–61(t)
Richards, C. P., 7n
Riots, race-motivated, 27, 29
Roads. *See* Highways
Robert R. Nathan Associates, Inc., 84, 85, 159n, 171n, 196n, 203n, 255n, 411n, 412n, 459n; arrival in Burma, 80; dismissal from Burma, 262–63; Draft Agreement recommendations, 538; and Economic and Social Board, 126, 555, 558–59; experience in Burma, 555–62; field staff in Burma, 659; and Japanese reparations, 57; and Ministry of National Planning, 126–27, 555, 560
Rosen, Martin, 242, 543
Rosenberg, Nathan, 592n
Rowe & Co., 261
Rubber industry, 281
Ruby production, 44
Rumania, trade with, 499
Rupee, exchange rate of, 36n
Rural health centers, 365(t)
Russia. *See* Union of Soviet Socialist Republics
Ryukyu Islands, trade with, 169–70(t)

S

S.A.M.B. *See* State Agricultural Marketing Board
S.C.S.C. *See* Standing Committee for Supervision and Coordination
"Sabape" loans, 43n
Saingdin Falls hydroelectric project, 66, 139, 139(t), 148, 326, 327

Salaries. *See* Wages

Sales tax, 122(t), 123

Salween (river), 6

San Lin, U, 167, 173n

Sanitation program, 104

Sao Pye, 539

Sapir, Pinchas, 243

Sapphire production, 44

Savings, attitude toward, 390–91

Sawmills: capacity, 322; labor, 37, 46, 46(t); proposed, 144(t), 319; sawyers, number of, 33(t); set up by S.T.B., 319–20

Saya San Rebellion (1930), 28

Schools. *See* Education

Schumacher, E. F., 379, 379n

Scott & Co., 261

Sebald, William J., 164

Secretariat, 107

Sector programs: implementation, 269–351; and K.T.A. Comprehensive Report, 134–49; weaknessess in, 378–79; *see also* Private sector

Security: and B.S.I., 386–87; defense expenditures, 51(t), 221(t), 352, 353–54(t), 421, 436; improvements, 274; and insurrection, 68–69, 382–87; and Ne Win Government, 259–60, 385–86; problems, 382–87; program implementation, 377

Seers, Dudley, 77n

Sein Win, 225n, 245n

Sesamum industry, 41(t), 339(t), 362(t)

Shan States, 5, 201, 289, 539

Shans (people), 4, 6n, 13

Shinpyu (ceremony), 12, 12n

Shipping: pre-World War II, 48; program, 332–33

Shipping Board. *See* Union of Burma Shipping Board

Silk industry, 301, 302(t), 313(t)

Silver production, 44, 341(t); *see also* Bawdwin Mines

Simon Commission, 27

Singapore, trade with, 169–70(t)

Sittang (river), 6

Soap industry, 344(t), 346(t)

Social services: financial data, 221(t), 353–54(t); improvements, 364–68, 365–66(t), 601–02; *see also* Education; Health; Housing

Socialist Party, 29

Soe, Thakin, 60

Soe Tin, U, 177, 177n, 254, 513

Soviet Union. *See* Union of Soviet Socialist Republics

Special assistance grant (1959), 532–34

Special Projects Implementation Board, 294, 300, 449

Specialists. *See* Foreign technicians and specialists

Specialized manpower. *See* Labor

Spinel production, 44

Spirits, propitiation of, 396

Spiritualists, influence of, 396

"Stable" faction (Swe-Nyein group), 245, 246, 264–65, 264n

Standing Committee for Supervision and Co-ordination (S.C.S.C.), 205n, 219, 309, 463, 471, 654

State Agricultural Bank, 111; and capital expenditures, 270; and credit needs, 498; expansion, 504; loans, 290–91, 292(t); and Ne Win Government, 263; and village banks, 124, 290–91, 292(t)

State Agricultural Marketing Board (S.A.M.B.), 449, 624; consultants' recommendations, 179–80; and Government finances, 226, 410, 415, 418, 421, 424–25, 428, 436–37; and gunnies, 181n; inventory accounts, 458; invoicing and collections, 175; and jute mill, 306, 457; and organization, 461, 462; personnel, 462; and price policy, 500; and rice exports, 91, 118, 122, 138, 162, 167, 176, 238, 255, 424–25; and rice milling, 144, 283–85; and rice storage, 282–83, 296; and U. S. loans, 529(t)

State boards. *See* Boards, state-owned

State Commercial Bank, 226, 343, 450

State Insurance Board, 345, 450

State Medical Stores Board, 456

State ownership of industries, 65; *see also* Nationalization; Public enterprises

State Sugar Board, 128, 280

State Timber Board, 449; financial data, 426(t); and forestry program, 319–23; potentials, 427; and profits, 122, 457; and timber exports, 455; and U. S. loans, 529(t)

Statistical and Economics Department, Central, 126, 154, 203, 560

Statistical data, inadequacy of, 443

Status, in Burmese society, 389–94, 395–96

Steam plants, 139(t), 140, 148, 326, 327

Steel Brothers mills, 319, 320, 350

Steel industry: financial data, 302(t), 313–14(t); mill, 301, 305–06, 312; products plant, 144(t), 145

Straits Settlements, trade with, 50(t)

Strikes: dock strike (1930), 27; students' (1920–21), 25; students' (1935), 29

Subsidy payments, 272

Suez Canal, 19

Sugar industry: cane production, 41(t), 278–80, 339(t); mills, 278, 301, 302(t), 304, 307–08, 312, 313–14(t), 492

Sulfuric acid plant, 144(t)

Supervision. *See* Public administration

Surplus-commodity sales, 197, 411, 524–25, 532, 606–07

Survey of Manufactures (1957), 345–46

Swe-Nyein group ("Stable" faction), 245, 246, 264–65, 264n

T

T.A.M.S. *See* Tippetts-Abbett-McCarthy-Stratton

Taikthugyis (circle headmen), 19, 20

Tariff Board, 128, 157, 158

Tariff policy, 499

Task Forces. *See* Foreign technicians and specialists

Taunggyi hospital, 535, 539

Taungpalu Dam, 286

Taungup-Prome road, 334

Tavoy District, 325, 385

Taxes: in British Burma, 21, 26, 27; enforcement, 599; and Government finances, 122(t), 421–25, 422(t), 428, 433, 444(t); income taxes, 51–52, 51(t), 122(t), 123, 123n, 422(t), 423, 444(t); and K.T.A. Comprehensive Report, 121–24; in pre-British Burma, 14; sales tax, 122(t), 123

Tea-packing industry, 301, 302(t), 313(t)

Teacher training, 403, 404

Teak industry: and Eight-Year Program, 319–22, 362(t); exports, 5–6; production, 43–44, 321(t), 660–61(t)

Technical and economic assistance program (1950–53), 508(t), 515–16

Technical assistance, problems of, 546–62; *see also* American consultants; Foreign technicians and specialists

Technical Assistance Administration, 548(t), 550

Technical Cooperation Administration Program, 80, 515–16 .

Technical Institute at Insein, 403

Technicians. *See* Foreign technicians and specialists

Technological Institute at Insein, 535

Telecommunications, 335; and K.T.A. Comprehensive Report, 135(t), 141, 141(t); radio facilities, 48; telegraph system, 48

Telecommunications Department, 335, 462, 529(t)

Telegraph system, 48

Telephone systems, 48, 141; Rangoon automatic dial system, 101, 141, 141(t), 335

Tenant farmers, 20, 35(t), 40–41, 293–94

Tenasserim coastal strip, 3; agriculture, 294; annexation, 17; climate, 4; fishing, 5; mining, 219, 323, 325, 342, 383; rice acreage, 18n

Textile industry: imports, 189(t), 191–92(t), 195–96, 198(t), 212(t), 219–20; labor, 33(t), 344(t), 346(t); production statistics, 344(t), 346(t), 348(t); spinning and weaving mill, 301, 310–12; *see also* Cotton industry

Textile-processing agreements, 197n, 202–03, 205, 522–24

Tha Kin, Thakin, 245

Thaketa housing program, 257, 367

"Thakin," meaning of, 29n, 574, 574n

Than Tun, Thakin, 60, 62, 68, 247

Thant, U, 164, 172, 176n, 473

Tharawaddy district, 244

Thayetmyo cement mill, 301, 492, 501

Thein Pe, Thakin, 60

Thet Su, U, 166n

Thet Tun, U, 270n, 374n

Thibauw, King, 17–18, 21

Thingangyun, 102

Thitson Dam, 287

Three-Year Plan (beginning 1956–57), 199–200, 210, 211n

Thugyis (village headmen), 19, 20

Tile. *See* Brick and tile plant

Timber Board. *See* State Timber Board

Timber industry, 43–44; exports, 5–6, 49(t), 660–61(t); production statistics, 321(t), 660–61(t); program implementation, 319–23, 362(t)

Tin, U, 125, 158, 171, 196, 239, 240, 241, 469n, 488, 574

Tin Maung, U, 176n, 177n, 202, 205n, 288, 473, 653, 654

Tin Pe, Brigadier, 254

Tin Pe, U, 126, 164, 177, 303, 475

Tin production, 44, 341(t); *see also* Mawchi Mines

Tin Tut, U, 63

Tin U, U, 296, 574n

Tinker, Hugh, 59n, 68, 100n

Tippetts-Abbett-McCarthy-Stratton, 287

Tobacco industry, 281; acreage, 41(t); financial data, 271(t); labor, 344(t), 346(t); production statistics, 339(t), 344(t), 346(t), 348(t)

Tractors, use of, 288–89

Trade, foreign. *See* Foreign trade

Trading companies, joint venture. *See* Joint ventures: trading companies

Trager, Frank N., 64n, 225n, 378, 378n

Transportation, 13–14; in British Burma, 19; financial data, 221(t), 352, 353–55(t); and insurrection, 382, 383; and K.T.A. reports, 91, 93, 94(t), 135(t), 140–42, 141(t), 331; labor, 33(t), 37, 401; pre-World War II, 33(t), 37, 47–48; private carriers, 345; program, 330–35; and Pyidawtha Conference, 100–01; and Two-Year Plan, 66, 67; *see also* Airways; Railways; Waterways transportation

Tun Thaung, U, 242, 245, 474

Tun Thin, Dr., 166n, 177n, 202, 536, 536n

Tun Tin, U, 328

Tun Wai, U, 43n

Tun Win, U, 245, 451n

Tungsten production, 44, 341(t); *see also* Mawchi Mines

Two-Year Plan of 1948, 64–68, 81, 148, 149

U

"U," meaning of, 574, 574n

U.B.A. *See* Union of Burma Airways Board
U.S.S.R. *See* Union of Soviet Socialist Republics
Unilever, 349
Union Bank, 162, 165, 167–68, 219, 226, 239, 330
Union Government. *See* Pyidaungsu Government
Union of Burma Airways Board, 448; financial data, 426(t), 427–28; flights, 333; and foreign specialists, 551(t); operating experience of, 452–53, 458–59, 459n; and Viscount aircraft purchase, 172n, 333–34
Union of Burma Investment Act, 351
Union of Burma Purchase Board, 426–27, 426(t), 449
Union of Burma Railways Board, 448; and budget allotments, 441; and coke and coal supplies, 181n, 326; financial data, 426(t), 427; freight rates, 345, 427; and private agencies, 243; training program, 403; and World Bank, 208, 542
Union of Burma Shipping Board, 448; financial data, 426(t); and K.T.A. Comprehensive Report, 140, 141(t); program, 140, 332; and timber exports, 455; and U. S. loan, 529(t)
Union of Civil Service Employees, 68
Union of Soviet Socialist Republics: aid to Burma, 194, 194n, 201, 219, 219n, 262, 508(t), 510–11(t), 534–40, 545; credits from, 204n, 206, 218, 411, 417(t), 539(t); technicians from, 403, 548(t), 549, 552; trade with, 169–70(t), 181n, 188(t), 191(t), 209, 498–99, 511, 512n, 534–37
Union Party. *See* Pyidaungsu Party
United Kingdom: British rule in Burma, 17–30, 56–60, 478; compensation payments from, 492; debt repayment to, 175, 419(t); economists from, 76–78; processing agreement with, 205; technicians from, 404, 548(t); trade with, 13, 50, 50(t), 169(t), 170(t)
United Nations: advice on public administration, 489; Food and Agriculture Organization, 282, 375, 548(t), 550; International Labor Organization, 548(t); International Monetary Fund, 185, 199, 200–01, 411, 417(t), 508(t), 510–11(t), 544; technical assistance from, 316, 402, 403, 462, 548(t), 549–51, 553–54, 607–08, 610; World Health Organization, 548(t), 549; *see also* World Bank
United States: aid to Burma, 76–77, 84–85, 508–11(t), 515–34, 605–07, 608–12; cotton purchase agreement, 197, 202, 519, 522–24; rice disposals, 201, 208, 499; surplus commodities from, 182, 197, 202, 209n, 411, 499, 524–25, 606–07; technical assistance from, 548(t), 549; trade with, 50(t); *see also under* Loans to Burma; *and* P.L. 480 programs

University Act of 1920, 25
University of Rangoon, 25, 29, 39–40, 176, 232, 366, 402, 538; Students Association, 29
University of Utah, 462
Upper Burma, 11, 21; agriculture, 41; annexation by British, 17; land tenure, 137

V

Vegetable production, 41(t)
Veterinary Department, 294
Veterinary research, 271(t)
Veterinary Research Institute, 295
Village banks, 124, 290–91, 292(t)
Village life, 14–16
Virginia tobacco. *See* Tobacco industry
Viscounts (planes), purchase of, 333–34
Von Monroy, Dr., 319

W

Wages: farm, 42n; Government pay scales, 481, 482(t); pre-World War II, 36–38, 37–38(t); in 1953 and 1957, 368
Wallboard plant, proposed, 144(t), 319, 320
War Damage Claims Commission, Burmese, 57
Was (people), 4
Water resources program, 92; *see also* Electric power; Irrigation; Waterways transportation
Waterways transportation: pre-World War II, 33(t), 47; and K.T.A. reports, 94(t), 135(t), 140–41, 141(t), 332; *see also* Inland Water Transport Board
Welfare. *See* Social services
West Germany: credits from, 218, 301; processing agreement with, 205; technicians from, 548(t)
Wheat production, 339(t)
White Flag Communists, 60, 68
White Paper, British (1945), 58
White Paper Report (1918), 24–25
Win, U, 126, 574
Win Pe, U, 205n, 653, 654
Wisara, U, 27
Women: and decision-making, 395; and jewelry, 389n, 390–91; in labor force, 32–34; literacy rate, 39; status of, 9, 15
Wood. *See* Timber industry *and* Wood products
Wood products, 344(t), 346(t), 348(t)
Work. *See* Labor
World Bank: aid program, 607, 610–11; and Canadian experts in Burma, 220, 462; missions of, 168–69, 185, 187, 194n, 242, 244, 378, 503, 540–43; relationship with Government, 244; *see also under* Loans to Burma
World Health Organization, 548(t), 549
World War II: and Burmese independence, 56–61; pre-World War II economy, 31–55
Worswick, G. D. N., 77n
Wundauks (officials), 11

Wungyis (ministers), 11
Wycelkowski, Mark, 434

X–Y–Z

Yadanabon mine, 324, 326
Yamethin District irrigation project, 139(t), 286, 287
Yeast tablets, distribution of, 303–04

Young, Kenneth, 200, 200n
Young Men's Buddhist Association, 24–25
Yugoslavia: technicians from, 403; trade with, 169–70(t), 188(t), 191(t)
Zeyawaddy sugar factory, 278, 307, 313(t), 492
Zinc industry: development projects, 142, 142(t), 324, 326; production, 44, 341(t); *see also* Bawdwin Mines